LEARNING EVIDENCE

FROM THE FEDERAL RULES TO THE COURTROOM

...

FOURTH EDITION

Deborah Jones Merritt

John Deaver Drinko/Baker & Hostetler Chair in Law
Moritz College of Law, The Ohio State University

Ric Simmons

Chief Justice Thomas J. Moyer Professor
for the Administration of Justice and Rule of Law
Moritz College of Law, The Ohio State University

WEST
ACADEMIC
PUBLISHING

© 2008, 2012 Thomson Reuters
© 2015 LEG, Inc. d/b/a West Academic
© 2018 LEG, Inc. d/b/a West Academic
    444 Cedar Street, Suite 700
    St. Paul, MN 55101
    1-877-888-1330

West, West Academic Publishing, and West Academic are trademarks of West Publishing Corporation, used under license.

Printed in the United States of America
ISBN: 978-1-63460-646-2

To Andrew and Daniel
DJM

To my parents
RS

PREFACE TO
THE FOURTH EDITION

The fourth edition of *Learning Evidence* updates the text to include all rule changes through December 1, 2017, as well as recent developments in the case law, including the most recent Confrontation Clause cases and cases involving racial discrimination in jury deliberation. This edition also includes a brand new learning tool for students: interactive trial videos in which students can take the role of a trial attorney or a judge during a simulated trial and make or rule on objections in real time. These are in addition to the thirteen explanatory videos that we added to the last edition, which allow students to listen to brief lectures on difficult subjects and then test their understanding of those subjects with self-assessments.

As always, the fourth edition preserves the chapter numbering, structure, and most examples from the first edition. If you used the third edition of *Learning Evidence*, this edition should feel quite familiar.

The book has an online presence which maintains a rich variety of quiz questions, simulations, writing assignments, and other learning exercises. These are available on the book's website, merrittevidence.com.

This book is unusual because students contributed so substantially to its preparation. For each successive edition, dedicated research assistants researched points of law, found examples, checked cites, proofread pages, and suggested formats. We offer special thanks to the outstanding work of our research team over these years. For the first edition: Abigail Andre, Courtney Cook, Daniel Corcoran, Katherine Everett, Christina Y. Han, Doug Hattaway, James Marra, Rex Miller, Megan Shepston Overly, Corrina Roy, Carla Scherr, Jillian Slinger, Ravi Suri, and Stephen M. Wolfson. For the second edition: Eric M. Bell, Timothy Brownrigg, Andrew DeFranco, Stephanie Fitos, Joe Griesmer, Douglas Hattaway, Chris Immormino, Caitlyn Nestleroth, and Joseph Saks. For the third edition: Joseph Case, Zach Horton, Scott McCormick, and Matthew Navarre. And for this edition: Kelsey Kornblut, Melissa Lenz, Mallory Murphy, and Chad Smith.

Our Evidence colleagues have suggested ideas that we incorporated in this edition or in the teaching materials associated with the book. We especially thank Michael

Avery, Leah Christensen, Andi Curcio, Michelle Madden Dempsey, Deborah M. Hussey Freeland, Judge Abraham J. Gafni, Mark Godsey, Jesse A. Goldner, Eileen Kaufman, Kenneth S. Klein, Jonathan (Jay) Koehler, Michael Mannheimer, John Mitchell, Brad Saxton, Martin A. Schwartz, Deirdre M. Smith, and Mark A. Summers for their helpful insights and thoughtful corrections.

We could not have completed any of the editions of this book without the dedicated, cheerful, and careful work of several office associates and other staff members at the College of Law. We thank Loraine Brannon, Susan Edwards, Allyson A. Hennelly, Dawn Parker, and Gabrielle Stephens for their superb support.

We are grateful, finally, for our supportive, engaging, and inspirational family members. They are true members of the *Learning Evidence* team, as well as partners in all of life's other adventures.

Deborah Jones Merritt
Ric Simmons

Columbus, Ohio
November 1, 2017

TABLE OF CONTENTS

DETAILED TABLE OF CONTENTS

STUDY GUIDE

How to Get the Most out of This Book

The study techniques you have developed in other courses will help you in this course as well. But this book approaches legal study differently than the typical casebook. Here are some tips on how to get the most out of this book:

1. Learning the Basics. The materials in this book teach the basic rules of evidence through textual discussion, analysis of the relevant rules, and concrete examples. The text does not require you to extract principles from cases, respond to questions, or solve problems to grasp these basics. By the end of each chapter, you should understand the basic features of the rule(s) discussed in that chapter.

 Key Concepts. Most chapters begin with a text box labeled "Key Concepts" and marked with this key icon. These boxes serve two purposes. First, they will alert you to the most important concepts that you should focus on when reading the chapter. Second, when you review the materials, you should be able to glance at the Key Concepts box for each chapter and readily recall the meaning of those concepts.

 **Quick Summary.** Each chapter ends with a "Quick Summary" of the contents, designated by the "summary folder" icon. These boxes do not contain all of the information you need to know from the chapter. You need to master details from the chapter, not just the summary principles. But these summaries will give you a mental framework for organizing the material in the chapter. After reading the chapter, look at the Quick Summary and see how many details you can recall to accompany each principle.

2. Reading Rules. The federal law of evidence has been codified in the Federal Rules of Evidence. To understand the law and practice it effectively, you need to read the rules! Rather than refer you to a statutory appendix or separate rulebook, these materials incorporate relevant sections of the rules in each chapter. The materials attempt to walk you through the rules, so that you will see how the language relates to the issues disputed in the courtroom.

To aid your understanding, we underline key words in the rules and arrange complex lists into bullets. This formatting is not part of the official rules; it is designed to introduce you to each rule. Here is how a hypothetical rule (one that is not part of any evidentiary code) might appear:

> ## HYPOTHETICAL RULE. Prohibited Conduct by Jurors.
>
> In any <u>civil or criminal</u> trial, <u>jurors</u> may not
>
> - Snore
> - Yawn, or
> - Roll their eyes
>
> during the presentation of a party's evidence, <u>except</u> when the judge engages in the same behavior.

The full text of the Federal Rules of Evidence appears in an appendix to this book. In addition to studying the rules in each chapter, you should look frequently at the full set of rules; that will help you understand how the rules relate to one another. You may want to annotate the rules in the appendix with notes from your reading and class. This is a good way to learn the rules.

3. Open Questions. Many points of evidentiary law are settled, but a surprising number are still open to dispute. Even when a principle is clear, its application may vary depending on the facts of the case. This book notes when legal issues are unresolved, as well as when application of a principle depends on the facts of the case. In addition to textual explanations, icons mark these points so they are easy to recognize:

 This icon indicates points of law that are still evolving. Evolving issues include (1) legal principles that most parties assume are settled, but that a thoughtful attorney might challenge; (2) issues on which a conflict exists among the federal circuits; (3) unsettled questions raised by recent Supreme Court decisions or rule changes; and (4) issues that no court has yet addressed. The "evolving rule" icon identifies these issues, which are discussed further in the text.

 This second icon marks issues on which the legal principle is clear, but the court's decision will depend on the facts of the case. Legal counsel's ability to apply the governing principle to the facts is particularly important in these situations. When you study these issues, the legal principle may seem straightforward. Think, however, about how you would apply the principle to a variety of factual situations. Applying the principle, rather than simply knowing it, is critical to these issues.

4. Organization. Each chapter in this book addresses a particular evidentiary principle. The chapters are self-contained, although later chapters build on earlier ones. True mastery of the Rules of Evidence, however, requires seeing relationships among the rules and using the rules in combination. To help you build that understanding, the book uses two techniques:

First, a **Table of Contents** and **Detailed Table of Contents** show how some of the rules relate to one another. The Table of Contents includes just the title for each chapter, while the Detailed Table of Contents incorporates the Key Concepts for each chapter. These tables may help you see the "big picture" and integrate the individual rules.

 Second, **Overview Chapters** and **Paragraphs** offer specific information about how rules relate to one another or to trials in general. When you see this overview icon at the beginning of a chapter, it means that the entire chapter is an organizational one, helping you relate rules to one another. When the icon appears beside a particular paragraph, it means that the paragraph positions the material within the broader Rules of Evidence.

5. How to Prepare for Class. You should read the assigned materials before class! All professors say that, but there is a particular reason to read these materials before class. With the case method, some students (especially in upper level courses) find that it is efficient to read the cases very lightly—or not at all—and wait for class to illuminate the principles contained in the cases. The materials in this book, however, teach the basics directly; there's no quicker way to learn them.

Your professor, moreover, may not review the basics in class. Instead, the professor may focus class on review questions, advanced problems, policy discussion, and simulations. If you haven't read the material, you will not benefit much from the classes.

 For some chapters, we have created short videos that review key concepts or give you a chance to test your understanding. You will find all of these videos online at http://www.merrittevidence.com/videos/, as well as in the videos module from the eBook on your eProducts bookshelf. Sidebars with this video icon will direct you to videos that complement specific chapters.

6. How to Prepare for Exams. You should find these materials helpful, both in preparing for the exam in this course and when reviewing for the bar exam. The techniques outlined below will help you prepare well for both exams:

a. Be sure that you understand the **Key Concepts** in each chapter. These appear both at the beginning of the chapter and in the **Detailed Table of Contents.**

b. Read over the **Quick Summary** for each chapter. In addition to understanding the summary, you should be able to recall details relating to each of the points in the summary.

c. Review the **Rules of Evidence** that you have personally annotated. Most of federal evidentiary law stems from those rules. The language of the Rules should help you track the basics, while your annotations flesh them out.

d. Review **Overview** chapters and paragraphs to be sure that you understand how the rules relate to one another. Reviewing the **Table of Contents** will also reveal important relationships.

e. Take special note of **Evolving Issues** and know how you would argue both sides of those issues. You may argue these issues some day in court and you almost certainly will have to argue some of them on an exam.

f.   Pay special attention to **Balancing Scale** principles as well. These rules often seem easy, but the essence of these rules lies in their application. You need to know how to apply these rules carefully to the facts of a problem, seeing arguments that both sides might raise.

Near the end of most chapters you will have the opportunity to **Test Your Understanding** with multiple choice questions that review the material you just learned. These questions can be found in the Quizzes module from the eBook on your eProducts bookshelf.

There are a total of two hundred of these questions throughout the book. After you respond to each question, the website will tell you the correct answer and explain why the answer is correct. You can use these questions to assess your understanding of the chapter you just read, or save them and take them all as a review at the end of the semester.

One final method of review is to engage with the **Evidence in Practice** interactive trial videos found after chapters 13, 22, 31, 43, and 56. You can access those videos through the Evidence in Practice module from the eBook on your eProducts bookshelf. In these interactive videos, you play the role of a trial attorney or judge during a witness examination at trial, and you make or rule on objections in real time as the trial unfolds. Each of these simulations will help you review a specific topic. In addition, there are two longer interactive simulations that review material from the entire course, which you can use at the end of the semester. Those videos are also available in the Evidence in Practice module from the eBook on your eProducts bookshelf.

Enjoy your study of evidence!

LEARNING EVIDENCE

FROM THE FEDERAL RULES
TO THE COURTROOM

FOURTH EDITION

1

Why Take This Course?

There are dozens of courses to take in law school, many more than you can fit into a three-year schedule. So why spend time in a class on the Federal Rules of Evidence? For some students, the answer is that they plan to litigate; mastering Evidence is essential to courtroom survival. Other students believe that Evidence is a basic area that every lawyer should know. Still others respond that the subject figures prominently on the bar exam. These are all good reasons to take an Evidence course, but there are other reasons why evidence matters, why the Federal Rules of Evidence matter, and why you will benefit from this course.

A. Why Does Evidence Matter? Evidence is the heart of persuasion. Humans do not respond to abstract, theoretical arguments as well as they respond to examples, details, and stories. Whenever we try to sway others, we cite evidence. Certainly this is true in the courtroom. A police officer who is called by the prosecutor to testify in a homicide case will show the jury the blood-stained knife found in the defendant's kitchen. A laboratory expert will then explain that the blood on the knife matches that of the deceased. The prosecutor will arrange pieces of evidence like these to tell a coherent tale about when, where, how, and why the defendant stabbed the victim. The jury will convict only if the prosecutor shows them evidence that tells a convincing story.

Evidence is central to every trial. Sometimes the evidence even determines whether there will **be** a trial. The question in many disputes is not what happened, but what the parties can prove. If two cars collide on an isolated highway, one of the drivers may be certain that the other crossed the center line and caused the collision. But if the other driver denies fault, there were no eyewitnesses, and the physical evidence of the crash is ambiguous, then the first driver has little chance of persuading a jury that the other driver was at fault. Without convincing evidence, even a truthful claim will fail.

Evidence matters outside the courtroom as well. Transactional lawyers, deal makers, negotiators, lobbyists, in-house corporate counsel, and attorneys of all stripes use evidence to analyze and advance their clients' causes.

- A real estate lawyer helping a client develop a new office complex will cite evidence of job growth, construction costs, traffic flow, environmental effects, and other factors during negotiations with lenders, zoning boards, tax authorities, and other decision makers.

- A lobbyist will emphasize evidence about the positive effects of a client's proposed legislation, while discrediting evidence offered by opponents.

- An in-house lawyer for a corporation, advising the company on the effect of new government regulations, will marshall evidence about the regulations' impact on the company's day-to-day operations.

Evidence, in other words, is vital to everything lawyers do. It is the essential counterweight to abstract legal rules. Without evidence to explain and persuade, legal principles have little meaning.

B. Why Do Rules of Evidence Matter? Lawyers use evidence in most tasks, but many of those uses fall outside formal evidentiary codes. An intellectual property lawyer negotiating a licensing arrangement, for example, may use evidence to show the other party how the proposed arrangement will generate profits for both sides. But this lawyer does not need to worry about whether the projected earning streams comply with evidentiary rules governing hearsay, expert opinion, or other matters. Formal evidentiary rules regulate courtroom evidence closely, but they may seem unimportant outside the courtroom.

In fact, however, the formal rules of evidence affect most aspects of legal practice in at least three ways. **First**, every action lawyers undertake, from informally advising a client to negotiating a contract, occurs in the shadow of possible litigation. Although much of what lawyers do is constructive, every human action has the potential to end in disagreement and conflict. Even when preparing a simple will, lawyers must think about what type of evidence will protect their client's interests if a disagreement generates a lawsuit.

Second, advances in technology have made evidence easier to gather for courtroom use. Even when the rules of evidence are the farthest thought from your mind, you may be generating evidence that could be used against your client in court. The e-mail you sent this morning might become evidence in a lawsuit; so might the notes you keep on your desk calendar or the files you dispatched to the storeroom. Savvy companies, law firms, and individuals keep track of changes in the rules of evidence so they know how the evidentiary trails they routinely create might affect them in the future.

Finally, the rules of evidence embody (mostly) sensible distinctions about what types of evidence support sound decision making and what types carry hidden risks of confusion. By learning the formal rules of evidence, you learn concepts that may help you and your clients make better decisions. No one, for example, wants to sign a long-term supply contract with a company that is unreliable. But how does a client judge reliability? Studying the rules of evidence will teach you that people sometimes attach more weight to secondhand reports than is rational. Learning the policies that surround formal evidentiary rules may help you make better decisions outside the courtroom.

C. How Will You Benefit from This Course? There are at least four ways in which you may benefit from this course.

First, you will learn the Federal Rules of Evidence. If you plan to litigate, a thorough knowledge of those rules is essential to your courtroom practice. Every trial plan depends on the Rules of Evidence for its success. The most brilliant strategy will fail completely if it is founded on hearsay, character evidence, unsupported lay testimony, or other evidence that your opponent successfully excludes. The best litigators know the Rules of Evidence so well that they incorporate those rules seamlessly into their strategies.

If you don't plan to litigate in federal court, the rules you learn in this course will still guide most adjudications in which you do take part. As we'll see in Chapter 3, most states have adopted principles from the Federal Rules of Evidence in their own evidentiary codes. Many administrative agencies also follow rules similar to the Federal Rules of Evidence.

Even when you settle disputes informally, the evidentiary rules you learn in this course will inform your negotiations. Parties settle disputes with an eye on both their underlying claims and what they are likely to prove in court. The admissibility of key evidence affects a party's bargaining position. So even if you hope to resolve all of your client's problems outside a courthouse, you are likely to encounter issues that turn on the Federal Rules of Evidence.

Second, this course will help you think about the role that facts play in conducting all kinds of legal business. Every appellate opinion you have read in law school began with a statement of the facts. But where did those "facts" come from? How does the prosecutor prove that the defendant intended to kill the victim, or that a car's passenger knew that the trunk contained packages of cocaine? How does the plaintiff in a contract action prove that the defendant provided defective goods or that the breach injured the plaintiff's business? In law school, we often take the facts for granted. But in practice, gathering, analyzing, and organizing facts are among the most important tasks a lawyer performs. Assembling evidence to prove the facts is inextricably interwoven with understanding a client's legal goals. In this course, we will spend more time on the "facts" than in any other course in law school.

Third, the course illuminates the strategies that lawyers use to create persuasive stories and arguments. What kinds of evidence do decision makers find most convincing? What types are likely to distract a decision maker? The basic Evidence course only scratches the surface of these issues: Courses on Trial Advocacy, Law and Psychology, and other subjects treat them in more depth. But the Federal Rules of Evidence rest on basic insights about how people weigh pieces of evidence and make decisions. Exploring why the Federal Rules permit some types of evidence and not others will help you understand how the human brain responds to evidence. You can apply those lessons to a wide range of tasks, from persuading a potential client to hire your firm to concluding a successful business deal.

Finally, this course confers several practical benefits. It **does** prepare you for an important bar exam subject, and it does fulfill a prerequisite for Trial Advocacy and some clinical courses. It will also give you useful insights into movies, television episodes, books, and news stories that feature courtroom evidence. When you watch courtroom dramas, you will no longer wonder why the lawyers are always objecting and proffering, while the judges are sustaining and overruling. What could be better than that?

2

Types of Courtroom Evidence

A. Introduction. Even if you've never attended a live trial, you already know something about courtroom evidence. In television and movie dramas, you've seen tense confrontations between witnesses and cross-examining attorneys. On the news you've heard about claims of privilege, from those asserted by cat burglars to those claimed by corporate CEOs and the President of the United States. You've probably read about seized narcotics, smoking guns, and blood-stained garments in both novels and news reports. You have seen and read about many types of evidence.

Before we plunge into the Federal Rules of Evidence, let's think more systematically about the kinds of evidence that attorneys present in the courtroom. Previewing the different types of courtroom evidence will expose you to words that lawyers commonly use when discussing evidence. If you don't know those words already, you will find it helpful to learn them now. A quick tour of the many kinds of evidence available to courtroom litigators will also help you see nuances in the rules and apply them more confidently.

In this chapter, we'll examine first the types of evidence that lawyers most commonly use in the courtroom. We'll then look at a typical case to see how a party draws upon different types of evidence and integrates them to tell a story. Finally, we'll discuss the concept of circumstantial evidence, a phrase that perplexes many lawyers and their clients.

B. Types of Evidence.
Lawyers and judges talk about evidence without defining the term. Even the Federal Rules of Evidence neglect to define "evidence." Chances are, you understand what evidence is without a formal definition. But for those who crave more certainty, the California Code of Evidence offers a useful definition of evidence:

> "Evidence" means testimony, writings, material objects, or other things presented to the senses that are offered to prove the existence or nonexistence of a fact.[1]

Evidence includes all the information given to the trier of fact during trial, except for the questions and statements made by the attorneys and judges. As this definition suggests, litigators can choose from a broad menu of evidence types when building a case in the courtroom. Evidence divides into six different categories:

1. Oral Testimony.
Most trials feature oral testimony by witnesses speaking from the witness stand. The witness takes an oath to testify truthfully, and then responds to questions posed by attorneys representing both parties. There are three types of witnesses:

a. **Fact Witnesses.** Many witnesses at a trial are fact witnesses. These are people who perceived facts related to the lawsuit and testify about those facts. Some fact witnesses directly perceived an event central to the trial, such as the alleged crime or disputed accident. Lawyers and jurors often call these individuals "eyewitnesses," but the law gives them no special status over other types of fact witnesses.[2] A fact witness may testify about facts even if they do not fit within the colloquial concept of being an "eyewitness." A coworker who heard the defendant admit that she caused an accident, for example, is a fact witness. A police officer who logs contraband into a secure locker at the police station is also a fact witness.

---

1   Cal. Evid. Code § 140 (West 2017).

2   In fact, controlled studies suggest that eyewitnesses often make mistakes. For good reviews of these studies, as well as discussion of some reform proposals, see Noah Clements, Flipping a Coin: A Solution for the Inherent Unreliability of Eyewitness Identification Testimony, 40 Ind. L. Rev. 271 (2007); Gary L. Wells, Eyewitness Identification: Systemic Reforms, 2006 Wis. L. Rev. 615.

b. Expert Witnesses. Expert witnesses use specialized knowledge to interpret evidence or explain it to the jury. A handwriting expert may testify that a kidnapper's ransom note was written by the defendant. An accident reconstruction expert may explain what the skid marks at an intersection reveal about how the accident occurred. A banker experienced in mortgage lending may describe the mechanics of home financing. Experts are increasingly common at trial. Parties sometimes even introduce expert testimony to explain the weight of other evidence. A psychologist who has studied eyewitness testimony, for example, might explain the circumstances under which that evidence is unreliable.

Unlike eyewitnesses, expert witnesses do not need to have any firsthand knowledge about the controversy in question—that is, they do not need to have directly seen or perceived the events that underlie the litigation. Many times experts simply review documents or data compiled by others and apply their expertise to this secondhand information.

c. Character Witnesses. These witnesses do not testify about facts directly at issue in the lawsuit. Instead, they offer information about the good or bad character of a party or witness. Like expert witnesses, character witnesses do not have to have perceived any fact related to the controversy; they need only have knowledge about the character of a party or a witness. As we will see, the Federal Rules of Evidence limit the use of character witnesses, but they still appear in some trials.

In addition to witnesses, there are other people or groups represented in the courtroom. The **parties** are the individuals or organizations who oppose each other at trial—the prosecutor and defendant in a criminal case, or the plaintiff and defendant in a civil case. The **victim** is the entity against whom a crime was committed or who suffered damages in a civil case.

The parties and victims frequently appear as fact witnesses in the case. As long as they perceived something relevant to the litigation and are competent to testify, the plaintiff and defendant in a civil case will appear as witnesses, each giving their version of the facts underlying the dispute. A corporation or a government entity can be a "party" in a civil case, even though they act through officers and employees; representatives of these entities will almost always testify as witnesses.

Criminal defendants sometimes appear as witnesses, but often choose not to do so. The Fifth Amendment privilege against self-incrimination and the constitutionally based presumption of innocence allow a criminal defendant to make this choice.[3]

The prosecutor in a criminal case is one "party" who does not appear as a witness. The government is an abstract entity that cannot take the stand to testify against the defendant. The prosecutor may call police officers and other government agents in making a case against the defendant, but they are not parties.

2. Real Evidence. "Real" evidence is any physical evidence that a party claims played a direct role in the controversy. The murder weapon is a classic example of real evidence; so is a blood-stained shirt that the police seized from the defendant's closet. A crude cartoon left on a female worker's desk might be real evidence in a sexual harassment case. And the sponge removed from a surgery patient's abdomen is real evidence in a medical malpractice action.

Despite its name, real evidence is no more "real" or important than other evidence. The Federal Rules of Evidence do not use the phrase "real evidence." However, all real evidence must be **authenticated**—that is, the proponent must offer some proof that the piece of physical evidence is what she claims it to be. This proof can be as simple as a witness testifying that the item is the same one she recovered from the defendant's office or removed from the victim's body.[4]

Juries are fascinated by real evidence, so good lawyers use this type of evidence whenever it is available. Real evidence makes a story more concrete—and more believable—to jurors.

3. Documents. Documentary evidence encompasses any type of writing or recording of information. Some documents, like contracts, bills of sale, real estate leases, and wills, directly determine the parties' legal rights in a lawsuit. Other documents bear more indirectly on disputed issues. An eyewitness to a bank robbery, for example, may note the getaway car's license plate on a scrap of paper. The prosecutor might try to use that "document" to establish that the defendant owned the getaway car.

Changes in technology and lifestyle constantly expand the types of documents that parties offer as evidence. Faxes, e-mails, tweets, text messages, blog posts, and

---

3   We discuss the privilege against self-incrimination in Chapter 68.

4   Rules 901–903 govern authentication procedures; we discuss those procedures further in Chapter 69.

computer printouts are all documents that parties may attempt to introduce in court. So are restaurant receipts, phone bills, envelopes addressed to a particular individual, and government reports.

Like oral testimony, documents stem from a variety of sources. Some are prepared by parties, some by eyewitnesses, and some by experts. Many derive from sources that have no direct connection to the litigation, like the businesses that generate bills and receipts.

Most documents are simply a subcategory of real evidence; they are physical evidence that played a direct role in the controversy. These documents must be authenticated to ensure that they are what the proponent claims them to be.

Documentary evidence is so common and so critical that a number of special rules govern its use. Some writings, for example, are "self-authenticating." This means that there is no need for a witness to confirm their authenticity.[5] On the other hand, a witness almost never may testify orally about the contents of a document; the Rules of Evidence require the party to admit the document itself into evidence unless all available copies have been lost or destroyed.[6]

4. Demonstrative Evidence. Demonstrative evidence is sometimes physical but, unlike real evidence, is not an object that played a role in the disputed events. Instead, parties create demonstrative evidence to illustrate concepts or facts to the jury. Charts, tables, pictures, maps, and graphs are common types of demonstrative evidence. Increasingly, lawyers use Power-Point slides and computer simulations as well. Demonstrative evidence may also substitute for objects relevant to the dispute. The prosecutor in a drug trial may display a plastic bag of powdered sugar to illustrate the package of cocaine found in the defendant's briefcase. The plaintiff in a patent infringement lawsuit might exhibit a scale model of a larger machine.

Parties may also stage a literal "demonstration" in the courtroom. Attorneys can use witnesses or even paid actors to show the jury where the participants of a fight stood and how they moved in relation to one another. A plaintiff's attorney in a personal injury case could ask the plaintiff to walk around the courtroom with his severe limp to demonstrate the extent of the injury caused by the defendant.

---

5   We discuss this concept, together with the other authentication rules, in Chapter 69.

6   Rules 1001–1008 codify this "best evidence" rule and its exceptions. We discuss those rules in Chapter 70.

In one recent case, a defense lawyer attempted to stage a particularly innovative demonstration. A local jail had mistakenly released a federal prisoner into the community. The United States recaptured the prisoner and prosecuted him for escape, claiming that he should have immediately placed a collect call to federal authorities in order to notify them of his release. During trial, the defense lawyer handed a cell phone to two different prosecution witnesses and asked them to dial the telephone number the prisoner was supposed to call. Dialing the number, the lawyer argued, would show that no live person ever answered the phone; a released prisoner attempting to call long distance to report his whereabouts would have encountered a bewildering array of automated menu choices refusing to accept a collect call.[7]

Demonstrative evidence sometimes poses special problems. Unlike real evidence, which is an object that was actually involved in the controversy, demonstrative evidence is a re-creation or imitation of some aspect of the controversy. As such, it is open to abuse: A party may re-create an item or interaction in a way that misrepresents the true nature of what happened. In addition, demonstrative evidence may become overly dramatic or theatrical, diverting the jury's attention from more probative evidence in the case. Trial judges carefully monitor demonstrative evidence to ensure that it does not mislead or distract the jury.

5. Stipulations. If both parties agree on a fact, they can stipulate that the fact is true for purposes of the litigation. To introduce a stipulation as evidence, both parties must agree to its exact language. The judge or proponent of the evidence then reads the stipulation to the jury. Parties usually stipulate to minor facts that would be cumbersome to prove in other ways, such as the authenticity of a document or other real evidence. Although stipulations are relatively straightforward, they occasionally raise interesting issues of relevance; we explore those problems in Chapters 6 and 7.

6. Judicial Notice. If a fact is indisputably true—such as the fact that Boston is in the state of Massachusetts—the trial judge can take judicial notice of the fact. To support judicial notice, the fact must either be "generally known" or "accurately and readily determined" by consulting an unimpeachable source. Rule 201 supplies these standards and governs other aspects of judicial notice; we examine that rule in Chapter 59.

---

7   United States v. Wilson, 70 F. App'x 120, 123 (4th Cir. 2003). Sadly, the trial judge did not allow the defense attorney to make this clever demonstration, finding that it was irrelevant because there was no evidence that the released prisoner ever attempted to make the call.

C. Photographs and Videos. The amount of video and photographic evidence has increased dramatically over the last two decades. Cell phones, surveillance monitors, and law enforcement cameras create many photos and videos for litigants to use at trial. Attorneys find these kinds of evidence especially effective with jurors because people react with special intensity to evidence they can see.

Photos and videos do not constitute their own category of evidence; depending on the context, they should be classified as either **real evidence** or **demonstrative evidence**. These media frequently appear as demonstrative evidence, because parties create them for trial to illustrate an aspect of the dispute. In a product liability suit, for example, a video of the plaintiff's daily activities may show how badly the defective product disabled the plaintiff. A prosecutor, similarly, may have photos taken of a crime scene and then show them to the jury to help the jurors understand where the victim's body lay in relation to other items in the room.

Some real video evidence is demonstrative?

But if a photo or video depicts the events of a controversy **directly**, it constitutes real evidence. Footage from a bank security camera that captured a robbery on tape—or video from a cell phone showing alleged police brutality—are depictions of the incident itself and are therefore real evidence.

This distinction matters because, as noted above, judges are more cautious about admitting demonstrative evidence than real evidence; attorneys can (and do) shade the truth when creating photos or videos for the purpose of litigation. Real evidence is more readily admissible than demonstrative evidence. Of course, even real photographic or video evidence may be excluded if it is unduly graphic or will provoke an unwanted emotional reaction among jurors. We will discuss in Chapter 7 the balancing test that judges conduct when weighing the admissibility of such evidence.

D. Evidence in Action. To help you picture the use of evidence in the courtroom, here is an outline of the evidence presented by the prosecution in an actual criminal case. This is a routine case rather than a famous one. It shows how a trial attorney will combine different types of evidence even in a simple case to tell the jury a coherent and persuasive story.

United States v. Myers[8]

The United States charged Carl Myers, a police captain, with using unreasonable force to subdue an arrestee named Cesar Yanez.[9] The prosecution presented the following evidence:

Patrol Officer James testified that he arrested Cesar Yanez in a parking lot for having an open can of beer in public. As James transported Yanez to the police station, he radioed ahead for help because Yanez was yelling obscenities. When they arrived at the police station, Yanez continued to yell obscenities and challenged several officers to a fight. The officers laughed at Yanez because he was only five foot, two inches tall; weighed about 115 pounds; and appeared drunk. Defendant Myers grabbed Yanez by the throat and told him to stop screaming at the officers. *(Oral testimony: eyewitness testimony about Yanez's behavior and Myers's initial encounter with Yanez)*

Police Officer Fleming testified that Myers told him to escort Yanez to the back area of the station, where he could be booked, searched, and processed. As Fleming escorted Yanez down the hall, Myers walked behind them with a stun gun aimed at Yanez's back between the shoulder blades. Yanez was turning his head and talking, but not engaging in any threatening behavior. As they walked, Myers fired the stun gun twice at Yanez's back. When they reached the back of the station, Fleming frisked Yanez, who complied with all of his orders and made no threatening moves. During the frisk, Myers fired the stun gun at Yanez's lower neck and upper back. Yanez flinched, then looked at Myers and said "If that is all you got, I can take some more." Yanez and Myers got into a shouting match, and Myers fired the stun gun a few more times. *(Oral testimony: eyewitness description of Myers's use of the stun gun)*

The prosecution introduced Myers's **stun gun** into evidence and asked Fleming to demonstrate how Myers had fired the gun. Fleming fired the gun

8   972 F.2d 1566 (11th Cir. 1992). The actual prosecution included evidence about two arrestees that the defendant allegedly mistreated. For simplicity, we outline only the evidence involving one of the arrestees. Other than reducing the evidence in that way and creating a name for one witness who was not identified by name in the official reports, the outline here tracks the actual trial evidence, as reported by the appellate court.

9   A police officer's use of unreasonable force violates 18 U.S.C. § 242 (2017), a civil rights statute that punishes individuals who act "under color of any law" to deprive any person "of any rights, privileges, or immunities secured or protected by the Constitution."

several times for the jury. *(Real evidence: stun gun; demonstrative evidence: using stun gun in a demonstration)*

Chief Everett, Myers's commanding officer, testified that Myers had purchased the gun several years before to use against "rowdy prisoners." Everett told Myers that the gun was unauthorized and directed him not to use it. *(Oral testimony of fact witness)*

The prosecution introduced a copy of the department's **written regulations**, which prohibited officers from using stun guns without official authorization. *(Documentary evidence)*

Lieutenant Welch, another member of the police department, testified that he observed Yanez's back four days after the arrest and saw six pairs of scabbed reddish burn marks approximately two and one half inches apart. He offered his expert opinion, based on nineteen years of police work, that the marks were consistent with those left by a stun gun. *(Oral testimony, including expert opinion)*

Police Officer Bobby Joe Baker, another police department member, described the methods he had learned in the police academy for handling verbally abusive arrestees like Yanez. These methods involved responding verbally to the arrestee, not using physical force. Baker also testified that these verbal methods had worked in his experiences with unruly prisoners and arrestees. He testified, finally, that he had observed Myers use the stun gun on Yanez and based on his expert knowledge of standard police procedure, Myers's use of the stun gun exceeded reasonable force. *(Oral testimony including expert opinion)*

Cesar Yanez, described the circumstances of his arrest, his unruly behavior at the police station, his verbal cursing of the officers, and Myers's use of the stun gun. *(Oral testimony by victim)*

Defendant Myers testified in his own defense, stressing Yanez's abusive language and continuous threats. He also testified that the battery in the stun gun was weak at the time he used it against Yanez, reducing its force. Myers presented the testimony of at least one other police officer, Robert Brown, who corroborated parts of Myers's testimony. Myers's testimony, however, was quite similar to the evidence presented by the government's witnesses, including Yanez. The parties differed little about what happened in this case; the decision turned on whether use of the stun gun was reasonable under the circumstances described above. The jury sided with the prosecutor on that issue, convicting Myers. The court of appeals affirmed the conviction.

Think about the many types of evidence that the prosecutor combined to prove the case against Myers: oral testimony from eyewitnesses and experts; documents; real evidence; and a courtroom demonstration. Each piece of evidence contributed a distinctive element to the story.

To learn the Federal Rules of Evidence, we will analyze each of the rules in isolation. It is necessary to understand each rule before trying to comprehend the whole. But as we study the rules, try to imagine how each rule and the evidence associated with it would fit into a full trial like the one described above. Thinking about how each evidentiary rule contributes to a trial will make the rules easier to understand.

E. Circumstantial Evidence.

Before we turn to the rules themselves, let's address a final category of evidence that often confuses students: circumstantial evidence. The Federal Rules of Evidence do not use the phrase "circumstantial evidence," but lawyers and judges frequently use this term. Circumstantial evidence is any evidence that requires the jury to make an inference connecting the evidence with a disputed fact. Direct evidence, in contrast, requires no inferential bridge; it directly establishes a contested fact.

An eyewitness who testifies that she saw the defendant plunge a dagger into the victim's chest offers direct evidence that the defendant stabbed the victim. A witness who testifies that he saw the defendant washing blood off his hands shortly after the victim was stabbed offers circumstantial evidence that the defendant did the stabbing. For the jury to use the latter witness's evidence to conclude that the defendant stabbed the victim, it must assume that (1) the blood came from the victim, and (2) the defendant got the blood on his hands when he stabbed the victim, rather than when he tried to aid the victim or perform some other act. This chain of assumptions makes the hand-washing evidence circumstantial rather than direct evidence that the defendant stabbed the victim.

In examples like this one, the difference between circumstantial and direct evidence is clear. But more ambiguous pieces of evidence muddy the distinction and make the concept of circumstantial evidence confusing. The confusion stems from the fact that these categories of evidence really are not distinct. In actuality, circumstantial and direct evidence are opposite ends of a spectrum rather than separate categories of evidence.

All evidence depends upon some inferences. Our brains function by gathering sense impressions, integrating those impressions into meaningful patterns, and drawing inferences from those patterns. Sometimes this process happens so quickly and intuitively that the inferences are hard to detect; we call the resulting evidence "direct" evidence. Other times, the inferences are more obvious and we call the evidence "circumstantial." But there is no clear line between direct and circumstantial evidence. Think about this example:

> **Example:** A witness in a homicide case testifies that she was standing near the defendant and victim while they argued on a street corner. The witness saw the defendant pull a knife from his pocket, raise the knife in the air, and swing the knife toward the victim. The witness turned away at that point and, fearing for her own safety, ran from the corner. As she ran, the witness heard the victim scream. Fifteen minutes later, the witness returned to the corner and found the victim dead from multiple knife wounds.

Is this witness's testimony direct evidence that the defendant stabbed the victim or circumstantial evidence that the defendant committed that act? Most lawyers and judges would call this witness an eyewitness and her testimony direct evidence of the defendant's guilt. The witness herself may believe that she "saw" the defendant stab the victim. Yet the witness did not actually see that act: She, and anyone who hears her testimony, infers that the defendant stabbed the victim from the facts that (1) the witness saw the knife moving quickly toward the victim, (2) the witness heard the victim scream, and (3) the victim died at that time and place from multiple knife wounds.

There is a circumstantial aspect, in other words, even to this "eyewitness" testimony. The natural inferences we draw from the witness's description, moreover, could be wrong. Perhaps just as the witness ran away, the defendant thought "the heck with it," threw the knife to one side, and ran off in a different direction. The victim may have screamed because he saw the knife, not because the defendant cut him. Maybe an unknown assailant showed up a few seconds later, picked up the knife, and stabbed the victim with it. Stranger things occasionally have happened.

The bottom line is that the distinction between direct and circumstantial evidence is gradual and fuzzy, not sharp and clear. Happily, it's not important to draw a sharp line between these types of evidence because **the distinction has no legal effect**. Here is a standard jury instruction that a trial judge reads to jurors just before they begin their deliberations:

> There are two types of evidence that are generally presented during a trial—direct evidence and circumstantial evidence. Direct evidence is the testimony of a person who asserts or claims to have actual knowledge of a fact, such as an eyewitness. Circumstantial evidence is proof of a chain of facts and circumstances indicating the existence of a fact. The law makes no distinction between the weight or value to be given to either direct or circumstantial evidence. Nor is a greater degree of certainty required of circumstantial evidence than of direct evidence. You should weigh all the evidence in the case.

Lawyers and judges find the terms "direct" and "circumstantial" evidence useful in some discussions, so you will hear them in the courtroom. In particular, trial attorneys sometimes disparage their opponent's evidence as "purely circumstantial," suggesting that the jurors should reject the evidence for that reason. But this is a rhetorical device rather than one based on any legal distinction.

The Rules of Evidence draw no distinction between direct and circumstantial evidence. Circumstantial evidence can support a verdict as effectively as direct evidence does; both civil judgments and criminal convictions may rest entirely on circumstantial proof. Conversely, juries are free to disregard direct evidence. Even eyewitnesses are wrong a surprising amount of the time; our eyes do deceive us on some occasions. This principle is now being vividly demonstrated in the criminal justice system, as hundreds of criminal defendants on death row—many placed there based on the testimony of eyewitnesses—have been exonerated by the circumstantial evidence of DNA matching.[10]

There frequently is no way to prove a person's state of mind, moreover, without using circumstantial evidence; people rarely say exactly what they know or intend when they commit an action. The most common circumstantial inference that we ask jurors to make is to assume that a person intends the consequences of her actions, an assumption that relies on an inferential leap. Since state of mind is an

---

10   For an overview of these cases, see Brandon L. Garrett, Judging Innocence, 108 Colum. L. Rev. 55 (2008).

element in almost every criminal case, prosecutors repeatedly use circumstantial evidence to prove a defendant's guilt.

In practice, it is more important to concentrate on the inferences that link your evidence to the disputed facts than to worry about the artificial distinction between direct and circumstantial proof. The longer the chain of inferences between a piece of evidence and a fact you need to prove, the less likely that the jury will reach the decision you desire. You should always search for evidence that requires the fewest possible inferences, whether you call that evidence "direct" or "circumstantial."

At the same time, you should think about hidden inferences that the jury may need to make even in response to eyewitness testimony and other types of "direct" evidence. Thinking about those inferences will remind you that even direct evidence is fallible; it will also prepare you to cross-examine an opponent's witnesses carefully. Who knows? Maybe a third party really did stab the victim while the "eye" witness ran from the scene.

Quick Summary

 Trial attorneys assemble a case from many types of evidence: oral testimony of fact witnesses, testimony from character witnesses, real evidence, documents, demonstrative evidence, stipulations, and judicial notice. Knowing the names for these types of evidence will make you more comfortable with cases discussing evidentiary rules.

Lawyers and judges often distinguish between circumstantial and direct evidence. These are not separate categories of evidence, but end points on a continuum. All evidence requires a fact finder to make some inferences. We call evidence that requires very quick, intuitive inferences "direct" evidence, and evidence that requires more conscious inferences "circumstantial." The distinction has no legal significance. Parties may introduce either type of evidence, and a verdict may rest entirely on circumstantial evidence. With any type of evidence, a trial attorney should consider the type and number of inferences that a decision maker would need to make to link the evidence to a favorable decision in the case.

3

Four W's of the Federal Rules of Evidence: Why, Who, Where, When

Key Concepts

- Policies Motivating the Federal Rules
- Drafting and Legislative History
- **Rules 101 & 1101:** Scope of the Rules

A. Introduction. Now that we've looked briefly at different types of evidence, it's time to focus on the Federal Rules of Evidence. What are these rules? The rules are **a set of restrictions that federal courts place on attorneys who wish to submit evidence to the trier of fact.**

For the rest of the course, we will discuss the specifics of **what** the Federal Rules of Evidence prescribe. But before examining the "what" of the rules, let's look briefly at four other introductory questions:

- **Why** do courts follow rules of evidence?
- **Who** wrote the Federal Rules of Evidence?
- **Where** do the Federal Rules of Evidence apply?
- **When** do the rules apply?

B. Why? Why do courts impose rules of evidence? Why don't they allow parties to present any and all information the parties believe would be helpful to their case? Why not admit all of the evidence, let opposing counsel point out any flaws, and let the jury decide how much weight to give each piece of evidence?

To some extent, modern evidence codes embrace the generous view implied by those questions. Under many circumstances, the Federal Rules of Evidence allow parties to introduce weak evidence for whatever it may be worth. The rules assume that opposing counsel will expose the flaws in this evidence or that jurors will discredit the evidence on their own. This permissive view guides many of the policy decisions underlying the Federal Rules.

The rules, however, do not give litigants complete control over the evidence they introduce at trial. If they did, wealthy litigants could prolong trials indefinitely, hoping to wear down their opponents. Parties could also introduce evidence that misleads juries in ways that are difficult to counter. Lay jurors, for example, sometimes attach too much weight to "expert" testimony, to lurid crime scene photos, or to evidence of a criminal defendant's prior convictions. Finally, parties might introduce evidence that compromises important social policies, such as our desire to protect confidential communications between spouses. For all of these reasons, evidentiary rules restrict the types of evidence that parties can introduce in court.

The Federal Rules of Evidence try to balance the competing policies identified above. The rules adopt a generous view of admissibility, giving parties as much leeway as possible to prove their cases. But they exclude evidence to achieve one or more of these ends:

Evidentiary Rules Exclude Evidence . . .

1. To protect the jury from misleading information.

2. To eliminate unnecessary delay and promote efficiency.

3. To protect a social interest, such as a confidential relationship.

4. To ensure that evidence is sufficiently reliable.

Advancing these ends, unfortunately, imposes a different type of cost on litigants. Evidentiary rules are too complex for most non-lawyers to use effectively in the courtroom, so parties hire lawyers to represent their interests. The state pays those costs for criminal defendants who face jail time,[1] but most civil litigants pay their own way. As you study the Federal Rules of Evidence, identify the policy objectives that each rule serves. Then consider whether the rule's complexity is necessary. Could the rule be simplified in a way that would make the courtroom more accessible to low-income litigants? Asking these questions will help you understand the competing polices behind the rules, as well as to master the details of those rules.

---

1   Argersinger v. Hamlin, 407 U.S. 25 (1972); Gideon v. Wainwright, 372 U.S. 335 (1963).

C. Who? Who wrote the Federal Rules of Evidence? Knowing the answer to this question will help you understand the sources that judges use to interpret these rules.

Courts initially developed most evidentiary rules as part of the common law. Although Congress and state legislatures supplemented or modified some of those rules, early statutes focused on discrete issues such as privilege. Attempts to produce a complete code of evidence did not succeed until the last third of the twentieth century.

During the 1960s, the Supreme Court appointed an Advisory Committee to draft an evidence code for the federal courts. The committee, which included practitioners, judges, and professors, labored for eight years on the Federal Rules of Evidence before presenting its final draft to the Supreme Court in 1972. The Court accepted those rules and transmitted them to Congress for approval.[2]

Neither the Supreme Court nor the Advisory Committee anticipated that Congress would display much interest in the Federal Rules of Evidence. But after the Watergate crisis, Congress was acutely worried about both questions of privilege and infringements on its power. Up until the 1970s, the rules of evidence had been fashioned by courts as part of the common law, and Congress was willing to defer to the courts' development of those rules. However, members of Congress viewed the codification of the rules as a matter of legislative prerogative. They accordingly held hearings on the proposed Rules of Evidence, drafted committee reports, and made numerous changes. Congress enacted its revised version of the Federal Rules of Evidence on January 2, 1975. Most of those rules still govern the federal courts.

In 1993, the Supreme Court appointed an ongoing Advisory Committee on Evidence Rules to oversee changes to the Federal Rules of Evidence. That committee has proposed numerous amendments, which the Supreme Court has transmitted to Congress for enactment. As with the original rules, Congress sometimes enacts these rules as proposed and sometimes modifies them. In addition, Congress has

---

2   The word "transmit" appears in the Rules Enabling Act, 28 U.S.C. § 2071 et seq. (2017). The Act gives the Supreme Court power to prescribe the Federal Rules of Evidence, as well as other procedural rules, that have been developed by the Judicial Conference. Section 2074 of the Act requires the Court to "transmit" proposed rules to Congress. If Congress does not act within a prescribed time, the rule takes effect. Congress, however, has the power to override the rule by enacting contrary legislation during the consideration period.

also occasionally amended the Rules on its own, without input from the Court or Advisory Committee.[3]

Legislative history illuminating the Federal Rules of Evidence, therefore, comes from two different sources:

- Notes written by the Advisory Committee
- Committee Reports and other legislative history from Congress

The relative importance of these sources depends on who initiated the rule and whether a rule was modified before enactment.

In addition to supplying a useful source for judicial construction of the rules, the Advisory Committee notes for each rule offer a nutshell explanation of that rule. Students and practitioners sometimes find these notes helpful in understanding basic applications of the rules, although the notes' utility has lessened with the passage of time. Today, more than thirty years after adoption of the Federal Rules of Evidence, court decisions more authoritatively address many of the issues originally discussed in the Advisory Committee notes. But you will still see references to the notes in judicial opinions, and this book incorporates some of the most useful insights from those notes.

In 2010, the Advisory Committee approved a stylistic revision of the Federal Rules of Evidence. The Supreme Court transmitted those revisions to Congress in April 2011 and, when Congress took no action, the restyled rules took effect on December 1, 2011. The restyled rules are much easier to read and apply than earlier versions of the rules.

The Advisory Committee notes to the 2011 revision declare that the "changes are intended to be stylistic only." The Committee did not change any operative words in the rules and it had "no intent to change any result in any ruling on evidence admissibility." Judges and lawyers who practiced under the old rules have made the transition to the new language. For you, starting with the new rules in this

---

3   Based on its concerns about evidentiary privileges, Congress also modified the Rules Enabling Act, discussed in the previous footnote, to provide that any "rule creating, abolishing, or modifying an evidentiary privilege shall have no force or effect unless approved by Act of Congress." 28 U.S.C. § 2074(b) (2017). If Congress fails to act on an Advisory Committee proposal concerning one of the evidentiary privileges, therefore, the proposal does not take effect. We discuss evidentiary privileges in Chapters 66–68.

text, invoking the new language will be even more natural. Beware, however, that rule language quoted in pre-2012 judicial opinions may differ from the text of the current, restyled rules.

D. Where? Where do the Federal Rules of Evidence apply? **Rule 101** defines the scope of the rules. That rule states very simply:

RULE 101. Scope; Definitions

(a) Scope. These rules apply to proceedings in <u>United States courts</u>. The specific courts and proceedings to which the rules apply, along with exceptions, are set out in <u>Rule 1101</u>.[4]

This rule establishes that the Federal Rules of Evidence apply broadly to proceedings in federal courts. Rule 1101 confirms this scope by listing the categories of federal courts subject to the rules:

RULE 1101. Applicability of the Rules

(a)   To Courts and Judges. These rules apply to proceedings before:

- United States <u>district courts;</u>
- United States <u>bankruptcy and magistrate</u> judges;
- United States <u>courts of appeals;</u>
- the United States <u>Court of Federal Claims</u>; and
- the district courts of <u>Guam</u>, the <u>Virgin Islands</u>, and the <u>Northern Mariana Islands</u>.

Thus the Federal Rules of Evidence apply to trial and appellate proceedings in almost all federal courts, including those held before bankruptcy judges and magistrates. The rules also apply to the Court of Federal Claims, a trial court that entertains civil suits against the federal government, and to district courts in the U.S. territories.

---

4   As explained in the Study Guide, we guide you through the text of each rule by underlining key phrases and, where appropriate, using indentations and other formatting. We also divide some long rules into multiple sections for closer study. The text we quote from the rules, however, is identical to the official wording. To read the full text of the rules without any special underlining or formatting, see the appendix.

Rules 101 and 1101, curiously, do not mention the Supreme Court of the United States; the Federal Rules of Evidence do not govern proceedings before that court. But this exception isn't very important, because the Supreme Court rarely holds proceedings that require evidentiary proof.[5]

The Federal Rules of Evidence do not apply by their own terms to administrative agencies; neither Rule 101 nor Rule 1101 includes those bodies. This result makes sense because most administrative hearings are less formal than federal court trials; strict application of the rules would exclude types of evidence that agency decision makers rely upon.

Agencies, however, are free to adopt the Federal Rules of Evidence if they choose to do so. Congress, moreover, has extended the Federal Rules to at least one administrative agency, the Tax Court. A provision of the Internal Revenue Code directs that court to apply the Federal Rules of Evidence in certain proceedings.[6]

Even within agencies that have not formally embraced the Federal Rules, decision makers follow some of the principles reflected in those rules. Lawyers practicing before administrative agencies, therefore, need to determine what formal rules of evidence—if any—apply to those hearings. Agency lawyers also must remember that adjudicators may find principles from the Federal Rules of Evidence persuasive when admitting and assessing evidence.

The Federal Rules have also influenced many state courts and legislatures. The rules apply only to federal courts, but more than forty states have adopted state codes that are very similar to the Federal Rules. Most of these states follow the same numbering system as the Federal Rules, aiding comparisons. A few states (such as California) have codified their own evidentiary rules, which differ somewhat from the Federal Rules in language but follow many of the same principles. A few remaining states have never fully codified their rules of evidence; they continue to develop common law rules. But in those states (which include New York and Virginia), judges regard the Federal Rules as powerful persuasive authority, much like the Restatements for other subjects.

---

5   The Court holds trial-type inquiries in only a small category of "Original Actions," such as land disputes between states. In these cases, the Justices appoint a Special Master (often a lower court judge) to receive evidence and submit a recommendation to the Court. Under Supreme Court Rule 17.2, the Federal Rules of Evidence may serve as "guides" in Original Action hearings, but they are not mandatory.

6   26 U.S.C. § 7453 (2017).

In short, by learning the Federal Rules of Evidence, you will learn almost all of the evidence rules for the state courts as well. You will also learn principles that decision makers follow in many administrative agencies.

E. When? The federal courts hear many types of cases. **Rule 1101(b)** confirms that the Federal Rules of Evidence govern all of these disputes, regardless of the underlying claim:

RULE 1101. Applicability of the Rules

(b) To Cases and Proceedings. These rules apply in:

- civil cases and proceedings, including bankruptcy, admiralty, and maritime cases;
- criminal cases and proceedings; and
- contempt proceedings, except those in which the court may act summarily.

The Federal Rules of Evidence thus govern all types of civil, criminal, bankruptcy, admiralty, and maritime cases. They also apply to contempt proceedings when those actions resemble a trial.

Contrary to what many people believe, however, the formal Rules of Evidence do not apply to every stage of adjudication in federal court. The rules apply only to the **main event** of litigation: the trial. Most other stages, even though they are adversarial in nature, need not follow the formal Rules of Evidence.

Rule 1101(b), for example, notes that courts may hold individuals in **summary contempt** without following the Rules of Evidence. Judges have the power to impose summary contempt when they directly witness contemptuous behavior; further adjudication under evidentiary rules is not necessary. **Rule 1101(d)** lists other adjudicatory stages that need not follow the Rules of Evidence:

RULE 1101. Applicability of the Rules

(d) Exceptions. These rules—<u>except</u> for those on <u>privilege</u>—do not apply to the following:

(1) the court's determination, under Rule 104(a), on a <u>preliminary question of fact</u> governing admissibility;

(2) <u>grand-jury</u> proceedings; and

(3) <u>miscellaneous</u> proceedings <u>such as</u>:

- <u>extradition</u> or <u>rendition</u>;
- issuing an <u>arrest warrant</u>, criminal summons, or search warrant;
- a <u>preliminary examination</u> in a criminal case;[7]
- <u>sentencing</u>;
- granting or revoking <u>probation</u> or supervised release; and
- considering whether to release on <u>bail</u> or otherwise.

Let's look quickly at the adjudicatory stages listed in Rule 1101(d). Subsection (1) relieves judges from applying the Rules of Evidence when deciding a **preliminary question of fact**. Judges make this type of determination whenever a party challenges the admissibility of evidence; those rulings may occur either before or during trial. Applying formal evidentiary rules to these preliminary determinations would unnecessarily complicate judicial decision making. A strict application of the rules, in fact, might prevent a judge from examining a piece of evidence to decide whether it was admissible.[8]

Second, Rule 1101(d)(2) recognizes that the Rules of Evidence do not govern **grand jury** proceedings. The prosecutor exerts considerable control over these proceedings, selecting what evidence to present. No judge presides over these inquiries, and in the federal system neither the potential defendant nor any defense attorney attends. Implementing the Federal Rules of Evidence, therefore, would be difficult even if the rules applied to grand jury hearings.

---

7   In a preliminary examination, the court determines whether there is "probable cause" to hold a defendant for trial. A preliminary examination has a similar function to that of a grand jury investigation, but the two are quite different procedurally. A preliminary examination occurs before a judge and is adversarial, while a grand jury meets only with the prosecutor and witnesses called by the prosecutor. The federal courts view the two processes as duplicative, so a defendant who has been indicted by a grand jury has no right to a preliminary examination.

8   We discuss preliminary determinations further in Chapter 34.

The prosecutor's power to choose evidence for the grand jury, moreover, reflects the early stage of the proceedings: When a grand jury returns an indictment, it does not convict a defendant. Granting flexibility at this stage allows prosecutors to build a case; after hearing evidence that might not be admissible in court, the grand jury can subpoena more reliable forms of evidence. On the other hand, the inapplicability of formal evidence rules can create abuses in the grand jury system.

Subsection 1101(d)(3), finally, exempts a large number of **miscellaneous proceedings** from the Federal Rules of Evidence. Some of these, like hearings to obtain search warrants, occur at such an early stage that it would unfairly hamper law enforcement to apply the formal Rules of Evidence. Others, such as sentencing proceedings, properly center on evidence that the Federal Rules would exclude. We will see, for example, that the Federal Rules greatly restrict evidence of a party's previous criminal record. That evidence is central during sentencing; application of the Federal Rules of Evidence would undercut the very nature of a sentencing proceeding.

Note that Rule 1101(d)(3) lists **examples** of miscellaneous proceedings exempt from the Rules of Evidence; it does not provide an exhaustive list of those proceedings. Judges may disregard the formal evidentiary rules during other hearings that resemble the ones listed in subsection 1101(d)(3).

Many stages of adjudication thus fall outside the scope of the Federal Rules of Evidence. Completely ignoring the formal rules during these proceedings, however, could impair judicial decision making. The Rules of Evidence exclude some types of proof (like hearsay) from trial because that information is weak or unreliable. The same considerations argue against relying on that type of proof in other stages of litigation. Many judges, therefore, continue to follow the Federal Rules of Evidence—to the extent practicable—in bail, sentencing, and other miscellaneous proceedings. Some litigants say that judges follow the rules "loosely" in those contexts. Even though the rules do not apply formally in many hearings, a litigant can invoke the rules' policies.

One set of evidentiary rules, however, applies in all federal court proceedings: the rules related to privilege. Section (d) signals this special treatment in its opening words ("except for [the rules] on privilege"), and section **1101(c)** confirms the special status accorded rules of privilege:

RULE 1101. Applicability of the Rules

(c) Rules on Privilege. The rules on <u>privilege</u> apply to <u>all stages</u> of a case or proceeding.

Even when the Federal Rules of Evidence do not apply in their entirety, the rules governing privilege apply. If the privilege rules did not apply to grand jury proceedings, bail hearings, and other proceedings exempted from the federal rules, the confidentiality promised by those privileges would be breached.

Example: A grand jury is investigating securities fraud by George Bluth. The jury subpoenas George's wife, Lucille Bluth, to probe details of George's business activities. Lucille invokes the spousal privilege, which shields a spouse from testifying against the other spouse. The privilege attempts to protect the confidentiality and harmony of marital relationships, as well as to avoid the unseemliness of convicting one spouse through the testimony of the other.

Analysis: The Federal Rules of Evidence do not govern grand jury proceedings. Without the special protection for privilege created by Rule 1101(c), Lucille Bluth could not invoke the spousal privilege; she would be forced to testify against her husband, thwarting the policies that underlie the privilege. Rule 1101(c), however, allows Lucille to invoke the spousal privilege even in a setting where the other Rules of Evidence do not apply.

Where and When Do the Federal Rules of Evidence Apply?
Rules 101 and 1101

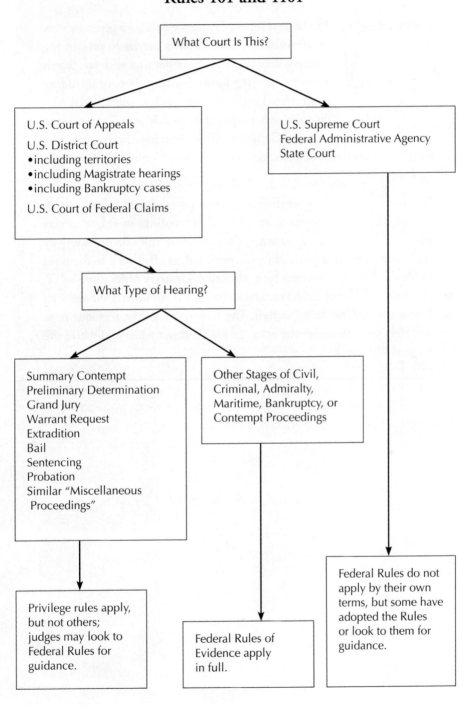

Quick Summary

The Federal Rules of Evidence balance a generous view of admissibility, which allows parties to present the evidence they believe to be important, with safeguards against confusing jurors, wasting time, or intruding on protected social interests such as confidential relationships. Most of the rules were proposed by an Advisory Committee of experts; a few originated in Congress. All of them have been enacted by Congress, sometimes with changes to the Advisory Committee's proposals.

The rules apply broadly to federal courts, although they govern just the "main event" of trial rather than most other proceedings in those courts. The privilege rules, however, apply to all proceedings in federal courts governed by the rules. Even when the remaining rules do not apply by their own terms to a proceeding or court, judges often look to them for guidance. Most of the states have adopted evidentiary codes modeled on the Federal Rules of Evidence, and some federal administrative agencies follow the Federal Rules as well. The flow chart on the previous page will help you remember the essential points about when and where the Federal Rules of Evidence apply.

4

Structure of a Trial

Key Concepts

- Pretrial Motions
- Opening and Closing Statements
- Cases-in-Chief
- Rebuttal and Rejoinder
- Jury Instructions

A. Introduction and Policy. At every trial, the parties tell competing stories. Those stories have a recognizable structure, determined partly by tradition and partly by the lawyers' strategy. The trial as a whole also has a familiar structure, one that allows the parties to present their competing stories without interrupting one another and confusing the jury. Before we look at the Rules of Evidence, let's look at the framework of a typical trial. Understanding the structure of a trial will make it easier to understand how the Rules of Evidence affect each party's ability to tell their story.

B. In the Courtroom. Here is the sequence for a typical jury trial, highlighting the role that evidence plays at each stage in the process. The sequence is the same for civil and criminal cases, with the prosecutor acting as the "plaintiff" in a criminal case.

1. Pretrial Motions. During the months before trial, the parties file motions on a variety of subjects. Some of these motions focus particularly on whether or not information is admissible under the Rules of Evidence. These motions are called **motions in limine**. "In limine" is a Latin phrase meaning "at the threshold"; the phrase signals the pretrial nature of these motions. A prosecutor, for example, may file a motion in limine to exclude evidence of a rape victim's sexual history. A civil plaintiff may file a motion in limine requesting permission to introduce evidence of the defendant's statements during a settlement conference.

Parties may file motions in limine either to exclude an opponent's piece of evidence or to secure permission to introduce a potentially contested piece of their own evidence. These pretrial motions carry at least three tactical advantages.

First, knowing ahead of time what evidence will be admitted and what will be excluded can help an attorney plan trial strategy. A criminal defense attorney who is trying to decide whether to put her client on the stand, for example, may want to know if the judge will admit evidence of her client's criminal record. A motion in limine allows her to make an informed decision about this crucial question before making an opening statement.

Second, because the motion in limine occurs before the trial, the attorneys can make more lengthy and sophisticated legal arguments, even submitting written motions and responses if necessary. Evidentiary arguments during trial usually are brief, taking place in hushed tones at a sidebar conference, with no time for the judge to evaluate fully the arguments on each side.

Third, if an attorney objects to an opponent's evidence at trial and loses, jurors jump to two conclusions: (1) The objecting attorney just lost a legal skirmish with opposing counsel; and (2) The disputed evidence must be particularly important, because it elicited an objection, so it deserves special attention. Neither of these conclusions helps the objecting attorney. If the attorney raises the objection through a motion in limine, the jurors may never know that the attorney attempted to keep them from hearing certain evidence. And if the attorney loses the motion, the jury never sees that defeat.

Two other types of pretrial motions are worth mentioning. Frequently in criminal cases, a defendant will file a **motion to suppress** certain evidence. A party filing a motion to suppress is not arguing that admitting the evidence will violate the Rules of Evidence; instead, she is claiming that the opponent's evidence was illegally obtained. If the judge grants the motion, then under the exclusionary rule, the opponent cannot use that evidence at trial. The legal issues surrounding these motions—which usually concern the legality of a search, a confession, or an identification procedure—are covered in classes on criminal procedure.

Finally, civil litigants may file pretrial motions for summary judgment. These motions argue "that there is no genuine dispute as to any material fact and the movant is entitled to judgment as a matter of law."[1] Since a motion for summary

---

1   Fed.R. Civ. P. 56(a).

judgment refers to evidence in the case, judges often make evidentiary rulings when deciding these motions. If a key piece of the plaintiff's evidence is inadmissible, then summary judgment for the defendant may be appropriate. Conversely, if the defendant's only defenses rest on inadmissible evidence, the judge may grant summary judgment for the plaintiff. Evidentiary issues can dramatically affect a party's fortunes in a summary judgment motion.[2]

2. Jury Selection. Before a trial formally begins, the parties must select a jury. Lawyers commonly call this process voir dire, a phrase that derives from a Middle French oath meaning to "tell the truth" or "give a true verdict." We won't discuss strategies of jury selection in this book, because parties don't present evidence during that process, but choosing the jury is an important stage of every jury trial.

3. Opening Statements. Before presenting evidence, lawyers for each side offer an opening statement to the jury. Each of these statements gives the jury an overview of the evidence that the party intends to present, explains why the jury should discount evidence presented by the opposition, and offers a theme that the jurors can use to organize the evidence they will hear. The best opening statements tell a coherent and compelling story, providing the jurors a framework that they can use to organize all of the evidence they hear at trial.

Psychology research suggests that most people "choose sides" very quickly when they hear about a dispute. Both inside and outside of the courtroom, most of us reach a tentative decision about any controversy before we hear all of the facts. And once we take that tentative position, we view all evidence through the lens of our decision. We pay attention to evidence that supports our initial inclination and discount evidence that conflicts with it.[3]

Because of this tendency, opening statements play a critical role in persuading jurors; each side vies to tell a story that will capture the jury's loyalty as early as possible.[4] But these statements are not empty rhetoric or creative fiction; their

---

2   In addition to these pretrial motions, parties to federal civil cases must note some objections to documents and other trial exhibits before trial begins. Fed.R. Civ. P. 26(a)(3). The parties, however, need not argue those objections before trial unless they choose to do so; the civil procedure rule serves as a filter, clarifying which exhibits will be admitted without objection.

3   For a highly readable summary of this tendency, see Carol Tavris & Elliot Aronson, Mistakes Were Made (But Not By Me): Why We Justify Foolish Beliefs, Bad Decisions, and Hurtful Acts (2007).

4   For good summaries of research on opening statements and jurors, see Paula L. Hannaford et al., The Timing of Opinion Formation by Jurors in Civil Cases: An Empirical Examination, 67 Tenn. L. Rev. 627 (2000); Valerie P. Hans & Krista Sweigert, Jurors' Views of Civil Lawyers: Implications for Courtroom Communication, 68 Ind. L.J. 1297 (1993). Recent studies suggest that opening statements do not, as some trial lore suggests, irrevocably commit

impact depends upon the evidence that the party will introduce. Jurors will discard the framework offered by an opening statement if the party does not produce the evidence promised to support it. An effective opening statement, therefore, (1) tells a compelling story, and (2) reflects the evidence that will unfold during trial.

Good trial lawyers think about their opening statement even during the early stages of assembling evidence for trial. The evidence helps define the story that the lawyer will tell. Conversely, if telling the story shows that part of the tale is missing, the lawyer must find evidence to fill the gap.

The party who bears the burden of proof—the plaintiff in a civil case and the prosecutor in a criminal one—delivers the first opening statement. This position confers a significant advantage: The civil plaintiff or prosecutor has the opportunity to frame the facts first for the jury. The defendant faces the more difficult task of dislodging that framework and persuading the jury to adopt an alternative perspective.

Most often, the defendant's lawyer makes an opening statement immediately after the plaintiff's or prosecutor's opening. Some court rules allow the defense to reserve its opening statement until the prosecution has finished presenting its evidence and the defense is about to present its case. This tactic is effective in some cases but most often lawyers choose to combat the opposition's story immediately with a story of their own.

The opening statements are not evidence, and the lawyers do not call witnesses during their statements. Lawyers, however, may use demonstrative evidence such as charts, slides, and other visual aids during the opening statement. Increasingly, lawyers use these aids to focus the jury's attention and convey a story that persuades visually as well as aurally. Research shows that the brain processes and remembers more information when it receives data simultaneously through visual and auditory channels. Pictures also engage a juror's emotions more effectively than words alone do. For these reasons, lawyers increasingly prepare opening statements that include demonstrative evidence.

4. Plaintiff's/Prosecutor's Case-in-Chief. After completion of opening statements, the plaintiff or prosecutor presents its case to the jury. The "case" consists of all of the evidence—witness testimony, real evidence, documents,

---

jurors to a verdict. The research confirms, however, that these statements are important in shaping jurors' views and offering a framework to interpret the evidence.

and demonstrations—that comprise the plaintiff/prosecutor's case. Usually the party decides the order in which it will present its evidence, although the judge occasionally influences that order. The examination and cross-examination of witnesses follow particular rules, which we will study in Chapter 15. Other rules, which we examine in Chapter 5, govern the process of objecting to evidence and defending admission of that evidence.

At the close of a civil plaintiff's case, the defendant will move for judgment as a matter of law.[5] Similarly, a criminal defendant will move for a judgment of acquittal at the close of the prosecutor's case-in-chief.[6] The judge will grant these motions only if, even after considering the plaintiff's or prosecutor's evidence in the best possible light, no reasonable jury could find for that side. Because of this high standard, these motions usually fail.

5. Defendant's Case-in-Chief or Case-in-Defense. The defendant then presents its case to the jury, calling witnesses and introducing evidence. Criminal defendants occasionally choose not to present a defense. The prosecutor's high burden of proof in a criminal case, combined with the fact that the judge will instruct the jury that a criminal defendant has no obligation to testify or otherwise present a defense, makes this a viable option. Criminal defendants are most likely to choose this route when offering evidence would open them to damaging cross-examination or impeachment, concepts we will explore in depth later in the course.

The rules that govern examination, cross-examination, objections, and offers of proof in the plaintiff's case also apply to the defendant's case.

6. Plaintiff's/Prosecutor's Case-in-Rebuttal. Some simple trials conclude after one round of proof, but many trials include at least some rebuttal evidence. In its rebuttal case, the plaintiff or prosecutor rebuts evidence introduced by the defense. The plaintiff or prosecutor may call new witnesses or introduce new evidence during this phase, but those witnesses and evidence must focus on issues raised by the defense. The plaintiff/prosecutor, for example, might introduce evidence to discredit one of the defendant's witnesses; we will study several rules governing this process later in the course.

---

5   Fed. R. Civ. P. 50. Some lawyers and judges refer to this motion as one for a "directed verdict," but the more modern terminology is "judgment as a matter of law." A 1991 amendment to the Federal Rules of Civil Procedure substituted the latter phrase for the older "directed verdict."

6   Fed. R. Crim. P. 29.

Apart from the narrower focus of the rebuttal case, this phase resembles the case-in-chief. The same rules govern examination and cross-examination of witnesses, objections to evidence, and offers of proof.

7. Defendant's Case-in-Rebuttal or Case-in-Rejoinder. Just as the plaintiff may respond to the defendant's case-in-chief, the defendant may respond to the plaintiff's rebuttal. This phase may also include new witnesses and evidence but, once again, it must respond to the new evidence produced in the preceding phase rather than simply revisiting the defendant's original case.

8. Further Rebuttal and Rejoinder. The trial judge has discretion to allow further rounds of rebuttal and rejoinder, although these usually are unnecessary. If these rounds occur, each one will be progressively narrower than the last, as the parties focus on evidence introduced in the preceding phase.

9. Closing Statements. Both the plaintiff/prosecutor and defendant have the opportunity to sum up their arguments in a closing statement. Closing statements, like opening ones, offer the jury a framework for assembling the evidence and delivering the verdict that the party favors. Lawyers do not call witnesses or introduce evidence during the closing statement but, as in the opening statement, they often use demonstrative evidence. They may also display documents and real evidence admitted during the trial. Many lawyers find real and demonstrative evidence particularly effective during closing argument. The jury is tired by the end of trial and needs well defined concepts to focus their attention. Visual aids, accompanied by an oral statement, often accomplish that goal.

10. Instructing the Jury. Judges traditionally instruct the jury after closing statements. Some judges, however, now instruct the jury before closing statements. Others provide a brief set of instructions to the jury at the beginning of the trial, giving them a general overview of the applicable law. If the judge provides this overview, he or she will also give the jury a more complete set of instructions at the end of the trial.

Most instructions to the jury include some directions about how to handle items of evidence. As we'll soon see, the rules allow the jury to use many types of evidence for one purpose but not another. Similarly, some pieces of evidence are admissible against one plaintiff or defendant, but not against other coplaintiffs or codefendants. Throughout the course, we will discuss ways in which judges attempt to shape the jury's use of evidence through instructions.

Judges deliver many of these evidentiary instructions during the trial itself. If evidence is admitted for one purpose but not another, for example, the judge usually explains that to the jury when the evidence is admitted. If the evidence is sufficiently important, however, the judge may repeat the instruction at the end of trial.

11. Deliberation. After receiving instructions, the jury retires to deliberate. Judges exercise discretion over what evidence, if any, the jurors may take to the jury room. Judges often allow the jury to take into the jury room real and documentary evidence that has been admitted into evidence. Sometimes they permit the jury to take demonstrative evidence, if it is particularly helpful in organizing the facts of a complex case and is not too argumentative. Juries, of course, cannot take witnesses with them into the jury room. If the jurors have difficulty recalling an important piece of oral testimony, they may ask the judge for a transcript of that testimony. Usually the judge responds to this type of request by calling the jury back into the courtroom and asking the court reporter to read the requested testimony back to them. Occasionally, the judge will send portions of the transcript itself into the jury room.

12. Verdict. The trial concludes with the jury's verdict and the court's entry of judgment on the verdict. Parties in both civil and criminal cases may file a variety of post-verdict motions, and disappointed parties (except for the prosecutor in a criminal case) may file an appeal. If a criminal trial ends in conviction, the judge will also hold a hearing to determine the defendant's sentence. We will not, however, devote much attention to these post-trial actions in this book.

This outline, like most of the examples we will consider in this text, assumes that the parties have elected a jury trial. Trials in which the judge is the decision maker follow the same sequence, except that there is no jury selection, no jury instructions, and no jury deliberation. After closing statements, the judge takes the case under advisement until she is ready to announce a judgment. The Federal Rules of Evidence govern both bench and jury trials, although some rules apply differently to the two.

Quick Summary

Most trials follow a common structure. Before trial, the judge entertains motions from the parties. Pretrial motions to exclude evidence often are called "motions in limine." Just before trial, the parties select a jury. The trial itself consists of opening statements, presentation of evidence, closing statements, jury instructions, deliberation, and verdict.

For opening statements, presentation of evidence, and closing statements, the plaintiff or prosecutor usually goes first. After each side has presented its case-in-chief, the parties may take turns presenting additional evidence in phases called "rebuttal" and "rejoinder." Evidence offered in these phases must focus exclusively on evidence presented in the preceding phase.

The opening and closing statements are not evidence, but they give counsel a critical opportunity to frame the evidence for the jury. Juries respond best to a simple, compelling story supported by evidence fitting clearly within the announced framework.

5

Raising and Resolving Evidentiary Objections

Key Concepts

- **Rule 103:** Objections and Motions to Strike
- Timeliness
- Specificity
- Offers of Proof
- Repeated Objections
- Jury's Presence
- **Rule 105:** Limiting Instructions
- Appellate Review

A. Introduction. The Federal Rules of Evidence trust the adversary system to identify inadmissible evidence. Trial judges rarely point out objectionable evidence on their own. Instead, judges rely on the parties to raise objections about an opponent's evidence.

In the last chapter, we discussed two pretrial motions that parties use to challenge an opponent's evidence: motions in limine and motions to suppress. These motions allow a party to attack—or defend—key pieces of evidence before trial. Litigants, however, continue to raise most of their evidentiary objections at trial.

In this chapter, we'll examine how parties object to evidence during trial, as well as how they defend the admissibility of challenged evidence. We'll also discuss how trial judges respond to evidentiary disputes. Finally, we'll consider the finality of most evidentiary rulings made at trial. The Federal Rules of Evidence allow very limited review of evidentiary rulings; appellate courts rarely reverse a trial judge's rulings on evidence.

These procedural rules set the stage for our exploration of the substantive Rules of Evidence. The procedural constraints also demonstrate why good litigators must thoroughly master those rules. Trial lawyers challenge and defend evidence on the spot in the courtroom, with few opportunities for a replay. A lawyer who knows the rules well, and who can defend a position persuasively, often carries the day.

B. Disputing and Defending Evidence. Rule 103 outlines the process that parties use to dispute and defend evidence at trial. The rule does so, however, from the standpoint of an appellate court. This perspective seems odd at first, but it reflects the strong deference that appellate judges show toward evidentiary rulings. Rule 103 outlines the procedural steps that an attorney must take at trial before a reviewing court will even consider the attorney's evidentiary objections on appeal. These hurdles to appellate review define the process that lawyers use to challenge and defend evidence at trial.

Reflecting its appellate perspective, Rule 103 opens with language referring to an appellate court's potential finding of evidentiary error on the part of a trial court:

Rule 103. Rulings on Evidence

(a) **Preserving a Claim of Error.** A party may claim error in a ruling to admit or exclude evidence only if . . . .

The rule then addresses four aspects of evidentiary disputes: (1) raising objections; (2) defending evidence; (3) maintaining objections; and (4) shielding the jury. We'll address each of those elements in turn.

1. Raising Objections. After the introductory language quoted above, Rule 103(a)(1) describes the process of challenging an opponent's evidence:

Rule 103. Rulings on Evidence

(a) **Preserving a Claim of Error.** A party may claim error in a ruling to admit or exclude evidence only . . .

    (1) if the ruling <u>admits</u> evidence, a party, on the record:

        (A) <u>timely objects or moves to strike</u>; and

> **(B)** states the <u>specific ground</u>, unless it was apparent from the context; . . . .

This subsection makes three important points about challenging evidence. **First,** the rule establishes **two mechanisms** for disputing evidence at trial: by objection and by a motion to strike. Both formats claim that evidence is inadmissible; they differ only in when they are made. A lawyer registers an objection before the opponent introduces a potentially inadmissible item into evidence. If the prosecutor calls an incompetent witness, for example, the defense will object to that witness testifying. Similarly, if the defense asks a witness an irrelevant question, the prosecutor will object to the question. An objection occurs before the potentially offending evidence emerges fully.

Motions to strike occur after disputed evidence has already entered the record. A witness, for example, may answer an irrelevant question so quickly that opposing counsel has no time to object. Opposing counsel will then move to strike the response. Or a witness may answer an innocuous question by raising an impermissible subject. Once again, opposing counsel will move to strike the response. Evidence, finally, may appear relevant when first introduced but lose its relevance in light of further trial developments. The opposing party may move to strike the evidence when its irrelevance emerges.

Second, Rule 103(a)(1) requires parties to challenge evidence in a **timely** manner. The rule does not define timeliness, but the word is well understood in practice: Lawyers must object to evidence as soon as the ground for objection is known or reasonably should be known. If a trial attorney fails to object promptly, an appellate court will not consider the evidentiary challenge:

> **Example:** The government indicted Guillermo Cerda Rodriguez for importing cocaine into the United States. At trial, the prosecutor introduced a record of telephone calls made from Rodriguez's residence; these showed numerous calls to Venezuela, where the cocaine originated. The trial judge admitted these records just before the parties rested, then released the jurors for the day. After the jurors had left the courtroom, the prosecutor and defense counsel discussed another matter with the judge. After concluding that discussion, defense counsel objected to introduction of the phone records as violating a provision of the hearsay rules.

Analysis: This objection—occurring after the government had introduced its evidence, the jury had left the courtroom, and the parties had discussed another issue—came far too late. An appellate court ultimately agreed that, under the circumstances of this case, introduction of the phone records violated the hearsay rules. Those records, moreover, were damaging to Rodriguez's defense. But the court affirmed Rodriguez's conviction despite the admission of this incriminating evidence because his attorney objected to the records too belatedly.[1]

The timeliness requirement allows trial judges to rule on objections before the jurors learn about potentially inadmissible evidence. Prompt objections also allow opponents to try to cure any evidentiary defect. Some courts refer explicitly to this policy when deciding whether an objection or motion to strike was timely. In a recent civil case, for example, the Court of Appeals for the Seventh Circuit observed:

"[A]n objection can still be deemed 'timely' if it is raised within a sufficient time after the proffer of testimony so as to allow the district court an adequate opportunity to correct any error."[2]

Careful trial attorneys, however, avoid pushing this envelope; they monitor an opponent's evidence closely and register any objection as soon as possible.

Finally, Rule 103(a)(1) requires trial lawyers to state "the **specific** ground" for any objection. The specificity requirement gives both the judge and opponent notice about the basis for an objection. The opponent can try to cure any defect in the evidence and, if that is not possible, the judge can more easily rule on admissibility.

If a trial attorney fails to offer a specific ground for an objection, an appellate court will not consider the evidentiary challenge:

Example: While standing outside Papa Don's tavern, Brian McGee struck Matthew Owen on the head. Owen suffered serious injury and sued the owner of Papa Don's, claiming that McGee worked as a bouncer for the tavern. At trial, the defendant cross-examined one of Owen's witnesses

---

1   United States v. Benavente Gomez, 921 F.2d 378, 383–86 (1st Cir. 1990).

2   Jones v. Lincoln Elec. Co., 188 F.3d 709, 727 (7th Cir. 1999).

about whether Owen had been drinking that evening. Owen's attorney objected to this line of questioning, saying, "I'm going to object to that, judge." The magistrate denied the objection and the jury returned a verdict for the defense.

Analysis: Counsel's generic objection failed to focus the magistrate's attention on any flaw in the question, leading to denial of the objection. Similarly, this generic objection failed to preserve any ground for appeal. Without a more specific objection, the appellate court refused to consider any error in the testimony.[3]

If an attorney sees multiple grounds for objecting to evidence, then the attorney should raise each of those specifics. Raising one specific objection will not prompt the trial judge to consider other grounds and will not preserve those other grounds for appeal.

Example: Customs Inspector Sergio Espinoza was stationed at Los Angeles International Airport. As he watched passengers disembark from a flight that originated in Bogota, Colombia, he noticed Jaime Leon Gomez-Norena, who "walked aimlessly down the concourse with a carry-on bag in his hand and a 'dumbfounded' look on his face." After talking with Gomez-Norena, Espinoza concluded that he fit the standard drug courier profile. Espinoza alerted other agents, who found cocaine in Gomez-Norena's bag. The government arrested Gomez-Norena and charged him with possession of the cocaine with intent to distribute. At trial, Espinoza testified about his conversations with the other airport agents, in which he identified Gomez-Norena as fitting the drug courier profile. Gomez-Norena's attorney objected to this testimony as hearsay and improper character evidence [two grounds that we will study later in the course]. The judge overruled these objections and a jury convicted Gomez-Norena.

Analysis: On appeal, Gomez-Norena abandoned his hearsay and character evidence objections, but argued that admission of this testimony was unfairly prejudicial under a different provision of the Rules of Evidence, Rule 403. The appellate court noted serious problems with admitting evidence of drug courier profiles, suggesting that it might have been sympathetic to

---

3   Owen v. Patton, 925 F.2d 1111, 1114 (8th Cir. 1991).

> Gomez-Norena's Rule 403 claim. But the court refused to consider that issue further, because Gomez-Norena's attorney had not raised a 403 objection in the trial court.[4]

The specificity rule also requires attorneys to designate the portion of a document or witness's testimony to which they object. If the entire document or testimony is objectionable, the attorney can object to the whole. But if just one part of the evidence is inadmissible, the attorney must specify that portion.

Rule 103 allows attorneys to forego specificity if the basis of an objection is "apparent from the context." In practice, most trial judges understand the grounds of an objection without further elaboration. Good litigators, however, always add at least one word or phrase to an objection; this assures the judge's understanding and preserves the issue for appeal. Rather than simply declare "objection" to a witness's testimony, an effective trial attorney will use words like "objection, hearsay" or "objection, beyond the scope." If the judge calls for more information, the attorney will cite specific rules and judicial authority.

2. Defending Evidence. After outlining the process for raising objections, Rule 103(a) turns to the process of defending evidence. When one party objects to introduction of evidence, the opponent makes an **offer of proof** to show the judge what the evidence entails. If the opponent fails to make this offer, then he waives any objection on appeal:

RULE 103. Rulings on Evidence

(a) **Preserving a Claim of Error.** A party may claim error in a ruling to admit or exclude evidence only . . .

    (2)   if the ruling <u>excludes</u> evidence, a party informs the court of its <u>substance</u> by an <u>offer of proof</u>, unless the substance was apparent from the context.

Like the timeliness and specificity requirements, the offer of proof gives the judge information needed to rule promptly and correctly on admissibility.

---

4   United States v. Gomez-Norena, 908 F.2d 497, 500–01 (9th Cir. 1990).

Judges have discretion to determine the form in which an attorney makes the offer of proof. Sometimes counsel simply describes the evidence that would be introduced, such as the answer a witness would give in response to the challenged question. Other times, an attorney may demonstrate with the witness the actual questions that would be asked and answered.[5]

A formal offer of proof is unnecessary if, as Rule 103(a)(2) provides, "the substance" of the evidence is "apparent from the context." Careful attorneys, however, usually make at least a brief offer of proof to buttress their argument for admissibility and to clarify the record for appeal.

3. Maintaining Objections. At common law, even a specific and timely objection wasn't enough to preserve an evidentiary point for appeal. If the judge overruled an objection, counsel had to announce an "exception" to that ruling. The exception confirmed that the attorney intended to preserve the issue for appeal.

Rule 103(b) abolishes the need for exceptions. Once trial counsel has made a specific and timely objection, and the judge has overruled the objection, the issue is preserved for appeal:

> ## RULE 103. Rulings on Evidence
>
> **(b) Not Needing to Renew an Objection or Offer of Proof.** Once the court <u>rules definitively</u> on the record—either before or at trial—a party <u>need not renew</u> an objection or offer of proof to preserve a claim of error for appeal.

The key phrase in this sentence is "rules definitively." When a litigant objects to evidence during trial, the judge usually disposes immediately of the issue. That decision allows the trial to continue and preserves any further arguments for appeal.

When a party files a motion in limine, the judge often "rules definitively" on that motion before trial. This is a major reason why litigants file these motions—to obtain decisions on key evidentiary issues before finalizing their trial strategies.[6]

---

5   Rule 103(c) explicitly refers to this option, noting that the court "may direct that an offer of proof be made in question-and-answer form."

6   For further discussion of motions in limine, see Chapter 4.

If a judge rules on a motion in limine, the losing party need not repeat any objection or offer of proof at trial. Rule 103(b)'s language preserves the issue for appeal without any further objection.

But judges sometimes defer ruling on a motion in limine, concluding that admissibility of the evidence will depend on other developments at trial. Under these circumstances, the judge has not ruled definitively, and the parties must renew their objections and offers of proof at trial.

4. Shielding the Jury. When litigants challenge the admissibility of evidence at trial, jurors might witness the debate, and they might be confused or misled by the legal arguments the litigants make to the judge. Rule 103(d) therefore requires the court to decide evidentiary issues in a manner that shields the jury, as much as possible, from hearing about inadmissible evidence:

RULE 103. Rulings on Evidence

(d) Preventing the Jury from Hearing Inadmissible Evidence. To the extent practicable, the court must conduct a jury trial so that <u>inadmissible evidence</u> is <u>not suggested to the jury</u> by any means.

Attorneys usually note their initial objection in the jury's presence, and the judge will rule on simple objections without further discussion or offers of proof. If an objection requires further explanation, attorneys will "approach the bench" for a sidebar to discuss the issues with the judge.

This prevents the jury from overhearing the discussion. If a more detailed argument is necessary, or if an attorney presents a detailed offer of proof, the judge will dismiss the jury from the courtroom or have the attorneys argue the point in chambers.

C. Response by the Judge. We've seen how the parties challenge and defend evidence. What options does a judge have in responding to evidentiary challenges? If the judge agrees with an evidentiary objection, she will **sustain** the objection and exclude the evidence. Conversely, if the judge disagrees with the objection, she will **overrule** it and admit the evidence.

The judge also has several options that fall between these two extremes. The judge may admit some of the challenged evidence, while excluding other portions. In the case of written documents, the judge may direct a party to **redact** (eliminate) portions of the document violating an evidentiary rule, while admitting the rest of the document. Similarly, the judge may direct the attorneys to avoid certain topics or questions in their examination of a witness, while allowing the witness to testify on other matters.

If inadmissible evidence has inadvertently reached the jury's ears, the judge may issue a **curative** instruction. This type of instruction tells the jury to disregard evidence, sometimes explaining why the evidence is misleading or inappropriate to consider. For example, a witness may volunteer irrelevant information before opposing counsel has time to object. In addition to sustaining counsel's motion to strike the irrelevant response, the judge will issue a curative instruction telling the jury to disregard the witness's answer.

Judges possess one other, particularly important tool for responding to evidentiary disputes: admission of evidence for limited purposes. As we'll see, many Rules of Evidence permit parties to introduce evidence for one purpose but not for others. Similarly, in cases involving multiple plaintiffs or defendants, evidence may be admissible against one plaintiff or defendant but not against others. Under these circumstances judges will admit evidence for specific, limited purposes. The judge usually gives the jury a **limiting instruction** to explain that the evidence may be used for some purposes but not for others. **Rule 105** governs limiting instructions:

> ## RULE 105. Limiting Evidence That Is Not Admissible Against Other Parties or for Other Purposes
>
> If the court admits evidence that is admissible against a party or for a purpose—but not against another party or for another purpose—the court, <u>on timely request,</u> <u>must</u> restrict the evidence to its proper scope and <u>instruct the jury</u> accordingly.

Note that Rule 105 uses the word "must." If evidence is admissible only for limited purposes or against particular parties, and a party requests an instruction making those limits clear, the judge must give that instruction. This is one of the few circumstances in which a judge does not have discretion over evidentiary matters.

1. Limiting Instructions in Practice. Here is a simple example of a case that used a limiting instruction to prevent a jury from considering irrelevant aspects of a piece of real evidence:

> **Example:** Floyd Raney was repairing a leaky pipe in the basement of an uninhabited house that the landlord was readying for tenants. When Raney lit his propane torch to solder the pipe, gas vapors in the house exploded; Raney was severely injured. Investigation showed that a gas control valve on the house's furnace had allowed gas to escape into the house. Raney sued the manufacturer of the furnace, Honeywell, claiming that the control valve was defectively designed.
>
> At trial, Raney introduced the defective valve from the house's furnace. The valve happened to contain a loose screw, which rattled when the valve was shaken. The parties agreed that the screw was irrelevant to the explosion. Honeywell asked the judge to remove the screw before admitting the valve into evidence, so that the jury would not be misled into thinking the valve was broken or defective because of this extraneous screw.
>
> **Analysis:** The judge denied Honeywell's motion, concluding that the valve should be admitted in its original condition. But the judge gave the jury a limiting instruction, telling them that the valve was admitted to show its condition at the time of the accident and that they should "disregard the loose screw because it had nothing to do with the cause of the explosion." The appellate court upheld the judge's decision and his use of a limiting instruction in this case.[7]

Judges also use limiting instructions to explain the role of demonstrative evidence:

> **Example:** The government charged John Scales, the business manager of a labor union, with embezzling union funds. At trial, the prosecution's case included 161 exhibits, the testimony of eight coconspirators who had pled guilty to the embezzlement, and testimony of seventeen other witnesses. To summarize this evidence, the government prepared a series of charts outlining the charges in the indictment and the evidence supporting each charge. Scales objected to these charts as unfairly argumentative.

---

7   Raney v. Honeywell, Inc., 540 F.2d 932, 935–36 (8th Cir. 1976).

> **Analysis:** The trial judge admitted the government's charts but gave the jury a limiting instruction to explain that the charts were not themselves evidence. The court of appeals affirmed this practice, noting that "[t]here is an established tradition . . . that permits a summary of evidence to be put before the jury with proper limiting instructions.[8]

We will see many other examples of limiting instructions as we study other Rules of Evidence.

2. Do Limiting Instructions Work? Many lawyers, clients, and judges are skeptical about the impact of limiting instructions. The notion of using evidence for one purpose but not others is difficult for jurors to understand. Even if jurors understand the instruction, it may be impossible for them to segregate their thoughts in the way that a limiting instruction directs. This is especially true when the disputed evidence has a strong emotional appeal.

Many lawyers, in fact, believe that limiting instructions often do more harm than good. The judge's instruction may simply highlight the impermissible purpose for the jury. For example, did the instruction telling the *Honeywell* jury to ignore the loose screw in the gas valve prevent the jury from drawing unfounded conclusions from that screw? Or did it simply focus the jury's attention on a small rattle they might otherwise have ignored?

Several empirical studies raise serious questions about the effectiveness of limiting instructions.[9] Those studies confirm the suspicion of many trial lawyers that limiting instructions often have a perverse effect: They may increase a juror's attention to the limited evidence rather than confining use of the evidence. Nonetheless, trial judges continue to rely on limiting instructions and appellate courts continue to approve them. As many courts have observed, much of the jury system depends upon the belief that jurors will follow instructions. Discarding that belief would raise serious questions about the system itself.

---

8   United States v. Scales, 594 F.2d 558, 561–64 (6th Cir. 1979).

9   See, e.g., Joel D. Lieberman & Jamie Arndt, Understanding the Limits of Limiting Instructions: Social Psychological Explanations for the Failures of Instructions to Disregard Pretrial Publicity and Other Inadmissible Evidence, 6 Psychol. Pub. Pol'y & L. 677 (2000); Roselle L. Wissler & Michael J. Saks, On the Inefficacy of Limiting Instructions: When Jurors Use Prior Conviction Evidence to Decide on Guilt, 9 Law & Hum. Behav. 37 (1985); J. Alexander Tanford, Thinking About Elephants: Admonitions, Empirical Research and Legal Policy, 60 UMKC L. Rev. 645 (1992). The same research demonstrates the limited utility of curative instructions.

Given the potential harm of limiting instructions, attorneys sometimes forego asking for them. Deciding whether to request a limiting instruction requires a careful calculation of whether the instruction will help the jury use evidence in permissible ways or will draw jurors' attention to harmful evidence. Attorneys may strike that balance differently in different cases.

D. On Appeal. To preserve an evidentiary objection for appeal, trial attorneys must follow the procedural steps described above. Even if an attorney complies with all of these requirements, appellate courts rarely reverse trial decisions based on evidentiary issues alone. There are two reasons for this.

First, appellate courts apply an **abuse of discretion** standard to most claims of evidentiary error. Some Rules of Evidence explicitly give the trial judge discretion to admit or exclude evidence. Others require the judge to apply a general principle to the facts of the case. Appellate judges are reluctant to reverse either type of decision, because the trial judge was more familiar with the evidence, evolving trial, and juror reactions. Even if the appellate judges believe they would have decided the issue differently at trial, they frequently defer to the trial judge's decision.

Second, Rule 103 allows appellate judges to reverse a trial decision for evidentiary error only if the error affected a "substantial right" of one of the parties. The very first sentence of Rule 103(a) declares:

RULE 103. Rulings on Evidence

(a) **Preserving a Claim of Error.** A party may claim error in a ruling to admit or exclude evidence only if the error <u>affects a substantial right</u> of the party . . . .

An evidentiary ruling affects a party's "substantial right" only if there is a reasonable probability that, if the judge had made the correct ruling, the outcome of the case would have been different. Since most evidentiary issues affect only a small part of the trial, it is unusual for any one mistake to affect the verdict. Therefore, even when an appellate court recognizes a trial judge's abuse of discretion in applying an evidentiary rule, the error rarely leads to reversal. Under Rule 103(a), most evidentiary missteps constitute **harmless error**.

The "substantial right" standard applies even when an appellate court reviews an evidentiary decision **de novo**. Appellate panels apply this standard, rather than the abuse of discretion one, when a trial judge misinterprets a Rule of Evidence or applies the wrong legal standard at trial. These instances are quite rare. Even when they occur, the error must have affected a substantial right of the party to produce reversal.

If a party fails to preserve an evidentiary objection at trial, appellate review of the challenge is even more limited. Under these circumstances, Rule 103(e) allows reversal only for "plain error":

RULE 103. Rulings on Evidence

(e) **Taking Notice of Plain Error.** A court may take notice of a <u>plain error</u> affecting a <u>substantial right</u>, even if the claim of error was <u>not properly preserved</u>.

Courts rarely find plain errors, especially in civil lawsuits. To reverse on this ground, courts require an error that is "clear and obvious under current law; . . . affects [a party's] substantial rights; and . . . would seriously affect the fairness, integrity or public reputation of judicial proceedings if left uncorrected."[10]

The limited appellate review of all evidentiary errors, even if a party made a timely objection, has three important consequences for students and practitioners:

First, appellate opinions on evidentiary issues often are less definite than decisions on other legal points. If an appellate panel concludes that a trial judge did not abuse his discretion in admitting a particular piece of evidence, a second trial judge might admit a similar piece of evidence without risking reversal. Counsel in the second case, however, could still persuade the judge to exclude the evidence. The first judge might have been **wrong**, even though he did not abuse his discretion. Appellate rulings on evidence give lawyers significant leeway for thoughtful advocacy.

---

10   Tompkins v. Cyr, 202 F.3d 770, 779 (5th Cir. 2000). This language draws upon the Supreme Court's description of plain error in a variety of criminal contexts. See, e.g., United States v. Olano, 507 U.S. 725 (1993). Other courts use different language to describe "plain error" under Rule 103(e), but all apply a rigorous standard that appellants rarely meet.

Second, evidentiary battles in practice are won and lost at the trial level. Trial lawyers must recognize evidentiary problems promptly and register appropriate objections. They usually must argue those positions on the spot, citing appropriate rules and case authorities. If the judge rules for an opponent, key evidence may be admitted or excluded, with little opportunity for appellate review.

Finally, students who seek to be litigators must internalize the Rules of Evidence as completely as possible. Effective litigators know the language, number, and policies of each rule. They are able to recognize when a rule applies, cite the rule by name or number, and make intelligent arguments about the rule on the spot. If you lose an evidentiary point in the courtroom, it is of little practical use to go back to your office, look up the rule, and craft a devastating response in your appellate brief: By then, nobody will be paying any attention.

Quick Summary

Rule 103 outlines the process for contesting evidence at trial: (1) Parties raise evidentiary challenges through objections or motions to strike; either type of challenge must be timely and specific. (2) The party introducing the disputed evidence responds with an offer of proof. (3) Once the judge rules definitively, the parties need not renew any objections or offers of proof. (4) To the extent possible, this process of evidentiary objections and offers of proof occurs outside the jury's hearing, so that jurors will not be exposed to inadmissible evidence.

A judge may respond to an evidentiary objection by overruling the objection, thus admitting the evidence; sustaining the objection (excluding the evidence); admitting a redacted or restricted form of the evidence; or admitting evidence for limited purposes or against limited parties. Under the latter circumstances, **Rule 105** requires the judge to issue a limiting instruction if a party requests that relief. Limiting instructions, however, are a double-edged sword. Under some circumstances they may draw the jury's attention to damaging evidence rather than restricting consideration of that evidence.

Appellate courts review evidentiary issues only if the complaining party complied with the procedural steps outlined above. In addition, appellate judges use a lenient "abuse of discretion" standard to review most evidentiary decisions. An appellate court will reverse a judgment on evidentiary grounds, finally, only if the trial judge's erroneous decision affected a "substantial right of the party."

Test Your Understanding

To assess your understanding of the material in this chapter, click here to take a quiz, or go to the Quizzes module from the eBook on your eProducts bookshelf.

6

Relevance

Key Concepts

- **Rule 402:** Evidence Must Be Relevant
- **Rule 401:** Defines Relevance
- Stipulations
- Unrelated Misdeeds
- Negative Evidence
- Hindsight
- Opening the Door

A. Introduction. The fundamental rule of evidence is relevance: Only relevant evidence is admissible. This requirement serves two different, but equally important purposes. First, the rule limits the amount of time that the parties, lawyers, jurors, and judge devote to the case. No one wants to waste time delving into extraneous matters. Second, the relevance requirement focuses the jurors on facts that the law deems important. By attempting to withhold irrelevant information—such as the parties' relative wealth—from the courtroom, we increase the odds that jurors will decide the case under the legal principles governing the dispute.[1]

B. The Rules. Rule 402 articulates the fundamental principle that only relevant evidence is admissible.

---

1   In many cases, of course, irrelevant matters cannot be kept from the jurors. A party's race, for example, often is visible. And litigants sometimes try to signal information about other irrelevant characteristics, such as an opponent's wealth, thinking that the information may influence the jury's decision. The extent to which irrelevant factors influence jury decision making is a fascinating branch of psychology research, one that is pursued in courses like Law and Psychology.

RULE 402. General Admissibility of Relevant Evidence

Relevant evidence is admissible unless any of the following provides otherwise:

- the United States Constitution;
- a federal statute;
- these rules; or
- other rules prescribed by the Supreme Court.

Irrelevant evidence is not admissible.

Note that, in addition to stating the basic relevance requirement, Rule 402 displays the Federal Rules' liberal approach to admissibility. If evidence **is relevant**, then it is **admissible unless** a specific rule, statute, or constitutional provision bars its admissibility. Relevance, therefore, is an essential gateway to the courtroom. If evidence fails the relevance test, the court cannot admit it. But if evidence is relevant, then it has cleared the first obstacle on the path to admissibility.

What is "relevant"? **Rule 401** complements Rule 402 by defining relevance.

RULE 401. Test for Relevant Evidence

Evidence is relevant if:

(a) it has <u>any tendency</u> to make a <u>fact more or less probable</u> than it be would without the evidence; and

(b) the fact is <u>of consequence</u> in determining the action.

As the underlining suggests, the Federal Rules' definition of relevance turns on three key phrases:

- any tendency
- more or less probable
- of consequence

1. "Any Tendency" to Make a Fact "More or Less Probable." These two phrases establish a very low threshold for relevance. The phrase **"more or less probable"** indicates that an individual piece of evidence can be relevant even if it does not conclusively establish any fact on its own. As many commentators have noted, pieces of evidence are like bricks. Together the bricks make up a wall, but each individual brick may contribute just a fraction of the wall's strength. A piece of evidence is relevant as long as it makes some fact of consequence "more or less probable." The "more" or "less" can be very slight indeed.

The words **"any tendency"** underscore this lenient standard. By stating that relevant evidence is evidence that has "any tendency" to make a fact "more or less probable," Rule 401 embraces evidence that could shift a fact finder's view of the facts even the smallest degree. Assume, for example, that plaintiff Polly wants to prove that defendant Donald ran a red light. Imagine that the scale below represents a juror's certainty that the light was red, ranging from 0% certainty to 100% certainty, and that the arrow indicates the jury's current level of certainty:

0%   25% ▲50%   75%   100%

Evidence that has **any tendency** to move the indicator slightly in one direction or another (to make the fact of a red light more or less probable) is relevant.

Here are a few examples of how these words create a generous definition of relevance:

Example: Thomas Walsh crossed the center line of a highway and hit an oncoming vehicle, seriously injuring Mary Hitchcock. Hitchcock sued Walsh for negligence, claiming that he was driving drunk. At trial, Hitchcock introduces the results of a blood alcohol test, taken shortly after the accident, showing that Walsh had an elevated level of alcohol in his blood. In response, Walsh introduces the testimony of his neighbor, Bill Chapman, who happened to see him walking down the street half an hour before the accident. Chapman testifies that Walsh was "walking normally and did not appear at all drunk." Hitchcock objects to this testimony as irrelevant, given the blood alcohol test.

Analysis: Chapman's testimony is much less persuasive than Hitchcock's evidence of the blood alcohol test, but it is still relevant. The testimony has **some tendency** to make Walsh's alleged drunkenness **less probable**. Walsh probably wishes he had stronger evidence, but this testimony clears Rule 401's low hurdle.

Example: In the same lawsuit, Walsh introduces the testimony of his 12-year-old daughter Shane. Shane testifies that she saw her father an hour before the accident and he did not seem drunk.

Analysis: This testimony may be even less persuasive than Chapman's evidence; given Shane's age and connection to Walsh, the jury may decide that she is a poor judge of drunken behavior or that her father pressured her to testify on his behalf. But, assuming Shane displays the usual capacity of a 12-year-old to perceive the world, articulate her recollection, and understand the necessity of truth telling, her evidence is still relevant. It has **some tendency** to make Walsh's drunkenness **less probable**; the jury can judge how great or small that tendency is.

2. Must Be a Fact "Of Consequence." The final highlighted phrase in Rule 401 imposes an important constraint on relevance. Evidence is not relevant simply because it makes **some** fact more or less probable. The fact itself must be related to the cause of action, that is, a fact that matters to someone who is trying to decide the case. The evidence, in other words, must tend to establish a fact that is "of consequence" to the lawsuit.

Rule 401's framers deliberately chose the words "of consequence" to establish a very low threshold for this part of the relevance rule. Before adoption of Rule 401, many appellate opinions required evidence to relate to a "material" fact, and trial judges interpreted this word to mean that the evidence had to make a significant difference in the dispute. Applying that standard, they excluded evidence that Rule 401's drafters thought should have been admitted. The words "of consequence" encourage judges to more readily find evidence admissible. The evidence must still connect to legal issues involved in the case, but the connection does not need to be as strong as the one connoted by the word "material."

Successfully attacking or defending evidence under this part of Rule 401 requires parties to articulate the legal principles of the case. Under one theory of a case, evidence may be relevant; under another theory or in a different case, the same evidence loses its relevance. Here are two examples:

Example: In Mary Hitchcock's lawsuit against Thomas Walsh, described above, Walsh's drunkenness is "of consequence" to the action. If Walsh was driving drunk, he was acting unreasonably; Hitchcock will use this evidence to show that Walsh breached a duty of care.

But suppose the evidence of Walsh's drunkenness arises in the context of a different lawsuit. Assume Walsh was injured in the accident and was transported to nearby New London Hospital. At the hospital, a nurse gave Walsh the wrong medicine and he suffered permanent paralysis. If Walsh sues New London Hospital for negligence, can the Hospital defend by introducing evidence that Walsh was drunk at the time?

Analysis: Is Walsh's drunkenness "of consequence" to this action? It is if New London can demonstrate that Walsh's drunkenness affected his care in some way. For example, if the medication harmed Walsh only because of his blood alcohol level, then the fact of his drunkenness is "of consequence" in this action. But if the nurse's mistake was not influenced in any way by Walsh's drunkenness, then that fact is not "of consequence" to this action. Whether Walsh arrived at the hospital as a sinner or a saint, he was entitled to the same level of reasonable medical care.[2]

Example: During a 1973 professional football game, Charles "Booby" Clark intentionally struck Dale Hackbart, a member of the opposing team, on the head. The blow occurred after play had ended and it was unprovoked; Clark explained later that he was frustrated because his team was losing. The blow fractured Hackbart's neck, and he sued Clark for battery. At trial, Clark attempted to introduce videos of Hackbart committing similar fouls in other games. Hackbart objected that the videos were irrelevant.

---

2   This variation of the Walsh example draws upon Walsh v. New London Hosp., 856 F. Supp. 22 (D.N.H. 1994).

Analysis: The trial judge admitted the videos, finding them relevant to Clark's legal theory that football players accept the risk of intentional torts on the field. Under this theory, Hackbart's behavior in prior games showed that he understood and accepted the risk of violent fouls. The court of appeals, however, rejected both Clark's legal theory and the videos. The appellate court concluded that players do not assume the risk of harmful contacts that violate the rules of the game; contact outside what the rules allow can form the basis for a battery claim. Given this ruling, Hackbart's behavior in previous games was no longer relevant. Unless there was evidence that Clark feared Hackbart was about to strike him—and Clark made no such claim—Hackbart's history of fouling other players was of no consequence to whether Clark committed a battery against him.[3]

 These examples illustrate how relevance depends upon the legal theory underlying a case. Under one theory, evidence is relevant; under another theory, it may be irrelevant. Rulings on relevance vary from case to case; they depend upon the legal principles governing the case, the disputed facts, and the lawyer's ability to articulate a persuasive connection between the two.

Sometimes one piece of evidence tends to prove several different facts of consequence within a single case. This flexibility assumes importance if the evidence is admissible to prove one of those facts but not others. An effective advocate often can introduce evidence to prove one fact, even if the opponent successfully objected to using the evidence for another purpose. Under these circumstances, the judge will give the jury a limiting instruction, as discussed in Chapter 5. The jury, however, still has an opportunity to consider the evidence. Here is a case in which one piece of evidence connected to two different facts of consequence:

Facts: Harry Ray borrowed his Uncle Stan's car to run some errands. While attempting to park at Kelly's Liquor Store, Harry plowed through the store's front window and smashed thousands of bottles of wine. A blood alcohol test showed that Harry was driving drunk. Kelly's Liquor Store sued both Harry and Stan for negligence. At trial, the store offered evidence that Harry had been arrested on three prior occasions for drunk

---

3   Hackbart v. Cincinnati Bengals, 601 F.2d 516 (10th Cir. 1979). Clark played for the Cincinnati Bengals, while Hackbart played for the Denver Broncos.

driving, that Stan knew about these arrests, and that Stan nonetheless loaned Harry his car. Stan and Harry objected to admission of any evidence related to Harry's previous arrests.

Analysis: The evidence of Harry's prior arrests tends to prove at least two facts of consequence to Kelly's claims: (1) that Harry was driving drunk when he crashed into the liquor store, and (2) that Stan knew Harry was an irresponsible driver. As we'll see when we study Rule 404(a) in Chapter 27, a judge probably would exclude this evidence if offered for the first purpose: The Rules of Evidence usually exclude evidence used to show that a person has a propensity to act in a particular way. Thus, the judge probably would prevent Kelly's from using evidence of the arrests to show that Harry was the type of person who frequently drove drunk, so he probably was driving drunk on this occasion.

On the other hand, evidence of the prior arrests almost certainly would be admissible to show that Stan was negligent when he loaned his car to Harry. If Harry had already been arrested three times for drunk driving, it is more likely that Stan knew (or should have known) that Harry was an irresponsible driver.

C. In the Courtroom. Here are some further examples of how courts have applied Rules 401 and 402 in a variety of contexts.

1. Controversy and Consequence. If a party concedes one element of a dispute, can the opponent still introduce evidence related to that element? Parties sometimes concede uncontroversial points, hoping to avoid the introduction of emotionally provocative evidence. A homicide defendant, for example, might stipulate that the victim died of a gunshot wound to the head, hoping to prevent the prosecution from presenting gory photos of the decedent's injuries. In the words of Rule 401, do images of a murder victim's wounds remain "of consequence in determining the action" if the defendant does not dispute the manner of death?

The Advisory Committee addressed this question in their notes to Rule 401, concluding simply: "The fact to which the evidence is directed need not be in dispute." Evidence, in other words, is relevant even if it addresses a matter that the opponent concedes.

A Supreme Court decision illustrates and confirms this principle:

Example: The United States charged Johnny Lynn Old Chief with violating a law that prohibits convicted felons from possessing firearms. Old Chief offered to stipulate that he had been convicted of a felony, because he did not want the government to present evidence about the specific crime he had committed. The government refused the stipulation and introduced evidence that Old Chief had been convicted previously of assault causing serious bodily injury. Old Chief objected that the evidence was irrelevant under Rule 401 because he had conceded his status as a convicted felon.

Analysis: The trial judge admitted the government's evidence, noting that "if [the prosecutor] doesn't want to stipulate, he doesn't have to." The court of appeals agreed that "[r]egardless of the defendant's offer to stipulate, the government is entitled to prove a prior felony offense through introduction of probative evidence." The Supreme Court also affirmed this ruling, concluding that concessions do not affect relevance under Rule 401.[4]

If evidence proves that a fact in consequence is more or less probable, that evidence is relevant even if an opposing party is willing to concede the truth of the fact. This principle allows parties to introduce direct evidence of damaging facts, despite an opponent's attempts to minimize the impact of the facts by conceding them. This aspect of Rules 401 and 402 places a powerful tool in the hands of some litigants.

2. Unrelated Misdeeds. Parties often attempt to influence the jury by introducing evidence that an opposing party has engaged in illegal or immoral behavior. The *Hackbart* case, described above, offers one example of this tactic; the opposing player attempted to show that Hackbart himself often fouled other players as evidence that he assumed the risk of violent hits by playing football. The appellate court in *Hackbart* rejected the assumption-of-risk theory, and so Hackbart's prior intentional hits were not relevant to the case.

---

4   Old Chief v. United States, 519 U.S. 172, 177, 179 (1997). The Supreme Court reversed Old Chief's conviction because, even though the evidence of his prior conviction was relevant, another rule barred its admission. We will return to the *Old Chief* case in the next chapter.

Here is another example in which a court rejected a party's legal theory of the case and thereby rendered certain evidence irrelevant.

Example: A rap group called "The Legend" composed and copyrighted a song with a distinctive chorus composed of the words "Uh-oh" sung in a particular rhythm and musical pattern. The famous musician M.C. Hammer later wrote and recorded a song, "Here Comes the Hammer," with a very similar chorus. The Legend sued Hammer for copyright infringement. In defense, Hammer claimed that The Legend had "unclean hands." This defense prevents a plaintiff from recovering if the plaintiff has acted wrongfully or unethically with respect to the disputed material.[5] To support the unclean hands defense, Hammer sought to introduce evidence that The Legend had incorporated portions of other composers' works in its song.

Analysis: The court determined that the small elements of other works used by The Legend were insufficient as a matter of law to establish unclean hands or any other legally recognized defense to Legend's copyright action. As a result, it precluded Hammer from introducing this evidence under Rules 401 and 402. Because Legend's actions did not establish any affirmative defenses, the court concluded, "proof of the facts surrounding [them] is not of consequence to the determination" of Legend's copyright claim.[6]

Courts seem especially reluctant to admit evidence of "unrelated" misdeeds in discrimination lawsuits. Plaintiffs in those cases sometimes try to prove intent by showing that the defendant engaged in a range of discriminatory behaviors. Here is an example:

Example: The DuPont Company dismissed Laura Barrios, an employee with a permanent disability that made it difficult for her to walk. The EEOC sued, claiming that DuPont could have easily accommodated Bar-

---

5   "Unclean hands" is a traditional defense to any claim that seeks an equitable remedy like an injunction. The defense derives from the principle that a court should not aid a party who has acted wrongfully or unethically, even when the party has been wronged by another. The defense arises in copyright and other intellectual property lawsuits because those claims often seek injunctions and other equitable (i.e., non-monetary) remedies.

6   Santrayll v. Burrell, 993 F. Supp. 173, 177 (S.D.N.Y. 1998).

rios's disability and that her dismissal violated the Americans with Disabilities Act. As part of its case, the EEOC attempted to introduce evidence that a DuPont employee sexually harassed Barrios ten years before her dismissal.

Analysis: The court refused to admit this evidence, finding that evidence of sexual harassment, even if true, was irrelevant to allegations of disability discrimination occurring ten years later.[7]

Several other courts have reached a similar conclusion. Psychology research, however, suggests that people who hold one type of bias are, in fact, more likely to harbor other biases.[8] Based on this research, plaintiffs' attorneys are pressing the courts to admit more varied evidence in discrimination suits. In the words of Rule 401, they argue, a defendant's history of sexual harassment has some "tendency" to make the alleged fact of disability discrimination "more probable."

3. Negative Evidence. Sherlock Holmes famously solved one case by noting that a dog did not bark.[9] Judges, however, frequently reject this type of negative evidence.

Example: The government discovered a substantial marijuana field on Robert Fuesting's property and charged him with possession of marijuana with intent to distribute. At trial, Fuesting attempted to introduce testimony by his banker and attorney that his bank accounts and tax returns showed no large sums of money. Fuesting argued that, if his finances *had shown* these kinds of transactions, the government would have introduced them to buttress its drug-dealing allegations. The absence of such transactions, Fuesting argued, was equally relevant to suggest that he was *not* engaged in drug dealing.

---

7   EEOC v. E.I. DuPont De Nemours & Co., No. Civ. A. 03–1605, 2004 WL 2347556 (E.D. La. Oct. 18, 2004).

8   See, e.g., Gordon W. Allport, The Nature of Prejudice (25th anniversary ed. 1979); Allison C. Aosved & Patricia J. Long, Co-Occurrence of Rape Myth Acceptance, Sexism, Racism, Homophobia, Ageism, Classism, and Religious Intolerance, 55 Sex Roles 481 (2006); James Sidanius, The Interface Between Racism and Sexism, 127 J. Psychol.: Interdisciplinary & Applied 311 (1993).

9   Arthur Conan Doyle, Silver Blaze, in The Memoirs of Sherlock Holmes 3 (Christopher Roden ed., Oxford University Press 2000).

> **Analysis:** The judge in Fuesting's case excluded this evidence, finding that there were too many conceivable explanations for the absence of large funds; the court of appeals upheld that ruling.[10]

 This is the type of case in which good advocacy could make the difference in admissibility. Another judge might be persuaded to admit this kind of negative evidence, because the lack of large sums in a defendant's financial records has **some** tendency to make drug dealing less probable. It also seems appropriate to rule generously in favor of evidence offered by criminal defendants; the jury can reject evidence it finds self-serving or unpersuasive.

4. Hindsight. One recurring fact pattern involves cases in which one individual uses deadly force against another, believing that the other poses a life-threatening danger. Liability in these cases depends on the defendant's subjective belief (his or her perception of the threat) rather than on the actual, objective threat. The actual threat posed by the victim, in other words, is **not** of consequence to the action. Recognizing this, courts try to eliminate the effect of hindsight (which incorporates knowledge of the actual threat) on a jury's decision.

Example: Police officers Willie Berry and Richard Klepfer stopped a car driven by Ronald Sherrod and carrying Gary Duckworth as a passenger. Berry believed that Sherrod and Duckworth had just robbed Ziggy's Plant and Gift Shop. The officers ordered the suspects to exit the car with their hands raised. Before the suspects complied with this direction, Berry saw Sherrod make "a quick movement with his hand into his coat . . . [as if] he was going to reach for a weapon." Berry shot Sherrod, killing him instantly. A subsequent search of Sherrod's body revealed that he had no weapon. Sherrod's father filed wrongful death and civil rights claims against Berry for using excessive force. Berry objected to introduction of the post-shooting evidence that Sherrod was unarmed.

---

10   United States v. Fuesting, 845 F.2d 664 (7th Cir. 1988).

Analysis: On the facts of this case, the court concluded that whether or not Sherrod was actually armed was not a fact of consequence in the litigation. Berry's liability depended on his reasonable belief at the time of the accident. The presence or absence of a weapon on Sherrod's person did not affect any of the facts known to Berry. The court noted, however, that in some cases the presence or absence of a weapon might be relevant to an individual's reasonable belief. "For example," the court observed, "if an officer testifies that 'I saw a shiny, metallic object similar to a gun or a dangerous weapon in the suspect's hand,' then proof that the suspect had neither gun nor knife would be material and admissible to the officer's credibility on the question of whether the officer saw any such thing (and therefore had a reasonable belief of imminent harm)." Since Berry testified only that he saw a quick hand movement, the absence of a weapon did not affect his credibility or the reasonableness of what he believed.[11]

5. Opening the Door. Irrelevant evidence sometimes becomes relevant to rebut claims made by another party. Lawyers and judges refer to this as "opening the door." Courts, for example, usually exclude evidence that a party was insured, since the presence or absence of insurance is generally irrelevant to the question of fault or damages.[12] If an insured plaintiff wins a judgment, the insurance company will get reimbursed from the judgment, and the jury need never know that their damage award is being partially used to reimburse the insurance company. Here is a case, however, in which one party "opened the door" to evidence of insurance, making that evidence relevant to the dispute:

Example: Six-year-old Sean Fitzgerald was injured while riding on a parade float. He and his parents sued Expressway Sewerage Construction, the float operator, for negligence. On direct examination, Sean's mother testified that her son's medical bills and related expenses had exceeded $20,000, and that Sean's accident had imposed "quite a strain both emotionally and financially" on the family. In response, the defendant introduced evidence that the family's health insurer had paid for most of Sean's medical care.

---

11 Sherrod v. Berry, 856 F.2d 802, 806 (7th Cir. 1988) (en banc).

12 Rule 411, which we discuss in Chapter 13, specifically addresses the admissibility of evidence related to some types of insurance.

Analysis: Although insurance usually is irrelevant to the issues disputed at trial, Sean's mother suggested that the family was suffering financial hardship due to Sean's medical bills. To rebut this impression, defendant Expressway was entitled to introduce evidence of the family's medical insurance. This insurance became "of consequence" to the action.[13]

In the terminology of evidence, the plaintiff created a new "fact of consequence" by testifying that she suffered emotional harm from the high medical bills. Before she testified to this fact, the question of who paid the medical bills was irrelevant to the issue of damages. But by claiming that the family suffered emotional strain due to the medical expenses, Sean's mother created a new fact of consequence: how much did the family suffer due to the strain of paying high medical bills? The presence or absence of insurance was relevant to that issue.

 The possibility of "opening the door" raises strategic issues for trial attorneys. A lawyer must consider carefully whether evidence is sufficiently important to outweigh the possibility of opening the door to undesirable opposing evidence. In addition, attorneys prepare witnesses carefully to insure that they don't inadvertently open the door to unwanted evidence while testifying on the stand. In the *Fitzgerald* case, for example, the attorney might have worked more carefully with Sean's mother to make sure that she didn't overstate the financial burden suffered by the family.

6. Case-by-Case Determination. As noted above, some courts define relevance narrowly in cases alleging racial, gender, or other types of bias. In employment discrimination suits, for example, trial judges often limit plaintiffs to proof of discriminatory acts committed by their own supervisor; they also impose temporal limits on which of these acts are relevant. In a 2008 decision, *Sprint/United Management Co. v. Mendelsohn*,[14] the Supreme Court reminded judges that they should not create "broad *per se* rules" excluding whole categories of evidence. Instead, the Court declared, questions of relevance under Rules 401 and 402 must always be "determined in the context of the facts and arguments in a particular case."

---

13   Fitzgerald v. Expressway Sewerage Construction, Inc., 177 F.3d 71 (1st Cir. 1999).

14   552 U.S. 379, 387 (2008).

Sprint's impact on employment discrimination cases remains uncertain. Some observers believe that the lower courts now apply Rules 401 and 402 more faithfully in those cases; others suggest that judges still use the relevance test to favor employers.[15] Outside that arena, *Sprint* is a useful opinion for trial attorneys who want to urge results under Rules 401 and 402 that differ from those reached by judges in similar cases. A well-prepared lawyer can stress the special facts and circumstances in her client's case and cite *Sprint* to underline the court's obligation to decide relevance on a case-by-case basis. However, as we will see in the next chapter, trial court judges must consider not only the probative value of evidence offered by a party, but also whether admitting that evidence will be unfairly prejudicial to the opponent.

---

15   Emma Pelkey, Comment, The "Not Me Too" Evidence Doctrine in Employment Law: Courts' Disparate Treatment of "Me Too" Versus "Not Me Too" Evidence in Employment Discrimination Cases, 92 Or. L. Rev. 545 (2013).

Quick Summary

Federal **Rule 401** adopts a very low standard for defining relevance. If a piece of evidence has **any tendency** to make a fact that is **of consequence** to the controversy **more or less probable**, then the evidence is relevant. Evidence remains relevant, moreover, even if the opposing party concedes the issue it illuminates. Under **Rule 402**, all relevant evidence is admissible unless some other rule, statute, or constitutional provision specifically precludes its admission.

In practice, judges do not view relevance quite this leniently. They sometimes exclude evidence that a reasonable person might view as satisfying Rule 401's low standard. Attorneys, therefore, should not overlook the possibility of objecting to evidence on relevance grounds. Conversely, trial lawyers should always be prepared to articulate a clear connection between evidence they offer and the legal theory of the case. Proving relevance depends on knowing the facts of the case, the Rules of Evidence, and the substantive law governing the lawsuit. Judges decide relevance based on a case-by-case examination of both the facts and the law.

Test Your Understanding

To assess your understanding of the material in this chapter, click here to take a quiz, or go to the Quizzes module from the eBook on your eProducts bookshelf.

7

Prejudice, Confusion, or Waste of Time

Key Concepts

- **Rule 403:** Exclusion of Evidence for Prejudice, Confusion, or Waste of Time
- Judge "May" Exclude
- Prejudice Must Be "Unfair"
- Prejudice or Other Concerns Must "Substantially Outweigh" Probative Value
- Stipulations
- Waste of Time

A. Introduction and Policy. In the last chapter, we saw that **Rule 402** broadly authorizes admission of relevant evidence, and that **Rule 401** defines relevance in expansive terms. These two rules offer litigants considerable leeway to introduce evidence that will build a persuasive case.

Rule 403 applies a counterweight to this generosity; it recognizes that some evidence, although relevant, might have unfair effects if introduced at trial. Some evidence provokes unwanted biases or irrational assumptions in the jury's mind. For example, some jurors may be more likely to convict a defendant if they learn that he is bisexual or practices an unpopular religion, even though the charged crime has no connection with either of those characteristics. Evidence may also mislead or confuse jurors when it injects a tangential issue into the case. If jurors hear evidence about a plaintiff's insurance policy, they may become confused about the role that insurance should play in their resolution of the dispute. Finally, some relevant evidence may simply waste time by repeating points that have already been made.

Rule 403 empowers judges to avoid these problems by allowing them to exclude relevant evidence that is problematic in any of these ways. While Rules 401 and

402 define relevance broadly, opening wide the courtroom doors, Rule 403 allows the trial judge to close the doors against some types of evidence.

Litigants invoke Rule 403 quite often. The rule's broad language makes it applicable to almost any evidentiary issue. In fact, as we'll see in later chapters, Rule 403 frequently serves as a backstop for unsuccessful objections under other, more specific rules. Rule 403's exclusionary power, however, remains limited. Even while exercising their broad discretion under this rule, trial judges remain cognizant of the federal rules' liberal attitude toward admitting evidence.

B. The Rule. The full text of **Rule 403** reads quite simply:

RULE 403. Excluding Relevant Evidence for Prejudice, Confusion, Waste of Time, or Other Reasons

The court <u>may</u> exclude relevant evidence if its probative value is <u>substantially outweighed</u> by a danger of one or more of the following:

- <u>unfair</u> prejudice,
- confusing the issues, misleading the jury,
- undue delay, wasting time, or needlessly presenting cumulative evidence.

All of the words in this rule are crucial to its meaning, but the words underlined above are particularly important. Let's consider them one by one.

1. May. The simple word "may" signals that judges possess considerable discretion under Rule 403. A judge "may" exclude evidence under that rule but, then again, a judge may not. Judges frequently differ in how they apply Rule 403; one judge will admit evidence that another judge would find prejudicial. The trial context also influences rulings under Rule 403. A judge might admit evidence in one trial and exclude very similar evidence in another trial posing different circumstances. The Supreme Court recently stressed that judges should apply Rule 403, like Rules 401–02, on a case-by-case basis.[1]

---

1   Sprint/United Mgmt. Co. v. Mendelsohn, 552 U.S. 379, 387 (2008). For further discussion of this case, see Chapter 6.

The role of judicial discretion under Rule 403 means two things for litigators. **First**, appellate courts rarely reverse Rule 403 rulings. Parties often include Rule 403 claims in their appeals, but appellate courts rarely agree with them. Rule 403's recognized grant of discretion insulates most rulings from reversal.

 **Second**, and equally important, the discretionary nature of Rule 403 offers opportunities for persuasive advocacy. Explaining prejudice or probative value concretely is the key to winning a Rule 403 motion. A trial attorney who focuses the judge's attention on the specific unfair harm stemming from a piece of evidence may block the evidence from admission. Conversely, an attorney who can forcefully articulate the probative value of the evidence may succeed in securing its admission.

2. Substantially Outweighed. The second key phrase in Rule 403 is "substantially outweighed." The balance between probative value and unfair prejudice that judges strike under the rule is not an even-handed one: The rule recognizes a firm tilt toward admissibility. For the judge to exclude relevant evidence, its unfair prejudice, confusion, or delay must "substantially" outweigh its probative value. Although judges may differ on whether a particular piece of evidence meets this standard, they all agree that the balance tips strongly toward admissibility. In other words, if the probative value and unfair prejudice are evenly balanced, or even if unfair prejudice somewhat outweighs probative value, the evidence must be admitted. Under these circumstances, the rules assume that the jury will weigh the evidence appropriately.

3. Unfair. Rule 403 authorizes judges to exclude evidence for several reasons, including unfair prejudice, confusing the issues, or undue delay. Parties, however, most often invoke the first basis for exclusion: that admitting the challenged evidence would cause unfair prejudice. The final key word underlined above clarifies that this prejudice must be "unfair" to allow exclusion.

All evidence is prejudicial in the sense that the party offering the evidence hopes that it will damage the opposing side. Judges won't exclude evidence simply because it accomplishes the job it was intended to do. Instead, the prejudice must be unfair in the sense intended by the rulemakers. As the Supreme Court has explained, "unfairly prejudicial" evidence "lure[s] the fact finder into declaring guilt [or liability] on a ground different from proof specific to the offense charged."[2] Unfairness

---

2   Old Chief v. United States, 519 U.S. 172, 180 (1997).

in this context means that the evidence will tempt the jury to decide the case on grounds different from those the law demands.

C. In the Courtroom. Rule 403 addresses a wide variety of evidence, from gruesome photographs to sophisticated DNA analysis. Evidentiary rulings depend heavily on the factual context and the advocates' arguments; it is impossible to articulate a common set of factors governing all Rule 403 cases. Five factors, however, frequently influence a judge's decision when applying this rule:

- The extent to which the evidence will arouse emotions or irrational prejudices among the jurors. Judges are more likely to exclude evidence that triggers strong emotional reactions.

- The extent to which the jury might overvalue the evidence—that is, take a piece of evidence which is only slightly relevant and give it undue weight.

- The strength of the connection between the evidence and the elements of the case. Judges are more likely to admit evidence that is closely related to essential elements of a case, even when that evidence is highly emotional.

- Whether the advocate can prove the same facts through less prejudicial or confusing means. If alternative routes are available, the judge is less likely to admit the challenged evidence.

- Whether it would be possible to reduce prejudice or other harm from introducing the evidence. If the judge can redact prejudicial components of the evidence or instruct the jury to refrain from improper uses of the evidence, he or she will be more likely to admit the evidence.

The examples below consider a number of common scenarios. Look for the courts' use of the above factors in the following contexts.

1. Damaging Evidence. Parties frequently claim that evidence is "unfair" simply because it will damage their case. Courts routinely reject these claims. Rule 403 permits exclusion of evidence that is unfair only in the sense that it inflames the jury's passions or otherwise introduces an improper basis for decision. Evidence that strongly supports the position of one party and damages the other is not "unfair," it is just persuasive.

Example: Jose Perez-Gonzalez participated in a riot that occurred at the former U.S. Naval base in Vieques, Puerto Rico. The base had been the target of considerable ill will and civil disobedience among Puerto Rican citizens. News broadcasters captured Perez-Gonzalez's behavior, along with that of other rioters, on videotape. The tape clearly "showed Perez-Gonzalez smashing a Humvee with a sledgehammer, scuffling with police, and repeatedly crashing a government water truck into [a] guard post until it collapsed." A jury indicted Perez-Gonzalez for damaging government property. At trial, Perez-Gonzalez objected to introduction of the videotape as unfairly prejudicial.

Analysis: The court readily dismissed Perez-Gonzalez's objection. The tape was properly authenticated and Perez-Gonzalez was able to cross examine the reporters about any editing. The video showed Perez-Gonzalez committing the very crimes with which he was charged. It undoubtedly was "damaging" to Perez-Gonzalez, but this was not "unfair prejudice" within the meaning of Rule 403.[3]

2. Videos and Photos. As the previous example shows, a real-time videotape of an event may be damaging evidence, but it is not unfair. As long as the affected party has an opportunity to cross-examine the filmmaker about perspective and editing, and to explain to the jury how the videotape might convey an erroneous impression, the tape seems to be as accurate as—or even better than—eyewitness testimony.

Prosecutors and other litigants, however, have long understood that photos, videotapes, and other visual displays do more than just show the details of an event. These visual media deliver an emotional punch that verbal testimony rarely conveys. Watching Perez-Gonzalez smash a Humvee with a sledge hammer, as in the previous example, stirs a juror's emotions more than hearing an eyewitness describe the same event. Seeing a photo of a homicide victim's dead body affects

---

3   United States v. Perez-Gonzalez, 445 F.3d 39, 47 (1st Cir. 2006).

jurors differently than hearing a police officer describe the same wounds. Seeing is believing and feeling, in a way that hearing is not.

For this reason, parties try to make their cases as visual as possible in the courtroom. Prosecutors routinely attempt to introduce photos of a victim's injuries, the gorier the better. Personal injury plaintiffs similarly exhibit their injuries on the witness stand, through photographs or with "day in the life" videos depicting their daily struggle with an injury. Are these visual techniques legitimate attempts to make a crime or injury "real" to the jury? Or do these images and videos risk inflaming juror emotions to the point where the jury feels compelled to hold *someone* responsible for a terrible wrong and chooses the defendant simply because he or she is convenient?

The video of Perez-Gonzalez posed little difficulty under Rule 403: The video showed the defendant himself committing the crime and there was little doubt that Perez-Gonzalez's smashing blows to the Humvee were intentional. It is difficult to argue that displaying the video to the jury was unfair.

But if a photo or video shows only the effects of the crime, giving no indication of how the crime occurred or who was responsible, the possibility of unfair prejudice is more substantial. The judge must decide whether the jurors' emotional reaction to the devastating effects of a crime will push them to blame the defendant, overlooking any exonerating evidence. This is the most unfair prejudice that photos, videos, and other visual aids may cause.

As a result of this concern, courts maintain an uneasy balance between allowing parties to make their cases "real" through visual evidence and preventing the parties from abusing the unrestrained emotions such evidence might unleash. Here is an example of how one court struck the balance:

> **Example:** The government charged Stephen McRae with shooting his wife, Nancy McRae. Stephen admitted shooting Nancy, but claimed it was an accident. The government introduced photographs of Nancy's corpse, taken soon after police arrived at the scene. One showed Nancy "clothed in her bloody garments, bent forward so as to display an exit wound in the back of her skull produced by part of [Stephen]'s dum-dum bullet, which exploded in her brain." Another showed "a front view of her body, seated in the chair where she died, her left eye disfigured by the bullet's entry

and her head broken by its force." Stephen objected to introduction of the photos as unfairly prejudicial.

Analysis: The court acknowledged that the photos were "not pretty even to the hardened eye." But, the court continued, "[n]either . . . was the crime" and the pictures were not "flagrantly or deliberately gruesome depictions of it." The government legitimately wanted to introduce the photos to counter Stephen's accident defense; they helped establish the position of the body and gun at the time of the shooting.[4]

Example: In the *McRae* case, the couple's children found their dead mother after the shooting. Some photos taken at the crime scene showed the victim's body along with bloody handprints made by the children as they attempted to aid their mother. The prosecution sought to introduce these photos.

Analysis: The district judge excluded these photos, and the court of appeals noted its agreement with that ruling. Photos that included the children's handprints did not add new information to that offered by other admitted photos. These photos would have simply outraged the jury, making it harder for them to weigh the evidence dispassionately.[5]

 The *McRae* case illustrates the line that judges often draw when faced with emotionally provocative photos. Courts will almost always admit some photos of the victim to illustrate elements of the crime, but will exclude photos like the ones showing the children's handprints, which greatly increase emotional reactions without adding new information. The case is also typical in that judges often attempt to "split the difference" by admitting some of the photos offered by one side while excluding the most prejudicial among them.

---

4   United States v. McRae, 593 F.2d 700, 707 (5th Cir. 1979).

5   Id. The reported case does not reveal why the prosecutor believed these particular photos were necessary. They passed the minimum relevance test by depicting the position of the body, as other photos in the series did. The prosecutor may have wanted to introduce the photos showing the children's bloody handprints precisely because they added outrage to the crime.

3. Socially Undesirable Behavior. Americans engage in a wide variety of lifestyles, and often disapprove of the lifestyles chosen by others. Parties sometimes attempt to introduce evidence of an opponent's unconventional lifestyle, hoping that the jurors' biases will lead them to view the opponent negatively. Judges exclude some of these attempts under Rule 402, because the evidence simply isn't relevant. In a negligence claim arising out of an auto accident, for example, the defendant's sexual orientation rarely is "of consequence" to the dispute. Other times, lifestyle evidence may have some bearing on issues in the case, especially given the broad definition of relevance under Rule 401. In these cases, parties may invoke Rule 403 on the ground that the unfair prejudice resulting from the evidence substantially outweighs any probative value.

Example: Ronald Bailie, Terri Bailie, and Nada Bailie operated the Bailie School of Broadcast. The government charged them with embezzling Perkins educational loan funds. At trial, the government introduced evidence of the Bailies' "opulent lifestyle, including homes, condos, expensive cars, and a chauffeured limousine." The Bailies objected to this evidence as unfairly prejudicial in arousing bias against their wealthy lifestyle.

Analysis: The district judge allowed the evidence, and the court of appeals affirmed. The courts accepted the government's argument that the evidence established the Bailies' motive for embezzlement. As such, any unfair prejudice did not substantially outweigh the probative value.[6]

Other courts have reached similar conclusions, allowing evidence of a lavish lifestyle to establish motive. But some courts are more skeptical. These courts acknowledge that sudden, unexplained wealth may suggest the fruits of criminal behavior, while heavy debts may establish a motive for that behavior. The criminal defendant's specific expenditures or debts, on the other hand, add little probative value while creating the possibility of unfair prejudice. As one district judge recently noted, it is irrelevant if a defendant "spent his fortune on lavish parties, instead of donating it to starving Malawian orphans."[7]

---

6   United States v. Bailie, 1996 WL 580350 (9th Cir. Oct. 8, 1996) (unpublished opinion).

7   United States v. Hatfield, 685 F. Supp. 2d 320, 326 (E.D.N.Y. 2010).

Recent cases also explore the admissibility of evidence revealing a party's racist attitudes and behavior. In some lawsuits, those attitudes are "of consequence" because they bear directly on claims of discrimination or other wrongdoing. In other cases, the evidence arises more tangentially and parties argue that the evidence of racism is more prejudicial than probative. Here are two contrasting examples:

Example: A grand jury indicted Harry Joseph Bowman, international president of the Outlaws Motorcycle Club, for racketeering, drug offenses, and conspiracy to murder members of the rival Hell's Angels Motorcycle Club. The trial revealed numerous unsavory details about the Outlaws, including their enthusiastic support of members who attempted murder, successfully committed murder, or exploded bombs on behalf of the Club. Bowman did not dispute these Club customs, but objected to introduction of a Club constitution limiting Club membership to white men. Bowman argued that, since the government alleged no racial motivation in any of the charged crimes, the reference to the Club's whites-only policy was unfairly prejudicial.

Analysis: The district judge refused to redact the whites-only clause from the Club constitution, allowing the jury to see it when the government introduced the constitution to prove other facts in the case. In a rare appellate ruling on a Rule 403 issue, the court of appeals held that the trial court's decision was an abuse of discretion.

Although the whites-only policy cleared the relevance hurdle, because it tended to show unity of purpose among the Club's chapters, sufficient other evidence was available to prove unity without exposing the Club's explicit racism. Under these circumstances, the unfair prejudice stemming from disclosure of the Club's highly offensive whites-only policy substantially outweighed any probative value. The court of appeals issued a stern warning that both the government and district judge "should have scrupulously avoided the possibility that the jury's verdict might be clouded by racial issues." Still, given the brief mention of the whites-only policy, and the substantial other evidence against Bowman, the court deemed the error harmless and upheld the conviction.[8]

---

8   United States v. Bowman, 302 F.3d 1228, 1239–40 (11th Cir. 2002).

Example: The government charged Leo Felton and Erica Chase with bank robbery, counterfeiting, and planned construction of an explosive device. At trial, the prosecutor introduced several pieces of evidence showing the association of Felton and Chase with white supremacist organizations. These included (1) a photo of Chase executing a Nazi salute while standing with Matthew Hale, a well known white supremacist who had been convicted of plotting to kill a federal judge; (2) an article written by Chase about white power rallies she had attended; and (3) a pamphlet describing "an apocalyptic 'future' in which white women were 'publicly gang-raped' by 'Negroids.' " Based on this and other evidence, a jury convicted Felton and Chase.

Analysis: On appeal, the court of appeals conceded that the evidence was "certainly inflammatory." It was, however, also quite relevant. The government alleged that Felton and Chase engaged in their criminal activities specifically to advance the ends of a white supremacist cell they had formed. Since the defendants disputed their involvement in these criminal acts, proof of motive was important to the government's case. And, since the defendants' motives were racist, the government had no less inflammatory evidence at its disposal. The court did express reservations about the prosecutor's tactic of having a witness read aloud the "lurid" gang-rape passage, but the trial court halted the reading as soon as the defense objected. Any error, therefore, did not affect the verdicts.[9]

Taken together, these cases illustrate that courts are sensitive to the prejudicial impact of evidence that a party has expressed racist attitudes. On the other hand, where that evidence relates directly to the crime or other litigated issue, courts will admit it.

 4. Flight. When a suspect flees or hides from the police, prosecutors frequently offer evidence of that conduct to show consciousness of guilt. For this evidence to be relevant, the government must show some link between the defendant's conduct and the charged crime. If the defendant simply left town for a scheduled vacation or business trip, her movements are not probative of guilt. But if the

---

9   United States v. Felton, 417 F.3d 97, 101–02 (1st Cir. 2005).

government offers "reasonable support" linking the defendant's conduct and the charged crime,[10]courts routinely admit flight evidence as relevant.

A defendant may still challenge this evidence as unfairly prejudicial under Rule 403. The defense may argue that the jurors will overestimate the possibility that flight signifies a guilty conscience, especially if the prosecutor's other evidence of guilt is particularly weak. Defendants may also point to the fact that some people run from the police because they fear a false conviction or police mistreatment. Non-white suspects in particular may experience those fears.[11]

Courts balance these factors, along with other evidence in the case, to determine whether any unfair prejudice substantially outweighs the probative value of the flight evidence. The following example illustrates how judges strike that balance; it also shows how the balance may shift as the case proceeds:

> **Example:** Pursuant to a valid warrant, state troopers searched Joseph Benedetti's Rhode Island apartment on November 19, 1998. They found a loaded handgun in the top drawer of a bedroom dresser. On March 10, 1999, a grand jury indicted Benedetti, a convicted felon, for unlawful possession of a firearm. Benedetti's lawyer, Paul DiMaio, told federal agents that his client would surrender on Monday, March 15. Instead, Benedetti disappeared and successfully evaded detection for more than four years. In 2003, government agents found him living in Florida under an assumed name and returned him to Rhode Island for trial on the weapon possession charge. Benedetti moved to exclude any evidence that he had left the state.

> **Analysis:** The court initially granted Benedetti's motion, finding it "plausible that the appellant, although innocent, might have fled because he feared that he would be unjustly convicted." Allowing the government to introduce evidence of Benedetti's travels in its case-in-chief raised too much danger that the jury would convict based on the flight alone; the unfair prejudice substantially outweighed the probative value of Benedetti's flight.

---

10   United States v. Myers, 550 F.2d 1036, 1050 (5th Cir. 1977).

11   See Commonwealth. v. Warren, 475 Mass. 530, 540, 58 N.E.3d 333, 342 (2016) (noting, in the context of a Fourth Amendment reasonable-suspicion ruling, that racial profiling "suggests a reason for flight totally unrelated to consciousness of guilt" because targeted minority members "might just as easily be motivated by the desire to avoid the recurring indignity of being racially profiled as by the desire to hide criminal activity").

Two incidents during trial, however, changed the trial court's decision. First, when cross-examining the government's witnesses, Benedetti's lawyer repeatedly stressed the long period of time that had elapsed between the search and the trial. Without evidence of Benedetti's flight, this conveyed a misleading impression that the government had acted too slowly.

Second, information about Benedetti's flight was relevant to testing the credibility of witnesses who testified on his behalf. One of Benedetti's friends testified that the gun belonged to him, and Benedetti's former wife corroborated that testimony. In testing whether these claims were true, the government was entitled to ask why these witnesses had not come forward at the time of Benedetti's indictment and whether they knew that he had fled the jurisdiction.

These factors altered the calculus under Rule 403 by increasing the probative value of the evidence relating to the flight. Thus, after the defendant had presented his case, the court allowed the government to cross-examine some of Benedetti's witnesses in a way that revealed the defendant's flight.[12]

We saw this "opening the door" phenomenon in the last chapter. Before the defense case, Benedetti's move to Florida only tended to prove one fact of consequence: that he knew he was guilty and thus fled the jurisdiction. Although this passed the low standard for relevance, the trial judge found that the unfair prejudice generated by the evidence substantially outweighed its probative value.

But by emphasizing the government's delay, the defense (perhaps inadvertently) created a new fact of consequence: Did the government act improperly by waiting so long to bring the defendant to trial? Similarly, by offering witnesses who claimed they knew the defendant was innocent, the defense created another fact of consequence: Were the witnesses credible when they said they knew that the defendant was innocent? The fact that the defendant left the jurisdiction and could not be located for four years was relevant to prove each of these facts of consequence. By creating these new facts of consequence, the defendant increased the probative value of the flight evidence to the point where it was no longer substantially outweighed by its unfair prejudice.

5. Stipulations. Our discussion of Rules 401 and 402 revealed that a party's stipulation does not eliminate the relevance of evidence offered by another party. Facts related to an element of a crime or civil claim, in other words, are "of con-

---

12   United States v. Benedetti, 433 F.3d 111, 114 (1st Cir. 2005).

sequence" even if the parties do not actually dispute that element. The presence of a stipulation, however, may affect the balance of unfair prejudice and probative value under Rule 403. The Supreme Court explored this issue in the *Old Chief* case discussed in the last chapter:

Example: The United States charged Johnny Lynn Old Chief with violating a federal statute that prohibits convicted felons from possessing firearms. Old Chief offered to stipulate that he had been convicted of a felony, because he did not want the government to present specifics about his prior crime. The government declined the stipulation and moved to introduce evidence that Old Chief had been convicted previously of assault causing serious bodily injury. The trial court refused to force the government to accept the stipulation, and admitted the government's evidence.

Analysis: The Supreme Court, as noted in our previous discussion, agreed that the government's evidence of a prior conviction was relevant. In a 5–4 ruling, however, the Court concluded that the district court abused its discretion in refusing Old Chief's stipulation and admitting the government's evidence of a prior conviction.[13] The *Old Chief* ruling includes three significant points related to Rule 403 generally and to the specific effect of stipulations under that rule:

First, the Court noted that Rule 403's balancing test requires the court to evaluate unfair prejudice and probative value in the context of the full evidentiary record. The availability of alternative evidence, including stipulations, affects the Rule 403 balance.

Second, the Court observed that with respect to most elements of a crime, the prosecution can choose to present detailed evidence rather than accepting a defendant's offer to stipulate. The probative value of a stipulation usually cannot match the "descriptive richness" and "coherent narrative" of conventional courtroom testimony. Jurors expect concrete evidence rather than abstract stipulations; if the prosecution disappoints this expectation, jurors may doubt the strength of the government's case. A full accounting of the defendant's thoughts and actions, as well as of the crime's consequences, may also be necessary to help the jury discharge its duty to convict or acquit. As Justice Souter wrote for the majority, "the

---

13   Old Chief v. United States, 519 U.S. 172 (1997).

evidentiary account of what a defendant has thought and done can accomplish what no set of abstract statements ever could, not just to prove a fact but to establish its human significance, and so to implicate the law's moral underpinnings and a juror's obligation to sit in judgment."[14]

Finally, however, the Court concluded that the calculus differs in the special context of the felon-in-possession statute. The statute itself does not distinguish among previous crimes; conviction of **any** felony bars the defendant from gun possession. The probative value of introducing evidence of the nature of the previous crime, therefore, is low. Nor is that evidence part of a detailed narrative like the ones described above. The choice in Old Chief's case was between introducing one abstract statement, a stipulation that he had been convicted of a felony, and admitting an equally abstract proposition, the documentary record of that conviction including the name of the previous crime.

Although these two pieces of evidence are equally abstract, the latter may cause substantial prejudice, especially when the previous conviction resembles misconduct charged in the current prosecution. That was true in Old Chief's case; his previous conviction was for assault causing serious bodily injury, while the current charges were for both assault and gun possession. Under these circumstances, the risk of prejudice was particularly high and the district court abused its discretion in admitting the government's evidence of the specific prior conviction rather than accepting Old Chief's stipulation.

The federal courts have applied *Old Chief* in the narrow manner these three points suggest. Trial courts have accepted a defendant's stipulation of felony status in gun possession cases, excluding other evidence of the prior conviction under Rule 403, but have not forced the prosecution to accept defendants' stipulations on elements of other crimes. Defendants still invoke *Old Chief* in other contexts, but they rarely succeed.

Conversely, the *Old Chief* opinion has provided surprising benefits to prosecutors. Although the decision aids defendants in one narrow class of cases, by allowing them to stipulate a prior felony conviction when charged with unlawful gun possession, the opinion eloquently articulates the probative value of detailed evidence in other types of prosecutions. Prosecutors have been able to invoke *Old Chief*'s language and reasoning to introduce detailed evidence of other criminal behavior, despite a defendant's offer to stipulate. In courtrooms today, prosecutors may cite

---

14   Id. at 187–88.

Old Chief's language more often than defendants cite its holding—*Old Chief* has become a very useful exception which proves the general rule.

6. Undue Delay, Wasting Time, and Cumulative Evidence. Although litigants focus on Rule 403's "unfair prejudice, confusing the issues, [or] misleading the jury" language, the rule also empowers trial judges to exclude evidence that would waste time, cause undue delay, or needlessly duplicate other evidence. With growing pressure on the federal dockets, district judges invoke these provisions to limit evidence they view as unnecessary or duplicative. Here is an example from the criminal prosecution of I. Lewis "Scooter" Libby, an advisor to former Vice President Dick Cheney:

Example: The United States charged I. Lewis Libby with lying to FBI agents and grand jurors in connection with an investigation into whether Libby had disclosed classified information to journalists. Libby defended in part on the ground that any misstatements to the FBI agents or grand jury were the result of faulty memory, not intentional deception. To buttress that defense Libby offered evidence about the more pressing matters that had occupied his attention on the days he made the disclosures to reporters. In pretrial proceedings, he identified hundreds of classified documents that he planned to introduce or describe while testifying. The government objected to introduction of many of these documents on the ground that they would waste time by disclosing a level of detail that was not necessary for Libby to make his memory defense.

Analysis: The trial judge sustained the government's objection with respect to many of the documents. One group of documents, for example, contained detailed discussion of small terrorist groups whose names would not be known to the jury. Admitting extensive information about these groups and why Libby might have been concerned about their activities, the judge concluded, would waste time and confuse the jurors. The judge had already permitted Libby to introduce voluminous evidence about his workload, and the government had announced that it would not contest the importance of matters occupying Libby's attention. The waste of time and confusion caused by introducing lengthy additional documents, therefore, substantially outweighed any probative value of that information.[15]

---

15   United States v. Libby, 467 F. Supp. 2d 1, 13–14 (D.D.C. 2006).

7. Bench Trials. Rule 403, like the other Federal Rules of Evidence, applies to both jury and bench trials. Application of the rules, however, sometimes differs when the judge is the fact-finder. Under Rule 403, it would be awkward to exclude evidence offered in a bench trial on the ground that the evidence is unfairly prejudicial or confusing; the judge would have to conclude that he or she could not fairly evaluate the evidence. Parties, therefore, do not invoke this objection when a judge serves as the fact-finder. They may, however, still object to evidence as a waste of time or unduly cumulative. Judges remain responsive to those motions in bench trials.

8. Discretion and Bias. Judges possess substantial discretion under Rule 403, especially when determining whether evidence is "unfairly" prejudicial or "needlessly" cumulative. This discretion allows judges to respond to the unique facts of each case, but it can also embody cultural prejudices and other unconscious biases.[16] As you review Rule 403 decisions in this chapter and class discussions, consider whether you see any evidence of unwanted bias. If the rule gives judges too much discretion, can you suggest narrower language?

16   See, e.g., 22A Kenneth W. Graham, Jr., Federal Practice and Procedure § 5215 (2d ed. Updated 2017); Victor J. Gold, Federal Rule of Evidence 403: Observations on the Nature of Unfairly Prejudicial Evidence, 58 Wash. L. Rev. 497 (1983); J. Alexander Tanford, A Political-Choice Approach to Limiting Prejudicial Evidence, 64 Ind. L.J. 831 (1989).

Quick Summary

 **Rule 403** gives judges the power to exclude evidence that is unfairly prejudicial, confusing, misleading, duplicative, or a waste of time. This provision counterbalances the low threshold for relevance set by **Rules 401** and **402**.

Judges frequently exercise their discretion under Rule 403 to exclude evidence that will unduly inflame the jury's emotions, distract it with tangential issues, or otherwise prevent fair consideration of the case. Under limited circumstances, Rule 403 may allow a criminal defendant to avoid the introduction of damaging evidence by stipulating to an element of the crime. Judges also invoke the rule to limit the time devoted to trial.

Despite this broad grant of discretion, Rule 403 honors the Federal Rules' generous view of admissibility by restricting the judge's power to exclude relevant evidence to those cases in which unfair prejudice or another concern "substantially outweighs" the evidence's probative value. When probative value more evenly matches prejudice, the rule favors admissibility.

Test Your Understanding

 To assess your understanding of the material in this chapter, click here to take a quiz, or go to the Quizzes module from the eBook on your eProducts bookshelf.

8

Fitting the Rules Together

 In the last two chapters, we looked at the three most fundamental Rules of Evidence: **Rules 401** and **402**, which require evidence to be relevant, and **Rule 403**, which gives the trial judge discretion to exclude evidence that is unfairly prejudicial, confusing, or a waste of time.

We still have dozens of other rules to study. But before we do, let's pause to consider how all of these rules fit together. Conceptually, how does a trial attorney navigate the many Rules of Evidence when presenting a case in the courtroom?

One helpful way to understand the overall plan of the Federal Rules of Evidence is to think about fish. Fish? Yes, fish. Imagine each piece of evidence as a fish swimming downstream, trying to reach a lake.

The Rules of Evidence are a series of nets that span the river, filtering out some of the fish before they swim into the lake. Only fish that avoid all of the nets and arrive at the lake are admitted into evidence.

At the start of the river is a net with a very wide mesh labeled "relevance." Almost all fish manage to swim through the holes in this net; most evidence offered by parties is relevant. But the relevance net does catch a few fish, stopping them from reaching the lake.

At the mouth of the river, just before it joins the lake, is a net marked "Rule 403: Prejudice, Confusion, and Waste of Time." This sieve represents the trial judge's last opportunity to trap a fish before it joins other admitted evidence in the lake. The mesh in the Rule 403 net is somewhat tighter than the weave in the relevance net; judges reject more evidence under Rule 403 than under Rules 401 and 402. But even this 403 net is woven loosely. Overall, the Federal Rules of Evidence remove relatively few "fish" from the stream of evidence offered by the parties.

Between the relevance net at the start of the river and the Rule 403 net at the end, there are dozens of other nets. Some of them look for very specific types of "fish," such as evidence that relates to insurance, plea bargains, or other topics. Others filter particular categories of evidence, such as unreliable expert testimony or out-of-court statements (hearsay). But the function of all of these nets is the same: to strain out evidence that the parties seek to admit.

We can build on this image of the fish, nets, and river to illustrate six essential principles about the Federal Rules of Evidence.

First, the evidence nets, like real fishing nets, don't activate themselves. Trial attorneys cast these nets into the river, hoping to catch and eliminate an opponent's evidence. Lawyers who understand the evidentiary rules wield those nets more effectively than those who don't. Just as some fishermen catch more fish than others, some trial attorneys trap and exclude more pieces of an opponent's evidence.

Second, almost all the Federal Rules tell us what evidence to **exclude**, not what evidence to admit. The party offering a piece of evidence sends it down the river, hoping it will reach the lake and be admitted. But no rule guarantees admission for any piece of evidence. Instead, each "fish" must evade all of the nets cast by opposing parties. If the fish avoids all of the nets, then it reaches the lake and is admitted into evidence. If an opponent traps the fish in one of its evidentiary nets, then the jury will not have a chance to consider it.

Third, with a few exceptions that we will study later in the course, evidence must survive scrutiny under **every** rule to gain admission. Testimony that overcomes the rule against hearsay might still run afoul of the rules against character evidence. Lawyers can cast multiple nets against an opponent's evidence; the fish must navigate around all of the traps to survive the downstream journey.

Fourth, a fish might get caught in the net because it is inadmissible for one purpose, but it still may be admissible for another purpose. In this case, the "game warden" (otherwise known as the trial judge) puts a tag on the fish explaining that it cannot be used for a certain purpose, and then throws the fish back into the river. This tag is a limiting instruction. When the fish reaches the lake and is admitted into evidence, the tag is read to the jury to ensure that the evidence is used for the proper purpose. Whenever that fish is mentioned throughout the trial, including in closing arguments, the tag must again be read to the jury to make sure the evidence is used properly.[1]

---

1   Thanks to Professor Mark Godsey for this addition to our analogy.

Fifth, the placement of the Rule 403 net at the end of the river is particularly significant. Many of the other, more specific rules attempt to exclude evidence that is prejudicial in some way. It is tempting to conclude that, if evidence survives all of those specific rules, it must be admissible. Rule 403, however, is an independent check on the suitability of evidence for courtroom use; with only a few exceptions, judges have discretion to reject evidence under this rule even if it has cleared other, more specific obstacles. Parties, therefore, often back up their narrow evidentiary nets with the broad 403 filter at the mouth of the river.

Finally, the evidentiary fish making their downstream journey do not travel alone. Each fish has a trial lawyer helping it navigate the stream. Skillful trial attorneys help their "fish" swim around an opponent's evidentiary net or find the holes (exceptions) in that net. Attorneys can also choose the type of fish they release into the stream. If one type of evidence (such as a particular document) is likely to get caught in a net, the attorney can choose a different piece of evidence (such as oral testimony on the same subject) to navigate the stream.

As we saw in Chapter 5, parties apply the Rules of Evidence through an adversary process. Each side attempts to exclude key evidence offered by the other side, while defending its own evidence. As we continue to explore this process, it will help to conceptualize the evidentiary contest as one of opponents casting nets into a stream, attempting to capture the other's evidence, while guiding their own evidence around the nets of the other.

9

Subsequent Remedial Measures

Key Concepts

- **Rule 407:** Evidence of Subsequent Remedial Measures
- Policy of Encouraging Prompt Repairs
- What is a "Measure"?
- Problems of Timing
- Repairs by Non-Parties
- Introducing Evidence for Other Purposes
- Defining "Impeachment" Under Rule 407

A. Introduction and Policy. Rules 407 through **411** are narrowly focused rules that exclude evidence related to five different subjects. **Rule 407** applies to subsequent remedial measures; **Rule 408**, to settlement negotiations; **Rule 409**, to payment of medical expenses; **Rule 410**, to plea bargaining; and **Rule 411**, to liability insurance. Each of these rules furthers goals of two types:

1. Each rule promotes a socially valuable activity, like plea bargaining or purchasing liability insurance, by protecting those who engage in that activity from evidence that might be used against them.

2. The evidence targeted by these rules tends to cause a high degree of unfair prejudice, while contributing little probative value. In other words, these rules apply **Rule 403**'s balancing approach to exclude particular categories of evidence.

Four of these narrowly focused rules share another characteristic: They exclude evidence only if a party offers the evidence for the purpose of proving liability or fault. If a litigant offers the same evidence for a **different** purpose, the judge may admit the evidence. This is one of the many circumstances in which a judge may use a limiting instruction; she will tell the jury to use the evidence for the admissible purpose, but not for the forbidden one.

 These rules require attorneys to identify the **purpose of the evidence** they and their opponents offer into evidence. An attorney who wants to admit evidence of subsequent remedial measures, insurance, or other subjects forbidden by Rules 407–411 will try to identify a permissible purpose for that evidence. His opponent, conversely, will argue that the evidence should be excluded because it is relevant only for a forbidden purpose. We will examine these opportunities for advocacy in greater detail as we discuss each rule.

We begin with **Rule 407**, which bars evidence of subsequent remedial measures. You may have heard about this concept when studying the law of negligence in Torts class. Sometimes after a plaintiff is injured, the defendant attempts to make conditions safer. If a plaintiff slips on the defendant's icy sidewalk, for example, the defendant might start putting salt on the sidewalk. Or if a plaintiff gets her arm caught in a factory machine, the manufacturer of the machine might change the machine's design to prevent future accidents. Evidence that the defendant made such a change is relevant to prove the plaintiff's case; the change tends to prove a fact of consequence, that the original condition or practice was unreasonably dangerous.

But there are two problems with admitting such evidence. **First,** it creates a perverse incentive for defendants. A defendant may postpone fixing a condition that injured the plaintiff, just so that the repair can't be used as evidence at trial. This hesitation may lead to additional injuries. Encouraging defendants to make repairs promptly, without worrying about the effects of those repairs on pending litigation, is an important social policy.

Second, juries may give too much weight to evidence of subsequent remedial measures. A defendant's post-accident conduct often bears little relationship to her pre-accident negligence. The plaintiff's accident may have revealed a previously unknown danger, one that no reasonable person would have predicted but that the defendant then remedies. Or a defendant who exercised reasonable care before the accident may respond to the plaintiff's injury by taking precautions beyond those required by law. In both of these situations, the defendant's initial conduct was fully reasonable, but the jury may interpret the defendant's subsequent repair as an admission of fault. Evidence of subsequent remedial measures, in other words, often causes unfair prejudice that substantially outweighs its probative value.

Rule 407 addresses these two problems by restricting the admissibility of subsequent remedial measures. The rule thus furthers an important social policy (encouraging prompt repairs), while also shielding defendants from unfair prejudice. Rule 407, however, does not **always** bar evidence of subsequent remedial measures. The rule precludes this evidence only if the plaintiff uses the repairs to show that a defendant was negligent or otherwise at fault. Plaintiffs may use evidence of subsequent remedial measures to prove other facts of consequence, such as the feasibility of repairs. Successfully advancing one of these permissible purposes is worth the effort for plaintiffs: As noted above, juries respond strongly to this evidence.[1]

B. The Rule. Rule 407 consists of two sentences. The first sentence spells out when a court will exclude evidence of subsequent remedial measures:

> ## RULE 407. Subsequent Remedial Measures
>
> When <u>measures</u> are taken that would have made an earlier injury or harm <u>less likely to occur</u>, evidence of the <u>subsequent</u> measures is not admissible to prove:
>
> * negligence;
> * culpable conduct;
> * a defect in a product or its design; or
> * a need for a warning or instruction.

The underlined phrases highlight issues that parties litigate when invoking this rule; we will address those in more detail in the Courtroom section below.

The second sentence of Rule 407 notes some circumstances under which subsequent remedial measures may be admissible. As noted above, the admissibility of this evidence depends on the **purpose** for which a party offers the evidence:

---

1   Throughout this chapter, we refer to "plaintiffs" using evidence of subsequent remedial measures against "defendants." Most often, the parties align this way in court. The rule, however, applies evenhandedly to all parties. Defendants sometimes offer evidence of a plaintiff's subsequent remedial measures; a defendant might offer that evidence, for example, to show that the plaintiff was contributorily negligent. In those cases, the plaintiff may use Rule 407 to oppose admission of the evidence offered by the defendant.

RULE 407. Subsequent Remedial Measures

But the court may admit this evidence for <u>another purpose</u>, <u>such as</u>

- <u>impeachment</u> or—
- <u>if disputed</u>—proving <u>ownership</u>, <u>control</u>, or the <u>feasibility</u> of precautionary measures.

This list is not meant to be exhaustive—subsequent remedial measures are admissible if they are offered to prove any fact in consequence other than the four listed in the first sentence of the rule. However, almost every instance of admissible subsequent remedial measures involves one of the underlined purposes in the rule's second sentence. We'll examine these purposes in more detail below.

C. In the Courtroom. Although the concept of subsequent remedial measures arose in tort cases, and continues to play a significant role in those lawsuits, courts now apply the rule in a wide range of other actions, from employment discrimination claims to intellectual property disputes. Evidence of subsequent remedial measures can significantly boost a plaintiff's likelihood of success in any of these contexts, so this evidentiary rule is assuming increased importance.

1. What Is a "Measure"? Rule 407 bars evidence of "measures . . . that would have made an earlier injury or harm less likely to occur." These actions are "remedial." But what kind of actions count as "measures"?

Putting salt on an icy sidewalk clearly is a measure. So is changing the design of a product that caused an injury. When a car manufacturer responds to gas-tank explosions by switching the tank's location, that is a measure. Adding a warning label to a product or changing an existing label is also a remedial measure.

But a defendant doesn't have to change a product or dangerous condition directly to engage in a remedial measure. Taking products off the market or issuing recalls are also measures that fall within Rule 407:

> **Example:** Betty Jo and Charles Chase purchased a Chevrolet Citation car in 1980. In 1982, the Chases were involved in a collision. Another car crossed the median and, when Charles applied the Citation's brakes, his car swung to the left and collided with the other car. Betty Jo suffered seri-

ous injuries and sued General Motors, claiming that the Citation's brakes were defective. In 1983, GM recalled its 1980 Citations to modify their brakes. The Chases introduced evidence of the recall at trial, arguing that it showed negligence in the original design of the brakes.

Analysis: The recall was a "measure" subject to Rule 407 and it occurred after the Chases' accident. The court of appeals, therefore, concluded that evidence of the recall should have been excluded.[2]

A policy change may also constitute a "measure" under Rule 407:

Example: Donna Peck worked on the custodial staff of the Hudson City School District. She sued the District, claiming that a maintenance worker had created a hostile work environment by sexually harassing her. After Peck's complaint, the District made changes in its sexual harassment policy, and Peck sought to admit evidence of these changes at trial.

Analysis: The court granted the District's motion in limine to exclude the changes, agreeing that the policy change was a "remedial measure" that occurred after Peck's injury. Rule 407, therefore, barred Peck from using the policy to establish the District's fault.[3]

Even firing or disciplining an employee who was responsible for the disputed injury may count as a remedial measure:

Example: George and June Specht sued the city of Steamboat Springs, claiming that city police had illegally searched their home. At trial, the Spechts attempted to prove culpability by introducing a city press release reporting that the police officers had exercised poor judgment and that appropriate disciplinary action would be taken. The city objected to this evidence under Rule 407.

---

2   Chase v. General Motors Corp., 856 F.2d 17 (4th Cir. 1988).

3   Peck v. Hudson City Sch. Dist., 100 F. Supp. 2d 118, 122 (N.D.N.Y. 2000).

Analysis: The trial judge excluded the press release and the court of appeals affirmed. The courts agreed that the press release simply reported remedial measures taken by the city. Disciplining the officers responsible for the disputed incident constituted a remedial "measure" that Rule 407 barred from admission.[4]

2. When Is a Remedial Measure "Subsequent"? Rule 407 applies only to measures that are taken after "an earlier injury or harm."[5] Defendants sometimes invoke the rule to protect remedial measures taken after sale of a product to the plaintiff, but before the plaintiff's injury. The rule, however, shields only measures taken after the injury itself:

Example: In the Chevrolet Citation litigation described above, the Chases could not introduce evidence of a recall issued by General Motors after Betty Jo Chase was injured in her car. That recall occurred after "an earlier injury." The Chases, however, also had evidence that GM modified the brakes on its Citation cars three months after the Chases purchased their model, but before the injury occurred.

Analysis: The court allowed the Chases to present evidence of the modifications GM made in its braking system. That potentially remedial measure occurred after the Chases purchased their car but before Betty Jo was injured. Rule 407 clearly defines subsequent remedial measures as those that occur after **injury**, not after purchase of a potentially defective product.[6]

Why does Rule 407 focus on the time of injury or harm, rather than earlier times such as the date of sale? Before a party has been injured, a potential defendant has sufficient motivation to make its products safe; by correcting dangerous defects, it will avoid both litigation and liability. The evidentiary rules need not give potential defendants any special incentives to act with care during this period. It is only after a potential plaintiff has been injured that a defendant faces conflicting pressures: Correcting a dangerous defect may avoid future injuries, litigation, and liability,

---

4   Specht v. Jensen, 863 F.2d 700, 701 (10th Cir. 1988), aff'd after remand, 936 F.2d 584 (10th Cir. 1991).

5   Congress amended the rule in 1997 to add this concept. Beware of any decisions issued before that date, which might conflict with the discussion in this text but have been superseded.

6   General Motors, 856 F.2d at 22.

but making that correction immediately might compromise the defendant's interests in any lawsuit filed by the injured party. Rule 407 thus tailors its protection to this situation.

The same reasoning means that parties injured after the first-injured plaintiff may be able to rely upon evidence that is unavailable to the initial plaintiff. A remedial measure that occurred after the first plaintiff's injury may occur before the injuries of other plaintiffs:

> **Example:** In the Chevrolet Citation case, the Chases purchased their car in April 1980. General Motors modified the design of the Citation's braking system in July 1980. Betty Jo Chase suffered her injury, allegedly due to defective brakes, in January 1982. GM issued its recall letter in February 1983. Rule 407 thus allowed the Chases to introduce evidence of the design modification (which occurred before Betty Jo's injury) but not of the recall (which occurred after the injury).
>
> Suppose that Michael Andretti purchased an identical Citation in May 1980 and suffered injuries in an accident that occurred in March 1983. If Andretti had sued GM, claiming that defective brakes in the Citation caused the accident, would Rule 407 have allowed him to introduce evidence of either the brake modification or the recall to show liability?
>
> **Analysis:** Andretti would have been able to introduce evidence of both measures; both occurred before his injury, so Rule 407 would not exclude this evidence in his lawsuit.

Why does Rule 407 distinguish between Betty Jo Chase and Michael Andretti, both of whom suffered similar injuries? If the recall were admissible in Chase's lawsuit, GM might have chosen to wait until after resolution of her claim before issuing its recall. Rule 407 eliminates this disincentive, encouraging defendants to take remedial measures as quickly as possible.

Andretti's lawsuit, however, did not discourage GM's recall in the same way that Chase's might have; Andretti had not even been injured at the time GM issued the recall. On the contrary, the possibility of preventing future injuries (and liability) should have encouraged GM to issue the recall. If the brakes were dangerous, then recalling vehicles and repairing those brakes was the best way to avoid further injuries and lawsuits. No social policy, therefore, prevents Andretti from introducing evidence of the recall. Rule 407 is not designed to shield defendants from liability; it targets only a very specific situation in which pending litigation may discourage remedial measures.

3. Negligence, Strict Liability, and Other Mental States. The classic case for application of Rule 407 is a tort claim for negligence, but the rule applies to all controversies, including those based on contract, intentional harm, and strict liability. Defendants increasingly invoke Rule 407 in a wide variety of contexts:

> **Example:** A research and risk assessment company, 21st Services, hired Vera Dolan as a consultant to write a manual for MedDiag, one of its software programs. Disagreements arose between Dolan and 21st Services, prompting a lawsuit in which Dolan claimed that the company had appropriated her work. Dolan's legal claims included breach of contract, fraud, conversion, and copyright infringement; her allegations suggested both negligence and intentional misconduct. At trial, Dolan offered evidence that shortly after she filed her lawsuit, 21st Services dropped some portions of the MedDiag manual that Dolan had written and added an explicit acknowledgement of her contributions in the manual's introduction. 21st Services objected under Rule 407 to introduction of this evidence.

> **Analysis:** The district judge excluded 21st Services' remedial efforts under Rule 407. The judge concluded that the company's "post-litigation efforts to redesign the MedDiag system in order to mitigate potential damages and/or potentially resolve the lawsuit . . . [were] precisely the type of evidence that must be excluded from consideration under Federal Rule of Evidence 407."[7]

Note that applying Rule 407 in a contract dispute invokes somewhat different policies than those that prompted the original common law rule. Courts devised the rule barring evidence of subsequent remedial measures in tort cases, hoping to encourage defendants to take steps that would protect other individuals from injury. A similar rationale applies in employment discrimination cases like the *Peck* example discussed above; if a company adopts remedial measures, it may protect

---

7   VFD Consulting, Inc. v. 21st Servs., 425 F. Supp. 2d 1037, 1052 (N.D. Cal. 2006). The parties subsequently settled this dispute and, pursuant to their settlement, the court vacated this order. VFD Consulting, Inc. v. 21st Servs., 2006 WL 870995 (N.D. Cal. Apr. 3, 2006).

other workers from harassment. The rationale for the rule in a contract action, however, is somewhat different. A remedial measure is unlikely to protect third parties from injury, but it may mitigate harm suffered by the plaintiff. The broad language of Rule 407 reaches all types of liability, and courts have adapted the rule's underlying policy to a wide variety of claims.

As courts broadened the applicability of Rule 407, a dispute arose about whether the rule applied to strict liability actions or only to ones based on "fault." Congress resolved this controversy in 1997 by amending Rule 407 to confirm that it applies to strict liability actions; the rule now explicitly includes claims based on "a defect in a product or its design; or a need for a warning or instruction."[8] In its revised form, Federal Rule 407 applies to any type of action regardless of the underlying theory of recovery.

Some states continue to limit their version of Rule 407 to fault-based cases. In those states, plaintiffs claiming injury under a strict liability theory may introduce evidence of subsequent remedial measures unless the evidence runs afoul of a different rule.

4. Remedial Measures by Non-Parties. The language of Rule 407 is quite broad. Read literally, the rule would bar admission of subsequent remedial measures adopted by any person or organization, even one who is not a party to the lawsuit. But the central policy behind the rule, to encourage prompt remedial measures, applies only when one party seeks to introduce evidence of a measure carried out by another **party**. Non-parties have no fear of implicitly admitting liability, so they don't need the incentive offered by Rule 407.

On this point, the courts have followed the policies motivating Rule 407, rather than its literal language; most federal courts have held that Rule 407 excludes evidence of subsequent remedial measures only when one party offers evidence of repairs made by another party:

> **Example:** Mark Fairweather owned pastureland in Oklahoma. He leased the land to the R.C. Drummond West Ranch Trust, which used the land to graze its cattle. Several of the Trust's cows broke through the fence surrounding the land and strayed onto an adjoining highway. William and

---

8   Be aware that this rule change supersedes any pre-1997 federal cases refusing to apply Rule 407 to strict liability claims.

Fredricka Mehojah, who were driving on the highway, rounded a curve and collided with the cows before they were able to stop. The Mehojahs suffered serious injuries and sued the Trust for negligence in placing their cattle in a field that was not properly fenced. The Trust filed a motion in limine to exclude any evidence that Fairweather installed a stronger fence the day after the accident.

Analysis: The appellate court held that Rule 407 does not apply to repairs made by non-parties to the litigation. The action taken by Fairweather thus was admissible.[9]

 Although the courts of appeals have uniformly held that Rule 407 does not apply to remedial actions by third parties, a few lower court judges and dissenting opinions have followed the rule's literal language to reach a different conclusion. An enterprising attorney might raise this contrary interpretation—especially in a circuit that has not yet adopted the majority view.

5. Other Purposes: Ownership and Control. As noted in the introduction, whether or not a subsequent remedial measure is admissible depends upon the purpose for which it is offered. If the plaintiff offers the subsequent remedial measure to prove negligence, culpable conduct, a defect in a product, a defect in a product's design, or a need for a warning or instruction—in other words, to prove liability on the part of the defendant—then the evidence is inadmissible. However, if the plaintiff offers the evidence for any other relevant purpose, Rule 407 does not bar admission. The second sentence of the rule lists a number of possible other purposes for which a party may introduce evidence of subsequent remedial measures.

Two of these other purposes are "ownership" and "control." If a defendant claims that it did not own or control the instrument that injured the plaintiff, the plaintiff may introduce evidence of subsequent remedial measures—not to prove that the original condition of the instrument was unreasonably dangerous, but rather as evidence that the defendant did own or control that instrument. Few people fix items that don't belong to them.

---

9   Mehojah v. Drummond, 56 F.3d 1213, 1214–15 (10th Cir. 1995). The court, however, affirmed the case even though the trial court had not admitted the evidence, on the ground that the trial court's error did not affect the "substantial rights" of the parties. See Chapter 5 to review the standards of review that appellate courts apply to evidentiary issues.

Example: Eric Clausen slipped on a ramp and injured his back while working at a fuel terminal. He sued both the company that owned the facility (Storage Tank) and the one that occupied it (Sea-3), claiming that the ramp was negligently maintained. At trial, Storage Tank argued that although they owned the facility, they had no control over the ramp, since it was occupied by Sea-3 at the time of the accident. In response, Clausen offered evidence that after the accident Storage Tank replaced the ramp with a set of steps. Storage Tank objected to this evidence under Rule 407.

Analysis: The appeals court upheld the admission of the evidence. Replacement of the ramp was a subsequent remedial measure, but Storage Tank had disputed its control of the ramp. By raising this issue, the company allowed Clausen to introduce Storage Tank's remedial step, not to show fault, but to demonstrate its control.[10]

6. Other Purposes: Feasibility. Rule 407 specifically permits a party to introduce evidence of subsequent remedial measures against a party who disputes "feasibility." A party disputes feasibility when it claims that it could not have remedied a dangerous situation because of economic, physical, or other constraints. Under these circumstances, evidence that the party did subsequently remedy the danger is strong evidence that the change was feasible. Rule 407 therefore allows litigants to introduce evidence of the subsequent remedial measure when an opponent disputes feasibility:

Example: Saundra Friedman suffered serious injuries when the cover blew off of a pressure cooker manufactured by National Presto Industries. Friedman sued National Presto, alleging negligence in the product's design. National Presto claimed that it was not physically possible to make the pressure cooker safer; some risk is inevitable when cooking under pressure. Friedman countered by offering evidence that later models of National Presto's pressure cookers featured a device that locked the cover of the cooker when its contents were under pressure. National Presto raised a Rule 407 objection.

---

10   Clausen v. Sea-3, Inc., 21 F.3d 1181, 1189–92 (1st Cir. 1994).

Analysis: The design change was a subsequent remedial measure, ordinarily inadmissible under Rule 407. But by claiming that it was not feasible to design a safer pressure cooker, National Presto opened the door to evidence of its new design. Friedman could offer this evidence, not to prove that National Presto's original design was negligent, but to counter the company's claim that a different design was not feasible.[11]

The distinction between "feasibility" and "liability" appears amorphous at best. Even if a judge instructs the jury to consider the subsequent measure only on the issue of feasibility, not liability, won't a jury necessarily conclude that feasibility of a safer design establishes fault in the earlier one? This is a strong possibility, which is why defendants vigorously resist introduction of subsequent remedial measures.

It is possible, however, to show feasibility without establishing liability. A change might have been physically feasible, but economically costly. In the pressure cooker case, for example, National Presto might show that it always manufactured cookers with and without locking devices—and that Friedman had her choice of the two—but that the locking cookers cost twice as much. Alternatively, a design might have become physically or economically feasible after the plaintiff's injury because of technological advances. Evidence of a subsequent remedial measure to show feasibility thus is damaging, but not necessarily conclusive.

Heated litigation over the admissibility of subsequent remedial measures to show feasibility occurs most often in cases involving unique actions or products. When the product has many marketplace equivalents, plaintiffs can readily use the conduct or products of other individuals to show feasibility. Remember that Rule 407 does not exclude evidence of any measures taken by non-parties.

If National Presto had not disputed the feasibility of making a safer pressure cooker, for example, Friedman would not have been able to introduce evidence of National Presto's subsequent design. But lots of companies make pressure cookers; Friedman could have introduced another company's design to show that National Presto's cooker was unsafe. Offering evidence of the defendant's own remedial

---

11   This example draws on Friedman v. National Presto Indus., Inc., 566 F. Supp. 762 (E.D.N.Y. 1983). The ruling in that case, however, occurred in response to the company's in limine motion to suppress evidence of the later design. The trial judge ruled that he could not resolve that issue until trial, when it would be clear whether National Presto disputed feasibility of an alternative design.

measure, however, packs a special punch with the jury. Even when the actions of nonparties provide usable evidence, therefore, plaintiffs like Friedman attempt to introduce evidence of the defendant's own remedial measures.

7. "If Disputed." Although Rule 407 explicitly recognizes that parties may prove subsequent remedial measures to show ownership, control, or feasibility, those exceptions carry a significant limit: They arise only if "disputed" by the opposing party.[12] In other words, the plaintiff cannot introduce evidence of subsequent remedial measures to prove ownership or control unless the defendant somehow denies that she owned or controlled the dangerous condition. Similarly, the plaintiff cannot use the defendant's design change to prove "feasibility" unless the defendant has argued that there was no feasible way to make the conditions safer.

This is a necessary limitation, because otherwise the exception would swallow the rule; plaintiffs would always offer subsequent remedial measures to prove ownership, control, or feasibility. But the limit creates a sometimes difficult question: When is a defendant "disputing" ownership, control, or feasibility? Sometimes the denial is obvious: The defendant corporation claims in the pleadings that the employee who caused the accident did not work for the defendant, or the defendant homeowner takes the stand and testifies directly that he does not own the land where the dangerous condition existed. But frequently the parties contest whether the defendant has disputed feasibility. Most tort defendants argue that their product or property was reasonably safe at the time of the incident, and it is difficult to make that argument without the defendant also claiming—sometimes inadvertently—that there was no feasible way to make it safer.

 The result is a battle between the plaintiff's attorney and the defendant's witnesses. The plaintiff's attorney tries to ask questions that will lead the defendant to dispute feasibility: "Isn't it true that there were safer ways to design the thresher?" "Isn't it true that you could have checked the patient's feeding tubes every fifteen minutes instead of every hour?" The defendant's witnesses try to defend the design, procedure, or conditions that caused the injury, without going too far and claiming that no safer method was feasible at the time. If the defendant's witnesses end up stating that no improvement was feasible, and yet the defendant later made such an improvement, then the plaintiff can admit evidence of that

---

12 Before 2011, Rule 407 used the phrase "if controverted" rather than "if disputed." The Advisory Committee updated the language to make the rule more readable; it intended no substantive change. Judicial decisions construing the "if controverted" phrase remain binding.

improvement under Rule 407. Here is a critical area in which good advocacy—either in cross-examining the witnesses or in preparing them properly ahead of time—can determine the admissibility of a significant piece of evidence.

8. Other Purposes: Impeachment. Rule 407 also allows a party to introduce evidence of subsequent remedial measures for the purpose of "impeachment." Impeachment is the process of discrediting a witness; we will study this concept in greater detail starting in Chapter 17. Rule 407, however, offers a good introduction to the process of impeachment.

One popular way to discredit a witness is to introduce evidence conflicting with the witness's testimony. If a witness testifies that the "day of the accident was bright and sunny," for example, an opponent may introduce testimony from other witnesses that the day was dark and cloudy.

One can easily imagine ways to discredit or "impeach" witnesses by using evidence of subsequent remedial measures. If, for example, a company's human resources manager testifies in an employment discrimination case that the company had "careful guidelines to assure fair evaluation of all job applicants," the plaintiff could discredit that testimony by introducing evidence that the company changed its evaluation procedures after the plaintiff sued. A change of procedure suggests that the previous guidelines were not as "careful" or "fair" as the manager claimed.

The problem with this interpretation of Rule 407's "impeachment" exception is that it would wipe out the entire rule. A party could always claim that evidence of subsequent remedial measures conflicted with or discredited some witness's testimony.

To avoid this result, courts have attempted to craft a narrow meaning of "impeachment" for the purposes of Rule 407. Trial judges look for a closer fit between the remedial measure and the testimony it is supposed to impeach. A judge is most likely to admit the evidence when (1) a witness makes a specific representation that conflicts with the subsequent remedial measure, (2) the witness makes an absolute declaration like "the product was perfectly safe," or (3) the witness making the statement was personally involved in implementing the remedial measure.

Here is a case illustrating the circumstances under which courts are most likely to admit evidence of a subsequent remedial measure to impeach a witness:

Example: James Dollar was crushed to death while operating a backhoe made by the Long Manufacturing Company. Dollar's mother sued Long, claiming that the backhoe was negligently designed. Max Saunders, the defendant's design engineer, testified at trial that in his opinion the backhoe was safe to operate while connected to a rollbar-equipped tractor; Dollar had been using the backhoe in that manner when he died.

The plaintiff then attempted to impeach Saunders with a memo that Saunders sent to all Long retailers after Dollar's death. In the memo, Saunders warned dealers that "[i]t has been determined that a backhoe operator can be crushed to death against the rollbar or safety cab where the backhoe is not rigidly mounted." Long Manufacturing objected to introduction of this memo as a subsequent remedial measure protected by Rule 407.

Analysis: The trial judge refused to allow the plaintiff to introduce Saunders's memo, concluding that Rule 407 protected the memo. Remember that a "measure" does not need to be a physical change in a product; it can consist of a warning to dealers like the one Saunders sent.

The court of appeals agreed that the memo was a subsequent remedial measure, but it held that the plaintiff properly attempted to use the memo for impeachment rather than to prove liability. Confronting Saunders with his own memo, which contradicted the opinion he voiced in court, qualified as impeachment. The specificity of Saunders' memo helped support this conclusion.[13]

The impeachment exception, like the feasibility one, puts the defendant in a difficult spot. The defendant wants to tell the jury that the original product was safe, but he opens himself up to impeachment if he has changed the product since the accident. One strategy is to avoid calling witnesses who were directly involved in remedial measures; these individuals, like Saunders, are particularly vulnerable to impeachment.

Another strategy is for defense witnesses to limit their testimony to general statements about safety. These statements usually will not support admission of subsequent remedial measures for impeachment:

---

13   Dollar v. Long Mfg. N.C., Inc., 561 F.2d 613, 618 (5th Cir. 1977).

Example: Joseph Kelly injured his back while dismounting from a forklift manufactured by the Crown Equipment Company. He sued Crown, claiming that the forklift was defectively designed. Crown's expert witness, Dr. Watkins, testified that the forklift was "properly designed." Kelly then offered evidence that Crown had modified the forklift, arguing that this impeached Watkins' testimony.

Analysis: The court rejected evidence of the remedial measure under Rule 407. Watkins' testimony was not inconsistent with redesign of the forklift. He maintained that the forklift used an "excellent and proper design," but he did not testify that the design was "the best or only one possible," say that the design could not be improved, or make other statements contradicting Crown's redesign.[14]

As these examples suggest, the exceptions for impeachment and proof of feasibility sometimes overlap under Rule 407. If a defendant claims that a product was "as safe as it possibly could have been," the plaintiff may argue that evidence of subsequent remedial measures is admissible both to impeach the witness and to show feasibility. A party may assert both grounds if both apply. And both of these grounds are ones that require fact-specific arguments by well-prepared advocates.

D. Rules 105 and 403: Limiting Instructions and Unfair Prejudice.

Rules 105 (limiting instructions) and 403 (unfair prejudice) complement Rule 407. If the judge admits evidence of subsequent remedial measures for a purpose other than proving liability, the defendant can request a limiting instruction. Under Rule 105, the judge must give that instruction if a party timely requests it. The instruction will attempt to explain the permissible uses of the subsequent remedial measure to the jury, while restraining them from using that evidence to establish liability.

As in other contexts, the defendant may believe that a limiting instruction is ineffective in preventing unfair prejudice. It is difficult to explain to jurors that evidence of the repairs they heard about can be used to impeach or prove feasibility, but is not evidence of liability.

---

14   Kelly v. Crown Equip. Co., 970 F.2d 1273, 1278 (3d Cir. 1992). If you read the Kelly opinion, note that the 1997 amendments to Rule 407 supersede some of the other discussion in this case, such as the court's ruling on post-manufacture, pre-accident changes in design.

To address this problem, defendants often urge the judge to exclude evidence of subsequent remedial measures under Rule 403, even if the evidence is admissible under Rule 407. Judges sometimes agree and exclude the evidence under Rule 403. On the other hand, Rule 403 requires the defendant to show that the evidence's unfair prejudice (the chance that the jury will inappropriately use the evidence as proof of liability) substantially outweighs its probative value (the utility the evidence has in proving disputed ownership, control, or feasibility). In most cases, judges decide that a limiting instruction will sufficiently reduce the unfair prejudice to admit the evidence.

Quick Summary

Rule 407 prevents litigants from introducing evidence of another party's subsequent remedial measures. The rule furthers an important social policy, encouraging potential litigants to remedy dangerous conditions promptly without fear of compromising their position in court. The rule also prevents unfairly prejudicial evidence from reaching the jury; jurors sometimes give undue weight to subsequent remedial measures, assuming that those repairs conclusively demonstrate that the original design or procedure was unreasonably dangerous.

Courts have applied Rule 407 to a wide variety of legal claims, including strict liability and contract actions. But the rule has important exceptions: It only excludes measures taken after an injury, measures adopted by another party to the lawsuit, and evidence introduced for the purpose of showing liability. When these exceptions apply, parties attempting to exclude evidence of subsequent remedial measures may turn to **Rules 105** (limiting instructions) and **403** (unfair prejudice) for possible relief.

Test Your Understanding

To assess your understanding of the material in this chapter, click here to take a quiz, or go to the Quizzes module from the eBook on your eProducts bookshelf.

10

Settlements and Offers to Compromise

Key Concepts

- **Rule 408:** Bars Admission of Civil Settlement Offers
- Also Protects Statements and Conduct from Negotiations
- Applies in Both Civil and Criminal Cases
- Exceptions

A. Introduction and Policy. Settlements are essential to the civil justice system: Courtrooms and judges could not begin to accommodate full trials on every civil claim. Full-fledged trials are expensive and time-consuming for litigants as well. As a result, most parties settle their claims before trial.

Rule 408, the second Article IV rule that we will study in this section, facilitates civil settlements and the negotiations that precede them. The rule protects settlement offers, as well as statements made during settlement discussions, from admission at trial. If those offers and statements were admissible, parties would be reluctant to discuss their claims candidly before trial and fewer settlements would occur.

Rule 408 also reflects concerns about the unfair prejudicial effect of settlement offers. Given the expense of litigation, some litigants offer to settle even if they believe they are not at fault. Jurors may not understand these decisions, and may greatly inflate the probative value of a party's offer to settle. Rule 408 exists, in part, to prevent juries from interpreting settlement offers as conclusive evidence of liability.

On the other hand, many statements made during settlement negotiations are highly probative; litigants may admit liability or make other significant concessions. These statements, moreover, are likely to be true: Their admission is unlikely to prejudice the parties **unfairly**.

The primary rationale behind Rule 408, therefore, is a policy justification: to ensure that parties are not inhibited from making offers or statements during the settlement negotiation process. To further the social policy favoring settlements, Rule 408 shields most of that process from admission at trial.

B. The Rule. The policy behind **Rule 408** is straightforward, but the rule is relatively complex. Rule 408 attempts to protect statements made during settlement discussions, while allowing parties to capitalize on admissions made by an adversary in other contexts. The rule also recognizes circumstances when justice requires introducing evidence from compromise negotiations. Incorporating these differing concerns generates a complex rule.

The best way to master Rule 408 is to focus first on the language that broadens the rule's reach, expanding the evidence **excluded** from trial. Following the metaphor of nets cast into a river of evidence, we'll look first at how large this net is and how tight its weave is. After exploring those aspects of the rule, we'll go back over the text to examine the features that restrict its scope and allow **admission** of some evidence related to settlements. In other words, we'll examine the holes in the net that allow some evidentiary fish to swim through.

1. Broadest Reach: What Is Excluded? Here is the first part of Rule 408, with the language expanding its scope underlined. The final part of the rule narrows its scope, so we'll postpone consideration of that text for now:

RULE 408. Compromise Offers and Negotiations

(a) **Prohibited Uses.** Evidence of the following is not admissible—on behalf of any party—either to <u>prove or disprove the validity or amount</u> of a <u>disputed claim</u> or to <u>impeach by a prior inconsistent statement or a contradiction</u>:

   (1) <u>furnishing</u>, promising, or offering—or accepting, promising to accept, or offering to accept—a valuable consideration in <u>compromising or attempting to compromise</u> the <u>claim</u>; and

   (2) conduct or a statement made <u>during compromise negotiations</u> about the claim . . . .

This language defines the reach of Rule 408 broadly in three ways:

(a) First, Rule 408 applies to **all parties**. This means that a party cannot introduce any evidence of settlement offers or negotiating statements, not even evidence of their **own** offers or statements. The drafters of the rule concluded that introducing any evidence from settlement negotiations might chill settlement discussions.[1]

> **Example:** The W Corporation fired Dirk Chaney, a 64-year-old vice president. Chaney sued for age discrimination. During settlement negotiations, W offered Chaney an alternative position as a salesperson. Chaney refused the offer and discussions broke down. At trial six months later, W attempts to introduce evidence of its offer to Chaney. The company argues that the offer shows that it lacked any discriminatory intent, while Chaney's refusal shows his failure to mitigate damages.

> **Analysis:** Rule 408 bars the company's evidence. Although W is attempting to introduce its own settlement offer, the rule prohibits this evidence when offered "on behalf of any party" to prove or disprove liability.

(b) Second, Rule 408 defines compromise **offers and acceptances** very broadly. The second underlined phrase encompasses offers, promises, acceptances, offers to accept, promises to accept, and any consideration extended as part of the settlement.

> **Example:** Barry drove through a red light and hit Hillary's car. Hillary suffered a broken toe and sued Barry. Their lawyers arrange a settlement conference. At the conference Barry says: "I'll give you $5,000 to settle the claim." Hillary refuses the offer and proceeds to trial, where she attempts to introduce Barry's offer.

[1] This phrase in Rule 408 is a recent addition. Acting on a recommendation from the Advisory Committee, Congress amended Rule 408 in December 2006 to clarify that the rule bars litigants from introducing evidence of their own statements or conduct during settlement discussions. Don't be misled by judicial decisions published before then that reach a contrary result; the amendment supersedes those decisions.

Analysis: Barry offered to furnish a valuable consideration ($5,000) to compromise the claim. Rule 408 prevents Hillary from introducing this offer.

(c) Finally, and most significantly, the rule protects all **conduct or statements** made during compromise negotiations, not just the operative offers and acceptances. This language greatly expands the protection that was available before adoption of the Federal Rules. The common law shielded settlement offers and acceptances, but not other statements made during negotiation. The drafters of Rule 408 believed that a broader rule would promote franker, more productive settlement discussions.

Example: To encourage Hillary to accept his offer of $5,000, described above, Barry says during their settlement conference: "Look, I know I ran the red light, and I'm sorry about that." Hillary refuses both the settlement and the apology, proceeds to court, and attempts to introduce Barry's statement about running the light.

Analysis: Barry's statement occurred during compromise negotiations regarding Hillary's claim. Rule 408 prevents Hillary from introducing it.

Example: A more forgiving Hillary, moved by Barry's apology, replies during their conference: "I appreciate that, and I wasn't all that badly injured. See, I've regained full use of my toe." She then wiggles her injured toe to show its full mobility. Barry, seeing how slight Hillary's injury was, decides to take his chances before a jury. He withdraws his settlement offer, proceeds to court, and attempts to introduce Hillary's statement as well as her conduct wiggling the toe.

Analysis: Hillary's statement and conduct occurred during compromise negotiations regarding her claim. Rule 408 stops Barry from introducing evidence of either one.

Example: At trial, Barry defends on the ground that he ran the red light because he was transporting a badly injured child to the emergency room. He attempts to introduce evidence of the statement he made to Hillary in the previous example ("I know I ran the red light, and I'm sorry about that") to substantiate his claim that he knowingly ran the red light but had justification for doing so.

> **Analysis:** Barry made his statement during settlement negotiations so, even though it is his own statement, he cannot introduce it. The drafters of Rule 408 decided to play it safe in promoting candid settlement discussions by preventing any party from introducing statements from those negotiations.

2. The Limits on Rule 408: What Is Still Admissible? Despite the broad reach of Rule 408, the rule incorporates several important limits. This evidentiary net, in other words, has several holes that evidence can wriggle through. Here is the first part of Rule 408 again, this time with its limiting features underlined:

> ## RULE 408. Compromise Offers and Negotiations
>
> **(a) Prohibited Uses.** Evidence of the following is not admissible—on behalf of any party—either to prove or disprove the validity or amount of a disputed claim or to impeach by a prior inconsistent statement or a contradiction:
>
> **(1)** furnishing, promising, or offering—or accepting, promising to accept, or offering to accept—a valuable consideration in compromising or attempting to compromise the claim; and
>
> **(2)** conduct or a statement made during compromise negotiations about the claim . . . .

This portion of Rule 408 includes four separate limiting features:

(a) First, the rule repeatedly uses the word **claim**. Although neither the rule nor its legislative history define this term, courts have used it to restrict the discussions that qualify for Rule 408's protection. For Rule 408 to apply, the disagreement between parties must have matured into a "claim." Parties often litigate this aspect of Rule 408; we'll discuss below how courts attempt to distinguish "claims" eliciting the rule's protection from disputes or disagreements that do not qualify for protection.

(b) Second, Rule 408 requires that the parties **dispute** some aspect of the claim. If both parties agree that liability exists and also agree on the extent of damages, Rule 408 doesn't shield their discussions:

Example: Elle Woods purchased a computer from the EZ-Pay Computer Company, promising to pay $100 per month for 15 months. After the first two months, Elle stopped making payments. EZ-Pay sent Elle a letter declaring that her payments were overdue and that she owed additional interest on the missed payments. Elle signed a form agreeing that she still owed $1300 plus the new interest; she also promised to resume payments immediately. When Elle defaulted again, EZ-Pay sued to recover the debt.

Analysis: In its lawsuit, EZ-Pay may introduce the form that Elle signed after missing the original payments. Elle did not dispute either her debt to EZ-Pay or the amount of that debt. The form, therefore, does not qualify as a settlement shielded by Rule 408.

(c) Third, to invoke Rule 408's shield, the statements or conduct must occur during "**compromise negotiations**" or while "compromising or attempting to compromise the claim." A formal settlement conference almost always qualifies as an attempt to compromise the claim, but courts often disagree about whether other communications are part of compromise negotiations. We'll explore litigation over this issue in the Courtroom section below.

(d) Finally, Rule 408 excludes statements and conduct made during compromise negotiations only when a party offers that evidence for one of the **three purposes** specified in the rule (and underlined above). Those purposes are: (1) to prove the validity or amount of a claim; (2) to disprove that validity or amount; and (3) to impeach a witness's testimony through a prior inconsistent statement or contradiction.[2] Like many evidentiary rules, Rule 408 excludes evidence only when a party attempts to use that evidence for particular purposes. As with almost every rule of evidence, a critical question to ask in evaluating admissibility under Rule 408 is: What is the party trying to prove by offering the evidence? We'll explore this issue further in the Courtroom section, after examining the final portion of Rule 408.

---

2   Congress, acting on the Advisory Committee's recommendation, added the third purpose to the rule in December 2006. Many courts recognized this purpose before the amendment, but some did not. The amendment supersedes any contrary decisions issued before that time.

3. Still More Limiting Language. For convenience, we have looked so far only at the first part of Rule 408. Here are the portions of the rule we have not yet examined, underlined and shown in context. All of this final text narrows the rule's scope even more, making still more evidence admissible:

RULE 408. Compromise Offers and Negotiations

(a) Prohibited Uses. Evidence of the following is not admissible . . . .

    (2) conduct or a statement made during compromise negotiations about the claim—except when offered in a criminal case and when the negotiations related to a claim by a public office in the exercise of its regulatory, investigative, or enforcement authority.

(b) Exceptions. The court may admit this evidence for another purpose, such as

- proving a witness's bias or prejudice,
- negating a contention of undue delay, or
- proving an effort to obstruct a criminal investigation or prosecution.

These portions of the rule include two different limits.

First, section (b) underscores the fact that Rule 408 prohibits introduction of evidence for some purposes but not others. Section (b) confirms that parties may introduce evidence from settlement negotiations for any **purpose other than the forbidden** ones specified in section (a). Section (b) also offers three common examples of other purposes. This list, however, is not exclusive; parties may introduce evidence from compromise negotiations for any purpose other than the explicitly prohibited ones.

Second, the text at the end of subsection (a)(2) allows some settlement statements to be used during criminal trials. Before 2006, courts divided on the question of whether Rule 408 barred admission of civil settlement evidence just in civil trials or in both civil and criminal trials.

To resolve this conflict, the Advisory Committee and Congress added the long "except when" clause to subsection (a)(2) in December 2006. On the one hand, by referring to criminal cases, the language recognizes that the protections of Rule 408 generally do apply in criminal prosecutions. Under most circumstances, neither the prosecutor nor the criminal defendant may rely on evidence from civil settlement negotiations that Rule 408 protects.

On the other hand, the new language in Rule 408 allows prosecutors and defendants in criminal cases to introduce evidence from one category of civil settlement negotiations. When the civil settlement discussions occurred in a civil proceeding that involved a "public office" exercising its "regulatory, investigative, or enforcement authority," the prosecutor and defendant may introduce evidence from those negotiations in a subsequent criminal case. The definitional list in Rule 101(b)(3) expands the meaning of a "public office" to include any government agency.

The rationale for this exception is weak, making the exception itself difficult to understand. The Advisory Committee explained that it was allowing introduction of evidence from these settlement discussions, despite the strong policies favoring confidentiality of settlement negotiations generally, because "[w]here an individual makes a statement in the presence of government agents, its subsequent admission in a criminal case should not be unexpected."[3] This undoubtedly is true but, absent Rule 408 **all** parties would expect their statements to be used against them in future proceedings. The exception for statements made during attempts to settle regulatory or quasi-criminal investigations cuts against the underlying rationale of Rule 408, which seeks to encourage uninhibited settlement discussions.

The fact that the drafters embedded this new exception in subsection (a)(2) adds to the confusion. Placement in subsection (a)(2) means that the exception applies only to that subsection, not to the prohibition in subsection (a)(1). The bottom line, therefore, is that subsection (a)(1) continues to prohibit prosecutors and criminal defendants from introducing evidence of civil settlement **offers, promises, and acceptances** in criminal proceedings, even if those offers, promises, or acceptances occurred when negotiating with a government agency exercising its regulatory, investigative, or enforcement authority. But the prosecutor and criminal defendant

---

3   Fed. R. Evid. 408 advisory committee's note. The Committee also suggested that individuals involved in these civil enforcement proceedings could "seek to protect against subsequent disclosure through negotiation and agreement with the civil regulator or an attorney for the government." Id. This, however, seems like a faint hope except for the largest corporate defendants. The government is one of the most difficult adversaries to negotiate with, given its size and prosecutorial power.

can introduce evidence of **other statements** made during settlement discussions related to the regulatory enforcement action.

We'll explore an example of this newest addition to Rule 408 in the Courtroom section below. But first, having explored all of Rule 408's twists and turns, let's quickly summarize what evidence the rule protects and what evidence it allows parties to introduce. The flow chart on the next page summarizes all of Rule 408's requirements. Note that the flow chart does not ask which party is offering the evidence because that question is unnecessary under this rule; the rule applies equally to all litigants.

C. In the Courtroom. Rule 408 is complex, but it is well worth mastering. The rule plays an important role in civil cases, because almost every civil trial occurs after failed settlement discussions. Parties often try to introduce admissions and other statements from those negotiations; understanding Rule 408 is essential to protect your client. The December 2006 amendments to the rule also give it increased prominence in criminal prosecutions. Government agencies pursue a large number of civil regulatory, investigative, and enforcement actions ranging from securities and tax probes to environmental ones. Counsel must understand Rule 408's implications for statements made during those civil negotiations; careless statements may lead to criminal liability.

Here are some further examples of the role Rule 408 plays in the courtroom, focusing on the issues that parties most often contest.

1. What Is a "Claim"? Courts agree that a "claim" arises once a complaint has been filed. Most judges also agree that a claim arises once a party has hired an attorney and threatened to sue. Without those features, courts are less likely to perceive a claim, even though the parties dispute an issue:

> **Example:** In February 1974, Big O Tire Dealers began marketing automobile tires under the "Big Foot 60" and "Big Foot 70" brands. Several months later, the Goodyear Tire & Rubber Company decided to use the word "Bigfoot" to promote a new series of its tires. Goodyear asked Big O for a letter consenting to Goodyear's use of the Big-foot trademark. Big O refused, indicating that it planned to continue using the Big Foot designation, that Goodyear's use would damage Big O's business, and that Goodyear should refrain from its proposed use. Goodyear nonetheless launched a national advertising campaign using the Bigfoot trademark.

Rule 408 Flow Chart

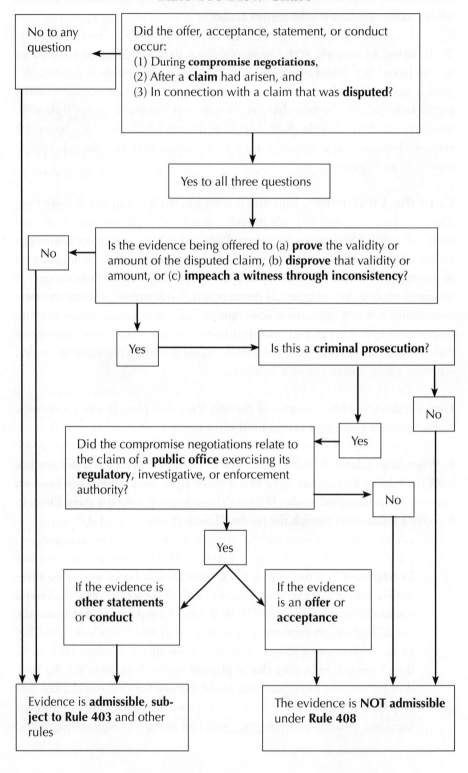

No to any question

Did the offer, acceptance, statement, or conduct occur:
(1) During **compromise negotiations**,
(2) After a **claim** had arisen, and
(3) In connection with a claim that was **disputed**?

Yes to all three questions

No

Is the evidence being offered to (a) **prove** the validity or amount of the disputed claim, (b) **disprove** that validity or amount, or (c) **impeach a witness through inconsistency**?

Yes

Is this a **criminal prosecution**?

No

Yes

Did the compromise negotiations relate to the claim of a **public office** exercising its **regulatory**, investigative, or enforcement authority?

No

Yes

If the evidence is **other statements** or **conduct**

If the evidence is an **offer** or **acceptance**

Evidence is **admissible, subject to Rule 403** and other rules

The evidence is **NOT admissible** under **Rule 408**

Big O sued for trademark infringement and sought to introduce evidence of the above discussions with Goodyear. The discussions tended to show knowledge, willful infringement, and other misconduct by Goodyear, all elements supporting its liability. Goodyear objected to introduction of the evidence under Rule 408.

Analysis: The district judge admitted the proffered evidence, ruling that no "claim" had arisen at the time the discussions occurred. Neither party had yet threatened litigation; these were business discussions exploring possible uses of the trademark. Rule 408, therefore, did not bar admission of the evidence. The court of appeals affirmed this ruling.[4]

2. When Do "Compromise Negotiations" Occur? Rule 408's protection hinges on the existence of both a claim and settlement negotiations. Formal negotiations, where both parties meet for the express purpose of discussing settlement, are easy to recognize. It is more difficult to determine whether other, less formal communications between parties are part of compromise negotiations. Here are some examples of how judges have drawn this line:

Example: The Lee Dolls Company produced an award-winning doll called the Millennium Angel. The Mann Company, another doll manufacturer, introduced a similar doll named My Special Angel. Lee Dolls sued Mann, claiming that Mann's doll copied the Millennium Angel and infringed several intellectual property statutes. Nine days after Lee Dolls served Mann with its complaint, Mann's president (Gideon Oberweger) approached Lee Dolls' president (Timothy Voss) at a trade show. Oberweger told Voss that he was "shocked that the Special Angel doll was not an original," that his company "would not intentionally copy another company's product," and that he hoped they could "work out the problem as businessmen." Voss did not respond to these overtures. At trial, Lee Dolls offered Oberweger's statements as admissions of liability. Oberweger objected, claiming that Rule 408 protected the statements because they occurred during a compromise negotiation.

---

4   Big O Tire Dealers, Inc. v. Goodyear Tire & Rubber Co., 561 F.2d 1365, 1372–73 (10th Cir. 1977). The district court's brief published discussion of this issue appears at 408 F. Supp. 1219, 1237 (D. Colo. 1976).

Analysis: The district judge rejected Oberweger's argument, concluding that no compromise negotiation occurred. Oberweger approached Voss unilaterally; Voss never signaled any openness to discussion. Nor did Oberweger make any concrete settlement offer. Rule 408 therefore permitted introduction of the statements.[5]

Example: The Harmonay Company was a subcontractor to the Binks Manufacturing Company on a construction project. Delays by Binks caused Harmonay increased costs; Harmonay sued Binks for breach of contract. One of Harmonay's lawyers sent Binks's lawyer a letter stating: "In accordance with our prior discussions and without prejudice to our clients' respective legal positions, I am taking the liberty of setting forth below summary of the damages suffered by Harmonay . . . ." After listing items of damage, the letter concluded by requesting "your client's earliest response."

At trial, Harmonay's witness claimed greater damages than those listed in the letter. Binks attempted to introduce the letter to impeach the witness by showing a prior inconsistent statement.

Analysis: The district judge concluded that the letter occurred during compromise negotiations. The reference to prior discussions, the phrase "without prejudice," and the request for a quick response all suggested ongoing attempts to settle the lawsuit. The judge excluded the letter under Rule 408.[6]

These two decisions suggest some of the factors that judges consider when deciding whether a statement occurred during compromise negotiations: (1) whether the statement was unilateral or occurred during bilateral discussions; (2) whether either party made a concrete offer; (3) whether attorneys were involved in the discussions; and (4) whether the parties used phrases (like "without prejudice") that are commonly used during settlement discussions. Judges, however, decide each case on its own facts; this issue is one that benefits from skillful advocacy.

---

5   This example is based on Lee Middleton Original Dolls, Inc. v. Seymour Mann, Inc., 299 F. Supp. 2d 892, 895–96 (E.D. Wis. 2004), although we have edited the parties' names for clarity and the conversation for brevity.

6   S. Leo Harmonay, Inc. v. Binks Mfg. Co., 597 F. Supp. 1014, 1023 (S.D.N.Y. 1984), aff'd mem., 762 F.2d 990 (2d Cir. 1985).

3. Settlements With Third Parties. Rule 408 applies to all settlement discussions, even those conducted by parties who are no longer involved in the case. If two plaintiffs sue a defendant, and the defendant settles with one of them, the remaining plaintiff cannot introduce the settlement as evidence of the defendant's liability. Likewise, if a plaintiff sues several defendants and settles with one of them, she cannot use that settlement against the other defendants at trial.

> **Example:** Hodari Sushi, a Japanese restaurant, mistakenly served four-day-old raw tuna to its customers one night. Two of its customers, Katy and Sarah, became severely ill from eating the tuna, and they each sued Hodari for negligently serving rancid food. Hodari offered each of the plaintiffs $10,000 and free sushi for a year if they agreed to drop their claims. Katy agreed to the deal, but Sarah rejected the offer and took her case to trial. At trial, Sarah called Katy to the stand and asked if Hodari had paid her $10,000 to settle the case. Hodari objected to the question.

> **Analysis:** The judge will sustain Hodari's objection and prevent Katy from testifying about her settlement. Rule 408 prohibits evidence of any settlements or settlement discussions, as long as the evidence is offered to show liability. Sarah seems to be offering the evidence for that purpose here.

As we'll see in the next two sections, evidence of Katy's settlement might be admissible if offered for other purposes. Applying Rule 408 to third-party settlements, however, makes sense as a policy matter. Otherwise, defendants in multi-party lawsuits would never be willing to settle a claim with any of the plaintiffs; the other plaintiffs would seize on that settlement as evidence of the defendant's liability.

Evidence of third-party settlements is also likely to confuse or unfairly prejudice the jury. A plaintiff who sues several defendants, for example, might settle for a small amount of money with one of the defendants. The plaintiff might believe that the one defendant is less culpable than the others, might need some immediate cash to pay medical expenses, or might be willing to give one defendant a discount for not continuing the expensive litigation process. Jurors may not understand the legal or strategic considerations that affect settlement amounts, and they might incorrectly interpret the low settlement as an accurate indicator of the plaintiff's injuries.

4. Other Purposes. Rule 408 broadly prohibits the use of settlement discussions to prove liability or damages, disprove those elements, or impeach a witness with inconsistencies. The rule, however, permits use of evidence from settlement discussions for other purposes. For example, a party may use evidence of settlement discussions to counter an argument that they delayed in pursuing their claim. Here is an example involving intellectual property:

Example: Emisphere Technologies, a medical research company, contracted with the pharmaceutical company Eli Lilly to collaborate in developing a new class of drugs. The contract required the companies to share research related to the project. Lilly breached this provision by conducting secret research, based on Emisphere's technology, and submitting its own patent application for the fruits of that research. When Emisphere discovered the patent application, it notified Lilly of the breach.

Lilly filed a suit for declaratory judgment to clarify the parties' rights under the contract. The two companies held a series of meetings attempting to settle the dispute. When those meetings failed, Emisphere terminated the contract and filed a counterclaim against Lilly for breach. Lilly defended against this claim by arguing that Emisphere had waived its claim for breach of contract by continuing to work with Lilly. Emisphere attempted to rebut this claim by introducing extensive evidence of its settlement negotiations with Lilly, arguing that it had not abandoned its claim but had attempted to settle it.

Analysis: The district judge admitted evidence of the settlement discussions. Since Lilly argued that Emisphere waived its rights by delaying termination of the contract, Rule 408 allowed Emisphere to introduce evidence from the settlement discussions to counter that claim.[7]

Emisphere behaved in this example like many parties do in response to breach of contract. When a breach occurs as part of a long-term relationship, parties often try to work the matter out rather than destroy the relationship through a courtroom battle. Attempting to resolve the breach without litigation leaves a party like

---

7   Eli Lilly & Co. v. Emisphere Techs., Inc., 408 F. Supp. 2d 668, 695 (S.D. Ind. 2006). The district court subsequently granted an injunction against Eli Lilly, although it did not discuss the Rule 408 issue further. Eli Lilly & Co. v. Emisphere Techs., Inc., No. 1:03-cv-1504-DFH-TAB, 2006 WL 1131786 (S.D. Ind. Apr. 25, 2006).

Emisphere open to the type of claim that Lilly made: that Emisphere had waived its breach of contract claim. Evidence of settlement discussions is an effective way to counter that claim, and Rule 408 allows using that evidence under these circumstances.

The list of other purposes in Rule 408 is not exclusive. Parties may introduce statements from settlement negotiations for any purpose other than the ones specifically prohibited by the rule. Courts, for example, have allowed parties to offer statements from settlement negotiations to support a claim that an opposing party engaged in frivolous or vexatious litigation.

Example: The Gen-X Company, an internet service provider, agreed to host websites and e-mail for the Veritas Media Group. Veritas failed to pay for the services; instead, it filed a federal lawsuit against Gen-X, claiming that the company had violated the antitrust laws, racketeering statute, and numerous other state and federal laws. The district judge dismissed most of these claims and, after a series of settlement discussions, Veritas voluntarily dismissed the remaining claim. Gen-X then moved for sanctions against Veritas, arguing that its lawsuit was a frivolous attempt to avoid paying amounts due under the parties' contract. As part of the sanctions case, Gen-X offered evidence from its settlement negotiations with Veritas.

Analysis: The district judge concluded that Rule 408 allowed consideration of the settlement evidence. Gen-X did not offer that evidence for any of the purposes prohibited by Rule 408. Although the rule does not explicitly list "evaluation of a sanctions motion" as "another" purpose, the rule's listing is not exclusive. Other courts, the judge noted, have also considered evidence from settlement negotiations when assessing the propriety of sanctions.[8]

5. Bias. One of the most common alternative purposes claimed by parties under Rule 408 is showing that a witness is biased. A witness who has settled a claim with one of the parties, for example, may develop a bias in favor of that party; other litigants may try to introduce evidence of the settlement to demonstrate that bias. Here is an example based on the Hodari Sushi hypothetical described above:

---

8   Joseph Giganti Veritas Media Group, Inc. v. Gen-X Strategies, Inc., 222 F.R.D. 299, 313 (E.D. Va. 2004).

Example: To defend against Sarah's claim, Hodari calls Katy as a witness at trial. On direct examination, Katy testifies: "The tuna that night was fine; I ate it and only felt a little stomach pain later in the evening." On cross-examination, Sarah's lawyer asks Katy: "Isn't it true that Hodari gave you $10,000 and free sushi for a year to settle your claim against them?" Hodari objects under Rule 408.

Analysis: In this context, the lawyer's question is permissible. By asking about Katy's settlement, Sarah's attorney is revealing that Katy may be biased in favor of Hodari. Out of gratitude for Hodari's generous offer, or because she wants to keep the restaurant in business to provide free sushi every night, Katy may shade her testimony to favor Hodari. Rule 408 allows parties to use evidence of settlements or settlement negotiations to show bias.

6. Impeachment: Inconsistency Versus Bias. In the previous example, Sarah used settlement evidence to discredit a witness (Katy) by showing possible bias. Another common way to impeach a witness is to show that the witness made an earlier statement that was inconsistent with the witness's testimony on the stand. It is important to understand the difference between these two types of impeachment, because Rule 408 allows parties to use settlement evidence for the first type of impeachment (bias), but not the second (inconsistency). A December 2006 amendment to Rule 408 clarified this point by specifically prohibiting the use of settlements or settlement negotiations to impeach witnesses with prior inconsistent statements or contradictions.[9]

The letter written by the Harmonay Company to the Binks Manufacturing Company, discussed in section 2 above, is one example of a prior inconsistent statement occurring during settlement that a party attempted to introduce at trial. Here is another example, based again on the hypothetical Hodari dispute:

Example: Sarah, like Katy, attempted to settle her claim with Hodari. During Sarah's settlement discussions with the restaurant, the restaurant's manager said: "I know that tuna was four days old; it got on the sushi counter by mistake." But after Sarah rejected the restaurant's offer, the case proceeded to trial. At trial, the same manager testifies: "That tuna was only four hours old. It was perfect for sushi." Sarah then moves to introduce evidence of the manager's contrary statement during settlement discussions.

---

9   As noted in footnote 2, any contrary rulings on this point issued before December 2006 are no longer good law.

Analysis: Rule 408 prevents Sarah from introducing this evidence. Although the manager's testimony contradicts statements he made during settlement negotiations, the drafters of Rule 408 concluded that it was more important to protect candor during those negotiations than to trap inconsistent witnesses in court. Sarah's counsel will have to try to undermine the manager's statements through cross-examination or other means.

Why does Rule 408 draw this distinction between discrediting a witness by showing bias (settlement evidence allowed) and impeaching the witness with prior inconsistent statements (settlement evidence disallowed)? The distinction derives from the rule's underlying goal of encouraging settlements. Introducing settlement-related evidence to show a witness's bias has little chilling effect on those compromise negotiations. The alleged bias often involves a third party who is no longer an active litigant. Bias of this nature, moreover, has strong probative value; if a witness has a financial stake or other strong interest in one party's recovery, the jury should know about that bias when evaluating credibility.

Allowing parties to introduce evidence of inconsistent statements made during settlement negotiations, on the other hand, would greatly impair Rule 408's goal. Parties would have to watch their words carefully during compromise discussions, shading every meaning to favor their legal claim. This restraint would significantly undermine the likelihood of settlement. Statements made during negotiations, moreover, may have weak probative value. Parties sometimes bargain for an apology; to secure agreement, a party might be willing to profess blame even when the law would not impose liability. Taken out of context, settlement talk might mislead the jury.

7. Preexisting Evidence. Can parties immunize evidence by discussing it during a settlement conference? Could a party, for example, bring a particularly damaging letter to the conference table and, by discussing it there, prevent the opposing party from introducing the letter at trial?

The answer to this question clearly is "no." Rule 408 was designed to promote settlement discussions, not to encourage shady strategies for withholding evidence. A previous version of Rule 408, in force through December 2006, included a sentence that attempted to make this clear. The sentence read:

> This rule does not require the exclusion of any evidence otherwise dis-
> coverable merely because it is presented in the course of compromise
> negotiations.

Courts and commentators found this sentence more clumsy than helpful. The
Advisory Committee recommended eliminating the sentence as unnecessary, and
Congress amended the rule to do so in December 2006. The stylistic change,
however, does not change the substantive rule. All courts agree that parties cannot
shelter preexisting evidence by discussing it during settlement negotiations.

8. Criminal Cases. The 2006 amendment to Rule 408 clarifies that the rule
applies to criminal as well as civil cases. Note that any criminal settlement negotiations (otherwise known as plea bargaining) are not covered by Rule 408. Rule
410, which we will consider in Chapter 12, sets out the rules for admitting offers
and statements made during plea bargaining. But occasionally a defendant will
face both civil and criminal liability for his actions, and he may make statements
relevant to the criminal case while trying to settle his civil dispute.

Rule 408 states that in most criminal trials, neither the prosecutor nor the accused
may introduce evidence from prior civil settlement negotiations for any of the
purposes prohibited by Rule 408. The rule, however, carves out an exception for
settlement discussions held during a civil regulatory, investigative, or enforcement
action conducted by a government agency. These are quasi-criminal proceedings,
and Rule 408 allows parties to introduce evidence from these settlement discussions
in a subsequent criminal prosecution:

Example: Joseph Smiley founded an investment company and solicited
$282,000 from elderly, naïve investors. He spent $281,000 of the funds
on himself, rather than investing the money as promised. The Securities
Division of the Indiana Secretary of State's Office initiated a civil investigation of Smiley's company and held several settlement negotiations with
Smiley. A federal grand jury subsequently indicted Smiley for mail fraud.
At the criminal trial, the prosecutor offered statements that Smiley made
during his discussions with the state Securities Division to prove that Smiley's conduct was fraudulent.

Analysis: Rule 408 allows introduction of this evidence. Although the rule applies in both civil and criminal lawsuits, so it ordinarily would protect Smiley's statements, the statements at issue here occurred during "negotiations related to a claim by a public office in the exercise of its regulatory, investigative, or enforcement authority." Rule 408(a)(2) specifically allows introduction of this evidence in a subsequent criminal proceeding.[10]

Note, however, that the prosecutor could not introduce evidence of any offers, acceptances, or promises from the civil settlement negotiations: The regulatory exception to Rule 408 applies only to other types of statements and conduct occurring during negotiations.

D. Rule 403 Again. Rule 408 establishes a fairly complex scheme governing the admission of evidence related to settlement negotiations. If the rule bars admission of proffered evidence, then the judge must exclude that evidence; no other rule trumps Rule 408 to guarantee admission. When Rule 408 allows introduction of evidence, however, a judge may still determine under **Rule 403** that admitting the evidence would cause unfair prejudice substantially outweighing any probative value. Rule 403 thus offers an important backup for parties seeking to exclude evidence related to settlement negotiations.

Rule 403 is particularly important when parties offer settlement evidence for a purpose other than those prohibited by Rule 408. Even though the evidence may further a legitimate other purpose, settlement evidence can seriously—and unfairly—harm the opposing party. Jurors may conclude, for example, that the party's willingness to participate in settlement discussions signaled a weak claim or that the party's statements constituted an admission of liability. The jury, in other words, may use statements admitted from settlement discussions to infer liability—one of the purposes prohibited by Rule 408—in addition to using that evidence for the legitimate other purpose.

For these reasons, parties can sometimes persuade a judge to exclude settlement evidence under Rule 403, even when Rule 408 clearly would admit that evidence:

---

10   These facts are based in part on United States v. Prewitt, 34 F.3d 436 (7th Cir. 1994), a decision that provided a model for the 2006 amendments.

Example: Jeremy Sweet was helping his aunt move furniture at her house. He fell while carrying a heavy bookcase down a staircase and sustained multiple injuries. Sweet sued both his aunt and Lays Home Improvement, a company that had recently renovated the stairs, claiming that the renovation was defective. Sweet settled the suit against his aunt for a small amount, but proceeded to trial against Lays. When Sweet called his aunt as a witness, Lays moved to introduce evidence of the settlement agreement. The company argued that, since the aunt no longer faced liability, she was likely to play down any of Jeremy's own carelessness and help him recover against Lays. Proving this bias, Lays argued, was "another purpose" expressly recognized by Rule 408.

Analysis: Although Rule 408 allows admission of this evidence, a judge might exclude it under Rule 403. Sweet's aunt might naturally favor a family member in a dispute with an unrelated company. But Lays's counsel can note that potential bias without referring to the settlement. Proving the settlement in this context adds little to the company's bias point. On the other hand, the jury might consider the small settlement as evidence either that Sweet considered his claim weak or that his damages were minor, both conclusions that would unfairly prejudice Sweet. In a case raising similar facts, a district judge excluded the settlement evidence.[11]

Keep Rule 403 in mind as a backup argument for excluding evidence related to settlement negotiations.

---

11   Sweeten v. Layson's Home Improvements, No. 1:04-CV-2771, 2007 WL 1189359 (M.D. Pa. Apr. 19, 2007). The judge in that case excluded the settlement evidence under both Rule 408 and 403. The Rule 408 ruling is questionable, but the decision seems sound as an application of Rule 403.

Quick Summary

Rule 408 encourages civil settlements by excluding evidence related to compromise negotiations from both civil and criminal trials. The rule encompasses offers, acceptances, and promises, as well as other statements or conduct occurring during settlement discussions. Rule 408 recognizes legitimate needs for admitting evidence by restricting its protection to statements made (a) after a claim arises, (b) during compromise negotiations, and (c) only when the statements are offered for one of three specified purposes. The rule also allows introduction at criminal trials of statements made during settlement discussions held with a government agency conducting a civil regulatory, investigative, or enforcement proceeding.

Test Your Understanding

To assess your understanding of the material in this chapter, click here to take a quiz, or go to the Quizzes module from the eBook on your eProducts bookshelf.

11

Medical Expenses

Key Concepts

- **Rule 409:** Offers to Pay Medical Expenses
- Protects Offer, Promise, or Payment, Not Other Statements
- Admission Allowed for Some Purposes

A. Introduction and Policy. Rule 409 is the simplest of the narrowly focused rules in Article IV. The rule excludes evidence of offers to pay medical expenses, as well as payment of those expenses, when offered to prove liability. Rule 409 thus encourages individuals and organizations to pay medical expenses for people who have been injured.

This principle serves a social goal and also protects parties from unfair prejudice. The rule furthers important humanitarian objectives by removing a factor that might discourage some potential litigants from paying the medical expenses of injured individuals. Good Samaritans shouldn't fear that their generous actions will be construed as admissions of liability if a lawsuit is filed. In this sense, Rule 409 furthers a worthwhile social policy.

The rule also advances important business and judicial purposes. Some businesses find it beneficial to pay immediately the medical expenses of individuals who are injured in connection with their business. These payments (1) promote good customer relations, (2) encourage rapid settlement of any legal claims that develop, and (3) sometimes reduce the extent of damages by treating injuries before they develop expensive complications.

Insurance companies respond to some of the same incentives. Liability for some injuries, such as those arising from auto accidents, is relatively straightforward. An insurance company may choose to pay immediately the medical expenses of a person injured by one of its insureds, because the company knows that it is likely to pay the claim eventually. Immediate payment may promote quick settlement while reducing the odds of expensive medical complications.

These business goals also serve the judicial system's interest in promoting settlements. To accommodate these social, business, and judicial ends, Rule 409 allows potential defendants to pay medical expenses without worrying about plaintiffs using evidence of those payments against them at trial to prove liability.

Rule 409 is also justified as a specific application of **Rule 403**. A party's offer to pay medical expenses often has limited value in proving liability, especially given the business motives for making some of those payments. Juries, however, may misunderstand the humanitarian or business interests and view these offers as clear admissions of fault. Introducing evidence of offers to pay medical expenses, therefore, may cause unfair prejudice that substantially outweighs the probative value of the evidence.

B. The Rule. Rule 409 is a very simple, one-sentence rule:

> ## RULE 409. Offers to Pay Medical and Similar Expenses
>
> Evidence of <u>furnishing, promising to pay, or offering to pay</u> <u>medical, hospital, or similar expenses</u> resulting from an injury is not admissible to <u>prove liability</u> for the injury.

As we will see below, Rule 409 is both broader and narrower than Rule 408, which covers settlement negotiations. Rule 409 is broader because it applies in **any** situation in which an individual or organization pays or agrees to pay medical expenses—unlike Rule 408, there need not be a "claim" or a "dispute," and the statement need not be part of any "compromise negotiations." However, Rule 409 is narrower than Rule 408 in that it **only** excludes the offer to pay or the furnishing of medical expenses; Rule 409 does not exclude any other statements that were made contemporaneously with the offer.

Rule 409, like Rules 407 and 408, bars admission of covered evidence only when offered to prove liability. If a party offers evidence of medical payments to prove some other fact of consequence, the evidence is admissible.

Although Rule 409 is relatively straightforward, the three phrases underlined above raise issues that parties sometimes dispute. We explore below how the courts have interpreted these phrases.

C. In the Courtroom.

1. Furnishing, Promising, Offering. Rule 409 bars admission of offers and promises to pay medical expenses, as well as actual payments of those expenses:

> **Example:** Mary Maverick, a motorist, collides with Peter Parker, a pedestrian. Parker falls to the ground and breaks his arm. Maverick calls an ambulance and waits with Parker until the ambulance arrives. She presses her business card into Parker's hand and says: "Just give me a call. I have good insurance that will cover all of your medical bills." Parker never calls Maverick, because he has adequate insurance of his own. Instead, he sues Maverick for his injuries and emotional distress. At trial, Parker seeks to introduce Maverick's statement as evidence of her fault.

> **Analysis:** Maverick's statement is an offer to pay medical expenses. It is inadmissible under Rule 409, even though Parker never followed up on her offer.

Rule 409 focuses quite narrowly on offers or promises to pay medical expenses. The rule does not protect any other types of statements, even if they occur in connection with offers to pay medical expenses. If Maverick, for example, had said: "Golly, that accident was entirely my fault. Just give me a call. I have good insurance that will cover all of your medical bills," Rule 409 would protect only the part of that statement containing her offer to pay Parker's medical expenses. The rule would not protect her first sentence, in which she admitted fault.

In this sense, Rule 409 offers very limited protection. The rule's narrow scope stems from the social policies that motivate it: Congress and the Advisory Committee wanted to encourage parties to pay the medical expenses of injured parties, not to immunize other statements suggesting fault. Here is a case illustrating this important principle:

Example: Joan Hughes slipped and fell on a restaurant floor. She sued the restaurant, claiming that an employee had left the floor slick with water after mopping. At trial, Hughes attempted to introduce two statements made by Roy Batson, the restaurant's assistant manager. Shortly after the accident, Batson said: "I have told the staff not to mop the floor like this when people are in the restaurant." Later, after he had driven Hughes to the hospital for treatment, Batson told Hughes's husband: "Go ahead and put your wife in a private room and get the best possible medical care. We will take care of it." The restaurant objected to admission of both of these alleged statements by Batson.

Analysis: Rule 409 bars admission of the second statement, which was an offer to pay Hughes's medical expenses. The rule, however, does not bar admission of the first statement; that comment did not relate to medical expenses in any way.[1]

As noted in the previous section, the narrow language of Rule 409 contrasts with the broad sweep of Rule 408, which covers not just offers to settle but also "conduct or a statement made during compromise negotiations about the claim." Thus, if Roy Batson made a similar statement during a compromise negotiation—"I know the accident was partly our fault. I have told the staff not to mop the floor like this when people are in the restaurant. Would you agree to settle the case for $50,000?"—Rule 408 would exclude all of the statements. The difference makes sense given the broader policy rationale of Rule 408, which attempts to foster open discussion during settlement negotiations.

2. Medical, Hospital, or Similar Expenses. Rule 409 only protects promises to pay "medical, hospital, or similar expenses resulting from an injury." Courts have construed "similar expenses" to include fees for all kinds of medical treatment and physical rehabilitation, but the rule does not encompass offers to pay lost wages, repair an automobile, or compensate an injured party for other types of economic or property damage:

---

1   This example draws on Hughes v. Anchor Enters., Inc., 95 S.E.2d 577, 582 (N.C. 1956), a case decided under state law before adoption of the Federal Rules.

Example: A trucker working for Great Coastal Express accidentally ruptured the fuel tank on his truck. He pulled into a truck stop for repairs. Before truck stop workers could repair the leaking tank, about 75 gallons of fuel leaked onto the ground. Cleaning up this fuel spill cost the truck stop more than $25,000; it sued Great Coastal for negligence. At trial, the truck stop introduced evidence that Great Coastal had already paid for some of the clean up, implicitly acknowledging their employee's negligence in rupturing the fuel tank. Great Coastal objected to introduction of this evidence.

Analysis: Rule 409 did not bar admission of this evidence. Although Great Coastal made a voluntary payment, it was not one for medical or "similar" expenses. Rule 409 does not apply to payments for property damage.[2]

Again, this limit reflects the very precise policy goals of Rule 409. The rule's drafters concluded that society's special concern for promoting payment of medical expenses justified excluding potentially relevant evidence from trial. Payments for other types of injuries did not seem as compelling, so those payments do not receive the same favored treatment.

3. To Prove Liability. As with many other evidentiary rules, Rule 409 only excludes evidence if it is offered for a particular purpose: to prove liability for the injury. If a party can establish some other purpose for the evidence, Rule 409 does not bar admission:

Example: Kerry King slipped on the ice in a Fall-Mart parking lot and sued Fall-Mart for negligence. At trial, Fall-Mart argued that King was feigning her injuries. King then sought to introduce evidence that, immediately after the accident, Fall-Mart's manager authorized payment for her medical treatment. Fall-Mart objected to the evidence under Rule 409.

Analysis: The manager's authorization constitutes a payment of medical expenses that Rule 409 embraces. But King is not introducing the evidence to show that Fall-Mart was negligent. Instead, she relies upon the evidence to show that the fall injured her; the manager's immediate authorization of

---

2   Great Coastal Express, Inc. v. Atlantic Mut. Cos., 790 So. 2d 966, 970 (Ala. Civ. App. 2000) (applying state rule analogous to federal one).

payment for medical treatment suggests that she was, in fact, injured. Fall-Mart's trial defense opened the door to using the evidence for this purpose; Rule 409 does not block its admission.

King may introduce evidence of the manager's offer to show that she was, in fact, injured, but she cannot rely upon that evidence to suggest that Fall-Mart was liable for her injury. King must introduce other evidence to prove Fall-Mart's negligence. To explain this distinction, Fall-Mart may ask the judge to give the jury a limiting instruction like this one:

You have heard evidence in this case that Fall-Mart's manager authorized payment for Kerry King's medical expenses after she notified the manger of her accident. You should consider this evidence **only** on the question of whether King suffered an injury from her fall, a fact that Fall-Mart has disputed. You should not consider the manager's authorization of payment for King's medical care on the question of whether Fall-Mart was negligent or otherwise responsible for any injury you find that King suffered.

The jurors may find this instruction puzzling. As discussed in Chapter 5, this kind of limiting instruction may even draw jurors' attention to the manager's authorization, prompting them to give that fact more weight than they otherwise would have. For these reasons, Fall-Mart's attorney may decide not to request a limiting instruction—instead, the company could simply have the manager or other company officer testify about why they authorize medical payments for customers who claim they have been injured on the store's premises. They may stress that this is a matter of routine customer relations rather than an admission of fault or injury. Fall-Mart's attorney can make the same argument in his closing statement.

D. Rule 403 Yet Again. Even if a medical payment is admissible under Rule 409, an attorney may attempt to exclude that evidence under **Rule 403**; Rule 403's balancing test serves as a backstop to Rule 409, just as it does for other rules.

Remember that if Rule 409 or any other rule **excludes** a piece of evidence, then Rule 403 has no role left to play; Rule 403 cannot rescue evidence that another rule has rejected. But when evidence passes through the Rule 409 "net," Rule 403 operates as a final check on the fairness of admitting the evidence. In other words,

Rule 403 is the final "net" filtering evidence before the judge allows the evidence in the courtroom.

Rule 403 is discretionary; there is no guarantee that a judge will exclude evidence under that provision. To illustrate how parties argue 403 motions in court, the table on the next page lists the contrasting arguments that Fall-Mart and King might make to exclude or admit the manager's authorization under Rule 403. The table also illustrates the kind of competing arguments you might make in response to an exam essay question raising a Rule 409/403 issue.

This evidence presents a close question under Rule 403; a judge might rule either way on the admissibility of the manager's authorization.

Quick Summary

Rule 409 encourages payment of an injured person's medical expenses by shielding those payments from admission as evidence of liability. The rule is quite narrow, applying only to **medical or similar expenses**, rather than lost wages, property damage, or other expenses; embracing only **offers, promises, and payments** rather than other statements made by a litigant; and excluding this evidence only when it is offered to establish liability. Evidence that is admissible under Rule 409 may still be excluded under **Rule 403** if it meets the latter rule's standards.

Test Your Understanding

To assess your understanding of the material in this chapter, click here to take a quiz, or go to the Quizzes module from the eBook on your eProducts bookshelf.

Fall-Mart Arguments to Exclude Evidence	King Arguments to Admit Evidence
• The authorization has little probative value; King might have suffered a minor immediate injury but be feigning her current injuries	• Fall-Mart has opened the door to this evidence by challenging the extent of King's injuries • The manager's authorization of medical expenses, immediately after the injury, is highly probative that King was injured
• If King's injuries are real, she can produce better evidence of those injuries, such as medical treatment records	• Although King may introduce medical records, this authorization has distinctive probative value because it establishes the origin and original scope of her injury
• Admitting the evidence will prejudice Fall-Mart unfairly by punishing it for its prompt offer to assist King • The authorization will mislead the jury because it will not understand a large company's incentive to treat minor customer injuries promptly, even if the company was not at fault	• Fall-Mart can explain its incentives for assisting customers to the jury
• A limiting instruction cannot cure the prejudice; it will only focus the jury's attention even more closely on this evidence	• To avoid any prejudice, Fall-Mart may request a limiting instruction, directing the jury to consider the authorization only for purposes of assessing whether King was injured, not on the question of Fall-Mart's liability

12

Criminal Plea Bargaining

Key Concepts

- **Rule 410:** Excludes Plea Bargaining Evidence
- Nolo Contendere Pleas and Withdrawn Guilty Pleas v. Finalized Guilty Pleas
- Protected Statements
- Only Defendant Protected
- Definition of "Plea Discussion"
- Exceptions
- Waiver
- Relationship to **Rule 403**

A. Introduction and Policy. Many observers believe that the criminal justice system could not function if every case went to trial. By 2012, fully 96% of federal prosecutions ended with a plea bargain; only 4% of defendants contested their guilt at trial.[1] Despite the prevalence of plea bargains, federal courtrooms remain crowded. The judicial system thus has a strong interest in encouraging criminal defendants to bargain with prosecutors and reach plea agreements.

At the same time, courts and commentators recognize that the plea bargaining system holds risks of unfairness for defendants. The government is almost always more powerful than an individual defendant, particularly if the defendant is young, nonwhite, or poor. While the judicial system has a stake in promoting plea bargains, it also has a policy interest in protecting defendants from any overreaching by prosecutors.

---

1   See Erica Goode, Stronger Hand for Judges in the 'Bazaar' of Plea Deals, N.Y. Times, Mar. 22, 2012 at http://www.nytimes.com/2012/03/23/us/stronger-hand-for-judges-after-rulings-on-plea-deals.html.

Rule 410 precludes some evidence of offers to plead guilty, as well as statements made during plea bargaining. In doing so, the rule advances both the social interest in plea bargains and the policy concern for protecting defendants who participate in the bargaining process.

Rule 410 also prevents the jury from hearing unfairly prejudicial information. Most jurors who hear that a defendant engaged in plea bargaining will assume that the defendant is guilty: After all, why would someone consider pleading guilty unless she had committed the crime? This inference—whether correct or not—may lead jurors to convict a defendant without proper consideration of other evidence. In criminal trials, where the prosecution must prove guilt beyond a reasonable doubt, this type of shortcut reasoning is particularly dangerous.

Rule 410 does not exclude evidence of **final guilty pleas** entered as the result of a plea bargain. A final guilty plea yields a conviction, which is a matter of public record. Finalized guilty pleas are admissible to the same extent as other criminal convictions, an issue we will study in Chapter 20 and later chapters.

Rule 410 is analogous to **Rule 408**, which governs the admissibility of settlement negotiations in the civil context. The two rules are similar in many ways: Both protect offers and statements made during settlement negotiations to encourage those settlements and to prevent unfairly prejudicial information from reaching jurors. But there are significant differences in the details.

B. The Rule. We'll examine **Rule 410** in three parts: (1) the opening language; (2) the prohibitions; and (3) the exceptions.

1. Opening Language. The opening text of Rule 410 reads:

> ## RULE 410. Pleas, Plea Discussions, and Related Statements
>
> **(a) Prohibited Uses.** <u>In a civil or criminal case</u>, evidence of the following is not admissible <u>against the defendant</u> who made the plea or participated in the plea discussions: . . .

As the underlined language reflects, the first part of this rule establishes two key points.

First, Rule 410 excludes evidence from both civil and criminal trials. The **evidence** protected by Rule 410 arises in criminal prosecutions. But the rule bars **admission** of this evidence in either civil or criminal trials.

Second, Rule 410 precludes this evidence only when introduced against the person who, as a criminal defendant, participated in the plea bargaining process. Most rules of evidence prohibit any party from introducing specified evidence against any other party. Rule 410, however, bars admission of evidence against only one type of party. The rule, as explained above, aims in part to protect the criminal defendant from overreaching during plea bargaining and prosecution. Consistent with that goal, the rule prohibits any party from introducing evidence **against** the defendant who participated in the plea bargaining but allows the **defendant** to introduce evidence from that process against others.

> **Example:** Sally Soprano engages in a series of financial transactions that appear to violate the federal money laundering laws. During a plea bargaining session, Soprano admits that she was "responsible" for the transactions. In return, the prosecutor acknowledges that Soprano had "good intentions" for some of her actions. Negotiations ultimately fail and Soprano proceeds to trial on the money laundering charges. Both Soprano and the prosecutor attempt to introduce statements made during the bargaining session.

> **Analysis:** The prosecutor cannot introduce Soprano's admission of responsibility; that would be introducing evidence "against the defendant who . . . participated in the plea discussions." Subject to the other rules of evidence, however, Soprano **can** introduce the prosecutor's acknowledgement of "good intentions." Rule 410 does not bar admission of that evidence because Soprano is introducing it against the prosecutor.

As we'll see below, the last portion of Rule 410 imposes some limits on this outcome: If Soprano introduces the prosecutor's statement, the judge may allow the prosecutor to introduce Soprano's admission in return. But this will depend upon the judge's discretion; the default position of Rule 410 is that the defendant may introduce protected plea-related evidence, but that other parties may not introduce this type of evidence against the defendant.

2. Prohibitions. The next portion of Rule 410 contains the rule's prohibitions. It lists four categories of evidence stemming from criminal plea bargaining that are not admissible against the defendant in any trial:

> ## RULE 410. Pleas, Plea Discussions, and Related Statements
>
> **(a)** . . . evidence of the following is not admissible . . . :
>
> **(1)** a guilty plea that was later withdrawn;
>
> **(2)** a nolo contendere plea;
>
> **(3)** a statement made during a proceeding on either of those pleas under Federal Rule of Criminal Procedure 11 or a comparable state procedure; or
>
> **(4)** a statement made during plea discussions with an attorney for the prosecuting authority if the discussions did not result in a guilty plea or they resulted in a later-withdrawn guilty plea.

Subsection (1) of the rule protects guilty pleas that a defendant withdraws. A criminal defendant who agrees to plead guilty retains complete discretion to withdraw that plea any time before the court accepts it. A defendant can also withdraw a guilty plea after acceptance but before sentencing if a "fair and just reason" exists for withdrawal.[2]

Rule 410 protects this right to withdraw a guilty plea by barring admission of a withdrawn plea against the defendant. If the prosecutor, or an opponent in a civil lawsuit, could introduce evidence of a withdrawn guilty plea, then the defendant would not be able to exercise this right of withdrawal effectively.

Subsection (2) shields an unusual type of plea known as a plea of nolo contendere or "no contest." In a plea of nolo contendere, the defendant allows the court to assume guilt for purposes of sentencing, but does not admit guilt for any other purpose. For this reason, a conviction based on a nolo plea does not establish liability by issue preclusion (also known as collateral estoppel) in a civil lawsuit. Through a plea of nolo contendere, the defendant allows himself to be criminally punished **as if he were guilty,** but he does not admit guilt.

---

2   This standard appears in Rule 11(d) of the Federal Rules of Criminal Procedure. We won't worry in this course about the standards courts apply in making that determination. For our purposes, we only need to know that guilty pleas can be withdrawn under certain circumstances.

Almost any criminal defendant would prefer a plea of nolo contendere to a guilty plea, but prosecutors are not always willing to offer a nolo plea. Although nolo pleas are uncommon, they help illustrate the preclusive effect of criminal prosecutions in civil lawsuits. Here is a series of examples showing the different effects of a criminal conviction based on a jury verdict, a guilty plea, and a plea of nolo contendere:

Example 1: While driving home from Joe's Bar, Zoe drives onto the sidewalk and hits Bart, seriously injuring him. A jury convicts Zoe of driving while intoxicated. Bart then sues Zoe for negligence and uses the conviction to establish through issue preclusion that Zoe was driving drunk. This significantly enhances Bart's ease of recovery against Zoe.

Example 2: On the same facts, Zoe pleads guilty to a charge of driving while intoxicated. Bart can use the conviction based on that plea in his negligence suit against Zoe in the same way he would have used a conviction based on a guilty verdict. The preclusive effect is identical.

Example 3: On the same facts, Zoe pleads nolo contendere to the charge of driving while intoxicated. The judge sentences her to prison as if she had pled guilty to the charge. Bart, however, cannot use Zoe's plea in his negligence suit to establish her drunk driving; the plea is inadmissible under Rule 410. He must prove negligence in some other manner.

Rule 410(a)(2) thus assures that civil litigants cannot use nolo pleas for preclusive effect.

Subsection (3) of Rule 410(a) protects statements made during a plea bargaining process if that process produced either a withdrawn guilty plea or a plea of nolo contendere. The Rule 11 "proceeding" referred to in this subsection encompass both the out-of-court bargaining process and any in-court discussions or acceptance of the plea. Suppose, for example, that a defendant negotiates a plea bargain and appears in court to enter the plea, but changes his mind before the judge accepts his plea. The plea is then "withdrawn" and is inadmissible against the defendant under Rule 410(a)(1). All statements that the defendant made as part of the plea negotiation process or during the aborted court appearance are also inadmissible against that defendant.

Subsection (4), finally, shields statements made during plea bargaining when no guilty plea results, including situations in which the defendant initially agrees to plead guilty but later withdraws the plea. The subsection limits its protection to plea discussions that occur "with an attorney for the prosecuting authority," a constraint that we will explore in the Courtroom section below. For now, focus on the fact that subsection (4) protects statements made during plea bargaining, but only when the bargaining produces no plea or a withdrawn one.

Subsections (3) and (4) overlap in an awkward manner, a fact that confuses some students. Both provisions protect statements made during guilty pleas that are later withdrawn. This duplication, however, results from the drafters' awkward composition rather than any substantive goal. Don't let the overlap concern you; simply focus on the statements and pleas that the rule protects under any of its subsections.

Remember that Rule 410 does **not** preclude evidence of a guilty plea that has been entered and finalized. Nor does the rule exclude evidence of any statements made during negotiations that produced the guilty plea. Once a plea has been accepted, of course, the defendant no longer faces trial on those charges. In that sense, protection of finalized pleas and statements underlying them is unnecessary. But a guilty plea, as well as statements made during bargaining sessions producing that plea, may provide damaging evidence against the defendant in other criminal proceedings or civil suits. Rule 410 does not prohibit use of that evidence if the defendant pled guilty.

The table below and on the next page summarizes the evidence that 410 does and does not protect.

Plea Type	Is the Plea Admissible?	Are Statements Made During Bargaining Admissible?	Are Statements Made During Plea-Related Court Proceedings Admissible?
Accepted Plea of Nolo Contendere	No 410(a)(2)	No 410(a)(3)	No 410(a)(3)
Withdrawn Guilty Plea	No 410(a)(1)	No 410(a)(3), (4)	No 410(a)(3)

Plea Type	Is the Plea Admissible?	Are Statements Made During Bargaining Admissible?	Are Statements Made During Plea-Related Court Proceedings Admissible?
Accepted Guilty Plea	Yes	Yes	Yes
No Plea	Not Applicable (no plea made)	No 410(a)(4)	Not Applicable (no proceedings)

3. Exceptions. The final section of Rule 410 establishes two exceptions to the preceding rules:

RULE 410. Pleas, Plea Discussions, and Related Statements

(b) Exceptions. The court may admit a statement described in Rule 410(a)(3) or (4):

(1) in any proceeding in which <u>another statement</u> made during the same plea or plea discussions has been introduced, if <u>in fairness</u> the statements ought to be considered together; or

(2) in a criminal proceeding <u>for perjury or false statement</u>, if the defendant made the statement

- under oath,
- on the record, and
- with counsel present.

The first point to note about this section is that Rule 410 does not base any exceptions on the **purpose** for which a party offers evidence covered by the rule. Rule 410 differs in this way from Rules 407–409, as well as from many other rules of evidence. The question, "What is the proponent of this evidence trying to prove?"—which is critical to applying most evidentiary rules—is irrelevant to Rule 410. Evidence relating to plea bargaining is inadmissible regardless of the purpose for which it is offered.

But Rule 410 does have two narrow, sensible exceptions. **First,** if a party introduces one statement from a plea bargaining session, another party may introduce additional statements from the same session when fairness requires consideration of those additional statements. This exception prevents a litigant from creating a misleading impression by introducing selected parts of a negotiation.[3]

To understand how this exception works, think back to the example of Sally Soprano, the alleged money launderer. At trial, the prosecutor cannot offer evidence in its case-in-chief that Soprano admitted during plea discussions that she was "responsible" for the financial transactions. But if Soprano introduces evidence during her defense that the prosecutor acknowledged during those same plea bargaining sessions that Soprano had "good intentions," then the prosecutor can argue that "in fairness" Soprano's admission of responsibility should be allowed into evidence.

The judge's decision on this point is discretionary and will depend on other evidence in the case, the degree of harm to the defendant, and whether the first statement is misleading without evidence of the second. In this example, the prosecutor's acknowledgement of "good intentions" seems to stand on its own; admission of Soprano's statement is not necessary to eliminate any misleading connotations. On the other hand, admitting Soprano's statement does not seem prejudicial under these circumstances. By introducing evidence that she had "good intentions" for some of her acts, Soprano seems implicitly to have acknowledged that she was responsible for them.

 The district judge could rule either way on this evidence. The important point is that the prosecutor has no **right** to introduce against the defendant statements that are otherwise protected by Rule 410; admission of those statements always depends on the judge's interpretation of "fairness."

The **second** exception recognized by Rule 410 is for perjury prosecutions. The government may introduce some statements otherwise protected by the rule when necessary to prosecute a defendant for perjury or false statement. For this exception to apply, the defendant must have made a statement "under oath, on the record, and with counsel present."

---

3   The exception is analogous to Rule 106, which establishes a "rule of completeness" for introduction of writings or recorded statements. We examine Rule 106 in Chapter 24.

Most plea bargaining discussions do not occur under those circumstances, so the exception is a limited one. This exception applies most often when a defendant appears in court to enter a plea and responds, under oath, to questions from the judge. If the judge rejects the plea or the defendant withdraws it, this final provision of Rule 410 allows the government to use statements from the in-court examination to prosecute the defendant for perjury. The government may claim that the defendant lied during the plea bargaining examination, or it may use that statement to show that the defendant lied under oath on another occasion.

Example: The government charged Ron Talbot with first degree assault, claiming that he knifed Nicky Chalmers. Talbot agreed to plead guilty to second degree assault and appeared in court, accompanied by his lawyer, to enter that plea. Under oath and on the record, Talbot stated: "I did it, your honor. I stuck Nicky with my knife and I'm sorry." The judge, however, rejected Talbot's plea, and the government proceeded to trial on the initial charge.[4] At his trial, Talbot took the stand and vigorously asserted that he "was nowhere near Nicky at the time of this unfortunate knifing." The jury acquitted Talbot, and the government filed perjury charges against him. The prosecutor now offers Talbot's admission, made during the plea hearing, at the perjury trial.

Analysis: Rule 410 allows the prosecutor to introduce this statement. The proffered statement was made "under oath, on the record, and with counsel present," and the government is offering the statement "in a criminal proceeding for perjury." Rule 410 explicitly permits this use.

C. In the Courtroom.
Statements made during plea bargaining often provide persuasive evidence of guilt. Parties, therefore, vigorously contest the admissibility of these statements. This section addresses some of the issues that arise under this rule.

1. What Are "Plea Discussions"? The most frequently disputed issue under Rule 410 centers on the definition of "plea discussions." The rule defines a "plea discussion" as one that occurs "with an attorney for the prosecuting authority." A formal session convened by the prosecutor specifically to discuss a plea clearly

---

4   The trial judge has no obligation to accept a guilty plea negotiated by the defendant and prosecutor. Indeed, the judge must reject a plea that she believes was involuntary or rests on no factual basis. Judges may also reject pleas for other reasons, although they accept the vast majority of guilty pleas offered by defendants.

qualifies as a "plea discussion" invoking Rule 410's protections. A suspect who volunteers an immediate confession to the arresting police officer, on the other hand, is not engaged in "plea discussions." That statement is admissible under Rule 410.

More ambiguous situations, however, arise between these two extremes. Prosecutors sometimes attend police interrogations. If a suspect makes an admission in the prosecutor's presence, hoping for leniency, is that statement made as part of a "plea discussion"? Even in the prosecutor's absence, police officers sometimes press a defendant to confess by suggesting that cooperation will lead to more lenient treatment. If the officer's language suggests that he has the prosecutor's authority to offer a plea, does that create a "plea discussion"?

A majority of courts use a **two-tiered approach** to analyze these ambiguous situations. Under this approach, a "plea discussion" occurs if:

    (a) the defendant displayed "an actual **subjective expectation** to negotiate a plea" and

    (b) that expectation was "**reasonable** given the totality of the objective circumstances."[5]

Application of this standard depends on the facts of the case and the skill of counsel in articulating persuasive arguments. Here are two examples illustrating some of the factors that courts consider when applying this standard:

Example: FBI Agent Hilley informed Danny Guerrero that the agency was investigating him for bribing Guam officials to obtain government contracts. Guerrero voluntarily attended a meeting with Hilley, said that he wanted to cooperate, and declined the opportunity to call an attorney. He asked Hilley what cooperation would mean; Hilley told Guerrero that courts usually consider whether a defendant has cooperated, but that U.S. Attorney Vernier would decide whether to charge Guerrero. Hilley stressed that he had no control over the courts or prosecutor, and could make no promises.

Guerrero asked to speak directly to Vernier, who came briefly to the FBI office. Vernier told Guerrero that his cooperation would be taken into

---

5   United States v. Robertson, 582 F.2d 1356, 1366 (5th Cir. 1978). Courts that have adopted a different legal standard still examine many of the same factors discussed in the examples below.

consideration in any future handling of cases involving him, that the decision whether to cooperate was his choice, and that he had the right not to cooperate. After Vernier left, Guerrero admitted paying kickbacks to several Guam officials. Five months later, the government indicted Guerrero for bribery and wire fraud. Guerrero moved to suppress the statements he made to Hilley, arguing they were part of "plea discussions."

Analysis: The district judge denied Guerrero's motion, allowing the government to use the contested statements at trial, and the court of appeals affirmed. The statements occurred before Guerrero had been charged with any crime. The U.S. Attorney appeared only briefly, and his statement that "cooperation would be taken into consideration" offered no particulars. The FBI agent stressed his inability to make any promises, and the U.S. Attorney emphasized Guerrero's right not to cooperate. Guerrero never manifested any **subjective belief** that he was engaged in plea bargaining and, under these circumstances, such a belief would not have been **reasonable**. The court thus found that neither prong of the two-tiered test was met in this case.[6]

Example: A grand jury indicted Riyaid Swidan for distribution of LSD. After the indictment, Swidan contacted a DEA agent and offered to set up a drug transaction that would help the agent obtain evidence against another individual. Swidan indicated that in return he "asked that something be done about the charges against him." The agent told Swidan that he was interested in the deal and would relay the offer to the prosecutor, but that the decision would be up to the prosecutor.

The agent did convey the proposal to the prosecutor who, in turn, told Swidan's attorney about it. The DEA agent then engaged Swidan in a second conversation about the proposed transaction. Despite these discussions, no plea bargain resulted. Before trial, Swidan moved to suppress the content of his two conversations with the DEA agent, arguing that they were part of a "plea discussion."

Analysis: The district judge agreed with Swidan and suppressed the evidence. Although the prosecutor did not participate directly in the discussions, and

---

6   United States v. Guerrero, 847 F.2d 1363 (9th Cir. 1988).

no specific terms were discussed, Swidan **subjectively believed** that he was participating in a plea discussion and the agent's behavior made that belief **reasonable**. By indicating his interest in Swidan's proposed deal, conveying the deal to the prosecutor, and returning to Swidan for further discussion, the agent created the impression that he was negotiating on behalf of the prosecutor—indeed, he may well have been doing so.[7]

2. Sentencing. Remember that the Federal Rules of Evidence do not apply to sentencing proceedings. Prosecutors frequently introduce statements from plea bargaining sessions to inform the court's sentencing decision, and judges consider that evidence when calculating a sentence.[8]

3. Waiver. Sometimes prosecutors refuse to engage in plea bargaining unless the defendant agrees to waive his rights under Rule 410, thus agreeing that his statements during the plea bargaining process will be admissible at trial if the negotiations break down. The Supreme Court upheld the constitutionality of a narrow version of a Rule 410 waiver in *United States v. Mezzanatto*,[9] and subsequent lower court decisions have interpreted that decision broadly, enforcing the most sweeping Rule 410 waivers. In particular, many waivers now allow the government to introduce statements made during plea bargaining even if the defendant does not take the stand at trial. The following example shows one of these waivers in operation:

> **Example:** The government charged Larry Burch with possession and distribution of cocaine. Burch negotiated a plea bargain in which he pled guilty to one of the four counts against him. At the same time, he signed a waiver allowing the government to use the plea as evidence against him if he withdrew the plea and proceeded to trial. Burch did, in fact, withdraw his plea and the government offered the contents of the withdrawn plea as evidence against him.

---

7   This example is based on United States v. Swidan, 689 F. Supp. 726 (E.D. Mich. 1988), aff'd on other grounds, 888 F.2d 1076 (6th Cir. 1989). The court's description of some of the facts in that case was sketchy, so we expanded them slightly for the example.

8   See, e.g., United States v. Upton, 91 F.3d 677 (5th Cir. 1996); United States v. Medina-Estrada, 81 F.3d 981 (10th Cir. 1996).

9   513 U.S. 196 (1995).

Analysis: The district judge allowed the government to introduce this evidence, finding that Burch knowingly and voluntarily waived his rights under Rule 410. The court of appeals affirmed. The court, like others confronting the same issue, stressed that criminal defendants may waive many of their most fundamental constitutional rights. A fortiori, the courts hold, they may waive rights given them by the Federal Rules of Evidence.[10]

D. Remember Rule 403.

Rule 403 complements Rule 410 in several ways. First, although Rule 410 only bars plea bargaining evidence that is offered against a **defendant**, courts often invoke Rule 403 to exclude similar evidence offered against the prosecution. Defendants sometimes attempt to introduce evidence of the prosecutor's willingness to plea bargain to suggest that the prosecutor considered the case weak. Similarly, defendants may attempt to introduce statements that the prosecutor made during plea bargaining sessions. Since prosecutors may offer to reduce charges during plea negotiations for any number of reasons unrelated to the defendant's actual guilt, courts often find that this evidence has little probative value, might confuse the jury, and would unfairly prejudice the prosecution in the eyes of jurors who do not fully understand the plea bargaining process.

Example: A grand jury indicted Abdul Ajami, Dagoberto Silva, Juan Delgado, and Henry Escobar on multiple drug trafficking charges. The defendants had been importing cocaine hidden in shipping containers that also held lawn furniture and other items. Before trial, Ajami pled guilty to charges of importing artifacts from Ecuador with false invoices, and the government dismissed the drug charges against him. At their trial, Silva, Delgado, and Escobar attempted to introduce evidence of this plea agreement, arguing that it showed that the government believed Ajami was innocent of the drug trafficking charges. If Ajami was innocent, the defendants argued, they must be innocent as well.

---

10   United States v. Burch, 156 F.3d 1315 (D.C. Cir. 1998).

Analysis: Although Rule 410 would allow admission of this evidence, the district judge excluded it under Rule 403. The judge noted that the government dismisses charges for many reasons unrelated to guilt or innocence. Often, as in this case, charges are dismissed in return for the defendant's cooperation in providing evidence against other potential defendants. The dismissal of charges has little probative value; introducing that evidence could confuse the jury and discourage plea negotiations.[11]

Defendants may also invoke Rule 403 when Rule 410 fails to exclude evidence offered against them. Under some circumstances, for example, a judge might exclude evidence of statements made during the process of negotiating a guilty plea that was finalized, even though Rule 410 does not protect statements under those circumstances. Counsel for both the government and defense should consider using Rule 403 when Rule 410 does not apply.

---

11   United States v. Delgado, 903 F.2d 1495 (11th Cir. 1990).

Quick Summary

Rule 410 encourages plea bargaining by shielding some pleas, as well as some statements made during plea discussions, from admission at trial. In practice, the protections of Rule 410 are rather narrow. The rule bars introduction of evidence against the defendant who participated in the plea discussions, not against other parties; it does not protect accepted guilty pleas or statements producing those pleas; both the rule's language and judicial decisions constrain when "plea discussions" occur; and federal prosecutors commonly require defendants to waive the rule's protections before beginning plea discussions.

The rule also includes two explicit exceptions, allowing the introduction of otherwise protected statements in certain perjury prosecutions and when necessary to correct a misimpression created by the selective introduction of statements from a plea discussion. Prosecutors and defense attorneys must understand these limits to protect their client's interests during plea negotiations and other interactions.

Test Your Understanding

To assess your understanding of the material in this chapter, <u>click here</u> to take a quiz, or go to the Quizzes module from the eBook on your eProducts bookshelf.

13

Liability Insurance

Key Concepts

- **Rule 411:** Liability Insurance
- What Is "Liability Insurance"?
- Admission of Evidence for Limited Purposes

A. Introduction and Policy. Rule 411 is the last of the narrowly focused rules in Article IV. Like Rules 407–410, Rule 411 advances an important social policy: encouraging individuals and organizations to obtain liability insurance. Liability insurance is good for society because it ensures that individuals and companies are able to compensate others for injuries they cause. It also spreads the cost of these injuries among an appropriate risk pool.

Rule 411 furthers these social ends by barring most evidence of liability insurance in lawsuits. Injured plaintiffs cannot introduce evidence of the defendant's liability insurance, hoping that the availability of insurance will persuade the jury to award a large recovery. Nor can defendants attempt to escape liability by arguing that they are uninsured and would go bankrupt if forced to compensate the plaintiff. Rule 411 tries to remove discussion of liability insurance from the courtroom.

In addition to advancing these social policies, Rule 411 reflects the prejudice/probative value analysis of **Rule 403**. In most lawsuits, the presence or absence of insurance has very low probative value. One could argue that a defendant's purchase of liability insurance suggests that she is a conscientious individual who acts carefully in all areas of her life and is therefore less likely to be negligent. Conversely, one could argue that the presence of insurance frees a defendant to act recklessly, secure in the knowledge that insurance will cover any harm.

In truth, neither of these arguments carries much probative weight; ownership of insurance bears little relationship to liability. Jurors, however, are likely to respond unfairly to evidence of insurance. If jurors believe that a large insurance company will pay the damages, they are likely to increase the plaintiff's award. The presence or absence of insurance, therefore, is another type of evidence that generates unfair prejudice substantially outweighing its probative value.

Rule 411 responds to these two concerns by broadly prohibiting any party from introducing evidence related to liability insurance. As with several of the rules we have just studied, however, Rule 411 only bars evidence of insurance if it is offered to prove negligence or some other wrongful behavior. If the evidence is relevant for some other purpose, it is admissible for that reason and the judge will give an appropriate limiting instruction.

B. The Rule. Rule 411 is relatively straightforward:

RULE 411. Liability Insurance

Evidence that a person was or was not <u>insured against liability</u> is not admissible <u>to prove whether the person acted negligently or otherwise wrongfully</u>. But the court may admit this evidence for <u>another purpose</u>, such as

- proving a witness's bias or prejudice or
- proving agency, ownership, or control.

The underlined phrases indicate the key concepts in this rule; we explore them further in the next section.

C. In the Courtroom.

1. What Is Liability Insurance? The phrase "insured against liability" includes two limits that restrict Rule 411's application. **First,** the rule only excludes evidence of **liability** insurance. This type of insurance compensates the policy holder for specified types of damages owed other people. Car insurance is the most common type of liability insurance: It covers liability that a motorist incurs when he or she injures other people and their property. Medical malpractice insurance is another type of liability insurance; it pays any damages that a doctor owes to an injured patient.

But health insurance, which compensates an individual for his or her own health care costs, is **not** a form of "liability" insurance. Disability insurance, life insurance, and many other types of insurance also fall outside the "liability" category. Although many states maintain common law or statutory provisions barring reference to these other types of insurance at trial, Federal Rule 411 refers only to liability insurance.

 Some judges and lawyers overlook this narrow aspect of Rule 411 and apply the rule to all types of insurance. The same policy rationales that preclude evidence of liability insurance—encouraging individuals and corporations to insure, and shielding the jury from information with low probative value but a high danger of unfair prejudice—apply with similar force to other types of insurance.

By its terms, however, Rule 411 applies only to liability insurance and courts should invoke it only in that context. Parties, of course, may urge the court to exclude evidence of other types of insurance under Rule 403. Under some circumstances, that evidence may cause unfair prejudice that substantially outweighs its probative value.

The **second** question raised by the phrase "liability insurance" concerns indemnity agreements. Several cases question whether these agreements qualify as liability insurance under Rule 411.

Indemnity agreements are similar to liability insurance in one respect: Under an indemnity agreement, one party agrees to reimburse ("indemnify") another party for damages if a specified form of liability arises. In other ways, however, indemnity agreements differ significantly from insurance. They are usually one-time agreements between parties, do not require the ongoing payment of premiums, and do not spread the risk of financial loss over a large number of people.

A common form of indemnity agreement occurs when one company purchases another; the seller may agree to indemnify the purchaser for liability arising from conduct that the selling company engaged in prior to the transfer of ownership. Another common form of indemnification occurs when companies agree to reimburse their employees for any liability they incur while engaged in company business.

 Courts have split over whether these types of agreements qualify as liability insurance under Rule 411. Some, stressing that one entity has agreed to compensate another for any liability, apply Rule 411 to exclude evidence of indemnity agreements.[1] Others, noting the differences between indemnity and classic liability insurance, limit the rule strictly to the latter.[2] In the latter courts, of course, a party can still argue for exclusion of the indemnity agreement under Rule 403.

Watch for this issue to gain importance, perhaps generating a clarifying amendment or a definitive judicial ruling, as indemnity agreements become even more common. The issue might be relevant to a case you prepare for trial.

2. For What Purpose Is the Evidence Offered? The most important limit on Rule 411 is a type of constraint we have already studied: Rule 411 only precludes evidence of liability insurance if it is offered to prove fault—that is, if offered "to prove whether the person acted negligently or otherwise wrongfully." Like several other rules we have studied, Rule 411 lists examples of other, permitted purposes: (1) "proving a witness's bias or prejudice," and (2) "proving agency, ownership, or control." But these examples are just illustrative; they do not comprise a complete list. **Any** purpose other than proof of liability is permissible under Rule 411 as long as the purpose is relevant to the dispute. Here are some examples of purposes for which courts have allowed parties to introduce evidence of insurance:

> **Example:** Roger Roux suffered complications from surgery performed by Gillian Cutter; he sued for malpractice. At trial, Cutter introduced the testimony of Joseph Egbert, a surgeon who testified that Cutter's surgery met all medical standards of care. Roux attempted to show that Egbert's opinion was biased by introducing evidence that Egbert worked for Cutter's insurance company. Cutter objected to this evidence under Rule 411.

Analysis: Roux may present this evidence. Although the evidence will reveal that Cutter has liability insurance, Roux is not introducing this information to prove that Cutter acted negligently. Instead, he is using the evidence to suggest that Egbert may be biased. As an employee of Cutter's insurance

---

1   See, e.g., Matosantos Commercial Corp. v. SCA Tissue N. Am., 369 F. Supp. 2d 191 (D.P.R. 2005).

2   See, e.g., DSC Communications Corp. v. Next Level Communications, 929 F. Supp. 239 (E.D. Tex. 1996).

company, Egbert has an incentive to defend Cutter's technique: Successful defense of the malpractice claim will save the company significant money.

Example: Posttape Associates purchased 105 rolls of Ektachrome Film from Kodak to use in shooting documentary films. Scratches appeared on the film after development, destroying its value. Posttape sued Kodak for breach of warranty, negligence, and strict product liability. Kodak defended on the ground that industry custom, as well as a notice attached to every roll of film, limited its liability to replacement of the film. To show Posttape's knowledge of this industry custom, Kodak offered evidence that Posttape had purchased insurance protecting it against other losses that might arise from defective film. Posttape objected to the evidence under Rule 411.

Analysis: The district judge excluded the evidence under Rules 411 and 403, but the court of appeals reversed. Kodak did not offer evidence of Posttape's insurance to suggest that Posttape "acted negligently or otherwise wrongfully," the purpose forbidden by Rule 411. Instead, Kodak presented the evidence to suggest that Posttape knew about the industry custom; otherwise, Posttape would not have purchased such specialized insurance. Rule 411 allows introduction of insurance evidence for "another purpose" like this. Nor should the trial judge have excluded the evidence under Rule 403: Posttape's insurance had significant probative value on a central disputed issue in the case, and revelations about insurance are unlikely to cause prejudice in commercial litigation between two companies.[3]

Notice that the insurance in the Posttape case was not "liability" insurance; it was insurance that Posttape had purchased to cover its own potential business losses, rather than to cover liability it might owe other individuals or businesses. Rule 411, therefore, did not apply to this evidence in the first place. The fact that both the trial judge and court of appeals overlooked this point illustrates how lawyers and judges sometimes forget this limitation in Rule 411. The outcome in Posttape, however, is sound; even if the insurance was "liability insurance," Kodak could introduce it for the purpose it claimed.

---

3   Posttape Assocs. v. Eastman Kodak Co., 537 F.2d 751, 758 (3d Cir. 1976).

When evidence of insurance is admitted for limited purposes, a party may request a limiting instruction. In the first case described above, for example, Dr. Cutter could ask the judge to instruct the jury that evidence of her insurance should be considered only for the purpose of evaluating Egbert's potential bias, not on the issue of her liability. On the other hand, she might forego requesting such an instruction, reasoning that the limiting instruction would only emphasize the presence of insurance to the jury. As we discussed previously, litigants sometimes conclude that a limiting instruction will cause more harm than good.

D. Don't Forget Rule 403. Remember that Rule 403 serves as a final "net," catching evidence that might unfairly prejudice the jury. Even when evidence is admissible under Rule 411—for example, to show ownership or bias—the judge might exclude that evidence under Rule 403. Evidence of insurance can be quite prejudicial and its probative value is often slight. An attorney who makes a convincing argument on these grounds might keep evidence of insurance out of the courtroom.

Evidence in Practice

To practice your knowledge of Article IV rules, take the role of a trial attorney in *Morris v. Blake*. Click here or access the **Evidence in Practice** module from the eBook on your eProducts bookshelf.

Quick Summary

 **Rule 411** promotes our social interest in insurance by barring evidence of a party's liability insurance. The rule also furthers the truth seeking goals of Rule 403; evidence of insurance has little probative value on the issue of liability and can cause significant unfair prejudice. As a general matter, therefore, it is appropriate to exclude evidence of liability insurance.

Rule 411, however, applies only to liability insurance, not to other forms of insurance; courts currently dispute whether the rule encompasses indemnity agreements. Rule 411 also contains several exceptions that parties use to introduce evidence of an opponent's liability insurance. Most important, the rule allows evidence of insurance when used for purposes other than proving liability. These purposes include proving a witness's bias, a party's knowledge, or a party's ownership of relevant property.

Test Your Understanding

 To assess your understanding of the material in this chapter, click here to take a quiz, or go to the Quizzes module from the eBook on your eProducts bookshelf.

14

Putting a Witness on the Stand

Key Concepts

- **Rule 601:** Competence
- State Law Exception
- **Rules 605** and **606:** Judges and Jurors
- **Rule 602:** Personal Knowledge
- Laying the Foundation
- **Rule 603:** Oaths and Affirmations
- **Rule 604:** Interpreters

A. Introduction. The last eight chapters focused on Article IV of the Rules of Evidence, which include the two most fundamental rules of courtroom evidence: **Rule 402**, which requires evidence to be relevant; and **Rule 403**, which allows the judge to exclude evidence when its unfair prejudice substantially outweighs its probative value. We also examined five more narrowly focused rules in Article IV, which under some circumstances exclude evidence of subsequent remedial measures, settlement negotiations, medical payments, plea bargaining, and liability insurance.

We now enter a different phase of our study. In the next series of chapters we will examine the process of how attorneys elicit evidence from witnesses and present that testimony to the jury. Article VI of the rules governs this process; it deals with qualifying witnesses, questioning them, and impeaching their credibility. The article contains fifteen rules, but many of them are quite simple.

In this chapter, we discuss the rules that qualify a witness to testify. To testify in court, a witness must (1) be competent (**Rules 601, 605,** and **606**); (2) have personal knowledge (**Rule 602**); and (3) take an oath or affirmation (**Rule 603**).

If an interpreter is necessary, the rules also provide for qualification of that person (**Rule 604**).

B. Competence: Who Can Testify? The common law strictly limited who could appear as a witness. At different times, courts excluded parties to the action, spouses of those parties, convicted felons, children, and atheists as "incompetent" to testify. Some nineteenth-century statutes declared nonwhite witnesses incompetent.[4]

The Federal Rules of Evidence swept away most vestiges of those ancient restrictions; like other modern evidentiary codes, the rules take a permissive view toward admitting evidence. The rules allow jurors to hear the testimony of almost any witness who has knowledge relevant to the case. If there is reason to doubt the witness's testimony, opposing counsel can raise those issues on cross-examination. The jurors, rather than inflexible rules, decide whether to believe the witness.

1. The Basic Rule: Everyone Is Competent. Rule 601 introduces the Federal Rules' permissive approach to competence by declaring:

RULE 601. Competency to Testify in General

Every person is competent to be a witness unless these rules provide otherwise . . . .

The default rule, in other words, is competence. Another rule must specifically deny competence to exclude a witness from the stand. And, as we'll see below, only a few provisions limit this general principle of competence. The Federal Rules allow even young children and mentally incompetent adults to appear as witnesses; it is up to the opposing counsel to expose any weaknesses in their credibility or testimony.

Here are some examples of the liberal approach embodied by Rule 601:

> **Example:** The United States charged Herman Harris and several codefendants with numerous drug-related crimes. Esker Dodson testified for the

---

4   See Gabriel J. Chin, "A Chinaman's Chance" in Court: Asian Pacific Americans and Racial Rules of Evidence, 3 U.C. Irvine L. Rev. 965 (2013); Jasmine B. Gonzales Rose, Toward a Critical Race Theory of Evidence, 101 Minn. L. Rev. 2243 (2017).

prosecution against the defendants. Dodson admitted that he had used "substantial" amounts of heroin for several years and that he had had a "fix" within two days of his testimony. After his first day of testimony, Dodson was hospitalized and received Demerol for pain relief. When he returned to the stand, the judge frequently had to remind Dodson to speak up; the witness was also "bouncing" and "nodding" on the stand.

Part way through Dodson's testimony, this colloquy occurred:

DEFENSE COUNSEL: This guy is flying now.

PROSECUTOR: That is your opinion.

DEFENSE COUNSEL: It is everybody's opinion.

THE COURT: It is not my opinion.

On appeal, the convicted defendants challenged Dodson's competence.

Analysis: The court of appeals rejected the defendants' claim. Rule 601 imposes no general competence requirement. Instead, opposing counsel may point out weaknesses in the witness's credibility; the jury will then assess credibility for itself. Here, defense counsel introduced evidence about the extent of Dodson's medications and their likely effect on his testimony. That, rather than a general finding of incompetence, is the appropriate method of raising credibility issues under the Federal Rules.[5]

Example: A jury convicted Roy Bonnet of sexually abusing his four- and six-year-old daughters; the trial occurred when the girls were six and seven. Bonnet argued that the children were incompetent to testify.

Analysis: Both the district judge and court of appeals rejected Bonnet's claim. The girls were able to testify about matters such as their age, grade in school, teacher, favorite subject, and the consequences of committing wrongful acts. Although the younger girl in particular failed to answer some of the prosecutor's questions, both satisfied the minimal competence requirements

---

5   United States v. Harris, 542 F.2d 1283, 1303 (7th Cir. 1976).

of Rule 601. Bonnet's attorney could point out weaknesses in the girls' testimony, but the daughters were not wholly incompetent to testify.[6]

Example: The government charged Diane Whited and others with conspiracy to possess cocaine with intent to distribute. Jerry Parks, an alleged participant in the scheme, had been found incompetent to stand trial for his own role in the conspiracy; he suffered from a history of auditory delusions and had spent time in mental health facilities. The prosecutor, however, called Parks to testify against Whited. Whited challenged Parks's competence to testify.

Analysis: The district judge allowed Parks to testify, and the court of appeals upheld that ruling. After referring to the generous competence rule embraced by Rule 601, the court of appeals observed: "As long as a witness appreciates his duty to tell the truth, and is minimally capable of observing, recalling, and communicating events, his testimony should come in for whatever it is worth. It is then up to the opposing party to dispute the witness' powers of apprehension, which may well be impaired by mental illness or other factors."[7]

As these examples suggest, the Federal Rules exclude few witnesses based on a lack of competence. Consistent with this approach, Rule 601 includes no standard for defining competence. On the contrary, it announces a broad default rule that "every person is competent" except as otherwise provided in the rules.

The components of competence mentioned by the court in the last example (appreciation of the duty to tell the truth and a minimal capacity to observe, recall, and communicate) do not appear in Rule 601. Instead, as we will see below, they incorporate aspects of **Rules 602** and **603**. Judges have drawn upon those rules to craft these minimum elements of competence.

---

6   United States v. Spotted War Bonnet, 882 F.2d 1360 (8th Cir. 1989), vacated and remanded on other grounds, 497 U.S. 1021 (1990), original decision reaff'd, 933 F.2d 1471 (8th Cir. 1991). Judge Lay authored a spirited dissent, but the majority's decision in this case represents a common perspective.

7   United States v. Phibbs, 999 F.2d 1053, 1070 (6th Cir. 1993).

2. State Law. Although the first part of **Rule 601** establishes a broad rule of competence, the second half of the rule introduces one important limit based on federalism:

RULE 601. Competency to Testify in General

. . . But in a <u>civil</u> case, state law governs the witness's competency regarding a claim or defense for which <u>state law</u> supplies the rule of decision.

The Federal Rules of Evidence apply to all civil trials in federal court, whether those claims are based on state law (as in diversity cases) or federal law (as in federal question ones). The portion of Rule 601 quoted above applies in those civil cases: Whenever state law supplies the elements of a civil claim or defense, which occurs most often in civil diversity actions, the court must determine competency under that state's law. This rule acknowledges that competency rules are sometimes interwoven with liability principles.

In practice, this exception has little effect. Most state evidentiary codes, like the federal rules, recognize almost all individuals as competent witnesses. Many states, however, maintain a few exceptions to the modern presumption of competence. Some declare children under a certain age incompetent to testify. Others retain "Dead Man's Statutes," which restrict evidence when a live person asserts a civil claim against a deceased one.

The federal rules do not contain any of these special rules of competence, and we will not study any of them further. When state law controls the substantive claims, however, the federal courts must apply these state rules of competence under Rule 601.

3. Can the Judge Testify? Although almost anyone qualifies to serve as a witness under the Federal Rules of Evidence, **Rule 605** recognizes an important exception: The judge who presides over a case cannot also testify as a witness, because the roles of testifying and presiding are incompatible. As the Advisory Committee's note to this rule observes: "Who rules on objections? Who compels him to answer? Can he rule impartially on the weight and admissibility of his own testimony?"[8]

---

8   Fed. R. Evid. 605 advisory committee's note.

The jury, moreover, might give the judge's testimony too much weight. **Rule 605** thus forbids a judge from testifying in any trial at which he or she presides:

RULE 605. Judge's Competency as a Witness

The <u>presiding judge</u> may not testify as a witness at the trial. A party <u>need not object</u> to preserve the issue.

The rule also recognizes that, as a practical matter, a party might withhold an objection to a judge's testimony, fearing that the judge might retaliate against a party raising this kind of complaint. Thus, the rule notes that no objections are necessary to preserve this issue for appeal.

Judges rarely, if ever, literally attempt to take the witness stand in a case where they are presiding. But Rule 605 also prohibits the judge from offering commentary from the bench that amounts to testimony. Here is an illustration of how that kind of "testimony" can arise:

Example: The United States charged Marc Nickl with aiding and abetting a bank employee in the misapplication of bank funds. The government alleged that Nickl worked with Paula Steward, the head bookkeeper at the National Bank of Andover, to channel almost $1 million of bank funds to a company owned by Nickl's domestic partner. Steward pled guilty to the charge against her, but Nickl's case went to trial.

To prove the charge against Nickl, the government had to prove that Steward intended to injure or defraud the bank. Steward gave conflicting testimony on this point at Nickl's trial, "first claiming she did not intend to injure the bank, then admitting she had pleaded guilty to having an intent to defraud." To suggest that Steward might have lacked the necessary intent, Nickl's attorney asked her whether she had pled guilty "just to 'get it over with.' " At that point, the trial judge interrupted and stated: "Well, I'll answer that question because I took her plea. We go through a very specific lengthy inquiry . . . . I would never have accepted her guilty plea unless she would have convinced me that . . . she intended [to injure the bank], and she did. And that's why I accepted her plea. And that's why she's in prison. Now, let's go on."

Analysis: The court of appeals held that this statement constituted impermissible testimony by the trial judge. The judge's comments added new information to the trial that the witnesses had not contributed. The error, moreover, required reversal. The judge's impermissible comments left little room for the jury to reach a decision on intent other than the one the judge suggested, and other evidence on this issue was equivocal. Nor, finally, did the judge attempt a curative instruction.[9]

Rule 605 similarly prohibits judges from reporting evidence related to experiments they have conducted or visits they have made to a site related to the case. The prohibition also applies to the judge's law clerks and other employees, as this unusual case shows:

Example: Edwin Kennedy, an 82-year-old shopper, broke his hip when he slipped and fell on the floor of an A&P grocery store. Kennedy sued the store, claiming that he slipped on a puddle caused by heavy rains outside the store. The first trial ended in a mistrial, and the judge scheduled a new trial. A few weeks before the new trial, the judge's clerk (James Madison) decided to visit the store. He stopped by the store after a heavy rain and saw a puddle of water on the floor near where Kennedy said he had fallen. At the second trial, the judge allowed Kennedy's lawyer to call Madison as a witness. Madison, after identifying himself as the judge's clerk, testified about the large puddle he had seen.

Analysis: The court of appeals concluded that this testimony violated Rule 605. Although that rule applies explicitly only to the judge, the same policy concerns apply to the judge's clerk in a situation like this one. Here, the jury almost certainly attached special weight to the clerk's testimony. The error, moreover, was too serious to be harmless; the court reversed the plaintiff's verdict.[10]

---

9   United States v. Nickl, 427 F.3d 1286, 1292–95 (10th Cir. 2005). We discussed curative instructions in Chapter 5.

10   Kennedy v. Great Atl. & Pac. Tea Co., 551 F.2d 593 (5th Cir. 1977).

4. What About Jurors? Jurors, like judges, cannot testify in a trial where they play a decision making role. Other jurors may not fairly weigh the credibility of one of their own colleagues. **Rule 606(a)** states this prohibition as a matter of competence:

RULE 606. Juror's Competency as a Witness

(a) At the Trial. A <u>juror</u> may not testify as a witness before the other jurors at the trial . . . .

This rule, analogously to Rule 605, recognizes that it may be uncomfortable for a lawyer to challenge the competence of a juror before other members of the jury. A lawyer must register an objection to a juror's proposed testimony, but may do so outside the presence of other jurors:

RULE 606. Juror's Competency as a Witness

(a) . . . If a juror is called to testify, the court must give a party an opportunity to <u>object outside the jury's presence</u>.

Occasionally, a party asks a juror to appear at a subsequent trial and testify as a witness about something he or she observed in the previous trial. Rule 606 does not bar this testimony, because it prohibits jurors from testifying only "at the trial" of the case in which the juror is sitting. If a juror in one case testifies as a witness in a different case, Rule 606(a) imposes no automatic bar.

> **Example:** In 1993, the government indicted Jose Barragan-Cepeda, claiming he was a deported alien who had reentered the United States in violation of federal law. Barragan-Cepeda moved to dismiss the indictment as a violation of double jeopardy. He argued that he had been charged with violating the same statute in 1980 and was acquitted of that charge. The 1980 jury, he argued, necessarily found that he was a citizen rather than an alien. To support this argument, Barragan-Cepeda introduced the affidavits of two jurors who served during his 1980 trial.

Analysis: The district judge rejected these affidavits as testimony from jurors, but the court of appeals held that they were admissible. The jurors were not testifying in the same trial at which they served, and their evidence was relevant. Indeed, relying in part on the affidavits, the court upheld Barragan-Cepeda's double jeopardy claim and ordered dismissal of the indictment.[11]

Notice, however, that counsel in this case did not use the former juror's testimony to attack the prior verdict. The Rules of Evidence impose strict limits on when jurors can offer testimony that would undermine the validity of a verdict they rendered. **Rule 606(b)** addresses that issue; we will explore that part of the rule in Chapter 72.

5. Can Counsel Testify? Although the Federal Rules of Evidence bar the judge and jurors from testifying in an ongoing trial, they do not restrict the lawyers who represent the parties. The federal rules leave open the possibility that a lawyer might testify on behalf of the party she represents, or that opposing counsel might call the lawyer to the stand. Ethical rules, however, discourage lawyers from testifying in cases in which they represent a party, and lawyers rarely take the stand in cases where they appear as counsel.[12]

C. Personal Knowledge

1. The Basic Rule. Although the federal rules adopt a liberal view of competence, they narrow the field of potential witnesses in one very important respect. **Rule 602** declares that witnesses may testify only about matters that they know about personally:

RULE 602. Need for Personal Knowledge

A witness may testify to a matter only if evidence is introduced sufficient to support a finding that the witness has personal knowledge of the matter. . . .

---

11   United States v. Barragan-Cepeda, 29 F.3d 1378 (9th Cir. 1994).

12   See Model Rules of Prof'l Conduct R. 3.7 (2004).

This rule means that witnesses can testify only about matters they have seen, heard, or otherwise sensed themselves. They cannot speculate about matters beyond their knowledge. An attorney, therefore, cannot ask a witness to guess at the motives or thoughts of another person. Questions like these probably call for answers beyond the witness's personal knowledge:

> When Ms. Jones signed the contract, what was she thinking?
>
> Why did he hit you?

Rule 602, however, does not limit witnesses to eyewitness accounts of the ultimate facts disputed at trial; remember that circumstantial evidence can also be relevant to a case:

Example: Darwin is on trial for stabbing Xavier to death on the evening of March 6. Darwin's neighbor Louise testifies that, at about 8 p.m. on March 6, she saw Darwin enter his home holding a knife. Darwin's counsel objects that Louise lacks personal knowledge of the stabbing.

Analysis: Louise lacks personal knowledge of the stabbing, but she has personal knowledge of a relevant piece of circumstantial evidence: the fact that Darwin was holding a knife around the time that the stabbing occurred. She can testify to that fact.

Some judges use the "personal knowledge" requirement as a limitation to **Rule 601**'s generous view of competence. Personal knowledge implies that a witness is capable of apprehending an event, remembering it, and describing it to others. If a witness lacks the ability to fulfill these functions—because of youth, mental impairment, or any other reason—the witness may not have sufficient personal knowledge to testify.

Even in such cases, however, the preference for admissibility usually prevails; the judge usually will let the witness testify, allowing opposing counsel to expose any flaws on cross-examination. The jury can then determine the extent to which the witness's condition affected his or her personal knowledge.

Example: The government indicted Jose Peyro for conspiring to distribute cocaine. Debra Anton provided some of the evidence against Peyro. Anton admitted on the stand that she had "some very substantial memory problems" and was "emotionally unbalanced." She also conceded on cross-examination: "I don't remember anything very well. There are, like, certain moments I know I remember, but nothing at all specific in any of it." Peyro objected to Anton's testimony, claiming she lacked sufficient personal knowledge to testify against him.

Analysis: Despite Anton's confused state and emotional problems, the district judge allowed her to testify; the court of appeals upheld that ruling. The district judge examined Anton outside the jury's presence and concluded that, although she could not remember details, "she [had] a broad, general recollection" that satisfied the personal knowledge requirement.[13]

In other words, personal knowledge establishes a threshold standard for competence, but it is a very easy standard to meet.

2. Establishing Personal Knowledge. Before witnesses start to testify, they must demonstrate that they have personal knowledge of the matters they will testify about. Establishing a witness's personal knowledge is part of the "foundation" that a lawyer must lay to support the witness's testimony. How does a lawyer show that a witness has sufficient personal knowledge to testify? **Rule 602** continues from where we left off above, offering some assistance on this point:

RULE 602. Need for Personal Knowledge

. . . Evidence to prove personal knowledge <u>may</u> consist of the witness's <u>own testimony</u>. . . .

Much of the time, a witness's own testimony provides the necessary foundation to establish personal knowledge. A witness may testify that she was at a certain place at a certain time and saw certain things. Unless it was physically impossible for the witness to have been where she claimed, or to have seen

---

13   United States v. Peyro, 786 F.2d 826, 830–31 (8th Cir. 1986).

what she claims to have seen, this kind of testimony is sufficient to establish personal knowledge.

Example: Arvin Adler and Betty Babcock collided in their automobiles at an intersection. Babcock sued Adler, claiming that she had the right of way and that he ran a red light. Babcock offers the testimony of Wilma Wilson, who was driving behind Adler at the time the accident occurred. Wilson testifies that she saw the light facing her and Adler turn red, and that Adler drove into the intersection after the light was red.

Adler's counsel objects that Wilson lacks personal knowledge of when the light turned red. To buttress his claim, he offers evidence that (a) it was a sunny day and Wilson would have been looking directly into the late afternoon sun while approaching the intersection, and (b) Wilson's cell phone records show that she was talking with a business customer at the time of the accident. For these reasons, he argues, Wilson could not possibly have noticed when the light turned red.

Analysis: Wilson's testimony that she was driving behind Adler at the time of the accident, and that she saw the light turn red, establishes her personal knowledge. Adler's counsel can cross-examine Wilson about her attentiveness while driving, and can introduce evidence about both the sunlight and the cell phone calls. The jury will weigh that evidence in determining Wilson's credibility. But Wilson's testimony that she was driving behind Adler and saw the light turn red is sufficient to establish her personal knowledge.

A judge will exclude testimony if the witness could not possibly have seen what he or she claims, but this is rare. The following example suggests how this unusual circumstance may arise:

Example: Jerry McCrary-El, a prison inmate, claimed that three prison guards beat him in his cell without provocation. He sued the guards and offered the testimony of Antonio Jones, who was housed in the neighboring cell. Jones claimed that a crack at the corner of his cell door, which measured about an inch and a half, allowed him to see into the prison corridor and witness part of the confrontation between McCrary-El and the guards.

Analysis: The district judge examined a diagram of the cells, listened to Jones's description, and concluded that Jones had not been able to see the relevant parts of the confrontation. No reasonable person, moreover, would believe that Jones could have seen "anything of relevance." The judge excluded Jones's testimony as lacking personal knowledge, and the court of appeals upheld this decision.[14]

Sometimes judges add commonly known facts to a witness's testimony to find that the witness has sufficient personal knowledge to testify.

Example: The United States prosecuted Hilton Lake for a carjacking that occurred in the Virgin Islands. As one element of the crime, the government had to prove that the affected car had traveled in interstate or foreign commerce before arriving in the Virgin Islands. To establish this element, the government relied upon the testimony of police officer Curtis Griffin. Griffin testified that he was a lifelong resident of the Virgin Islands, that no vehicles are manufactured on the islands, and that all cars on the islands have been shipped there. Lake's counsel objected that Griffin lacked personal knowledge to support these statements.

Analysis: The district judge concluded that, as a lifelong resident and police officer within a small territory, Griffin possessed sufficient personal knowledge to make this claim. The court of appeals, in an opinion authored by then Circuit Judge Alito, affirmed; the court noted that the Virgin Islands consist of only 136 square miles total. It would be difficult for a car manufacturing plant to hide from a lifelong resident and police officer under those circumstances.[15]

3. Experts and Personal Knowledge. A final sentence of **Rule 602** notes the connection between this rule and **Rule 703**, which governs opinion testimony by experts:

---

14   McCrary-El v. Shaw, 992 F.2d 809, 811 (8th Cir. 1993).
15   United States v. Lake, 150 F.3d 269 (3d Cir. 1998).

RULE 602. Need for Personal Knowledge

. . . This rule does not apply to a witness's expert testimony under Rule 703.

As we will see later in Chapter 63, expert witnesses are allowed to offer opinions related to a controversy even if they lack personal knowledge of the underlying facts. Indeed, experts usually learn about a controversy by speaking to eyewitnesses or studying reports compiled by others. Rule 602, combined with Rule 703, allows jurors to benefit from expert opinions based on this secondhand knowledge.

D. Oaths and Affirmations. The first words out of any witness's mouth are not testimony, but an oath or affirmation. You have probably seen countless witnesses—in real courtrooms, on television, or in movies—swear to "tell the truth, the whole truth, and nothing but the truth." The oath or affirmation impresses the witness with the seriousness of courtroom testimony and reminds him of the obligation to speak truthfully. The oath or affirmation also lays the basis for a perjury prosecution if a witness lies on the stand.

Rule 603 governs oaths or affirmations in federal court. The rule is quite open-ended, allowing witnesses to choose between an oath or affirmation and imposing no particular format for either. An "oath" traditionally includes the word "swear" and a reference to God; an "affirmation" is a promise to tell the truth that omits religious references and uses the word "affirm" rather than "swear." But there is no legal distinction between these two forms.

RULE 603. Oath or Affirmation to Testify Truthfully

Before testifying, a witness must give an oath or affirmation to testify truthfully. It must be in a form designed to impress that duty on the witness's conscience.

Judges sometimes invoke this rule to prevent a very young or mentally infirm witness from testifying. If the witness lacks the ability to understand the truth or to appreciate the seriousness of testifying in court, then the judge may find that the witness is incapable of taking the oath or affirmation required by Rule 603. Like the personal knowledge requirement, Rule 603 establishes a minimal standard of competency that all witnesses must meet.

As with other issues touching on competency, however, judges use this power very sparingly. They are more likely to allow the witness to testify, leaving it to opposing counsel to raise questions about the witness's ability to testify truthfully.

If a witness refuses to make an oath or affirmation that satisfies Rule 603, then the judge will exclude the witness's testimony.

Example: E.L. Fowler, a gravestone dealer, did not file tax returns for more than 20 years. The IRS finally detected Fowler and the government indicted him for willful failure to file tax returns. Fowler represented himself at trial and, apparently continuing his anti-government streak, refused to take any of the oaths offered by the judge, including a simple one that "I state that I will tell the truth in my testimony." Instead, Fowler "was willing to do no more than laud himself in such remarks as 'I am a truthful man,' and 'I would not tell a lie to stay out of jail.' "

Analysis: The district judge held that Fowler's proposed statements were insufficient to satisfy Rule 603, and prevented him from testifying. The court of appeals upheld that ruling.[16]

On the other hand, Rule 603 does not require a witness to utter particular magic words to satisfy its requirement. The drafters attempted to craft a requirement that would accommodate any set of religious beliefs or nonbelief. Even if these beliefs are unfamiliar to trial judges, they should try to find a way to accommodate them.

Example: The IRS investigated Betty Ann Ferguson for tax evasion. At a Tax Court hearing, Ferguson refused to use the words "oath," "affirm," or "swear" in promising to tell the truth. Citing Biblical passages, she argued that all three of these words violated her religious beliefs. Ferguson offered to state: "I, [Betty Ann Ferguson], do hereby declare that the facts I am about to give are, to the best of my knowledge and belief, accurate, correct, and complete."

---

16   United States v. Fowler, 605 F.2d 181, 185 (5th Cir. 1979).

> **Analysis:** The Tax Court judge refused to accept Ferguson's statement, but the Court of Appeals for the Fifth Circuit reversed. Ferguson's formula satisfied the needs of Rule 603 and would support a perjury prosecution if she lied on the stand. She did not need to use the words "swear" or "affirm" if those violated her religious beliefs.[17]

E. Interpreters. With a multi-lingual population, global trade, immigration, and increased recognition of communication disabilities, courtroom interpreters have become common. The Federal Rules of Evidence do not confer the right to an interpreter or specify when interpreters should be appointed. The Rules of Civil and Criminal Procedure, various statutes, and (in criminal cases) constitutional provisions govern those issues.

Rule 604 of the Federal Rules of Evidence, however, sets the standard for judging an interpreter's competence.

RULE 604. Interpreter

An interpreter must be <u>qualified</u> and must give an <u>oath or affirmation</u> to make a true translation.

Under this rule, an interpreter's competence rests on two factors. First, the interpreter must be qualified. Second, the interpreter must make an oath or affirmation, not to tell the truth (as a witness would) but to "make a true translation."

---

17   Ferguson v. Commissioner, 921 F.2d 588 (5th Cir. 1991). Recall that, although the Federal Rules of Evidence do not apply by their own terms to the Tax Court, Congress directed in a separate statute that the Tax Court use those rules. See Chapter 3.

Quick Summary

 The Federal Rules of Evidence adopt a very generous view of competence. Under **Rule 601**, almost all witnesses are competent to testify, regardless of their youth or mental impairment. The rules assume that opposing counsel will highlight a witness's shortcomings and that the jury will assess the witness's credibility. The only categories of witnesses barred completely from testifying are judges (**Rule 605**) and jurors (**Rule 606**); they may not testify in cases in which they perform those roles. Ethical rules likewise restrict attorneys from testifying at a trial in which they represent a party, although the Rules of Evidence do not address this issue.

The federal rules impose just three other limits on competence: (1) A witness may only testify about matters within her personal knowledge (**Rule 602**); (2) A witness must make an oath or affirmation to testify truthfully (**Rule 603**); and (3) When state law supplies the rule of decision, as in a civil diversity case, state law also determines competence (**Rule 601**). The latter rule rarely affects a witness's competence, although states maintain some idiosyncratic competence rules.

The Federal Rules of Evidence also set a competence threshold for interpreters (**Rule 604**); an interpreter must be qualified and must make an oath or affirmation to render a true translation.

15

Examining Witnesses

Key Concepts

- Taking Turns: Direct, Cross, Redirect, and Recross Examinations
- **Rule 611** Guidelines
- Leading Questions
- Beyond the Scope
- Impeachment
- Rehabilitation
- **Rule 614:** Judicial Questions and Witnesses
- **Rule 615:** Excluding Witnesses During Testimony

A. Introduction and Policy. In this chapter we look at another three straightforward rules in Article VI: **Rules 611, 614,** and **615**. These three rules establish the basic structure for examining witnesses. The structure allows lawyers to elicit admissible testimony from witnesses while focusing them on the facts related to the dispute. The process also accommodates the adversarial nature of the courtroom by allowing opponents to question each other's witnesses.

Parties take turns examining a witness at trial, following this sequence:

- **Direct Examination** by the attorney who called the witness

- **Cross-Examination** by attorneys for other parties

- **Redirect Examination** by the attorney who called the witness, if necessary

- **Recross-Examination** by attorneys for other parties, if necessary

- **Additional Rounds of Redirect and Recross** (although these are rare)

Rule 611 is a broad provision that sets out different rules for each of these stages. It is worth looking at the rule as a whole before we analyze it piece by piece:

RULE 611. Mode and Order of Examining Witnesses and Presenting Evidence

(a) Control by the Court; Purposes. The court should exercise reasonable control over the mode and order of examining witnesses and presenting evidence so as to:

    (1) make those procedures effective for determining the truth;

    (2) avoid wasting time; and

    (3) protect witnesses from harassment or undue embarrassment.

(b) Scope of Cross-Examination. Cross-examination should not go beyond the subject matter of the direct examination and matters affecting the witness's credibility. The court may allow inquiry into additional matters as if on direct examination.

(c) Leading Questions. Leading questions should not be used on direct examination except as necessary to develop the witness's testimony. Ordinarily, the court should allow leading questions:

    (1) on cross-examination; and

    (2) when a party calls a hostile witness, an adverse party, or a witness identified with an adverse party.

The first part of the rule gives the judge the general power to control how witnesses are examined during any stage of the witness's testimony. This allows a judge to prevent an attorney from badgering a witness or confusing the witness with complex or compound questions.

The second and third parts of the rule work together to ensure that a witness uses his own words to tell the story about what happened. Thus, leading questions are generally not allowed on direct examination; the attorney must use the witness's own words to build her case. But these questions are allowed on cross-examination, when the opposing attorney is limited to exploring topics covered on direct rather than developing a new case.

In order to understand this process more completely, let's look more closely at each of the phases of witness examination, drawing on the applicable provision of **Rule 611** as we go.

B. Direct Examination.
Through direct examination, an attorney constructs a story that presents the client's case. The attorney may preview this story during opening statement, but she must build the case with pieces of evidence. In most trials, witness testimony recounts most of the story; the attorney reveals that story through direct examination.

Direct examination begins with the matters we discussed in the last chapter. The witness first takes an oath or affirmation, as required by **Rule 603**. If an opponent objects to the witness's competence, the judge will address that issue under **Rule 601**. The attorney presenting the witness will then lay a foundation for the witness's testimony, establishing under **Rule 602** that the witness has personal knowledge of the matters they will describe. For most witnesses, these preliminaries cause little difficulty.

If the witness is an expert, the attorney will lay a further foundation for the expert's opinion. We will explore that process separately when we examine the expert opinion rules in Chapters 61–65.

After these foundational matters are satisfied, the lawyer elicits the witness's testimony through a series of questions and answers. The question-and-answer format allows the attorney to focus the witness's attention on relevant and otherwise admissible facts. If left to their own devices, witnesses can confuse and lengthen trials by discussing tangential issues and multitudes of irrelevant facts. Here, for example, is a witness who began to stray from helpful testimony on direct examination:

> **Q:** All right. So the day they came to your mother's house you saw Johnny talking to Chino; is that correct?
>
> **A:** No. When I got there, I was at my sister's home. They were waiting for me at the house, so I came from my sister's house and they left my mother's house to go to my sister's house, but I was already coming to my mother's house, so they got to my sister's house, and they called over at the house, and I was there at my mother's house. They came back.[1]

---

1   Disorder in the Court 215 (foreword by Richard Lederer, National Court Reporters Association, 1996).

This witness's testimony is not so unusual. Psychology research shows that people remember incidents by reliving them as they speak. Details of movement, sensory impressions, and even thoughts that occurred during the earlier event are embedded in those memories. Extraneous detail like this tends to confirm the accuracy of the memory and the truthfulness of the speaker.[2]

But trials require more focused narratives. Through witness preparation and direct examination, the trial attorney tries to cut through the witness's natural tendency to supply unnecessary detail. Direct examination questions help focus the witness on the facts that matter for the courtroom controversy.

1. Leading Questions. When a lawyer constructs a story through direct examination, the witness—rather than the lawyer—should tell the story. If the lawyer puts words in the witness's mouth, the jury may doubt the witness's memory or honesty. On direct examination, therefore, good advocacy requires lawyers to give witnesses a chance to tell their own stories.

The justice system also has an interest in letting witnesses speak for themselves. If a lawyer leads a witness by asking him questions that suggest a particular answer, the witness may give those answers out of deference or confusion. Even if the witness's recollection differs from the attorney's words, the witness may assume that the attorney must be right.

For these reasons, Rule 611(c) restricts the use of leading questions during direct examination:

> ## RULE 611. Mode and Order of Examining Witnesses and Presenting Evidence
>
> **(c) Leading Questions.** Leading questions should not be used on direct examination except as necessary to develop the witness's testimony. . . .

A leading question is one that suggests a certain answer to the witness; it "leads" the witness to that answer. A classic example of a leading question is a statement followed by a request for confirmation that the statement is true:

---

2   See Pär Anders Granhag & Aldert Vrij, Deception Detection, in Psychology and Law: An Empirical Perspective 43 (Neil Brewer & Kipling D. Williams eds. 2005).

> **Q:** The defendant shot the victim in the head, didn't he?

If asked on direct examination, this question almost certainly would prompt an objection from opposing counsel. And as noted above, this type of question can undermine the lawyer's own witness by suggesting that the witness lacks sufficient knowledge or confidence to testify independently.

But don't jump to the conclusion that any question that guides a witness's answer is an improperly leading one. Instead, think of questions as lying on a continuum, from completely open-ended to leading. As questions approach the "leading" end of the spectrum, they become more and more closed; that is, they may suggest a certain type of answer, or ask the witness to choose between different options.

For example, the most open-ended question would offer no guidance at all to the witness:

> **Q:** What happened next?

Or an attorney could try to focus the witness with a question that is a little less open:

> **Q:** What did the defendant do at that point?

Or close the question even more:

> **Q:** Did you see the defendant do anything to the victim?

A judge probably would not consider any of these questions leading. But once an attorney places specific facts into the question, suggesting a particular answer to the witness, the question may become a leading one. Even then, much depends on context. If the question repeats specific facts that the witness has already stated and asks for more detail, the question simply follows up on the witness's answer; it does not suggest an answer. To identify a leading question, always ask: In this context, does the question suggest a specific answer? For example, consider the following exchange:

> **Q:** What happened next?
>
> **A:** I saw the defendant come into the room.
>
> **Q:** Did the defendant shoot the victim in the head?

The last question almost certainly is leading, because it suggests a "yes" answer. The witness has not yet described anything about the defendant's actions in the room, and in this context the lawyer is the one who is suggesting that the defendant shot the victim in the head. In a different context, however, the same question probably is not leading:

> **Q:** What happened next?
>
> **A:** I saw the defendant shoot the victim.
>
> **Q:** Did the defendant shoot the victim in the head?

This question seeks clarification, and requests a "yes" or "no" answer, but the question in this context does not imply that "yes" is the only correct answer.[3] But some judges might disagree, finding this question leading. To avoid any chance of an objection sustained by the judge, the attorney might open up the question somewhat:

> **Q:** What happened next?
>
> **A:** I saw the defendant shoot the victim.
>
> **Q:** What part of the victim's body did the bullet hit?

This question provides the witness with guidance about the level of detail that the attorney wants, but would never be called a leading question. If the witness requires more guidance, the attorney could list a number of options, like a multiple choice test:

---

3   A leading question in this context might be: "In fact, the defendant shot the victim in the head, isn't that correct?"

> **Q:** What part of the victim's body did the bullet hit: the head, the chest, the arms, or the legs?

This question is quite closed because it restricts the range of possible answers, but it is not leading because it does not suggest that any specific answer is correct.

2. Permissible Leading on Direct. Although **Rule 611** restricts the use of leading questions during direct examination, the rule gives judges discretion to allow leading questions when they are "necessary to develop the witness's testimony." There are four contexts in which judges most often allow attorneys to lead witnesses on direct examination:

To Establish Pedigree Information. The witness's pedigree includes uncontested points like educational background and occupation. Leading questions establish these points efficiently:

> **Q:** And Dr. Davidson, you are the Chief Surgeon at St. Luke's Hospital, is that correct?

To Direct a Witness's Attention to A Relevant Place and Time. Leading questions about place and time can help the attorney shift a witness's attention to a new chapter of the testimony. These questions are particularly useful if the direct examination covers a number of incidents over a long period of time:

> **Q:** Now directing your attention to Monday, December 3rd, did you attend the board meeting at the Chicago office on that day?

To Help a Witness Who Is Hesitant, Confused, or Has Trouble Recalling. Judges allow lawyers to lead witnesses who have difficulty testifying because of youth, nervousness, illness, memory problems, or other characteristics. Many witnesses find the format of courtroom questioning unfamiliar and have difficulty responding to the attorney's questions. A leading question can get a flustered witness back on track, as in this example from a San Diego case:

Q: What do you do as a clerk?

A: I work as a cashier and, you know, sometimes I make the orders and, you know, deliveries sometimes. Everything in the store.

Q: Now, directing your attention again to June 16, did something unusual happen inside the liquor store on that day?

A: No. Everything was regular.

Q: Everything was normal?

A: Normal. Yeah.

Q: Well, was there a body found inside the liquor store on that day?

A: Yeah, that's right.[4]

Leading questions can play a particularly important role in cases involving young children and/or victims of physical or sexual abuse. These witnesses sometimes are reluctant to testify directly, and find it easier to answer yes-or-no questions. In the following example, a prosecutor is conducting the direct examination of an eleven-year-old child:

Q: And what happened next, Emily?

A: My nose got hurt.

Q: How did it get hurt?

A: It was hurt with a kick. Someone kicked me in the face.

Q: Emily, who kicked you in the face?

[No answer]

Q: Emily, was it your mother who kicked you in the face?

A: Yes.

---

4   Charles M. Sevilla, Disorder in the Court 238–39 (W.W. Norton & Co. 1992).

The prosecutor's final question is leading, because it strongly suggests the expected answer. But the judge probably would allow the question, because there is no other way to elicit the information from this reluctant witness. Remember, however, that even though this question may be permissible, it is not as effective as an open-ended one. The jury will understand that the attorney suggested the answer to the witness, which diminishes the persuasive power of the testimony.

Hostile Witnesses. Finally, Rule 611 explicitly recognizes that leading questions are appropriate on direct examination when a party calls a witness who is likely to resist that party's position. Litigants usually call witnesses who they know will support their position, but a party sometimes must call to the stand the adverse party or a person identified with that party to present a coherent case. In a dispute growing out of an automobile collision, for example, a passenger of one of the drivers may have been the only eyewitness to the accident. If the other driver calls that passenger as a witness, the witness may be reluctant at best and antagonistic at worst.

In other cases, parties discover that a witness they thought would be favorable has changed perspectives and offers damaging testimony on the stand. A party will ask the judge to declare this type of witness a hostile witness. Do not be misled by the term "hostile witness," or by the common portrayal in television and movies of hostile witnesses as antagonistic and rude. A "hostile witness" is any witness who is evading questions or otherwise being uncooperative to such an extent that it is interfering with the eliciting of testimony. A hostile witness might be very kind and polite to the attorney conducting the direct examination—she simply does not give direct answers to the questions put to her. As long as the witness is sufficiently evasive or uncooperative, the judge will declare the witness hostile.

Rule 611(c) sets out a special rule for hostile witnesses, witnesses who are adverse parties, or witnesses identified with adverse parties, allowing them to be interrogated during direct examination with leading questions:

RULE 611. Mode and Order of Examining Witnesses and Presenting Evidence

(c) Leading Questions. . . . Ordinarily, the court should allow leading questions: . . .

    (2) when a party calls a <u>hostile witness</u>, an <u>adverse party</u>, or a <u>witness identified with an adverse party</u>.

3. Other Rule 611 Objections. Apart from the restriction on leading questions, the federal rules do not define the form of direct examination. Instead, Rule 611(a) gives the trial judge broad discretion to control that form and the overall order of the trial:

RULE 611. Mode and Order of Examining Witnesses and Presenting Evidence

(a) Control by the Court; Purposes. The court should exercise <u>reasonable control</u> over the mode and order of examining witnesses and presenting evidence so as to:

    (1) make those procedures effective for determining the truth;

    (2) avoid wasting time; and

    (3) protect witnesses from harassment or undue embarrassment.

This rule is the basis for the overwhelming majority of objections at trial. Any objection to the **form** of a question is an objection based on Rule 611(a). But for these objections, nobody cites the actual rule. Instead, lawyers note the reason why the form is objectionable. Those objections fall into categories that all trial lawyers and judges recognize. We list the most common Rule 611 objections at the end of this chapter. Here are just two examples:

P's Attorney: Do you really expect us to believe that, Mrs. Davis?

D's Attorney: Objection, Your Honor, harassing the witness.

. . . .

> **P's Attorney:** When you signed the contract, did you forge your part-ner's signature and alter the amount you both promised to pay?
>
> **D's Attorney:** Objection, compound question.

C. Cross-Examination. Cross-examination differs from direct examination in two important ways: (1) leading questions are allowed, but (2) the cross-examiner may ask questions only about issues covered during the direct examination. In trial terminology, the cross-examining attorney cannot ask any questions that are "beyond the scope" of the direct examination. Let's explore each of these limits.

1. Leading Questions on Cross. On direct examination, lawyers construct a story by allowing witnesses to tell what they know. But the primary purpose of cross-examination is not to construct a story; it is to limit or discredit the story told by the witness. Lawyers can most effectively test the bounds of a witness's knowledge, as well as the witness's credibility, by controlling the witness's answers. That is exactly what leading questions do, so Rule 611(c) allows lawyers to use leading questions during cross-examination:

> ## RULE 611. Mode and Order of Examining Witnesses and Presenting Evidence
>
> **(c) Leading Questions.** . . . Ordinarily, the court should allow lead-ing questions:
>
> **(1)** on cross-examination; . . .

Leading questions are the norm during cross-examination. Lawyers conducting cross-examination usually ask witnesses very specific questions, sometimes requir-ing them to give only "yes" or "no" answers. This allows the lawyer to control the witness's testimony; witnesses can't answer questions they haven't been asked.

Rule 611 qualifies its permission of leading questions on cross-examination with the word "ordinarily," because attorneys sometimes question a friendly witness on cross-examination. If the plaintiff calls the defendant as a witness, for example, the judge will not allow the defendant's lawyer to use leading questions as freely on cross-examination.

2. Beyond the Scope. The use of leading questions on cross-examination raises a different problem: What will stop the cross-examining lawyer from using those questions to construct a new story, one told by the lawyer rather than any witness? Skillful trial lawyers may begin to suggest a competing story during cross-examination; chipping away parts of the opponent's story may reveal the outlines of a new story. But lawyers are not allowed to tell a completely new story through their own questions posed on cross-examination. Rule 611(b) implements this limit by restricting the "scope" of cross-examination to the subject matter of the direct examination and the witness's credibility:

> ## RULE 611. Mode and Order of Examining Witnesses and Presenting Evidence
>
> **(b) Scope of Cross-Examination.** Cross-examination should not go beyond the <u>subject matter of the direct examination</u> and matters affecting the witness's <u>credibility</u>. The court may allow inquiry into additional matters <u>as if on direct examination</u>.

This provision makes three important points. **First,** lawyers conducting cross-examination usually cannot ask a witness about topics or incidents that were not addressed during direct examination. Cross-examination is not the time to construct a new story; it is the time to probe the opponent's story. If a lawyer wants to use a witness to construct a new story, the lawyer must call the witness during his own case and ask questions on direct examination. Unless the witness is an adverse party or other hostile witness, the lawyer will not be able to use leading questions on direct examination; that assures that the new story comes from the witness instead of from the lawyer.

Second, the rule gives the judge discretion to expand the scope of cross-examination. If the witness is about to leave town, for example, and it would be difficult to recall the witness during another part of the case, the judge may allow the attorney to ask about new matters on cross-examination. But under these circumstances, the cross-examiner must inquire about the new matters "as if on direct examination." In other words, the attorney must use non-leading questions.

Finally, parties are allowed on cross-examination to ask questions affecting the witness's credibility. This is known as "impeaching" the witness. As we'll see in upcoming chapters, this is one of the most important functions of cross-examination. Opposing counsel may cross-examine a witness about the accuracy of the perceptions underlying her testimony, about factors (such as drunkenness or drug use) that might have affected that perception, about prior criminal convictions, and about a host of other discrediting matters.

 Parties frequently dispute whether a topic raised on cross-examination is beyond the scope of the direct examination. The judge has discretion to interpret the subject matter of direct examination narrowly or broadly: If a security guard testifies for the prosecution that she saw the defendant shoplift DVDs at 11:00 AM on June 21st, can defense counsel cross-examine the guard about what she was doing at 2:00 PM on that same day? Can counsel ask about what the guard was doing at 10:30 AM that day? How about other shoplifting incidents the guard witnessed on other days? Good advocacy may persuade the judge to rule that these questions fall inside or outside the subject matter explored on direct examination.

But one subject **always** falls within the scope of cross-examination. Rule 611(b) explicitly allows questions designed to test the credibility of the witness. Questions related to impeachment are always fair game on cross-examination, regardless of the subject matter of the direct testimony or the number of questions the witness was asked on direct.

D. Redirect Examination. The Federal Rules of Evidence do not refer to redirect examination, but most judges allow this additional "turn" in witness examination. On redirect examination, the lawyer who initially called the witness will explore issues that were raised during cross-examination. Questions asked on redirect may clarify responses the witness gave during cross-examination, flesh out parts of the story that the cross-examiner ignored, and otherwise illuminate the cross-examination. If the cross-examiner impeached the witness by showing bias, prior felony convictions, or other matters (all of which we'll explore in upcoming chapters), the opponent may use redirect to "rehabilitate" that witness. Rehabilitation may include eliciting exonerating details or otherwise combating the negative information.

Judges are more tolerant of leading questions on redirect examination than on direct. Since the lawyer is following up on specific matters raised by the cross-examiner, leading questions often are more efficient than open-ended ones. Still, the attorney conducting redirect avoids leading questions as much as possible, allowing the witness to tell his own story.

Redirect examination must focus on matters raised during cross-examination, just as cross-examination concentrates on matters raised on direct. Each phase of examination is progressively narrower than the last. Judges, in fact, may grow impatient during redirect examination; they are less tolerant of repetition or tangential inquiries than on direct examination or cross.

E. Recross-Examination.

Recross, like redirect, receives no official sanction from the Rules of Evidence. Once again, however, most judges will allow recross-examination if new issues arose on redirect and if the recross is brief. The same rules apply as during cross-examination: The lawyer may use leading questions, but must stay within the scope of the previous examination (in this case, the matters explored on redirect). As with redirect examination, judges display increasing impatience with delay or tangential matters during recross.

F. Additional Rounds of Redirect and Recross.

In theory, rounds of redirect and recross-examination could continue indefinitely, as long as each inquiry raises a new matter that requires response. In practice, however, judges are unlikely to allow the parties to continue beyond recross-examination. By that phase, each side should have brought out relevant detail and further inquiry would be repetitive. Sometimes, however, recross-examination will reveal a new fact that is sufficiently important that the opposing party should have an opportunity to examine the witness further about that fact.

G. Miscellaneous Issues.

The Federal Rules include several other provisions related to the examination of witnesses. We explore most of those in upcoming chapters. But before concluding this chapter, we note two other rules related to witness examination that arise sometimes in court but require little discussion.

First, Rule 614 authorizes the judge to call her own witnesses and to interrogate witnesses called by parties. Judges rarely call their own witnesses, but they frequently ask questions of witnesses called by the parties. Many of these judicial questions are minor ones seeking clarification or asking the witness to repeat an answer that the court reporter did not hear. Occasionally, however, judges will ask witnesses more substantive questions. Rule 614 allows the judge to assume this active role:

RULE 614. Court's Calling or Examining a Witness

(a) Calling. The court may call a witness on its own or at a party's request. <u>Each party is entitled to cross-examine</u> the witness.

(b) Examining. The court may examine a witness regardless of who calls the witness.

As the rule indicates, all parties are entitled to cross-examine any witnesses called by the judge. They may also object to any of the judge's questions, or even to the competency of the witnesses that she calls. As noted earlier, a jury may disapprove of an attorney objecting to a judge's questions, so Rule 614(c) suspends the general rule requiring that all objections be made immediately:

RULE 614. Court's Calling or Examining a Witness

(c) Objections. A party may object to the court's calling or examining a witness either at that time or at <u>the next opportunity when the jury is not present.</u>

The **second** witness examination rule we will note briefly is **Rule 615,** which governs the exclusion of witnesses from the courtroom while other witnesses are testifying. If witnesses were permitted to hear what earlier witnesses said on the stand, they might change their testimony in response to what the earlier witnesses said. This danger is especially acute (1) when witnesses offer conflicting accounts of an event or (2) when a party's position depends on persuasive corroborating testimony. Under the first circumstance, exclusion of witnesses prevents them from hearing the testimony of opposing witnesses and then tailoring their stories specifically to negate the claims made by opponents. Under the second circumstance, excluding the witness may make their independent corroboration more persuasive.

RULE 615. Excluding Witnesses

<u>At a party's request</u>, the court <u>must</u> order witnesses excluded so that they cannot hear other witnesses' testimony. Or the court may do so <u>on its own</u>. But this rule does not authorize excluding:

(a) a <u>party</u> who is a natural person;

(b) an officer or employee of a party that is not a natural person, after being designated as the party's representative by its attorney;

(c) a person whose presence a party shows to be essential to presenting the party's claim or defense; or

(d) a person authorized by statute to be present.

This rule has three important provisions. **First,** the rule can be invoked by either party or by the judge herself. **Second**, the rule gives the judge no discretion: Once either party makes a request to exclude witnesses, the judge must exclude them from the courtroom. In the real world, witnesses are almost always excluded from the courtroom as a matter of course; there is no need to make any kind of formal request.

Third, the rule makes exceptions for several categories of witnesses who cannot be barred from the courtroom. Two categories are especially important:

- Parties to the case are allowed to watch the entire trial, even though they may be (and usually are) called as witnesses. If the party is an organization, then an officer or employee represents the organization in the courtroom. Criminal defendants have a constitutional right to confront the witnesses against them, and basic principles of fairness suggest that civil parties should be able to attend their trials as well.

- A witness "whose presence a party shows to be essential to presenting the party's claim or defense" can watch the trial. This provision refers primarily to expert witnesses, who sometimes observe the testimony of other witnesses in order to gather data to support their expert opinion.

Quick Summary

Attorneys examine witnesses in "turns" known as direct examination, cross-examination, redirect examination, and recross-examination. Under **Rule 611**, the trial judge exercises discretion to control these examination phases, assuring that the attorneys offer the jury helpful information without wasting time or harassing witnesses. Rule 611 discourages leading questions on direct examination, but allows them on cross-examination. The rule also restricts the scope of cross-examination to matters covered during the direct exam and matters affecting the witness's credibility. Similarly, any redirect or recross-examinations should focus only on matters raised during the preceding examination.

Rule 614 allows judges to question witnesses called by other parties as well as to call their own witnesses. Judges frequently exercise the former power, but rarely engage in the latter. **Rule 615** allows the judge to exclude witnesses from the courtroom during the testimony of other witnesses, either sua sponte or in response to a party's motion. But parties, as well as witnesses acquiring the foundation for their testimony, cannot be excluded from the courtroom under this rule.

Test Your Understanding

To assess your understanding of the material in this chapter, click here to take a quiz, or go to the Quizzes module from the eBook on your eProducts bookshelf.

Common Rule 611 Objections

Objection	Examples
Argumentative: The attorney is drawing inferences or making conclusions that should be reserved for closing argument. These questions may also constitute harassing the witness, but not necessarily.	Q: Isn't it difficult to believe that you could see the defendant clearly when there were no streetlights on the entire block? Q: Don't you think it's incredibly improbable that the eyewitness would have 'mistakenly' picked you out of a line-up and then it turns out that your fingerprints were found at the scene? **BUT** the attorney may challenge the witness: Q: Could you really see the defendant clearly given the fact that there were no streetlights on the entire block? Q: Since you claim that the identification was improper, can you explain why your fingerprints were found at the scene?
Asked and Answered: The attorney has already asked the question and the witness has already answered.	Q: And what did Mr. Biswell do next? A: He approached me with a knife in his right hand. Q: Could it have been a cell phone in his hand? A: No, I'm sure it was a knife. Q: But it's possible that it could have been a cell phone?

Objection	Examples
Assumes a Fact Not in Evidence: These questions include a factual assertion that is imbedded into the question.	Q: When did you stop beating your wife? Q: As you sped through the red light at a high rate of speed, did you see the plaintiff's car before you hit it? **BUT** if the witness has already testified to the facts imbedded in the question, the question is proper.
Beyond the Scope: Cross-examination topic is beyond the scope of direct, **OR** redirect is beyond the scope of cross.	
Calls for Narrative: The question is too broad; the witness will tell a story instead of answering a specific question.	Q: What happened to you on January 24th? Q: Tell me about the car accident. **BUT** the judge has discretion to allow broad questions like these. Very broad questions sometimes are useful, especially near the beginning of direct testimony: Q: Describe the collision for me. Q: What happened next?

Objection	Examples
Calls for Speculation: The question asks the witness what other people may have been thinking or what might have been happening beyond the realm of the witness's perception. This objection is based on both Rule 602 (which requires the witness to have personal knowledge) and Rule 611 (because the form of the question calls for speculation). These questions can sometimes be rephrased so that it is clear that they are asking for information that the witness personally perceived.	Q: And when Ms. Jones was signing the contract, what was she thinking? Q: Why did Steve hit you at that point? Q: After Terri left the building, where did she go? (Objectionable if the witness has no personal knowledge as to where Terri went). **BUT** if the questions are re-phrased, they do not call for speculation: Q: Did Ms. Jones tell you what she was thinking when she signed the contract? Q: Had you done anything at all that you think might have given Steve a reason to hit you? Q: After Terri left the building, did you see her out the window? A: Yes Q: Where did she go?
Compound Question: The question tries to elicit more than one fact at a time.	Q: When you saw the police, did you run away and drop the drugs?

Objection	Examples
Harassing/Badgering the Witness: The lawyer is asking the same question repeatedly in different ways, insulting the witness for no purpose, or arguing with the witness about his answer.	Q: It looks like you can't be trusted to ever tell the truth, can you Mr. Jones? Q: You expect us to believe that you never read contracts before you sign them?
Improper Characterization of Testimony/Misstates the Testimony: The attorney is pretending to repeat testimony back to the witness as the basis for the next question, but is altering the testimony. The attorney may use a more powerful word or change the facts themselves. This affects the witness's testimony and can also make it difficult for the jury to remember the original testimony. The misstatement may occur immediately or much later in the trial, when it will be harder for the judge and opposing counsel to detect.	W: I sometimes go for walks late at night when I'm bored. Q: And when you go out casing the neighborhood late at night, where do you usually go? W: Then my car struck Mr. Smith's car. Q: And after you smashed into Mr. Smith's car, did you get out of your car? W: I ran for about fifteen minutes and then finally hid behind the dumpster. Q: So after you ran for nearly half an hour, you finally decided it was better to hide?

Objection	Examples
Leading Question: The attorney is asking a question that suggests a specific answer.	Q: Did he hit you in the face next? **BUT** the attorney usually may suggest multiple answers, as long as she doesn't suggest which one the witness should choose: Q: Where did he hit you next, the face or the body?
Non-Responsive Answer: This usually occurs on cross-examination. The attorney who asked the question can object to the witness's answer as non-responsive, ask the judge to strike that answer, and force the witness to answer the question posed.	Q: You had four beers at the bar before you got behind the wheel that night, isn't that right? W: The guy driving the other car looked a lot more drunk than I was. He could barely stand up.
Vague: The question does not give enough detail to allow the witness to respond properly OR a term in the question has an unclear meaning.	Q: How many cars did you sell from your lot? (Without a specific timeframe, witness can't give a meaningful response.) Q: You were far away from the bank when the robbers ran out into the street, correct? (There is no clear definition of "far away.")

16

Refreshing a Witness's Memory

Key Concepts

- Process of Refreshing Recollection
- Testifying from Refreshed Memory, Not Reciting Content of Document
- **Rule 612:** Rights for Adverse Parties During Refreshment
- Limited Use of Documents Admitted Under Rule 612
- Writings Include Photographs, Videotapes, and Other Media

A. Introduction and Policy. Trials occur months or years after the event giving rise to a criminal charge or civil claim. During that time, memories fade. Even if a lawyer prepares a witness to testify shortly before trial, the witness may not be able to recall key details in court. And sometimes a witness is called upon to testify about complicated data, such as a series of license plate numbers or a long list of items that were stolen or damaged. Even a witness with a strong memory may not remember all of this information on the stand.

As we noted in the last chapter, a lawyer can jog a witness's memory by using leading questions. If a witness recalls the general outlines of an incident but is having trouble reciting details, the judge may allow the lawyer to "lead" the witness even on direct examination. Here is an example of a lawyer using leading questions to help a witness remember property damage that she witnessed when one car backed into another:

> **Q:** Did you notice any damage to the plaintiff's car?
>
> **A:** It's hard for me to remember. It was a long time ago.
>
> **Q:** Take your time and think. Was there any damage to the headlights?
>
> **A:** I think so. Yes, I remember seeing a lot of glass on the ground and I noticed that both headlights were smashed.
>
> **Q:** And what about the front of the car? Was it damaged also?
>
> **A:** Yeah, the front of the car was pretty smashed up. The bumper, the hood, things like that.

Leading questions expanded the witness's recollection significantly in this example. But they diminish the persuasive impact of the witness's testimony because the jury hears the attorney suggesting answers to the witness. And suppose that the witness still has not volunteered an item of damage that is important to the plaintiff's case. The plaintiff's car, for example, might have had an expensive custom hood ornament that was destroyed in the accident. How can the lawyer prod the witness to remember that particular item?

The lawyer might ask a series of increasingly specific questions ("Did you notice anything special about the hood? Was there anything on the hood? Was there an ornament on the hood that might have been damaged?") Questions like these, however, will make the witness seem even less credible. An extended game of twenty questions is unlikely to impress the jury.

Rule 612 gives the attorney another option: She can refresh the witness's recollection with a document or other item. The document could be something that the witness herself wrote—such as notes that she took or a form that she filled out—but it need not be. **Any** document can be used, as long as the witness states that it will help her remember the necessary information.

In the example discussed above, the witness might have provided a report to the plaintiff's insurance agent shortly after the accident. If that report detailed all of the damage that the witness saw, the plaintiff's lawyer could use that report to refresh the witness's recollection. Or if the witness herself did not write down any information, the attorney might have a report filled out by a police officer, or an insurance agent, or perhaps a picture of the car itself. Any of these documents, if shown to the witness, would help her remember what was damaged.

If the lawyer uses a report filled out by the witness, the testimony recounted above might continue:

Q: Did you notice anything special about the bumper or hood?

A: I just don't remember. I'm not that good when it comes to cars.

Q: Would seeing the insurance report that you filled out help you to remember what happened to the car?

A: Yes it would.

Q: Your honor, may I approach the witness?

Court: You may.

Q: I'd like to show you this report and ask you to look at it for a minute. I'd also like the record to reflect that I have shown this document to opposing counsel and have given that counsel a photocopy. [Hands paper to witness]

Have you had a chance to look at that paper?

A: Yes, I have. [Hands paper back to the questioner]

Q: Has looking at the report helped you to remember any other damage to the car?

A: Yes. There was a special ornament on the hood. It looked like an animal of some kind. But it had been completely smashed by the accident.

If the witness made no written record of her own (or if the attorney has no copy of a written record that the witness made), the attorney could use a writing made by someone else. But whatever kind of writing is used, the witness must first state that (1) she does not remember the answer to the question being asked; and (2) seeing the writing will "refresh her recollection." These two statements lay the foundation for the writing being used to refresh recollection.

After the witness reviews the writing, the examining attorney will ask whether the writing has refreshed her recollection. This question is meant to ensure that the witness testifies only about what she remembers—not about things she read but can no longer recall.

Rule 612, which we'll examine in this chapter, acknowledges that judges often allow witnesses to refresh their recollection in this way. The rule establishes several procedural guidelines for this process.

B. The Rule. Using a writing to refresh a witness's recollection is an efficient and persuasive way to improve live testimony. Rule 612 facilitates this process by allowing the opposing party to use the writing in various ways; this ensures that the attorney who is refreshing recollection does not abuse the process.

Rule 612 distinguishes between a witness who refreshes recollection while testifying and one who refreshes memory before taking the stand:

> ## RULE 612. Writing Used to Refresh a Witness's Memory
>
> **(a) Scope.** This rule gives an adverse party certain options when a witness uses a writing to refresh memory:
>
> **(1)** <u>while testifying</u>; or
>
> **(2)** <u>before testifying</u>, if the court decides that justice requires the party to have those options.

The provisions in Rule 612 apply primarily to the first situation, when a witness refreshes recollection while testifying. Although subsection (2) gives the judge discretion to apply the rule to pre-testimony preparation, judges rarely do so. We'll explore this issue further in the Courtroom section.

The core language of **Rule 612** gives adverse parties the right to (1) inspect any writing the witness uses to refresh recollection, (2) cross-examine the witness on the writing, and (3) introduce the relevant portions of the writing into evidence:

RULE 612. Writing Used to Refresh a Witness's Memory

(b) Adverse Party's Options; Deleting Unrelated Matter. . . . an adverse party is entitled

- to have the writing produced at the hearing,
- to <u>inspect</u> it,
- to <u>cross-examine</u> the witness about it, and
- to <u>introduce in evidence</u> any portion that relates to the witness's testimony. . . .

Attorneys, in other words, may refresh a witness's recollection but only at a price: The opposing party will be able to see the writing used for refreshment, cross-examine the witness about the writing, and introduce portions of the writing into evidence.

Note that the adverse party may introduce a writing used for refreshment into evidence even if the writing **would not otherwise be admissible**. Rule 612, in other words, trumps other rules of evidence when an adverse party invokes it; the rule gives the adverse party the right to introduce the writing for the limited purpose of assessing the witness's credibility.

The "refreshing" party may also introduce the writing into evidence, but only if the writing is already admissible under the rules; Rule 612 does not offer any help. Often the writing is not admissible by the refreshing party because, as we'll see starting in Chapter 35, most documents are hearsay. To admit the writing, therefore, the refreshing party would have to identify an exception to the hearsay rules.

Let's apply these rules to the car damage example discussed above. In that case, the plaintiff's lawyer refreshed the witness's recollection by showing her a report she made to an insurance adjuster. As the transcript notes, the lawyer gave a copy of the writing to opposing counsel. On cross-examination, opposing counsel could question the witness further about both the report and her current recollection of the accident. Information in the report might undermine the witness's testimony by suggesting some uncertainty in her recollection. If it does, the defendant's cross-examination can expose that uncertainty to the jury.

The defendant might also choose to introduce those portions of the report into evidence so that the jury will see them. As an adverse party, the defendant has a right to introduce relevant portions of the report for the purpose of assessing the witness's credibility, even if the report would not be admissible for other purposes. If the plaintiff wants to offer the report as evidence, he would have to comply with other evidentiary rules.

* * *

The remainder of Rule 612 addresses **three procedural issues** that may arise when writings are used to refresh recollection. Apart from noting them, we won't focus on these aspects of the rule. They are covered more completely in courses on Trial Advocacy or Criminal Procedure.

First, the rule outlines procedures for determining which portions of a writing to admit when only part of the document relates to a witness's testimony:

RULE 612. Writing Used to Refresh a Witness's Memory

(b) Adverse Party's Options; Deleting Unrelated Matter. . . . If the producing party claims that the writing includes unrelated matter, the court must examine the writing in camera, delete any unrelated portion, and order that the rest be delivered to the adverse party. Any portion deleted over objection must be preserved for the record.

Second, the rule discusses remedies if a party refuses to produce a writing used to refresh recollection:

RULE 612. Writing Used to Refresh a Witness's Memory

(c) Failure to Produce or Deliver the Writing. If a writing is not produced or is not delivered as ordered, the court may issue any appropriate order. But if the prosecution does not comply in a criminal case, the court must strike the witness's testimony or—if justice so requires—declare a mistrial.

Finally, the rule makes clear in its opening phrase that it is subject to the Jencks Act, which governs discovery in federal criminal trials:

Rule 612. Writing Used to Refresh a Witness's Memory

(b) Adverse Party's Options; Deleting Unrelated Matter. Unless 18 U.S.C. § 3500 provides otherwise in a criminal case . . . .

C. In the Courtroom.

1. Method of Refreshing Recollection. In order to use a writing to refresh a witness's recollection, the attorney should follow five steps:

(A) Establish that the witness does not recall the answer to a question.

> **Q:** What else was stolen from your store?
>
> **A:** I don't remember.

(B) Describe the writing she wishes to use to refresh the witness's recollection and ask if that writing would refresh the witness's recollection.

> **Q:** I have here a copy of the police report that you filed the day after the burglary. Would seeing this help refresh your recollection as to what else was stolen?
>
> **A:** Yes, I think it would.

(C) Show the writing to the witness. The witness will examine the writing and put it aside (usually giving it back to the attorney).

(D) Ask whether the writing has refreshed the witness's recollection or helped her to remember. The witness should answer yes, and then she can answer the original question from her refreshed recollection.

(E) Either before or during this process, the attorney must be sure to give the opposing counsel a copy of the writing.

2. Testifying from Original Memory. Rule 612 rests in part on a legal fiction. The rule assumes that a witness will jog her memory by looking at a writing, and then testify from the "refreshed" memory rather than from what the writing itself said. This is why the witness puts the writing aside or hands it back to the lawyer before continuing to testify.

Often, however, it is obvious that the witness is not really testifying from a refreshed memory; instead, she is parroting information quickly memorized from the writing. A witness who sees the license plate of a robber's car, for example, may memorize the eight digits and quickly write them down on a scrap of paper. When the witness testifies at trial six months later, she may have no memory of the license plate number—not even one she can jog. When the prosecutor refreshes the witness's recollection by showing her the scrap of paper, the witness may "remember" the numbers and relate them. But she probably is just reciting the numbers she saw on the scrap of paper.

In this type of situation, opposing counsel can ask to "voir dire" (examine) the witness on her recollection. By posing a series of questions to the witness, opposing counsel will try to show the judge that the witness does not independently recall the events recorded in the writing. If the opponent persuades the judge that this is the case, the judge will not allow the witness to testify further on the matter; a witness with no independent recollection lacks the personal knowledge required by **Rule 602** to testify.

This type of voir dire is unusual, however, because distinguishing refreshed recollection from new memorization is difficult. If the witness refreshes memory from a credible source, and the refreshed portions of testimony are brief, the opposing counsel usually does not challenge the witness. Here is a case in which a judge used voir dire to measure the extent of a witness's recollection on a more complex series of events:

> **Example:** Margaret Lindsey sued the M&M Restaurant Supply Company for employment discrimination. During the five years she worked at M&M, Lindsey made notes about crude comments and other sexist behavior directed toward her. She later transcribed these notes into a "book" of incidents that she relied upon in her lawsuit. In a pretrial motion, M&M attempted to block Lindsey from relying upon her book to refresh her recollection while testifying at trial.

Analysis: The judge rejected M&M's motion, finding that Lindsey could refer to the book to assist her recollection of the many events that had occurred during her employment. He noted, however, that he would voir dire Lindsey before her testimony to distinguish memories that she could recount after refreshment from events that she no longer recalled. Lindsey could testify to the former, but she could not "in effect, read[] excerpts from her notebook into the record" to introduce evidence of the latter.[1]

Why does memory matter so much? Why do we care whether a witness testifies from a refreshed memory or recites information that she recorded earlier but no longer recalls? In the latter situation, the witness is not really testifying; the document is "testifying" through her. As we'll see starting in Chapter 35, the hearsay rules limit the ability of parties to introduce documents into evidence. Judges often admit documents under exceptions to the hearsay rules, but parties shouldn't be able to circumvent those carefully tailored exceptions by having a witness pretend to refresh recollection and then recite information contained in a document.

3. What Type of Writing? Rule 612 does not limit the type of writing a witness may use to refresh recollection. The writing may be a handwritten note on a napkin or a deposition transcript. The writing does not even have to be one that the witness prepared; an attorney could refresh a witness's recollection with a newspaper article or a record written by a third person.

Indeed, the writing does not have to be a "writing" at all. Trial judges have allowed attorneys to refresh the memory of witnesses with audiotapes, photographs, and other media.[2] The irrepressible Judge Learned Hand once declared that "[a]nything may in fact revive a memory: a song, a scent, a photograph, an allusion . . . ."[3] The definition of "written material" in **Rule 101(b)(6)**, finally, makes clear that attorneys may use "electronically stored information" to refresh recollection.

But there are two practical limits on an attorney's creativity when choosing ways to refresh a witness's recollection: (1) the jury's perception, and (2) opposing counsel's Rule 612 rights. In theory, an attorney could refresh a witness's recollection with a newspaper article or a police report filled out by a third party, but neither

---

1   Lindsey v. M&M Restaurant Supply, 170 F. Supp. 2d 788, 791 (N.D. Ohio 2001).

2   See, e.g., 20th Century Wear, Inc. v. Sanmark-Stardust Inc., 747 F.2d 81, 93 n.17 (2d Cir. 1984) (audiotape); Fernandez v. Leonard, 963 F.2d 459, 466 (1st Cir. 1992) (photographs).

3   United States v. Rappy, 157 F.2d 964, 967 (2d Cir. 1946).

technique will impress the jury. Instead, it will appear as though the attorney is feeding answers to the witness. It will also signal to the jury that the witness's own perception was unreliable. On the other hand, refreshing a witness's recollection with her own handwritten notes or with an insurance report she filled out herself is unlikely to damage her credibility in the eyes of the jury.

Judges, moreover, have construed Rule 612's reference to "a writing" to encompass any object that counsel uses to refresh recollection. If an examining attorney refreshes recollection with a photograph, or an object, or a statement written by a third party, then the adverse party has the right to examine that item, cross-examine the witness about it, and introduce the item into evidence. These guarantees, like the jury's perception, constrain counsel's choice of objects used to refresh recollection. Most often, the "writings" used under Rule 612 are documents that genuinely help the witness and buttress her credibility.

4. Refreshing Memory Before Testifying. At common law, adverse parties could examine only documents that a witness used to refresh recollection while testifying. Rule 612 liberalized this rule by granting parties access to documents that a witness reviews for refreshment before taking the stand if "justice requires" that access. Courts, however, tend to limit an adverse party's right to see documents that a witness reviews before testifying. It is common practice for witnesses to review all of their own documents and notes on a case prior to testifying, and if judges were to grant the opposing counsel extensive rights to review this information, they would legitimize endless fishing expeditions through the opposing counsel's files.

> **Example:** The government charged John Sheffield and Dennis Crowder with conspiring to defraud an insurance company by falsely claiming that Sheffield's car had been stolen. Clay Thomas, the detective who investigated the case, testified extensively for the prosecution. Thomas noted that he had reviewed his case file before coming to testify, and the defendants requested access to the file under Rule 612.

> **Analysis:** The district judge denied this request and the court of appeals upheld the lower court ruling as "well within its discretion." Rule 612, the appellate court continued, "is not a vehicle for a plenary search for contradictory or rebutting evidence that may be in a file."[4]

---

4   United States v. Sheffield, 55 F.3d 341, 343 (8th Cir. 1995). The facts in the example simplify those from the case slightly.

5. Adverse Parties. The phrase "adverse party" in Rule 612 allows any party who did not initiate the refreshment of a witness's recollection to claim the rule's protection. If a party refreshes a witness's recollection on direct examination, then other parties may invoke Rule 612 for cross-examination. Conversely, if a lawyer refreshes a witness's recollection during cross-examination, then the party that called the witness may invoke Rule 612 to examine the materials used by the cross-examiner.

> **Example:** Annette Rush sued the Illinois Central Railroad on behalf of her nine-year-old son Johnathan, who injured himself while playing with several friends in the Railroad's train yard. Rush called one of the other boys, Doyle Lockett, who testified about how the injury occurred. On cross-examination, the Railroad's attorney asked Lockett if he remembered making a statement to the police after the accident. When Lockett could not recall his statement, the cross-examiner showed him a transcript to refresh his recollection. Rush then requested under Rule 612 to see the transcript.

> **Analysis:** Rush was entitled to view the document used to refresh Lockett's recollection. Although Rush initially called Lockett as a witness, the Railroad initiated the refreshment of Lockett's recollection. Rush, therefore, was the "adverse party" for purposes of invoking Rule 612.[5]

6. Effect of Introducing the Writing. If the adverse party chooses to admit the writing into evidence, courts have held that—unless the writing is admissible on other grounds—the jury may use the writing only to assess the witness's credibility.[6] The jury, in other words, cannot use the document to establish substantive matters referred to in the document. This principle prevents parties from evading other Rules of Evidence, such as the restrictions on use of written hearsay, by introducing documents under Rule 612 that would not otherwise be admissible.

When a party introduces a document under Rule 612 and the document is not independently admissible under other rules, the judge will give the jury a limiting instruction explaining how to use the document. In the hood ornament example described in the Introduction, the judge's instruction might sound like this if the

---

5   This example draws from Rush v. Illinois Central R.R. Co., 399 F.3d 705, 710–11 (6th Cir. 2005), although that case raised additional issues under Rule 612.

6   See, e.g., United States v. Hugh, No. 05–4260, 2007 WL 1705629 (3d Cir. July 18, 2007); United States v. Harris, 908 F.2d 728, 738 (11th Cir. 1990).

defendant introduced into evidence the witness's report to the insurance agent, but the report was not independently admissible:

> At defendant's request, I admitted into evidence a report to an insurance agent that the plaintiff used to refresh Ms. Johnson's recollection. You may use that document only to assess Ms. Johnson's credibility. The report itself is not evidence of any of the matters written in it. For evidence of those matters, you must rely only on Ms. Johnson's oral testimony and other evidence presented in this case.

If the document used to refresh recollection is otherwise admissible, then an instruction like this is not necessary; the jury may use the document for any permitted purpose.

Quick Summary

 Trial judges often allow parties to refresh a witness's recollection by showing the witness a document or other reminder. Once memory has been refreshed, the witness must testify from memory rather than reading aloud from the document. **Rule 612** allows parties who did not initiate the refreshment to inspect any document used in this manner, to cross-examine the witness about the document, and to introduce into evidence portions of the document related to the testimony. Documents introduced under Rule 612, however, may only be used to assess a witness's credibility; the jury may not use them as independent evidence of matters asserted in the documents unless the documents are also admissible under other rules. If a document admitted under Rule 612 is not otherwise admissible, the judge will give the jurors a limiting instruction directing them to use the document only to assess credibility.

Test Your Understanding

 To assess your understanding of the material in this chapter, click here to take a quiz, or go to the Quizzes module from the eBook on your eProducts bookshelf.

17

Impeaching Witnesses

Key Concepts

- Toolbox of Ten Tactics
- **Rule 607:** Any Party May Impeach
- Drawing the Sting

A. Introduction. Discrediting or "impeaching" witnesses is an essential part of many trials. Most trials center on the testimony offered by live witnesses; documents and real evidence often assume meaning only in the context of a witness's testimony. To prevail in court, it usually is not enough for a litigant to present a convincing case of his own to the jury. The litigant often must discredit at least some of the opponent's witnesses to win. Here is a colorful example of a successful impeachment:

> **Q:** Is it true that your laboratory for which you work is jokingly known as "Malfunction Junction"?
>
> **A:** It is?
>
> **Q:** I am asking you.
>
> **A:** I have not heard it. They have more sense than to say it to my face.
>
> **Q:** Was there not a sign on your door that said for a long time "Malfunction Junction"?
>
> **A:** How do you know these things?
>
> **Q:** Here's a picture of your front door, right?
>
> **A:** I'll be damned. Okay. That's been gone for at least a year.
>
> **Q:** When you said earlier that it wasn't known as that—

A: I forgot.

Q: That wasn't true?

A: I forgot. What is truth? It was taken off the door. Could I see that door? I don't even think it is in the present laboratory.

Q: It was taken off the door right after I took this picture.

A: Oh, is that when it was taken off?

Q: Yes. The flash woke somebody up in there.

A: Well, somebody has a strange sense of humor. It says: "Nothing works here." That's nasty.[1]

This is the kind of cross-examination that lawyers dream about. Not only does the cross-examining attorney bring out evidence that the witness's laboratory is known for shoddy work, but—equally important—he demonstrates to the jury that the witness was lying to them on the stand.

 The Federal Rules of Evidence regulate the impeachment methods that are available to attorneys. **Rule 608** discusses how to attack a witness's character for credibility; **Rule 609** describes when a witness's prior criminal convictions are admissible to impeach her; and **Rule 610** forbids an attorney from impeaching a witness because of her religious beliefs or opinions. We discuss each of those rules in future chapters. To place those rules in context, we pause in this chapter to catalogue the different ways in which litigants can impeach a witness. We'll also look at **Rule 607**, which allows parties to impeach any witness, including one of their own.

B. A Toolbox of Ten Tactics. A trial lawyer who confronts damaging testimony from an opponent's witness can draw upon ten different tactics to combat that evidence. Let's explore those ten tools in the context of a simple hypothetical: Imagine a routine personal injury case in which an injured bicyclist (Brandon) claims that a motorist (Molly) ran a red light and hit him. Defendant Molly's key witness is Eli, who testifies that he was standing at the intersection when the

---

1   Charles M. Sevilla, Disorder in the Court 91–92 (1992).

accident occurred and he noticed that the traffic light facing Molly was green at the time she entered the intersection. If the jury believes Eli, then defendant Molly had the right of way, she did not act negligently, and Brandon's case fails.

Brandon therefore needs to attack Eli's testimony in order to prevail in the case. What are the different ways that Brandon can respond to Eli's potentially devastating testimony? Here are the ten techniques that his lawyer may use:

1. Exclude the Evidence Through a Specialized Rule. Brandon may attempt to exclude Eli's testimony, invoking any of the dozens of Rules of Evidence. Potential grounds for exclusion include those we have already learned (relevance, competence, personal knowledge, medical expenses, insurance, subsequent remedial measures) as well as the many we will study soon (hearsay, bad acts, unsupported opinion). Unfortunately, none of these objections are likely to exclude Eli's testimony. He is a classic eyewitness, testifying to a simple fact that he observed.

2. Claim Unfair Prejudice, Confusion, or Delay. Rule 403 gives the trial judge discretion to exclude evidence based on prejudice, confusion, delay, or related grounds. After considering objections under the other, more specific Rules of Evidence, trial lawyers always evaluate the possibility of a Rule 403 objection. Unfortunately, that rule is not likely to exclude Eli's rather straightforward testimony.

3. Complete the Story. Sometimes additional information reduces or eliminates the negative effect of testimony. Eli, for example, may be correct that the light facing Molly was green. But Eli may have observed some additional facts that could help Brandon's case. Perhaps he observed how badly the accident injured Brandon, and could describe the extent of his injury for the jury. Or maybe he saw that Molly was looking at her passenger in the backseat as she drove through the intersection; this might show that Molly was negligent in failing to keep a proper lookout, despite having the green light. Sometimes counsel can use cross-examination to elicit positive information from a witness, completing the story in a way that helps her client. Other times, counsel may introduce the positive information through a direct or rebuttal witness of her own.

4. Clarify the Ambiguous Testimony. Cross-examination is particularly useful to clarify the words used by a witness on direct examination; attorneys often overlook this opportunity. If Eli testified on direct that he saw Brandon biking "really fast" through the intersection, Brandon's attorney might ask Eli what he means by "really fast." Is that faster than a person can walk? Faster than a person can run? As fast as cars drive? Jurors may differ in the way they interpret Eli's words; cross-examination could resolve the ambiguity in a way that helps Brandon.

Similarly, if Eli testified on direct that Molly was driving "very cautiously," Brandon's attorney might challenge Eli's use of that phrase. What did he mean by "very cautiously"? Can Eli offer any specific observations to support this assertion? If he can't, then the cross-examination will expose Eli's damaging statement about Molly's caution as a baseless opinion with little probative value.

In civil cases, parties depose most witnesses extensively before trial. That information helps an attorney decide when to clarify a witness's testimony and when to leave it alone. If Eli did notice specific facts demonstrating Molly's caution, or if he saw Brandon tearing through the intersection with his head down, Brandon's attorney won't try to clarify those statements on cross-examination.

5. Show Impairment of Perception or Recollection. A lawyer may try to show that an opponent's witness perceived an event incorrectly or recalls it inaccurately. Eli, for example, might have been standing far away from the intersection, he might have been looking at a newspaper rather than the light, or he might have just emerged from a local bar after having consumed several beers. Similarly, if Eli left the scene shortly after the accident and offered his first recollection months later, he may not correctly recall the color of the light. Brandon's lawyer can try to reveal factors like these through cross-examination. She might also offer independent proof of a factor that would have impaired Eli's perception or recollection.

Brandon's lawyer could even attempt to show more pervasive forms of impairment, such as those stemming from drug use or a disability. Some of these points raise questions of unfair prejudice under Rule 403 or problems under other rules, but they are still potential tools for impeachment.

6. Demonstrate Inconsistencies. Opposing counsel may try to undermine a witness's testimony by showing that the testimony is internally inconsistent or contradicts earlier statements made by the witness. Cross-examination is one way to reveal these inconsistencies. When pressed, for example, Eli may give a series of conflicting answers that undermine his claim that the light was green. Brandon's attorney, however, will pursue this route only if she has some reason to suspect inconsistency or confusion; eliciting Eli's vehement confirmation that the light was green will not help Brandon.

Brandon's lawyer may also try to introduce evidence that Eli made earlier, contrary statements about the light. If Eli initially told a police officer that the light facing Molly was red, that is strong evidence that Eli is confused or lying. The earlier statement also directly supports Brandon's claim. We will study several rules that govern when a party can introduce prior inconsistent statements and how they can be used.

7. Rebut the Evidence. A party may introduce evidence that contradicts a witness's testimony. Brandon, for example, may present another eyewitness (Winnie) who testifies that the light facing Molly was red. In these circumstances, the jury will have to decide which witness it believes. Each party, of course, will attempt to persuade the jury to believe its witness by employing other techniques from the toolbox to discredit the opposing witness.

8. Show Bias. Juries understand that bias—either for or against a party—may taint testimony. Brandon's lawyer, therefore, may attempt to reveal ways in which Eli is biased against Brandon or in favor of Molly. Is he Molly's friend? Do they work for the same company? Does Eli work for Molly's insurance company? Did Brandon get a job that Eli wanted? Does Eli have any other grudge against Brandon?

Revealing a witness's bias is so important that courts will admit otherwise prejudicial information to show the extent of that bias. When an expert witness testifies, for example, the judge will allow the opposing party to elicit not just the fact that the expert is being paid but how much she is being paid. Or consider this case:

> **Example:** John Abel was on trial for robbery. He called Robert Mills as a witness, and Mills testified that a key prosecution witness was lying. In response, the prosecution wanted to introduce evidence that Mills and Abel both belonged to the Aryan Brotherhood, a prison gang that required its members to lie on each other's behalf. The trial judge ruled that admitting the name of the organization was unfairly prejudicial, but he allowed the prosecutor to elicit testimony that Mills and Abel belonged to a "secret type of prison organization" that required members to "deny its existence and lie for each other." The defense objected to this testimony, claiming that it was unfairly prejudicial under Rule 403.

> **Analysis:** The Supreme Court upheld admission of the evidence, noting that bias is a powerful impeachment tool. The Court specifically approved the

testimony describing the gang's tenets, noting: "If the prosecutor had elicited that both [defendant Abel] and Mills belonged the Book of the Month club, the jury probably would not have inferred bias . . . . The attributes of the Aryan Brotherhood—a secret prison sect sworn to perjury and self-protection—bore directly not only on the fact of bias but also on the source and strength of Mills' bias."[2]

Several evidentiary rules make special exceptions to accommodate proof of bias. **Rule 411**, for example, specifically allows parties to introduce evidence of liability insurance when the insurance is relevant to establish a witness's bias. Other rules, like **Rule 407** (subsequent remedial measures) and **Rule 409** (medical expenses), do not include express exceptions for bias but implicitly allow proof of otherwise inadmissible evidence when offered to show a witness's bias. Later chapters will explore still more rules affecting proof of bias.

9. Attack the Witness's Character for Truthfulness. Trial attorneys sometimes try to discredit a witness by showing that the witness is a generally untruthful person. If the witness has lied in other situations, the jury may conclude that the witness is lying on the stand. Witnesses rarely admit that they are habitual liars, so lawyers attempt to prove a witness's untruthful character in other ways. Brandon's lawyer, for example, might ask Eli about lies he has told in the past. Or she might demonstrate that Eli has a reputation for dishonesty. If Eli has been convicted of any crimes, Brandon's lawyer might try to introduce evidence of those convictions to show that Eli has a dishonest character. The Rules of Evidence limit the ways in which parties can prove a witness's general character for truthfulness; we will study those rules in an upcoming chapter.

10. Introduce Expert Testimony About Evidence. Expert testimony can aid several of the techniques listed above. An expert in accident reconstruction, for example, might testify that Eli could not have seen the color of the light facing Molly from where he was standing. Increasingly, however, parties also call experts to testify about the limits of evidence itself. Psychologists, for example, have shown that eyewitness testimony is much less reliable than most people believe.[3] Brandon might try to call one of these experts to explain that, although Eli was looking right at the traffic light and is a truthful person honestly reporting what he thinks

2   United States v. Abel, 469 U.S. 45, 54 (1984).

3   See the sources cited in footnote 2 of Chapter 2 for an introduction to the extensive studies on eyewitnesses.

he saw, his recollection may still be wrong. Courts understandably approach this type of testimony with great caution, but we will consider its admissibility when we study the rules governing expert testimony.

* * *

Summary. We can group these ten tactics into three sets, making them easier to remember. The groups suggest the competitive nature of a trial, separating the tactics into offensive, defensive, and refereeing categories. First, there are four **offensive** techniques a party may employ, offering new evidence that combats a witness's damaging testimony:

1. **Rebut** the Evidence.

2. **Complete** the Story.

3. **Clarify** the Ambiguous Testimony.

4. Introduce **Expert Testimony**.

Next, counsel can draw upon four **defensive** techniques. These are tactics that attack the "messenger" or witness:

5. Show **Impairment of Perception or Recollection.**

6. Demonstrate **Inconsistencies.**

7. Show **Bias.**

8. Attack the Witness's **Character for Truthfulness**.

Finally, there are two tactics with which a party appeals to the **"referee" or judge** to exclude the witness's testimony:

9. **Exclude** the Evidence Under a **Specific Rule.**

10. **Exclude** the Evidence by Demonstrating **Unfair Prejudice, Confusion, or Delay.**

As we study the Rules of Evidence, think about how they relate to these strategies.

C. Counter Moves. As one lawyer seeks to discredit another's witness, the other will use strategies to rehabilitate the witness. In the above example, as Brandon attempts to undermine Eli's testimony, Molly will work to bolster that evidence. All of the tools discussed above are available to Molly as well as Brandon. Molly may offer another witness's testimony to substantiate Eli's story, introduce evidence of his truthful character, or show that his statements have been consistent over time. At the same time, she will use the ten tactics to discredit Brandon's witnesses. This series of moves and countermoves gives trials their complex texture.

We will see that the Federal Rules of Evidence limit the availability of these countermoves to some extent. A party, for example, may not introduce evidence of a witness's truthful character until that character has been challenged. Trial judges will also cut off prolonged disputes over tangential issues. Viewing trial tactics in the context of moves and countermoves will help you understand these limits when we reach them.

D. Which Witnesses? Parties usually want to impeach witnesses called by an opponent. Sometimes, however, a party's own witness offers damaging evidence. Cross-examination may uncover negative facts, or a witness may equivocate in a harmful way. Some witnesses recant prior positions, telling a different story on the stand than they did before trial. May a party impeach its own witness?

The common law prohibited parties from impeaching their own witnesses, but the Federal Rules of Evidence changed that practice. **Rule 607** allows any party to impeach any witness:

RULE 607. Who May Impeach a Witness

Any party, including the party that called the witness, may attack the witness's credibility.

Here is an example of a party impeaching its own witness:

Example: The government prosecuted Mark Carter for conspiracy to distribute cocaine. The prosecutor called Cedric Scott, a conspiracy member who had pled guilty to a lesser charge in exchange for a promise to testify truthfully against Carter. On the stand, however, Scott testified inconsistently with information he had previously given the police. He denied, for example, that Carter had ever given him any cocaine to sell.

Analysis: The court allowed the prosecutor to impeach Scott, who obviously had testified differently than the government expected. Rule 607 allows parties to impeach their own witnesses.[4]

Parties sometimes impeach even a favorable witness as a way of preempting or "drawing the sting" of negative information that an opponent most likely will raise on cross-examination. By introducing this negative information on direct examination, the lawyer attempts to gain the jury's trust and downplay the potentially harmful information. Rule 607 allows parties to impeach their witnesses in this manner:

Example: The government charged Eric Marroquin with participation in a fraudulent scheme to submit inflated insurance claims for a number of horses. Michael McKinney pled guilty to several crimes related to the same scheme; he then provided testimony against Marroquin. On direct examination, the prosecution asked McKinney about his involvement in other equine insurance frauds. The defendant Marroquin had not been involved in those frauds, but the government suspected that defense counsel would ask McKinney about them on cross-examination in order to impeach him. The prosecutor attempted to draw the sting of that anticipated impeachment by revealing the witness's flaws on direct examination.

Analysis: The district judge permitted the prosecution to impeach its witness in this manner, and the court of appeals affirmed. The appellate court observed that trial attorneys frequently anticipate cross-examination this way, hoping to gain the jury's trust and defuse the negative impact of any impeaching evidence.[5]

---

4   United States v. Carter, 973 F.2d 1509, 1512 (10th Cir. 1992).

5   United States v. Marroquin, 885 F.2d 1240, 1246–47 (5th Cir. 1989).

Quick Summary

 Trial attorneys draw upon at least ten techniques to rebut damaging testimony. These tactics include offensive, defensive, and refereeing strategies. Both plaintiffs and defendants can invoke these tactics. Rule 607, moreover, allows a party to discredit its own witness when necessary. Even when a witness testifies favorably, a trial attorney may decide to "draw the sting" of cross-examination by revealing a witness's potential bias or other flaws on direct examination.

18

Using Prior Statements to Impeach Witnesses

Key Concepts

- Powerful Impeachment Tool: Showing Inconsistency in a Witness's Statements
- Extrinsic Evidence and Collateral Matters
- **Rule 613:** Procedural Guidelines
- **Rules 403** and **611:** Prejudice, Delay, and Confusion
- Impeachment Versus Proof
- Limiting Instructions

A. Introduction and Policy. One of the most powerful impeachment techniques in a trial lawyer's toolbox is to show that a witness made inconsistent statements at different times. If an attorney can show that a witness's courtroom testimony conflicts with statements the witness made outside the courtroom, the attorney will significantly undercut the witness's testimony. Unless the witness can offer a plausible explanation for the inconsistency, the jurors are likely to conclude that the witness is confused, unreliable, or even lying.

Suppose, for example, that Wilma Flintstone testifies for the prosecution that she saw the defendant, Barney Rubble, hit his wife Betty with a golf club. If Barney's counsel proves that Wilma previously told a friend that **Fred** hit Betty with the golf club, the jury probably won't put much stock in Wilma's testimony. Some jurors may think that Wilma is lying on the stand; others may think she lied earlier to her friend. In either case, the jurors will generally find Wilma less credible based on the fact that she has changed her story.

Although prior inconsistent statements are an effective impeachment tool, they raise problems of their own. Some witnesses make many inconsistent statements. Proving that the witness made each of these statements is time-consuming and could distract the jurors from the important issues in the case. The Rules of Evidence, therefore, restrict how parties use prior inconsistent statements.

To understand these restrictions, we need to introduce two new courtroom phrases. The first is the term **extrinsic evidence**. Extrinsic evidence is any evidence **other than** testimony from the witness currently on the stand. Suppose, for example, that Barney's counsel wants to show the jury that Wilma previously blamed Fred for hitting Betty. The attorney could cross-examine Wilma by asking, "Isn't it true that you told your friend, Sharon Stone, that Fred hit Betty?" This question doesn't introduce extrinsic evidence; it merely asks Wilma for more testimony. Wilma may admit or deny the prior statement to Sharon; either way, she responds with testimony rather than evidence beyond her words.

But if Barney's lawyer introduces evidence other than Wilma's testimony, that is extrinsic evidence. If the lawyer calls Sharon Stone to the stand and asks her to recount Wilma's previous statement, that is extrinsic evidence. If the lawyer introduces an email that Wilma sent Sharon, complaining that Fred hit Betty, that is extrinsic evidence as well.

The evidentiary rules distinguish between extrinsic and non-extrinsic evidence because extrinsic evidence takes more time to present and causes more distractions. If Barney's lawyer adds a few questions to his cross-examination of Wilma, that produces little delay in the trial. But if he calls Sharon to the stand or introduces a document to impeach Wilma, those new pieces of evidence cause more disruption. The prosecutor may claim that the document is a forgery or that Sharon is a liar; each new witness or piece of evidence causes ripples in the trial. As we'll see, the evidentiary rules allow impeachment with extrinsic evidence under some circumstances, but they place more restrictions on that type of impeachment.

The second new phrase is **collateral matter.** A collateral matter is relevant to the case **solely** because it impeaches a witness. A non-collateral matter, in contrast, proves a fact in consequence other than impeachment. If a piece of evidence both proves a fact in consequence and impeaches a witness, then it is non-collateral. Some prior inconsistent statements are collateral, because they only serve to impeach a witness; others are non-collateral because they prove at least one fact in consequence.

In the Flintstone case, for example, assume that Wilma testified on the stand that she walked to the golf course and, ten minutes after arriving, she saw Barney hit Betty with the golf club. Barney's counsel knows about the prior statement mentioned above, that Wilma told her friend Sharon that she saw **Fred** hit Betty with the golf club. But counsel also has a copy of a statement Wilma gave to the police shortly after the assault. In that statement, Wilma said that she **drove** to the golf course and, ten minutes after she arrived, she saw Barney hit Betty with the golf club.

Wilma has made two inconsistent statements. The one she made to the police contradicts her trial testimony about how she got to the golf course: She told the police that she drove, while she testified on direct examination that she walked. But the jury doesn't care how Wilma got to the golf course that day—this detail does not prove any fact of consequence to the assault charges against Barney. This inconsistency is relevant only because it shows that Wilma changed her story and is less credible. Thus, it is a collateral matter.

Wilma's inconsistent statement to Sharon, however, is relevant for two reasons. It impeaches Wilma by showing that she has changed her story, **and** it tends to show that Fred, not Barney, committed the assault. The identity of Betty's attacker is a fact of consequence to the case, so this inconsistency is not collateral.

Collateral matters, like extrinsic evidence, consume time and distract the jury. The combination of extrinsic evidence and collateral matters is the most disruptive of all. Calling a police officer to the stand simply to testify that Wilma said she drove, rather than walked, to the golf course would be wasteful.

For this reason, judges use their discretion under **Rules 403** and **611** to prohibit **extrinsic** evidence of a prior inconsistent statement on a purely **collateral** matter. Evidence of this nature causes delay and confusion that substantially outweighs its probative value (Rule 403) and disrupts the orderly presentation of evidence (Rule 611).

The rules, on the other hand, allow parties to present extrinsic evidence of prior inconsistent statements related to non-collateral matters. **Rule 613** imposes modest procedural requirements on this process, which we will study in this chapter. But demonstrating inconsistencies in a witness's statements about a fact of consequence to the litigation is central to the truth-finding function of trials. The rules, therefore, allow this process.

Attorneys may also explore inconsistent statements on cross-examination. They may use this non-extrinsic evidence to probe both collateral and non-collateral matters. At some point, a judge may halt extended cross-examination on collateral matters. But judges give lawyers some latitude to probe collateral inconsistencies on cross-examination.

Before we discuss the details of this process, here is a summary of how the rules treat these different types of impeachment with prior inconsistent statements:

	Non-Extrinsic Evidence	Extrinsic Evidence
Non-Collateral Matter	Cross-examiner asks Wilma, "Didn't you tell your friend Sharon that Fred hit Betty?" **Allowed.**	Sharon testifies that Wilma told her that Fred hit Betty. **Allowed**, subject to procedures in **Rule 613.**
Collateral Matter	Cross-examiner asks Wilma: "Didn't you tell the police that you drove to the golf course that day?" **Allowed**, subject to some outer limits under **Rules 403** and **611.**	Police officer testifies that Wilma told him she drove to the golf course. **Prohibited** under **Rules 403** and **611.**

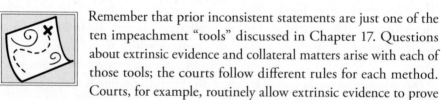 Remember that prior inconsistent statements are just one of the ten impeachment "tools" discussed in Chapter 17. Questions about extrinsic evidence and collateral matters arise with each of those tools; the courts follow different rules for each method. Courts, for example, routinely allow extrinsic evidence to prove a witness's bias. The Supreme Court approved this principle in *United States v. Abel*, the Aryan Brotherhood case described in the last chapter.[1] Although evidence of bias must comply with other rules (such as the rule against hearsay), bias is

---

1   469 U.S. 45 (1984).

never collateral. Instead, it is one of the "favored forms of impeachment" allowing extrinsic evidence.[2]

Similarly, parties can rely upon extrinsic evidence to show that a witness's perception was impaired. A party may call a witness's friend to testify that the witness always wears eyeglasses. Or the party may introduce the witness's medical records, showing that the witness has poor hearing. These types of evidence are extrinsic—they go beyond questioning the witness on the stand—but they do not violate Rules 403 or 611 because of their strong probative value.

The bar on extrinsic evidence for collateral matters, in fact, only applies to a few types of impeachment. The first is prior inconsistent statements, discussed in this chapter. The second is impeachment by contradiction, in which an attorney uses evidence other than a witness's prior statement to show that the witness lied on the stand. After Wilma testifies that she walked to the golf course in the above hypothetical, for example, Barney's lawyer might offer testimony by the club's parking attendant to show that Wilma arrived by car. A court would not allow this testimony, just as it wouldn't allow evidence of Wilma's prior statement, to contradict the collateral matter of how Wilma arrived at the golf course.

Finally, as we'll see in Chapters 19 through 22, courts limit the use of extrinsic evidence to prove a witness's character for untruthfulness. But before we turn to those rules, let's complete our exploration of impeachment through prior inconsistent statements.

B. The Rules. **Rule 613** outlines two procedural steps that parties must follow when impeaching a witness with a prior inconsistent statement. Neither of these steps is onerous; indeed, the rule loosens common-law restrictions that often hampered effective use of these statements. **Rules 403** and **611** impose substantive constraints on the use of extrinsic evidence to impeach witnesses with prior inconsistent statements; these rules largely bar that evidence when it relates to collateral matters.

1. Disclosing the Prior Statement. The common law required trial lawyers to disclose a prior inconsistent statement to a witness before impeaching her with it.[3] This prevented lawyers from surprising witnesses with inconsistencies, but it

---

2   Id. at 52.

3   This doctrine, called the "Rule in Queen Caroline's Case," arose from a notorious 19th century English controversy. Queen's Case, 129 Eng. Rep. 976 (1820). The trial stemmed from King George IV's attempt to divorce his unpopular and estranged wife, Queen Caroline. The divorce action did not succeed, and England's Parliament

also lessened the impact of cross-examination. Mandatory disclosure also gave witnesses time to formulate stories—sometimes disingenuous ones—to reconcile their inconsistent statements.

Rule 613(a) abolishes this common-law convention. Lawyers now may surprise witnesses by asking them without warning about prior inconsistent statements. The rule requires only that the lawyer disclose the statement to opposing counsel immediately before the lawyer brings up the statement on cross-examination:

RULE 613. Witness's Prior Statement

(a) Showing or Disclosing the Statement During Examination.
When examining a witness about the witness's prior statement,

- a party <u>need not show it</u> or disclose its contents to the witness.
- But the party must, on request, <u>show it</u> or disclose its contents to an <u>adverse party's attorney</u>.

The required disclosure to opposing counsel gives that lawyer a chance to raise any evidentiary objections, as well as to prepare to rehabilitate the witness. Opposing counsel, however, has no right to see the impeaching statement before cross-examination begins; thus, the opposing counsel cannot prepare the witness unless she knows about the statement from her own investigation.

Here is an example of how an attorney might surprise Wilma Flintstone with one of the prior inconsistent statements mentioned above:

On direct examination, Wilma Flintstone testified for the prosecution that she saw Barney Rubble hit his wife Betty over the head with a golf club. Barney's lawyer is now cross-examining Wilma:

Defense: Ms. Flintstone, you testified on direct examination that you saw the defendant Barney Rubble hit his wife Betty Rubble over the head with a club. Is that correct?

Flintstone: Uh huh, that's right.

---

abolished the rule limiting impeachment in 1854. The rule, however, took hold in the American judicial system and persisted until enactment of the Federal Rules of Evidence and similar codes in the states. A few states still follow the rule from the *Queen's Case*, requiring lawyers to show the inconsistent statement to a witness before impeaching the witness.

Defense: And you're positive it was Barney who hit Betty?

Flintstone: Absolutely—I was looking right at him when it happened.

Defense: And you were able to recognize Barney easily?

Flintstone: That's what I just said! I've known him for about 15 years. I was looking right at Barney when he hit poor Betty.

Defense: [Walking over to the prosecutor's table and handing the prosecutor a copy of Wilma's prior statement]. But just an hour after Betty was hit, didn't you send an email to your friend Sharon Stone, telling her that your own husband Fred was the person who hit Betty?

Flintstone: I—I don't think I said that . . .

Defense: You don't think so? Isn't it true that at 8:11 p.m. on March 5, 2014, you sent an e-mail to Ms. Stone in which you wrote, quote, "Sharon, we're in big trouble. Fred just hit Betty with a club"?

Rule 613(a) allows lawyers to surprise witnesses in this manner. Many lawyers, however, choose to show the witness an inconsistent statement before asking about it. Handing a document to the witness can draw the jury's attention, signaling that something dramatic is about to happen. Some judges and jurors also perceive an attorney's cross-examination as more "fair" if the attorney shows an inconsistent statement to the witness before asking questions about the statement. Barney's lawyer could have conducted the cross-examination this way:

Flintstone: That's what I just said! I've known him for about 15 years. I was looking right at Barney when he hit poor Betty.

Defense: [Walking over to prosecutor's table and handing him a copy of the statement]. Your Honor, may I approach the witness?

Court: You may.

Defense: Ms. Flintstone, I am handing you a document that has been marked as Defense Exhibit 12 for identification. Do you recognize this document?

Flintstone: Well, it looks like an email that I sent my friend Sharon Stone.

Defense: Did you in fact write this e-mail?

Flintstone: Yes, I did.

Defense: And what is the date and time on that email?

Flintstone: Uh, it says 8:11 p.m. on March 5, 2014.

Defense: And doesn't that email read—I'm quoting here: "Sharon, we're in big trouble. Fred just hit Betty with a club"?

The point of Rule 613(a) is that lawyers may choose either strategy to impeach a witness with a prior inconsistent statement. The lawyer may show the statement to the witness before asking about it, or the lawyer may ask about the inconsistency without showing the statement directly to the witness.

Note that Barney's lawyer did not admit the prior inconsistent statement into evidence in either of these examples; in the second example, he marked it for identification only. Rule 613(a) applies even when a party relies upon non-extrinsic evidence. Even if a party simply cross-examines a witness about a prior inconsistent statement, the party must disclose the statement to opposing counsel if requested to do so.

If Barney's lawyer wants to introduce the email into evidence, rather than just asking Wilma about it, then he must comply with the rules governing extrinsic evidence of prior statements. We explore the procedural and substantive limits on that evidence in sections (2) and (3) below.

2. Procedural Constraints on Extrinsic Evidence. The Federal Rules of Evidence allow extrinsic evidence of some prior inconsistent statements, but **Rule 613(b)** establishes procedural rules for admission of this evidence. If a party offers extrinsic evidence of a prior inconsistent statement, the witness who made the prior statement must have an opportunity to explain the inconsistency, and opposing counsel must have a chance to question the witness about that inconsistency.

RULE 613. Witness's Prior Statement

(b) Extrinsic Evidence of a Prior Inconsistent Statement. <u>Extrinsic evidence</u> of a witness's prior inconsistent statement is admissible only

- if the witness is given an <u>opportunity to explain or deny</u> the statement and an adverse party is given an opportunity to <u>examine the witness</u> about it, or
- if <u>justice so requires</u>.[4]

These conditions are easy to satisfy. In many cases, a lawyer introduces an impeaching statement while cross-examining a witness. The witness is on the stand and has an opportunity to explain or deny the statement immediately. Opposing counsel will have a chance to ask questions—and give the witness further opportunities to respond—on redirect. This common process satisfies Rule 613(b).

Rule 613(b) raises potential problems only when a lawyer introduces evidence of a prior inconsistent statement after a witness has left the stand. Rule 613(b) allows the lawyer to do this, as long as opposing counsel can recall the witness to the stand. We will explore this option, as well as the "if justice so requires" exception, in the Courtroom section below.

3. Substantive Constraints on Using Extrinsic Evidence. Judges give parties considerable freedom to **ask** witnesses about prior inconsistent statements. Inconsistencies are relevant to a witness's credibility, and questions posed on cross-examination take little court time. But if a party wants to introduce **extrinsic evidence** of a prior inconsistent statement, judges are more restrictive. As explained above, judges usually exclude extrinsic evidence of a prior inconsistent statement that relates solely to a collateral matter.

In the example of Wilma's e-mail to Sharon, this constraint poses no problem. The question of who hit Betty with the golf club is not collateral; it is central to the case. But Wilma's statement to the police officer that she drove to the golf course is collateral; so are comments about what outfit she was wearing when she went to the course that day. The judge would allow Barney's counsel to ask Wilma

---

4   A final sentence of Rule 613(b) provides an exception for statements of an opposing party that are governed by Rule 801(d)(2). We will examine that exception when we explore Rule 801(d)(2) in Chapters 53–55.

about these inconsistencies, but he would not let counsel waste the court's time by calling other witnesses to prove these collateral inconsistencies.

Judges precluding extrinsic evidence of collateral inconsistencies often refer loosely to excluding the evidence under Rule 613. In reality, the decision rests on Rule 403's balancing test or on the judge's Rule 611 authority to create an orderly trial. Loose references to Rule 613 in this context can confuse students and new lawyers, who wonder how that rule can exclude evidence of collateral matters when it doesn't even use the phrase.

C. In the Courtroom.

1. Inconsistent Statements. Rule 613's title and section 613(a)'s text refer broadly to prior statements rather than prior **inconsistent** statements. Judges, however, usually allow parties to cross-examine witnesses only on their inconsistent statements—not on consistent ones. This limit rests, not on Rule 613, but on Rules 401–403. A prior consistent statement adds little to a trial; it doesn't discredit a witness or add new information. A prior consistent statement might reinforce the witness's testimony, but that probative value is minor compared to the delay and confusion the statement might cause.

Except in the unusual circumstances described in the next section, therefore, courts do not allow attorneys to examine witnesses about prior consistent statements. Sometimes, however, a dispute arises about whether a prior statement is sufficiently "inconsistent" to support examination:

> **Example:** The government charged Rodney Heslip and three other individuals with conspiracy to possess and distribute cocaine. Detective Moore, who investigated the conspiracy, provided key testimony against Heslip and his codefendants. Heslip moved to impeach Moore's testimony by introducing an affidavit that Moore had executed to obtain a search warrant early in the investigation. In this affidavit, Moore named the other defendants but not Heslip. Heslip argued that the affidavit was admissible as a prior inconsistent statement, which impeached Moore's trial testimony that Heslip participated in the conspiracy.

Analysis: The trial judge refused to admit Moore's affidavit, noting that the evidentiary rules allow impeachment only with prior **inconsistent** statements. The affidavit, executed a year and a half before the trial, did not satisfy that requirement. Moore broadened his view of the conspiracy as his investigation matured; the affidavit executed at an early stage in the inquiry was not inconsistent with his later testimony. The prior statement, therefore, was not admissible to impeach Moore. The court of appeals affirmed this ruling.[5]

The trial judge and appellate panel referred to Rule 613 in excluding Moore's affidavit. Those references are consistent with the shorthand that lawyers use to discuss the admissibility of prior statements for impeachment. Rule 613 itself, however, does not prohibit impeachment with consistent (or marginally consistent) prior statements; you will be confused if you search the rule for this prohibition. The affidavit in Heslip's case was inadmissible under Rule 403; the potential for prejudice, confusion, and delay substantially outweighed any probative value.

2. Prior Consistent Statements for Rehabilitation. Prior consistent statements are most likely to assist the fact finder, warranting admission under Rules 402 and 403, when parties use them to rehabilitate a witness who has been discredited on cross-examination. Even when offered for rehabilitation, judges exclude most of these prior consistent statements as duplicative and confusing. Under limited circumstances, however, judges allow parties to use prior consistent statements to rehabilitate witnesses.

Judges most often admit these statements when the prior statement occurred **before** an event that allegedly changed a witness's testimony. For example, if the government persuades one member of a criminal conspiracy to testify against the others at trial, the remaining defendants may challenge the turncoat's credibility. The defendants may argue that their former coconspirator manufactured evidence simply to please the government and obtain a favorable plea. In response to this type of cross-examination, the trial judge might allow the prosecution to introduce consistent statements made by the witness before any contact with the government. These statements have special probative force in negating the suggestion that the witness concocted testimony to negotiate a favorable deal.

---

5   United States v. Misher, 99 F.3d 664, 669–70 (5th Cir. 1996).

Once again, parties and judges sometimes refer to introducing these prior consistent statements as "rehabilitating a witness under Rule 613." Since Rule 613 does not refer to this practice, the customary reference is confusing. Although you may adopt that parlance in court, it is easier to remember that the admissibility of these statements really turns on the relevance and balancing requirements of Rules 402 and 403. Rule 613 merely outlines the procedural requirements surrounding the use of prior statements.

3. Showing the Statement to the Witness. Although Rule 613(a) specifically allows a party to examine a witness about a prior inconsistent statement without showing the statement to the witness, attorneys sometimes show the statement to the witness for the strategic reasons noted above. Judges, moreover, sometimes exercise their general authority under Rule 611 to **require** a cross-examining attorney to show the statement to the witness. A judge will do this when the cross-examination might otherwise create an unfair or inaccurate impression. Here is an example of a case in which a trial judge made that decision:

> **Example:** The government charged Marshall Marks with conspiring to distribute marijuana. Ernest Poland, one of Marks's alleged coconspirators, testified against Marks at trial. Marks's attorney cross-examined Poland by highlighting inconsistencies between Poland's courtroom testimony and statements he previously made to FBI investigators. The cross-examination began in the style suggested by the hypothetical transcript from the Flintstone case discussed above: Marks's attorney read aloud portions of Poland's statement to the FBI agents, pausing after each portion to ask whether Poland had made those comments.
>
> The trial judge halted this procedure and required Marks's attorney to show the written FBI report to Poland, then ask whether Poland adopted the statement made in that report. The judge took this course because the FBI report was not a transcript of Poland's previous comments; it was the agent's personal summary of what Poland had said. Under these circumstances, counsel's cross-examination technique might confuse the jury by suggesting that he was reading from an actual transcript of Poland's remarks.
>
> Marks challenged this ruling on appeal, complaining that it violated Rule 613(a) and interfered with his right to cross-examine Poland effectively.

Analysis: The court of appeals rejected Marks's argument and upheld the trial judge's ruling. Although Rule 613(a) generally allows counsel to cross-examine a witness about a prior statement without showing the statement to the witness, that rule does not eliminate the trial judge's discretion under Rule 611 to structure testimony in a way that avoids misleading the jury. The possibility of confusion was clear in this case and the trial judge acted appropriately to avoid that confusion. Showing the statement to Poland at the start of cross-examination, and asking him to confirm or deny the agent's notes of his previous statements, prevented jury confusion.[6]

4. When Is An Issue Collateral? If an inconsistency relates solely to a collateral issue, then the potential for prejudice, delay, or confusion substantially outweighs the probative value of admitting extrinsic evidence of the previous statement.

 Often the line between collateral and non-collateral matters is obvious, as in the Flintstone examples used earlier. But as with any issue of relevance, the question of whether a statement is collateral depends on the facts of the case and the persuasiveness of counsel.

In our earlier discussion, for example, Wilma Flintstone's conflicting statements about walking or driving to the golf course seemed collateral to the assault charges against Barney. The fact of consequence was whether Wilma saw Barney hit Betty, not how she arrived at the golf course. But what if Barney's counsel has evidence that Wilma drove to the golf course with Fred as her passenger? If Wilma brought Fred to the golf course, and Barney claims that Fred was the person who hit Betty, then Wilma's means of arrival at the golf course is more consequential. The judge might allow Barney to introduce extrinsic evidence of this inconsistent statement.

5. Witness Denials. The rule against using extrinsic evidence to prove inconsistent statements on collateral issues prevents trials from getting bogged down tangential issues. But what if a witness denies making a prior statement that the attorney knows the witness made? In her police statement, for example, Wilma might have mentioned that she wore old golfing shoes to the course. On the witness stand, she notes that she was wearing brand new pink Crocs. Barney's lawyer asks Wilma on cross-examination: "Didn't you tell the police that you

---

6   United States v. Marks, 816 F.2d 1207, 1210–11 (7th Cir. 1987).

were wearing your old golfing shoes that day?" If Wilma responds, "No, I never said any such thing. I'm sure I told the police I was wearing my new pink Crocs, just like I testified today," can Barney's lawyer prove that Wilma really made a different statement to the police?

The answer is no. Barney's lawyer is stuck with Wilma's answer and must move on. Even if he has an audiotape of Wilma making the inconsistent statement, and three police officers are willing to take the stand and testify that she referred to golfing shoes, the court will not waste time on this extrinsic evidence. At most, Barney's lawyer could ask one more question, perhaps reading from a document in front of him: "Ms. Flintstone, are you sure that when you spoke to Officer Pebbles at 7:30 PM that night, you didn't say, quote, I was wearing my old golfing shoes and my feet were very sore, unquote?" But if Wilma denies the statement again, the matter is closed. Her choice in footwear isn't consequential enough to waste more court time.

6. Extrinsic Evidence and Rule 613(b). If extrinsic evidence of a prior inconsistent statement clears the material/collateral hurdle described above, the party offering the statement must also satisfy the procedural steps outlined in Rule 613(b): The witness must have an opportunity to "explain or deny" the earlier statement, and the opposing party must have a chance to "examine" the witness about the statement.

Notably, however, Rule 613(b) does not mandate a particular sequence for these events. This laxity overrules the common-law tradition, which required attorneys to show an inconsistent statement to a witness before demonstrating the inconsistency. Indeed, an attorney may even impeach a witness with a prior inconsistent statement after the witness has left the stand. Under some circumstances, this technique delivers a devastating surprise blow to the witness's credibility. Here is one case in which a defense attorney used this tactic:

> **Example:** A grand jury indicted Stephen Rose, an attorney, with procuring false identification documents for clients. The prosecution's star trial witness was Richard Britz, who testified that Rose helped him obtain a driver's license in another name after his own license was suspended. On cross-examination, Rose's counsel asked Britz if he knew a man named Dennis Ilenfeld and if Ilenfeld, rather than Rose, had obtained the fake license for him. Britz answered "no" to both questions. Defense counsel did not pursue the matter further at that time.

But as part of the defense case, Rose's attorney called Frank DeFrancesco as a witness. DeFrancesco testified that Britz told him that he had obtained a fake license from Dennis Ilenfeld and that, if DeFrancesco ever needed a fake document, "Ilenfeld was the guy to see." Rose's attorney thus introduced extrinsic evidence of Britz's prior statement (his comments to DeFrancesco) without first reminding Britz of the statement. DeFrancesco's testimony significantly undermined Britz's credibility because Britz had claimed on cross-examination that he didn't even know Ilenfeld. The inconsistency suggested, as defense counsel hoped, that Ilenfeld rather than Rose might have obtained the false IDs for Britz.

The prosecutor objected to DeFrancesco's testimony, claiming that Rose should have laid a foundation for the testimony by first asking Britz about any statements he had made to DeFrancesco.

Analysis: The trial judge granted the prosecutor's motion, finding that Rose's attorney should have laid a foundation for DeFrancesco's testimony. The court of appeals, however, reversed this ruling. The appellate court held that Rose's presentation of DeFrancesco's testimony complied fully with Rule 613(b). That rule does not require a party to lay any particular foundation before introducing extrinsic proof of a witness's prior inconsistent statement. The witness must have an opportunity to explain or deny the statement, and opposing counsel must have a chance to interrogate the witness about the statement, but those tasks are easily accomplished by recalling the witness. The prosecutor was able to cross-examine DeFrancesco and could recall and interrogate Britz as part of the government's rebuttal case. Rule 613(b), the appellate court concluded, requires no more.[7]

 The example teaches two important lessons. First, as the court of appeals concluded, Rule 613(b) allows parties to pursue the strategy that Rose's attorney employed above. Under most circumstances, the opposing party can recall the witness whose testimony has been impeached, affording the opportunities guaranteed by Rule 613(b). Second, however, the case demonstrates that trial judges often frown on this strategy. An attorney who plans to impeach a witness with extrinsic proof of an inconsistent statement, without first asking the witness

---

7   This example is based on United States v. Della Rose, 403 F.3d 891, 903 (7th Cir. 2005), although we have simplified the facts somewhat.

about the statement, should be prepared to cite appropriate appellate authorities to the trial judge.

7. "If Justice So Requires." Rule 613(b) provides that in unusual circumstances, when "justice so requires," a party may introduce extrinsic evidence of a witness's prior statement even when the witness will not have an opportunity to explain or deny the statement, and opposing counsel will not have a chance to interrogate the witness. This exception is designed for the case in which a witness becomes unavailable after testifying but before introduction of the prior inconsistent statement. Under these circumstances, justice might support admitting the statement despite the lack of opportunity for the witness to explain or deny the inconsistency.

Trial judges, however, are very reluctant to apply this exception. They are more likely to rule that the party attempting to impeach should have confronted the witness with the prior statement while he or she was on the stand. Partly for this reason, many attorneys follow that practice even though Rule 613(b) does not require it; confronting the witness with a prior statement during the initial testimony assures that the party does not lose the opportunity if the witness suddenly becomes unavailable.

8. Limiting Instruction. This chapter discusses the use of prior inconsistent statements to **impeach** a witness. The prior statement, in other words, shows that the witness has told conflicting stories at different times. The very fact of inconsistency casts doubt on the witness's memory, accuracy, and truthfulness. Rules 401–403 support cross-examination about inconsistencies, as well as introduction of extrinsic evidence about inconsistent statements that touch material issues. Rule 613 imposes only modest procedural constraints on the use of these prior inconsistent statements to impeach witnesses.

But parties often want to do more than simply impeach a witness with a prior inconsistent statement; litigants frequently want to persuade the jury to accept the **content** of a prior statement. Asking the jury to base its decision on the content of a prior, out-of-court statement, however, often violates the hearsay rules.

We will study the hearsay rules in much greater depth later in the course. For now, note this interplay of impeachment and hearsay: Sometimes a statement is admissible to discredit a witness by showing an inconsistency, but not to prove the content of the statement.

In the prosecution of Barney Rubble discussed above, for example, Barney's attorney showed that Wilma's courtroom testimony (that Barney hit Betty) conflicted with her previous email (that Fred hit Betty). This inconsistency casts doubt on Wilma's credibility: Is she confused about which man hit Betty? Does she know that Fred hit Betty, but is lying to protect him? Based simply on Wilma's conflicting statements, the jury may decide to disregard Wilma's testimony. If the prosecution's case rests on Wilma's testimony, and if Barney's lawyer shows that Wilma's testimony has changed over time, that vacillation alone may create a reasonable doubt about Barney's guilt.

When a party offers a prior statement solely for impeachment purposes, however, the jury cannot rely upon the substance of the prior statement. To understand this difference, imagine that Betty files a civil suit against Fred for battery. In defense, Fred offers the same testimony from Wilma—who testifies that she saw Barney, not Fred, hit Betty.

Betty may now impeach Wilma by introducing evidence of Wilma's previous email to Sharon Stone. In that email, Betty can point out, Wilma said that Fred hit Betty. This inconsistency impeaches Wilma's testimony; if she told Sharon one thing, and testified in court to another, how believable is she? Betty's counsel may argue that the jury should ignore Wilma's testimony as completely unreliable.

Unless the email qualifies for admission under the hearsay rules, however, Betty cannot argue that the jury should believe the **content** of Wilma's email to Sharon Stone. Wilma's courtroom testimony, in other words, may not offer **credible evidence** that Barney hit Betty. But her email provides **no evidence** that Fred hit Betty.

To explain this distinction to the jury, the judge may give a limiting instruction. A sample instruction for this context is:

> Evidence that, at some other time while not under oath a witness . . . has said or done something inconsistent with the witness' testimony at the trial, may be considered for the sole purpose of judging the credibility of the witness. However, such evidence may never be considered as evidence of proof of the truth of any such statement.[8]

---

8   3 Kevin F. O'Malley, Jay E. Grenig, & Hon. William C. Lee, Federal Jury Practice & Instructions § 105:09 (6th ed. 2016).

This type of instruction is very difficult for lay jurors to understand; indeed, law students often struggle to master the distinction between using a statement for impeachment and using it for substantive proof. Judges sometimes try to make the instruction more clear by linking it to specific evidence in the lawsuit. In the case of Wilma Flintstone, for example, the judge might instruct the jury:

> During this trial, you heard testimony from Wilma Flintstone. You also heard about an email that Ms. Flintstone sent to her friend Sharon Stone on the evening of the alleged assault. Ms. Flintstone's email was a statement that occurred outside the courtroom, and she did not make it under oath. You may not, therefore, use that email to decide whether facts stated in the email are true or not. You may only consider the email to help judge Ms. Flintstone's credibility at trial.

Even with this type of specificity, jurors may find it difficult to distinguish between using a prior statement to assess credibility and using the content of that statement for other purposes. The law, however, often requires this distinction; it is one we will return to when we study the hearsay rules.

Quick Summary

Parties often try to impeach witnesses with prior inconsistent statements. **Rules 401–403** allow parties to ask witnesses about these statements, because any inconsistency casts some doubt on a witness's credibility. Questions about prior inconsistent statements are relevant, and they rarely cause delay that substantially outweighs their probative value.

Litigants, however, face greater constraints if they offer extrinsic evidence of a witness's prior inconsistent statement. If these statements relate to a collateral matter, rather than a material issue in the case, judges will exclude them under Rules 403 or 611. Extrinsic evidence of a witness's prior statement about a collateral matter would delay the trial and confuse the jury.

Rule 613 complements this framework by requiring parties to follow two procedural steps when impeaching witnesses with prior inconsistent statements. First, the attorney must disclose the statement to opposing counsel if the opponent requests that disclosure. The attorney, however, need not show the statement to the witness before asking about it. This requirement applies whether the attorney uses extrinsic or non-extrinsic evidence. Second, if the judge permits extrinsic evidence of a prior inconsistent statement, the party offering that evidence must give (a) the affected witness an opportunity to explain or deny the statement, and (b) opposing counsel a chance to examine the witness about the statement.

The evidentiary rules draw a sharp distinction between evidence admitted to prove a substantive matter and evidence admitted solely for impeachment. This chapter discusses admission of prior inconsistent statements for impeachment. To introduce a statement for substantive purposes (that is, to prove the truth of what the statement asserts), a party must also comply with the hearsay restrictions and other rules. When a party uses a prior inconsistent statement solely for impeachment, the judge will give the jury an instruction limiting their use of the statement.

Test Your Understanding

 To assess your understanding of the material in this chapter, click here to take a quiz, or go to the Quizzes module from the eBook on your eProducts bookshelf.

19

Revealing Untruthful Character on Cross-Examination

Key Concepts

- **Rule 404(a):** General Prohibition of Character Evidence
- **Rule 608(b)(1):** Limited Exception for Proving a Witness's Character for Truthfulness or Untruthfulness
- Cross-Examination on Specific Incidents
- Good Faith Belief and Judicial Discretion
- Extrinsic Proof Prohibited

A. Introduction and Policy. In the last chapter we explored the use of inconsistent statements to impeach witnesses. Another effective way to discredit a witness is to demonstrate that the witness has an untruthful character. If the jurors learn that the witness has a reputation for lying, or that the witness engaged in dishonest behavior in the past, the jurors may discount the witness's testimony.

Discrediting a witness in this manner involves using "character evidence," a type of evidence we will discuss in great detail in upcoming chapters. Character evidence suggests that, because an individual has a particular character trait (e.g., mendacity, aggressiveness, violence), the person was likely to have acted in a particular way during a specific incident. Arguing that a homicide defendant probably killed the victim because the defendant is a violent, aggressive person is a classic use of character evidence.

However, as we'll see in later chapters, the Rules of Evidence generally exclude character evidence. Parties must focus on the events they dispute, not on one another's general character. So a medical malpractice plaintiff usually cannot introduce evidence that the doctor treated other patients carelessly in the past;

the plaintiff must focus on how the doctor acted on this occasion. Similarly, a prosecutor usually cannot introduce evidence that a homicide defendant has a violent temper or a history of attacking others; the prosecutor must focus on facts showing that the defendant committed this particular murder.

The Federal Rules of Evidence, however, make several exceptions to this general prohibition against the use of character evidence. One of these exceptions allows evidence about a witness's character for telling the truth. Within certain carefully defined limits, parties in both civil and criminal cases may offer evidence that a witness has an untruthful nature. The jury may then consider that evidence when assessing the witness's testimony. If the jurors believe that the witness is a generally untruthful person, they may reject or discount that witness's words in the courtroom.

In this chapter we'll focus on the simplest way to introduce evidence of a witness's untruthful character: by asking the witness questions on cross-examination. In the next three chapters, we'll probe other ways to demonstrate a witness's proclivity for lying.

B. The Rule. Rule 404(a), which we will study in greater detail starting in Chapter 25, contains a general prohibition against the use of character evidence. The rule opens by stating:

RULE 404. Character Evidence; Crimes or Other Acts

(a) Character Evidence.

    (1) *Prohibited Uses.* Evidence of a person's character or character trait is not admissible to prove that on a particular occasion the person acted in accordance with the character or trait.

On its own, this rule would prevent litigants from suggesting that a witness is a generally untruthful person. Untruthfulness is a character trait, so Rule 404(a)(1) prohibits a party from arguing that, because the witness is a generally untruthful person, the witness probably lied on the stand (i.e., acted in conformity with that trait while testifying in the courtroom).

Rule 404(a), however, continues by noting several exceptions. Subsection 404(a)(3) provides:

> ## Rule 404. Character Evidence; Crimes or Other Acts
>
> **(a) Character Evidence. . . .**
>
> > **(3)** *Exceptions for a Witness.* Evidence of a <u>witness's character</u> may be admitted under Rules 607, 608, and 609.

Rule 404(a), in other words, is an evidentiary net that excludes most character evidence from the courtroom. The net, however, has several important holes, and one of those allows introduction of evidence related to a witness's character.

To learn more about revealing a witness's character flaws on cross-examination, we turn to **Rules 608** and **609.**[1] In this chapter we will discuss **Rule 608(b)(1)**, which covers methods of establishing untruthful character by offering proof of a witness's prior specific instances of conduct:

> ## Rule 608. A Witness's Character for Truthfulness or Untruthfulness
>
> **(b) Specific Instances of Conduct. . . .** <u>extrinsic evidence</u> is not admissible to prove <u>specific instances of a witness's conduct</u> in order to attack or support the witness's character for truthfulness. But the <u>court may</u>, on cross-examination, allow them to be inquired into if they are <u>probative of the character for truthfulness or untruthfulness</u> of:
>
> > **(1)** the <u>witness</u> . . . .

This section of Rule 608 establishes four important points, signaled by the underlined phrases above.

First, a party may ask a witness about "specific instances of conduct" on cross-examination to suggest that the witness has an untruthful character. Cross-examin-

---

1   We discussed Rule 607, which allows any party to impeach a witness, in Chapter 17.

ing attorneys may ask witnesses a host of unpleasant questions to establish their general character for untruthfulness. Questions that attorneys have asked include:

> **Q:** When did you use the name Pedro Flores Vera [a name different from the one the witness was using on the stand]?[2]
>
> **Q:** Is it true that you lied on two employment applications filed in 1974 and 1975?[3]
>
> **Q:** Did you lie on loan applications to the Stephenson National Bank?[4]
>
> **Q:** Have you filed any tax returns during the last eight years?[5]

All of these questions inquire about specific acts related to the witness's general character for telling the truth.

Second, attorneys must limit these questions to actions that are "probative of the [witness's] character for truthfulness or untruthfulness." An attorney cannot probe other aspects of a witness's character such as drunkenness, slothfulness, messiness, or meanness. This rule reinforces the general rule of relevance; a witness's laziness or table manners are not relevant to the truthfulness of his testimony in court. The rule also reduces harassment of witnesses. Imagine how unpleasant it would be to testify if witnesses had to answer questions like, "Is it true that you have six slices of moldy pizza on the bottom shelf of your refrigerator?" or "How often do you yell at your spouse?" We will explore further in the Courtroom section the kinds of questions that are probative of truthfulness and those that are not.

Third, the judge has discretion to prevent questions cross-examining a witness about specific acts that reveal untruthful character; Rule 608(b) states that the court "may" allow these questions. This discretion complements the freedom that trial judges already have under **Rule 403** to exclude unfairly prejudicial evidence and under **Rule 611** to control the presentation of courtroom testimony. As we'll see in the Courtroom section, judges often invoke this authority to restrain extensive cross-examination of witnesses on character issues.

---

2   United States v. Ojeda, 23 F.3d 1473, 1476–77 (8th Cir. 1994).

3   United States v. Howard, 774 F.2d 838, 844–45 (7th Cir. 1985).

4   United States v. Chevalier, 1 F.3d 581, 582, 583–84 (7th Cir. 1993).

5   Chnapkova v. Koh, 985 F.2d 79, 82–83 (2d Cir. 1993).

Finally, Rule 608(b) bars proof of these specific instances by extrinsic evidence. We discussed the concept of extrinsic evidence in the last chapter. Rule 608(b)'s prohibition means that attorneys may **cross-examine** witnesses about acts that suggest an untruthful character, but they may not introduce **other evidence** of those acts, such as disciplinary reports or testimony from other witnesses.

Rule 608(b) imposes this limit for the same reason that judges forbid use of extrinsic evidence to prove prior inconsistent statements about collateral matters. If parties could introduce extrinsic evidence of untruthful acts by witnesses, trials would bog down in tangential disputes about the prior conduct of those witnesses. If an attorney cross-examines a witness about committing an untruthful act, therefore, the attorney must accept the witness's answer and move on. Even if the witness denies an act that the attorney could easily prove with extrinsic evidence, the attorney cannot introduce that evidence.

We'll explore this distinction between cross-examination and extrinsic evidence further in the Courtroom section. And in the next chapter, we will examine one very important exception to the bar on extrinsic evidence.

C. In the Courtroom.

1. Probative of Character for Truthfulness or Untruthfulness. Rule 608(b)(1) allows parties to establish a witness's character for untruthfulness by asking on cross-examination about specific examples of conduct suggesting that character. To fit within the rule, however, the acts must "be probative of the [witness's] character for truthfulness or untruthfulness." As the examples listed in the previous section show, using a false name, lying on an employment or loan application, and failing to file tax returns are all acts that are probative of untruthfulness.

Many other actions, although immoral or illegal, are not related to truthfulness, so parties cannot cross-examine witnesses on them under this rule. Some of the many actions that courts have prevented attorneys from asking about under Rule 608(b)(1) are murder, drug use, sexual proclivities, and driving over the speed limit. Here is a case that illustrates the type of line the courts attempt to draw on this issue:

Example: The United States charged Vasiliy Ermichine and Alexander Nosov with kidnapping and murdering Sergei Kobozev. Alexander Spitchenko provided much of the evidence against the defendants at trial. Ermichine and Nosov attempted to impeach Spitchenko's credibility by cross-examining him on a number of acts related to a scheme he developed to produce pornographic films with women brought to the United States from Estonia. Spitchenko's film business was unrelated to the alleged kidnapping and murder.

Analysis: The trial judge allowed the defendants to cross-examine Spitchenko on aspects of the scheme that involved dishonesty. These included questions about bribing officials in Estonia to secure the women's emigration and about illegally seizing the women's passports to make sure they carried out their contracts. The judge, however, did not let the defendants ask about the pornographic nature of the films. That aspect of Spitchenko's behavior was not relevant to his truthfulness and it posed substantial danger of inflaming the jury.[6]

2. Good Faith Belief. Before asking a witness about a specific incident suggesting untruthfulness, an attorney must have a good faith belief that the incident occurred. Otherwise, parties could attack witnesses simply by asking wildly incriminating questions based purely on imagination. Even if the witness denied the accusation, the jury might believe that there was some basis to the attorney's inquiry. Innuendo is hard to combat.

A good faith belief is one that rests on some evidence, even if the evidence would not be admissible in court. Some writers analogize the good faith belief requirement of Rule 608(b) with the probable cause standard for obtaining a search warrant. Here is one example of a cross-examination that lacked a good faith belief:

Example: The United States charged Tom and Penny Crutchfield, who operated a business selling exotic reptiles, with illegally importing an endangered species of iguana. One of the Crutchfields' former employees, Robert Harding, testified for the defense. On direct examination, Harding admitted that he occasionally smoked marijuana. On cross-examination, the prosecutor questioned Harding this way:

---

6   United States v. Nosov, 221 F. Supp. 2d 445, 448–51 (S.D.N.Y. 2002), aff'd, 119 F. App'x 311 (2d Cir. 2004).

Q: Are you aware of the mullet boats coming in at night without lights around that area carrying the square grouper[7] off of the boats there?

[Defense counsel objected, but before the court could rule the prosecutor continued]

Q: Do you know what a square grouper is?

[Defense counsel objected again and the judge sustained the objection. But the prosecutor interrupted the judge mid-sentence to ask a final question of Harding]

Q: Weren't you involved in obtaining bales of pot?

The Crutchfields were convicted and, on appeal, they challenged the prosecutor's questions to Harding as lacking any good faith basis.

Analysis: The court of appeals agreed that the prosecutor's questioning of Harding was "unquestionably out of line and an obvious violation of Federal Rule of Evidence 608(b)." The prosecutor offered no basis for believing that Harding was involved in drug trafficking other than unsubstantiated references to "suggestions to that effect." Nor did Harding's reference to occasional personal use of marijuana suggest that he was a drug smuggler. Based on this error and other instances of misconduct by the prosecutor, the court reversed the conviction.[8]

Even if the prosecutor had possessed firm evidence of Harding's drug dealing, the court probably would have rejected the questions outlined above. Drug dealing is illegal, but it does not suggest a character for untruthfulness. Most courts have barred questions about drug dealing under Rule 608(b)(1), just as they preclude questions about other illegal acts that lack an element of deceit.

---

7   For those who aren't current on drug jargon, "square grouper" is a slang term for bales of marijuana. The phrase reputedly originates from members of the U.S. Coast Guard in Southern Florida making communications like "Base we've got some square groupers floating outside of Miami harbor." Urban Dictionary, Square Grouper (Nov. 6, 2004), www.urbandictionary.com/define.php?term=square+grouper.

8   United States v. Crutchfield, 26 F.3d 1098, 1101–02 (11th Cir. 1994).

3. Judicial Discretion. Even when a cross-examiner demonstrates a good faith belief in conduct bearing on a witness's untruthful character, the trial judge has substantial discretion to preclude inquiry into that behavior. **Rule 403** authorizes judges to exclude evidence when its unfair prejudice substantially outweighs its probative value, and **Rule 611** allows the court to "exercise reasonable control over the mode . . . of examining witnesses . . . to . . . protect witnesses from harassment or undue embarrassment." **Rule 608(b)** confirms these protections by providing that the court "may" allow cross-examination about specific instances of a witness's conduct. Here is one case in which a trial judge exercised that discretion to preclude questioning:

Example: Stephanie Vincent, a midshipman at the Kings Point Merchant Marine Academy, accused fellow midshipman Francis Crowley of sexual assault. The government prosecuted Crowley on several counts related to this charge. At trial, Crowley attempted to cross-examine Vincent on other complaints that she had filed against fellow students at the Academy. Crowley's attorney planned to ask Vincent whether she had "lied about what happened" in these complaints or "falsely accused" the other students.

Analysis: After hearing Crowley's offer of proof (in which he cross-examined Vincent outside the jury's presence) and reviewing Vincent's student file, the trial judge refused to allow this cross-examination. He concluded that the questioning would be unfairly prejudicial, would elicit little of value since Vincent responded "no" to all of Crowley's incriminating questions, and would sidetrack the trial. He also noted that Vincent's student file contained no evidence that her prior claims were false. School officials reached "equivocal" conclusions on those claims, giving Crowley a good faith belief sufficient to support cross-examination, but on balance the record persuaded the judge to preclude the cross-examination.

The jury convicted Crowley and he appealed, claiming error in this ruling. The court of appeals judges noted that they "might have taken a different course in the position of the trial judge," but upheld the judge's decision as falling within his discretion.[9]

---

9   United States v. Crowley, 318 F.3d 401, 416–18 (2d Cir. 2003).

The court's decision in *Crowley* demonstrates the latitude that trial judges have to prevent cross-examination about specific acts under Rule 608(b)(1). The conviction in *Crowley* turned on whether the jury believed defendant Crowley or his alleged victim, Vincent. Vincent's credibility, therefore, was critically important. There was at least some evidence, moreover, that she had made false accusations in the past. The court of appeals nonetheless held that it was within the trial judge's discretion to preclude the cross-examination proposed by Crowley's counsel. Another trial judge might have exercised his discretion differently; the availability of cross-examination under 608(b)(1) turns on the views of the judge, the facts of the case, and the persuasiveness of counsel.

4. Extrinsic Evidence. Rule 608(b)(1) lifts the general bar on character evidence by permitting attorneys to cross-examine witnesses about acts that demonstrate a character for untruthfulness. The rule, however, prohibits extrinsic evidence on these matters. The cross-examiner, in other words, must accept whatever answer the witness gives. The opposing party cannot pursue the matter by introducing additional evidence to establish the witness's untruthful acts.

In the *Crowley* case, for example, suppose that the judge had allowed Crowley's attorney to cross-examine Vincent about her previous complaints against other students. The defense attorney had a good faith basis for asking these questions, they were relevant to her character for trustworthiness, and Rule 608(b)(1) allows the attorney to question the witness herself about incidents of untruthfulness.

Crowley's offer of proof suggested that the cross-examination would have gone like this:

> **Q:** Ms. Vincent, do you know a student named Theresa James?
>
> **A:** Yes.
>
> **Q:** And did you ever file a complaint with school authorities about Ms. James?
>
> **A:** Yes, I did.
>
> **Q:** That complaint involved Ms. James's alleged cheating on an exam?
>
> **A:** Yes.

> **Q:** Weren't your allegations against Ms. James proved false?
>
> **A:** No, they were not.
>
> **Q:** Did you lie to anyone about any aspect of what Ms. James did?
>
> **A:** No, certainly not.

At this point, the defense would probably want to prove Vincent's false claims with extrinsic evidence. For example, he would probably want to call Theresa James to testify about the complaint that Vincent filed against her. Or perhaps he might want to introduce school records related to the complaint or call an authority from the school to discuss it. Rule 608(b), however, would prevent the attorney from doing any of these things. Any such proof would be extrinsic evidence about a specific incident relating to Vincent's character for truthfulness.

Rule 608(b)'s bar against extrinsic evidence seems harsh when applied to a witness whose word will put a defendant in jail, but the rule prevents trials from detouring too far into unrelated controversies. The jury in the *Crowley* trial had to decide whether it believed Vincent's testimony about Crowley. The best way to assess Vincent's credibility on that issue was to listen to her responses on direct and cross-examination, to view her demeanor, and to compare her story with other evidence offered in the case.

Some information about Vincent's character for truthfulness might provide context for assessing her credibility, but too much detail would simply embroil the jury in deciding other disputes. If the jury became too deeply involved in questions of whether Theresa James really cheated on the exam, whether Vincent lied in making that allegation, or whether school authorities rejected Vincent's complaint because they were trying to cover up rampant cheating in their academy, the jurors would lose sight of Crowley's case.

The potentially explosive nature of character evidence provides an additional justification for the extrinsic evidence ban in this context. Remember that Rule 404(a)(1) generally prohibits the use of evidence to suggest that a person committed a particular act simply because that would be consistent with her character. Rule 608(b)(1) establishes an exception to that rule for testing the truthful character of witnesses. But the underlying policy of the bar on character evidence is sound: People have some tendency to act according to "character," but they are also unpredictable. Trials should not turn on how parties generally behave, but on how they acted on a particular occasion. Even if Vincent did lie about James, she might be telling the truth about Crowley. We want to focus the jury on the latter incident, not on the overall "character," truthfulness, or deservingness of Vincent.

5. Rule 608(b)(1) and Other Rules. The cross-examination of witnesses on incidents related to their truthful character rests at the intersection of several important evidentiary doctrines. It is worth pausing for a moment to consider how this rule fits with other rules we will study in upcoming chapters. In the next chapter, we will explore **Rule 609**, which establishes one very important exception to the extrinsic evidence rule: Under certain circumstances, parties may introduce extrinsic evidence of a witness's prior criminal convictions. This rule plays a critical role in impeaching some witnesses.

After probing Rule 609, we will return in Chapter 21 to **Rule 608** to explore another method of establishing a witness's untruthful character: through reputation or opinion testimony. In that chapter, we will see that Crowley was able to use reputation testimony as an alternative way of suggesting Vincent's untruthful character. In Chapter 22 we'll examine the special rules that govern cross-examination of witnesses who offer opinion or reputation evidence about character. And finally, in Chapter 23 we'll look at **Rule 610**, which prohibits parties from using a witness's religious beliefs to attack the witness's credibility. That will complete our discussion of impeaching witnesses, and we'll move on to other uses of character evidence in trials.

For a further explanation of the concepts discussed in this chapter, click here to see the video "Impeaching with Prior Dishonest Actions" or go to the Videos module from the eBook on your eProducts bookshelf.

Quick Summary

Rule 608(b)(1) allows parties to suggest a witness's untruthful character by cross-examining the witness on specific acts related to untruthfulness. Parties must have a good faith belief to support their questions and may only ask about matters related to truthfulness or untruthfulness. Judges exercise considerable discretion in controlling this type of cross-examination. Parties, moreover, must accept the witness's response to questions on cross-examination; they may not introduce extrinsic evidence to prove that the witness committed particular acts showing untruthfulness. These rules prevent trials from getting bogged down in tangential issues and further the underlying policies restricting the use of character evidence.

20

Using Criminal Convictions to Impeach Witnesses

Key Concepts

- **Rule 609:** Evidence of a Witness's Prior Criminal Convictions Is Admissible
- Limited Purpose: To Attack Truthfulness
- Special Treatment of Criminal Defendant
- Crimes Involving Dishonesty
- Time Limits
- Other Limits

A. Introduction and Policy. Under **Rule 608(b)**, parties may cross-examine witnesses about incidents that suggest an untruthful character. But as we learned in the last chapter, Rule 608(b) prohibits the cross-examiner from introducing extrinsic evidence of the conduct if the witness denies the untruthful conduct.

Rule 609 establishes a very important exception to the rule against extrinsic evidence: Under the circumstances described in Rule 609, parties **may** introduce evidence of a witness's prior criminal convictions.

The admissibility of criminal convictions to impeach a witness's character for truthfulness has deep roots in the law of evidence. At one time, courts prevented convicted felons from offering any testimony in court; the law declared them incompetent to testify. Modern evidentiary codes like the Federal Rules of Evidence no longer take that view; convicted felons, like almost everyone else, are competent to appear as witnesses. But the Federal Rules retain the assumption that a witness's criminal record is **relevant** to his truthfulness. The rules assume, as the common law did, that a witness who has been convicted of a crime is more likely to lie in court than a witness who has never been convicted.

Counterbalancing this assumption, however, Rule 609 recognizes that admission of a witness's criminal record can unfairly prejudice a party under some circumstances. Jurors may place more weight than they should on a witness's prior criminal conduct. The eyewitness to a murder might have been convicted of drunk driving several years before. How much weight should the jurors attach to that drunk driving conviction? Should the prosecution's case suffer because of the misfortune that the only eyewitness has a criminal record?

The risk of unfair prejudice is even higher when the impeached witness is a party to the lawsuit. The jurors, after learning of the conviction, may do more than simply discount the party-witness's testimony; they may decide that the convicted party is a "bad person" who doesn't deserve to prevail in court. But that type of reasoning contradicts the principles of our justice system. A government "of laws" is one in which even convicted felons may recover damages if they are injured by a reckless driver, a careless doctor, or a discriminatory employer. A party's character, especially as reflected by a criminal conviction for which they have already paid a penalty, should not determine his success or failure in unrelated lawsuits.

The shadow cast by evidence of prior criminal convictions, finally, is most worrisome when the prosecution uses those convictions to impeach a criminal defendant who testifies in his own defense. If jurors learn that the defendant was convicted of a previous crime, they are more likely to believe that the defendant committed the current offense as well. That reasoning undermines the presumption of innocence, as well as the judicial system's commitment to punishing defendants for particular bad acts rather than for a history of being a bad person.

Rule 609 attempts to address these concerns by creating a detailed scheme for when parties may use evidence of prior criminal convictions to attack the truthfulness of witnesses. As we'll see, the rule balances the competing policy concerns by drawing a series of distinctions based on the nature of the prior crime, when the crime was committed, and the witness's role in the trial.

B. The Rules. Rule 608(b) explicitly acknowledges that **Rule 609** creates an exception to the extrinsic evidence rule:

> ## RULE 608. A Witness's Character for Truthfulness or Untruthfulness
>
> **(b) Specific Instances of Conduct.** <u>Except for a criminal conviction under Rule 609</u>, extrinsic evidence is not admissible to prove specific instances of a witness's conduct in order to attack or support the witness's character for truthfulness. . . .

Rule 609 then elaborates that exception. This rule is a lengthy one because it attempts to balance the competing concerns described in the introductory section. Let's look at the rule section by section.

1. Opening Provision. Rule 609 begins by setting a very important limit on the rule's scope:

> ## RULE 609. Impeachment by Evidence of a Criminal Conviction
>
> **(a) In General.** The following rules <u>apply to attacking a witness's character for truthfulness</u> by evidence of a criminal conviction:

Rule 609, in other words, applies only when a party uses a criminal conviction for a particular purpose: to suggest that a witness has an untruthful character. If a party attempts to introduce a criminal conviction for a different reason, the rule does not apply. A prior conviction, for example, is an element of some crimes.[1] If the government charges a defendant with violating one of those laws, it can prove the prior conviction without worrying about Rule 609. We will consider these and other uses of prior convictions when we address **Rule 404** beginning in Chapter 25.

When a party does rely on Rule 609 to introduce evidence of a prior conviction, the jury may consider that conviction **only** to assess the witness's character for

---

1   One frequently charged federal statute prohibits convicted felons from possessing guns. This was one of the crimes charged in the *Old Chief* case, discussed in Chapters 6 and 7.

truthfulness. If the witness is also a party in the case, the jury should not use the conviction as evidence of guilt or liability. In this sense, Rule 609 parallels other rules we have studied, which allow introduction of evidence for one purpose but not others. But it can be particularly difficult for a juror to distinguish truthfulness and liability, as required by Rule 609, when a party is impeached with a prior conviction. We will consider this practical difficulty further in the Courtroom section below.

2. Three Rules for Three Categories. Rule 609 continues by articulating three different rules for specific categories of witnesses and prior convictions:

a. The first rule governs prior **felony convictions** used to impeach any witness **other than the defendant in a criminal case**.

b. The second applies to prior **felony convictions** used to impeach a witness who **is the defendant in a criminal case**.

c. The third addresses prior convictions for any crime involving a **dishonest act or false statement**, regardless of the witness's role or the crime's felony status.

Let's look more closely at each of these categories and the rules that govern them.

a. Felony Convictions/Any Witness Except a Criminal Defendant. Rule 609 first addresses the use of prior felony convictions, defined as crimes that are "punishable by death or by imprisonment for more than one year."[2] Some felonies, like embezzlement and fraud, involve a type of illegal conduct that is quite similar to lying on the stand. Others, like assault, murder, and drug use, are less analogous to lying under oath. The drafters of Rule 609 believed that commission of any felony was serious enough to affect a witness's courtroom credibility; they wanted parties to be able to introduce these convictions to impeach an opponent's witness. On the other hand, the drafters recognized that evidence of prior felony convictions could be very damaging to an accused criminal defendant. They distinguished, therefore, between criminal defendants and other witnesses in allowing the use of prior felony convictions. For all witnesses **other than** a criminal defendant, the rule provides:

---

2   Rule 609 does not use the word "felony," but lawyers use that word as a shorthand for crimes "punishable by death or by imprisonment for more than one year." The specific definition rather than the name "felony" controls when applying Rule 609.

RULE 609. Impeachment by Evidence of a Criminal Conviction

(a) In General. The following rules apply to attacking a witness's character for truthfulness by evidence of a criminal conviction:

(1) for a crime that, in the convicting jurisdiction, was <u>punishable by death or by imprisonment for more than one year</u>, the evidence:

(A) <u>must be admitted</u>, subject to <u>Rule 403</u>,

- in a <u>civil case</u> or
- in a <u>criminal case</u> in which the witness is <u>not a defendant</u>;

. . . .

Prior felony convictions, in other words, are generally admissible to impeach witnesses other than criminal defendants. The judge, however, retains the usual discretion under **Rule 403** to exclude a conviction if a party persuades the judge that the conviction's unfair prejudice will substantially outweigh its probative value.[3]

b. Felony Convictions/Criminal Defendant. For criminal defendants who appear as witnesses, the Advisory Committee and Congress crafted a slightly different rule. This rule recognizes the risk, discussed above, that a jury will improperly use evidence of a criminal defendant's prior convictions to conclude that the defendant must also be guilty of the charged crime. To reduce that risk, this part of Rule 609 makes it harder to introduce evidence of a criminal defendant's prior felony conviction than to introduce the same evidence against other witnesses:

---

3   Before 1990, some courts ruled that judges could not apply Rule 403's balancing test to the proposed use of felony convictions to impeach witnesses in civil cases. A 1990 amendment to Rule 609(a)(1) introduced this explicit reference to Rule 403, superseding those cases. Don't be misled by any of those older decisions.

RULE 609. Impeachment by Evidence of a Criminal Conviction

(a) In General. The following rules apply to attacking a witness's character for truthfulness by evidence of a criminal conviction:

(1) for a crime that, in the convicting jurisdiction, was <u>punishable by death or by imprisonment for more than one year</u>, the evidence: . . .

(B) <u>must be admitted</u> in a <u>criminal case</u> in which the witness is a <u>defendant</u>, if the <u>probative value of the evidence outweighs its prejudicial effect to that defendant</u> . . . .

Prior felony convictions, in other words, are admissible against a criminal defendant who takes the stand only if the judge makes a distinctive finding that probative value outweighs prejudicial effect. This special Rule 609(a)(1)(B) standard differs from Rule 403's more general test in three ways:

First, the standard weighs the prejudicial effect of the prior conviction only on "that defendant," not on any other person. A testifying defendant cannot tip the prejudice scale by counting harms to codefendants as well as himself; Rule 609(a)(1)(B) considers only prejudice against the testifying defendant. In this sense, Rule 609(a)(1)(B) is narrower than Rule 403, which considers unfair prejudice to any person.

On the other hand, Rule 609(a)(1)(B) sets a lower threshold for excluding evidence than Rule 403 does. The language of 609(a)(1)(B) bars evidence of a prior conviction whenever prejudicial effect equals or exceeds probative value—not only when prejudice substantially exceeds that value. Rule 609(a)(1)(B), in other words, tilts its balance toward exclusion, while Rule 403 favors admission. The following table illustrates this **second** difference between the two standards:

When Prejudicial Effect . . .	Rule 403	Rule 609(a)(1)(B)
Is less than probative value	Admits the evidence	Admits the evidence
Equals probative value	Admits the evidence	**Excludes** the evidence
Somewhat outweighs probative value	Admits the evidence	**Excludes** the evidence
Substantially outweighs probative value	**Excludes** the evidence	**Excludes** the evidence

Finally, Rule 609(a)(1)(B) places the burden on the prosecutor to demonstrate that probative value outweighs prejudicial effect so that evidence of a prior conviction should be admitted.[4] Rule 403, in contrast, puts the burden on the party opposing admission to prove that prejudicial effect substantially outweighs probative value.

We will consider some of these issues further in the Courtroom section below. Meanwhile, let's examine the final category of conviction/witness covered by Rule 609.

c. Crime Involving a Dishonest Act or False Statement/Any Witness. Conviction of a crime involving a dishonest act or false statement is highly probative of a witness's character for truthfulness. For that reason, Rule 609 allows litigants to use **any** conviction for a crime of dishonesty or false statement, no matter what the sentence, to impeach **any** witness's character for truthfulness:

---

4   Technically, Rule 609(a)(1)(B) places this burden on any party attempting to impeach a criminal defendant with evidence of a prior conviction. That party almost always is the prosecutor, although a codefendant might also attempt to impeach an accused with evidence of a conviction. See, e.g., United States v. Milloway, No. 99–4377, 2000 WL 14220 (4th Cir. Jan. 10, 2000). In that situation, the codefendant would bear the same burden.

RULE 609. Impeachment by Evidence of a Criminal Conviction

(a) **In General.** The following rules apply to attacking a witness's character for truthfulness by evidence of a criminal conviction: . . . .

    (2) for any crime regardless of the punishment, the evidence <u>must be admitted</u> if the court can readily determine that establishing the elements of the crime required proving—or the witness's admitting—<u>a dishonest act or false statement</u>.

Subsection (a)(2) is notable because it does not include any balancing test or reference to Rule 403. Congress discussed Rule 609 at length and decided that a balancing test was inappropriate for evidence of these prior convictions. According to the Conference Report on the final version of the rule:

> The admission of prior convictions involving dishonesty and false statement is not within the discretion of the Court. Such convictions are peculiarly probative of credibility and, under this rule, are always to be admitted.[5]

Courts have consistently enforced this interpretation of Rule 609(a)(2), holding that trial judges have no discretion (even under Rule 403) to exclude prior convictions for dishonesty or false statement when they are offered to impeach a witness.[6]

Because prior convictions for crimes of dishonesty or false statement are automatically admitted for impeachment under Rule 609(a)(2), it is particularly important to distinguish those crimes from other crimes, which are subject to the more stringent requirements of 609(a)(1). We'll look more closely at how judges differentiate these two categories in the Courtroom section. First, let's look at a few concluding provisions of Rule 609.

---

5   H.R. Rep. No. 93–1597 (1974) (Conf. Rep.), reprinted in 1974 U.S.C.C.A.N. 7098, 7103.

6   See, e.g., United States v. Tracy, 36 F.3d 187, 192 (1st Cir. 1994); United States v. Morrow, 923 F.2d 427, 431 (6th Cir. 1991).

3. Time Limits. When weighing prejudice and probative value under Rule 403 or 609(a)(1)(B), a judge almost certainly would consider the length of time that has elapsed since the prior conviction. An older conviction is less probative of a witness's current truthfulness than a recent one. Section (b) of Rule 609 strengthens this tendency by imposing special requirements for admission of convictions that are more than ten years old:

RULE 609. Impeachment by Evidence of a Criminal Conviction

(b) Limit on Using the Evidence After 10 Years. This subdivision (b) applies if <u>more than 10 years</u> have passed since the witness's conviction or release from confinement for it, whichever is later. Evidence of the conviction is admissible only if:

    (1) its probative value, supported by <u>specific facts and circumstances, substantially outweighs</u> its prejudicial effect; and

    (2) the proponent gives an adverse party <u>reasonable written notice</u> of the intent to use it so that the party has a fair opportunity to contest its use.

This provision imposes three special barriers to using convictions that are more than ten years old:

(1) The party seeking to use the conviction must give the adverse party reasonable written notice.

(2) The judge must find specific facts and circumstances supporting the conviction's probative value.

(3) The judge must determine that the probative value of the conviction "substantially outweighs its prejudicial effect."

The last hurdle is the **reverse** of the one used under Rule 403, which admits evidence unless prejudicial effect substantially outweighs probative value. We can amend our previous chart to illustrate this difference:

When Prejudicial Effect . . .	Rule 403	Rule 609(a)(1)(B) [for conviction less than ten years old]	Rule 609(b) [any conviction more than ten years old]
Is substantially less than probative value	Admits the evidence	Admits the evidence	Admits the evidence
Is somewhat less than probative value	Admits the evidence	Admits the evidence	**Excludes** the evidence
Equals probative value	Admits the evidence	**Excludes** the evidence	**Excludes** the evidence
Somewhat outweighs probative value	Admits the evidence	**Excludes** the evidence	**Excludes** the evidence
Substantially outweighs probative value	**Excludes** the evidence	**Excludes** the evidence	**Excludes** the evidence

Rule 609(b), in other words, adopts a particularly tough standard for admitting evidence of convictions that are more than ten years old. It is even harder to satisfy this standard than to satisfy the special balancing test established for criminal defendants under Rule 609(a)(1)(B).

4. Pardons, Annulments, and Certificates of Rehabilitation. Section (c) of Rule 609 deals with convictions that have been pardoned, annulled, or subject to a certificate of rehabilitation.[7] In most cases, a conviction that has been subject to one of these procedures cannot be used for impeachment under Rule 609. The only exception (allowing such a conviction to be used under the rule) is when the witness has since committed another felony and the original conviction was pardoned for reasons other than innocence:

---

7   A certificate of rehabilitation is a document restoring some of a convicted offender's rights and privileges of citizenship. States vary widely in whether they offer these certificates and, if they do, the conditions under which they are available. Certificates usually are obtained from a court or parole board.

RULE 609. Impeachment by Evidence of a Criminal Conviction

(c) Effect of a Pardon, Annulment, or Certificate of Rehabilitation. Evidence of a conviction is not admissible if:

(1) the conviction has been the subject of a <u>pardon, annulment, certificate of rehabilitation</u>, or other equivalent procedure based on a finding that the person has been rehabilitated, and the person has <u>not been convicted of a later crime punishable by death or by imprisonment for more than one year</u>; or

(2) the conviction has been the subject of a pardon, annulment, or other equivalent procedure <u>based on a finding of innocence</u>.

It is easier to understand the operation of this portion of Rule 609 through a diagram:

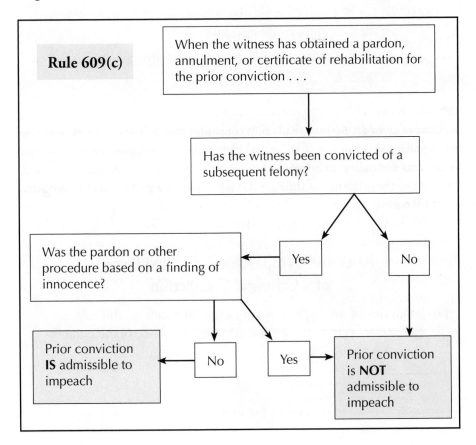

5. Juvenile Adjudications. Section (d) of Rule 609 addresses juvenile adjudications. These convictions are **never** admissible against the accused in a criminal case. Most of the time, they are not admissible to impeach the character of any other witness; the law promotes the rehabilitation of juvenile offenders by limiting disclosure of their convictions. But Rule 609(d) recognizes one limited exception. Evidence of juvenile convictions is admissible in criminal cases when offered to impeach a witness other than the accused and when the evidence is necessary to fairly determine the defendant's guilt:

RULE 609. Impeachment by Evidence of a Criminal Conviction

(d) Juvenile Adjudications. Evidence of a juvenile adjudication is admissible under this rule <u>only if</u>:

   (1) it is offered in a <u>criminal case</u>;

   (2) the adjudication was of a <u>witness other than the defendant</u>;

   (3) an adult's conviction for that offense would be admissible to attack the adult's credibility; and

   (4) admitting the evidence is <u>necessary to fairly determine guilt or innocence</u>.

6. Pendency of an Appeal. Rule 609 concludes (finally!) with a brief provision noting that the pendency of an appeal from a prior conviction does not bar the use of that conviction to impeach the character of a witness. On the other hand, evidence of the pendency of the appeal is admissible if a party wishes to note that fact to the jury.

RULE 609. Impeachment by Evidence of a Criminal Conviction

(e) Pendency of an Appeal. A conviction that satisfies this rule is admissible even if an appeal is pending. Evidence of the pendency is also admissible.

C. In the Courtroom. Rule 609 is a lengthy rule, but it is an important one. The rule plays a key role in criminal cases because many criminal defendants and witnesses at criminal trials have prior convictions. As we'll see when we study **Rule 404**, starting in Chapter 25, the Federal Rules severely restrict the introduction of an opposing party's prior convictions to prove guilt or liability. If a criminal defendant does not take the stand, therefore, the prosecutor will probably not be able to introduce evidence of the defendant's prior convictions. But if the defendant does testify, then Rule 609 gives the prosecutor an avenue for introducing evidence of the defendant's convictions. The judge will instruct the jury to use the convictions only to assess the defendant's truthfulness, not to decide whether he is guilty of the charged crime, but jurors may have difficulty following that instruction. Both prosecutors and defendants know that prior convictions can sway a jury's decision.

Rule 609 thus plays a substantial role in determining whether a criminal defendant will testify at trial. Even if a defendant is innocent and has useful testimony to offer, the revelation of prior convictions is a significant deterrent to testifying. Many defense attorneys fear that evidence of those convictions will overshadow any exonerating testimony that the defendant can offer. Empirical research shows that this dynamic sometimes contributes to the wrongful conviction of innocent defendants.[8]

Rule 609 also affects the strength of the prosecutor's case in a criminal trial. In criminal investigations, the government often relies upon informers, codefendants who plead guilty, and other witnesses who have themselves faced criminal charges. When deciding whether to charge a defendant or what type of plea bargain to propose, the prosecution must consider the credibility of its own witnesses in court. The defense almost certainly will try to impeach any prosecution witnesses with evidence of prior convictions, reducing their credibility before the jury.

Rule 609 also applies in civil cases, although fewer civil litigants and their witnesses have criminal records. For those who do, however, Rule 609 may play a key role in strategic decisions about which individuals to call as witnesses.

Given its complexity and its importance in all types of litigation, Rule 609 has generated considerable controversy over some of its provisions. In this section, we explore the most important of those disputes.

---

8   John H. Blume, The Dilemma of the Criminal Defendant with a Prior Record—Lessons from the Wrongfully Convicted, 5 J. Empirical Legal Stud. 477 (2008).

1. Defining Felonies. Rule 609(a)(1) defines felonies as crimes "**punishable** by death or by imprisonment for more than one year." The witness need not **receive** such a sentence for impeachment to occur.

> **Example:** The government charged Clyde Hall with distribution of heroin. Hall testified at trial, and the prosecutor introduced evidence under Rule 609(a)(1) of two previous convictions for heroin distribution and possession. Hall received suspended sentences for both of those prior convictions.

> **Analysis:** Despite the suspended sentences, both convictions qualified for impeachment under Rule 609(a)(1). The crimes were punishable by imprisonment of more than a year, even though Hall did not receive sentences of that nature. The district judge allowed the government to use the convictions for impeachment, and the court of appeals affirmed.[9]

2. Special Balancing Test for Criminal Defendant. Rule 609(a)(1)(B) creates a special balancing test, more stringent than the one established by Rule 403, to determine when prior felony convictions are admissible to impeach a criminal defendant who takes the stand. Several circuits have articulated five factors that may guide a district judge's discretion in resolving the 609(a)(1)(B) balancing test. Some of these factors affect the probative value of the prior conviction, others relate to its prejudicial impact:

- **Impeachment Value of the Former Crime.** A crime that relates to truth telling has more probative value than one that does not.

- **Timing of the Prior Conviction and Subsequent Criminality.** Convictions that occurred long ago have less probative value, unless they are part of a pattern of criminality.

- **Similarity Between the Prior Crime and the Charged One.** When the prior crime is similar to the charged one, the likelihood of prejudice is particularly high, because the jury may use the prior conviction not just to judge credibility but to reason that the defendant has a tendency to commit this type of crime.

---

9   United States v. Hall, 588 F.2d 613, 615 (8th Cir. 1978).

- **Importance of the Defendant's Testimony.** The risk that a defendant will forego testifying should always count as an element of prejudice. In some cases, that testimony may be particularly important to help the defendant present his case.

- **Centrality of Credibility.** If guilt turns on a swearing match between the defendant and the prosecution's witnesses, the prosecutor's interest in impeaching the defendant is higher and the jury may have greater need of that testimony.[10]

Courts acknowledge these factors, but stress that they are merely guidelines.[11] District judges have wide discretion to weigh factors under Rule 609(a)(1)(B) and appellate courts rarely reverse those decisions. As with many other evidentiary disputes, well-reasoned arguments by a skillful trial counsel may persuade the judge.

Rule 609 has come under heavy criticism from scholars, many of whom reject its underlying premise that the fact of a prior conviction provides the jury with useful evidence about the witness. The critics also argue that some jurors misunderstand the judge's limiting instruction and use the prior convictions—at least unconsciously—as evidence that the defendant has a criminal disposition. The critics, finally, point out that admitting prior convictions disproportionately affects nonwhite and low-income defendants. Racial profiling, heightened neighborhood surveillance, and implicit bias subject those defendants to more criminal prosecutions than other citizens. Low-income defendants who cannot pay bail are often pressured into pleading guilty rather than contest the charges against them. Once these defendants have a prior conviction from these pleas, Rule 609 makes future convictions easier to obtain—perpetuating a cycle of disadvantage.[12]

For these and other reasons, an increasing number of scholars have urged courts and legislatures to restrict the use of prior convictions to impeach criminal defendants. The rule, however, remains firmly embedded in current practice.

---

10   See, e.g., United States v. Hernandez, 106 F.3d 737, 739–40 (7th Cir. 1997).

11   Id.

12   See, e.g., Michelle Alexander, The New Jim Crow: Mass Incarceration in the Age of Colorblindness (2010); Anna Roberts, Impeachment by Unreliable Conviction, 55 BC L Rev. 563 (2014).

3. Crimes Involving a Dishonest Act or False Statement. Rule 609(a)(2) admits prior convictions for crimes of dishonesty or false statement, even if they were misdemeanors and without any consideration of undue prejudice. Students (and some courts) sometimes have trouble with this provision: after all, many crimes include some element of deceit. Is burglary a crime that involves a dishonest act? What about murdering a victim by offering her a "refreshing glass of beer" that is laced with cyanide? All law breaking, for that matter, is dishonest in the broadest sense of that word. Which crimes involve the narrower type of dishonesty required by Rule 609(a)(2)?

Rule 609(a)(2) answers this question with a strict test: a prior conviction is admissible under this subsection only if "the court can readily determine that establishing the elements of the crime required proving—or the witness's admitting—a dishonest act or false statement." This test focuses on the **elements** of the prior crime. If the statutory language requires proof of a dishonest act or false statement, then the crime qualifies as one of "dishonesty." A relatively small number of crimes (such as perjury, fraud, and embezzlement) meet this requirement.

The rule expands its reach slightly to include prior convictions in which the judge can "readily determine" that the prosecution used a dishonest act or false statement to satisfy a more general element. That information may come from the indictment, a statement of admitted facts, or a companion crime; the judge will not delve into the history of the prior conviction to determine whether it included some dishonest act.

> **Example:** The government charged Kevin Rankin with illegal possession of a handgun. The prosecutor filed a motion in limine, seeking permission to impeach Rankin, if he took the stand, with his prior convictions for making a false statement to a federal agency and endeavoring to obstruct justice.

Analysis: The district judge granted the prosecutor's motion, finding that both convictions were for crimes of dishonesty or false statement. Making a false statement to a federal agency is a crime that, on its face, requires proof of a defendant's false statement. And although defendants may obstruct justice through both deceitful and nondeceitful means, it was clear from the companion charge that Rankin's conviction was for making false statements in an affidavit submitted under oath to a judge. Under these circumstances, the court could "readily determine" that a dishonest act or false statement was an element of Rankin's obstruction of justice.[13]

Courts have adhered to Rule 609's strict definition of crimes involving dishonesty. Ordinary theft does not qualify; neither does poisoning. When in doubt, check precedent for a particular crime.

4. Time Limits. Section (b) of Rule 609 establishes a presumption against allowing impeachment with crimes that are more than ten years old. This provision is especially important with respect to convictions for crimes of dishonesty or false statement; remember that judges otherwise lack any discretion to exclude evidence of those convictions when offered for impeachment.

Section (b) ties its ten-year limit to the date of the witness's "conviction" **or** "release from confinement for" that conviction, **whichever is later**. Notice that the inclusion of jail time significantly extends the period for which convictions escape the 609(b) hurdle: An attorney could impeach a witness who served a ten-year jail term with a conviction that occurred as much as twenty years earlier, without having to meet 609(b)'s stringent standard.[14] Violations of probation that result in re-incarceration can extend the period even further:

Example: Linwood Gray threatened his lawyer with bodily harm if he did not refund the fees Gray had paid. The government charged Gray with extortion, and the case came to trial in 2004. Gray took the stand and the prosecutor impeached him under Rule 609(a) with a 1977 bank robbery conviction. Gray objected to use of this conviction as beyond the ten-year limit established by Rule 609(b).

Analysis: Gray had been paroled from prison on the robbery charge in 1982, but his parole was revoked in 1989 and he returned to prison to serve the remainder of his term. He was released again in 1995. His release from confinement thus occurred less than ten years before he took the stand in 2004. The district judge did not have to apply Rule 609(b)'s presumption against

---

13   United States v. Rankin, Criminal No. 05–615, 2007 WL 1181022 (E.D. Pa. Apr. 18, 2007).

14   For example, if a defendant was convicted in 2000 and remained in jail until 2010, that conviction would still be admissible without consideration of Rule 609(b)'s special balancing test until 2020—ten years after the release from jail.

admissibility. Instead, the conviction was admissible under the more lenient standards of Rule 609(a).[15]

When a conviction does exceed Rule 609(b)'s ten-year limit, judges must apply that rule's stringent balancing test to decide whether to admit evidence of the outdated conviction. The Senate Judiciary Committee, which drafted 609(b)'s balancing test, suggested that this test was so strict that "convictions over 10 years old will be admitted very rarely and only in exceptional circumstances."[16] Implementing that perspective, judges consider older convictions very carefully before deciding to admit them.

In making this determination, they use the same factors we discussed earlier in the chapter for weighing the admissibility of prior felony convictions to impeach an accused under 609(a)(1)(B).[17] The prosecution, however, bears a heavier burden under 609(b) than under 609(a)(1)(B).

Despite this heavy burden, judges sometimes do admit evidence of older convictions. Here is one case in which the trial judge concluded that the probative value of the conviction substantially outweighed its prejudicial effect:

> **Example:** The United States charged Edward Gilbert with conspiring to manipulate the market price of shares in a publicly traded company. Gilbert had previously been convicted of mail fraud, but had been released from prison more than ten years before commencement of the stock manipulation prosecution. Gilbert's attorney asked the judge to rule that, if Gilbert took the stand, evidence of this prior conviction would not be admissible to impeach him.

> **Analysis:** The judge denied Gilbert's request, ruling that the conviction would be admissible. The judge found that (1) if Gilbert testified his credibility would be a "crucial issue"; (2) the impeachment value of a fraud conviction is high; (3) the two crimes were dissimilar enough to reduce Gilbert's preju-

---

15   This example draws upon United States v. Gray, 852 F.2d 136, 139 (4th Cir. 1988), in which an ungrateful defendant did attempt to extort repayment of his lawyer's fee and the court allowed impeachment of the witness with a prior robbery conviction. We have modified the case slightly and extended the time periods for illustration.

16   S. Rep. No. 93–1277 (1974), reprinted in 1974 U.S.C.C.A.N. 7051.

17   See, e.g., United States v. Sloman, 909 F.2d 176, 181 (6th Cir. 1990).

dice; and (4) "the age of the prior conviction and the defendant's subsequent history did not suggest that he had abandoned his earlier ways." The court of appeals upheld this finding as "well within" the trial judge's discretion.[18]

5. Limiting Instructions. Remember that courts admit evidence of prior convictions under Rule 609 for a limited purpose: to suggest that a witness has an untruthful character. The jury should not use the conviction to determine guilt, liability, or any other substantive matter. When a party impeaches another party under Rule 609, the judge gives the jury an instruction explaining this difference. Here is a sample instruction used by district judges in the Sixth Circuit:

1) You have heard that before this trial the defendant was convicted of a crime.

2) This earlier conviction was brought to your attention only as one way of helping you decide how believable his testimony was. You cannot use it for any other purpose. It is not evidence that he is guilty of the crime that he is on trial for now.[19]

Despite this type of instruction, jurors probably find it difficult to restrict their consideration of a party's prior criminal convictions. The parties to any lawsuit, particularly to a criminal prosecution, recognize that evidence of a prior criminal conviction may substantially affect the jury's consideration of the case. Rule 609, therefore, plays a major strategic role in any trial involving parties or other key witnesses who have criminal records.

---

18 United States v. Gilbert, 668 F.2d 94, 97 (2d Cir. 1981).

19 Pattern Criminal Jury Instructions: Sixth Circuit, Instruction No. 7.05A (2013), reprinted in, 1A Kevin F. O'Malley, Jay E. Grenig, & Hon. William C. Lee, Federal Jury Practice & Instructions § 11.12 (6th ed. 2008).

Quick Summary

Rule 609 establishes a complex scheme governing evidence of prior criminal convictions offered to impeach a witness's character for truthfulness. This rule allows introduction of this evidence (a) only against witnesses, and (b) only to impeach character for truthfulness. As reflected in the limiting instruction above, the jury should not use this evidence to decide guilt, innocence, or other substantive issues. Within these overall constraints, Rule 609 establishes a series of rules that vary depending on whether the witness is the defendant in a criminal case, the nature of the prior crime, and the time elapsed since the prior conviction. The rule also includes special provisions for pardons, juvenile offenses, and convictions pending appeal. Rule 609 may substantially affect trial strategy in any case involving a party or key witness with a criminal record; critics have noted the disproportionate impact of this rule on some categories of criminal defendants.

The table on the next page sums up Rule 609, showing which convictions are admissible to impeach witnesses. Note that as you move down the table, it becomes easier to admit evidence of the conviction.

Test Your Understanding

To assess your understanding of the material in this chapter, click here to take a quiz, or go to the Quizzes module from the eBook on your eProducts bookshelf.

Rule 609: Using Convictions to Impeach a Witness

Type of Conviction	Type of Witness	Outcome
Misdemeanor that did not involve dishonest act or false statement	Any	**Automatically EXCLUDE** all of these convictions: No balancing test applies.
Crime pardoned or annulled based on finding of innocence	Any	
Crime for which witness obtained pardon, annulment, or certificate of rehabilitation, without finding of innocence, but has no subsequent felony convictions	Any	
Crime committed as a juvenile	Defendant in Criminal Case	
	Anyone Other than the Defendant in a Criminal Case	Admit in a criminal case IF conviction would be admissible against an adult AND the evidence is necessary to fairly determine guilt or innocence.
Crime for which witness was released from confinement (or convicted, if no confinement) more than ten years ago	Any	Exclude unless probative value substantially outweighs prejudicial effect.
Felony that did not involve dishonest act or false statement	Defendant in Criminal Case	Admit if probative value outweighs prejudicial effect to that defendant.
	Anyone Other than the Defendant in a Criminal Case	Admit unless Rule 403 (unfair prejudice substantially outweighs probative value) dictates exclusion.
Felony or misdemeanor involving a dishonest act or false statement that (a) was committed as adult and (b) for which confinement ended (or conviction occurred), ten years ago or less	Any	**Automatically ADMIT.** No balancing test—not even Rule 403—applies.

21

Reputation or Opinion Evidence
of Untruthful Character

Key Concepts

- **Rule 608(a):** Reputation or Opinion Evidence About a Witness's Character
- Limited to Character for Untruthfulness or Truthfulness
- Evidence of Truthful Character Admissible Only After Character Has Been Attacked

A. Introduction and Policy. As we have seen, the Federal Rules of Evidence allow an attorney to attack an opposing witness's character for truthfulness in order to persuade the jury that the witness and her testimony are not trustworthy. We have already examined **Rule 608(b)**, which allows an attorney to ask the witness questions about specific instances of conduct that demonstrate untruthfulness, and **Rule 609**, which regulates when an attorney can admit evidence of a witness's prior criminal convictions. In this chapter we examine an additional method for suggesting a witness's untruthful character: presenting a separate witness, a "character witness" who testifies that the original witness has an untrustworthy character. We will also examine the opposite strategy: presenting a character witness who opines that the original witness is a truthful person.

Rule 608(a) allows both of these strategies, but with three important caveats. First, the rule only allows general **reputation or opinion** evidence of character, not testimony giving specific instances of conduct related to a witness's truthfulness or deceit. We'll discuss this essential distinction in more detail below. Like the bar against using extrinsic evidence to prove a witness's character for truthfulness or untruthfulness, the focus on reputation or opinion evidence prevents parties from overloading trials with too many extraneous details about witnesses' lives and pastimes.

Second, just as parties may cross-examine witnesses only on acts related to their character for **truthfulness or untruthfulness,** not on other types of acts, character witnesses may only offer reputation or opinion evidence about another witness's character for truthfulness or untruthfulness. Witnesses may not discredit another witness by offering their opinion that the other witness is a glutton or a slut, or by offering testimony that the witness has a reputation for violence or aggression.

Finally, a party may introduce evidence of a witness's **truthful** character only after that character has been attacked. Litigants may not waste courtroom time by routinely bolstering their witnesses' evidence with testaments to the witnesses' truthfulness.

Let's look now at the specific ways in which Rule 608(a) achieves these ends.

B. The Rule. Remember that **Rule 404(a)**, which we examined briefly in Chapter 19, generally prohibits parties from introducing character evidence to suggest that a person acted consistently with his or her character on a particular occasion. That general rule would prevent litigants from offering evidence about a witness's character for veracity in order to argue that, because the witness has a generally untruthful nature, the witness must be lying on the stand.

We've already seen, however, that **Rules 608(b)** and **609** carve exceptions to the prohibition on character evidence contained in Rule 404(a). **Rule 608(a)** establishes yet another exception to that rule—another hole in the evidentiary net—that allows parties to introduce opinion or reputation evidence about a witness's character. Here is the language from Rule 608(a):

> ## RULE 608. A Witness's Character for Truthfulness or Untruthfulness
>
> **(a) Reputation or Opinion Evidence.** A witness's credibility may be attacked or supported by testimony about the <u>witness's reputation</u> for having a <u>character for truthfulness or untruthfulness,</u>
>
> or by testimony in the <u>form of an opinion</u> about that character.
>
> But evidence of <u>truthful character is admissible only after the witness's character for truthfulness has been attacked</u>.

As the underlined language shows, the rule incorporates the three limits identified in the introductory section: the evidence must be in the form of reputation or opinion only; the evidence must relate to the witness's character for truthfulness or untruthfulness; and testimony about a witness's character for truthfulness can only be elicited after his character has been attacked. Let's look now in more detail at those limits and other aspects of the rule in courtroom practice.

C. In the Courtroom. Rule 608(a) allows one witness to offer testimony about another witness's character for truthfulness or untruthfulness. Discussing these interactions can be confusing because of the need to refer to two different witnesses. To simplify matters, many lawyers distinguish between the "fact witness" and the "character witness." Parties present fact witnesses to establish facts related to the underlying legal dispute. They introduce character witnesses to offer evidence about the truthful or untruthful character of a fact witness. We'll use these terms in the discussion that follows to help distinguish the different types of witnesses.

1. Reputation or Opinion Evidence. What does reputation or opinion evidence sound like? Both types of testimony are quite simple. When a character witness offers an **opinion** about a fact witness's character for truthfulness, the attorney will first lay a foundation by showing that the character witness knows the fact witness well enough to have formed an opinion about the fact witness's truthful or untruthful nature. The attorney will then ask the character witness to voice her opinion about the fact witness's character. A typical examination of a character witness (Ms. Ware) with respect to a fact witness (Faris Ford) would proceed like this:

> **Q:** Ms. Ware, are you acquainted with Faris Ford?
>
> **A:** Yes, I am.
>
> **Q:** In what context do you know Mr. Ford?
>
> **A:** He has been my neighbor for more than 10 years.
>
> **Q:** So you have known Mr. Ford for more than 10 years?
>
> **A:** Yes.
>
> **Q:** In that time, have you formed an opinion of Mr. Ford's character for truthfulness or untruthfulness?

A: Yes, I have.

Q: And what is your opinion of Mr. Ford's character for truthfulness or untruthfulness?

A: In my opinion, he is a very untruthful person.

An examination designed to elicit information about a fact witness's **reputation** for truthfulness or untruthfulness is quite similar. The attorney first establishes that the character witness has a basis for knowing the fact witness's reputation. The attorney then will ask the character witness to state that reputation.

In the Crowley case, which we discussed in Chapter 19, the defense was not able to cross-examine the alleged victim, Stephanie Vincent, about specific incidents of conduct that might reveal her untruthful character. The defense, however, was allowed to present a character witness, Shannon Pender, who testified about Vincent's reputation for untruthfulness. Here is a reconstruction of Pender's testimony:

Q: Ms. Pender, you were a student at the Kings Point Merchant Marine Academy?

A: Uh huh, yes I was.

Q: Was Stephanie Vincent enrolled at the Academy during the time you were a student?

A: She sure was.

Q: Did you know Ms. Vincent?

A: Yes, we had several classes together. And everyone at the Academy pretty much knew everyone else. It's a small place.

Q: Did you ever discuss Ms. Vincent's character for truthfulness or untruthfulness with other people at the Academy?

A: Oh, lots of times. It was a pretty big issue there.

Q: With what types of people did you discuss her character?

A: With other students. And also with some of the officers who managed things at the Academy.

> **Q:** Did you discuss Ms. Vincent's character for truthfulness with both male and female students?
>
> **A:** Yes, both men and women.
>
> **Q:** And what was Ms. Vincent's reputation for truthfulness or untruthfulness among students and officers at the Academy?
>
> **A:** She had a reputation for untruthfulness.[1]

As you read Pender's testimony, you may be tempted to ask the logical next question: "Can you give us some specific examples of Vincent's untruthfulness?" A generalized reputation for untruthfulness is a hazy concept; we want specifics to understand what the witness means.

Rule 608, however, prohibits that next question, logical though it seems. Rule 608(a) allows testimony only "about the witness's reputation" or "in the form of an opinion." The rule does not allow parties to ask character witnesses questions on direct examination that focus on specific examples of a fact witness's untruthfulness.

This rule seems counterintuitive; surely specific examples of untruthful behavior are more probative than a general opinion about untruthfulness. The rule, however, attempts to keep trials focused on the underlying controversy that motivated the lawsuit. Parties are allowed to cross-examine fact witnesses about incidents that might reveal untruthfulness, and they may present character witnesses who offer opinion or reputation evidence about the fact witness's truthfulness, but they may not elicit specific details from the character witnesses on direct examination. The details would be juicy, and perhaps informative, but they would distract the jury and consume too much time.

2. Character for Truthfulness and Untruthfulness. When examining a character witness under Rule 608(a), parties must limit their inquiry to the fact witness's character for truthfulness or untruthfulness. This limit parallels the one we examined under Rule 608(b). Character witnesses may offer their opinion about a fact witness's untruthfulness under 608(a), but not other qualities:

---

1   This is a hypothetical rendition of Pender's testimony, based on the information given in the opinion affirming Crowley's conviction. *United States v. Crowley*, 318 F.3d 401, 416 (2d Cir. 2003).

Example: In a homicide prosecution, the government calls Frank Fogel as a key witness. To impeach Fogel, the defense attempts to call Fogel's wife, who is willing to offer her opinion that Fogel is a "Louse, dog, long-nose, dirty bald head, fat slob [and] . . . tightwad." She will also testify that Fogel has a reputation for these qualities in the community.

Analysis: Fogel may suffer from these negative traits, and the community may share his wife's view, but Mrs. Fogel's testimony is not admissible under Rule 608(a). That rule allows only opinion or reputation testimony about a witness's character for truthfulness or untruthfulness. None of the characteristics described by Mrs. Fogel affect Mr. Fogel's truthfulness as a witness.[2]

3. Limited Purpose. Evidence of untruthful character admitted under Rule 608(a), like questions posed on cross-examination under Rule 608(b) or evidence of a criminal conviction admitted under Rule 609, is admissible only to assess the credibility of the witness's courtroom testimony. The evidence is not admissible for other purposes, such as establishing guilt or innocence.

This distinction is most problematic when a criminal defendant takes the stand. Once the defendant testifies, the prosecution can present a character witness to testify about the defendant's untruthful nature. A witness's assertion that the defendant has a "reputation for untruthfulness" properly casts doubt on the veracity of the defendant's testimony. The jury, however, may be tempted to use the evidence for an additional, prohibited purpose, to conclude that the defendant committed the charged crime. The risk is particularly great when the charged crime involves dishonesty.

The trial judge may give the jurors a limiting instruction to help them understand the proper use of character evidence on truthfulness. When the unfair prejudice stemming from this type of character evidence substantially outweighs the probative value of the evidence, moreover, the judge may exclude the evidence under **Rule 403.**

4. When Has Character Been Attacked? Rule 608(a) allows parties to bolster a fact witness's credibility with evidence of a truthful character, but only after the

---

2   These insults, allegedly spoken by a real Mrs. Fogel, appear in Fogel v. Fogel, 54 A.2d 844, 845 n.1 (Pa. Super. Ct. 1947). The testimony, however, was given in the context of a divorce action rather than to impeach Mr. Fogel under Rule 608.

witness's character for truthfulness "has been attacked." If an opponent presents a character witness who testifies about the fact witness's lack of truthful character, then character clearly has been attacked. Likewise, if the opponent conducts a cross-examination of the fact witness and asks questions about specific acts of dishonesty under Rule 608(b), or if the opponent introduces evidence of a conviction under Rule 609, the opponent has attacked the fact witness's character for truthfulness. But are there any other situations in which a fact witness's character for truthfulness has been attacked?

Generally, the answer is no. To understand this distinction, focus on the difference between a witness's **character** for truthfulness and the witness's credibility when testifying about a particular matter. Aggressively cross-examining a witness about her testimony, or pointing out inconsistencies in that testimony, does not attack the witness's general character for truthfulness. This type of cross-examination may cast substantial doubt on the witness's testimony; it may even suggest that she lied on direct examination. But these suggestions relate to the particular case; they do not attack the witness's general character for truthfulness.

Likewise, demonstrating that a witness has an interest in the outcome of a case, or is biased against a particular party, are attacks on the witness's credibility in the context of the case. Once again, they are not general attacks on the witness's character for honesty. Rule 608(a) allows a party to call a positive character witness only when a fact witness's character for truthfulness has been attacked.

Example: The government prosecuted Carl Drury for plotting to procure the murder of his wife. Drury testified in his defense, and the prosecutor cross-examined him, presenting evidence of numerous inconsistencies in his testimony and prior statements. Drury then offered six witnesses who would testify about his truthful character.

Analysis: The district court excluded testimony by the six character witnesses, and the court of appeals affirmed. The prosecutor's cross-examination did not constitute an attack on Drury's character for truthfulness, and no prosecution witness testified that he had an untruthful character. Under those circumstances, Drury could not offer evidence that he had a truthful character.[3]

---

3   United States v. Drury, 396 F.3d 1303, 1314–15 (11th Cir. 2005).

5. Applicable Only to Witnesses. Rule 608(a) only admits evidence related to a witness's character. If an individual does not testify in court, parties cannot rely upon this rule to attack that person's credibility:

> **Example:** Detective Guy Penn and several other police officers conducted narcotics surveillance at the St. Louis airport. Based on an informant's tip, they identified Donald McGauley as a suspect who might be carrying narcotics. A specially trained dog smelled narcotics in McGauley's suitcase, and a search revealed more than 500 grams of cocaine in the bag. The government charged McGauley with possession of cocaine with intent to distribute. The prosecutor did not call Detective Penn at trial, relying instead on testimony from other officers who had participated in the arrest. McGauley attempted to introduce evidence that Penn's reputation for truthfulness was poor; indeed, Penn had resigned from the police force after perjuring himself in two other drug cases.

> **Analysis:** The trial judge properly excluded this testimony. Penn did not testify at trial, so McGauley could not offer evidence impeaching his character for truthfulness.[4]

The McGauley case illustrates the strategic decisions parties make when choosing witnesses. If no other officer had participated in McGauley's arrest, the prosecutor might have been forced to call Detective Penn as a witness. Given a choice among possible witnesses, however, the government picked witnesses who could not be impeached with opinion or reputation evidence about their untruthfulness. Other parties make similar decisions when they have a choice of potential witnesses.

---

4   United States v. McGauley, 786 F.2d 888, 892 (8th Cir. 1986).

Quick Summary

Rule 608(a) allows any party to offer opinion or reputation evidence to attack a fact witness's character for truthfulness. The rule, however, strictly limits both the form of this evidence (a statement of reputation or opinion) and its focus (character for truthfulness rather than other traits). Once a fact witness's character for truthfulness has been attacked, a party may rehabilitate that witness by offering evidence of the witness's character for truthfulness.

22

Cross-Examining the Character Witness

Key Concepts

- **Rule 608(b)(2):** Cross-Examining the Character Witness
- Inquiry Into Specifics
- Good Faith Belief
- Judicial Discretion
- No Extrinsic Evidence

A. Introduction and Policy. The process for impeaching witnesses with evidence of an untruthful character balances the parties' interest in offering that evidence with the judicial system's concern for focused and efficient trials. So far we have seen that a party who wishes to challenge a fact witness's character for truthfulness may do so in any of three ways:

- Cross-examine the witness about specific incidents suggesting a character for untruthfulness under **Rule 608(b)(1)**

- Offer evidence of the witness's criminal convictions under **Rule 609**

- Present a character witness who offers reputation or opinion testimony about the fact witness's character for untruthfulness under **Rule 608(a)**

A character witness offered under Rule 608(a), however, may not give specific examples of the fact witness's untruthful behavior. And apart from introducing evidence of criminal convictions, the party may not offer extrinsic evidence, such as documents or testimony from other witnesses, to show specific instances of a fact witness's untruthfulness. These rules prevent the trial from becoming embroiled in tangential issues about a fact witness's character.

Once a fact witness's character for truthfulness has been attacked, a party may introduce evidence to show the witness's truthful character. That evidence takes three primary forms:

- Explanation of any extenuating circumstances related to specific incidents of untruthfulness raised by the opponent during cross-examination. The party usually elicits these details from the fact witness on redirect examination.

- Explanation of any extenuating circumstances related to prior convictions. Once again, the party usually elicits these details from the fact witness on redirect examination.

- Introduction of reputation or opinion evidence suggesting a character for truthfulness. The party offers this testimony through a rebuttal character witness.

Rule 608(b)(2) throws a final wrinkle into this scheme, one that many students and practitioners find bizarre. This subsection of the rule allows parties to ask character witnesses **on cross-examination** about specific incidents of a fact witness's behavior. Although the party who calls a character witness may not ask the witness questions about specific incidents on direct examination, an opposing party may ask about specifics on cross-examination. This provision rests on longstanding courtroom practice, as well as on the general policy of allowing some discussion of a witness's character for truthfulness without derailing the main focus of the trial.

An attorney who cross-examines a negative character witness, for example, can ask that witness whether she knows about various truthful acts committed by the fact witness. If the character witness has never heard of these truthful acts, she appears not to know the fact witness as well as she claimed during the direct examination. If the character witness has heard of these truthful acts, she has to explain why, in spite of them, she still believes that the fact witness has an untruthful character.

The cross-examiner cannot ask these questions on cross-examination unless she has a good faith basis for believing that the specific acts occurred. And, just as with other specific act evidence covered by Rule 608(b), the cross-examining attorney cannot offer extrinsic evidence of the specific act; she is stuck with the character witness's answer on cross.

B. The Rule. Rule 608(b)(2) contains one of the most obscure statements in the Federal Rules of Evidence. Here is the text of the Rule:

RULE 608. A Witness's Character for Truthfulness or Untruthfulness

(b) Specific Instances of Conduct. Except for a criminal conviction under Rule 609, extrinsic evidence is not admissible to prove <u>specific instances of a witness's conduct</u> in order to attack or support the witness's character for truthfulness. But the court may, <u>on cross-examination</u>, allow them to be inquired into if they are <u>probative of the character for truthfulness or untruthfulness</u> of:

(1) the witness; or

(2) <u>another witness whose character the witness being cross-examined has testified about.</u>

. . . .

An attorney, in other words, may not ask a witness on direct examination about specific instances of conduct. Nor may an attorney ask a character witness on direct examination about the fact witness's specific instances of conduct. However, on cross-examination the opposing counsel can ask the fact witness about his own specific instances of conduct, and on cross-examination she can also ask a character witness about the underlying fact witness's specific instances of conduct. Let's see how this plays out in the courtroom.

C. In the Courtroom.

1. Cross-Examination of the Character Witness. Recall from the last chapter the testimony that Shannon Pender offered about Stephanie Vincent in the Crowley case. Pender concluded her testimony by stating that Vincent "had a reputation for untruthfulness" among the students and officers at the Merchant Marine Academy. The defense attorney, who called Pender, could not ask her about specific incidents buttressing this reputation for untruthfulness; defense counsel had to settle for Pender's general statement.

Under Rule 608(b)(2), however, the prosecution could cross-examine Pender on specifics. If the prosecutor knew of specific instances when Vincent had been truthful, or had a good faith belief about those instances, he could rehabilitate Vincent by asking Pender about those incidents. If a commanding officer had awarded Vincent a commendation for her truthfulness, for example, the prosecutor could ask: "Ms. Pender, are you aware that Ms. Vincent's commanding officer awarded her a commendation for her truthfulness?"

The theory behind these questions is that the cross-examiner is entitled to test the basis of the character witness's opinion or recital of reputation. A character witness who testifies about a fact witness's character should be aware of relevant incidents. Asking about these incidents creates a win–win situation for the cross-examiner. If the witness admits knowing about the incident, the incident casts doubt on the substance of her opinion or reputation testimony. If Pender admitted knowing about the commendation, for example, that would undermine her testimony that Vincent had an untruthful character. Conversely, if the character witness denies knowing about the specific incident, that weakens the foundation supporting her testimony: If Pender denies having heard about Vincent's commendation, how much does she really know about Vincent?

In practice, however, it is hard to effectively cross-examine a character witness who has offered negative testimony about a fact witness's character. Very few people receive specific commendations for their truthfulness, or commit acts (such as returning a wallet full of cash to its rightful owner) that dramatically demonstrate their honest character. Without an incident like this, the cross-examination is likely to fall flat. Even if the character witness admits that the fact witness was truthful on a variety of occasions, that does little to undermine the general assertion that the fact witness is untruthful. Few liars lie all the time. Evidence that a fact witness was occasionally truthful offers a weak rebuttal to testimony that the witness is generally untruthful.

Cross-examination of a character witness can be much more devastating when the witness testifies about the fact witness's **truthful** nature. Imagine, for example, that after Pender testified in the Crowley case, the prosecution called another student—Tom Jencks—to offer his opinion that Vincent was generally truthful. Once Jencks stated that opinion, the defense could cross-examine him about specific instances of Vincent's untruthfulness. Defense counsel could ask Jencks questions like: "Are you aware that other students charged Ms. Vincent with filing false accusations against them?" or "Did you know that Ms. Vincent cheated on an exam?"

This type of cross-examination faces just two limits. First, cross-examiners may only ask questions for which they have a good faith supporting belief. And, second, the trial judge has discretion to exclude questions when they will create unfair prejudice substantially outweighing their probative value. Parties, however, can often find evidence of some untruthful behavior that taints a witness's character; few people lead blameless lives. And judges are much more likely to allow cross-examination about untruthful acts when a character witness is on the stand than when the questioner directly faces a fact witness. By presenting a character witness, a party invites cross-examination on specifics. Thus, even though the trial judge in Crowley precluded cross-examination of Vincent about her previous accusations against other students, the judge might well have allowed those questions on cross-examination of a character witness who claimed that Vincent had a truthful character.

Because of the damaging questions that can be asked on cross-examination, parties are much less likely to present character witnesses who testify about truthfulness than they are to offer witnesses who testify about untruthfulness. Cross-examination of the latter witness with specific instances of truthfulness usually is ineffectual. But cross-examination of a positive character witness with specific questions about untruthful behavior can seriously undermine an opponent's position.

2. Extrinsic Evidence. Parties may cross-examine character witnesses about a fact witness's specific conduct, but they may not offer extrinsic evidence of that conduct. Just as when a party cross-examines a fact witness on specifics, the cross-examiner must accept the character witness's denial. The trial moves on without allowing additional witnesses or other evidence to prove the specific conduct.

But even without the opportunity to offer extrinsic evidence, the cross-examination of character witnesses about specific incidents usually is a win–win tactic for the cross-examiner. The character witness either admits the existence of behavior undercutting his opinion or makes a denial that suggests he is uninformed. Under these circumstances, an opportunity to offer extrinsic evidence is less important.

For a further explanation of the concepts discussed in this chapter, click here to see the video "Using Character Witnesses to Impeach" or go to the Videos module from the eBook on your eProducts bookshelf.

Evidence in Practice

To practice your knowledge of impeachment, take the role of a criminal defense lawyer in *People v. Young.* Click here or access the **Evidence in Practice** module from the eBook on your eProducts bookshelf.

Quick Summary

Rule 608(b)(2) allows parties to cross-examine character witnesses about specific conduct that would contradict the opinion or reputation they have asserted. These questions test the basis of the character witness's knowledge or opinion. If the character witness does not know about the conduct, that raises questions about the scope of his knowledge; if the witness does know about the conduct, that undercuts the contrary opinion or reputation he has expressed.

Cross-examiners must have a good faith belief to support the questions they ask, and judges have discretion to preclude these questions as unfairly prejudicial. The strategy is also difficult to use against witnesses who testify that a fact witness has an untruthful character. When a character witness claims that a fact witness has a truthful character, however, this cross-examination technique can be devastating.

Test Your Understanding

To assess your understanding of the material in this chapter, click here to take a quiz, or go to the Quizzes module from the eBook on your eProducts bookshelf.

23

Religious Beliefs and Impeachment

Key Concepts

- **Rule 610:** No Impeachment or Bolstering with Religious Beliefs
- But Religious Beliefs Are Admissible for Other Purposes

A. Introduction and Policy. A witness's religious beliefs might seem to offer some evidence of the witness's character for truthfulness. After all, most courtroom witnesses take a religious oath to tell the truth. If we rely upon a religious oath to encourage honest testimony, shouldn't evidence of a witness's regular church attendance or devout beliefs be admissible to enhance the witness's credibility? Conversely, couldn't parties introduce evidence that a witness violates the principles of a religion to which he claims allegiance, to suggest an untruthful nature?

Whatever the connection between religious beliefs and truthfulness, introducing evidence of religious beliefs to prove a witness's truthfulness would undermine our constitutional and cultural commitment to religious freedom. Evidence of a witness's religious beliefs, when offered to prove a truthful or untruthful character, would encourage jurors to credit some faiths more than others. Jurors might believe witnesses who shared their personal religious beliefs while discounting testimony from witnesses adhering to other faiths or to no religion.

To avoid this result, **Rule 610** prohibits parties from using a witness's religious beliefs to attack the witness's credibility. The rule also bars parties from using religious beliefs to enhance credibility. Bolstering a witness's credibility with evidence of particular religious beliefs would, by implication, discredit witnesses of other faiths.

Rule 610 thus furthers an important social policy. The rule is growing in importance, moreover, as the nation's religious diversity increases.

B. The Rule. Rule 610 provides:

> # RULE 610. Religious Beliefs or Opinions
>
> Evidence of a witness's religious beliefs or opinions is not admissible to attack or support the witness's credibility.

This straightforward language raises few issues of interpretation. To illustrate the rule's application, however, here is an interesting example involving Rule 610's intersection with **Rule 603**, which governs the oath or affirmation requirement:

Example: The government prosecuted Bedros Kalaydjian and Akram Hayat for distribution of heroin. Haji Karim and Sultan Ahmad, who had both participated in the heroin transactions charged against the defendants, testified for the government at trial. Before Karim and Ahmad testified, the defendants' counsel requested that they be sworn on the Koran rather than the Bible, because the witnesses were practicing Muslims and would take the oath more seriously if sworn on the Koran.

After the district judge granted this request, Karim and Ahmad elected to make affirmations of truthfulness, as **Rule 603** allows, rather than to swear religious oaths on the Koran. The defendants' counsel then sought to cross-examine Karim and Ahmad about why they were unwilling to swear oaths on the Koran. Counsel argued that this cross-examination would show the witnesses' lack of credibility; the fact that they, as devout Muslims, were unwilling to swear on the Koran before testifying suggested that their testimony was false.

Analysis: The district judge barred this cross-examination under Rule 610, and the court of appeals affirmed. The defendants' attempted cross-examination hinged on demonstrating that Karim and Ahmad were devout Muslims. If they were not believers in that faith, their failure to swear an oath on the Koran was meaningless. But Rule 610 properly precludes any inquiry into a witness's religious beliefs for purposes of attacking or supporting credibility. The court, moreover, rejected the defendants' attempt to distinguish conduct based on a religious belief (such as swearing an oath) from the belief itself. At least in this context, Rule 610 prohibited inquiry into either form of religious devotion.[1]

C. In the Courtroom.

As with most of the other rules we have studied, Rule 610 forbids introduction of evidence for one purpose, but allows that evidence when offered for other purposes. In this case, Rule 610 bars evidence of religious beliefs only when offered to attack or buttress a witness's credibility. The rule, however, does not preclude evidence of religious beliefs when they are relevant to other matters, such as bias, damages, or motive. Here is a case illustrating this distinction:

Isn't bias attaching credibility?

Example: In 1984, mailroom employees at the White House opened a letter to President Reagan that read: "Ronnie, Listen Chump! Resign or You'll Get Your Brains Blown Out." A crude drawing of a pistol accompanied these words. Investigators identified David Hoffman as the letter's author, and the government charged Hoffman with threatening the life of the President.

To secure conviction on this charge, the prosecutor had to prove that Hoffman's words constituted a "true threat" rather than a joke or political hyperbole. To establish that element, the government offered evidence that Hoffman had been a follower of the Reverend Sun Yung Moon and that he was upset with Reagan for failing to pardon Moon and release him from prison. Hoffman objected to introduction of this evidence under Rule 610.

Analysis: The district judge rejected Hoffman's argument and the court of appeals affirmed. Proving motive was essential to the government's case; without exploring Hoffman's reason for writing the letter, the government could not show that the letter was a true threat. Rule 610 bars evidence of religious belief when offered to impeach a witness's credibility, but not when introduced for other purposes such as establishing motive.[2]

---

1   United States v. Kalaydjian, 784 F.2d 53, 56–57 (2d Cir. 1986).

2   United States v. Hoffman, 806 F.2d 703, 708–11 (7th Cir. 1986).

Prosecutions for religious hate crimes offer another example of a situation in which religious beliefs may be relevant for a purpose other than credibility. In those prosecutions, an element of the crime is that the defendant committed the offensive act because of the victim's religion.

Quick Summary

Rule 610 prohibits parties from introducing evidence of a witness's religious beliefs to attack or defend that individual's credibility. The rule protects an important social interest in religious freedom. If evidence of religious beliefs is relevant to other matters, however, parties may offer the evidence for those purposes.

Test Your Understanding

To assess your understanding of the material in this chapter, click here to take a quiz, or go to the Quizzes module from the eBook on your eProducts bookshelf.

24

Rule of Completeness

Key Concepts

- **Rule 106:** Rule of Completeness
- Applies Only to Writings and Recordings
- Rule of Timing or Admissibility?

A. Introduction and Policy. When a litigant uses a document to impeach a witness, that litigant may offer just part of the document into evidence. A few pages from a thousand-page deposition may suffice to contradict a witness's courtroom testimony. The whole deposition is unnecessary and might simply confuse the jury.

Parties introduce portions of documents in other contexts as well. A lengthy contract, for example, may contain just a single disputed clause. In cases like these, admitting just part of a document may focus the jury's attention and speed the trial.

Selectivity, however, can also be an adversarial tool. A prosecutor might introduce only the most incriminating portions of a defendant's confession, omitting more exculpatory statements. Another party might impeach an opponent's witness with a few carefully selected lines from a lengthy deposition. Read in isolation, those lines might contradict the witness's trial testimony; viewed in context of the full deposition, the apparent inconsistency might disappear.

To prevent litigants from misleading the jury through piecemeal use of documents, **Rule 106** establishes a rule of completeness. If one party introduces part of a document, Rule 106 allows the opponent to immediately introduce other portions "that in fairness ought to be considered at the same time" as the first portion. The rule applies the same principle to recorded statements, as well as to documents and recordings that are pieces of a larger series. Understanding a letter from Anna to Zoe, for example, may require knowledge of both Anna's letter and a prior one written by Zoe to Anna.

B. The Rule. Rule 106 appears in Article I of the Federal Rules of Evidence; it applies to all documents and recorded statements:

RULE 106. Remainder of or Related Writings or Recorded Statements

If a party introduces all or part of a <u>writing or recorded statement</u>, an adverse party may require the introduction, <u>at that time</u>, of any <u>other part</u>—or <u>any other writing or recorded statement</u>—that in <u>fairness</u> ought to be considered <u>at the same time</u>.

There are four important aspects to this rule. First, Rule 106 allows a party to introduce qualifying portions of a writing or recorded statement **as soon as** the opponent offers the first portion. The party does not have to wait until presentation of its case-in-chief or rebuttal to offer the clarifying information. Rule 106 recognizes that reading portions of a document in isolation may confuse or mislead the jury. A litigant, therefore, may invoke this rule to offer clarifying portions of a writing or recorded statement "at the same time" as the jury hears the opponent's evidence.

Second, Rule 106 applies only to **writings** and **recorded statements**; it does not apply to other forms of evidence, such as oral conversations, photographs, and physical objects. Rule 106 articulates a special rule for writings and recorded statements because these types of evidence pose special problems of confusion if parties introduce them piecemeal.

Third, although parties most often invoke Rule 106 to introduce remaining portions of a single writing or recording, they may also use the rule to introduce **whole** writings or recordings when necessary to understand another document offered by the opponent. If the plaintiff in a contract action introduces a letter that she wrote to the defendant, for example, the defendant may offer additional letters from the correspondence to interpret the plaintiff's letter.

Finally, Rule 106 uses a **fairness principle**; it admits portions of writings or recorded statements "that in fairness ought to be considered at the same time" as those offered by an opponent. This is a flexible standard that allows exercise of the trial court's discretion. Judges apply the standard to achieve the goal articulated by the Advisory Committee: Rule 106 exists to correct a "misleading impression created by taking matters out of context."[1]

C. In the Courtroom.

1. Oral Statements. Although Rule 106 applies only to writings and recorded statements, courts sometimes invoke other rules to create a similar completeness principle for other evidence. Some courts use **Rule 403** to admit missing portions of an oral statement when necessary to avoid unfair prejudice or confusion. Other courts use **Rule 611(a)**, which gives the trial judge power to control the presentation of evidence:[2]

> **Example:** The government prosecuted Arthur Pless and 14 other members of the "Boobie Boys" gang for drug trafficking. In addition to distributing cocaine, gang members allegedly murdered more than a dozen individuals. Detective Simmons offered some of the most persuasive evidence against Pless by describing numerous incriminating statements Pless made orally after arrest. The defense attempted to cross-examine Simmons about several exculpatory statements that Pless made during the same post-arrest discussion.

> **Analysis:** The trial court denied the defendant's motion because the statements were neither written nor recorded. The court of appeals, however, held that the trial court should have used its power under Rule 611(a) to admit the exculpatory statements. Several circuits have "extended Rule 106 to oral testimony in light of Rule 611(a)'s requirement that the district court exercise 'reasonable control' over witness interrogation and the presentation of evidence."[3]

---

1   Fed. R. Evid. 106 advisory committee's note.

2   See Chapter 7 for discussion of Rule 403, and Chapter 15 for discussion of Rule 611.

3   United States v. Baker, 432 F.3d 1189, 1223 (11th Cir. 2005). Although the court held that the district court abused its discretion in failing to allow introduction of Pless's exculpatory statements, the court found the error harmless in light of the substantial evidence against Pless.

 Courts differ in their willingness to expand Rule 106's completeness principle through Rules 403 and 611. Advocates, however, successfully invoke these rules before some judges.

2. Timing or Admissibility. When Rule 106 applies, it allows a party to introduce portions of a writing or recorded statement as soon as the opponent offers the initial piece of the evidence. The party stops the proceedings and introduces the "completing" evidence immediately, rather than waiting for its own case or rebuttal. This right prevents the opponent from misleading the jury through selective use of documents.

 Some courts hold that Rule 106 affects only the **time** at which parties introduce otherwise admissible evidence.[4] These courts apply Rule 106 only if the document portions offered under that rule comply with all other Rules of Evidence. Other courts, however, have interpreted Rule 106 much more broadly; they read the rule as one of admissibility.[5] Under this interpretation, Rule 106 gives parties an avenue for admitting portions of a document that would not otherwise be admissible. As always, Rule 403 restricts this avenue when it would cause unfair prejudice, confusion, or delay.

The Supreme Court has not resolved this fundamental conflict about interpretation of Rule 106, and the issue remains open in some circuits. Knowledgeable counsel may draw upon these conflicting views of Rule 106 to urge adoption or exclusion of documentary evidence.

---

4   See, e.g., United States v. Costner, 684 F.2d 370, 372–73 (6th Cir. 1982).

5   See, e.g., United States v. Sutton, 801 F.2d 1346 (D.C. Cir. 1986).

Quick Summary

 When a party offers part of a document or recorded statement, **Rule 106** allows the opponent to introduce any remaining portions "that in fairness ought to be considered at the same time" as the original portion. Some courts interpret this rule simply to affect timing; the opponent may offer the remaining portions of the statement immediately, but those portions may not violate any other Rules of Evidence. Other courts read Rule 106 as a rule that broadens admissibility; if a party introduces one part of a document or recorded statement, the opponent may offer other portions regardless of their admissibility under other rules

Although Rule 106 applies only to writings and recorded statements, some courts apply a similar rule of completeness to oral conversations and other types of evidence. These courts rely upon **Rule 403** or **611(a)** to achieve that result.

25

Character Evidence and the Rules

Key Concepts

- "Character Evidence" Includes Many Kinds of Evidence
- Character, Reputation, and Acts Are Distinct Concepts
- When Evidence Relates to Character, Ask **What** the Proponent Is Trying to Prove and the **Inferences Relied Upon**
- Four Categories of "Character" Evidence Help Determine Admissibility

---

A. Introduction. In the last few chapters, we examined how parties use evidence of character, reputation, and specific acts to suggest that a witness lied on the stand. The evidentiary rules, as well as lawyers and judges, refer to these types of proof as "character evidence." But this label is misleading: Character, reputation, and actions are related but distinct concepts. The phrase "character evidence," moreover, fails to focus on the **purposes** for which parties offer this evidence. The admissibility of any evidence related to character depends on **what** the proponent is trying to prove and the **type of inferences** the proponent relies upon when using that character evidence.

In this chapter, we disentangle the concepts of character, reputation, and actions. We'll also examine four different purposes for which parties offer this evidence. These four categories, rather than the unhelpful label of "character evidence," help separate evidence that is admissible from evidence that is not.

B. Character, Reputation, and Actions.
Character, reputation, and actions are related to one another, but they are distinct concepts.

Character traits are internal; they reside within a person. We can't see character directly, but people seem to possess traits that incline them to act in particular ways. Some people tend to respond angrily to the slightest provocation; others are calm no matter what happens. Some people spend money freely, without tracking their outlays; others count every penny carefully. These differences, we assume, stem from variations in character.

Reputation is external; it reflects what other people think about an individual. Reputation often corresponds to character, but the two sometimes differ. A lawyer may have a reputation for being cold and unfriendly, while his internal character is warm and sociable. The lawyer's brusque manner may reflect stress or an attempt to represent clients aggressively. Reputation is not always a reliable guide to character.

Actions, finally, lie between character and reputation. Since we can't see character, we deduce it from an individual's actions. If a legislator responds rudely to a question, we assume that she has an unfriendly character: We reason backwards from the action to the character. At the same time, we use actions to construct an individual's reputation: We reason forward to assemble reputation from the actions we see.

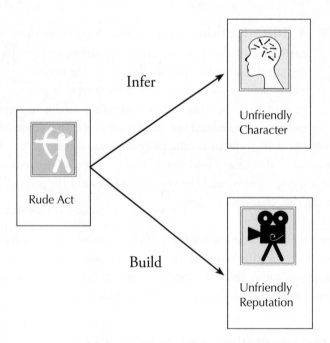

Character is difficult to prove directly: Brain scans don't reveal character, and neither do blood tests. In the courtroom, therefore, parties usually use acts and reputation to show character. **Rule 609**, which we discussed in Chapter 20, allows parties to prove that a witness was convicted of crimes of dishonesty. A party will use those specific acts to argue that the witness has an untruthful character.

Similarly, **Rule 608** allows a party to introduce evidence that a witness has a reputation for untruthfulness. Since reputation often corresponds to character, a party can use that evidence to argue that the witness has an untruthful nature. In the courtroom, therefore, reputation and specific acts often appear as circumstantial evidence of character.[1]

Character, reputation, and acts thus are linked, both inside and outside of the courtroom. The concepts, however, are distinct. And, as we'll see in the next section, evidence of reputation or specific acts can play roles wholly separate from proving character. These multiple roles cause some of the confusion surrounding "character" evidence.

C. Four Categories of "Character Evidence."

Let's look now at why parties introduce evidence of character, reputation, or specific acts related to those concepts. What do litigants hope to prove by introducing this type of evidence? Parties offer this evidence to prove four different types of facts. The admissibility of the evidence depends on what the litigant is attempting to prove, so it is essential to understand these four categories. We studied the first category in Chapters 19–23, and we'll examine the other three in the next series of chapters. First, though, let's outline all four categories briefly.

1. Proof of a Witness's Propensity to Lie or Tell the Truth. We have already seen one reason why parties introduce evidence related to character: to suggest that a witness lied on the stand. Under some circumstances, **Rules 608** and **609** allow parties to introduce evidence related to a witness's character for untruthfulness. Based on this evidence, the party asks the jury to make this chain of inferences:

---

1   As we saw in Chapter 21, Rule 608 also allows parties to prove character through opinion testimony. Opinion testimony is the most direct evidence of character available to parties.

1. This witness has an untruthful character.

2. A person with an untruthful character has a tendency to lie.

3. Therefore, this witness lied on the stand.

It is helpful to use symbols to represent these links in the inferential chain:

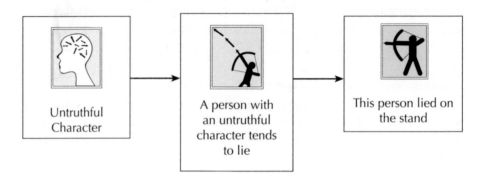

In this diagram, the first symbol represents any type of character trait. The second symbol represents a tendency—or propensity—for people with that trait to act in a particular way. And the third symbol represents the conclusion that a person acted consistently with their character on a particular occasion.

Parties usually use evidence of a dishonest reputation or a criminal conviction to suggest an untruthful character, so the chain of inferences really has four links:

1. This witness has a reputation for untruthfulness. Alternatively, this person has committed a crime that involves dishonesty.

2. Someone with a reputation for untruthfulness (or who has committed a crime of dishonesty) probably has an untruthful character.

3. A person with an untruthful character has a tendency to lie.

4. Therefore, this witness lied on the stand.

By adding the symbols for action and reputation used above, we can also illustrate this more complex chain of inferences:

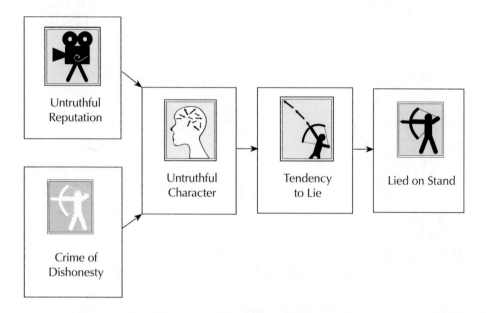

Rule 608 allows parties to rebut this evidence with proof of a witness's truthful character. The process for proving a witness's truthful nature is similar to the process for suggesting an untruthful disposition. A trial lawyer usually establishes truthful character by asking about instances of truthful behavior on cross-examination or by introducing evidence of a truthful reputation. The attorney then asks the jury to conclude that, since the witness has engaged in truthful acts or has a reputation for truthfulness, the witness has a truthful character. People with truthful characters, the lawyer further urges, tend to tell the truth; therefore, the witness must have told the truth on the stand.

This first category of "character" evidence depends on the notion of **propensity**. Parties introducing evidence of a witness's untruthful character urge the jury to conclude that the witness's propensity to lie produced lies on this occasion. Similarly, a litigant who offers evidence of a witness's truthful character maintains that the witness's propensity to tell the truth yielded truthful testimony on this occasion. In either case, the parties contend that the witness acted consistently with her character while testifying in the courtroom. This consistency—or propensity to act in a particular way—lies at the heart of all evidence relating to a witness's character to lie or tell the truth.

The final two symbols used above illustrate this crucial concept of propensity reasoning. Propensity reasoning from character evidence consists of two steps: (1) an assumption that someone with a particular character tends to act in a particular way, and (2) a conclusion that the person acted consistently with that tendency on a particular occasion.

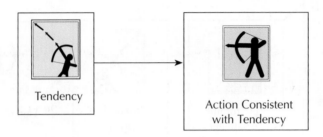

As we continue to study character evidence, look for this "propensity inference." It often determines whether evidence is admissible or inadmissible.

2. Proof of Conduct by Propensity. The second category of character evidence, like the first, depends on the concept of propensity. Parties often argue that, just as witnesses testify consistently with their character for truthfulness or untruthfulness, people act in other ways that are consistent with other character traits. A prosecutor, for example, might try to prove that David assaulted Victor on January 10 by showing that David engaged in many violent acts both before and after January 10. The prosecutor would then urge the jury to reason:

1. David has committed many violent acts.

2. Someone who has committed many violent acts probably has a violent character.

3. A person with a violent character has a tendency to commit assaults.

4. Therefore, David assaulted Victor on January 10.

Using our action, character, and propensity symbols, we can illustrate this chain of inferences like this:

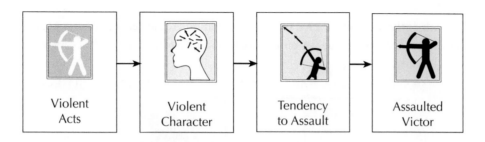

| Violent Acts | Violent Character | Tendency to Assault | Assaulted Victor |

As we'll see in Chapter 26, **Rule 404(a)** bars most attempts to prove conduct by propensity. But the rule recognizes a few exceptions, which we'll examine in Chapter 27. And as we saw in Chapter 19, the use of evidence to suggest a witness's character for truthfulness or untruthfulness is itself an exception to this general rule against the use of evidence to show propensity.

3. Proof of Character or Reputation as Elements. A party may offer evidence of character or reputation for reasons that do **not** depend on an inference of propensity. Some crimes, civil claims, or defenses require proof of character or reputation to establish an element of that claim or defense. Defamation plaintiffs, for example, usually must prove that the defamatory statement was false. If the statement referred to a character trait, then both parties will introduce evidence about the plaintiff's character:

> **Example:** Jasper, a third-year law student, posted a note on his Facebook webpage saying that his classmate Linda was "lazy as a slug." Linda sued Jasper for defamation. At trial, Linda will offer evidence of her industrious nature while Jasper attempts to prove that Linda is, in fact, quite lazy.

Defamation plaintiffs often must also show injury to reputation. To establish that element, Linda may offer evidence that she had a reputation for being a hard-working person before Jasper posted his note, but that now people view her as a slacker. Reputation itself is an element of her claim, not just a way of proving character.

In both of these examples, character and reputation are elements of the action; the parties need not engage in any propensity reasoning to make the evidence relevant:

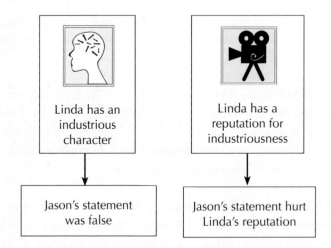

Legal claims or defenses that require proof of character or reputation to establish an element are rare, but a few exist. When parties offer evidence of character or reputation to establish an element in this manner, **Rule 405** allows that evidence. We will explore this category of evidence further in Chapter 26.

4. Proof of Other Acts for Non-Propensity Purposes. In the first two categories described above, parties offer evidence of specific actions to establish a person's character. They then argue that this character shows a propensity to act in a particular way. Evidence of a person's actions, however, can establish facts **other than** character and can support inferences **other than** one based on propensity.

Indeed, every action a person takes can support multiple inferences. If Sam exceeds the speed limit while driving down a main avenue, a judgmental observer might infer that Sam has a reckless, impatient, or law-breaking character. This observer might point to Sam's speeding and argue that he has a propensity to drive recklessly or to break the law.

A more compassionate observer might infer that Sam was transporting a heart attack victim to the emergency room. Still another might conclude that he was trying to escape a dangerous sniper or that his speedometer was broken. A single action can support dozens of different inferences about character traits, mental states, or circumstances.

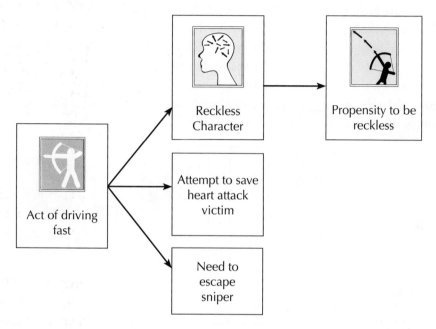

When parties offer evidence of an action for a purpose other than to prove character and a propensity to act in a particular way, **Rule 404(b)** often allows that evidence. We will explore this category of evidence in detail in Chapter 30. But to help you start thinking about this concept, here is one example of courtroom evidence that could be used in multiple ways:

> **Example:** Gloria is on trial for stealing money from a locked safe on June 25. The prosecutor offers evidence that Gloria broke into the same safe on March 19 and took the money it held at that time.

The prosecutor could try to use the evidence of Gloria's March 19 conduct to prove that Gloria has a dishonest character; that this character trait established a propensity to break into safes and steal the money inside of them; and that Gloria acted consistently with this propensity by breaking into the safe on June 25. If the prosecutor offers the evidence for these purposes, the evidence of Gloria's March 19 conduct will fall into the second category described above. As we'll see in Chapter 27, the judge probably would exclude the evidence under **Rule 404(a)** if the prosecutor offers the March 19 theft for these purposes.

But the prosecutor in this case can argue that evidence of Gloria's March 19 theft serves an entirely different purpose. Safecracking is an unusual skill; not everyone could have broken into this safe on June 25. The fact that Gloria stole money from the same locked safe on March 19 suggests that she either knows the combination or knows how to break into locked safes. The evidence, in other words, proves that Gloria had the **knowledge** to accomplish this crime. Evidence of her March 19 behavior, the prosecutor may argue, is no different than showing that Gloria possessed a slip of paper with the safe's combination written on it. The evidence simply shows that she had essential knowledge to commit the crime.

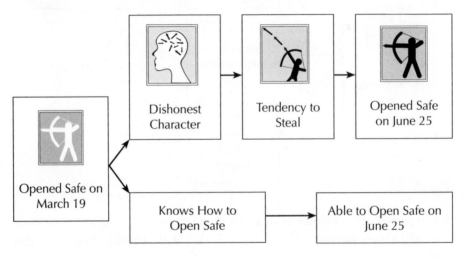

As the above diagram shows, the same action (breaking into the safe on March 19) can support two entirely different chains of reasoning. In one, the prosecutor asks the jury to use the type of propensity inference we discussed above: The prosecutor argues that, because Gloria had a dishonest character, she had a tendency to steal and, consistent with that tendency, broke into the safe on June 25.

The second chain of reasoning, however, avoids the propensity inference. Instead, the prosecutor argues that Gloria's action demonstrates a knowledge that gave her the ability to commit the June 25 crime. This type of reasoning falls into this fourth category of "character evidence." The trial judge may admit evidence of Gloria's March 19 action if it falls into this category. In Chapter 30, we'll examine more closely the process that the judge will employ in deciding whether to admit this evidence and in instructing the jury if it is admitted.

For a further explanation of these concepts, <u>click here</u> to see the video "Introduction to Character Evidence" or go to the Videos module from the eBook on your eProducts bookshelf.

Quick Summary

"Character evidence" is a complex subject involving the interplay of several different rules. To understand the rules in this area, it is best to set aside the vague and misleading phrase "character evidence." Instead, focus on the distinct roles that character, reputation, and specific acts play in the courtroom. In addition, when determining the admissibility of any evidence related to these concepts, ask what the party offering the evidence is trying to prove with that evidence and what type of inferences the party is urging the jury to make. The answers to those questions will place the evidence in one of four categories:

1. Proof of a witness's propensity to lie or tell the truth

2. Proof of conduct by propensity

3. Proof of character or reputation as elements

4. Proof of other acts for non-propensity purposes

Once you have placed the "character evidence" into its proper category, you can refer to the appropriate rule to determine whether it is admissible.

26

Evidence to Prove Character as an Element

Key Concepts

- Character May Be an Element of a Charged Crime, Civil Claim, or Defense

- **Rule 405:** When Character Is an Element, Evidence of Specific Acts, Reputation, and Opinion Are All Admissible

- **Rule 403** and Other Rules Still Apply

A. Introduction and Policy. In this chapter, we look more closely at the third category of "character" evidence identified in the previous chapter: evidence used to prove character as an element of a crime, civil claim, or defense. This category does not arise very often, because a person's personality trait usually is not an element of a claim or defense. In a personal injury case, for example, the plaintiff must prove that the defendant was negligent on a particular occasion, not that the defendant has a careless character. Similarly, the defendant in a personal injury case cannot escape liability by proving that he has a cautious, careful character. If the defendant was negligent on one occasion and his negligence harmed the plaintiff, the defendant is legally responsible for the injury regardless of his general character.

But there are a few situations in which an individual's character is itself an element of the claim or defense. Character, for example, sometimes is an element in a defamation lawsuit:

> **Example:** W. Bradley Poore III, a mathematics professor, opposed construction of low-income housing near his home. Jim Frank, the housing developer, published ads in two local newspapers claiming that Poore was "wrongly named because he's an elitist who hates the poor." Frank also charged that Poore had a "miserly and tight-fisted nature." Poore sued Frank for libel. Since truth is a defense to libel, Frank defended by claim-

ing that his characterization of Poore was truthful. In response, Poore presented witnesses who testified that Poore was a generous, fair-minded, and caring person who treated the poor with compassion.

Analysis: Frank's statement attacked Poore's character, so character became a central element of this dispute. Frank argued that his assertions about Poore's character were true, while Poore contended they were false. To resolve the defamation claim, the jury had to decide whether Poore really was a miserly, tight-fisted elitist who hated the poor. If those assertions were true, then Frank's ads were not defamatory.[1]

Character can also become an essential element of a child custody claim, in which the court must determine the "best interest of the child." As this example shows, the child's best interest often depends on what the judge believes about the character of each parent, step-parent, or other adult interacting with the child:

Example: J.M. and C.F. divorced in 1999, and C.F. (the mother) was awarded sole custody of their child. In 2003, J.M. sought to gain custody of the child because of the character of C.F's new husband (the child's new stepfather), a man named "Mike." J.M. presented evidence from Mike's former wife that he had been physically abusive towards her during their marriage, and also evidence that the child's grandmother had witnessed Mike choking C.F. in front of the child.

Analysis: In this custody dispute, determination of the child's best interest requires scrutiny of Mike's character. The acts Mike committed suggest that he has a violent and abusive character toward women. That character, in turn, predicts that he will commit additional acts of domestic violence against C.F. that could harm the child. To protect children, judges consider character as an essential element of custody decisions. In this case, the court determined that given Mike's lack of moral fitness to be a parent, his presence in the home constituted a material and adverse change in circumstances, and thus the court awarded custody to the father J.M.[2]

---

1   This example was inspired by Fleming v. Moore, 275 S.E.2d 632 (Va. 1981), a case with somewhat similar facts that did not address the evidentiary issue.

2   This example is based on C.A.M.F. v. J.B.M., 972 So. 2d 656, 665–66 (Miss. App. 2007). Because this case, like most custody cases, was a bench trial, the judge ruled on the evidentiary issue and then later, as the trier of fact,

The Rules of Evidence impose few limits on proving character when character is an element of a crime, claim, or defense. Parties may prove character with the type of reputation and opinion evidence we studied in Chapter 21; in addition, they may introduce evidence of specific acts to show character as an element. As we learned earlier, the Rules of Evidence prohibit evidence of specific acts to prove the untruthful character of a witness, because that evidence would distract the jury from the parties' central dispute. But when character is an element of a crime, claim, or defense, then **all** evidence related to that character is central to the case.

B. The Rule. The Federal Rules of Evidence do not specifically authorize admission of character evidence to prove an element of a crime, civil claim, or defense, but the structure of the rules makes this explicit authorization unnecessary. **Rule 402** states that all relevant evidence is admissible unless otherwise provided, and evidence used to prove an element of the case easily meets the relevance definition of **Rule 401.** To exclude this type of character evidence, we would have to identify another rule barring its admission. But **Rule 404(a)**, which we looked at in Chapter 19 and will explore further soon, only prohibits character evidence when it is used to suggest that a person acted consistently with their character on a particular occasion. This prohibition does not affect the admissibility of evidence proving character as an element.

The main question with this type of evidence is the method of proving the relevant character trait: In other words, how may a litigant present this evidence? Recall that **Rules 608** and **609** restrict the types of evidence used to prove the character of a witness. **Rule 405** outlines the permissible ways to prove character as an element of a crime, claim, or defense. The first part of that rule confirms the approach we studied under Rule 608; it allows proof of character through opinion or reputation evidence.

RULE 405. Methods of Proving Character

(a) **By Reputation or Opinion.** When evidence of a person's character or character trait is admissible, it may be proved by testimony about the person's reputation or by testimony in the form of an opinion. . . .

---

determined that given the evidence about Mike's character, the best interest of the child mandated an alteration of the custody order.

In a trial of the child custody dispute described above, for example, the father could present testimony from Mike's ex-girlfriends and ex-wives. After establishing their knowledge of Mike, these witnesses could offer their personal opinion that Mike is violent towards women. Similarly, neighbors or former babysitters could testify that they know Mike's reputation in the community as someone who physically abuses his wife.

Rule 405(a) continues by recognizing another technique we studied under Rule 608. On cross-examination, the opposing party may ask one of these character witnesses about specific acts:

RULE 405. Methods of Proving Character

(a) **By Reputation or Opinion.** . . . On cross-examination of the character witness, the court may allow an inquiry into relevant specific instances of the person's conduct.

So if the father offered a character witness who testified that, in her opinion, Mike was "vicious towards women," the child's mother could attempt to undermine that testimony by cross-examining the witness about incidents negating that character. She might, for example, ask that witness whether she knew of the occasion when a girlfriend slapped Mike in the face and he calmly walked away instead of hitting her back.

For our purposes, however, the most striking part of Rule 405 lies in section (b):

RULE 405. Methods of Proving Character

(b) **By Specific Instances of Conduct.** When a person's character or character trait is an <u>essential element</u> of a charge, claim, or defense, the character or trait may also be proved by relevant <u>specific instances</u> of the person's conduct.

When character is an element of a crime, civil claim, or defense, therefore, the Rules of Evidence do not limit parties to opinion or reputation testimony. In addition to those forms of proof, the parties may introduce specific evidence demonstrating the disputed character. In our child custody case, for example, the defendant did not present mere opinion or reputation evidence about Mike's character. Instead, he offered evidence that Mike had choked the child's mother and abused a former wife. This was dramatic proof of Mike's violent character.

The Rules of Evidence usually tell us what evidence is excluded, not what evidence is admissible. Rule 405(b) is a necessary exception to that general approach. Since the rules often limit character evidence to reputation or opinion testimony, as in Rule 608, Rule 405(b) explicitly confirms that specific instances of conduct **are** admissible to prove character as an element of a crime, claim, or defense.

Evidence of specific conduct offered under Rule 405(b) must satisfy the other Rules of Evidence. A party cannot, for example, prove specific instances of conduct through a witness who lacks personal knowledge of those instances. But Rule 405 makes clear that parties may prove character through specific actions, as well as through more general reputation or opinion testimony, when character is a disputed element of the case.

C. In the Courtroom. Proof of character through specific instances of conduct usually is much more persuasive than proof through opinion or reputation testimony. Parties proving character as an element of the case, however, may decide to use all of these avenues to prove character. In this section, we explore issues that arise under each of these approaches.

1. Foundation for Opinion or Reputation Testimony. The foundation required for opinion or reputation testimony offered under **Rule 405(a)** is the same as that needed under **Rule 608(a)**. As we saw in Chapter 21, the examining attorney must first establish that the witness knows the person whose character is at issue or knows that person's reputation. After establishing that knowledge, the witness will offer a brief opinion or reputation report about the person's character. In the child custody case, for example, the mother's attorney might have attempted to counter the negative evidence about the stepfather by offering evidence that he had a peaceful, nonaggressive character and that he seemed to be a good stepfather:

> **Q:** Ms. Travers, do you know Mike?
>
> **A:** Yes, I do.
>
> **Q:** In what connection do you know Mike?
>
> **A:** Mike used to take his children for walks in the park near my house.

Q: When was that?

A: Starting about five years ago, I guess, and continuing until he moved away last year.

Q: Did you see Mike often during that time?

A: Oh, yes. I walk my dog at the same time every day, and I would frequently see him in the park with his kids. We would talk while his kids played on the playground.

Q: And based on those contacts, have you formed an opinion about Mike's character for violence or aggressiveness?

A: Yes, I have. Mike was never aggressive or violent. He was just the sweetest man.

Q: And have you formed any opinion about whether he is a good caregiver for his children?

A: Yes, I think he had an excellent disposition with his children and stepchild. He was always very calm and kind to them.

2. Good Faith Belief for Cross-Examination on Specifics. If a party uses opinion or reputation testimony to show a character trait, Rule 405(a) allows the opponent to cross-examine the witness about specific incidents related to that character trait. As with cross-examinations conducted under Rule 608(b)(2), the cross-examiner must have a good faith belief that the incidents actually occurred.[3] In the child custody case, the father's attorney had interviewed the grandmother and ex-wife who informed him about Mike's violent actions. The father's attorney, therefore, had a good faith belief that Mike beat his wife and ex-wife and could have asked the hypothetical Ms. Travers this question on cross-examination:

---

3 For further discussion of cross-examination under Rule 608(b)(2), the rule governing a witness's character for truthfulness, refer back to Chapter 22.

> **Q:** Ms. Travers, did you know that Mike choked his wife in front of his eight-year old stepson?

This is a devastating question on cross-examination. In addition to the shock of the question itself, the witness has no satisfactory way to answer. If she admits knowing about the incident, her opinion of Mike as the "sweetest man" appears ludicrous. If she denies knowledge of it, the basis of her opinion seems unbearably weak.[4]

3. Proof of Specific Incidents. Rule 405's primary value to parties proving character as an element of their case is section (b)'s provision allowing evidence of specific instances of conduct. When character is at issue in the case, the parties need not limit themselves to general statements of opinion or reputation. Nor are they limited to probing specific acts on cross-examination; they can introduce the latter evidence in their case-in-chief through direct examination of their own witnesses. They may also prove character with other types of evidence related to specific acts, such as a certificate of conviction, which proves the individual committed a given crime.

In the child custody case, for example, the father's attorney offered eyewitness testimony from Mike's ex-wife about how Mike physically abused her. If Mike had ever been convicted of a crime of violence, the father's attorney could have also admitted the certificate of conviction showing that Mike was guilty of those acts. Rule 405(b) allows evidence of these specific acts in any form, because Mike's allegedly violent character is an element of determining the best interest of the child.

4. Relationship to Rule 403 and Other Rules. Remember that even though Rules 404 and 405 do not bar character evidence used to prove an element, another rule may still prohibit the proffered piece of evidence. Parties, for example, must comply with the rules governing hearsay and authentication of documents, which we will study later in the course. Perhaps most important, **Rule 403** limits a party's ability to offer character evidence. Even when character is a centrally disputed element of the case, a judge may exclude some types of character evidence because the danger of confusion, delay, or unfair prejudice substantially outweighs any probative value.

---

4   Because of this prospect, it is unlikely that the mother offered any evidence of Mike's good character in this case. Even if the mother's attorney had been able to find a witness who believed in Mike's gentle disposition, the attorney would have known about Mike's violent outbursts and would have avoided setting up his own witness for this type of attack. The Travers testimony and cross-examination are purely imaginary.

5. What Is "Character"? Rule 405 does not define "character" or "character trait." Nor do any of the other rules referring to these concepts. Litigants, however, rarely dispute the meaning of character, and judges seem confident that they understand what "character" means. Character seems to include almost any personality trait, including honesty, mendacity, cautiousness, recklessness, aggressiveness, and passivity or peaceableness. Philosophers and psychologists may debate the meaning of character, but judges and litigants seem to share a broad consensus about the traits that contribute to character.

6. When Is Character an "Element"? The most difficult issue that arises in applying Rule 405(b) is determining whether character truly is an element of the controversy. As we have already discussed, the Rules of Evidence do not allow character evidence to prove conduct through propensity. Determining whether character is an element of a charge, claim, or defense, therefore, is an important issue.

Relatively few legal controversies fall into this category. Just four categories of cases account for almost every lawsuit in which character is an element. Defamation cases, as noted in the introduction, form the first of these categories. If the allegedly defamatory statements concern the plaintiff's character, then the parties will dispute whether those statements were true. Even if the defendant's assertion did not concern character directly, defamation law often requires the plaintiff to prove an injury to reputation. Proving reputation often overlaps with showing character.

Second, child custody cases frequently involve deciding whether each of the litigants is a "good parent" or a "bad parent." Because the court must determine the best interest of the child, a judge might hear evidence about the character of each parent. A father might call character witnesses to testify about their poor opinion of the mother's abilities as a caregiver, while the mother might call witnesses to testify about specific times when the father left their young children alone in a public place or drove drunk with them in the car. Each would try to prove the unfitness of the other.

Third, character arises in criminal cases when the defendant claims entrapment. At least in some circuits, the entrapment defense requires the defendant to prove that she lacked a predisposition to commit the crime. In these circuits, the defendant's criminal or noncriminal character is an essential element of the defense.[5]

---

5   See, e.g., United States v. Thomas, 134 F.3d 975, 980 (9th Cir. 1998).

Negligent entrustment claims, finally, include character as an element of a civil case. In a negligent entrustment case, an injured plaintiff argues that the defendant carelessly entrusted a car, gun, or other potentially dangerous instrument to a person that the defendant had reason to know would misuse that instrument. The plaintiff, in other words, argues that the defendant knew something about a third party's character and negligently ignored that knowledge. Here is one example of a negligent entrustment claim:

Example: A Pan Am flight crashed in Bali, Indonesia, killing more than 100 passengers. Representatives of the deceased passengers sued Pan Am, claiming that the airline negligently entrusted the plane to a pilot who had a reckless character while flying. To show both the pilot's poor character and Pan Am's knowledge of that character, the plaintiffs offered evidence of multiple mistakes the pilot had made in his ongoing training.

Analysis: The court of appeals ruled that this evidence was admissible. By claiming that Pan Am negligently allowed the pilot to fly, the plaintiffs made the pilot's character an element of the case. Rule 405(b) then allowed proof of specific incidents—like the mistakes the pilot made during training—to prove the pilot's character.[6]

Other negligent entrustment cases involve defendants who loan cars to drivers they know are careless or who give guns to individuals they know are violent and lawbreaking.

---

6   In re Aircrash in Bali, 684 F.2d 1301, 1315 (9th Cir. 1982), aff'd on other grounds, 871 F.2d 812 (9th Cir. 1989).

Quick Summary

In some lawsuits, a party's character is an element of the charged crime, civil claim, or defense. This occurs most often in civil actions for defamation or negligent entrustment, or during a child custody case when each parent tries to prove that the other is unfit to be the primary caregiver. When character is an element of the case, **Rule 405(b)** allows the parties to prove that element by introducing evidence of specific actions. Under **Rule 405(a)**, these parties may also prove character through opinion or reputation testimony.

Rule 403 does constrain evidence used to prove character as an element of the case. Under some circumstances, judges may exclude that evidence as confusing, repetitive, or unfairly prejudicial. Character evidence must also comply with other evidentiary rules, such as those governing hearsay.

27

Using Character Evidence to Prove Propensity

Key Concepts

- **Rule 404(a)(1):** Bars Character Evidence When Used to Prove Propensity
- Policy Rationale: Liability Based on Specific Acts, Not General Character
- Includes Proof of Good or Bad Character
- Bars Evidence of Any Person's Character

A. Introduction and Policy. So far, we have examined two categories of character evidence. In Chapters 19–22 we considered the use of this evidence to show a witness's untruthful nature. Then in Chapter 26 we looked at cases in which character forms an element of a charged crime, civil claim, or defense.

In this chapter and the next two, we will discuss a third use of character evidence: to prove an element of the case by arguing that, because a person has a particular character trait, she probably acted in a particular way. A defendant claiming self defense, for example, might offer evidence that the alleged victim had a violent temper. This character trait would support the defendant's story that the victim threatened him with a gun. People with violent tempers are more likely to threaten others with guns; the character trait is circumstantial evidence lending some support to the defendant's story:

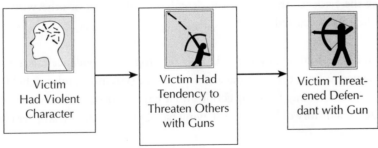

As explained in Chapter 25, this is a "propensity" use of character evidence. Character evidence offered to show propensity does not prove an element of the case directly. Instead, the evidence suggests that, because a person had a tendency to act in a particular way, the person was more likely to have committed a particular act on a specific occasion. Violent people have a propensity to strike others, dishonest people are prone to steal, and clumsy people are likely to fall over furniture.

We use propensity reasoning frequently in our own lives. If a friend frequently drives drunk, we don't allow our children to ride in that friend's car; we worry that the friend might endanger our children by driving drunk with them on board. If we receive undercooked food several times at a restaurant, we take our business elsewhere; we assume that a chef who cooks badly on several occasions will continue to do so. And if we find a shattered dish on the living room floor, we suspect the clumsiest member of the household of breaking the dish. In everyday life, propensity reasoning saves time and keeps us safe.

In the courtroom, however, propensity arguments create a problem. Propensity evidence usually is relevant: Most of us believe that the person with a careless disposition is more likely than other housemates to have been broken the dish. Most judges and evidence scholars, however, believe that this evidence is unfairly prejudicial.

Precisely because propensity arguments are so common in everyday life, a jury hearing those arguments in the courtroom may base its verdict on general propensities rather than on specific evidence about the disputed incident. If jurors hear that a criminal defendant beat up five people during the past year, they may give that evidence more weight than it deserves. They may assume that, because the defendant has a violent disposition, he must be guilty of the assault charged on this occasion. The jurors may ignore other equally probative evidence about the specific incident because they know "the kind of person the defendant is." Similarly, jurors might hold a defendant responsible for injuries arising out of a car crash simply because the defendant has a reputation for drunk driving, not because the evidence shows that the defendant was drunk or otherwise careless when the crash occurred.

This tendency of jurors to rely too heavily on propensity evidence raises a serious policy concern. Both the criminal and civil justice systems promise to hold defendants responsible only for their actions on a particular occasion, not for an evil character or a history of bad acts. Allowing parties to introduce character evidence and make propensity arguments based on that evidence would run a serious risk of compromising this fundamental principle of justice.

For this reason, **Rule 404(a)(1)** broadly prohibits the use of character evidence when offered to show propensity.[1] As we discussed in Chapter 24, "proof of conduct by propensity" is only one of the four categories of character evidence. The Rules of Evidence more freely admit character evidence falling in the other three categories. Even this most restricted category of "proof of conduct by propensity" harbors some exceptions that we will examine in the next two chapters. The basic principle of Rule 404(a)(1), however, declares that parties may not use character evidence to prove that, because a person had a propensity to act in a certain way, the person was more likely to have acted in that way on a particular occasion.

Litigants frequently want to make propensity arguments, because they are so appealing to juries. Recognizing and excluding character evidence that is used to prove conduct by propensity, therefore, is an important part of evidence law. In this chapter, we will focus on that task.

B. The Rule. Rule 404(a) begins with this general statement:

Rule 404. Character Evidence; Crimes or Other Acts

(a) Character Evidence.

    (1) Prohibited Uses. Evidence of a person's character or character trait is <u>not admissible</u> to prove that on a particular occasion the person <u>acted in accordance with the character or trait</u>.

As noted in Chapter 25, the key element to applying this rule is identifying the purpose for which a party is offering evidence. If the evidence is being offered to prove that "the person acted in accordance with the character or trait," it is being offered as propensity evidence and will almost always be barred.

---

1   Until December 2011, this prohibition was numbered simply 404(a). When reading cases published before 2012, look carefully at the portion of Rule 404(a) cited by the court.

The remainder of the rule articulates several exceptions, which we will study in upcoming chapters. For the remainder of this chapter, let's focus on the general prohibition of Rule 404(a)(1).

C. In the Courtroom.

1. Good Character and Bad. Parties most often attempt to introduce evidence of an opponent's bad character. Rule 404(a)(1), however, bars evidence of both bad and good character if that evidence is offered to prove that a person acted consistently with their character on a particular occasion:

Example: Angelita Kettles sued Vernon Bonner for defrauding her of the government benefits she was entitled to receive as a war veteran's widow. Kettles presented several witnesses who testified about her good character. Dean Blake, for example, testified that Kettles was "an honest mother" and "a good wife." Kettles also offered witnesses who testified about Bonner's "deceptive, shady, evasive, and manipulative" character.

Analysis: Rule 404(a)(1) barred both of these lines of testimony. Neither Kettles's good character nor Bonner's bad one was an element of this fraud claim. Instead, Kettles offered evidence about her honest, virtuous character to suggest that, because that was her general nature, she was duped by Bonner. Similarly, Kettles introduced evidence of Bonner's bad character to suggest that, because he was a deceptive and shady person, he more likely than not defrauded her of the benefits due to her. Rule 404(a)(1) prohibits the propensity use of character, whether the character traits are good or bad.[2]

2. Any Person. Rule 404(a)(1) bars the use of character evidence to prove the propensity of any person to act in a particular way. Unlike **Rules 608** and **609**, which limit their scope to proof of a **witness's** character, Rule 404(a)(1)'s prohibition applies even to people who never appear in the courtroom.

Example: Cordelia Chase was riding in a car driven by her friend Spike.

---

2   This example draws upon the facts in United States v. Bonner, 302 F.3d 776, 780–82 (7th Cir. 2002), a criminal prosecution based on these circumstances.

They collided with a car driven by Rupert Giles, a mild mannered high school librarian, and Chase suffered serious injuries. Chase sued Giles, claiming that he carelessly rammed the car driven by Spike. Spike, who passed out immediately after the accident, was neither a party to the lawsuit nor a witness. At trial, Giles attempts to introduce evidence that Spike has a reckless character while driving; he argues that Spike caused the accident.

Analysis: Giles's evidence about Spike violates Rule 404(a)(1). Giles is offering this evidence to make a propensity argument: He wants the jury to reason that, because Spike often drives recklessly, he probably drove carelessly on this occasion and caused the accident. Even though Spike is neither a party nor a witness in the lawsuit, Rule 404(a)(1) bars Giles's evidence. That rule prohibits all uses of character evidence to prove that a person acted consistently with his character on a particular occasion.

The fact that Rule 404(a)(1) prohibits propensity evidence with respect to any person, even nonparties, underscores its broad policy rationale. The rule aims to focus trials on particular disputed actions, not on the character of the parties. This goal, in turn, serves our fundamental commitment to imposing civil or criminal liability only for particular actions proven in court.

Quick Summary

 **Rule 404(a)(1)** prohibits the use of character evidence to prove that a person acted consistently with their character on a particular occasion. The prohibition applies to proof of good or bad character; it also applies to evidence offered about any person, even nonparties and nonwitnesses. The rule helps assure that jurors base verdicts on evidence about particular events, not about the parties' general characters or proclivities.

Rule 404(a)(1) includes several exceptions. One, which we studied in Chapters 19–22, allows parties to prove a witness's character for truthfulness or untruthfulness under **Rules 608** and **609**. We will examine an additional exception in the next two chapters. Remember also that **Rule 404(a)(1)** only bars character evidence when it is offered to prove particular conduct through propensity reasoning. When character itself is an element of a claim or defense, parties may prove character.

28

Character Evidence to Show Propensity in Criminal Prosecutions

Key Concepts

- **Rule 404(a)(2)** Allows Some Character Evidence to Prove Propensity in Criminal Cases
- Exceptions Derive from the "Mercy Rule"
- Character Traits Must Be Pertinent
- Prosecutor May Only Match Defendant's Evidence

A. Introduction and Policy. Rule 404(a)(1) bars propensity evidence—that is, character evidence used to prove that a person acted consistently with their character on a particular occasion. Subsection **404(a)(2)** sets out three related exceptions to this rule, which we explore in this chapter.[1]

These three exceptions to the "no propensity" rule apply **only to criminal prosecutions**. Both constitutional doctrine and common law support the principle that criminal defendants should have as much latitude as possible to present a defense. Courts sometimes refer to this principle as the "mercy rule." If a criminal defendant believes that proof of his good character, or of an alleged victim's bad one, would help defend his innocence, then the mercy rule weighs in favor of the defendant presenting this evidence.

Following this reasoning, the common law developed a series of exceptions to the no-propensity rule; those exceptions allow criminal defendants to introduce some

---

1   Subsection 404(a)(3) deals with propensity evidence used to establish the character of a witness. Although this type of evidence technically is another exception to the bar on propensity evidence, it is easier to think of "character of a witness" evidence as one of the four categories of character evidence. That category has its own set of rules for how and when character evidence can be admitted; we explored those rules in Chapters 19–23.

types of character evidence for propensity purposes. To maintain a fair balance in the adversarial process, courts also allow prosecutors to use character evidence to make propensity arguments, usually in situations where they are responding to the defendant's use of propensity evidence. Rule 404(a)(2), which we'll examine in this chapter, incorporates these common law exceptions.[2]

B. The Rule. The exceptions for criminal prosecutions outlined in **Rule 404(a) (2)** are among the most complicated provisions in the Federal Rules of Evidence. Here is the full text with the most significant phrases highlighted:

RULE 404. Character Evidence; Crimes or Other Acts

(a) Character Evidence.

. . . .

   (2) Exceptions for a Defendant or Victim in a Criminal Case. The following exceptions apply in a <u>criminal case</u>:

      (A) a <u>defendant</u> may offer evidence of the defendant's <u>pertinent trait</u>, and if the evidence is admitted, the <u>prosecutor</u> may offer evidence to <u>rebut</u> it;

      (B) subject to the limitations in <u>Rule 412</u>, a <u>defendant</u> may offer evidence of an <u>alleged victim's pertinent trait</u>, and if the evidence is admitted, the <u>prosecutor</u> may:

         (i) offer evidence to <u>rebut</u> it; and

         (ii) offer evidence of the <u>defendant's same trait</u>; and

      (C) in a <u>homicide</u> case, the <u>prosecutor</u> may offer evidence of the <u>alleged victim's</u> trait of <u>peacefulness</u> to rebut evidence that the victim was the <u>first aggressor</u>.

There are four key points to note about these provisions:

---

2   Until December 2011, these exceptions appeared in Rule 404(a)(1) and (2). When restyling the rules, Congress renumbered these provisions 404(a)(2)(A) through (C). Be aware of these changes when reading cases published before 2012. Examples in this chapter all use the current numbering system, even when they draw from cases published before 2012.

- **First,** these exceptions to the no-propensity rule apply only in criminal cases.

- **Second,** the exceptions allow only proof of "pertinent" character traits. We will explore that limit in the Courtroom section below.

- **Third,** these subsections of Rule 404(a)(2) allow proof about both the defendant's character and the alleged victim's character.

- **Finally,** the subsections distinguish between when the defendant may introduce these types of evidence and when the prosecutor may do so.

The complicated text of the rule stems from the intersection of the last two points. When may each party introduce each type of evidence? It is easier to see these relationships in a table:

Character Evidence Admissible to Prove Propensity in Criminal Trials—Rule 404(a)(2)

Type of Character Evidence	When May the Defendant Offer this Evidence?	When May the Prosecution Offer this Evidence?
Pertinent Trait of the Defendant	Any time	To rebut character evidence of the same trait offered by the defendant, OR to match character evidence that the defendant offered about the alleged victim
Trait of Peacefulness of Alleged Victim	Not applicable: Defendant would not introduce this evidence	In a homicide case: To rebut any evidence that the alleged victim was the first aggressor In other cases: To rebut character evidence that the victim was not peaceful
Other Pertinent Trait of Alleged Victim	Any time, unless barred by Rule 412 (the rape shield law)	Only to rebut evidence of the same trait offered by the defendant; evidence must comply with Rule 412 (the rape shield law)

As this table shows, the accused has considerable freedom to introduce character evidence about herself or the alleged victim. The only limits on the defendant's ability to introduce character evidence are (1) the evidence must relate to a "pertinent" character trait, a requirement we'll discuss further below; and (2) the evidence must comply with **Rule 412**, the rape shield law. We will examine the provisions of that rule in Chapter 32.

The prosecutor, on the other hand, may introduce character evidence under these exceptions only **in response to** an action taken by the defendant. The prosecutor's permitted responses fall into three categories.

First, if the defendant offers character evidence about herself, the prosecutor may rebut that evidence with proof that the defendant lacks that trait or holds an opposite one. For example, a defendant charged with killing another person in a barroom brawl might offer evidence of her nonviolent nature. The prosecutor could then present evidence that the defendant has a violent character.

Second, if the defendant introduces character evidence about the alleged victim, the prosecutor may rebut that evidence by showing that the victim lacked that trait or held the opposite one. Under these circumstances, the prosecutor may **also** introduce evidence that the defendant held the trait that the defendant attributes to the victim. The defendant charged with killing a person during a barroom brawl, for example, might introduce evidence that the decedent had a violent character. This evidence would support a self-defense claim. In response to this evidence, the prosecution could offer evidence that the victim was peaceful. The prosecutor could **also** introduce evidence that the defendant is a violent person.

Finally, in a homicide case the prosecutor may offer evidence that the deceased victim was a peaceful person in response to **any** evidence that the deceased was the first aggressor. Under these limited circumstances, the prosecutor does not have to wait for the accused to introduce character evidence; the government may respond to any evidence that the deceased attacked first. The defendant charged with killing a person during a barroom brawl, for example, might present an eyewitness who testifies that the victim struck the defendant first. This testimony, suggesting that the deceased was the first aggressor, would allow the prosecutor to present evidence that the deceased had a peaceful character, even if the defendant has introduced no character evidence at all.

Once again, a table may help you understand when and how the prosecutor can respond to the defendant's evidence:

Character Evidence Admissible to Prove Propensity in Criminal Trials—How the Prosecutor Can Respond

If the Defendant . . .	Then the Prosecutor Can:
Introduces evidence of his own good character . . .	Introduce evidence of the defendant's bad character for the same character trait.
Introduces evidence of the victim's bad character . . .	Introduce evidence of the victim's good character for the same character trait AND evidence of the defendant's bad character for the same character trait.
Introduces evidence that the victim in a homicide case was the first aggressor . . .	Introduce evidence of the victim's peaceful character.

These rules, which limit the prosecutor's ability to introduce character evidence until the defendant has taken some action, reflect the underlying policy of the exceptions. They allow a criminal defendant latitude to present the defense of her choice, while limiting the use of propensity arguments based on character evidence. At the same time, the rules maintain fairness by allowing the prosecutor to use character evidence to show propensity when the defendant has done so.

The final exception, allowing the prosecutor to present evidence of the victim's peaceful nature in homicide cases, also redresses possible unfairness in the adversary process. A dead victim cannot respond to evidence suggesting that he was the first aggressor in a fight. The rules, therefore, allow the prosecutor to respond to this type of claim with a small dose of character evidence.

The next section offers several examples to illustrate these patterns and several other points of courtroom practice involving Rule 404(a)(2).

C. In the Courtroom.

1. Pertinence. Character evidence admitted under Rule 404(a)(2)(A) or (B) must be "pertinent" to the crime or defense. A classic example of pertinent evidence occurs when the defendant in a homicide trial claims self defense and supports that claim by offering evidence that the alleged victim had a violent character:

Example: The government charged James Gregg with killing James Fallis. Gregg, Fallis, and several other friends were drinking together when a dispute erupted between Gregg and Fallis. The dispute became a physical fight, which ended when Gregg shot Fallis five times in the back. Gregg claimed self defense, arguing that he shot Fallis only after Fallis started running towards his truck to obtain a gun. To support his self-defense claim, Gregg offered evidence of Fallis's violent character.

Analysis: Gregg's evidence of Fallis's character was admissible under Rule 404(a)(2)(B). The character trait of violence is pertinent to whether a homicide victim acted aggressively and provoked the confrontation ending in his death.[3]

Other examples of pertinent character traits include: (a) the defendant's peaceful character in a prosecution charging assault, battery, homicide, or other violent acts; (b) the defendant's honest character in a prosecution for fraud; or (c) the defendant's aversion to risk and gambling in a gambling prosecution.

Here, on the other hand, are some examples of character traits that were not pertinent to the charged crime or a defense to that crime:

Example: The government charged Dr. Jennifer Berry with submitting false Medicare claims. Berry attempted to introduce evidence of her excellent skill in treating patients.

Analysis: The court excluded this evidence, finding that it was not "pertinent" to the charges filed against Berry. Medical competence and honesty are

---

3   United States v. Gregg, 451 F.3d 930, 933 (8th Cir. 2006). The Federal Rules, however, restricted the form in which Gregg could offer this evidence. We will explore that point in the next chapter.

two different traits. Berry "could be the most competent, skilled physician in the world," and still commit fraud.[4]

Example: A grand jury indicted Ramon Santana-Camacho with illegally bringing citizens from the Dominican Republic into the United States. Santana-Camacho's daughter sought to testify that her father was a "kind person" and a "good family man."

Analysis: The district judge excluded this evidence as not "pertinent" and the court of appeals affirmed. A kind-hearted, good family man was just as likely to help immigrants enter the country illegally as an unkind man who neglected his family.[5]

Many courts say that Rule 404(a)(2)'s "pertinent" standard is the same as **Rule 401**'s definition of relevance.[6] Judges, however, sometimes apply Rule 404(a)(2) more rigorously than Rule 401; that is, they reject evidence as not pertinent even when the evidence probably satisfies Rule 401's generous definition of relevance. This tendency reflects the law's overall distaste for character evidence. Appellate courts, moreover, give trial judges especially broad discretion to determine when character evidence is pertinent. These tendencies lead to the exclusion of some character evidence that seems at least marginally relevant to the charged crime or its defenses:

Example: Richard Nazzaro, a Boston police officer, stood trial as part of a federal prosecution of Examscam, a Massachusetts scandal in which a group of police officers sold advance copies of civil service exams and answer sheets to other officers seeking promotions. The government charged Nazzaro with purchasing two separate exam/answer sets for $3000 apiece. As part of his defense, Nazzaro attempted to introduce evidence of commendations he had received in the military and in the police force, including a medal for special valor. The trial judge rejected this evidence as "not pertinent."

---

4   United States v. Berry, Crim. No. 4:06CR104-P-B, 2007 WL 324027, at *1 (N.D. Miss. Jan. 31, 2007).

5   United States v. Santana-Camacho, 931 F.2d 966, 968 (1st Cir. 1991).

6   See, e.g., id. To review Rule 401's definition of relevance, see Chapter 6.

Analysis: The court of appeals affirmed the trial judge's decision, noting its wide deference to trial rulings on this issue. The court also concluded that the qualities shown by this evidence, "bravery, attention to duty, perhaps community spirit," were not pertinent to the fraudulent behavior charged against Nazzaro. Evidence of an honest character would have been most pertinent to this crime.[7]

 Another judge might have ruled that the "attention to duty" represented by Nazzaro's commendations was pertinent to a charge of circumventing his duties by cheating on a promotion exam. Pertinence is one of the many areas in which effective advocacy may sway a judge's decision.

2. Matching Traits. When the prosecution introduces character evidence under the exceptions outlined in Rule 404(a)(2), it must offer evidence on traits that match those raised by the defendant. This is a tougher standard than mere pertinence. If a defendant offers evidence on one of two pertinent character traits, the prosecutor can respond only by offering evidence related to the trait raised by the accused. The prosecutor cannot offer evidence on the second trait, even though it might be pertinent.

Example: The government charged Randall Dahlin with robbing a bank. Dahlin claimed that he was babysitting his infant niece at the time and that he never would have left the baby alone because he was "deeply devoted to his niece and his family." To support these claims, Dahlin presented several character witnesses who testified about his devotion to his family.

In response, the prosecutor offered two types of character evidence: (1) that Dahlin got along poorly with his family; and (2) that Dahlin tended to take things that didn't belong to him. Dahlin objected to both lines of evidence as exceeding the bounds of Rule 404(a)(2).

Analysis: The district judge properly admitted testimony about Dahlin's poor relationship with his family. Since Dahlin buttressed his alibi defense with character evidence suggesting family devotion, Rule 404(a)(2)(A) al-

---

7   United States v. Nazzaro, 889 F.2d 1158, 1168 (1st Cir. 1989).

lowed the government to respond with evidence of a contrary character. The prosecutor, however, could not introduce evidence that Dahlin was prone to theft. Although this character trait was pertinent to the crime charged against Dahlin, the defendant had not introduced any evidence suggesting a generally honest character. The government may rebut only traits that the defendant has raised.[8]

3. Homicide Cases. In most trials, the prosecution can introduce character evidence to show propensity only after the defendant has done so. Remember, however, that Rule 404(a)(2)(C) loosens this restriction slightly in homicide prosecutions. If a homicide defendant claims that the alleged victim was the first aggressor, the prosecutor may introduce evidence of the victim's peaceful character regardless of whether the defendant used character evidence to raise this issue:

> **Example:** The government prosecuted Michael Garibaldi for stabbing Zack Allen to death. Garibaldi claimed that Allen attacked him, and that he stabbed Allen in self defense. To support this claim, Garibaldi presented the testimony of his girlfriend, Lisa Edgars, who testified that she saw Allen attack Garibaldi and strike the first blow. The prosecutor then offered testimony from Allen's neighbors and coworkers that he had a "peace-loving, nonaggressive nature."

> **Analysis:** Rule 404(a)(2)(C) permits Allen's neighbors and coworkers to testify. Garibaldi has not introduced any evidence about Allen's character, but he offered eyewitness testimony suggesting that Allen was the first aggressor. In homicide cases, the prosecutor can offer evidence of the victim's peaceful character whenever the defense offers evidence that the victim was the first aggressor, even if the defense did not rely upon character evidence.

---

8   This example draws on United States v. Dahlin, 734 F.2d 393, 394–95 (8th Cir. 1984).

Quick Summary

Rule 404(a)(2) establishes a series of exceptions to the rule against using character evidence to prove particular conduct through propensity reasoning. Under these provisions, the accused in a criminal case may introduce evidence of his own pertinent character traits or of pertinent traits of the alleged victim. The prosecutor may rebut this evidence with contrary character evidence on the same trait. In homicide cases, the prosecutor may also offer evidence of the victim's peaceful nature whenever the defendant introduces evidence suggesting that the victim was the first aggressor. These rules give the defendant latitude to present a defense while maintaining the adversarial balance in court.

29

Methods of Proving Propensity in Criminal Cases

Key Concepts

- **Rule 405(a):** Character Evidence About Accused or Alleged Victim Is Limited to Opinion or Reputation Testimony
- Cross-Examiner May Ask About Relevant Specific Acts
- Good Faith Belief
- No Extrinsic Evidence
- Limiting Instructions
- Rebuttal Character Witnesses

A. Introduction and Policy. As we saw in the last chapter, **Rule 404(a)(2)** allows the parties in a criminal case to offer evidence about some character traits of the defendant or alleged victim. Our previous discussion, however, did not address **how** parties present evidence of those traits.

We have already seen that the first two categories of character evidence have different rules governing how this evidence is presented:

1. Proof of a Witness's Propensity to Lie or Tell the Truth. For this first category of character evidence we studied, parties can attempt to show a witness's truthful or untruthful nature in three different ways:

(A) **Rule 608(b)**, discussed in Chapter 19, allows parties to **cross-examine witnesses** about conduct that suggests a truthful or untruthful character. The questioner, however, must accept the witness's answer; the cross-examiner cannot introduce extrinsic evidence proving that the conduct occurred.

(B) **Rule 608(a)**, discussed in Chapters 21–22, allows parties to offer **reputation or opinion testimony** about a witness's truthful or untruthful character. The party offering the testimony cannot ask the character witness to cite specific examples of conduct supporting her opinion, but the opponent may inquire about them on cross-examination. Once again, neither side may offer any extrinsic evidence of conduct asked about on cross-examination.

(C) **Rule 609**, discussed in Chapter 20, allows parties to introduce extrinsic evidence of some **prior criminal convictions** to suggest a witness's character for untruthfulness.

2. Proof of Character or Reputation as Elements. For this second category of character evidence, discussed in Chapter 26, parties may offer proof in any way. **Rule 405** allows parties to present both opinion/reputation testimony and extrinsic evidence of specific instances of conduct related to character. The opposing party may also ask about specific instances of conduct during cross-examination.

Let's return now to the category of character evidence we have been examining in the last two chapters: proof of conduct by propensity. For this category, **Rule 405** allows proof of character in a way that draws upon methods 1(A) and 1(B) above. A criminal defendant attempting to show his peaceful character, for example, may present witnesses who offer opinion or reputation testimony about his peacefulness. On cross-examination the prosecutor may then ask those witnesses about specific instances when the defendant was not peaceful. But neither party could try to prove, or disprove, these specific acts with additional evidence. Nor could the prosecutor introduce evidence of the defendant's prior criminal convictions—method 1(C) above—unless the defendant took the stand as a witness.

These rules significantly reduce the appeal of invoking the **Rule 404(a)(2)** exceptions to offer propensity evidence in criminal cases. Defendants providing evidence of their good character risk devastating cross-examinations in which the prosecution asks the character witness about specific instances of misconduct. Even a relatively upstanding citizen may have one or two blemishes on his life history;

the prosecutor will seek those out and attempt to raise them. And even if the character witness denies knowledge of any misconduct, the jury may remember the unrebutted negative questions better than they recall the witness's general testament to the defendant's good character.

Most judges and commentators recognize the peculiarities in this process. The evidentiary rules give an accused the opportunity to present a character defense, but limit the defense to the least persuasive type of evidence. If the defendant takes advantage of the opportunity, moreover, the prosecutor may counter with a cross-examination that leaves the defendant worse off than if she had never presented the initial character witness. The defendant's decision to call a character witness also allows the prosecutor to present contrary character witnesses who will give opinion or reputation testimony about the defendant's bad traits.

This structure, however, is firmly rooted in both common law and the Federal Rules. It rests in part on the law's general dislike of using character evidence to show propensity; courts tolerate that evidence, but without much enthusiasm. Thus, the Rules of Evidence allow propensity evidence, but only under narrow conditions, and only by using the easiest and simplest method—calling character witnesses to give opinion or reputation evidence. Allowing parties to try to prove or disprove specific instances of conduct would lead to countless mini-trials about whether the defendant or the victim did or did not commit some specific action months or years earlier.

The courts have also stressed the voluntary nature of a defendant's decision to introduce character evidence. If a defendant does not want to open the door to cross-examination on particular instances of misconduct, he can forego presenting character witnesses. In the leading common-law decision on this issue, *Michelson v. United States*, the Supreme Court observed that "the law foreclose[s] this whole confounding line of inquiry" into character issues, "unless [the] defendant thought the net advantage from opening it up would be with him."[9] Having opened the door on character, the defendant cannot complain about the type of evidence that enters.

B. The Rule. Rule 405, which we first examined in Chapter 26, outlines the methods of proving character traits at trial; these include the method for introduc-

---

9   335 U.S. 469, 485 (1948). Although decided decades before adoption of the Federal Rules, *Michelson* affirmed the process of allowing cross-examination of character witnesses about specific instances of misconduct. Courts and commentators still cite *Michelson*'s discussion of this process.

ing character evidence to show propensity in criminal cases. Section (a) of the rule sets out a process that we have already studied in the context of **Rule 608**: proof of character by reputation or opinion testimony, followed by cross-examination on specifics.

> ## RULE 405. Methods of Proving Character
>
> **(a) By Reputation or Opinion.** When evidence of a person's character or character trait is admissible, it may be proved by testimony about the person's <u>reputation</u> or by testimony in the form of an <u>opinion</u>. On <u>cross-examination</u> of the character witness, the court may allow an inquiry into relevant <u>specific instances</u> of the person's conduct.

The remainder of Rule 405, section (b), applies only when character is an element of the criminal charge, civil claim, or defense. We discussed that section in Chapter 26; it allows proof of specific acts to show character, but only when character is an element.

C. In the Courtroom. Most of the issues that arise under Rule 405(a) will be familiar to you; they are similar to those that arise under Rule 608(a), discussed in Chapters 21–22. These two rules establish an identical process for presenting character evidence, although in different contexts. Rule 608(a) controls proof of a witness's propensity to lie or tell the truth, while Rule 405(a) governs situations in which Rule 404(a)(2) allows parties to make other propensity arguments in criminal trials. In other words, Rule 405(a) applies to proof of a defendant's or victim's propensity in criminal cases.

To review the mechanics of this process, let's examine the testimony of a character witness from a prominent criminal prosecution: the trial of Kenneth Lay, CEO of the Enron Corporation, on charges of securities fraud, wire fraud, and making false statements.

As part of his defense, Lay offered several character witnesses. The first of these witnesses was Bob Lanier, the former mayor of Houston. After laying a foundation, in which Lanier explained the contexts in which he had known Lay, defense counsel examined Lanier in this way:

Lewis [Defense Counsel]: Let me ask you a couple of pointed questions about your opinions on Ken Lay's character. Based on your close friendship and working with Mr. Lay on various community projects, do you have an opinion as to his character for being an honest man?

Lanier: He was just straight as a string with me. And he's—all my dealings with him were—were straight up. He was very frank. He was a man of his word. I relied on him. He had this others focus that I think is good in—is almost essential in a public servant.

He didn't come into a deal thinking of—I didn't see him coming in as a hard case. It was constructive, trying to find constructive solutions. And I found him very, very pleasant to work with in all the different roles where I came in contact with him, and there were quite a few.

Lewis: Let me ask you about any opinion you might have formed. There have been allegations levied that Ken Lay is a greedy man. What do you have to say about that, Mayor?

Lanier: Well, I don't think he's indifferent to money; but at the same time, I wouldn't characterize him as—in my experience with him, he never showed a greedy side to me. I—I don't recall him ever doing anything I would call selfish.[10]

Lay and his character witnesses were sophisticated, articulate people, so this is one of the most detailed testaments to character you will see. The prosecutor and trial judge in this case also gave Lay's attorney significant latitude in conducting his examination. Since they were involved in a highly publicized and closely scrutinized trial, they may have wanted to give Lay every opportunity to present an effective defense. Under other circumstances, the prosecutor might have objected to Lanier's testimony that he didn't recall Lay ever doing anything selfish; testimony about the **absence** of specific acts, just like evidence of their presence, violates Rule 405. Character evidence in less notable trials, delivered by less prominent or articulate witnesses, is often even briefer and more general than the testimony reproduced above.

---

10   Trial Transcript at 16,397–98, United States v. Skilling, No. H-04–025ss, 2006 WL 213904 (S.D. Tex. May 2, 2006) (direct examination of Bob Lanier).

The prosecutor did object under Rule 405(a) when Lay's character witnesses strayed too far toward specific instances of Lay's conduct. Here's an example from the testimony of Robert Drayton McLane, Jr., another one of Lay's character witnesses:

> **McLane:** . . . I saw the kindness of his heart, the respect of his heart. An incident that I remember later is that after Ken's father passed away—
>
> **Strickland [the Prosecutor]:** Excuse me, Mr. McLane. Excuse me. Your honor, I'd object under 405, Your Honor.
>
> The Court: We shouldn't go into prior incidents if you can avoid it.
>
> **Lewis [Defense Counsel]:** Certainly, your Honor.[11]

The prosecutor conducted little cross-examination of Lay's character witnesses. Given the prominence of the individuals and the contexts in which they had known Lay, it would have been difficult to score points against these witnesses by asking if they knew about various misdeeds that Lay might have committed. Instead, the prosecutor used cross-examination primarily to gain the witnesses' acknowledgement that they knew nothing about the internal workings or finances of Enron.

Let's look more closely now at a few of the issues that arise under Rule 405(a).

1. Laying a Foundation. An attorney examining a character witness must lay a foundation showing that the witness has sufficient knowledge to offer an opinion about character or reputation. The process for laying a foundation under Rule 405 is the same as that under Rule 608; the examples in Chapter 21 show how this is done.

Laying a foundation under either of these rules is not just a formality. It is also a question of advocacy: It is imperative that the jury believe the character witness knows the individual well enough to have an informed opinion about his character. Under some circumstances, moreover, attorneys can use the foundation questions to reveal positive information about the defendant or alleged victim to the jury—despite Rule 405's prohibition against evidence related to specific acts. The trick lies in choosing witnesses who know the defendant or victim in a context that conveys those acts.

---

11   Id. at 16,428 (direct examination of Robert McLane).

If defense counsel calls the defendant's minister to offer an opinion on the defendant's character, for example, the attorney will lay the foundation by asking the minister in what context he knows the accused. If the minister responds that he knows the accused "extremely well because the defendant has attended church every week for the last twenty years," the jury will learn about the defendant's regular church attendance.

Similarly, Ken Lay's character witnesses knew him through a variety of philanthropic, civic, and other "good works" projects. Their responses to foundation questions allowed the defense counsel to remind the jury of the civic projects Lay had supported, even though the witnesses were able to offer only general opinions about Lay's character. This opportunity to inject specific information through foundation questions is one of the reasons why parties continue to call character witnesses.

2. Cross-Examination on Specific Acts. Parties in criminal cases run a serious risk if they call a character witness to testify about a defendant's or victim's good character. On cross-examination, the opposing party may decimate that witness by asking questions related to specific bad acts. In theory, as explained in Chapter 22, these questions simply test the witness's knowledge of the defendant's or victim's character. In practice, these questions dangle damaging innuendos before the jury. Here is just one of many cases in which the cross-examination of a character witness caused significant damage:

> **Example:** John and Michelle Sandalis operated Dalis Painting, a company that performed paint jobs for the University of Virginia. The Sandalises failed to report revenue from the painting business on their tax returns, leading to prosecution for tax fraud and evasion. John Sandalis called six character witnesses who each testified about his character for truthfulness. On cross-examination the government asked one of these witnesses, "Did you know that Mr. Sandalis within the last few years attempted to persuade [a witness] to testify falsely in a judicial proceeding?"

> **Analysis:** The district judge permitted the question. Since the witness testified to Sandalis's character for truthfulness, the government could ask about a specific incident bearing on that character.[12]

---

12   United States v. Sandalis, 39 F. App'x 798, 803 (4th Cir. 2002).

3. Relevant Acts. Although Rule 405 allows attorneys to cross-examine character witnesses about specific acts, the examiners may ask only about acts that are relevant to the character trait described by the witness. This limit reflects **Rule 611(b)**'s restriction of cross-examination to subjects raised on direct examination, a rule we discussed in Chapter 15. It is also consistent with the courts' narrow approach to presenting character evidence. Here are two cases illustrating this requirement:

> **Example:** The government charged Alfred Grady with attempting to pass counterfeit money. A witness testified that Grady had a good reputation in the community for truth and honesty. On cross-examination, the prosecutor asked this witness if he knew that Grady had been arrested for filing a false employment security claim as well as for making a false statement to the police.

> **Analysis:** The district judge allowed these questions, and the court of appeals affirmed. Both arrests related to crimes of dishonesty, and the witness testified to Grady's truth and honesty. Opposing counsel thus could raise these specific incidents during cross-examination.[13]

> **Example:** The government prosecuted Samuel George for beating Herman Kellywood to death. In response to George's claim of self defense, the government presented a character witness who testified to Kellywood's peacefulness. George's counsel attempted to cross-examine the witness about his knowledge of Kellywood's numerous arrests for speeding, driving without a license, disorderly conduct, driving while intoxicated, endangering the welfare of a minor, and public intoxication.

> **Analysis:** The district judge precluded inquiry into these arrests, finding that none of them related sufficiently to peacefulness or violence. One factor that might have influenced the trial judge's ruling is that the character witness had already testified on direct that "he occasionally drank with Kellywood and on no occasion, either drunk or sober, did he see Kellywood get violent." If the witness had not already discussed Kellywood's drinking, the trial judge might have allowed inquiry about the arrests for driving while intoxicated

---

13   United States v. Grady, 665 F.2d 831, 834 (8th Cir. 1981).

and public intoxication. Intoxication induces violence in many people, so knowledge of those arrests might affect a witness's opinion of peacefulness.

The trial judge may also have been influenced by the fact that Kellywood was a victim rather than a defendant. Judges tend to be more protective of a victim's reputation—especially that of a deceased one—than of a defendant's reputation. If the defendant George had presented a character witness testifying to his peacefulness, the judge might have allowed cross-examination about a similar arrest record.

The court of appeals affirmed the trial judge's ruling in this case, but the appellate court probably would have affirmed a contrary ruling as well. Trial judges have wide discretion on the questions they allow on cross-examination of a character witness.[14]

As the George case suggests, the question whether a particular act relates to a character trait does not always generate a straightforward answer. This is an issue on which persuasive advocacy may make a difference.

4. Good Faith Belief. As in other contexts, a cross-examiner cannot ask a character witness about speculative or imaginary acts; the attorney must have a good faith belief that the incidents occurred. Here is an example of the good faith requirement under Rule 405:

Example: A grand jury indicted Oneyda Zambrana and ten other individuals for a series of narcotics offenses. Zambrana presented two character witnesses, who both opined that she was peaceable and law-abiding. The government asked the witnesses whether they knew that Zambrana had helped her husband, a convicted drug dealer, escape from state prison. Zambrana challenged the government's good faith belief that she had acted in such a manner.

---

14   United States v. George, 778 F.2d 556, 564–65 (10th Cir. 1985).

Analysis: In response to Zambrana's challenge, the prosecutor told the district judge that Zambrana had confessed her role to an FBI agent. The government also obtained an affidavit from the agent confirming that confession. This was sufficient to establish a good faith belief, and the judge allowed the questions.[15]

The standard for good faith is not very high. In particular, courts do not require cross-examiners to prove good faith with evidence that would itself be admissible in court. Attorneys frequently demonstrate good faith through hearsay and other weaker forms of evidence. And of course the evidence that proves good faith is never shown to the jury, because this would violate the ban on extrinsic evidence. Instead, the attorney who is attempting to prove good faith will present the evidence to the judge at a sidebar, or (if a sidebar conference on the question would be unwieldy) in open court after the jury has been excused from the courtroom.

5. Extrinsic Evidence. A party who cross-examines a character witness about specific conduct under Rule 405(a) must accept the witness's response. If the witness denies knowledge of the conduct, the cross-examiner cannot introduce evidence that the conduct really occurred. Nor can the opposing party offer evidence disputing whether the conduct occurred. Either type of evidence would be proof of a "specific instance[] of the person's conduct," which Rule 405 allows only when character is an element of the case.

This limit parallels Rule 608(b)'s restriction on extrinsic evidence. Under both rules, the courts prevent parties from straying too far from the main controversy by disputing the existence of prior acts.

Example: Imagine that in the Zambrana case, the character witness responded to the prosecution's question by saying: "No, I've never heard anything about Zambrana helping anyone escape from prison. That would be completely inconsistent with her character." The prosecutor then attempts to call the FBI agent to prove that Zambrana admitted to helping her husband escape from prison.

---

15   Unites States v. Alvarez, 860 F.2d 801, 828 (7th Cir. 1988). For other discussions of the need for good faith when cross-examining a witness, see Chapter 19 (revealing untruthful character on cross-examination) and Chapter 22 (cross-examining the character witness).

Analysis: A judge would not allow the prosecution to call this witness; the agent's only role would be to offer extrinsic evidence of the specific act raised on cross-examination. The agent's information gave the prosecutor a good faith belief sufficient to ask a character witness about the incident. But once the witness denies knowing about this incident, counsel must let the matter drop.

The same reasoning usually bars a party from attempting to prove that an incident raised during this type of cross-examination did **not** occur. In the Zambrana case, for example, the defendant had admitted giving her husband money to facilitate his escape from prison; she argued that the prosecutor's cross-examination suggested she played a more active role in the prison escape. Zambrana, however, could not introduce testimony clarifying this point. Admitting this type of evidence would sidetrack trials and confuse the jury. Only the character witness's response to the question, moreover, is relevant to the character inquiry—the actual facts of Zambrana's previous conduct are not relevant.

Under unusual circumstances, when a mistaken inference of bad behavior would be highly prejudicial, the judge might allow the affected party to introduce extrinsic evidence disproving the incident. These cases, however, are rare. Judges more often avoid this type of prejudice by requiring cross-examiners to demonstrate their good faith belief outside the presence of the jury before the question is asked. At that point, the opposing party can argue that inquiry into the matter would seriously mislead the jury or cause substantial unfair prejudice.

6. Limiting Instructions. The Rules of Evidence allow counsel to cross-examine character witnesses on specific acts as a way of testing the knowledge underlying the witness's opinion or reputation testimony. The act itself, therefore, is not relevant to the case; only the fact of the witness's knowledge is relevant.

When parties cross-examine character witnesses, the judge will attempt to explain this fine distinction to the jurors. Here is an instruction, for example, that the judge might have offered in the Zambrana case:

You will recall that after witness Evans testified about the defendant's character for peacefulness and law-abidingness, the prosecutor asked the witness some questions about whether he knew that the defendant had helped her husband escape from prison. Those questions were asked only to help you decide if the witness really knew about the defendant's character for peacefulness and law-abidingness. The information developed by the government attorney on that subject may not be used by you for any other purpose.

That the defendant may have helped her husband escape from prison is not evidence that she committed the crime charged in this case.[16]

The jury may have great difficulty understanding or following this instruction. In fact, reiterating the government's questions may simply highlight them in the jurors' minds. In theory, however, the jury should only consider these cross-examination questions to assess the knowledge of the character witness; they should not assume the truth of the acts inquired about and use them to make judgments about whether the defendant has the type of character that would cause someone to commit the charged crimes. In fact, if (as is usually the case) the character witness denies that the specific act occurred or simply states that she has no knowledge of the specific act, there is no evidence that the specific act ever did occur, since the attorney's questions do not constitute evidence.

7. Rebuttal Witnesses. In addition to cross-examining a character witness, the parties in a criminal case may present rebuttal character witnesses. These character witnesses testify that the defendant or victim has a character trait contrary to one presented by another character witness. In the Zambrana case, for example, the government could also have refuted the testimony of Zambrana's character witnesses by calling its own character witnesses. Those witnesses, if available to the government, would have testified that Zambrana had an unpeaceful and law-breaking character. A party does not have to choose between cross-examination and the presentation of rebuttal witnesses; both avenues are available.

A rebuttal character witness is treated exactly the same as any other character witness: The party calling the witness can ask only about opinion or reputation, not about specific acts. The opponent may ask about specific acts on cross-exam-

---

16   Eighth Circuit Manual of Model Jury Instructions § 2.10 (2014). This is the model instruction used in the Eighth Circuit, with specifics from the Zambrana case inserted.

ination to test the witness's knowledge, but she cannot prove these specific acts with extrinsic evidence; the cross-examiner is stuck with the witness's answer.

For a further explanation of these concepts, <u>click here</u> to see the video "How to Prove Character Evidence" or go to the Videos module from the eBook on your eProducts bookshelf.

Quick Summary

In criminal cases, **Rule 404(a)(2)** gives both the prosecution and defense limited ability to present propensity evidence about the accused and alleged victim. **Rule 405(a)** further constrains that opportunity by restricting a character witness's direct testimony to opinion or reputation evidence. On cross-examination, opposing counsel may ask a character witness about specific acts related to the character traits discussed on direct examination. The cross-examiner must have a good faith belief that the acts occurred, but neither party may offer extrinsic evidence related to those acts. When this type of cross-examination occurs, the judge will instruct the jury to consider evidence of specific acts only in assessing the character witness's knowledge and credibility, not in determining the underlying issue of guilt or innocence.

30

Crimes, Wrongs, or Other Acts

Key Concepts

- **Rule 404(b):** Admission of "Character" Evidence for Purposes Other Than Proof of Propensity
- Relationship of **Rules 404(b)** and **404(a)**
- Non-Exclusive List of Other Purposes
- Prior or Subsequent Acts
- Civil and Criminal Cases
- Good and Bad Acts
- Application of **Rule 403**
- Limiting Instructions

A. Introduction and Policy. We have separated "character evidence" into four different categories. First there is evidence used to show a witness's propensity to lie or tell the truth. **Rules 608 and 609** allow such attacks, but restrict the types of evidence parties can employ for that purpose. The second category includes evidence used to prove other types of conduct through propensity arguments. **Rule 404(a)** prohibits most uses of this evidence, and **Rule 405** restricts the methods that can be used to prove general propensity when it is admissible. The third category comprises evidence used to prove a character trait when that trait is an element of the crime, charge, or defense. As long as the character trait is relevant, this evidence is admissible in any form.

We now turn to the fourth and final category of character evidence, evidence of specific acts that reveal an individual's character but are also relevant to prove some other fact of consequence in the case. The phrase "character evidence" is particularly misleading as applied to this category, because this evidence is not offered to prove character. Instead, parties present this evidence to prove some other fact relevant to the case. The concern about character evidence arises with this category because the jury might **also** use this evidence impermissibly to infer an individual's character and then, based on that inference, conclude that the individual had a propensity to act in a particular way. This type of propensity reasoning undercuts our commitment to judge individuals based on their acts rather than their general character.

Here is an example of a piece of evidence that could be used both to show a propensity to commit crimes (an impermissible purpose) and the identity of a defendant (a permissible purpose):

Example: Warren Pindell, a police officer, developed an illicit method of supplementing his income. Pindell patrolled a neighborhood populated with female prostitutes. When Pindell observed a prostitute get into the car of a male customer, he would follow the car until it parked. Pindell, dressed in his police uniform, would then approach the car, demand that the man show identification, and order him out of the car. Once the would-be customer had left the car, Pindell would threaten him with a gun or billy club, handcuff him, and take all of his cash. Pindell then released his victims, assuming they would be unlikely to report a robbery that occurred while attempting to use the services of a prostitute.

The government ultimately caught Pindell and prosecuted him. Among other evidence, two prostitutes identified Pindell as the man who had robbed several of their customers. Over Pindell's objection, the trial judge allowed these prostitutes to testify that they knew Pindell because he had previously purchased their sexual services.

Analysis: Evidence that Pindell had hired prostitutes, which was illegal in his city, could be used to show that he had a bad character. The actions suggest that Pindell was a lawbreaker; some jurors would also condemn his acts as immoral. The prosecutor, however, did not elicit this evidence to prove that Pindell was a lawbreaker and, consistent with that character, that he had robbed the prostitutes' customers. Using evidence of Pindell's prior lawbreaking in that manner would have violated Rule 404(a)(1), which prohibits using character evidence "to prove that on a particular occasion the person acted in accordance with the character."

Instead, the prosecutor introduced this testimony to support the prostitutes' identification of Pindell. Because the prostitutes had served Pindell as a customer, they knew his identity. Evidence of Pindell's illegal actions, therefore, was admissible to prove identity, a purpose allowed by Rule 404.[1]

This diagram summarizes the two types of inferences that a jury could have drawn from Pindell's action of hiring prostitutes:

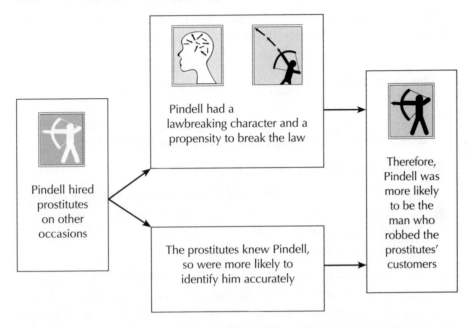

The top line represents an impermissible way of using the evidence that Pindell had hired prostitutes: to make a propensity inference. As we saw in Chapter 27, Rule 404(a)(1) bars this type of reasoning. The bottom line, however, uses the same evidence for a different purpose: to show that the prostitutes could accurately identify Pindell as the man who robbed their customers. This line of reasoning does not include the propensity inference, so it does not violate Rule 404(a)(1).

Notice that Rule 404(a)(1) resembles many other rules we have studied by admitting evidence for some purposes but not others. **Rule 409**, discussed in Chapter 11, bars evidence of an offer to pay medical expenses if a party presents that evidence to show liability. But the rule allows introduction of the same evidence for other purposes, such as to prove that the plaintiff was injured. Rule 404(a)(1) has

---

1   United States v. Pindell, 336 F.3d 1049, 1056–57 (D.C. Cir. 2003).

the same structure: A party may introduce "character evidence" for any purpose **other than** to prove that a person acted consistently with their character on a particular occasion.

Rule 404(b), which we'll study in this chapter, underscores this distinction and expands upon it. The rule also addresses the relationship between specific acts and character. Rule 404(b) recognizes that actions that reveal a person's character may also prove a variety of facts material to the lawsuit. As long as the actions are used to prove one of those facts, rather than to show a propensity to act in a particular manner, Rule 404 allows their admission.

B. The Rule. Rule 404(b) is relatively simple to read:

> # RULE 404. Character Evidence; Crimes or Other Acts
>
> **(b) Crimes, Wrongs, or Other Acts.**
>
> > **(1)** *Prohibited Uses.* Evidence of a crime, wrong, or other act is <u>not admissible</u> to prove a person's character in order to show that on a particular occasion the person acted in accordance with the character.
> >
> > **(2)** *Permitted Uses; Notice in a Criminal Case.* This evidence <u>may</u> be admissible for <u>another purpose</u>, <u>such as</u> proving motive, opportunity, intent, preparation, plan, knowledge, identity, absence of mistake, or lack of accident. On request by a defendant in a <u>criminal case</u>, the prosecutor <u>must</u>:
> >
> > > **(A)** provide <u>reasonable notice</u> of the <u>general nature</u> of any such evidence that the prosecutor intends to offer at trial; and
> > >
> > > **(B)** do so before trial—or during trial if the court, for good cause, excuses lack of pretrial notice.

Here are six initial points to note about this rule. **First,** the opening subsection restates the principle established by **Rule 404(a)(1):** Character evidence is not admissible to prove that a person acted "in accordance with" their character. Section (b) expands upon this principle by noting that a party may not evade this prohibition by introducing evidence of specific acts that prove character, which in turn is used to show propensity.

Second, the section affirms that evidence of these other acts may be admissible for other purposes. The use of the word "may," however, is significant. This evidence is not automatically admissible, like proof of a recent conviction for a crime of dishonesty.[2] A judge may exclude the evidence under **Rule 403** if its unfair prejudice, potential for confusion, or other negative qualities substantially outweighs its probative value. As we'll see below, the risk of unfair propensity reasoning is one of the factors that the judge will weigh under Rule 403.

Third, the section lists nine specific examples that qualify as "another purpose" for which evidence of other acts may be admitted. The words "such as," however, make clear that these are only examples and that other purposes are possible. If a party can cite any purpose for character-related evidence other than raising the forbidden propensity inference, Rule 404 supports admission of the evidence.

Fourth, the section applies to both criminal and civil cases. Unlike section 404(a), which explicitly limits the exceptions in subsection (2) to criminal cases, nothing in the text of section 404(b) restricts its application in that way. To the contrary, the special notice requirement for criminal cases appearing within subsection 404(b)(2) suggests that the remainder of the section applies to both civil and criminal suits.

Fifth, the final provisions of Rule 404(b) require the prosecution to provide reasonable notice in criminal trials of its intent to introduce evidence of crimes or other acts in the manner sanctioned by this rule. This type of evidence, as we'll see below, can significantly enhance the prosecutor's case. Because of the potency of the evidence, it is fair to give the accused notice and an opportunity to prepare.

In a sense, **finally,** Rule 404(b) is a completely unnecessary provision; courts could reach the result contemplated by that section even without its text. Rule 404(a)(1) bars evidence that tends to prove a person's personality trait only **if** a party uses that evidence for a propensity purpose: to suggest that the person acted consistently with their character on a particular occasion. Rule 404(a)(1) does not prohibit admission of evidence related to personality **traits** when a party offers that evidence for **another purpose**. Nor does any other rule bar admission of evidence related to personality traits when the evidence is offered for non-propensity

---

2   Recall the discussion in Chapter 20 about Rule 609, which automatically admits evidence of a witness's conviction for a crime of dishonesty that occurred within ten years as defined by that rule.

purposes. Rule 402, meanwhile, declares that all relevant evidence is admissible. So if a party offers evidence related to character for any relevant purpose other than proving propensity, that evidence would be admissible even without Rule 404(b).

Rule 404(b) is similar to the final section of **Rule 408** or to the concluding sentences of **Rules 407** and **411**. Like those provisions, Rule 404(b) underscores the admissibility of evidence offered for purposes other than the one barred by the first part of the rule. Rule 404(b) also assures reasonable notice to criminal defendants when the prosecutor uses this powerful evidence.

Perhaps most important, Rule 404(b) helps litigants make the distinction between permissible and impermissible uses of character-related evidence by suggesting some permissible uses of that evidence. Evidence of conduct related to character may be admissible to prove motive, opportunity, intent, preparation, and the other facts noted in Rule 404(b). The list of purposes recited by the rule, however, is not exclusive: If a party can find any use of character evidence other than one that relies upon propensity reasoning, she has a chance of admitting the evidence.

C. In the Courtroom. Rule 404(b) is one of the most frequently invoked

provisions in the Federal Rules of Evidence. The example of Warren Pindell, outlined above, indicates why. The rule allows parties to introduce evidence that delivers two separate blows. First, the evidence accomplishes its stated purpose, to prove identity, intent, motive, or a similar fact. Second, assuming that the evidence shows a prior act that is bad or immoral, the jury may develop a negative view of the person. Although the judge will instruct the jury to use the evidence only for its intended purpose, the jurors are likely to engage in propensity reasoning as well. The rules forbid that, but few people doubt that it happens.

 Given these realities, parties work hard to find ways to introduce evidence of an opposing party's bad or immoral acts. The opponents try just as hard to exclude this evidence. Judges, however, tend to construe the "another purpose" phrase in Rule 404(b) rather broadly. In many cases it will seem that a very small dog tail (a purported other purpose) is being used to admit a rather large dog (evidence of a bad character that the jury will use as propensity evidence). Rule 404(b), more than any other rule of evidence, creates a contest of wits in which opposing attorneys seek to admit or exclude evidence that carries particularly high stakes.

We first explore below some of the other purposes that Rule 404(b) and the courts have recognized to support admission of crimes, wrongs, and other acts. We then examine some more general issues, such as the limiting instructions that judges offer when admitting this evidence.

1. Motive. A prosecutor sometimes argues that a previous crime or other bad act is admissible because it motivated the charged crime. We saw one example of this in the Felton case discussed in Chapter 7. The government in that case charged Felton and his codefendant Chase with robbery, counterfeiting, and planned construction of an explosive device. Over the defendants' objection, the court allowed the government to show that Felton and Chase had engaged in a number of white supremacist activities. Their commitment to a white supremacist agenda, the government successfully argued, established the motive for their robbery and other crimes. The evidence thus was admissible, despite its bad character overtones, under Rule 404(b). Also, as we saw in Chapter 7, the judge permitted the evidence under **Rule 403**.

Here is an example of a case in which a crime, rather than an antisocial act, was admissible to establish motive:

> **Example:** The government charged Gary DeCicco with setting his commercially unsuccessful warehouse on fire and fraudulently collecting insurance proceeds on the building. At trial, the prosecutor planned to show that DeCicco torched the warehouse in part to obtain money to pay off more than one million dollars in back taxes. DeCicco's debt arose from years of illegal tax evasion recently uncovered by the Internal Revenue Service. DeCicco filed a motion in limine to exclude evidence of his tax evasion and resulting liability, arguing that Rule 404(a)(1) barred this evidence.

> **Analysis:** The district judge agreed with DeCicco and excluded the evidence. This judge concluded that, since the government had not charged DeCicco with any tax crimes, it was attempting to show that DeCicco was the kind of bad person who would commit arson and other crimes—just the type of propensity inference that Rule 404(a)(1) forbids.

> But the prosecutor appealed this pretrial ruling, and the court of appeals reversed. The appellate court held that the trial judge abused his discretion by focusing exclusively on the differing nature of the charged and prior crimes.

Although the government had not charged DeCicco with tax violations, his accumulated tax liabilities provided a motive for the charged arson. Arson is a crime in which financial motives play a significant role, making this evidence particularly relevant. The evidence, therefore, was admissible to prove a fact—motive—that did not depend on the propensity inference forbidden by Rule 404(a)(1).[3]

2. Plan. The DeCicco prosecution included another bad act that the government offered for a different "other" purpose under Rule 404(b). This act, the government argued, established a common plan or scheme:

Example: In the prosecution described above, the government charged DeCicco with setting two separate fires in his warehouse during July 1995. The prosecutor also offered evidence that DeCicco tried to burn the same warehouse in March 1992. The earlier fire was set in a similar manner to one of the 1995 fires, it occurred just hours before DeCicco's insurance policy was due to end, and DeCicco was also facing financial pressures at that time. A quick response from the fire department prevented much damage to the building in 1992, and DeCicco submitted no insurance claims for that fire. The government, however, argued that the earlier fire showed DeCicco's ongoing plan to burn the financially unsuccessful warehouse and collect insurance proceeds.

Analysis: The district judge excluded evidence of the 1992 fire in a pretrial ruling, but the court of appeals held that this decision was also an abuse of discretion. The appellate court found that the existence of similar suspicious fires occurring in the same building suggested a common plan. The three-year gap, moreover, was not too long to preclude evidence of commonality. On the contrary, the three-year delay supported the common plan. DeCicco's 1992 insurer had cancelled the policy due to misrepresentations, and he had to wait three years to apply for a new policy without disclosing the earlier cancellation. The 1995 fires occurred just two months after DeCicco's insurance resumed.[4]

---

3   United States v. DeCicco, 370 F.3d 206, 213–14 (1st Cir. 2004).

4   Id. at 210–13.

3. Identity. In the Pindell case, the court admitted evidence of the defendant's other bad acts (hiring prostitutes) because participants in those acts were able to identify the defendant and link him to the charged crime. Using the bad acts for that purpose avoided the propensity inference prohibited by Rule 404(a)(1).

"Signature elements" of a crime may also allow the prosecutor to prove identity by introducing evidence of the defendant's other crimes or bad acts. If a charged crime has an unusual feature, and if the defendant has engaged in other acts incorporating that feature, then these common characteristics tend to show the defendant's identity as the perpetrator of the charged crime. This use of bad acts also avoids any forbidden propensity inference.

 Determining whether the features of one crime are similar enough to those of another to constitute proof of identity requires judges to scrutinize the facts closely. Here is an example of a case in which the court found sufficient similarity to admit the evidence:

Example: Leo Alonzo, an undercover police agent, purchased 83 milligrams of heroin from a man who had parked a primer gray Volkswagen bug in front of a house at 4906 Buena Vista Avenue. The dealer sold Alonzo the drugs packaged in two pink balloons. Alonzo did not know the name of the dealer when he purchased the heroin, but he later identified Rudy Sanchez as the dealer from a photograph. The government charged Sanchez with selling heroin.

At trial, defendant Sanchez claimed that Alonzo mistakenly identified him as the dealer. In rebuttal, the prosecutor called police officer Erasmo Martinez as a witness. Martinez testified that he visited 4906 Buena Vista Avenue a week after Alonzo's "buy," approached a primer gray Volkswagen bug parked in the driveway, and purchased two pink balloons containing heroin from a man seated in the car. Martinez also testified that (1) the man in the car was Sanchez, and (2) the Volkswagen bore the same license plates as the car Alonzo had seen a week earlier. Sanchez objected to Martinez's testimony under Rule 404.

Analysis: The district judge allowed Martinez's testimony as relevant to establish Sanchez's identity, and the court of appeals affirmed. The court noted that the purchase of heroin in pink balloons was not as distinctive as it might first appear. Heroin dealers often package the drug in balloons so that they can swallow the balloons if they spot a police officer. But the purchase of bags of heroin from the same address, sold in the same manner by a man who controlled the same car, was sufficiently distinctive to allow introduction of the evidence as proof of identity. The fact that the sales occurred only one week apart further buttressed the case for introducing this other crime evidence.[5]

Although prosecutors frequently attempt to use the "identity" prong of Rule 404(b), this argument works only if two conditions are met: (1) identity must be at issue, and (2) there must be strong similarities between the charged and other crimes. Both of these conditions existed in the Sanchez case. In the following example, however, both conditions failed:

Example: The government charged Kristen Gilbert, a nurse at a veteran's hospital, with killing four patients by injecting epinephrine in the patients' intravenous lines. Excessive doses of epinephrine can cause a fatally rapid heartbeat; the patients who died under Gilbert's care all suffered cardiac arrests.

The government filed a pretrial motion, seeking permission to introduce evidence that Gilbert previously tried to kill her husband by injecting him with an excess dose of potassium. Excess potassium, like epinephrine, can cause cardiac arrest; the government contended that this evidence established Gilbert's identity as the person who killed the patients. Gilbert opposed the motion, arguing that the government was using the evidence to create a forbidden propensity inference: that she had a tendency to murder people and thus had killed these patients.

Analysis: The district judge excluded evidence about any attempt Gilbert might have made to kill her husband, citing two reasons:

First, even if Gilbert had tried to kill her husband in the manner described by the prosecution, the judge concluded that the similarities between the crimes

---

5   United States v. Sanchez, 988 F.2d 1384, 1392–94 (5th Cir. 1993).

were too slight to support admission for the purpose of proving identity. In a hospital context, the use of injections on different occasions was not particularly distinctive. In addition, Gilbert's alleged attempt on her husband's life employed a different medication than the one used in the charged crimes.

Second and most important, the judge observed that identity was not an issue in the case. Gilbert did not defend against the charges by arguing that someone injected epinephrine in the patients' intravenous lines, but it was not her. Instead, she contended that no crime had occurred, that these patients died of natural causes. Under those circumstances, the government's effort to introduce evidence of Gilbert's alleged attempt to kill her husband did not realistically support proof of identity. Instead, the government wanted to introduce the evidence to support a forbidden propensity inference: that Gilbert was the type of person who was capable of murder.[6]

4. Opportunity. Commission of a crime sometimes requires a particular opportunity, such as access to a protected place or to special tools. To prove that the defendant had the opportunity to commit a crime like this, the prosecutor may offer evidence that the defendant enjoyed access to the protected place or special tools on another occasion. That "other occasion" might consist of a prior crime or bad act, leading to an objection that the evidence violates Rule 404(a)(1). But as long as the evidence establishes a needed opportunity, it avoids the propensity inference forbidden by the latter rule:

Example: The government charged Basil Fawlty, a motel owner, with breaking into one of his motel rooms at night and sexually assaulting a guest. The guest testified that she had locked the door from the inside, and that her assailant entered the room with a key. But investigators found no extra keys to the room, and Fawlty testified that he had no passkey or other means to enter guest rooms. To rebut Fawlty's claim, the prosecutor offered evidence that a year before the sexual assault, Fawlty pled guilty to breaking into another room at the motel and stealing a guest's wallet. That room was also locked from the inside when the crime occurred.

---

6   United States v. Gilbert, 229 F.3d 15, 21–25 (1st Cir. 2000). Although the government lost this evidentiary motion, it won the case. A jury convicted Gilbert of four homicides and two attempted murders; she is serving four consecutive life sentences.

Analysis: The jury could use the evidence of Fawlty's guilty plea to make a forbidden propensity inference. They might infer that Fawlty has a tendency to break into his guests' rooms for illegal purposes, and that—as a result of this tendency—he committed the charged assault. The prosecutor, however, has another, permissible purpose for the evidence: It demonstrates that Fawlty had the opportunity to commit the charged crime. He must own a passkey or other means giving him access to locked guest rooms. The judge might admit the guilty plea to show Fawlty's opportunity to commit the charged crime.

5. Knowledge. We considered one example of knowledge as a permissible purpose for "bad acts" evidence in Chapter 25: Gloria's successful theft of money from a safe in one month showed that she possessed the necessary knowledge to break into the same safe three months later. This type of knowledge could also be called "opportunity" evidence; without the knowledge to break into the safe, Gloria would not have had the opportunity to steal its contents. For the purpose of 404(b) admissibility, the difference is merely semantic. As long as the other act evidence proves a relevant fact without using the propensity inference, the evidence is admissible regardless of what it is called.

Prosecutors often cite "knowledge" as a purpose for introducing evidence of other crimes or bad acts when knowledge of a particular fact is an element of the crime. Evidence of another crime sometimes demonstrates that the defendant possessed that knowledge:

Example: London Hylton tried to shoplift three t-shirts from a local Gap Store. The manager caught Hylton and forbade her from returning to the store. When Hylton entered the store the following week, the manager had her arrested and charged with trespass.

Analysis: To prove trespass under these circumstances, the prosecutor must show that Hylton knew that the store had revoked her privilege to enter the premises. To do this, the prosecutor could elicit testimony from the manager that he caught Hylton shoplifting the previous week and told her that she could no longer enter the store. Although evidence of the shoplifting might prompt the jury to conclude that Hylton has a lawbreaking character, it also establishes the knowledge necessary for the charged crime.

Example: Donovan New was driving his father and cousin down the highway at 89 miles per hour when he lost control of the car, causing it to run off the highway and roll over twice. New's father and cousin were both killed in the crash. New was taken to the hospital and his blood alcohol content was measured at .320. The government charged New with two counts of involuntary manslaughter, which requires proof that the defendant knew, or reasonably could have foreseen, that his conduct was a threat to the lives of others. At trial, the government offered evidence that New had two prior convictions for driving under the influence of alcohol. New objected to the evidence under Rule 404(a).

Analysis: The district court admitted the prior convictions, and the appellate court affirmed. The prior convictions were not admitted to prove that the defendant had a propensity to drive drunk or to act recklessly, but instead to show that he was aware of the risks of drunk driving and therefore knew that driving while intoxicated threatened the lives of others: "One who drives a vehicle while under the influence after having been convicted of that offense knows better than most that his conduct is not only illegal, but entails a substantial risk of harm to himself and others."[7]

6. Intent. Evidence of other crimes, wrongs, or acts may also be admissible to prove that a defendant possessed the intent necessary to commit a crime.

Example: J.R. is charged with killing his elderly father, Jock, by running him over with his Mercedes. J.R. claims that the incident was an accident, that Jock wandered out into the driveway and J.R. was not paying attention while parking the car. The prosecution wishes to call Sue Ellen, J.R.'s wife, to the stand. She will testify that the day before the killing, she caught J.R. trying to put arsenic in his father's bourbon.

Analysis: The fact that J.R. attempted to put arsenic in Jock's bourbon is evidence that J.R. has a propensity to commit crimes of violence. But it is also probative to prove that J.R. had the intent to kill Jock, which tends to prove that when he actually did kill Jock the next day, it was not an accident.

---

7   United States v. New, 491 F.3d 369, 375 (8th Cir. 2007) (quoting United States v. Tan, 254 F.3d 1204, 1210 (10th Cir. 2001)) (emphasis original).

Therefore, Rule 404 does not bar the evidence; the judge may admit it to prove J.R.'s intent.

In J.R.'s case, the prosecution's case for admissibility is strengthened by the fact that the earlier bad act was so close in time to the charged crime. If the attempted poisoning happened two years earlier, it would be more difficult (though not impossible) for the prosecutor to argue that J.R.'s intent to kill his father still existed at the time of the driveway killing. The prosecutor's case is further strengthened by the fact that the prior act involved an intent to commit the very same crime that J.R. is now charged with, thus making the evidence less about J.R.'s general propensity to commit violent crimes and more about his specific mental state with respect to this specific crime.

All too often, however, courts broaden their use of the "intent" purpose to include evidence that is little more than propensity evidence. Consider this example:

Example: During 1990, the FBI mounted "Operation Lost Trust," an investigation of corruption in the South Carolina legislature. The Bureau persuaded Ronald Cobb, a registered lobbyist who had been caught purchasing cocaine, to serve as an informant. At the Bureau's direction, Cobb offered several legislators cash payments if they would support a bill legalizing betting on horse and dog racing. Legislator Kenneth Bailey accepted $500 from Cobb, allegedly for this purpose.

When the government charged Bailey with accepting a bribe, Bailey admitted receiving cash from Cobb but claimed that the money was a legitimate campaign contribution. To prove that Bailey accepted Cobb's money with the intent to commit his vote on the betting bill in return, the prosecution presented testimony from Robert Kohn. Kohn testified that during the same legislative term that Bailey accepted his "contribution" from Cobb, Kohn paid Bailey $200 to authorize pavement of a dirt road used by a boating company.

Analysis: The district court admitted Kohn's testimony, and the court of appeals affirmed. Both courts concluded that the government relied on this evidence to prove intent, which Bailey clearly disputed. The court of appeals, in fact, noted that intent was the "crux of the case" because Bailey admitted taking the money. Bailey's sale of his legislative services for a similar sum during the same time period offered important evidence of his unlawful intent when he accepted Cobb's payment.[8]

Bailey's acceptance of Kohn's bribe does have some tendency to make it more likely that he had a similarly unlawful intent when he accepted Cobb's money. The problem with this reasoning, however, is that it relies on exactly the type of propensity inference that Rule 404(a)(1) forbids. Unlike most of the other examples we have examined so far in this chapter, this evidence gives rise to only one chain of inferences, not two:

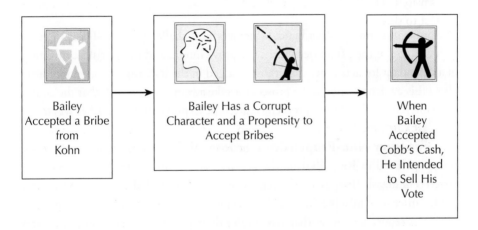

| Bailey Accepted a Bribe from Kohn | Bailey Has a Corrupt Character and a Propensity to Accept Bribes | When Bailey Accepted Cobb's Cash, He Intended to Sell His Vote |

Despite the clear presence of propensity reasoning in this chain, courts frequently accept this type of evidence of intent. Their willingness to overlook the propensity inference may represent confusion about the meaning of Rule 404. It may also derive in part from the difficulty of proving intent for some crimes through other types of evidence; there are no eyewitnesses to a defendant's thoughts, and many defendants are wise enough to avoid explicitly incriminating statements.

The use of prior acts to prove intent, despite the presence of propensity inferences, is particularly well established in drug cases. To prove a defendant's intent to distribute illegal narcotics, rather than mere possession of the drug, prosecutors frequently rely upon evidence that the defendant sold narcotics on previous occasions. This evidence often follows the same propensity path as the one marked out in Bailey—a defendant sold narcotics to others in the past; he therefore has a

---

8   United States v. Bailey, 990 F.2d 119, 124 (4th Cir. 1993).

tendency to sell narcotics; and thus he probably intended to sell the narcotics in his possession when he was arrested.

Many courts are willing to accept this argument, despite the propensity reasoning. This willingness raises challenges for both prosecutors and defense counsel. Defense counsel must determine how much effort to devote to challenging propensity evidence offered to prove intent. The evidence appears to violate Rule 404(a)(1), and the government often has other evidence of intent, such as possession of equipment used to package and sell drugs. These factors give defense counsel a good basis to challenge evidence of the defendant's prior drug sales. But defense lawyers know that the judge probably will reject the challenge; the admissibility of "prior sale" evidence is well established in most circuits.

The prosecutor, on the other hand, faces an ethical challenge. Rule 404(a)(1) seems to forbid use of the prior sale evidence to prove intent, and its use risks conviction of a defendant for acts other than those charged in the indictment. Yet most courts allow this evidence. Should the prosecutor take advantage of a path that the courts have offered, or should the prosecutor attempt to prove intent in other ways?

7. Any Other Non-Propensity Purpose. We've discussed six of the nine purposes listed in Rule 404(b). The other three are similar to the ones we have covered in detail. "Preparation" overlaps with plan, knowledge, and opportunity, while "absence of mistake" and "lack of accident" both overlap with intent, motive, and knowledge. The issues that arise under these purposes are similar to the ones we have discussed above, including the courts' tendency to lapse into propensity reasoning when applying some of the purposes.

Even these nine listed purposes, however, do not exhaust the potential of Rule 404(b). The rule offers a non-exclusive list of permissible purposes for evidence of other crimes, wrongs, or acts. As long as the litigant can come up with a purpose that is relevant to the case and avoids the propensity inference, the evidence is not barred by Rule 404.

Example: Police officers in Tahlequah, Oklahoma, routinely collect the serial numbers of firearms pawned in their jurisdiction and try to match the numbers to serial numbers of stolen firearms. During one of these checks the officers learned that a shotgun left at a pawnshop a day earlier had been stolen. The officers examined the pawnshop records and discovered that the gun had been pawned by a man named "Shaun James." The officers put a hold on the gun so that it could not be reclaimed and left their contact information with the pawnshop owner. A few months later, a man named Shaun James began calling the police station, demanding his gun back. He explained that he had bought the gun from a neighbor and had no way of knowing it was stolen.

The police did not have sufficient evidence of James's knowledge to charge him with possession of a stolen firearm. However, they checked their records and found that James had a prior felony conviction. They subsequently arrested James for possessing a firearm as a convicted felon. At trial, the police officers sought to testify that the shotgun James possessed had been stolen in order to explain how the shotgun had first come to their attention and why they placed a hold on the shotgun. James objected to this evidence, arguing that the jury would be unfairly prejudiced against him if they heard that the firearm he owned had been stolen.

Analysis: The trial court admitted the evidence, and the appellate court upheld the admission. Although the fact that the defendant possessed a stolen firearm tended to prove he had a bad character, it was impossible for the government witnesses to tell their story without explaining that the shotgun had been stolen: "without inclusion of the fact the shotgun was stolen, the testimony of [the law enforcement officers] may have been confusing and incomplete, as the jury would have been left in a void as to the circumstances leading to confiscation of the shotgun and Mr. James's incriminating statements to both of them." The fact that the shotgun was stolen was "inextricably intertwined" with the witness's narrative, and so it had to be disclosed to the jury.[9]

Judges and attorneys refer to the type of evidence introduced in James as res gestae, which means evidence necessary to complete the story. This is a relatively common purpose for other act evidence under Rule 404(b). But the possible arguments for

---

9   See United States v. James, 217 F. App'x 776, 779–82 (10th Cir. 2007).

admission under 404(b) are as diverse as the many different fact patterns that arise in litigation. Here is just one more example; this case is interesting because it was the defendant rather than the government who wanted to introduce evidence of other acts under Rule 404(b):

Example: Police searched a car driven by Hugo Garcia and Juan Castro. On the floor of the back seat they found a jacket that belonged to Castro and that contained more than 100 grams of heroin. The government charged both men, and Castro pled guilty to conspiracy to traffic heroin. Garcia claimed no knowledge of the drugs and proceeded to trial.

At Garcia's trial, the government called Castro as a witness. Castro testified that Garcia was the drug dealer and that he "was just along for the ride." Castro further claimed that he pled guilty because Garcia pressured him repeatedly to take the blame. The prosecutor built upon this testimony by telling the jury that Castro was "really, really stupid," "as dumb as a box of rocks," and "a fool." Given Castro's limited abilities, the government contended, Garcia must have masterminded the drug transaction.

In response, Garcia offered evidence that Castro had been previously convicted of selling cocaine and heroin to an undercover agent on six separate occasions. Garcia argued that this evidence rebutted the government's claim that Castro was too dumb to deal drugs on his own. Garcia himself had no prior drug convictions.

Analysis: The district judge excluded evidence about Castro's prior drug convictions, apparently concluding that the evidence violated Rule 404(a)(1) and did not fit within Rule 404(b). But the Ninth Circuit Court of Appeals reversed. The appellate court noted that Castro's alleged incompetence was central to the government's theory of the case. Castro's prior conviction, based on repeated drug sales, was quite relevant in rebutting that argument. Nor did the evidence require an impermissible propensity inference. Garcia offered the evidence to show that Castro had the knowledge and ability to conduct the charged drug sale on his own, not merely to suggest that he had a tendency to sell drugs.[10]

---

10   United States v. Cruz-Garcia, 344 F.3d 951, 954–55 (9th Cir. 2003).

The use of Castro's prior conviction might fall into the knowledge or opportunity categories of Rule 404(b), but the context gives the purpose a somewhat different focus. The case is useful, not only in illuminating the existence of other purposes under Rule 404(b), but in stressing that Rule 404(a)(1) bars only evidence offered to prove that an individual acted consistently with his character on a particular occasion. If a party offers evidence for another purpose, as Castro did here, the evidence is admissible.

8. Subsequent Crimes, Wrongs, and Acts. Most of the acts offered as evidence under Rule 404(b) occur before the charged crime. For this reason, judges and attorneys sometimes refer to introduction of "prior" acts under Rule 404(b). The rule, however, imposes no time constraints on this evidence. In the Sanchez case, discussed above as an example of proving identity, the other heroin purchase occurred a week after the charged one. Unless the timing of the actions affects their relevance, both prior and subsequent acts are admissible under Rule 404(b).

9. Civil Cases. The majority of cases arising under Rule 404 are criminal ones, but the rule applies to both civil and criminal actions. Rule 404(a)(1) prohibits the use of propensity evidence in civil cases, just as in criminal ones. Rule 404(b), similarly, confirms that character-related evidence is admissible in civil cases if the proponent identifies a non-propensity purpose for the evidence.

Example: The Green Acres Contracting Company fired Harry Ansell, a 45-year-old laborer and truck driver. Ansell sued, claiming age discrimination. At trial, Ansell offered evidence that Green Acres fired at least one other worker in his forties around the time that Ansell was fired, and that the company hired several much younger workers during the same period. In response, Green Acres offered evidence that it fired Ansell because of several incidents of insubordination. Based on this evidence, the issue for the jury was whether Green Acres' claimed reason for firing Ansell was its true reason or whether the claims of insubordination were a pretext for age discrimination.

To address this issue, Green Acres offered evidence that it hired Anthony Beddington, a 45-year-old worker, about 18 months after the company laid off Ansell. This evidence, the company claimed, showed that it had no animus toward older workers. Ansell objected to this evidence under Rule 404.

Analysis: The district court admitted the evidence about Beddington, and the appellate court affirmed. Green Acres offered the evidence to illuminate its intent or motive when it fired Ansell, both purposes that Rule 404(b) approves.

The court of appeals noted that both plaintiffs and defendants in employment discrimination suits frequently offer evidence about the treatment of other workers. In this case, Ansell had introduced evidence about another older worker who was terminated, while Green Acres offered evidence about a similar worker who was hired. Neither side, the court suggested, offered this evidence to prove that, because the company had a particular intent on other occasions, it must have had acted with the same intent on the disputed occasion. Indeed, the company's intent on all of these occasions was unknown. Rather than making a propensity argument, the parties urged the jury to infer motive from the overall pattern of actions.[11]

In addition to showing the application of Rule 404(b) to civil cases, the Green Acres decision further elucidates the difference between permissible and impermissible uses of prior act evidence to show intent. At first glance, both Ansell and Green Acres seem to be making propensity arguments about the company's intent. Ansell argued that the company had fired other older workers and hired young ones, suggesting that it had a propensity to favor the young. Green Acres, conversely, stressed that it had hired a worker as old as Ansell, suggesting that it had a propensity to treat workers of all ages fairly.

The evidence offered by both parties in Green Acres thus seems to rely upon the same type of propensity reasoning that Bailey's evidence of a prior bribe invoked. Under all of these circumstances, the parties appear to use an opponent's intent on one occasion to prove the opponent's propensity to act in a certain way; they then use that propensity to argue that the opponent must have held the same intent on the disputed occasion.

There is a reasonable argument, however, that the prior acts in Green Acres showed intent without invoking the propensity inference used in Bailey. Ansell and Green Acres disputed the company's intent on **all** of the occasions presented in evidence. Ansell argued that the company held a discriminatory intent when it hired and

---

11   Ansell v. Green Acres Contr. Co., 347 F.3d 515 (3d Cir. 2003).

fired all of the workers referred to by the evidence. Green Acres, on the other hand, claimed that it had a benign intent on all of those occasions.

Neither party, therefore, argued that the jury should use a known intent from one occasion to infer intent at another time. That is the type of propensity reasoning Rule 404(a)(1) forbids. Instead, both parties claimed that the jury should consider the entire history of events to infer the company's intent when firing Ansell. Examining a pattern of actions is somewhat different from using one act to infer responsibility for another act.

This distinction—reasoning from an overall pattern rather than reasoning by propensity—is a subtle one. Most courts haven't focused on the distinction because they overlook the propensity inference in cases like Bailey. If the evidence in Bailey (of a prior bribe) was admissible, then the evidence in Green Acres clearly was admissible as well. Criticizing the result in Bailey requires drawing finer lines to explain cases like Green Acres.

 The courts' current position with respect to the admissibility of prior acts to show intent, in both civil and criminal cases, is relatively clear: Judges rather freely admit this type of evidence under Rule 404(b), even when the evidence seems to rely upon a forbidden propensity inference. In that sense, rulings are fairly predictable in these areas. The analysis supporting these decisions, however, often is questionable. Sophisticated attorneys may challenge some of the courts' reasoning in this area, leading to changes in judges' willingness to admit evidence of prior acts to show intent. This is an area to watch for future developments.

10. Good Acts. As the Green Acres case shows, Rule 404 applies to both bad and good acts. The employer in Green Acres sought to introduce evidence of a prior good act, that it had hired an older worker. If the company had offered that evidence to make a propensity argument, Rule 404(a)(1) would have barred the evidence of this good act in the same way that it prohibits evidence of bad acts offered to show propensity.

Here is another case illustrating the treatment of good acts under Rule 404:

Example: The government charged Thomas Hayes, a Vice President of Saybolt, Inc., with participating in a company-wide conspiracy to fabricate the results of petroleum tests. The prosecutor's evidence included testimony from Saybolt employees that Hayes had pressured them to obtain good test results and to fabricate negative ones. In response, Hayes offered testimony from other employees that, during the time of the alleged conspiracy, he had never pressed them to fabricate results and that he consistently directed them to follow proper testing procedures.

Analysis: The district judge rejected Hayes's evidence under Rule 404, but the court of appeals reversed. The appellate court concluded that Hayes was not trying simply to show a good character through the evidence he offered. Instead, in response to the government's charge that Hayes had participated in a company-wide conspiracy, Hayes offered evidence of acts that tended to negate his participation in that conspiracy. Just as the government offered specific acts to suggest Hayes's participation, Hayes could present specific acts to show his non-participation. Indeed, it was difficult to see how else Hayes could have defended against the government's charges.[12]

11. Rule 403. The evidence that litigants offer under Rule 404(b) is relevant for at least two purposes: one permissible purpose (knowledge, intent, motive, etc.) and one inadmissible purpose (propensity). In deciding whether the unfair prejudice of the propensity inference substantially outweighs the probative value of the permissible purpose, the trial judge will turn to Rule 403.

Application of Rule 403's balancing test to evidence of bad acts is so important that several circuits require district judges to apply Rule 403 closely before admitting any evidence under Rule 404(b). Appellate courts have reversed trial judges, not only for admitting evidence that is unfairly prejudicial, but for failing to conduct a proper Rule 403 inquiry. Here is a recent example of a verdict reversed on that ground:

Example: Kevin Curtin, a 42-year-old man, met an individual who claimed to be a 14-year-old girl on an internet chat channel called "ltgirlsexchat." After exchanging four hours of sexually explicit messages, Curtin and the girl agreed to meet in the bowling alley of a Las Vegas casino. Their messages contemplated spending the night together and engaging in

---

12   United States v. Hayes, 219 F. App'x 114, 115–16 (3d Cir. 2007).

sexual acts. Unfortunately for Curtin, the "girl" was really a male Las Vegas Police Detective. When Curtin arrived at the bowling alley at the specified time, he was arrested and charged with traveling across state lines with the intent to have sex with a minor.

Curtin's defense was that he never believed he was chatting with a minor; he thought he was corresponding with a woman in her 30's or 40's pretending to be a 14-year-old girl. Curtin further claimed that he intended to have sex with her while they both pretended that she was a 14-year-old girl; he assumed that both of them wanted to role-play "daddy/daughter incest."

To counter this defense, the prosecutors sought to admit stories that they found on Curtin's personal digital assistant (PDA) when he was arrested. These stories, downloaded by Curtin, described a variety of incestuous relationships between adults and children. Since Curtin's subjective intent was the only contested issue in the case, the government urged that the stories were both relevant and essential to establish that intent. Curtin opposed admission of the stories, claiming they would unfairly prejudice the jury against him.

Analysis: The trial court admitted five of the stories, concluding that they were relevant to establish Curtin's intent, properly offered for that purpose under Rule 404(b), and sufficiently probative to survive Rule 403's balancing test. But the court of appeals reversed, finding that the trial judge's Rule 403 determination was flawed because he read only portions of the admitted stories.

The appellate panel sympathized with the trial judge's distaste for reading the "inflammatory," "reprehensible," and "abhorrent" stories, but that was exactly why he had to read them. To weigh the prejudicial nature of the stories against their probative value, the trial judge had to understand the full extent of the potential prejudice. One of the stories, for example, included a graphic description of a young girl engaged in sexual acts with a dog. This passage had no relevance to the government's case and was highly prejudicial; if the judge had read the stories in their entirety, he could have excised this passage.[13]

---

13   United States v. Curtin, 489 F.3d 935, 956–58 (9th Cir. 2007) (en banc).

In addition to noting the procedural requirements that courts impose on the admission of evidence under Rule 404(b), it is instructive to consider how a trial judge might weigh probative value and prejudice in any retrial of Curtin. On the one hand, the prosecution hinged on proof of Curtin's intent; the stories seemed to bear on that element; and the government had few other avenues for showing intent. On the other hand, the stories were highly inflammatory; even with redaction and a limiting instruction, the jurors might conclude that anyone reading such filth deserved punishment. The stories, moreover, may not have been as probative of intent as the prosecution contended. Curtin clearly was not planning to have sex with his own daughter; these fictional descriptions of incest might have appealed to a man who engaged in role-plays with other consenting adults as well as to one who sought sex with minors.

These concerns suggest the difficult task that judges face when evaluating evidence of other acts under Rule 403. In addition, advocates have noted that evidence offered under Rule 404(b) can be particularly prejudicial when it activates racial, ethnic, or other stereotypes.[14] Rule 403 offers an avenue for counsel to raise those concerns. Counsel in all cases must pay careful attention to the intersection of Rules 403 and 404(b).

12. Limiting Instructions. When a judge admits evidence under Rule 404(b), he or she gives a limiting instruction to the jury. This instruction explains that the jury should use the evidence of another crime, wrong, or act only for the purpose for which the evidence was admitted, not to draw inferences about the individual's character or propensity to act in conformity with that character. Here is an example of the instruction used in one federal trial:

> Ladies and gentlemen of the jury, the [certified copy of defendant's prior conviction] provides evidence of other crimes, wrongs, or acts. It is not admissible to prove the character of a person in order to show action in conformity therewith. It may, however, be admissible for other purposes such as proof of intent. With the admission of [the conviction], you have heard evidence of acts of the defendant other than those charged in the indictment. You may consider this evidence only on the question of

14   Chris Chambers Goodman, The Color of Our Character: Confronting the Racial Character of Rule 404(b) Evidence, 25 Law & Ineq. 1 (2007).

intent. You should consider this evidence only for this limited purpose and for no other purpose.[15]

As is always the case with limiting instructions, it is questionable whether jurors are able to understand and follow this type of instruction.

Quick Summary

Rule 404(b) reinforces and clarifies **Rule 404(a)** and **Rule 402.** Evidence of some actions may prompt jurors to infer that an individual has a particular character and a propensity to act consistently with that character. Under most circumstances, Rule 404(a) bars parties from using evidence for that type of propensity purpose. But if the evidence is also relevant to prove a fact of consequence to the case, the judge may admit the evidence to prove that fact. Rule 404(b) gives examples of the kinds of purposes that are permissible, but the list is not exclusive; any purpose—other than propensity—can be used to admit this evidence.

Rule 404(b) applies to both civil and criminal cases. It also governs evidence of good acts as well as bad ones. Judges admitting evidence under Rule 404(b) usually conduct a Rule 403 balancing test to compare the probative value of the evidence for its permissible purpose with the unfair prejudice of its propensity overtones. If the evidence survives the balancing test, it is admitted with a limiting instruction.

Test Your Understanding

To assess your understanding of the material in this chapter, click here to take a quiz, or go to the Quizzes module from the eBook on your eProducts bookshelf.

15   United States v. Jones, 455 F.3d 800, 804 n.2 (7th Cir. 2006).

31

Habit

Key Concepts

- **Rule 406:** Evidence of Habit or Routine Practice Is Admissible to Show Action on a Particular Occasion
- "Habit" Is Specific, Repeated Conduct in Response to Certain Situations
- Corroboration Not Needed
- Proof by Any Means
- Habit Alone May Support Verdict

A. Introduction and Policy. In the last chapter we saw that evidence of other acts may prove both a character trait and a fact of consequence to a dispute. Gary DeCicco's tax evasion, one of the examples discussed in that chapter, suggested that he had a dishonest, lawbreaking character. Those dishonest acts, however, also provided a motive for the crime of arson charged against him. The court of appeals held that the prosecutor could use the bad act of tax evasion to establish motive in the arson prosecution of DeCicco.

Rule 404(b) provides a non-exhaustive list of facts, such as motive, that parties may prove through evidence of other acts. Proof of these facts does not require propensity reasoning, so it does not violate **Rule 404(a)(1)**. **Rule 406** adds another permissible purpose to the list of non-propensity uses recognized in Rule 404(b): use of other acts to prove an individual's habit or an organization's routine practice.

Like Rule 404(b), Rule 406 is somewhat superfluous; it merely gives another example of a use for prior act evidence that is permissible because it does not rely on propensity. But Rule 406 is helpful because it focuses attention on the tricky distinction between habit and propensity. Habit gets its own rule to underscore the difference between these concepts.

To explore this distinction, let's begin by defining the term "habit." That word has a special meaning in the Federal Rules of Evidence. Lay people commonly use the word "habit" in one of two ways: (1) to denote a type of unconscious behavior like chewing fingernails when under stress, or (2) to describe a general tendency or addictive behavior such as "he has a habit of getting drunk at night," or "she has a bad habit of smoking cigarettes."

As it is used in the Rules of Evidence, "habit" means something much broader than unconscious behavior but more narrow than a general tendency. In the Rules of Evidence, habit refers to **specific, repeated responses to a particular situation or stimulus**. Habit, in other words, means that an individual who is placed in a particular situation will respond over and over again with the same specific behavior. Rule 406 allows litigants to present past examples of this specific behavior to prove that an individual behaved the same way during the incident that is the subject of litigation.

A good example of habit as used in the Rules of Evidence is a mechanic who always follows the same steps in changing the oil of a car. The mechanic probably changes oil many times in a week, and has probably worked out a set routine for completing the task. If the mechanic's colleague can testify that she has seen the mechanic change oil dozens of times, and he always uses a wrench to tighten the oil plug when he is finished, the jury can consider this fact as evidence that he used a wrench to tighten the oil plug on a specific occasion, even if the witness was not present on that occasion.

Why is habit evidence admissible if propensity evidence is not? Courts give two reasons. First, habit evidence tends to be **morally neutral**, so there is less chance of unfair prejudice resulting from its admission. Jurors tend to react emotionally, and thus inappropriately, toward propensity evidence that an individual has a reputation for lying, cheating, or stealing. They are likely to respond with similar emotion toward evidence that an individual has a propensity to donate money to charity. Evidence that a person habitually orders a double espresso decaf cappuccino at Starbuck's every morning is unlikely to have such an emotional impact.

The second, more important reason why habit evidence is admissible is that this evidence has a higher **probative value** than propensity evidence. The fact that a defendant has a reputation for starting bar fights is somewhat helpful when trying to determine if he started a fight on a specific occasion, but it is not very strong evidence. Even highly aggressive individuals pick fights on some occasions and choose to enjoy their beer on others. On the other hand, if a store employee testifies that every evening for three years she has seen the manager lock the door when he closes down for the night, the odds are pretty strong that he locked the door on the specific occasion that gave rise to the litigation.

Despite these distinctions, the line between habit and propensity can be difficult for courts to draw. The extremes are easy: Evidence that an individual has a violent disposition is propensity, while testimony that a person always brushes his teeth, flosses, and takes his vitamins before going to bed at night is habit. But in between these extremes the answers are murkier. How specific and how repetitive does conduct have to be before it transforms from inadmissible propensity to admissible habit?

To distinguish habit from propensity, focus on three factors:

- The specificity of the conduct

- The distinctiveness of the situation producing the conduct

- The regularity of the conduct

Very specific conduct that arises regularly in an identifiable context is most likely to constitute habit. A judge might rule that a defendant who ran the same stop sign every day for the last six months had a habit of disregarding that sign. Proof that the defendant ran ten different stop signs, each on a single occasion, would be less likely to show habit. The latter evidence suggests that the defendant is a careless driver with a tendency to disregard stop signs, but that is a propensity argument forbidden by Rule 404. The first example, in which the defendant regularly repeated the same behavior in the same context, is more likely to establish habit.

 But the line between habit and propensity is a fuzzy one. Good advocacy may spell the difference between admissible evidence of habit and inadmissible evidence of character.

B. The Rule.

> # RULE 406. Habit; Routine Practice
>
> Evidence of a person's <u>habit</u> or an organization's <u>routine practice</u> may be admitted to prove that on a particular occasion the person or organization acted in accordance with the habit or routine practice. The court may admit this evidence <u>regardless of whether it is corroborated</u> or whether there was an eyewitness.

There are three points to note about this rule. **First,** the rule does not define the terms "habit" or "routine practice." Instead, courts have turned to the Advisory Committee's note, which explains that habit is "one's regular response to a repeated specific situation."[1] The notes also clarify that routine practice is the equivalent of habit for an organization. These definitions have guided the courts' application of Rule 406, as these two examples show:

Example: Paul Babcock was driving alone in his truck when he went off the road and hit a tree, suffering injuries that led to his death. Babcock's estate sued General Motors, the manufacturer of the car, claiming that Babcock had been wearing his seatbelt at the time of the accident, but that it released on impact due to a design defect known as "false latching."

At trial, General Motors argued that there was no defect in the seatbelt, and that Babcock simply was not wearing his belt at the time of the accident. General Motors pointed out that nobody saw Babcock wearing his seatbelt during his fatal drive, and that there was no seatbelt fastened around him when the emergency responders arrived at the scene.

Babcock's estate called three witnesses to testify about Babcock's habit of wearing a seatbelt. The first testified that he had ridden with Babcock at least ten to twenty times a year for the past sixteen years. The second had ridden with Babcock about a dozen times in the eighteen months prior to the accident. The third had ridden with him eight to twelve times over the last few years before the accident. All three witnesses testified that Babcock

---

1   Fed. R. Evid. 406, advisory committee's note (quoting McCormick on Evidence § 162, at 340).

always wore his seat belt, regardless of whether he was the driver or a passenger and regardless of the length of the trip.

Analysis: The district judge properly admitted this evidence. The appellate court noted that evidence of a person's habitual seat belt use should be admissible to suggest that he was wearing a seat belt on a particular occasion, but that the same evidence probably would not be admissible to prove that the person had a more general disposition to act safely.[2]

In the *Babcock* case, the estate did not use Babcock's regular seatbelt use to show that he had a general propensity to act safely. It did not, for example, argue that Babcock's seatbelt use suggested that he must have been driving below the speed limit when the accident happened. Instead, the estate provided many examples of a specific act (using a seatbelt) to suggest that Babcock engaged in that specific, regular conduct on the disputed occasion. Contrast that argument with the reasoning of the plaintiff in this case:

Example: A Southern Pacific Railroad train collided with a pickup truck at a train crossing, killing the driver and injuring the passenger. The passenger sued Southern Pacific, claiming that the operator of the train was driving too fast, failed to blow his whistle, and failed to brake properly. The plaintiff sought to admit the train operator's prior safety record, which included nine violations over the course of his twenty-nine-year career. The infractions included speeding, failure to display headlights, and failure to properly identify himself on the radio.

Analysis: The court excluded this evidence under Rule 404 as improper propensity evidence. The plaintiff's claim that the violations proved "habit" was rejected for two reasons. First, the number of infractions over the course of such a long time did not constitute repeated conduct. And second, the conduct described in the safety record varied widely and for the most part did not match up with the alleged conduct by the operator at the time of the train crash.[3]

---

2   Babcock v. GMC, 299 F.3d 60, 62, 65 & n.2 (1st Cir. 2002).

3   Jones v. Southern P. Railroad, 962 F.2d 447 (5th Cir. 1992). The court noted that the plaintiff in this truck–train case did not try to show that Southern Pacific was negligent in continuing to employ the train operator. If the plaintiff had asserted that type of legal claim, the operator's character would have been an element of the case. See

The **second** point to note about Rule 406's language is that it allows admission of habit evidence "regardless of whether it is corroborated or whether there was an eyewitness." A person can testify about her own habit even if no one else has ever seen her act in that way. The opposing attorney will cross-examine the witness about the regularity and consistency of the claimed habit, and the jury is then free to reject uncorroborated testimony if it chooses to do so.

In these cases, the existence of habit is a question of **credibility**: Rule 406 allows a party to present uncorroborated evidence to the jury, but the jurors do not have to accept it. Many juries do reject self-serving claims of habit; evidence from a third party supporting the repeated and regular nature of a habit makes a claim much more persuasive.

Finally, Rule 406 is silent about how to prove habit. Because the rules do not restrict the manner of proof, courts allow attorneys to prove habit through both opinion testimony and specific instances of conduct. However, because habit evidence is admissible only if the proponent can show that the habitual behavior is specific and frequently repeated, attorneys usually offer evidence of specific conduct. An attorney probably would find it difficult to prove habit through opinion testimony alone. Babcock's estate, for example, presented testimony from witnesses who had seen Babcock buckle his seatbelt regularly; those witnesses testified about the specific incidents rather than offering an opinion about Babcock's seatbelt use.

C. In the Courtroom. Parties opposing the introduction of habit evidence frequently contest whether the evidence proves habit or propensity. Resolving that issue, which we discussed above, absorbs much of the courts' attention under Rule 406. We review below two other points that arise in courtroom practice.

1. Not Just Admissible, But Possibly Sufficient. Sometimes the only information about what happened on a particular occasion is evidence of habit. A person may have done a task so many times that he cannot possibly remember whether he did it a certain way on the day in question. A laboratory technician who tests dozens of substances a day for the presence of drugs, for example, is unlikely to remember the specifics of a single test. Mechanics who conduct routine weekly maintenance on a machine and police officers who frequently perform breathalyzer tests may fall in the same category. In these situations, judges and juries routinely

Chapter 26. Instead, the plaintiff argued that the operator was negligent and the railroad company was vicariously liable for that negligence. Character is not an element of that type of negligence claim, so the special rules governing proof of character as an element did not apply.

conclude that the habit evidence is sufficient to establish that the witness performed the disputed action in accordance with long-standing habit. The fact finder does not have to accept the habit evidence, but it can be compelling in cases like this.

Fact finders may accept uncorroborated habit evidence as conclusive even when the disputed actions are not as routine as laboratory testing or regular machine maintenance:

> **Example:** A few weeks after undergoing dental surgery, Katherine Meyer learned that she had suffered nerve damage in her tongue and gums. She sued the dental clinic, claiming that the dentist who performed the surgery failed to warn her that the procedure could result in nerve damage. The dental surgeon, Kent Aitkin, could not remember the exact conversation he had with Meyer, but he testified that his standard procedure with any patient undergoing surgery was to advise the patient of all risks that the surgery entailed.

> **Analysis:** The district court admitted Aitkin's testimony, noting that he had been in practice for over three years and had developed a "long established habit and custom" of informing all patients of the risks involved. Two of Aitkin's dental assistants also testified that the dentist gave all patients such warnings. Given this evidence of Aitkin's habitual practice, the court (sitting as the trier of fact in a bench trial) concluded that the defendant did advise Meyer about the risks of her surgery, even though there was no direct evidence about what he said to her.[4]

Juries frequently find habit evidence sufficient even in criminal cases. In other words, habit may be all that is needed to prove beyond a reasonable doubt that a person acted a certain way on a certain occasion.

2. Routine Practice of an Organization. Routine practice is the organizational equivalent of personal habit. Corporations and other institutions often have standard procedures for dealing with particular situations. A firehouse may have a set of steps that it always follows—in the same order—when an alarm reaches the

---

4   Meyer v. United States, 464 F. Supp. 317, 320–21 (D. Colo. 1979), aff'd, 638 F.2d 155 (10th Cir. 1980). Meyer used an Air Force dental clinic, so the "clinic owner" in this case was the United States. She sued under the Federal Tort Claims Act, which authorizes tort suits against the government.

station. A software company may always respond to the report of a program bug by creating a patch and posting it on their website. If a litigant can show that an organization always (or frequently) acts a certain way under designated circumstances, then a court will accept that practice as evidence that the organization acted that way on a particular occasion.

 Courts generally are more willing to accept routine practice evidence from a corporation than habit evidence from an individual because "the need for regularity in business and the organizational sanctions which may exist when employees deviate from the established procedures give extra guarantees that the questioned activity followed the usual custom."[5] Even with organizations, however, judges may disagree about the admission of routine practice evidence. Here is a case in which a district judge rejected such evidence, but the court of appeals reversed:

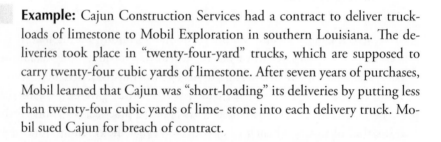

Example: Cajun Construction Services had a contract to deliver truckloads of limestone to Mobil Exploration in southern Louisiana. The deliveries took place in "twenty-four-yard" trucks, which are supposed to carry twenty-four cubic yards of limestone. After seven years of purchases, Mobil learned that Cajun was "short-loading" its deliveries by putting less than twenty-four cubic yards of lime- stone into each delivery truck. Mobil sued Cajun for breach of contract.

Cajun had destroyed all records of how much limestone they loaded on the trucks sent to Mobil, so Mobil offered more than 3,400 loading records of Cajun trucks that delivered limestone to Cajun's own sites and to other third-party customers. The records showed that the average load for deliveries in twenty-four-yard trucks was about seventeen and a half yards. Cajun argued that evidence of how it loaded trucks bound for its own sites or other third parties was irrelevant to the question of how it loaded trucks sent to the plaintiff.

---

5   McCormick on Evidence § 195, at 786 (Kenneth S. Broun ed., 6th ed. 2006).

Analysis: At a bench trial, the district judge agreed with Cajun that the records were irrelevant and excluded the evidence. As a result, the judge concluded that there was insufficient evidence to prove that Cajun had short-loaded the trucks to Mobil.

The appellate court reversed, noting that in order to establish the routine practice of an organization, a party had to show "a sufficient number of specific instances of conduct to support that inference . . . Evidence of the defendant's actions on only a few occasions or only in relation to the plaintiff are not enough; the plaintiff must show regularity over substantially all occasions or with substantially all other parties with whom the defendant has had similar business transactions."

But in this case, Mobil had over 3,400 records of how Cajun loaded its trucks. Mobil's lawyers, moreover, had elicited testimony from Cajun employees that they always loaded a twenty-four yard truck the same way, regardless of where the truck was going. Thus, Mobil had established that Cajun had a routine practice of short-loading its trucks and the evidence should have been admitted under Rule 406.[6]

This is an example of routine practice evidence used by a corporation's opponent to prove that the corporation acted in accordance with a routine practice when it cheated the plaintiff. As with evidence of an individual's habit, evidence of an organization's routine practice can serve as both a sword and a shield. An organization may offer evidence of its routine practices to show that it acted properly on a particular occasion. But, as in the Mobil case, an opponent may present evidence of routine practices that were improper.

Evidence in Practice

To practice your knowledge of character evidence, take the role of a judge in *State v. Newhouse*. Click here or access the **Evidence in Practice** module from the eBook on your eProducts bookshelf.

---

6   Mobil Exploration & Producing U.S. v. Cajun Constr. Servs., 45 F.3d 96, 97–101 (5th Cir. 1995).

Quick Summary

Rule 406 provides another way to admit evidence of other acts to show a relevant fact rather than to prove propensity. If the other act evidence shows repeated, specific conduct taken in response to repeated, specific situations, the evidence is admissible to show that the individual or organization acted in conformity with that habit on the disputed occasion.

The greatest challenge under Rule 406 lies in distinguishing propensity evidence, which is used to prove a general character trait, from habit evidence, which is used to prove that the individual always takes a specific kind of action. To distinguish between the two, focus on: (1) the specificity of the conduct in the proffered evidence; (2) the specificity of the situation or stimulus that gives rise to the individual's conduct; and (3) the regularity of the conduct. The more specific the act and the stimulus, and the more predictable the response, the more likely that the evidence is permissible habit instead of impermissible propensity.

Test Your Understanding

To assess your understanding of the material in this chapter, click here to take a quiz, or go to the Quizzes module from the eBook on your eProducts bookshelf.

32

Rape Shield Law

Key Concepts

- **Rule 412:** Bars Most Evidence of an Alleged Victim's Prior Sexual Acts or Sexual Reputation
- Applies Only in Cases of "Sexual Misconduct"
- Criminal Case Exceptions:
  - Prior Sexual Conduct Explains Physical Evidence
  - Prior Sexual Conduct Between Defendant and Alleged Victim
  - Necessary to Protect Defendant's Constitutional Rights
- "Reverse 403" Standard for Civil Case Exceptions

A. Introduction and Policy. Rule 412, popularly known as the "rape shield law," restricts the kind of evidence that can be introduced in sexual assault cases. In those cases, the rule prohibits almost all evidence of an alleged victim's prior sexual encounters or sexual reputation.

This rule is another one of the "character evidence" rules, barring use of an individual's specific actions or reputation to suggest that the person has a propensity to act in particular ways. Given that **Rule 404** generally prohibits propensity evidence, why is Rule 412 necessary? Doesn't Rule 404 already prohibit any evidence about the sexual reputation or prior sexual encounters of a rape victim if used to show that the victim had a propensity to consent to sexual acts?

The answer is no. Rule 404 provides two opportunities for defense attorneys to admit evidence of a rape victim's sexual reputation or past sexual history. First, Rule 404(a)(2)(B) expressly allows the defendant in a criminal case to offer "evidence of an alleged victim's pertinent trait." This language applies to sexual assault prosecutions, as well as to those for homicide, robbery, fraud, or any other criminal act. The Advisory Committee's note to Rule 404, in fact, points to a rape victim's character as an example of evidence that is admissible under this subsection: "an accused may introduce pertinent evidence of the character of the victim as in . . . consent in a case of rape."[1]

Second, although Rule 404(a)(1) prohibits evidence of other acts when offered solely to prove propensity, Rule 404(b) allows admission of other acts when offered to prove some other relevant fact. Thus, before the adoption of rape shield laws, judges could admit evidence of a victim's prior sexual activity under Rule 404(b) whenever defense attorneys convinced them that the activity was relevant to prove some fact other than propensity.

Defense attorneys often took advantage of these opportunities to attack a rape victim's character, either by introducing opinion or reputation evidence under Rule 404(a)(2)[2] or by offering evidence of prior sexual encounters under Rule 404(b). In the latter cases, defense attorneys ostensibly offered the evidence for purposes other than proving propensity, but they usually hoped that the jury would conclude that the victim was sexually promiscuous and therefore that she probably consented to a sexual act with the defendant.[3] Until the 1970s, when Congress and the states began adopting rape shield laws, many rape trials followed this pattern:

> **Example:** Pauline met Zach in a bar and asked him back to her apartment. Once there, the couple had a few more drinks. The next day, Pauline claimed that Zach raped her: She told police that she asked Zach to leave after a "pleasant nightcap" but he refused to go and forced her to have sex. Zach denied raping Pauline, claiming that she never asked him to leave and consented to their sexual acts.
>
> At trial, the defense attorney called Greg, who frequented the bar where Pauline met Zach. Greg testified that everyone who went to the bar reg-

---

1   Fed. R. Evid. 404 advisory committee's note. For further discussion of the criminal prosecution exceptions to Rule 404, see Chapter 28.

2   Remember that Rule 405(a) allows only reputation or opinion evidence when pursuing Rule 404(a)(2)'s exceptions for the use of character evidence in criminal cases. Chapter 29 reviews this concept.

3   The majority of sexual assault cases involve female victims and male defendants, so we use those pronouns in most examples. As discussed in the Courtroom section, however, Rule 412 is gender neutral, and cases involving male victims and/or female defendants arise. Likewise, the rule applies to both heterosexual and homosexual assaults.

ularly knew that Pauline was "easy" and that she was "always available for sex." The defense attorney also called Ronald, who testified that one week earlier, Pauline invited him back to her apartment for drinks and then the two of them had consensual sex.

Analysis: In the absence of rape shield laws, judges often admitted both types of evidence. Greg's testimony was admissible under 404(a)(2) and 405(a) as reputation evidence showing that Pauline had a propensity to consent to sex, and therefore she was more likely to have consented to sex with Zach. Ronald's testimony probably would have been admitted under 404(b) to suggest that when Pauline invited Zach back to her apartment, she intended to have sex with Zach because that was her intent with Ronald one week earlier.

Courts offered other justifications for allowing evidence of a victim's sexual reputation and history. Some courts held that "unchaste" women were less credible, so evidence of sexual promiscuity was a proper method of impeachment;[4] while other judges held that sexually promiscuous women were more likely to have "rape fantasies" and thus were more likely to fabricate a rape charge.[5]

These rationales are patently illogical. Promiscuity, for example, was never used to impeach the credibility of male witnesses—or even to discredit female witnesses outside the rape context.[6] We include these examples to illustrate the mindset of many judges in the era before adoption of rape shield rules. Any prosecutor seeking to preclude this kind of evidence under Rule 404 or Rule 403 faced an uphill battle.

This began to change in the 1970s. The feminist movement fed a growing dissatisfaction with the harsh treatment of rape victims in court. Rape victims were reluctant to come forward for fear that their past sexual history would be exposed in open court. And society itself changed, viewing the sexual reputation and history of a woman as less relevant—if it was relevant at all—to the likelihood that she would consent to sex on any given occasion.

Michigan adopted the first rape shield law in 1974; Federal Rule 412 took effect four years later. Today the federal courts and every state judicial system have some form of rape shield law. These laws reflect a consensus that (1) a victim's sexual

---

4   See, e.g., Packineau v. United States, 202 F.2d 681, 685 (8th Cir. 1953).

5   See, e.g., People v. Smallwood, 306 Mich. 49, 53–54, 10 N.W.2d 303, 305 (1943).

6   To review the types of conduct that courts accept to impeach the credibility of witnesses, see Chapters 17–23.

reputation and prior sexual history usually are not relevant to prove whether the victim consented to a particular sexual act; (2) this kind of evidence often is unduly prejudicial to the prosecutor or other party who calls the alleged victim as a witness; and (3) robust protection of sexual assault victims is necessary to encourage them to come forward and testify.

Despite this consensus, there remain some circumstances when other sexual acts by the victim are highly probative, while unfair prejudice can be minimized. Suppose, for example, that the defendant denies ever having had intercourse with the complainant, while the prosecutor has undeniable physical evidence that somebody had intercourse with the complainant on the night of the alleged rape. Should the defendant be allowed to produce evidence that the alleged victim had sex with someone else that night? This avenue of proof could be essential to an effective defense, with very little unfair character implications for the complainant. A rape shield law that barred all mention of the alleged victim's sexual history would preclude this evidence.

Rape shield laws like Rule 412 thus strike a difficult balance. The rules try to preclude evidence of sexual reputation and prior sexual acts when that evidence aims primarily at tarnishing the alleged victim's character. At the same time, the rules allow defendants to offer exonerating evidence when used for a proper purpose.

B. The Rule. Reflecting the balance that rape shield laws strike, **Rule 412** divides into three parts. Section (a) declares a general prohibition against using evidence of an alleged victim's past sexual behavior or sexual reputation; section (b) recognizes several exceptions to that general rule; and section (c) establishes procedural guidelines to protect privacy while judges determine the admissibility of evidence under the exceptions. We'll examine each part of the rule separately.[7]

1. The General Prohibition. Rule 412 opens with its general prohibition:

RULE 412. Sex-Offense Cases: The Victim's Sexual Behavior or Predisposition

(a) Prohibited Uses. The following evidence is not admissible in a civil or criminal proceeding involving alleged sexual misconduct:

---

7   A final section of Rule 412 clarifies that all of the rule's references to a "victim" include "an alleged victim."

> **(1)** evidence offered to prove that a victim engaged in <u>other sexual behavior</u>; or
>
> **(2)** evidence offered to prove a victim's <u>sexual predisposition</u>.

There are four points to notice about Rule 412(a). **First,** the rule encompasses both civil and criminal proceedings. In its initial form, Rule 412 applied only to criminal prosecutions. But in 1994 Congress expanded the rule's protection to include civil cases, noting that these cases raise similar privacy and stereotyping concerns as those marking criminal trials.

Second, in both the civil and criminal context, Rule 412 applies only to trials "involving alleged sexual misconduct." Witnesses, therefore, cannot use Rule 412 in other types of cases to exclude relevant inquiries about sexual history.

On the other hand, the rule's reference to any "proceeding involving alleged sexual misconduct" is a generous one. In criminal cases, Rule 412 may apply even if the prosecutor does not charge a sex crime directly. The Advisory Committee, for example, suggested that the rule would apply to a kidnapping case in which the prosecutor argued that the defendant intended to molest the victim sexually.[8] In civil cases, the committee noted that the rule would govern both sexual battery and sexual harassment claims.[9]

Third, Rule 412 bars both types of evidence that rape defendants previously offered to show propensity: It prohibits evidence both of specific acts ("other sexual behavior") and of reputation or general character ("sexual predisposition").

Finally, the rule broadly bars evidence of sexual behavior or predisposition regardless of the purpose for which a litigant offers that evidence. In this way Rule 412 differs from almost every other rule in Article IV. Most of those rules forbid particular types of evidence only when offered to prove a specific fact. Rule 408, discussed in Chapter 10, prohibits evidence drawn from settlement discussions only when offered to prove fault, and Rule 404 prohibits other act evidence only when offered to prove propensity.

---

8   See Fed. R. Evid. 412 advisory committee's note.

9   Id.

Rule 412 is like Rule 410, the rule barring evidence related to plea bargaining. Rather than prohibiting evidence only when offered for a particular purpose, these rules bar their designated types of evidence when offered for **any** purpose **except** those outlined in a few narrow exceptions.

2. The Exceptions. Section (b) of Rule 412 recognizes several exceptions to section (a)'s general prohibition. Because different policies arise in criminal and civil cases, the rule establishes different exceptions for each of those categories. We'll examine each of those briefly here.

(a) Criminal Cases. Subsection (b)(1) covers the exceptions for criminal cases:

RULE 412. Sex-Offense Cases: The Victim's Sexual Behavior or Predisposition

(b) Exceptions.

  (1) Criminal Cases. The court may admit the following evidence in a criminal case:

    (A) evidence of specific instances of a victim's sexual behavior, if offered to prove that someone other than the defendant was the source of semen, injury, or other <u>physical evidence</u>;

    (B) evidence of specific instances of a victim's <u>sexual behavior with respect to the person accused</u> of the sexual misconduct,

      • if offered by the defendant to prove consent or
      • if offered by the prosecutor; and

    (C) evidence whose exclusion would violate the defendant's <u>constitutional rights</u>.

Note that none of these exceptions admit evidence if a rule other than Rule 412 bars the evidence. If the proffered evidence violates Rule 404's bar against propensity evidence, the rule against hearsay, or any other rule, these exceptions do not override those prohibitions. In particular, all evidence offered under Rule 412's exceptions remains subject to Rule 403's balancing test.

We will explore the three 412(b)(1) exceptions at greater length in the Courtroom section. For now, note the general focus of each exception. The first exception allows proof of a complainant's prior sexual conduct when that evidence suggests that someone other than the accused was responsible for semen or other **physical evidence.** This exception covers the hypothetical described in the Introduction, when the defendant argued that another person was the source of semen found on the complainant.

The second exception admits evidence of **prior sexual encounters** between the complainant and the defendant. The structure of this exception is particularly notable: The defendant may offer this kind of evidence for just one purpose, to prove consent, but the prosecutor may offer this evidence for any purpose.

By allowing the defendant to try to show consent through evidence of prior sexual encounters, Rule 412 does not imply that these encounters inevitably **prove** consent. The Federal Rules of Evidence set a low standard for relevance: Evidence that has any tendency to make a fact of consequence to the action more or less probable is relevant. Prior sexual contact between the accused and complainant makes the fact of consent at least a little more likely than the absence of that contact. By limiting this exception to evidence of prior sexual contacts between the complainant and the defendant, the rule strikes a balance between the victim's privacy interests and the defendant's right to offer a legitimate defense.

In striking that balance, moreover, Rule 412 allows the prosecutor to offer evidence of prior sexual encounters between the accused and complainant for any purpose. The prosecutor, therefore, can offer evidence of other non-consensual encounters between the accused and the victim in order to show a defendant's motive, intent, identity, or any other relevant fact recognized by Rule 404(b).[10]

The third exception, finally, is a **catchall** exception; it allows evidence of sexual acts or reputation in criminal cases if excluding them "would violate the defendant's constitutional rights." This exception reflects the tension underlying the rape shield rule: We want to protect the privacy of victims and encourage them to come forward, but we also want to give all criminal defendants a fair opportunity to defend themselves.

---

10   As we'll see in the next chapter, Rule 413 permits prosecutors to admit propensity evidence about defendants in sexual assault cases. Without this second exception to Rule 412, the rape shield law would have the perverse effect of preventing prosecutors from showing that a defendant had raped the same victim on previous occasions.

Unfortunately, the plain language of this exception is not very helpful; it merely begs the question. Under what circumstances would excluding evidence of a victim's sexual acts or reputation violate the defendant's constitutional rights?[11] Defendants frequently invoke this exception when they claim that the alleged victim made prior allegations of sexual assault that were false. However, there are other circumstances under which a defense attorney might use this exception. We will examine those possibilities further in the Courtroom section.

(b) Civil Cases. Rule 412 proposes a single exception for civil cases, allowing introduction of an alleged victim's sexual acts or reputation under these circumstances:

RULE 412. Sex-Offense Cases: The Victim's Sexual Behavior or Predisposition

(b) Exceptions.

. . . .

(2) *Civil Cases.* In a civil case, the court may admit evidence offered to prove a victim's sexual behavior or sexual predisposition if its <u>probative value substantially outweighs</u> the danger

- of harm to any victim <u>and</u>
- of unfair prejudice to any party.

The court may admit evidence of a victim's reputation only if the <u>victim has placed it in controversy</u>.

There are four key points to this exception.

First, just as in criminal cases, evidence fitting this civil exception remains subject to all other Rules of Evidence. Litigants, therefore, cannot offer evidence of an alleged victim's sexual acts or reputation to prove propensity; that evidence would violate Rule 404.

---

11   Read literally, in fact, this exception is superfluous. The federal Constitution trumps any statute or rule; a litigant can override any rule of evidence if it conflicts with a constitutional provision.

Second, evidence of sexual acts or sexual predisposition faces a "reverse 403" test in civil cases: The evidence is admissible only if its probative value substantially outweighs the unfair prejudice to any party.[12]

Third, the rule ensures that the court weighs the danger to the alleged victim, whether or not she is a party to the litigation. Rule 412(b)(2) accomplishes this goal by directing the judge to weigh the "harm to any victim" as well as the "unfair prejudice to any party." This furthers the general policy of Rule 412 to protect victims of sexual assault from embarrassment or harassment in court.

Finally, reputation evidence is admissible in civil cases involving alleged sexual misconduct only if the alleged victim has "opened the door" by presenting evidence of her own reputation. Note that this constraint applies only to reputation evidence, not to evidence of sexual conduct.

3. Procedures. The third part of Rule 412, section (c), details a two-step procedure for determining the admissibility of any evidence of an alleged victim's sexual activity or reputation. First, a party intending to offer this evidence must give notice to the court, opposing counsel, and the alleged victim fourteen days before trial. Second, the court must hold a secret, sealed proceeding involving both parties and the alleged victim in order to determine whether the evidence is admissible. These procedures ensure that parties do not violate the privacy protected by the rule during the process of determining admissibility.

C. In the Courtroom. Most of the litigation arising under Rule 412 centers on the three exceptions that apply in criminal cases. During the last twenty years, however, Rule 412 has played an increasingly important role in civil claims involving sexual harassment. In this section, we'll look first at each of the criminal case exceptions and then examine recent developments in civil suits.

1. Physical Evidence. The first criminal case exception to the rape shield rule allows the defendant to introduce evidence of the victim's sexual acts when relevant to show that another person was "the source of semen, injury, or other physical evidence." Here is a widely publicized example of this exception:

---

12   This standard is similar to the one used by Rule 609(b) to determine the admissibility of convictions that are more than ten years old. See Chapter 20 for discussion of the standard and its nuances in the context of that rule.

Example: Kobe Bryant, the basketball star, was charged with raping a hotel employee in his hotel room. Bryant conceded that he had sexual intercourse with the complainant, but claimed that the sex was consensual. At a preliminary hearing, the prosecution called a doctor to testify that he examined the complainant shortly after the incident and found cuts and abrasions in the vaginal area consistent with forcible sex. On cross-examination, Bryant's attorney asked whether the injuries the doctor observed were consistent with multiple acts of consensual intercourse with different men over a short period of time. The prosecution objected, citing the rape shield law.

Analysis: The question was admissible under Rule 412, because it sought evidence that might show that a person other than the accused caused the physical injuries to the complainant.[13]

2. What Is "Sexual Behavior" Under 412(b)(1)(B)? The second exception for criminal cases allows the defendant to admit evidence of "specific instances of a victim's sexual behavior" between the complainant and the accused to prove consent. Courts have interpreted this phrase very liberally: "sexual behavior" includes any kind of intimate contact between the complainant and the accused.

The exception even covers statements that the complainant made about the defendant. The Advisory Committee opined that "sexual behavior" includes "statements in which the alleged victim expresses an intent to engage in sexual intercourse with the accused, or voiced sexual fantasies involving the specific accused."[14] The courts agree:

Example: Barry Young was an officer in the city police department, where he had met the complainant on several occasions. The complainant claimed that Young stopped her for a traffic violation, and then used his authority as a police officer to force her to have sex with him. Young contended that the complainant flagged him down while he was on the way

---

13   See Howard Pankratz & Steve Lipsher, Experts Say 'Bomb' Aids Bryant, Denver Post, Oct. 10, 2003, at A-16. The Bryant case took place in Colorado state court, so the judge applied the Colorado rape shield law. Federal Rule 412 and most state rape shield laws do not apply to preliminary hearings, but judges usually follow those rules in these pretrial proceedings. Prosecutors ultimately dropped the case when the complainant decided not to proceed.

14   Fed. R. Evid. 412 advisory committee's note.

home from work, that the two of them talked, and that they then engaged in consensual sexual intercourse.

Young sought to introduce evidence that (1) the complainant frequently came by the police department and flirted with him; and (2) the complainant told a friend that she "wanted to engage in sex with Young to such a degree that it would melt the ice in the water cooler." The prosecution argued that since the complainant did not act on these desires or fantasies at the time she talked about them, they were only evidence of general sexual predisposition and thus were barred by Rule 412.

Analysis: An appellate court upheld admission of both pieces of evidence relating to the complainant. When the defendant, as in this case, claims consent as a defense, then sexual thoughts and fantasies that are directed towards the defendant are admissible under Rule 412(b)(1)(B).[15]

3. The "Catchall" Exception. As noted above, criminal defendants frequently invoke the "catchall" exception (412(b)(1)(C)) to show that the alleged victim has made prior false claims of sexual assault. Defendants rely upon this evidence to argue that the current charges likewise are false:

Example: Dewayne Stamper was a dispatcher in the Cherokee Police Department; he was recently married and his wife was expecting their first child. During the summer of 1990, a friend's twelve-year-old daughter alleged that Stamper engaged in sexual acts with her, violating statutory rape laws.

At his criminal trial, Stamper offered evidence that (1) in 1989 the complainant had accused her stepfather and two other men of sexually molesting her; (2) as a result of those accusations, she was removed from her mother's custody and placed with her father; and (3) she later admitted that the allegation against her stepfather was false, and the police dropped the charges against all three men. The prosecution sought to preclude this evidence, arguing that Rule 412 barred any mention of the complainant's prior sexual activity.

---

15   Commonwealth v. Young, 182 S.W.3d 221 (Ky. Ct. App. 2005) (applying Kentucky's version of Rule 412).

Analysis: The district court admitted the evidence, holding that the defendant had a "substantial interest in presenting an adequate defense," and that he was offering evidence of a "scheme of fabrication" that tended to show that the alleged victim was lying in the instant case. Noting that the prosecution's case rested solely on the complainant's testimony, the court stated that "[d]efendant's right of confrontation is paramount to Rule 412's policy of shielding a rape victim from potential embarrassment."[16]

Applying the catchall exception may not be necessary to admit prior false allegations of sexual assault: The Advisory Committee's note on Rule 412 implies that the rule does not bar this evidence because prior allegations are not "sexual behavior" under 412(a)(1), and many courts agree.[17] But as the above case shows, even if a court assumes that Rule 412 applies to this situation, the evidence is admissible under 412(b)(1)(C) because it is so critical to the defendant's case.

Another way in which defense attorneys attempt to use the catchall exception is to argue that the complainant manufactured a rape claim to protect an existing intimate relationship:

Example: Susan Francis and Vernon Laughlin were driving together when Ferlin Platero, a private security guard, pulled them over. Francis claimed that Platero pretended to be a police officer, separated her from Laughlin, handcuffed her, drove her a few miles away to a deserted location, and raped her in his car. Platero then drove Francis back to her car, where Laughlin was waiting. Laughlin saw Francis emerge from Platero's car buttoning up her blouse and fixing her clothes. Francis immediately told Laughlin that she had been raped, and Platero was charged with the crime.

At trial, Platero claimed that Francis engaged in consensual intercourse with him, and that when Laughlin saw her getting out of his car and buttoning up her blouse, Francis decided to concoct a story about a rape so that Laughlin would not think she had willingly had sex with Platero. To bolster this theory, Platero offered evidence that Laughlin and Francis

---

16   United States v. Stamper, 766 F. Supp. 1396, 1041 (W.D.N.C. 1991).

17   See, e.g., United States v. Cournoyer, 118 F.3d 1279, 1282 (8th Cir. 1997), judgment vacated on other grounds, 522 U.S. 1102 (1998).

were engaged in an intimate relationship, which gave Francis a motive to lie about what happened. The prosecution argued that Rule 412 barred any evidence about the relationship between Francis and Laughlin.

Analysis: The appellate court held that, under the circumstances of this sexual encounter, the existence of an intimate relationship between Francis and Laughlin gave Francis a motive to lie about her encounter with Platero; therefore Platero had a constitutional right to present this evidence to the jury.[18]

Some students are surprised that courts allow evidence for this purpose, because it seems unlikely that a woman would falsely accuse a man of rape—thereby ruining his life and sending him to prison—just to explain away an act of sexual intercourse. But courts tend to stretch the catchall provision to protect the defendant's rights. And of course, the jury need not accept the defendant's arguments. Indeed, in cases like Platero the jury may conclude that a false accusation is unlikely.

This tendency to read the catchall exception liberally, however, has limits. Defense attorneys occasionally offer evidence of the alleged victim's "promiscuous" reputation to prove that the defendant reasonably believed that she consented to sexual contact with him. Most courts reject the evidence when offered for this purpose:

Example: Patricia Duckett accused Henry Saunders of rape. Saunders' defense was that he procured crack cocaine for Duckett and reasonably believed that she consented to the sexual acts in return. To support this defense, Saunders offered evidence that Duckett was known as a "skeezer"—or prostitute—and that because Saunders knew of Duckett's reputation, he reasonably believed that she consented to sex with him.

Analysis: The district court excluded the evidence, and the appellate court affirmed. The court acknowledged that "a defendant's reasonable, albeit mistaken, belief that the victim consented may constitute a defense to rape," but observed that it nonetheless "is unreasonable for a defendant to base his belief of consent on the victim's past sexual experiences with third persons."

---

18   United States v. Platero, 72 F.3d 806 (10th Cir. 1995).

Admitting Saunders's evidence, the court concluded, would "eviscerate the clear intent of the rule."[19]

Although a few courts have allowed evidence of the alleged victim's reputation to show the defendant's "state of mind,"[20] most courts agree with the Saunders opinion that doing so would "eviscerate" Rule 412.

4. Civil Cases. Rule 412 plays an increasingly important role in sexual harassment and other civil cases. When a civil plaintiff complains about sexual assault, defendants may try to offer evidence of the plaintiff's sexual history and reputation for purposes similar to those asserted in the criminal cases described above. Rule 412 applies to these civil conflicts, although it gives the judge somewhat greater discretion to admit the contested evidence. Remember that Rule 412's exception for civil cases allows the judge to admit evidence if its probative value substantially outweighs both any unfair prejudice to the parties and harm to the alleged victim:

> **Example:** B.K.B., a female officer employed by the Maui police department, sued the department for sex discrimination, claiming that (1) pornographic magazines and films were routinely displayed at the police station; (2) male officers compared her to females in the magazines and asked her if she could perform acts depicted in the movies; and (3) Lanny Tihada, the Deputy Chief of Police, raped her on three occasions. On the first of those occasions, B.K.B. claimed that Tihada told her that she "was just a fucking woman, no one will believe you and your career will be over" if she complained about the rape or other treatment.
>
> At trial, the department offered testimony from Jamie Becraft, another male officer, to attempt to prove that B.K.B. expressed her own sexuality in ways that welcomed this treatment. Becraft testified that after a party at B.K.B.'s house, she modeled lingerie for him, told him that she thought he would be fun in bed, and described how she stimulated herself sexually while thinking of him. B.K.B.'s counsel objected to this testimony under Rule 412.

---

19   United States v. Saunders, 943 F.2d 388, 392 (4th Cir. 1991).

20   See, e.g., Doe v. United States, 666 F.2d 43, 48 (4th Cir. 1981).

Analysis: The trial and appellate courts agreed that Becraft's testimony violated Rule 412. The defendant in a sexual harassment suit may attempt to show that the disputed workplace conduct was welcome. But Becraft's testimony, relating statements that B.K.B. uttered outside of work and that did not refer to the individual who committed the alleged rape, did not have sufficient probative value to outweigh their harm to B.K.B.[21]

Rule 412 applies to sexual harassment suits even when the plaintiff claims no sexual assault or other physical contact:

Example: Dujuana Socks-Brunot sued the Hirschvogel company, claiming that her superior—Charles Bentz— created a hostile work environment that forced her to resign. Socks-Brunot alleged that Bentz repeatedly referred to the size of her breasts; asked her what type of condoms she used; told her that a coworker wanted to have sex with her; asked her to bring him a videotape of her son's birth so he could "see another side of her"; and suggested "you want me . . . why don't you just admit it." Socks-Brunot also introduced evidence that Bentz had harassed another employee, Cindy Lehman; that Socks-Brunot and Lehman complained about Bentz's conduct to Hirschvogel's president; and that the president responded by creating a new sexual harassment program and designating Bentz as a contact person to receive complaints.

Hirschvogel defended on the ground that Socks-Brunot engaged in equally crude workplace conduct and thus welcomed Bentz's behavior. The company offered evidence that (1) Socks-Brunot had a consensual affair with Richard Head, another company employee; (2) Socks-Brunot asked a female colleague what she thought about blow jobs; (3) another coworker thought Socks-Brunot's body language toward Bentz was flirtatious; and (4) Socks-Brunot frequently used profanity, "including a four letter word beginning with the letter 'f' and a five letter word beginning with the letter 'b.' "

---

21   B.K.B. v. Maui Police Dep't, 276 F.3d 1091, 1103–06 (9th Cir. 2002).

Analysis: Although the district judge initially allowed this evidence, he concluded after trial that Rule 412 prohibited its admission; on that ground, the judge granted Socks-Brunot a new trial. Applying Rule 412(b)(2)'s "reverse 403" test, the judge noted that: (1) The alleged harasser, Bentz, did not know about Socks-Brunot's affair with Head, so the affair had little relevance to whether Bentz thought Socks-Brunot welcomed his comments; (2) Bentz likewise did not know about Socks-Brunot's question to a female colleague, and there was no evidence that she made similar comments to Bentz or other male workers; (3) Bentz himself did not describe Socks-Brunot as flirtatious, so the perception of another coworker had weak probative value; and (4) the widespread use of profanity in the workplace, combined with the loss of any sexual connotations in the common use of those terms, made Socks-Brunot's use of profanity weak evidence that she welcomed Bentz's more explicit comments.[22]

Note that most of the evidence rejected in *Socks-Brunot* was relevant under Rule 401. The fact that Socks-Brunot asked a female colleague about a sexual act, for example, made it slightly more likely that she signaled her willingness to talk about similar issues with Bentz; the relevance threshold is very low.

The judge in *Socks-Brunot*, however, readily concluded that the probative value of the defendant's evidence was very slight, while the unfair prejudice and harm to Socks-Brunot were high. Rule 412's "reverse 403" standard highlights the low probative value of most evidence related to a plaintiff's sexual conduct in sexual harassment cases. The standard also helps judges identify the unfair prejudice posed by this evidence: Much of the evidence rests on an unstated assumption that any indication of a woman's sexuality signals her openness to all sexual approaches in the workplace.

5. Gender and Sexual Orientation. Rule 412 applies regardless of the alleged victim's gender or sexual orientation. Here is one example of a male plaintiff invoking Rule 412 as part of a sexual harassment suit involving a male coworker:

---

22   Socks-Brunot v. Hirschvogel Inc., 184 F.R.D. 113 (S.D. Ohio 1999).

Example: A.W., a male worker, sued his employer, the I.B. Corporation, claiming that another male worker engaged in a series of sexually harassing acts. These actions included (1) grabbing A.W.'s buttocks or groin; (2) rubbing his groin into A.W.'s buttocks; (3) flashing A.W. by dropping his pants; and (4) shoving his hands into A.W.'s pants to touch A.W.'s genitals. During discovery, the I.B. Corporation attempted to question A.W. about any sexual conduct with other men. A.W.'s counsel objected under Rule 412.

Analysis: The district judge sustained A.W.'s objection, refusing to compel answers to these questions. The judge noted that "these are precisely the types of intrusive generalized questions about past, private, consensual sexual conduct that courts readily have found marginally (if at all) probative to sexual-harassment claims, highly prejudicial and likely to harm the plaintiff." The judge permitted the defendant's counsel to ask A.W. in discovery whether he had committed any sexual acts at the workplace, but prohibited other inquiries into sexual conduct under Rule 412.[23]

6. State Rules. The federal courts do not conduct many rape trials because state law governs most violent crime. However, all fifty states and the District of Columbia have adopted some form of Rule 412; in fact, some states passed their version of a rape shield law before the federal rule took effect. Unlike most of the other rules of evidence, the federal rule differs significantly from many state laws. Because of the dominance of state law in this area, and the continued evolution of rape shield laws, it is worthwhile to look briefly at developments in the states.

Rape shield laws in the states fall into three categories:[24]

a. Broad Prohibition with Specific Exceptions. Most states have adopted rape shield laws that follow the federal pattern of generally prohibiting evidence of prior sexual conduct or sexual reputation, then listing specific instances in which such evidence can be admitted. The exceptions vary from state to state but include provisions such as:

---

23   A.W. v. I.B. Corp., 224 F.R.D. 20 (D. Me. 2004).

24   For further discussion of these categories and the evolution of rape shield laws, see Michelle Anderson, From Chastity Requirement to Sexuality License: Sexual Consent and a New Rape Shield Law, 70 Geo. Wash. L. Rev. 51 (2002).

- Evidence of prior sexual conduct between the complainant and the accused

- Evidence of an alternative source of semen, pregnancy, or injury

- Evidence of a pattern of prior sexual conduct by the complainant

- Evidence of bias or motive to fabricate the sexual assault

- Evidence offered to prove that the accused had a reasonable but mistaken belief in the complainant's consent

- Evidence of prior false accusations of sexual assault by the complainant

- Evidence of prior prostitution

In addition, some of these states include a "catchall" provision like the federal one, admitting evidence when its exclusion would violate the defendant's constitutional rights.

b. Barring Evidence Offered for a Specific Purpose. A number of state rape shield laws use a more traditional structure for evidentiary rules: They bar evidence of sexual reputation or conduct only if it is offered for a specific purpose. The two most common prohibited purposes are (1) to prove the alleged victim's consent, and (2) to attack the alleged victim's credibility.

c. Judicial Discretion. Some states have no codified rape shield law, but give courts broad discretion to admit or preclude any evidence of the victim's prior sexual conduct or sexual reputation.

 Rape shield laws are still relatively new; Arizona did not adopt its law until 2003. The manner in which states structure rules, and courts enforce those rules, remains in flux. Courts and legislatures struggle to balance the defendant's constitutional rights against the state's interest in protecting victim privacy and overcoming outdated stereotypes. The growing prominence of civil claims for sexual harassment has added new complexities to the application of rape shield laws.

Quick Summary

Rule 412 generally bars any evidence of an alleged victim's sexual reputation or prior sexual acts in cases involving sexual misconduct. In those cases, Rule 412 trumps **Rule 404(a)(2)**'s exception for propensity evidence. Under Rule 412, the defendant cannot offer evidence of an alleged victim's sexual reputation to prove "propensity to consent."

Rule 412 allows evidence of reputation or prior sexual acts under certain circumstances. In criminal cases: (1) Evidence of specific instances of sexual behavior is admissible if offered to provide an alternate explanation for physical evidence such as injuries or semen; (2) Evidence of prior sexual conduct between the defendant and the alleged victim is admissible when offered by the prosecution for any purpose or by the defendant to prove consent; and (3) Evidence of either sexual behavior or predisposition is admissible when necessary to protect the constitutional rights of the defendant. Courts most often admit evidence under the final catchall provision when a defendant offers it to attack the complainant's credibility.

In civil cases, Rule 412 allows evidence of an alleged victim's sexual behavior or predisposition only if the offering party can pass a "reverse 403 test" by showing that the probative value of the evidence substantially outweighs its unfair prejudice to the parties and harm to the alleged victim.

Test Your Understanding

To assess your understanding of the material in this chapter, <u>click here</u> to take a quiz, or go to the Quizzes module from the eBook on your eProducts bookshelf.

33

Propensity in Sexual-Assault and Child-Molestation Cases

Key Concepts

- **Rules 413–415:** Propensity Evidence Is Admissible in Cases Involving Sexual Assault or Child Molestation
- The Rules Override **Rule 404's** General Bar on Propensity Evidence
- **Rule 403** Still Applies

A. Introduction and Policy. Although **Rule 404(a)** prohibits character evidence when used to prove propensity, that rule recognizes three exceptions: (1) when a criminal defendant offers evidence to prove his own propensity or that of his victim; (2) when a prosecutor responds by offering evidence to prove the defendant's or victim's propensity; and (3) when any party offers evidence to prove a witness's propensity to lie or tell the truth, as governed by **Rules 608 and 609**. We studied these exceptions in Chapters 19–22 and 27–28.

In 1995, Congress created another exception to the propensity rule: the use of character evidence to prove a defendant's tendency to commit sexual assaults or child molestation. **Rules 413**, **414**, and **415** codify this exception. In criminal prosecutions for sexual assault, Rule 413 allows prosecutors to introduce evidence of other sexual assaults committed by the defendant and to use that evidence for any purpose, including to suggest that the defendant has a propensity to commit sexual assaults. Rule 414 achieves the same result in prosecutions for child molestation: The prosecutor may introduce evidence of other molestations and argue that the defendant has a propensity to molest children. Rule 415, finally, allows the same evidence and propensity reasoning in civil cases involving sexual assault or child molestation.

These rules create significant advantages for prosecutors and civil plaintiffs claiming sexual assault or child molestation.[1] These parties may introduce evidence of a defendant's other sexual misdeeds without identifying a non-propensity purpose for the evidence under **Rule 404(b)**. Equally important, they may use the evidence to argue explicitly that the defendant has a propensity to commit sexual assaults or molest children. Rules 413–415, moreover, contain no exceptions or special balancing tests to modify their impact. **Rule 403** applies to evidence admitted under these rules but, as we'll see below, even that balancing test raises special problems in this context.

The procedure for adopting Rules 413–415 was unorthodox. The Advisory Committee did not propose these rules; instead, Congress drafted them in 1994 as part of its Violent Crime Control and Law Enforcement Act.[2]

The bill's supporters offered two arguments to support the new evidentiary rules. **First**, they claimed that individuals who commit sexual assaults or child molestation possess a distinctive disposition—the desire to commit violent sexual acts or sexual acts with children—so that prior acts of this kind are unusually probative. **Second**, they noted that cases of sexual assault and child molestation are particularly hard to prove because they frequently turn on the credibility of the victim and the defendant. In child-molestation cases, moreover, the victim may have difficulty testifying or lack credibility. Thus, the bill's supporters argued that sexual assault and child molestation were distinctive crimes that required an exception to the ban on propensity evidence.[3]

Congress deferred the effective date of Rules 413–415 so the Advisory Committee could provide feedback. That feedback was nearly unanimous: Of all the Committee members, including judges, practicing lawyers, and academics, all but one opposed adopting Rules 413–415. The sole dissenter, who supported the rules, was a representative of the United States Justice Department.

The Advisory Committee offered three objections to Rules 413–415. **First,** Rule 404 already allowed parties to admit evidence of a defendant's sexual misconduct if it proved anything other than propensity. **Second,** the proposed rules increased

---

1   Rule 415 allows both plaintiffs and defendants to introduce evidence of sexual assaults or child molestation to prove propensity, but plaintiffs are most likely to invoke the rule.

2   To review the usual process for drafting the rules, see Chapter 3.

3   See, e.g., Concerning the Prior Crimes Evidence Rules for Sexual Assault and Child Molestation Cases, Cong. Rec. H8991–92 (daily ed. Aug. 21, 1994) (statement of Rep. Susan Molinari).

the danger that a criminal defendant would be convicted based on his past conduct rather than the charged crime. **Third,** because the rules allowed the prosecutor or plaintiff to offer evidence of sexual misconduct even if the defendant had not been convicted of any crime for those acts, the rules would produce a number of distracting and time-consuming mini-trials in which each side attempted to prove or disprove that the prior offense occurred.[4]

The ABA's Criminal Justice Section noted another flaw: since most sexual assault and child molestation cases are prosecuted in state court, the new federal rules would apply primarily to crimes charged on Native American reservations. "Other questions of fairness aside," the Section asked in its report, "should such a significant and controversial rule change be adopted which will primarily impact Native Americans?"[5]

Ignoring all of this advice, Congress allowed the new rules to take effect in 1995.

B. The Rules. Rules 413 and **414** are structured identically; the only difference is that Rule 413 allows evidence of a defendant's other "sexual assaults" in criminal prosecutions for sexual assault, while Rule 414 permits evidence of other acts of "child molestation" in child-molestation cases. Section (a) of each rule contains the central principle of that rule:

> ## RULE 413 [414]. Similar Crimes in Sexual-Assault [Child-Molestation] Cases
>
> **(a) Permitted Uses.** In a criminal case in which a defendant is accused of a sexual assault [child molestation], the court may admit evidence that the defendant <u>committed any other sexual assault [child molestation]</u>. The evidence may be considered on <u>any matter to which it is relevant</u>.

There are three points to note about Rules 413(a) and 414(a):

---

4   See Report of the Judicial Conference of the United States on the Admission of Character Evidence in Certain Sexual Misconduct Cases, Feb. 9, 1995.

5   Myrna S. Raeder, ABA Criminal Justice Section Report to the House of Delegates, 22 Fordham Urb. L.J. 343, 352 (1995)

First, the rules apply only in criminal cases in which the defendant is currently being charged with either sexual assault or child molestation.

Second, each rule allows admission of a single type of evidence: evidence showing that the defendant committed another offense of sexual assault (Rule 413) or child molestation (Rule 414).

And **third**, this evidence is admissible for any relevant purpose, including propensity. Rules 413 and 414 thus override Rule 404(a)(1)'s bar on propensity evidence for sexual-assault and child-molestation cases.

Section (b) of each rule requires the government to follow a special disclosure procedure if it plans to introduce evidence under the rule. Given the unusual nature of evidence admitted under this rule, as well as its potency, the government must give the defendant notice of the evidence it plans to present.

Section (c) of each rule provides:

> ## RULE 413 [414]. Similar Crimes in Sexual-Assault [Child-Molestation] Cases
>
> **(c) Effect on Other Rules.** This rule does not limit the admission or consideration of evidence under any other rule.

This section emphasizes that, although Rules 413 and 414 supersede Rule 404's general propensity bar, they do not override other rules such as hearsay and privilege. In particular, this section preserves the application of **Rule 403** when a party offers evidence under Rules 413 or 414. As we discuss further in the Courtroom section, the judge must decide whether the unfair prejudicial effect of Rule 413/414 evidence substantially outweighs its probative value.

Section (d) of Rule 413, finally, defines "sexual assault" for the purpose of that rule, while section (d) of Rule 414 similarly defines "child molestation." The rules enumerate all federal statutes covering these crimes, and also include state offenses that meet specified definitions. For sexual assault, Rule 413 focuses on physical, rather than verbal conduct. For child molestation, Rule 414 defines a child as a person below the age of fourteen.

Rule 415 simply refers back to Rules 413 and 414, and applies its language to civil cases:

> ## RULE 415. Similar Acts in Civil Cases Involving Sexual Assault or Child Molestation
>
> **(a) Permitted Uses.** In a civil case involving a claim for relief based on a party's alleged sexual assault or child molestation, the court may admit evidence that the party committed any other sexual assault or child molestation. The evidence may be considered as provided in Rules 413 and 414.

Thus, Rule 415 allows the plaintiff in a civil case involving sexual assault or child molestation to introduce other, similar conduct of the defendant to prove propensity or any other relevant fact. **Rule 415(b)** articulates the same notice provision found in Rules 413 and 414, and **Rule 415(c)** offers the same proviso acknowledging application of other evidentiary rules.

C. In the Courtroom.

1. Prior Crime Need Not Be Proven. Rules 413, 414, and 415 do not require that the prior act resulted in a criminal charge or conviction. Any conduct that constitutes sexual assault or child molestation is admissible under these rules, regardless of whether formal charges were ever brought for the prior conduct.

> **Example:** Wilbur Gabe was on trial for molesting his adopted daughter. The abuse allegedly began in 1988, when the adopted daughter was in first grade, and continued until she was fifteen years old. At trial, the adopted daughter testified against Gabe, as did a doctor who had examined her. In addition, the government offered the testimony of Holly Thompson, a female relative of Gabe's. Thompson testified that Gabe had molested her 20 years earlier, when she was seven years old.

> **Analysis:** Thompson's evidence was admissible under Rule 414. The conduct described by Thompson constituted an offense of child molestation under Rule 414's definition. Although Gabe was never arrested for that offense,

and it occurred two decades before prosecution for the alleged molestation of his daughter, Rule 414 includes acts that meet the Rule's definition of child molestation.[6]

Note that Gabe's alleged conduct with Thompson was admissible to prove his propensity to commit such an offense even though it occurred twenty years before the offense for which he was on trial. Rules 413–415 have no time limit, although a judge may exclude conduct that occurred many years ago under **Rule 403**. We explore the interaction of that rule with Rules 413–15 in the next section.

2. Rule 403. Although Rules 413–415 include no exceptions, the rules remain subject to Rule 403's balancing test. A judge may, in her discretion, decide that evidence of a prior sexual assault or child molestation is so unduly prejudicial to the defendant that its unfair effect substantially outweighs the probative value.

Courts, however, find it difficult to apply Rule 403's balancing test in the context of Rules 413–415. Rules 413–415 explicitly require judges to recognize the probative value of prior sexual assaults and child molestations to show the defendant's propensity to commit these types of acts. Because the rules favor the probative value of these acts, despite their prejudicial effect, judges have struggled to articulate the proper relationship between Rule 403 and Rules 413–415.

 Some courts have suggested that trial judges should apply Rule 403 lightly in these cases, deferring to Congress's decision to allow propensity evidence of sexual assault and child molestation. Other courts have fashioned special criteria to govern application of Rule 403 to evidence offered under Rules 413–415. Still others have declared that trial judges should apply Rule 403 to this evidence using the same standards that govern all other cases.[7]

Despite this disagreement, most courts consider similar factors when applying Rule 403 to evidence of prior sexual assaults or child molestation. These factors are similar to ones that courts apply to other Rule 403 decisions:

---

6   United States v. Gabe, 237 F.3d 954, 959–60 (8th Cir. 2001).

7   For a review of these different approaches, see Martinez v. Cui, 608 F.3d 54 (1st Cir. 2010).

- The length of time that has passed since the other acts

- Reliability of the witness testifying about the other acts

- Similarity of the other acts to those charged

- Whether the government could make similar points with less prejudicial evidence

Here is a case in which the court used considerations like these to exclude evidence under Rule 403:

Example: Betsy Sue Johnson sued her former high school guidance counselor, Wayne Stevens, claiming that he sexually harassed and abused her while she was a high school student. Johnson alleged that during her freshman and sophomore years, Stevens sent her cards, roses, and flowers; frequently tried to hug and kiss her without her consent; and once fondled her breasts and vagina.

To support her allegations, Johnson offered testimony from Karen Radwanski, a friend and coworker of Stevens, about an incident in which Stevens picked Radwanski up and threw her over his shoulder during a lunch break at work. Radwanski was wearing a skirt and "Stevens's hand went up her skirt and touched her in the crotch area while he raised her off the floor." Radwanski gave conflicting testimony about whether she believed the touching was intentional. Johnson argued that the evidence was admissible under Rule 415.

Analysis: The trial court precluded the evidence, and the Third Circuit upheld the ruling. The court of appeals concluded that when the other act of sexual assault is proven with reliable testimony and is substantially similar to the actions under dispute, Rule 415 tips the prejudice/probative value balance in favor of admissibility. In this case, however, the evidence that the prior action was an intentional sexual assault was "equivocal," and the action was not very similar to the actions Johnson complained about. Therefore, the trial court properly excluded Radwanski's testimony under Rule 403 as unfairly prejudicial, confusing, and a waste of time.[8]

But when the facts of another assault or molestation more closely resemble the charged crime, courts seem more reluctant to exclude the evidence under Rule 403:

Example: In the Gabe case described above, the defendant argued that Rule 403 should bar the evidence that he had molested Thompson, because the alleged conduct took place twenty years earlier.

Analysis: The Eighth Circuit upheld the trial court's admission of the evidence, noting that "[t]he abuse alleged by Thompson was almost identical to the abuse of [Gabe's daughter] alleged in Count I. Both were young girls of six or seven years at the time of the offenses; both were related to Gabe; and the sexual nature of the offenses was similar." The court observed that the similarity of the incidents enhanced the probative value of the prior conduct while reducing its inflammatory nature; the jury would not be distracted by lurid and distasteful acts of a different sort.[9]

Example: The government charged David Mann with sexually molesting his grand niece, who was six or seven years old. The government introduced the evidence of R.K., another one of Mann's grand nieces, who testified that Mann had molested her when she was that age. At the time of trial, R.K. was seventeen.

Analysis: The court of appeals upheld admission of R.K.'s testimony under Rules 414 and 403, noting that the prior acts were very similar to the charged ones and that R.K. was a credible witness. Mann's prominence in the community explained why R.K. did not come forward earlier, and her age at the time of trial added probative value to her statements compared to those of the much younger alleged victims.[10]

---

8   Johnson v. Elk Lake School District, 283 F.3d 138, 156–59 (3d Cir. 2002).

9   Gabe, 237 F.3d at 959.

10   United States v. Mann, 193 F.3d 1172 (10th Cir. 1999).

3. States Not Following Suit. Unlike Rule 412, which has been adopted in some form by all fifty states, only a minority of state courts and legislatures have embraced Rules 413–415. About twelve states have statutes embodying some form of Rule 413 and/or 414, and a few others have common-law exceptions for propensity to engage in this conduct.[11] A smaller number of states have adopted some version of Rule 415. But at least thirty states lack any provision like 413–415. In addition, courts in five states have struck down state versions of Rule 413 or 414 as unconstitutional.[12]

In states without these rules, some courts find creative ways to admit evidence of prior sexual assaults or child molestations, frequently stretching their application of Rule 404(b) to admit this evidence as proof of "intent" or "motive" or "common plan or scheme."[13] States that have an analogue to Rules 413–415, however, allow the prosecutor or civil plaintiff to argue overtly that the defendant has a propensity for sexual assault or child molestation.

4. Are Civil Cases Different? Although commentators widely condemn Rules 413 and 414, which apply to criminal cases, a few have defended Rule 415's provision for civil suits.[14] These scholars argue that Rule 415 helps plaintiffs overcome cultural biases in sexual harassment cases. According to these scholars, jurors in those cases often assume that the plaintiff invited the defendant's behavior; evidence that the defendant engaged in similar behavior with others can challenge that assumption.

---

11 See Tamara Rice Lave & Aviva Orenstein, Empirical Fallacies of Evidence Law; A Critical Look at the Admission of Sex Crimes, 81 U. Cin. L. Rev. 795, 800–01.

12 Id. at 801.

13 Id. at 802.

14 See, e.g., Jane H. Aiken, Leveling the Playing Field: Federal Rules of Evidence 412 & 415, 21 QLR 927 (2003).

Quick Summary

 If a criminal defendant is charged with sexual assault, **Rule 413** allows the prosecutor to introduce evidence of other sexual assaults to prove that the defendant had a propensity to commit the crime. **Rule 414** adopts the same approach in prosecutions for child molestation; the prosecutor may introduce evidence of other molestations to show propensity. **Rule 415** grants private parties the same freedom in civil cases involving sexual assault and child molestation. These rules thus create another exception to **404(a)(1)**'s general ban on propensity evidence.

The prior offense of sexual assault or child molestation need not produce a formal charge or conviction; any accusation of prior conduct meeting the elements of these crimes satisfies Rules 413–415. Rule 403, however, still applies to this evidence: The court will balance the probative value of the evidence against its prejudicial effect.

But Rule 403 is difficult to apply to evidence admitted under Rules 413–415. For evidence of bad acts admitted under other rules, such as Rule 404(b) or Rule 609, the possibility of using the evidence to prove propensity counts as prejudice. Rules 413–415, conversely, embrace this possibility as a positive aspect of the evidence's probative value. In applying Rule 403 to evidence admitted under Rules 413–415, therefore, courts look to (1) the amount of time that has passed since the prior incident; (2) the reliability of the evidence relating to that prior incident; (3) the similarity between the past incident and the charged crime; and (4) whether the government could prove its point using less prejudicial evidence.

Test Your Understanding

 To assess your understanding of the material in this chapter, click here to take a quiz, or go to the Quizzes module from the eBook on your eProducts bookshelf.

34

Preliminary Questions

A. Introduction and Policy. During any trial, the judge makes dozens—even hundreds—of decisions to admit or exclude evidence. We have already examined some of the procedural steps associated with those decisions: motions in limine, objections, and trial rulings.[1] In this chapter we take a closer look at the standard that a judge applies when deciding whether a challenged piece of evidence is admissible.

Admissibility sometimes depends on a question of law. Rule 609, for example, requires the judge to determine whether a witness's prior conviction was for a "dishonest act or false statement."[2] Characterization of the prior conviction is a question of law for the court. Judges applying Rule 411's bar against evidence of liability insurance, similarly, must decide as a matter of law whether indemnity agreements fall within the rule's prohibition.[3] Issues like these are legal ones that the judge decides by reading the rule's language, applying judicial precedent, and considering the rule's legislative history and policy rationale. The jurors play no role in deciding questions of law that govern admissibility.

---

1   See Chapters 4–5.

2   Refer back to Chapter 20 for further discussion of Rule 609.

3   See Chapter 13 for further discussion of Rule 411.

But many questions of admissibility depend on **contested facts**. The prosecutor in a sexual assault case, for example, may invoke **Rule 413** to offer evidence that the defendant previously assaulted another victim.[4] If the defendant claims that the previous sexual encounter was consensual, should the judge resolve that disputed fact and admit the evidence only if she decides that the previous incident was, in fact, a nonconsensual assault? Or should the jury hear conflicting evidence about the previous encounter and decide whether that encounter was consensual?

A different type of factual issue can arise under **Rule 407,** which bars admission of subsequent remedial measures.[5] If the parties dispute when a repair occurred, who resolves that factual controversy? Does the judge decide the issue, admitting evidence of the repair only if it occurred before the plaintiff's injury? Or does the jury resolve the timing issue along with other factual issues arising in the case?

Rule 104 establishes a process for resolving disputed issues—both legal and factual—that relate to admissibility. The rule refers to these decisions as "preliminary questions" because they affect the admissibility of evidence rather than disposition of the underlying charges or claims.

Rule 104(a) assigns most of these preliminary questions to the judge: The judge resolves all legal issues affecting admissibility, as well as most factual ones. But Rule 104(b) limits the judge's authority when resolving one category of preliminary factual issues. These are factual issues that affect whether evidence is **relevant**.

In the sexual assault example given above, the consensual nature of the defendant's prior sexual encounter affects whether the evidence is relevant to the charged assault. If the defendant previously assaulted another victim, that evidence suggests some tendency to commit sexual assaults, and Rule 413 permits the prosecutor to introduce that evidence. But if the previous encounter was consensual, it is irrelevant to the assault prosecution. A defendant's consensual sex with one person tells us nothing about whether the defendant assaulted a different person.

Some lawyers call this type of preliminary factual question a matter of **conditional relevance**: The evidence is relevant if a factual predicate is true, but not if it is false. The Federal Rules describe these questions with a simpler phrase, **"relevance that depends on a fact."** Whatever words you use, the key to this

---

4   See Chapter 33 for further discussion of this rule.

5   See Chapter 9 for further discussion of Rule 407.

subset of preliminary questions is the connection between a disputed factual issue and relevance: The proffered evidence is relevant only if the disputed fact is true.

Rule 104(b) recognizes that the jury should resolve this type of factual dispute. When relevance depends on the existence of a fact, the trial judge performs only a screening function before admitting the contested evidence. The judge will ask whether enough evidence exists that a reasonable jury **could** resolve the factual dispute in a manner that makes the evidence relevant. If the evidence passes that low threshold, the jury will decide the preliminary factual question and, if the decision favors relevance, will use that relevant evidence in deciding the case. We will look more closely at application of this standard in the Courtroom section below.

In the other category of preliminary factual controversies, the dispute does not relate to the relevance of the evidence. Instead, the factual disagreement affects whether one of the many rules of evidence will exclude an otherwise relevant piece of evidence.

When the parties contest whether a defendant's remedial measure occurred before or after the plaintiff's injury, for example, that disagreement does not affect the repair's relevance. Subsequent remedial measures are just as relevant—perhaps more so—than repairs completed before a plaintiff's injury. Instead, the repair's timing affects whether Rule 407 applies to the case. That rule encourages defendants to make prompt repairs by assuring them that those repairs will not be admissible to prove liability in a pending lawsuit. Judges, accordingly, exclude repairs made after the plaintiff was injured but admit ones made before the injury occurred.

Under these circumstances, when resolution of the factual issue does not affect relevance, Rule 104(a) directs the judge to decide the factual issue without deferring to the jury. The judge will review the evidence presented by the parties, resolve any credibility issues, and decide the factual question. Based on that ruling, the judge will admit or exclude the evidence. The jury plays no role in resolving these preliminary factual issues.

Although the distinction between these two categories sounds complex, the distinction makes sense as a practical matter. Factual issues that affect relevance often determine both the admissibility of evidence and its weight. Since jurors determine the weight of admitted evidence, it makes sense for them to decide whether the evidence deserves any attention at all—as long as the proffered evidence clears Rule 104(b)'s low hurdle.

Jurors, conversely, are not familiar with the legal principles that govern most rules of evidence. They would not understand why the timing of a repair affects its admissibility; asking them to resolve that preliminary issue would distract them from the primary issues in the case. Giving that job to the jury would also expose them to evidence that ends up excluded. The judge alone, therefore, resolves disputes related to whether a party has laid the required factual foundation to admit or exclude a particular a piece of evidence.

B. The Rule. Rule 104 contains five sections, although the first two are most important for our purposes; those sections include the rules governing resolution of the two types of factual disputes described above.

1. Section (a). The first section of Rule 104 establishes the general rule for all preliminary questions:

> ## RULE 104. Preliminary Questions
>
> **(a) In General.** <u>The court must decide</u> any preliminary question about whether a witness is qualified, a privilege exists, or evidence is admissible. In so deciding, the court is <u>not bound by evidence rules</u>, <u>except those on privilege</u>.

This section establishes three points. **First,** the section announces a default rule that the judge decides preliminary questions related to admissibility. These questions include both issues of law and matters of fact.

Second, the section confirms that the Rules of Evidence do not apply to the information a judge can hear when making a preliminary determination. We noted this point when we discussed **Rule 1101** in Chapter 3. The judge may consider any evidence—even evidence that violates evidentiary rules—when deciding whether evidence is admissible. Any other approach would prevent the judge from looking at evidence to decide whether it is admissible.

Finally, section (a) recognizes the same exception to this principle that Rule 1101 acknowledges: The rules of privilege do apply to preliminary determinations. If judges could override those privileges when deciding whether to admit evidence, parties would lose the confidentiality that privileges protect.

2. Section (b). The second section of Rule 104 governs preliminary factual questions that fall into the special category discussed above: questions of fact that determine whether a piece of evidence is relevant. Section (b) tells judges to screen just for the sufficiency of this evidence to establish relevance. If the evidence survives this threshold scrutiny, the jury will resolve the factual dispute:

RULE 104. Preliminary Questions

(b) Relevance That Depends on a Fact. When the <u>relevance</u> of evidence depends on whether a fact exists, proof must be introduced <u>sufficient to support a finding</u> that the fact does exist. The court may admit the proposed evidence on the condition that the proof be introduced later.

Two aspects of this language sometimes confuse readers. **First**, the section's reference to "relevance" prompts some readers to conclude that the section applies only to issues raised under **Rules 401** and **402**, the rules that expressly address relevance. But, as we saw with the example of a disputed prior assault, relevance issues lurk in the application of other rules as well. We will explore further in the Courtroom section the different contexts in which relevance depends on resolution of a factual dispute.

Second, the instruction that "proof must be introduced sufficient to support a finding," is an unduly vague description of the judge's role. The phrase refers to a standard that judges and litigators sometimes call the prima facie standard. It means that the judge should let the jury decide the factual issue if enough evidence exists that a rational jury **could** resolve the factual dispute either way.

This is a very low standard for screening evidence. The judge herself might well resolve the factual dispute in a way that would exclude the contested evidence. Nine out of ten juries might reach the same conclusion. But as long as **some** rational jury **could** resolve the issue the other way, the judge will let the jury weigh the disputed facts. In particular, the judge will allow the jurors to assess the credibility of the evidence presented by the parties.

3. Section (c). Judges resolve many evidentiary issues quickly, without the need to receive additional information or argument from the parties. But some admissibility disputes require a hearing. Fairness, moreover, sometimes requires holding this hearing outside the jury's hearing; otherwise, discussion of the evidentiary issues might prejudice the jury's understanding of the case. Section (c) of Rule 104 addresses this need to hold hearings outside the jury's hearing. It is a straightforward section requiring little interpretation:

RULE 104. Preliminary Questions

(c) Conducting a Hearing So That the Jury Cannot Hear It. The court must conduct any hearing on a preliminary question so that the jury cannot hear it if:

(1) the hearing involves the admissibility of a confession;

(2) a defendant in a criminal case is a witness and so requests; or

(3) justice so requires.

4. Section (d). The fourth provision of Rule 104 allows the accused in a criminal case to testify on preliminary matters, such as the voluntariness of a confession, without subjecting himself to cross-examination on other issues in the case.

RULE 104. Preliminary Questions

(d) Cross-Examining a Defendant in a Criminal Case. By testifying on a preliminary question, a defendant in a criminal case does not become subject to cross-examination on other issues in the case.

This safeguard allows the accused to contest potentially unreliable evidence without waiving the privilege against self-incrimination. We will return to this concept when we study the privilege against self-incrimination in Chapter 68.

5. Section (e). The final section of Rule 104 recognizes that, even if the judge admits evidence, the parties may dispute the evidence's weight at trial. The rule specifically acknowledges the right of parties to introduce evidence related to the weight or credibility of other evidence that has been admitted:

RULE 104. Preliminary Questions

(e) Evidence Relevant to Weight and Credibility. This rule does not limit a party's right to introduce before the jury evidence that is relevant to the weight or credibility of other evidence.

We have already discussed many of the ways in which parties impeach the credibility of witnesses;[6] we don't need to explore this section further here.

C. In the Courtroom. We'll look more closely now at the difference between resolving preliminary factual disputes under Rule 104(a) and deciding those questions under Rule 104(b). We'll begin by looking at examples from each category. Then we'll examine a few broader questions, such as the standard of proof that judges apply to these decisions and the relationship of Rule 104 to **Rule 403**.

1. Rule 104(b): Relevance That Depends on a Fact.

a. Personal Knowledge Under Rule 602. Rule 602, which requires witnesses to testify from their personal knowledge, offers a straightforward example of an evidentiary rule that can generate factual disputes governed by Rule 104(b):[7]

Example: A man entered a small neighborhood store, ordered the employees and customers to lie face down on the floor, and stole all of the store's cash. One of the customers, Martha Magon, told police that she lifted her head slightly and saw the robber. Magon identified Butch Cavendish in a line-up and the state prosecuted Cavendish for robbery.

In a pretrial motion, Cavendish challenged Magon's personal knowledge under Rule 602. Cavendish introduced evidence that Magon had very poor eyesight, even with corrective lenses. Cavendish's attorney argued that this circumstance, combined with the fact that Magon admitted lying face down during the robbery, made it impossible for Magon to see the robber clearly. The attorney claimed that Magon lacked personal knowledge of the robber's identity.

---

6   Look in particular at Chapters 17–22.

7   To review Rule 602 and the concept of personal knowledge, see Chapter 14.

Analysis: Magon's personal knowledge is a disputed factual issue: She claims that she saw the robber clearly enough to identify him, while Cavendish contends she could not. Resolution of this issue determines the relevance of Magon's testimony. If she saw the man who robbed the store, then her identification of Cavendish is highly probative; if she could not see the robber, then it is unfounded and irrelevant. In the language of Rule 104(b), the relevance of Magon's testimony "depends on whether a fact exists."

A reasonable jury could resolve this dispute either way. The jury might believe Magon's claim that she could see the robber, or they might believe Cavendish that Magon could not have possibly seen the robber. But based on this conflicting testimony, a reasonable jury **could** believe Magon's claim that she saw the man who robbed the store; this would give her sufficient personal knowledge to testify.

Because there is evidence "sufficient to support a finding" that Magon had personal knowledge, the judge will admit her testimony under Rule 104(b). But the jury will still decide whether Magon really did see the robber and, if so, whether her identification of Cavendish is reliable. In the jury room, these two issues will merge into a single question of whether the jury believes that Magon correctly identified Cavendish.

Sometimes the absence of personal knowledge is so clear that a judge will exclude the testimony, even after applying Rule 104(b)'s liberal standard. Remember this example from Chapter 14:

Example: Jerry McCrary-El, a prison inmate, claimed that three prison guards beat him without provocation. He **sued** the guards and offered the testimony of Antonio Jones, an inmate housed in a neighboring cell. Jones claimed that a crack at the corner of his cell door, which measured about an inch and a half long, allowed him to see into the prison corridor and witness the initial confrontation between McCrary-El and the guards. The nature of this confrontation was relevant to whether the guards beat Mc-Crary-El without provocation. The guards objected to Jones's testimony, claiming that he physically could not have seen the part of the corridor where the confrontation occurred.[8]

---

8   McCrary-El v. Shaw, 992 F.2d 809 (8th Cir. 1993), discussed in Chapter 14. It is not clear if Jones could

After listening to testimony from Jones and examining a prison floor plan, the judge concluded that Jones could not possibly have seen the confrontation. Given the physical layout of the prison, no reasonable person would believe Jones's claim. There was no evidence, accordingly, that would "support a finding" that Jones had personal knowledge of the confrontation between McCrary-El and the guards. After resolving this factual issue under Rule 104(b), the judge excluded Jones's testimony under Rule 602.

b. Evidence of Other Acts Under Rule 404(b). Rule 404(b), which governs admission of "other acts" to prove facts like motive or knowledge, also generates questions in which relevance depends on resolution of a factual dispute.[9] Indeed, Rule 404(b) produces a large number of hotly contested, preliminary factual contests.

Recall, for example, the case of Gloria the safe-cracker that we discussed in Chapters 25 and 30. We suggested that a prosecutor might try to prove Gloria's knowledge of safe-cracking by introducing evidence that Gloria had broken into locked safes on previous occasions. But what if Gloria disputes her role in those previous safe-crackings? Can the prosecutor introduce evidence of a previous crime that the defendant disputes? How does the judge resolve that preliminary factual controversy?

The Supreme Court answered these questions in a case with these facts:

> **Example:** The government prosecuted Guy Huddleston for selling stolen videotapes. Huddleston conceded that he sold the tapes but claimed that he didn't know they were stolen. To show knowledge, the government offered evidence that Huddleston previously sold suspiciously low-priced television sets obtained from the same source as the videotapes. Two months before the videotape sale, Huddleston had offered to sell several thousand black-and-white television sets for just $28 apiece; he had no bill of sale for the televisions.[10] These circumstances, the government argued, showed that the television sets were stolen and that Huddleston knew

---

hear the confrontation, but the parties did not focus on that issue. The significance of Jones's testimony turned on whether he was able to see certain details that he claimed to see.

9   To review Rule 404(b), see Chapter 30.

10   Today black-and-white television sets are collector's items. In 1985, when Huddleston sold his sets, this was a remarkably low price.

they were stolen. The previous sale of stolen television sets, the prosecutor further claimed, provided evidence that Huddleston knew the videotapes (obtained from the same source) were also stolen.

Huddleston challenged admission of this evidence on the ground that the government offered insufficient proof that the televisions were stolen. Huddleston argued that, before admitting this potentially prejudicial evidence, the district judge should have determined under Rule 104(a) that the televisions were in fact stolen.

Analysis: The Supreme Court acknowledged that the television-set evidence was relevant only if the sets were stolen. If the televisions were stolen, then Huddleston's previous sale of stolen merchandise obtained from the same source made it more likely that he knew the videotapes were also stolen. The Court, however, rejected Huddleston's claim that the district judge should determine under Rule 104(a) whether the television sets were stolen.

Instead, the Court applied Rule 104(b)'s more lenient screening standard to this preliminary determination about "other act" evidence. To admit the government's evidence, the trial judge only had to find that a reasonable jury **could find** that the television sets were stolen. Huddleston's inability to produce a bill of sale, combined with the suspiciously low price at which he offered to sell the televisions, was sufficient to allow a reasonable jury to make that finding.[11]

 For a review of the *Huddleston* standard, as well as some issues related to character evidence, <u>click here</u> to see the video "Character Evidence in Civil Cases" or go to the Videos module from the eBook on your eProducts bookshelf.

Trial judges, in other words, admit "other act" evidence as long as a reasonable jury could find the factual condition that makes the evidence relevant. The jury then determines both whether the factual condition is met and, if it is, how the evidence affects its decision in the case. In Huddleston, for example, the jury had to decide (1) whether the television sets Huddleston previously sold were stolen;

---

11   Huddleston v. United States, 485 U.S. 681 (1988).

and, if they were, (2) whether the previous sale of stolen television sets showed that Huddleston knew that the videotapes were also stolen.

c. Factual Determinations Under Rule 412. In sexual misconduct cases, Rule 412 bars most evidence of the alleged victim's sexual acts or predisposition. The rule, however, allows the defendant to introduce that evidence under specified circumstances.[12] Those exceptions frequently generate preliminary factual disputes. The defendant, for example, may claim that he engaged in previous consensual acts with the victim, while the victim denies the consensual nature of those encounters. Or the defendant may argue that physical evidence (semen, bruising) stemmed from the victim's sexual acts with another person, while the victim denies those acts.

These disputes affect the relevance of the proffered evidence, so Rule 104(b) governs their disposition. Here is one example, based on a case we examined in Chapter 32. The defendant in this case invoked Rule 412(b)(1)(C), the "catchall" exception, as grounds for introducing the evidence:

> **Example:** The government charged Ferlin Platero with raping Susan Francis. Platero argued that Francis consented to sex with him and that she claimed rape to avoid embarrassment in front of Vernon Laughlin, with whom she was having an intimate affair. Francis and Laughlin both denied that they were romantically involved at the time of the alleged rape; indeed, Francis was married to another man. Francis and Laughlin, however, were intimately involved by the time of Platero's trial, and Laughlin's former girlfriend claimed that the two had carried on a secret affair for many years. Francis, moreover, referred to Laughlin as her "boyfriend" in statements made to police and doctors immediately after the alleged rape.

> **Analysis:** The court of appeals concluded that Platero presented sufficient evidence of Francis's relationship with Laughlin to "support a finding" that the two were having an intimate affair when Francis accused Platero of rape. Rule 104(b) required the jury to decide that preliminary issue.[13]

---

12   See Chapter 32 for discussion of Rule 412 and its exceptions.

13   United States v. Platero, 72 F.3d 806 (10th Cir. 1995), discussed in Chapter 32.

d. Other Sexual Assaults by Defendant Under Rules 413–415. As suggested in the Introduction, Rules 413–415 raise preliminary factual issues that affect relevance. If a prosecutor or plaintiff offers evidence of other sexual assaults committed by the defendant, and the defendant denies those assaults, the conflict affects the relevance of the proffered testimony. Applying Rule 104(b), the judge will determine whether a reasonable jury could find that the other assault occurred. If the evidence meets that threshold, the judge will allow the jury to determine both the existence and probative value of the alleged assault.

2. Rule 104(a): Questions of Admissibility Unrelated to Relevance.

a. Timing of Remedial Measures Under Rule 407. The question of whether a remedial measure occurred before or after the plaintiff's injury raises a different type of factual issue than the ones discussed in the previous sections. As explained in the Introduction, a remedial measure may be relevant whether it occurred before or after the plaintiff's injury. But if the defendant adopted the remedy after the plaintiff's injury, the plain language of **Rule 407** bars admission of the evidence.

Deciding a dispute over the timing of a remedial measure under Rule 407 does not affect relevance, so the court decides that issue without deference to the jury.

Example: Robin Straley, a trash collector, was standing on the rear step of the truck while helping the driver back the truck into an alley. Straley fell off the step and his legs were crushed beneath the truck's wheels. Straley sued the manufacturer of the truck, claiming that the truck was poorly designed and that the rear step lacked sufficient handgrips. Before trial, the manufacturer moved under Rule 407 to exclude evidence of warnings it had issued to all purchasers of the truck, notifying them about the dangers of riding on the truck's rear step. The parties disputed whether the manufacturer issued those warnings before or after Straley's accident.

Analysis: After examining the parties' conflicting evidence, the trial judge concluded that the manufacturer issued the warnings before Straley's injury. Accordingly, Rule 407 did not bar evidence of the warnings and the judge ruled them admissible.[14]

---

14   This example is very loosely based on Straley v. United States, 887 F. Supp. 728 (D.N.J. 1995).

b. Whether Repeated Conduct Is Propensity or Habit Under Rule 406.
Many preliminary decisions that judges make under Rule 104(a) present mixed
questions of law and fact. The judge, for example, determines whether an individual's conduct was sufficiently regular and specific to constitute a habit admissible
under Rule 406. Separating an admissible habit from inadmissible propensity
evidence may depend on answers to a host of factual questions. When determining
whether a plaintiff's seatbelt use was a habit, for example, a judge might ask: How
often did the plaintiff wear a seatbelt? Did the plaintiff use a seatbelt for all types
of journeys or just for certain types? Did the plaintiff use a seatbelt in all vehicles
or just in her own car? These are all factual issues that will inform the decision.

At the same time, characterizing conduct as a habit involves policy concerns that
give the question a legal cast. Some judges would say that determining the admissibility of evidence under Rule 406 is a question of law rather than one of fact. But
the distinction doesn't matter: Even if the question is one of "fact," it is one that
the judge will resolve under Rule 104(a). Admissibility of habit evidence depends
on whether the proponent has laid a sufficient factual foundation to satisfy Rule
406. If that foundation is lacking, the jury should not hear about the evidence.

c. Other 104(a) Determinations. Other issues that judges resolve under Rule
104(a) include the existence of a dispute or compromise negotiations sufficient
to invoke **Rule 408**; whether a defendant offered to pay "medical, hospital, or
similar expenses" excluded under **Rule 409**; whether plea discussions occurred
that would shield statements under **Rule 410**; and whether a questioner has a
good faith belief for questions posed on cross-examination under **Rule 608** or
Rule 405. We will see further examples of factual issues decided by judges under
Rule 104(a) as we progress through the course.

3. Standard of Proof. Whether the judge resolves a factual issue independently
under Rule 104(a) or determines merely the sufficiency of the evidence "to support
a finding" under Rule 104(b), Rule 104 is strangely silent about the standard
of proof applicable to those decisions. Does a judge apply the preponderance
standard to the determinations required by Rules 104(a) and (b)? Do different
standards govern the two sections? Does the beyond-a-reasonable-doubt standard
apply in criminal cases? The language of the rule offers no guidance on these
important issues.

Fortunately, the Supreme Court has already answered these questions. In a series of cases beginning with *Bourjaily v. United States*,[15] and including the Huddleston case we discussed above, the Court has held that a simple preponderance standard applies to all preliminary factual issues resolved under Rule 104. The preponderance standard governs both civil and criminal cases; and it applies to issues resolved under both Rule 104(a) and 104(b).

A judge who resolves a preliminary factual issue under Rule 104(a), therefore, will ask whether the fact governing admissibility has been established by a preponderance of the evidence. A judge deciding whether Rule 407 bars admission of a particular repair, for example, will weigh conflicting testimony on when the repair occurred and decide whether the remedial measure more likely than not occurred before the plaintiff's injury.

Similarly, under Rule 104(b), the judge will ask whether a reasonable jury could find by a preponderance of the evidence that a fact governing admissibility exists. When applying Rule 602's personal knowledge requirement, for example, a judge would ask: Based on the evidence, could a reasonable jury find by a preponderance of the evidence that the witness saw the event he claims to have seen?

Use of the preponderance standard means that a trial judge can admit evidence under Rule 104(b) even when a previous jury has rejected the evidence under a reasonable doubt standard:

> **Example:** The government charged Reuben Dowling with robbing a bank in St. Croix, Virgin Islands. The robber wore a ski mask (a more unusual disguise in the Virgin Islands than elsewhere) and carried a small pistol. After fleeing the bank, the robber "scurried around in the street momentarily, and then commandeered a passing taxi van." The police and prosecutor believed that the robber had an accomplice, Delroy Christian, who had been parked in a getaway car outside the bank but was frightened away when police happened to notice the car. Hence, the robber improvised by commandeering the taxi.
>
> An eyewitness identified Dowling as the bank robber, but the government wanted to buttress that identification. To do so, the prosecutor offered

---

15   483 U.S. 171 (1987). The Court's ruling on standards of proof under Rule 104 applies to resolution of all factual disputes in preliminary determinations.

testimony from Vena Henry that Dowling and Christian attempted to rob her home two weeks after the bank robbery. Henry testified that one of the men who attempted to rob her home wore a ski mask and carried a small gun; she pulled the mask off the man and identified him as Dowling. The prosecutor linked this testimony to the bank robbery by arguing that (1) the primary perpetrator wore a ski mask and carried a small gun in both robberies; and (2) the perpetrator worked with Delroy Christian on both occasions. Since Henry identified the home robber as Dowling, this reasoning corroborated the identification of Dowling as the bank robber.

Dowling opposed introduction of Henry's testimony on the ground that a jury had already acquitted him of robbing her home. Thus, he argued, the government lacked sufficient evidence of this other act to present it to the jury.

Analysis: The trial court allowed Henry to testify about the home robbery, and the Supreme Court upheld that decision. The jury in the home robbery case acquitted Dowling, but that meant only that the jury entertained a reasonable doubt of his guilt. The jury in the bank robbery case, the Court reasoned, could still find by a preponderance of the evidence that Dowling committed the home robbery. If so, the home robbery was relevant to the bank robbery for the reasons that the government articulated. Under Rule 104(b), the trial court could allow the jury to hear Henry's testimony about the home robbery as long as some reasonable jury could find by a preponderance of the evidence that Dowling attempted to rob Henry's home.[16]

4. Burden of Proof. In close cases governed by the preponderance standard, allocation of the burden of proof is dispositive. Yet Rule 104 offers no guidance on which party bears the burden of proof on admissibility, and judicial decisions provide surprisingly little discussion of this important matter.

Although few opinions discuss the issue at length, judges usually place the burden of proof on the party offering evidence. This occurs because, once the opponent raises a plausible objection to the evidence, the proponent usually possesses the information needed to demonstrate admissibility. The practice also seems consistent with Rule 104(b)'s instruction that "proof must be introduced sufficient to support a finding that the fact does exist."

---

16   Dowling v. United States, 493 U.S. 342 (1990).

In the Dowling case, for example, the prosecutor offered Vena Henry's testimony that Dowling had robbed her home; Dowling challenged admission of that evidence. Dowling's challenge placed the burden of proving admissibility on the prosecutor. To meet that burden, the prosecutor had to produce sufficient evidence to persuade a reasonable jury by a preponderance of the evidence that Dowling robbed Henry. That is a low standard to meet; Henry's testimony alone would suffice unless Dowling offered irrefutable evidence that he could not have committed the previous robbery.

5. Rule 403. Rule 403's concern for confusion, delay, and unfair prejudice may affect a judge's fact finding decisions under both Rules 104(a) and 104(b). If a preliminary factual dispute falls within Rule 104(a), the judge usually resolves the factual issue at the same time that he applies Rule 403. A judge who finds the factual case for admissibility weak will be more inclined to exclude the evidence under Rule 403.

If the timing of a remedial measure is ambiguous, for example, the judge may conclude that the potential unfair prejudice (in penalizing the defendant for the repair) substantially outweighs any probative value. Similarly, a judge may exclude evidence that presents a close factual question under Rule 406 (habit), because of the significant danger that the jury will use the evidence for propensity purposes.

The merger of Rule 403 with factual determinations is even more common under Rule 104(b). Rule 104(b)'s low threshold for admissibility allows parties to present a wide range of weakly supported, but damaging, allegations to the jury. Under Rule 404(b), the prosecutor may offer evidence of prior criminal acts that have never been prosecuted; indeed, as the Dowling case suggests, the prosecutor may offer evidence of crimes for which a defendant has been acquitted. Even if the jury decides that the evidence fails to establish the existence of these acts, it may conclude that the defendant must have done something or the prosecutor would not file so many charges.

Similarly, a rape defendant may invoke Rule 412's exceptions to present certain types of arguments about the complainant's sexual behavior, even when the evidence supporting those arguments is slim. Even if the jury rejects the defendant's specific claims about the complainant, finding those allegations unfounded, the jurors may remain suspicious of the complainant's character.

In many situations, in other words, jurors may not be able to completely disregard evidence that they have rejected under the preponderance standard; shadows of that evidence may still color the jury's judgment. To address this problem, courts often combine a Rule 104(b) assessment with their Rule 403 balancing. Even if sufficient evidence exists to support a finding of a prior act, the weakness of that evidence may argue in favor of exclusion under Rule 403. Recall this case from Chapter 33:

Example: Betsy Sue Johnson sued her former high school guidance counselor, Wayne Stevens, claiming that he sexually harassed and abused her while she was a high school student. Johnson attempted to support her case by offering evidence under Rule 415 that Stevens had sexually assaulted Karen Radwanski, a coworker, by touching her crotch during lunchtime horseplay. Radwanski provided conflicting testimony about whether she thought this touching had been intentional, which was necessary for it to qualify as a prior "sexual assault" under Rule 415.

The court concluded that, although Radwanski's ambivalent testimony might "support a finding" of a previous sexual assault, the ambiguous nature of the evidence weighed in favor of exclusion under Rule 403. As discussed in Chapter 33, the court precluded the evidence under the latter rule.

Courts similarly consider the strength of evidence demonstrating the existence of prior acts offered under Rule 404(b) or of evidence tendered under the exceptions to Rule 412. If significant doubt exists about the truth of this evidence, those doubts reduce the probative value of the evidence and support exclusion under Rule 403.

Quick Summary

Rule 104 establishes procedures for resolving both legal and factual disputes involving the admissibility of evidence. The judge decides all questions of law, as well as many factual disputes, under Rule 104(a). But if a dispute relates to **relevance**, Rule 104(b) assigns the judge only a screening function. The judge determines whether sufficient evidence exists to "support a finding" of the evidence's relevance. If the evidence passes that low threshold, the jury resolves the factual issue.

Preliminary factual disputes that determine whether a rule applies fall within Rule 104(a). Under that section, the judge decides the factual issue governing admission without any deference to the jury.

Rule 104 does not assign the burden of proof on these preliminary factual determinations or articulate a standard of proof to govern them. The Supreme Court has held that the preponderance standard governs all preliminary factual determinations under Rule 104. Courts have less clearly articulated which parties bear the burden of proof under different rules, but judges usually impose the burden on the party attempting to introduce the evidence.

Rule 403 enjoys a close relationship with preliminary factual determinations under Rule 104. Even if a judge concludes that evidence survives scrutiny under Rule 104(a) or (b), the judge is more likely to exclude weakly supported evidence under Rule 403.

Test Your Understanding

To assess your understanding of the material in this chapter, click here to take a quiz, or go to the Quizzes module from the eBook on your eProducts bookshelf.

35

What Is Hearsay and Why Don't We Like It?

Key Concepts

- In Daily Life, We Prefer Firsthand Reports to Secondhand Ones
- Courts Strongly Share This Preference
- **Rule 802:** Most Hearsay Is Barred from Trial
- **Rule 801:** Defining Hearsay
- A Declarant Is a Person Who Makes a Statement Based on Firsthand Knowledge
- Any Statement Is Potential Hearsay, Unless It Is Made by a Declarant on the Witness Stand in the Current Proceeding

---

A. Introduction and Policy. Everyone dreads hearsay. Students fear they will never master its mysteries. Witnesses chafe at its constraints. Even seasoned trial lawyers shudder when asked to describe hearsay. In the words of two trial advocacy experts, "the rule against hearsay ranks as one of the law's most celebrated nightmares."[1]

But hearsay's reputation is much worse than its reality. Hearsay is difficult, but not impossible. If you focus on the policies underlying the rule and its exceptions, you will find them much easier to master. Judges developed the hearsay ban and all of its exceptions to force litigants to present the best possible testimony in the courtroom. If you keep your eye on that goal, the hearsay rules will seem more sensible and less mysterious.

---

1   Peter Murphy & D. Barnard, Evidence and Advocacy 19 (1984).

All of hearsay doctrine stems from one simple idea: Firsthand reports are more reliable than secondhand ones. Here is a mundane example that illustrates the value of a firsthand report. Suppose that you want to meet a law firm partner who is on campus talking informally about opportunities to practice patent law, but you don't know where the partner is holding her talk. You see your friend Greg in the hallway and ask if he knows where the partner is. He responds: "I saw her near the auditorium just about ten minutes ago."

Can you rely on Greg's report? As an evidence student, someone who views testimony critically, you know that there are four reasons to question Greg's information:

- First, there is the problem of **perception**: Greg might have thought he saw the law firm partner near the auditorium, but he really saw a new assistant dean and mistook her for the partner.

- Second is the problem of **memory:** Greg may have forgotten what he saw; even though he saw the partner only ten minutes ago, the detail may have been unimportant to him and he may have confused the auditorium and the student lounge in his memory.

- Third is the problem of **clarity:** Greg says he saw the partner "near the auditorium," but what does he mean by "near"? At the doorway of the auditorium? In a classroom four doors down? In the hallway walking away from the auditorium? And what does he mean by "about ten minutes ago?" Could that actually be twenty minutes ago?

- Finally, there is the problem of **sincerity:** To put it bluntly, Greg may be lying to you. Maybe he doesn't want you to practice patent law, or he is getting even for a stunt you pulled on him last week.

Luckily, Greg is still standing in front of you. If you doubt his information, you can ask him questions: How did you know it was the partner from the patent law firm? Do you remember other details about seeing the partner: how she was dressed, what she was holding? When you say "near the auditorium," where exactly do you mean? You can also look at Greg's demeanor when he gives his answers: Does he look like he may be trying to mislead you, or that he's playing a joke?

After asking a few follow-up questions and observing Greg as he responds, you should have a fairly good idea about whether to head for the auditorium. That is the value of a firsthand statement: You can test the speaker's perception, memory, clarity, and sincerity. Even the best-intentioned speakers make mistakes.

Now let's rewind the scenario and assume that instead of meeting Greg, you see another friend named Lisa while searching for the patent law partner. You ask Lisa if she knows where the partner is, and she replies: "I don't know, but Greg told me that he saw her near the auditorium about ten minutes ago."

Once again, you must decide whether to head across the building to the auditorium. How reliable is Lisa's report? There are the same four concerns about Lisa that we had about Greg in the first hypothetical:

- **Perception**: Lisa may not have heard Greg correctly; he might have said that a litigation lawyer, rather than the patent law partner, was near the auditorium.

- **Memory**: Lisa might have spoken to a lot of people in the last ten minutes and she might not accurately recall what Greg said.

- **Clarity**: Is Lisa repeating Greg's statement word for word or is she changing some of the words when she reports the statement?

- **Sincerity**: Lisa might want to practice at the firm herself, so she sends you running off to the auditorium on a wild goose chase.

But with Lisa's report, these concerns are only part of your problem. Even if you are able to convince yourself that Lisa's perception, memory, clarity, and sincerity are all positive, you still have the same set of concerns about Greg's information. Just as before, Greg could have misperceived, remembered incorrectly, been unintentionally vague about his description, or lied to Lisa. Secondhand reports double the risk of unreliable information.

And that's not all. With Lisa's secondhand report, you face an even bigger problem than the double risk of error. Remember that when you spoke to Greg directly, you could ask him questions and observe his demeanor as he answered; you could check his perception, memory, clarity, and sincerity. Here you can question Lisa in the same way to check her perception, memory, clarity, and sincerity: How long ago did she talk to Greg? Was that exactly what he said? Did he say anything else about what the partner was doing, where she was going? You can question Lisa and observe her demeanor to assess her credibility.

But this assessment only gets you halfway. When Lisa relays Greg's information to you, there is no way for you to check **Greg's** accuracy and sincerity. You cannot cross-examine Greg or assess **his** demeanor. No matter how extensively you question Lisa, the most you will know is that Greg said certain words to her, at a certain time and place; you will be no closer to knowing whether or not Greg's words were true.

For all of these reasons, firsthand reports are more reliable than secondhand ones. That is the basic idea behind the ban on hearsay: Courts prefer firsthand reports to secondhand ones. Indeed, the rule against hearsay completely bars most secondhand reports from the courtroom.

The Rules of Evidence impose this result for the same reasons that you prefer Greg's firsthand information to Lisa's secondhand report. Secondhand testimony doubles the risk of faulty perception, memory, clarity, and truthfulness. Secondhand reports also eliminate the fact finder's opportunity to cross-examine the original speaker. And those reports deprive the fact finder of the opportunity to observe the initial speaker's demeanor, directly assessing his credibility.

Trials depend on cross-examination and assessment of witness demeanor to yield the truth. Opponents question witnesses to expose defects in their observation and memory, as well as to clarify their statements and reveal lies. Jurors observe the witness closely during this courtroom questioning. Does the witness make eye contact with the questioner? Does she seem nervous or shifty-eyed? Does she seem confident in her responses? The conventional wisdom is that individuals can more easily evaluate the truth and accuracy of a statement if they observe the person making the statement.[2] Secondhand reports eliminate effective cross-examination and credibility assessment.

---

2   Social science research has cast considerable doubt on this assumption; even trained investigators have difficulty separating liars from truth tellers. See, e.g., Pär Anders Granhag & Aldert Vriij, Deception Detection, in Psychology and Law: An Empirical Perspective 43 (Neil Brewer & Kipling D. Williams eds. 2005). Courtroom trials, however, still proceed on the assumption that firsthand observation helps to assess credibility. Whatever the limits of human ability to distinguish liars and truthtellers, it is easier to judge credibility firsthand than through secondhand reports.

The final advantage of firsthand testimony in the courtroom is that witnesses testify under oath, during a formal proceeding with a judge and a jury listening to what they have to say. Statements made under these conditions are more likely to be true than are casual statements made in everyday life. A witness who swears formally to tell the truth opens himself to a perjury prosecution if he lies. The solemnity of the occasion also encourages truthfulness.

A courtroom witness who reports information secondhand swears only to the truth of what she heard, not to the truth of what the firsthand reporter said. The oath and solemnity of the occasion give us no additional confidence that the reported event actually happened.

In summary, we prefer firsthand testimony to secondhand reporting because:

1. Secondhand testimony doubles the possibility that one of the reporters is mistaken or lying.

2. Firsthand testimony can be tested by cross-examination.

3. The finder of fact can better evaluate the confidence and sincerity of the information if they can watch the individual report it firsthand.

4. At trial, firsthand testimony is made under oath in a formal, solemn setting.

It is important to remember these reasons behind the hearsay ban; knowing the reasons will make it easier to understand which statements are hearsay, as well as why some hearsay statements are admissible under exceptions to the rule.

B. The Rules. The Federal Rules of Evidence devote a full article to the hearsay ban and its exceptions. The basic prohibition against use of hearsay, contained in **Rule 802**, is straightforward:

RULE 802. The Rule Against Hearsay

Hearsay is not admissible <u>unless</u> any of the following provides otherwise:

- a federal statute;
- these rules; or
- other rules prescribed by the Supreme Court.

We won't worry in this course about the first and last of these exceptions; Congress and the Supreme Court rarely create hearsay exceptions in statutes or other sets of rules. Most of the federal law of hearsay appears in Rules 801–807 of the Federal Rules of Evidence. Rule 802 states the general rule, that hearsay is NOT admissible except as otherwise provided in the rules.

To apply this prohibition, we have to know what hearsay is. **Rule 801(c)** provides that definition:

RULE 801. Definitions That Apply to This Article; Exclusions from Hearsay

(c) Hearsay. "Hearsay" means a <u>statement</u> that:

(1) the <u>declarant</u> does not make <u>while testifying at the current trial or hearing</u>; and

(2) a party offers in evidence to prove the <u>truth of the matter asserted</u> in the statement.

There are three important parts to this definition. First, hearsay requires a **statement**. Second, the statement must be made by a **declarant** in a context other than testimony at the current trial or hearing. And, third, a party must offer the statement to prove **the truth of the matter asserted.** In the remainder of this chapter we will talk about who is a declarant; in Chapter 36 we will discuss what we mean by "the truth of the matter asserted," and in Chapter 37 we will explore the meaning of the word "statement."

Rule 801(b) offers a simple definition of declarant:

RULE 801. Definitions That Apply to This Article; Exclusions from Hearsay

(b) Declarant. "Declarant" means the person who made the statement.

This definition, unfortunately, is deceptively simple; it leaves unstated a key aspect of the relationship between declarants and their statements. We'll explore that element, as well as the important distinction between declarants and witnesses, in the next section.

C. In the Courtroom. Rule 801(b) defines a declarant as "the person who made the statement." But the "statement" described in Rule 801 is a special one: It is a communication that reflects the speaker's personal knowledge.

Remember that Rule 602 allows witnesses to testify only about things they know personally. Rule 801(b) silently incorporates this requirement, assuming that the "statement" made by each declarant contains only what that person knows personally.[3] Reading Rule 602's concept of personal knowledge into Rule 801(b) will help you better understand the hearsay doctrine. If we combine these pieces, Rule 801(b) defines declarant as "the person who made the statement based on personal knowledge." To see why this matters, let's return to the example of Greg and Lisa.

1. Who Declared What? Greg and Lisa, the two friends we discussed at the beginning of the chapter, are both declarants; both of them are people who made statements. But look more closely at the focus of their statements.

When asked about the patent law partner, Greg said: "I saw her near the auditorium just about ten minutes ago." Greg had personal knowledge of the partner's

---

3   See Chapter 14 to review Rule 602.

whereabouts, so his statement encompasses that knowledge. The hearsay rules consider Greg a declarant whose statement referred to the partner's location.

When asked the same question, Lisa said: "I don't know, but Greg told me that he saw her near the auditorium about ten minutes ago." Lisa did not have personal knowledge about the partner's location; she only had personal knowledge that Greg spoke to her. The hearsay rules consider Lisa a declarant, but her "statement" refers only to the fact that Greg spoke certain words to her.

Lisa, in other words, is a declarant who made a statement about another declarant. The diagram below illustrates that peculiar sounding relationship. In the diagram, the heavy lines outline the "statement" made by each declarant. The statement, remember, reflects only the speaker's personal knowledge. So Greg made a statement about the partner's location; Lisa made a statement that another declarant said something.

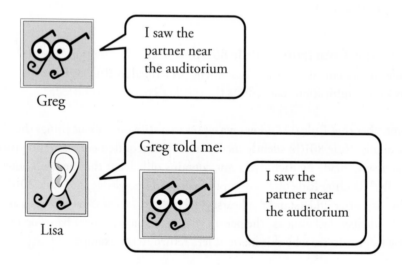

2. Declarants and Witnesses. Rule 801(c) distinguishes between statements made by declarants "while testifying at the current trial or hearing" and all other statements. A declarant who testifies at a trial or hearing is a witness; a declarant who speaks outside the courtroom is just a declarant. In other words:

> • All witnesses are declarants.
>
> • But declarants are witnesses only when they testify under oath at a trial or hearing.

In the example given above, Greg and Lisa are declarants but not witnesses. They spoke to a friend in the law school; they did not testify under oath at trial. What would happen if Greg and Lisa did make their statements at trial? How would the hearsay rules treat their statements?

Suppose that, on the same day that the patent law partner visited the law school, someone vandalized the law school auditorium. After investigating the incident, the police arrested the partner for the crime. At trial, the prosecutor calls Greg as a witness and asks him if he saw the partner on the day of the crime. Greg responds: "Yes, I saw the partner near the auditorium at about 2:30."

Greg is still a declarant: He is a person making a statement based on personal knowledge. But now he is also a witness, because he is making his statement under oath at trial. Most important, Greg's statement is **not hearsay** at that trial. Rule 801(c) defines hearsay as a statement "the declarant does not make while testifying at the current trial or hearing." In our new example, Greg offers his statement while testifying at trial, so it is not hearsay within that proceeding.

Now suppose that Greg is unable to attend the trial and the prosecutor calls Lisa as a witness instead. When asked if she saw the partner on the day of the crime, Lisa says: "No, but Greg told me that he saw her near the auditorium."

Lisa is a declarant and she has made a statement at trial. But remember the nature of Lisa's statement. As Lisa's testimony reveals, she has no personal knowledge of the partner's whereabouts; she only has personal knowledge of Greg's statement. The piece of Lisa's testimony that reports the **fact** that she spoke to Greg is not hearsay; that report is a statement based on personal knowledge that Lisa made while testifying at trial.

But the simple fact that Greg spoke to Lisa isn't relevant to the vandalism prosecution. The prosecutor wants Lisa to testify about **what** Greg said; the prosecutor, moreover, claims that Greg spoke the **truth**. If Greg really saw the patent law partner outside the auditorium, that fact helps the prosecutor prove the partner's guilt.

Greg, however, is the one who saw the partner outside the auditorium; he is the person with personal knowledge about that fact. Lisa knows that Greg spoke to her, but she has no personal knowledge of whether Greg's statement was true. Greg's statement about the partner, moreover, occurred outside the courtroom. Under Rule 801(c), that out-of-court statement is hearsay. Unless Greg's statement falls within one of the hearsay exceptions, which we study in upcoming chapters, the prosecutor cannot ask Lisa to recount Greg's statement.

This result fits with the policies discussed above. When a declarant makes a statement while testifying at trial, the declarant speaks under oath in a formal setting. The jury can assess the declarant's credibility, and opponents can cross-examine him. Since the declarant speaks from personal knowledge, finally, errors of perception or memory are reduced.

If a witness recounts a declarant's out-of-court statement, on the other hand, the declarant takes no oath of truthfulness. The jurors have no opportunity to assess the declarant's credibility, and opponents have no chance to cross-examine him. The secondhand nature of the witness's report multiplies the possibility of error.

For all of these reasons, the hearsay rules distinguish between statements made at trial and all other statements. A statement made by a declarant while testifying at trial is not hearsay for purposes of that trial. All other statements constitute poten-tial hearsay:

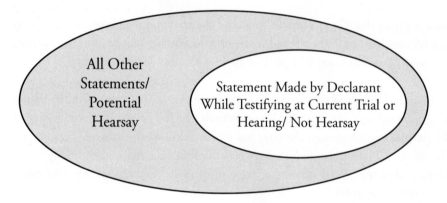

As we'll soon see, the Rules of Evidence recognize many exceptions to the hear-say prohibition. But the first step in applying the hearsay rules is to suspect **any** testimony that refers to a statement made anywhere but on the witness stand in the current proceeding.

3. Recognizing Declarants. Here are two more examples to illustrate the role of declarants in defining hearsay:

> **Example:** Former Judge Robert Bork fell as he tried to mount the dais at the Yale Club and sued the Club for his injury. A year after filing his claim, Bork settled the lawsuit for an undisclosed amount.[4] Imagine, however, that the parties proceeded to trial and disputed whether Bork was contributorily negligent in mounting the dais. In this hypothetical trial, Ellsworth "Ellie" Rawls VI, a long-time member of the Yale Club, testifies: "I was at the Club for lunch that day and saw Bork. He rushed toward the dais without even glancing down. The man tripped over his own feet."

Analysis: In this example, Rawls is a witness giving a firsthand account at trial of what he saw at the Yale Club. Rawls, therefore, is a declarant making a statement while testifying at trial and his statement is not hearsay.

Now vary the facts slightly:

> **Example:** Suppose that Bork's claim against the Yale Club proceeds to trial, but Rawls has gone to France for his annual holiday and is unable to testify at trial. Rawls's good friend, Punky Brewster, appears as a witness instead and testifies: "Ellie Rawls told me that he was at the Yale Club the day that Bork fell, and he saw Bork run toward the dais without looking where he was going. Ellie says that Bork fell over his own feet."

Analysis: In this example, Rawls is still a declarant; he made several statements to Brewster. But Rawls made those statements outside the courtroom. When Brewster repeats Rawls's statement in the courtroom, she is offering hearsay.

Once again, the policies animating the hearsay rules explain why Rawls's testimony is admissible, while Brewster's testimony is hearsay. When Rawls testifies as a witness, he does so under oath, the jurors can assess his credibility, Bork's attorney

---

4   Bork did fall in this manner, filed a lawsuit against the Yale Club, and settled the claim. Alan Feuer, Bork v. Yale Club: Jurist Seeks Redress Over a Fall, N.Y. Times, June 8, 2007, at B1; Isaac Arnsdorf, Robert Bork Settles $1 Million Lawsuit with Yale Club, Yale Daily News, May 12, 2008. The other details suggested above are fictional.

can cross-examine him, and he minimizes the possibilities of error. When Brewster repeats Rawls's out-of-court statement, all of those safeguards disappear.

This simple distinction between Rawls's testimony and that of Brewster resolves a large number of potential hearsay claims. Congratulations, you have mastered the basics of the rule! A declarant is a person who has firsthand information about a fact relevant to the lawsuit. If the declarant offers that information while testifying at trial, the statement is not hearsay. If the declarant makes a statement based on that information outside the courtroom, and someone repeats the statement at trial, it is hearsay. It really is that simple.

4. The Witness's Prior Statement. Let's return to the state's prosecution of the patent law partner and Greg's testimony about seeing the partner near the auditorium. Suppose the prosecutor's direct examination of Greg goes like this:

> **Prosecutor:** Did you see the defendant anywhere in the law school on the afternoon of March 8th?
>
> **Greg:** Yes, I did.
>
> **Prosecutor:** Please tell us where you saw the defendant.
>
> **Greg:** Well, my friend Lisa asked me if I'd seen the patent law partner—that is, the defendant—and I told Lisa that I saw the defendant near the auditorium.

What is wrong with Greg's statement? He has turned his direct testimony into hearsay. Instead of testifying about what he **perceived**, Greg is testifying about a prior **statement** that he made. Greg has changed his firsthand testimony into a secondhand report. As a witness, Greg is referring to himself in the third person; he is not telling us what he saw, but what he said that he saw. Remember, the hearsay definition includes **any** statement that is not made on the witness stand in the current proceeding. Greg's statement to Lisa was not made on the witness stand at trial, so it is hearsay, even though the declarant (Greg) is now on the stand.

Fussing about this seems like a silly technicality. Greg clearly saw the partner near the auditorium and is simply conveying that information in a slightly awkward manner. Why allow an opponent to interrupt the flow of testimony with a hearsay objection?

As we will see in Chapter 39, there are good reasons to treat a witness's prior statements as hearsay. Rule 801(d)(1) exempts some of those statements from the hearsay rule but others—like Greg's testimony in the last example—remain inadmissible. We will explore these issues further in Chapter 39. The important point to understand for now is that **all** out-of-court statements are hearsay when offered to prove the truth of the matter asserted. Even if a witness quotes her own out-of-court statement, that statement is hearsay.

Quick Summary

The hearsay rules impose a general ban on secondhand testimony. This prohibition exists for four reasons: (1) Secondhand testimony has double the chance of error because the fact finder must rely on the accuracy and credibility of two different people; (2) Firsthand testimony can be more fully tested by cross-examination; (3) When a witness reports another person's statement secondhand, the fact finder cannot observe that other speaker and evaluate his sincerity; and (4) Statements made outside the courtroom usually lack the oath and formal setting that encourage honesty and careful statements.

To articulate these concepts, the hearsay rules introduce special terms. A **declarant** is a person who makes a statement based on firsthand knowledge. A **witness** is a person who testifies in the current proceeding. The hearsay bar applies to any statement made by any declarant unless that declarant offers the statement while testifying in the current proceeding. Even if the witness and the declarant are the same person, any prior statements by the witness are potentially hearsay because they were not made under oath during the current proceeding.

36

The "Truth of the Matter Asserted"

Key Concepts

- Statements Are Only Hearsay if Offered to Prove the Truth of the Matter Asserted
- Out-of-Court Statements Often Prove a Fact Other than the Truth of the Matter They Assert
- When Offered for These Other Purposes, Statements Are Not Hearsay

---

A. Introduction and Policy. You now understand the basic principles of hearsay: (1) that the courts prefer firsthand testimony based on personal knowledge, and (2) that any testimony referring to a statement made outside the courtroom is potentially hearsay. But why do we say "potentially"? What factor determines whether an out-of-court statement is inadmissible hearsay?

As with many other rules of evidence, the answer depends on the **purpose** for which a party introduces an out-of-court statement. If a litigant offers the statement to prove **the truth of the matter asserted**, it is inadmissible hearsay. If the party offers the statement for any other purpose, it is not hearsay. When trying to determine whether an out-of-court statement is hearsay, you must ask: What is the proponent trying to prove with the statement?

Luckily, you have already mastered the tools required to make this determination. Many of the rules we have studied so far require you to identify the proponent's purpose for offering evidence. **Rule 407** excludes evidence of subsequent remedial measures when offered to prove negligence or fault, but not when introduced for other purposes. **Rule 404** prohibits evidence of "other acts" when offered to prove propensity, but not when introduced to prove knowledge, plan, or some other relevant fact.

Applying the hearsay rule requires you to make the same inquiry about out-of-court statements. Parties attempt to introduce out-of-court statements for many purposes. Often, the party wants the fact finder to believe the truth of the statement's **content**. If a party offers an out-of-court statement for this purpose, it is hearsay.

Other times, however, a party introduces an out-of-court statement only to demonstrate that the statement was **made**. The truth of the statement is irrelevant to the party's purpose. Under these circumstances, the statement is not hearsay.

One way to make this distinction is to focus on the **personal knowledge** of the speaker, as we did in the previous chapter. Remember one of the examples from that chapter: The state prosecuted a patent law partner for vandalizing the law school auditorium. Suppose at trial, the prosecutor called Lisa as a witness and examined her like this:

> **Prosecutor:** Did you see anyone in the law school hallway at around 2:30?
>
> **Lisa:** Yes, I saw my friend Greg.
>
> **Prosecutor:** And did Greg tell you anything?
>
> **Lisa:** Yes, he said that he saw the partner near the auditorium.

What part of Lisa's statement reflects her personal knowledge? She knows that Greg was alive at 2:30 on the day that the law school was vandalized, that he was in the law school hallway, and that he spoke to her. She also knows that Greg claimed he had seen the partner.

Lisa knows all of these things from the simple fact that Greg made the statement she recounts. She has personal knowledge of these facts, so reporting them is not hearsay. If the prosecutor wanted to prove that **Greg** was in the law school that afternoon, Lisa's statement would not be hearsay. Under those circumstances, the prosecutor would be offering Lisa's statement for a purpose that reflects her personal knowledge.

Unfortunately, the prosecutor in this case is trying to prove that the **partner** was near the auditorium. Lisa has no personal knowledge of that fact; she is simply reporting what Greg told her. The content of Greg's statement does not fall within

Lisa's personal knowledge; it is hearsay. To use Greg's knowledge about the partner's whereabouts, the prosecutor must call Greg to the stand.

What if the facts of the case were different? Suppose, for example, that the partner was a crime victim rather than a perpetrator: The career services director found her strangled to death in the auditorium. Police discovered that Greg held a grudge against the partner for failing to give him a job offer; they arrested Greg and charged him with the murder. At trial, Greg claims that he had no idea that the partner was anywhere near the law school on the day of the crime. In rebuttal, the prosecutor calls Lisa to the stand and elicits the same testimony as above:

> **Prosecutor:** Did you see anyone in the law school hallway at around 2:30?
>
> **Lisa:** Yes, I saw my friend Greg.
>
> **Prosecutor:** And did Greg tell you anything?
>
> **Lisa:** Yes, he said that he saw the partner near the auditorium.

Lisa's testimony is the same as in the previous example, and she reports the identical statement by Greg. This time, however, the prosecutor is not trying to prove the truth of the matter asserted by Greg. Greg's statement is not necessary to prove that the partner was near the auditorium; the location of the dead body proves that fact. Instead, the prosecutor is using Greg's statement to prove (1) that Greg was in the law school building at the time of the murder, and (2) that Greg claimed to know where the partner was. Because the prosecutor is not offering Greg's statement for the truth of the matter he asserted, but only for the fact that he made the statement, it is not hearsay.

Another way to put this is to say that Lisa has firsthand knowledge of (1) the fact that Greg was in the law building, and (2) that he claimed to know where the law partner was. Lisa can establish the first fact without even disclosing the substance of her conversation with Greg. She can testify that she saw Greg in the law school hallway at about 2:30 p.m. on the day of the crime. She can add that she knows the man she saw was Greg, because she had a brief conversation with him.

Lisa's ability to establish the second fact is a little trickier. To show that Greg claimed to know where the partner was, the prosecutor must ask Lisa to recount the substance of Greg's comment. Greg's words, telling Lisa that he had seen the partner near the auditorium, suggest that he knew where the partner was.

In this example, however, the prosecutor is not asking Lisa to recount these words to establish the **truth** of the partner's location. Regardless of where the partner was located, Greg claimed that he had seen the partner. Lisa has personal knowledge of that claim and may testify that Greg made the representation. The prosecutor may then use Greg's words as circumstantial evidence that Greg had seen the partner on the day of the murder. The fact that Greg claimed to know the partner's location is some evidence that he had seen the partner recently.

Note how the policies behind the hearsay rule support this result. Lisa is testifying about what Greg said, without regard to whether the truth of his statement was correct. She has firsthand knowledge of Greg's words, so we don't have to worry about a communication chain with multiple points of error. Defense counsel can cross-examine Lisa about how accurately she heard and remembers Greg's statement. The jury can judge Lisa's truthfulness. And Lisa is making the statement under oath and in a formal courtroom setting, so it is more likely that she will truthfully tell us what she heard Greg say.

 For further explanation of these concepts, click here to see the video "Truth of the Matter Asserted" or go to the Videos module from the eBook on your eProducts bookshelf.

We'll explore more examples of the "truth of the matter asserted" in the Courtroom section below. First, however, let's look back at Rule 801.

B. The Rule. In the last chapter we examined **Rule 801**'s definition of hearsay, which contains the reference to proving "the truth of the matter asserted." Here is that provision again:

RULE 801. Definitions That Apply to This Article; Exclusions from Hearsay

(c) Hearsay. "Hearsay" means a <u>statement</u> that:

(1) the <u>declarant</u> does not make <u>while testifying at the current trial or hearing</u>; and

(2) a party offers in evidence to prove the <u>truth of the matter asserted</u> in the statement.

Unlike **Rule 404(b)** and some of the other rules in Article IV, which offer examples of permissible purposes for disputed evidence, Rule 801(c) gives no such guidance. Here, however, are some common purposes for out-of-court statements that do not depend on the truth of the matter asserted. Statements like these are not hearsay if offered for the purposes identified below:

- **Knowledge** of the speaker. The defendant in a personal injury case might have mentioned to a neighbor that a dangerous condition existed on his property. The statement is hearsay if offered to show that the condition existed, but it is not hearsay if offered simply to show the defendant's knowledge

- **Notice** to a listener. In a medical malpractice action, a nurse might testify that she heard the surgeon explain the risks of surgery to the plaintiff, showing that the patient was fully aware of the dangers.

- **Publication** in a defamation case. To recover for defamation, the plaintiff must prove both that the defendant made a defamatory statement and that at least one other person heard or read the statement. The statement need not be true; indeed, the plaintiff claims that it was false.

- **Effect** on the listener. If the defendant in a prosecution for menacing said to a victim "I hid a dozen venomous rattlesnakes in your house," it doesn't matter whether the defendant really hid the rattlesnakes. The elements of this crime require only that the defendant make the statement and the words give the victim a reasonable fear of bodily harm.

> • **Legally Binding Statements.** In a contract case, the fact that the defendant said "I accept" is relevant to prove that he agreed to a contract. Similarly, in a trespass case, the fact that a property owner said "I give you permission to come onto my property" is relevant to prove that the defendant entered with consent. The truth of these statements doesn't matter; even if the speaker was lying, the words establish acceptance or consent.

As with the other purposes suggested in Rule 404(b), this is not an exclusive list. As long as the other purpose is relevant to the dispute, an out-of-court statement is admissible to prove any fact that does not depend on the truth of the matter asserted.

C. In the Courtroom.

1. Evidence Relevant for Multiple Purposes: Many out-of-court statements are relevant to prove more than one fact. Consider this hypothetical:

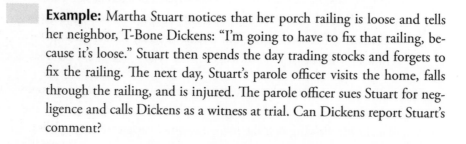

Example: Martha Stuart notices that her porch railing is loose and tells her neighbor, T-Bone Dickens: "I'm going to have to fix that railing, because it's loose." Stuart then spends the day trading stocks and forgets to fix the railing. The next day, Stuart's parole officer visits the home, falls through the railing, and is injured. The parole officer sues Stuart for negligence and calls Dickens as a witness at trial. Can Dickens report Stuart's comment?

Analysis: The parole officer could try to use Dickens's report of Stuart's comment for two different purposes. First, he could introduce the comment to show that the railing was in fact loose. This is a hearsay use of the comment; the parole officer would be offering it for the truth of what Stuart said. But the parole officer could also introduce this evidence for a non-hearsay purpose: to prove that Stuart knew about the loose railing and was negligent in failing to fix it. Thus, the statement is hearsay for one purpose, and not hearsay when used for another purpose.

Similarly, in a murder case, the defendant might claim that he stabbed the victim in self defense because the victim threatened to pull a gun from her pocket. The defendant could not offer the victim's statement for the truth of its assertion, to prove that the victim did have a gun. But the defendant could introduce the statement for a non-hearsay purpose, to show that he reasonably feared that the victim had a gun. To show reasonable fear, the truth of the victim's statement doesn't matter. The defendant might have reasonably feared imminent bodily harm even if the victim was bluffing. Once again, the same statement would be hearsay if used for one purpose, but not hearsay if used for another.

We have seen dual purposes like this in several other contexts. Just as in those contexts, the judge will admit evidence that is admissible for one purpose as long as any unfair prejudice does not substantially outweigh probative value. To discourage the jury from using the evidence for an impermissible purpose, the judge will offer a limiting instruction. In the murder case described above, for example, the court might instruct the jury:

> You have heard evidence that the victim told the defendant that she had a gun in her pocket and was about to shoot the defendant. You are only to consider this statement for its effect on the defendant; in other words, whether hearing this statement, along with all the other evidence put forward by the defendant, was sufficient to put the defendant in reasonable fear for his life. You are not to consider the statement as evidence that the victim did in fact actually have a gun in her pocket.

The hearsay rules, like Rule 404, often prompt game-playing by litigants. A litigant may have an out-of-court statement that is extremely probative if used for the truth of the matter asserted. The hearsay rules forbid the litigant from using the evidence for that purpose, so the attorney seeks a non-hearsay purpose to support introduction of the evidence. The opposing counsel will point out that the non-hearsay purpose is a Trojan horse hiding the proponent's real purpose for offering the evidence. If the court admits the out-of-court statement, the opponent will argue, the jury will be unable to ignore the truth of the matter asserted.

The judge will resolve this conflict by balancing the probative value of the non-hearsay purpose against the unfair prejudice of the hearsay purpose. This Rule 403 balance, however, tilts in favor of admissibility and often admits evidence with both hearsay and non-hearsay purposes.

Example: Tim O'Reilly sued Officer Farley for using excessive force when arresting him. O'Reilly's evidence shows that Farley beat him ten times with a nightstick before handcuffing him. Farley claims in defense that he believed O'Reilly was high on PCP, which would make him extremely violent. Farley testifies that as he approached O'Reilly to make the arrest, O'Reilly's companion (John Hannity) said: "Be careful officer. This guy just took two tabs of PCP and he's been acting real angry."

Analysis: Hannity's statement is relevant for two purposes. First, it is relevant for the truth of the matter asserted, to show that O'Reilly really was high on PCP and probably reacted violently to Farley's arrest. This is an improper hearsay purpose. Hannity is not in court, so O'Reilly's attorney cannot attack the accuracy and credibility of the statement. If Hannity were present, the attorney could ask him: "How do you know O'Reilly took PCP rather than aspirin? What do you mean when you say real angry? Are you jealous of O'Reilly for any reason?" Likewise, the jury cannot assess Hannity's credibility as he makes the statement. And Hannity was not in court and under oath when he made this statement; he may not have considered the comment as carefully on the street as he would under oath during a trial.

Hannity's statement, however, is also relevant for a non-hearsay purpose: to show that Farley had reason to believe that O'Reilly was high on PCP and might react violently to arrest. For this purpose, all that matters is that the statement was made and that it was reasonable for Farley to believe it, not whether it was true. Farley can testify firsthand about the fact that the statement was made; O'Reilly's attorney can cross-examine him on that claim and the jury can determine whether Farley really heard such a statement.

The judge will have to balance the probative value of this non-hearsay purpose against the unfair prejudice of the hearsay one. In making the determination, the judge will consider the availability of a limiting instruction, as well as other evidence in the case.

This is another situation in which good lawyering can spell the difference between the admission of critical evidence and its exclusion.

2. Hearsay Puzzles. Hearsay puzzles abound in both published cases and professors' minds. Here is a sampling of cases and hypotheticals to help you practice the concepts of declarant, hearsay, and "truth of the matter asserted." The first two examples are variations of hypotheticals that many professors recount.

Example: As a joke, Roseanne shouts "killer bees!" in a crowded restaurant. All of the other customers rush from the restaurant, causing significant damage and loss of revenue. The state prosecutes Roseanne for malicious mischief. At trial, the restaurant's manager testifies that he saw and heard Roseanne shout "killer bees!" just before all of the customers rushed from the restaurant. Is this hearsay?

Analysis: This is **not hearsay**. The prosecutor is not trying to prove the truth of the matter asserted—indeed, the prosecutor's case depends in part on the fact that Roseanne's statement was false. The statement is being offered to prove that (1) Roseanne made a statement that was likely to have the effect of causing a panic; and (2) immediately after the statement (and thus apparently in response to it), the other customers did in fact panic. The prosecutor will use this testimony to prove only that the statement was made and that others were able to hear it. The manager perceived both of these facts firsthand, so his testimony does not violate the hearsay rule.

Roseanne's prank is unusual, but the concept conveyed by this hypothetical recurs frequently. The occurrence of a statement and its effect on listeners usually do not depend on the truth of the statement's content.

Here is another unusual hypothetical that demonstrates a useful concept:

Example: A brother and sister are in a car crash together, and both die within minutes of the crash. They shared a trust fund given to them by their parents, and by the terms of the fund, the principal reverts to the family of the sibling who dies last. The spouses of the brother and sister sue each other, each claiming that their spouse outlived the other. At trial, the brother's wife calls as a witness the first medic on the scene. The medic testifies that he took the sister's pulse, determined that she was dead, and then went to the brother. When the medic leaned over the brother's inert body, he heard the brother say, "I am still alive." The sister's husband objects that this statement by the brother is hearsay.

Analysis: The statement is **not hearsay**. The problem is tricky because although the brother's wife is trying to prove the truth of the matter asserted, this is only a coincidence. We care both that the statement is true and that the statement was made; if the brother said anything else, the statement would be equally probative. The statement can be admitted for a non-hearsay purpose: to prove that the brother was still able to speak and therefore was still alive at the time.

This dying siblings example, like the killer bees one, demonstrates that the occurrence of a statement may have legal significance regardless of its content. The example of the dying brother also illustrates that, even when the matter asserted is relevant, we can look beyond that content to identify a non-hearsay use of the words. And in this case any unfair prejudice is minimal because the brother's act of speaking so clearly demonstrates that he was alive; reliance on the content of the words is unnecessary.

Here is an example of a hearsay issue that often arises in commercial cases:

Example: The United States promised to ship soybean oil to India under its "Food for Peace Program," and hired Central Gulf Lines to deliver the oil. When the cargo arrived in India, auditors discovered that 54,128 pounds of soybean oil were missing. The government sued Central Gulf to recover damages for the lost oil. At trial, the government introduced a letter of protest that it had sent to Central Gulf which described how much oil was lost and informed Central Gulf that it was in breach of the contract because of the shortfall. Central Gulf objected that the letter was hearsay.

Analysis: As a preliminary matter, this problem illustrates a point that we will explore further in the next chapter: Written, as well as verbal, statements may constitute hearsay. In this case, however, the letter is **not hearsay**. The government did not introduce the letter to prove the truth of any matter asserted within its text. The letter mentioned that the oil was missing, but the government introduced independent evidence of that fact. Instead, the government used the written statement to prove that it had given Central

Gulf notice of the breach, as required under the contract. The fact of the letter, rather than truth of its contents, was the relevant information.[1]

Many commercial cases involve the notice problem raised in Central Gulf. Notices of breach are hearsay if introduced to prove the underlying facts of the breach, but are not hearsay if offered to prove that notice was given.

Here is an example of a different type of hearsay problem. The issue here focuses on how an individual responds to a statement made by someone else:

Example: Fred arrives at a party carrying a folded umbrella. Police receive a reliable tip that cocaine will be sold at the party; they search the premises during the party and find cocaine inside Fred's umbrella. Fred is arrested and charged with possession of cocaine with intent to distribute. At trial, he takes the stand and testifies that he had no idea that the cocaine was in his umbrella; his testimony suggests that someone must have hidden the drug there.

Fred's counsel then asks him why he took the umbrella to the party. Fred responds: "Because I heard the weather forecaster on the radio say that it would rain." Is this statement hearsay?

Analysis: This statement is **not hearsay**. Fred is reporting an out-of-court statement made by the weather forecaster, but he is not offering the statement to prove the truth of the matter asserted. The jury does not care whether the forecaster's statement was true or not. In other words, it makes no difference to the case whether or not it rained that evening. Instead, Fred offers the forecaster's statement to show why he took the umbrella with him to the party; he wants to rebut the prosecutor's theory that he took the umbrella to carry the cocaine secreted inside. The forecaster's statement matters only because Fred heard it and reacted by carrying his umbrella. Fred can testify directly about the fact that he heard the statement.

Fred's testimony raises a common hearsay problem: Many witnesses testify that another person's statement prompted them to act in a particular way. Most of the

---

1   United States v. Central Gulf Lines, Inc., 747 F.2d 315, 319 (5th Cir. 1984).

time, this testimony is not hearsay. Witnesses in these cases, like Fred, are not offering the other person's statement to prove the truth of what the other person said. Instead, the witness describes a signal in the environment that caused them to act a particular way. The signal might have been emitted by an inanimate object (such as a thermometer displaying the outside temperature) or by another person making a statement. In either case, the signal existed as a fact that the witness can describe.

Here, finally, is an example derived from a famous English case. The case illustrates yet another way in which words may convey meaning other than the truth of the matters they assert:

Example: Tabitha Tatum, an elderly widow, died leaving a substantial estate. Her will left all of her property to the Museum of Beverage Containers in Goodlettsville, Tennessee. Tatum's grandchildren challenged the will, claiming that their grandmother lacked mental capacity when she made the will. At trial, Tatum's executor defended the will by introducing a variety of letters written by different people to Tatum around the time she made the will. These letters discussed a variety of everyday and business matters. The executor argued that the letters showed that Tatum's correspondents believed she was of sound mind; otherwise they would not have written letters of this nature. Tatum's grandchildren objected to the letters as hearsay.

Analysis: The letters were **not hearsay**. Tatum's executor did not offer these letters to prove the truth of their content. The outcome of the trial did not turn on whether Tatum wished to attend a board meeting for a local nonprofit, whether she agreed that the local politicians were corrupt, or any other matters asserted within the letters. Instead, the letters were offered to prove that people who knew Tatum well believed that she would understand and respond to topics like these. That belief was relevant because it tended to prove that Tatum was mentally competent at the time.[2]

As we saw in the very first hypothetical involving Lisa and the law partner, a person's statement can be used to prove many different things. Each of the above

---

2   Wright v. Doe d. Tatham (1837), 112 Eng. Rep. 488 (Exchequer Chamber). The English court held that letters like these were inadmissible hearsay, but the Federal Rules of Evidence dictate a different result.

hypotheticals and cases underscores that point. When analyzing a hearsay problem, the key question is often: What is the litigant attempting to prove by offering this statement?

Quick Summary

The hearsay rules only bar out-of-court statements if they are offered for the "truth of the matter asserted." Thus, a critical question to ask about any out-of-court statement is: What is the proponent trying to prove by offering the statement into evidence? If she is trying to prove that the content of the out-of-court statement is true, then the statement is hearsay because secondhand reports are inherently unreliable and we have no way of testing the accuracy and truth of the out-of-court statement.

But if we only care about the fact that the out-of-court statement was made, not the truth of its content, then the statement is not hearsay. The witness who heard the statement can testify from firsthand knowledge about the fact that the statement was made, as well as about who made the statement, its exact wording, and any other relevant details. Opposing counsel can test the witness's accuracy and credibility through cross-examination and the jury can assess those issues directly in the courtroom. When offered for this purpose, the statement falls outside **Rule 801**'s hearsay definition and does not raise any of the policy concerns we identified in the last chapter.

Test Your Understanding

To assess your understanding of the material in this chapter, click here to take a quiz, or go to the Quizzes module from the eBook on your eProducts bookshelf.

37

What Is a Statement?

A. Introduction and Policy. We have discussed the policies underlying the hearsay rule, the concept of an out-of-court declarant, and the distinction between statements introduced to show the "truth of the matter asserted" and statements offered for another purpose. We now turn to the final element of defining hearsay: What is a "statement"?

A declarant can make a statement either orally or in writing. A person who says, "I inspected the farm machinery and it was in good working condition at the time of the sale," has made a statement. A criminal defendant who writes a confession also has made a statement. The hearsay rules apply to both written and oral communications.

Declarants can also make statements through actions: A patient who nods her head when asked if she is sick, or points to a nurse when asked who gave her an injection, has also made a statement. These assertive behaviors are statements subject to the hearsay rules.

Attorneys applying the hearsay rule, however, are sometimes too quick to read statements into actions. Most of an individual's actions are not meant to assert a fact; those actions are not statements so they raise no hearsay issues. The confusion arises because we often **infer** facts from observing the conduct of others. If we look out the window and see pedestrians bundled up in overcoats, we infer that the weather is chilly. The overcoats are circumstantial evidence of cold weather; we infer the temperature from their existence.

Pedestrians who wear overcoats, however, are not communicating with others; they are simply keeping themselves warm. Non-assertive behaviors like wearing an overcoat are not statements, so the hearsay rules do not apply to them.

Here are some more examples of conduct that are **not statements**. Because they are not statements, they raise no hearsay problems if reported in the courtroom:

- Samantha testifies that she noticed the defendant reach into his pocket at 2:00 p.m., take out his cell phone, and immediately begin to talk. The prosecutor offers Samantha's testimony as evidence that the defendant received a call at 2:00 p.m. Samantha's report of the defendant's conduct does not violate the hearsay rules; the defendant did not intend to communicate any meaning through his action, so his action was not an out-of-court statement. Samantha, the jurors, and others who hear about the defendant's conduct may infer from the defendant's action that he received a call.

- Edward testifies that he was sitting at an intersection behind a large truck that was so big it obscured the stoplight. After a few seconds, Edward reports, the truck began to move forward. The plaintiff in a personal injury case offers Edward's testimony to show that the light turned green when the truck moved. The truck driver did not intend to assert any fact by driving forward; his conduct contained no statement. Edward may report the out-of-court conduct, allowing the jury to draw the inference that the light turned green.

- Alice testifies that she walked into the living room of her house and found her brother in tears, crying and sobbing. The brother offers Alice's testimony in his action against a debt collection agency to show that he suffered severe emotional distress from the agency's actions. The brother's tears were not intended to communicate any fact to others; he had started crying before Alice even entered the room. Instead, the brother's conduct offers circumstantial evidence of his mental distress. Alice can describe that out-of-court conduct

> • without violating the hearsay rules because her brother's tears were not a statement.

Another way to solve hearsay problems involving conduct is to remember that the hearsay rule only prohibits statements offered for the truth of the matter asserted. Actions like moving forward at a green light or answering a telephone are non-assertive behavior. They do not assert anything, so there is no truth of any matter to assert.

Actions like nodding or pointing, on the other hand, do assert something. These examples of assertive conduct convey matters that have a truth. You could replace these actions with words like "yes, I am sick" or "that nurse gave me the injection." These actions are statements because a party could offer them to prove the truth of the matter they assert.

A good rule of thumb for distinguishing between assertive and non-assertive conduct is to ask: Do we need to assess the actor's **sincerity** in order to rely upon the conduct? If we do, the conduct contains an assertion and the hearsay rule applies. If not, the actor was not trying to assert any fact, and the jury is free to draw any reasonable inference from the reported conduct.

This distinction makes sense when we think about the policies motivating the hearsay rule. We exclude hearsay from the courtroom primarily because we worry whether the out-of-court declarant spoke honestly. We can't observe an out-of-court declarant's demeanor; we cannot cross-examine her; and we can't rely on the formal courtroom setting and oath to induce honesty. But if the declarant did not intend to make any assertion, we don't need to worry that she lied.

The hearsay rule also responds to concerns about perception, memory, and clarity. But in the case of non-assertive behavior, we can satisfy those concerns by cross-examining the witness who reports the behavior and observing that witness's demeanor.

In the examples given above, we may wonder whether the coworker really answered the phone; whether the truck could have moved before the light turned green; and how upset Alice's brother really was. But we can answer these questions by cross-examining Samantha, Edward, and Alice and by observing their demeanor on the stand.

Samantha, Edward, and Alice, in other words, have **personal knowledge** about the coworker talking into a phone, the truck moving forward, and the brother crying. Their reports about these actions are no different than reports about any other phenomenon. After listening to Samantha, Edward, and Alice, a jury can decide whether to infer from their reports that the coworker received a call (because he began talking into the phone); the light turned green (because the truck moved forward); and the brother was upset (because he was crying and sobbing).

B. The Rule. Rule **801(a)** defines "statement" as an "assertion" that can be made with or without words:

> ## RULE 801. Definitions That Apply to This Article; Exclusions from Hearsay
>
> **(a) Statement.** "Statement" means
>
> - a person's <u>oral assertion</u>,
> - <u>written assertion</u>, or
> - <u>nonverbal conduct</u>,
>
> if the person intended it as an assertion.

What does Rule 801(a) mean by an "assertion"? We have already explored that concept by thinking about the policies behind the hearsay rule. An assertion is any action undertaken by the declarant **that is intended to communicate a fact.** Any time a person asserts a fact, she makes a statement. Saying or writing words almost always makes an assertion, but **conduct** can also make an assertion. The key is whether the declarant intended to communicate a fact through her conduct.

C. In the Courtroom.

1. Assertive v. Non-Assertive Conduct. Individuals almost always intend certain gestures, such as nodding and finger-pointing, as assertions. But other gestures are more ambiguous. Often the court must look at the context to see if the declarant intended to assert a fact through her actions:

Example: The outcome of a personal injury lawsuit turns on whether it had started raining by 6 p.m. on April 2. The parties vigorously contest this issue. Wilbur, a witness for the plaintiff, testifies that Dora visited him at 6 p.m. on April 2 and he asked Dora whether it was raining outside. In response, Wilbur testifies, "Dora said nothing but shook a wet umbrella at me." The defendant objects to this testimony as hearsay.

Analysis: Wilbur's testimony contains hearsay. Although shaking an umbrella usually is not an assertion, the action carried an assertive meaning in this context. In response to Wilbur's question, Dora's action was equivalent to the verbal statement, "Yes, it's raining, you fool—that's why I'm carrying an umbrella." Dora made this assertion outside the courtroom, and Wilbur is offering the assertion as proof of the matter asserted (that it was indeed raining).

But consider similar evidence in a different context:

Example: Suppose that in the previous example Wilbur did not ask Dora about the weather. Instead Wilbur testifies: "I never looked outside that evening, but my friend Dora arrived at 6 p.m. As she came in the door, she was folding a dripping wet umbrella. The umbrella left water on the floor of my entrance way." Is this hearsay?

Analysis: This example is very similar to the previous one. In both cases, Wilbur reports Dora's conduct with a wet umbrella. But the testimony in this second example is not hearsay. In this variation, Dora did not assert any fact when she folded her wet umbrella. She may not even have known that Wilbur was watching her. Instead, Wilbur reports firsthand what he saw Dora do. The fact finder can make any reasonable inferences based on Dora's actions.

Another example distinguishing assertive and non-assertive conduct comes from a famous nineteenth century English case, *Wright v. Doe d. Tatham:*[1]

---

1   (1837), 112 Eng. Rep. 488 (Exchequer Chamber). The dispute in this case centered on the problem discussed in the previous chapter of an allegedly incompetent testator who received ordinary business and personal letters. The court proposed this example, discussed by courts ever since, in its opinion.

Example: A commercial ship sinks at sea, with no survivors to explain the loss. A subsequent lawsuit disputes the seaworthiness of the ship at the time it left port. The party claiming seaworthiness offers evidence that the ship's captain inspected the ship, then sailed off in it with his wife and children on board. Is this hearsay?

Analysis: The captain's conduct was not hearsay because he did not intend to assert anything to anyone when he set sail with his family. He was simply going about his business. The captain's conduct is circumstantial evidence that he believed the ship was seaworthy; otherwise he probably would not have risked his life and those of his family members. But he was not, through his actions, declaring or asserting anything to anyone.[2]

2. Implicit Assertions. One has to look carefully at some actions for assertions that may be hidden within them. Here is an example of a partially hidden assertion:

Example: Lillian Keller was stabbed to death on December 2. Police discovered a wallet containing John Stevenson's driver's license that was lying near Keller's body. A few days later, police officer Schultze visited the address printed on the license. John Stevenson was not home, but Schultze spoke with Stevenson's wife. He asked Mrs. Stevenson to give him the clothing that Stevenson had been wearing on December 2. Mrs. Stevenson gave Schultze a pullover shirt. Laboratory tests showed bloodstains on the shirt that were the same general type as the victim's blood. The stains, however, were too small to allow more precise typing.

The state prosecuted Stevenson for homicide. At trial, the prosecutor introduced the shirt as evidence, together with testimony by Schultze about how he had obtained the shirt. Stevenson objected to both the testimony and the shirt as hearsay.

Analysis: The shirt was not hearsay, but Mrs. Stevenson's conduct in handing over the shirt was. Mrs. Stevenson gave Schultze the shirt in response to his request for the clothing that Stevenson had worn on December 2. Under

---

2   The nineteenth-century English judges who posed this hypothetical suggested that the testimony *was* hearsay. They reasoned that the captain's action was a kind of declaration that the ship was seaworthy. Modern courts and commentators have rejected that analysis; current thinkers agree that the captain's conduct was not hearsay.

those circumstances, Mrs. Stevenson's silent gesture of handing over the shirt included the implicit assertion: "This is the shirt that John Stevenson wore on December 2." This implicit assertion occurred outside of court, and the state offered it for the truth of the matter asserted (that John did wear the shirt that day). The prosecutor could attempt to elicit Mrs. Stevenson's direct testimony about John wearing the shirt that day, but they could not introduce her statement secondhand through Schultze.[3]

How does this example differ from the myriad cases in which the government introduces evidence seized from a defendant's home? Police officers who execute search warrants routinely testify that they found certain items at a defendant's residence, in his car, or in other places linked to the defendant. There is no hearsay problem in those cases because the police testify solely about their own actions; they do not quote third parties. The prosecutor then relies upon an inference to tie the defendant to the items: The items were found in the defendant's home, so the prosecutor asks the jury to infer that the items belonged to the defendant.

In the example given above, Officer Schultze could have testified that he obtained the shirt from John Stevenson's apartment, and the lab technician could have testified that the shirt had a blood stain of a type that matched the victim's blood. However, the prosecutor went further and used information derived solely from Mrs. Stevenson's production of a particular shirt in response to Schultze's specific question. Since Mrs. Stevenson's act of handing the shirt over in response to that question was an assertion, Schultze's secondhand reporting of the act was hearsay testimony.

The policies behind the hearsay rule confirm the difference between the typical case in which an officer seizes a shirt from the defendant's home and the one in which Mrs. Stevenson produced a specific shirt in response to Schultze's question. In the typical case, the officer who seized the evidence will appear in court to testify that he took the evidence from a particular place at a particular time. Defense counsel can cross-examine the officer to test whether he is certain that this shirt came from that place. Counsel can also point out defects in the inferences that the prosecutor draws from the seized shirt. The defendant, for example, might share

---

3   Stevenson v. Commonwealth, 218 Va. 462, 465–66, 237 S.E.2d 779, 781–82 (1977). Note that Mrs. Stevenson probably invoked the spousal privilege, which we will study later in the course, and refused to testify against her husband at trial. Hearsay problems often arise when the witness with firsthand knowledge is unwilling to testify.

his home with several other people; perhaps the shirt belongs to one of them. The jury, finally, can evaluate the police officer's credibility: Is there any chance that he planted the shirt?

Once these questions have been raised, the defendant in the typical seizure case has no other inquiries to make. There is no missing witness who could provide further information about seizure of the shirt and what that seizure might mean.

In the *Stevenson* case, in contrast, the crucial information lay in Mrs. Stevenson's choice of this particular shirt to hand over to Officer Schultze. That act signified that the shirt had been worn on December 2, the day Keller was killed. Unless Mrs. Stevenson testifies, the defendant has no way to test the accuracy of that assertion. How certain was Mrs. Stevenson that her husband wore this shirt on that day? Could she have mistaken the day or shirt? Could she have been lying? Did she purposely give Schultze the wrong shirt for some reason known only to herself? Pursuing these questions is essential to assessing the value of Mrs. Stevenson's implicit assertion that the shirt was worn on December 2. Counsel's inability to pursue those questions through Schultze's testimony confirms that this aspect of the testimony was hearsay.

3. Audiotapes. Most audiotapes contain verbal assertions by human actors. Those assertions are statements; the tape is analogous to a witness who repeats out-of-court assertions. Although the tape is present in the courtroom, the recorded declarants are not. Jurors cannot fully assess the declarants' demeanor; nor can adverse parties cross-examine the recorded declarants.

Recorded statements, of course, are hearsay only if a litigant offers them for the truth of the matter asserted. An audiotape of an accident might demonstrate that the plaintiff received a warning ("watch out!") just before the accident occurred. If the defendant introduces the tape to show the existence of the warning, the recorded words would not be hearsay.

4. Photographs and Videotapes. The hearsay status of photographs and videotapes, like that of audiotapes, depends on what they portray. Unlike audiotapes, however, most photos and videotapes shown in the courtroom **do not** portray human assertions. Instead, these media usually depict physical objects or non-assertive human conduct. Security cameras that record the defendant pulling a gun on a store clerk, for example, produce a video of that event; they do not report an assertion. Likewise, pictures of crime scenes or drug transactions usually do not portray an assertion by any individual.

Even if a videotape or photo includes spoken or written words, the proponent rarely introduces the evidence for the truth of what the words assert. A security videotape that shows the defendant demanding that a store clerk "hand over all of your cash" is not offered to prove some fact about the cash; the prosecutor offers the tape simply to show that the defendant spoke those words.

But if a photo or a videotape does convey verbal assertions or assertive behavior, offered for the truth of the matter asserted, then those assertions are statements subject to the hearsay rule:

Example: Stacey Dutch sues the International House of Pancakes for negligence, claiming that she slipped in a puddle of maple syrup that the restaurant carelessly allowed to accumulate on its floor. Dutch claims that she suffers permanent paralyzing pain in the left leg from her injury. She offers a videotape of her nurse describing the great difficulty that Dutch has walking, caring for herself, and living independently as a result of this injury. IHOP objects that the videotape is hearsay.

Analysis: The videotape is hearsay. Although the jury can evaluate the nurse's words for themselves, rather than through the testimony of another witness, IHOP has no opportunity to cross-examine the nurse about her testimony. Careful questioning might reveal that Dutch's disability is much less than the nurse originally claims or even that the nurse is lying about some of the difficulties she reports. The statements in the videotape are assertions, they were made outside the courtroom, and Dutch offers them for the truth of what they say (that she is disabled in particular ways).

5. Machine Readouts. Information conveyed by a machine usually is not a statement. When a watch reveals the time, or a thermometer indicates the temperature, no human has made an assertion. Thus, if a witness testifies: "I looked at my watch when I heard the crash and it was quarter to five," the witness has not recounted an out-of-court statement.

More complex devices, such as polygraph machines, breathalyzers, and radar guns, similarly use automated processes to report information to law-enforcement personnel and other people outside the courtroom. These devices do not make statements, so witnesses may recount information gleaned from them. Opposing counsel can challenge the reliability of these machines, but that inquiry differs from the hearsay rule.

If, on the other hand, a machine conveys a human assertion, the assertion qualifies as a statement. Comments uttered over the telephone or transmitted via e-mail are assertions made by individuals. Likewise, if a bank teller pushes a silent alarm button to signal a hold up, the alarm is an assertion. A security officer who hears the alarm understands the meaning of the signal and responds to it. If the security officer testifies that the robbery began at 10:30 a.m. because he heard the alarm at that time, his reference to the alarm would be hearsay.

In short, when evidence consists of information conveyed by a machine, the judge will explore whether that information incorporates a human assertion. If a person communicated a fact through a machine, then the assertion is a statement subject to the hearsay rule. If the machine generated information according to its own internal processes, then the machine's output is not an assertion by a person.

Here is a contemporary example of machine-generated information that is not hearsay:

Example: The government charged Kenneth Hamilton with uploading child pornography to an internet newsgroup. The prosecutor introduced 44 images that Hamilton allegedly had posted on the internet. Each of the images included a computer-generated header that revealed the unique IP address of the computer where the images originated. That address corresponded to Hamilton's computer. Hamilton objected to introduction of the headers as hearsay.

Analysis: The court concluded that the headers were not hearsay. The computer generated these headers automatically, without input from any human. They were analogous to the time shown on a clock or a temperature reading on a thermometer. The prosecutor, therefore, could introduce the headers without violating the hearsay rules.[4]

---

4   United States v. Hamilton, 413 F.3d 1138, 1142–43 (10th Cir. 2005). Tracing the IP address in the actual case was slightly more complicated than the example suggests because Hamilton used an internet service provider (Earthlink) rather than his own server. Earthlink, however, had records of which IP addresses were assigned to users at particular times and the IP addresses in these headers linked to Hamilton's usage.

The policies underlying the hearsay rules support this result. Machines sometimes are inaccurate; parties often contest the accuracy of breathalyzers and other mechanical devices. But machines do not consciously lie as humans sometimes do. Courtroom cross-examination, therefore, does not add to the reliability of a machine-generated report. We need the assurances of a courtroom appearance and cross-examination only when information transmitted by a machine originated with a human decision maker.

Quick Summary

The hearsay rules bar only admission of out-of-court statements, not other types of evidence gathered outside the courtroom. A statement is an assertion through which an individual intends to convey information. The assertion may be oral, written, or displayed through which an individual intends to convey information. The assertion may be oral, written, or displayed through conduct. The key to determining whether conduct is a statement is to ask whether the actor intended to communicate information through that conduct.

Photos, videotapes, audiotapes, and machine-generated data constitute statements under some circumstances but not others. Focusing on the policies underlying the hearsay rules helps determine when these media contain statements. If one of these types of evidence transmits an assertion by a human, then the evidence contains a statement. If a party offers the statement for the truth of the matter asserted, then it is hearsay. Under the latter circumstances, we want to cross-examine the human declarant in the courtroom and assess that individual's credibility.

Test Your Understanding

To assess your understanding of the material in this chapter, click here to take a quiz, or go to the Quizzes module from the eBook on your eProducts bookshelf.

38

Admissible Hearsay

Key Concepts

- Reliability and Need Are Keys to Hearsay Exceptions
- 31 Exceptions in Four Categories
- The Judge Decides Admissibility, Including Factual Issues, Under **Rule 104(a)**
- Sixth Amendment Limits Some Exceptions, but Only in Criminal Cases

A. Introduction and Policy. The hearsay rule is well known for its many exceptions: thirty-one of them, to be exact. While this number seems daunting at first, many of the exceptions rarely arise; we will cover them only briefly in this course. Most of the exceptions, moreover, are straightforward if you understand the reasoning behind them. Once you appreciate the policies supporting the exceptions, you will find it easy to understand and apply them.

All of the hearsay exceptions rest on two axioms. First, some hearsay statements are **more reliable** than others. Although all secondhand reports are less trustworthy than firsthand ones, some circumstances boost the reliability of hearsay statements. A statement made under oath in another proceeding, for example, technically is hearsay because it is not a statement made on the stand in the current proceeding. But the oath and formal setting of the prior proceeding offer assurances of reliability that more informal out-of-court statements lack. Nearly every exception to the hearsay rule rests in part on special indicia of reliability.

Second, some hearsay statements are **more needed** than others. A murder victim's deathbed moan that "Joe did it" may be the victim's only pronouncement on the issue. The victim cannot testify in court, and the evidence has special probative value. In a situation like this, the court must choose between letting the jury consider the hearsay statement with appropriate warnings or losing the evidence altogether. Many hearsay exceptions strike this balance in favor of admissibility, especially if circumstances suggest that the needed statement is more reliable than other types of hearsay.

The bottom line, therefore, is that hearsay statements are not all created equal. Due to variations in reliability and probative value, courts are willing to admit some types of hearsay. And they have created thirty-one exceptions to do so.

B. Four Categories of Exceptions. The Federal Rules of Evidence group the hearsay exceptions into four categories. Understanding the categories will help you work your way through the exceptions as we explore them in upcoming chapters. Here is a brief tour.

First, Rule 801(d) defines two types of out-of-court statements as "not hearsay." These are (1) prior statements by witnesses, and (2) statements made by opposing parties. Labeling these statements "not hearsay" is unhelpful: The statements clearly **are** hearsay, and courts admit them only because special considerations trump the rule against hearsay. The drafters' decision to call these two exceptions "not hearsay" has confused many lawyers and judges.

But these two kinds of hearsay arise frequently in litigation, and the rationales supporting their admission differ somewhat from those that the courts offer for the other twenty-nine hearsay exceptions. For these reasons, it is useful to consider the two 801(d) categories as a distinct class of admissible hearsay. To honor the rule's identification of these statements as "not hearsay," we will call them **exemptions** rather than exceptions. But many lawyers simply refer to prior statements by witnesses, as well as those made by opposing parties, as exceptions to the hearsay rule.

We will explore each of these exemptions in detail, the first in Chapter 39 and the second in Chapters 53–55. For now, simply note these as the first category of hearsay exemptions.

Second, Rule 804 recognizes five exceptions to the hearsay rule. The drafters grouped these exceptions together because they apply only if the declarant is unavailable to testify in court. The archetypal, and most colorful, of these exceptions is the dying declaration described above. The rule also includes several exceptions that assume importance when a key witness claims a privilege that shields her from testifying at trial. Invocation of the privilege sometimes makes the declarant's direct courtroom testimony "unavailable."

The five exceptions grouped under this rule rely heavily on the need for a declarant's statement. Whether a declarant is unavailable due to death, claim of privilege, or other cause, the court can obtain the declarant's perspective only by admitting a hearsay statement. Although each of these five exceptions rests on a particular type of reliability, the need for the declarant's statement plays a strong role in admitting all hearsay in this category.

The **third** and largest category of hearsay exceptions appears in **Rule 803**. That rule lists twenty-three different exceptions to the hearsay rule. These exceptions apply whether or not the declarant is available to testify. A party, in other words, may rely upon one of these exceptions even if a declarant could testify live—and even if the declarant actually takes the stand.

Parties may also rely upon most of these exceptions when a declarant is unavailable to testify. A deceased declarant, or one who has claimed a privilege during the trial, may have made hearsay statements that are admissible under Rule 803.

The rationales for the Rule 803 exceptions depend substantially on reliability rather than need for the evidence; in at least some cases, firsthand testimony could be obtained. But high indicia of reliability allow admission of these statements regardless of the declarant's availability.

The circumstances generating that reliability are quite varied, so the exceptions appearing under this rule are diverse as well. They cover a broad range, including excited utterances, market reports, commercial publications, and learned treatises. We will explore some of these exceptions at length and others more briefly in upcoming chapters.

Rule 807, finally, creates a residual exception that allows courts to admit some statements that fall outside the other thirty exceptions but have similar guarantees of trustworthiness. Courts use this rule infrequently; the other thirty exceptions cover most of the situations in which reliability is sufficient to admit hearsay. But this residual exception constitutes a fourth category of hearsay exceptions.

The chart on the next page lists the thirty-one hearsay exceptions, grouping them into the four categories.

Hearsay Exceptions: Thirty-One Flavors

Rule 801(d): Exemptions	Rule 803: Availability of Declarant Varies
• Prior statement by witness • Statement of opposing party	• Present sense impression • Excited utterance • Then-existing mental, emotional, or physical condition • Statement made for medical diagnosis or treatment • Recorded recollection • Records of a regularly conducted activity • Absence of a record of a regularly conducted activity • Public records • Public records of vital statistics • Absence of a public record • Records of religious organizations concerning personal or family history • Certificates of marriage, baptism, and similar ceremonies • Family records • Records of documents that affect an interest in property • Statements in documents that affect an interest in property • Statements in ancient documents • Market reports and similar commercial publications • Statements in learned treatises, periodicals, or pamphlets • Reputation concerning personal or family history • Reputation concerning boundaries or general history • Reputation concerning character • Judgment of a previous conviction • Judgments involving personal, family, or general history, or a boundary
Rule 804: Declarant Unavailable	
• Former testimony • Statement under the belief of imminent death ("dying declaration") • Statement against interest • Statement of personal or family history • Statement offered against a party that wrongfully caused the declarant's unavailability ("forfeiture by wrongdoing")	
Rule 807: Residual Exception	
• Other statements having equivalent circumstantial guarantees of trustworthiness, when admission will serve the interests of justice	

C. Who Decides? Whether a statement fits into a hearsay exception often depends upon the existence of specific facts: Every exception has its own conditions to fulfill before the exception applies. Who decides whether these factual conditions exist? Does the judge decide under **Rule 104(a)**? Or are these questions that the jury resolves under **Rule 104(b)**?

For the reasons explored in Chapter 34, the judge decides these preliminary factual disputes. Remember that Rule 104 assigns most preliminary factual questions to the judge; the jury plays a role only when the factual dispute affects relevance. But neither the hearsay bar nor its exceptions affect relevance. Instead, these rules implement policy concerns about the reliability of secondhand statements.

The judge, therefore, decides both whether a statement is hearsay and whether one of the exceptions applies. If the parties dispute whether the necessary facts exist to support an exception, the judge will resolve that factual question under Rule 104(a). The party offering the statement must persuade the judge by a preponderance of the evidence that the facts exist to support a hearsay exception. As with other preliminary determinations, the preponderance standard applies in both civil and criminal cases. We will explore this process in more detail as we examine specific exceptions in upcoming chapters.

D. A Word About the Sixth Amendment. Exceptions to the hearsay rule can raise constitutional issues in criminal trials. The Sixth Amendment guarantees a criminal defendant the right "to be confronted with the witnesses against him." When the court admits an out-of-court statement, the defendant often lacks an opportunity to cross-examine the declarant who made the statement. Courts, therefore, have struggled in determining when the hearsay exceptions violate the Sixth Amendment.

Until recently, courts viewed most traditional hearsay exceptions as consistent with the Sixth Amendment. Historical pedigree supported the constitutionality of these exceptions. That changed in 2004 when the Supreme Court decided *Crawford v. Washington*.[1] That decision raises new constitutional questions about some of the hearsay exceptions.

We will examine *Crawford* and several other Sixth Amendment rulings in Chapter 58. We address first the hearsay exceptions as articulated in the Federal Rules,

---

1   541 U.S. 36 (2004).

without considering any constitutional challenges, for two reasons. First, despite the importance of *Crawford*, the majority of hearsay exceptions remain unchanged. Second, *Crawford* applies only against the **prosecution** in criminal cases. Even when the Sixth Amendment limits application of a hearsay exception, civil litigants and criminal defendants may still rely upon the traditional exception. It is easier to learn the exceptions first, knowing that all of them will apply fully to at least some evidence, and then add the constitutional caveats.

Quick Summary

The hearsay rule has thirty-one exceptions, which rest primarily on two principles. First, some secondhand statements are more reliable than others; circumstances give them extra credibility. Second, some hearsay statements are more needed than others; without the declarant's out-of-court statement the fact finder would lack needed evidence.

The Federal Rules divide the hearsay exceptions into four categories: (1) Two exceptions that Rule 801(d) defines as "not hearsay" or exemptions from the rule; (2) Five Rule 804 exceptions that depend on the declarant being unavailable; (3) Twenty-three Rule 803 exceptions that apply whether the declarant is available or unavailable; and (4) a residual exception offered by Rule 807.

The proponent of a hearsay statement bears the burden of proving by a preponderance of the evidence that the statement meets one of the exceptions. The trial judge determines whether the proponent has met this burden, resolving any factual issues under Rule 104(a).

In criminal cases, some hearsay exceptions violate the defendant's Sixth Amendment right to confront the witnesses against him. We will discuss these Sixth Amendment issues after mastering the basic hearsay exceptions. All of the exceptions remain viable in civil cases, and the Sixth Amendment affects only some exceptions in criminal trials.

39

Hearsay Exemption—
Prior Statements by Witnesses

Key Concepts

- **Rule 801(d)(1):** Exempts Some Prior Statements by Witnesses from the Hearsay Ban
- Witness Must Be Subject to Cross-Examination
- Inconsistent Prior Statements
- Consistent Prior Statements
- Identifications

A. Introduction and Policy. Many students are surprised to learn that a witness's out-of-court statements are hearsay. If the witness is on the stand, sworn to tell the truth, and available for cross-examination, why draw a distinction between the witness's direct testimony and statements that the witness made at a previous time?

Suppose, for example, that Cynthia is a witness in a kidnapping trial. She lives across the street from the victim, John, and saw him shortly before he disappeared. The prosecution calls Cynthia to help establish the time of John's disappearance. If Cynthia says on the stand, "I looked out of my window at 8:00 a.m. on December 19th and saw John leaving his house," that is direct testimony.

The prosecutor can present this direct testimony without raising any hearsay issues. But even with Cynthia appearing on the stand, all of the following statements are hearsay if the prosecutor introduces them to prove when John left his house on December 19:

- Cynthia's courtroom testimony: "After John disappeared, I told my husband Bill that I saw John leaving his house at 8:00 a.m. on December 19."

- Bill's courtroom testimony: "After John disappeared, Cynthia told me that she had seen him leaving his house at 8:00 a.m. on December 19."

- Bill's courtroom testimony: "At 8:00 a.m. on December 19, I heard Cynthia exclaim, 'There's John leaving his house!' "

- A police report noting that during questioning after John's disappearance, Cynthia told police that she had seen John leave his house at 8:00 a.m. on December 19.

- Cynthia's recorded statement, made under oath to a grand jury, that she saw John leave his house at 8:00 a.m. on December 19.

All of these statements occurred outside the current courtroom; Cynthia's appearance on the stand doesn't alter their hearsay character. These statements remain hearsay because the safeguards that we apply to courtroom testimony—the oath, opportunity to cross-examine, and ability to assess the witness's credibility—don't fit the timing of these statements. Cynthia has taken an oath to tell the truth now, the defense counsel can cross-examine Cynthia now, and the jury can see Cynthia's demeanor now, but those safeguards didn't all apply at the time Cynthia made the statements listed above. The timing of the safeguards, in other words, doesn't match the timing of the statements.

This problem is more than a minor technicality. Usually when a party attempts to introduce a witness's prior statement instead of asking the witness to testify directly, it is because the witness cannot—or will not—make the same statement on the stand. In the above example, if Cynthia is able to testify directly about seeing John, the prosecutor will simply elicit her direct testimony and have no need to rely upon her prior statements. On the other hand, if the prosecutor is forced to rely on Cynthia's prior statements to prove when John left his house, it is probably because Cynthia is unable or unwilling to testify about the incident directly.

In short, parties usually resort to a witness's prior statement when the witness's direct testimony is insufficient. Under these circumstances, the witness is unable to endorse the prior statement, and the credibility safeguards of the trial are no longer effective: The opposing party cannot effectively cross-examine the witness on that statement; the courtroom oath does nothing to enhance the reliability of the earlier statement; and the jury has no opportunity to observe the witness's demeanor when making the statement.

Although these are good reasons to treat a witness's out-of-court statements as hearsay, there are some circumstances under which the reliability of the prior statement is sufficiently high, and the need for the statement is sufficiently great, that the hearsay rules recognize an exception for a witness's prior statement. The very fact that the declarant is available in the courtroom seems to add **some** reliability to these prior statements.

Rule 801(d)(1) allows admission of some prior statements by witnesses. As noted in the previous chapter, the rule defines these statements as "not hearsay" or as exemptions from the rule against hearsay. Whatever we call it, however, the exemption for prior statements of witnesses is fairly narrow.

B. The Rule. Rule 801(d)(1) first establishes two conditions that must be met to admit any statement under that subsection: The declarant must testify at the trial, and the declarant must be subject to cross-examination on the statement:

> ## RULE 801. Definitions That Apply to This Article; Exclusions from Hearsay
>
> **(d) Statements That Are Not Hearsay.** A statement that meets the following conditions is <u>not hearsay</u>:
>
> **(1)** *A Declarant-Witness's Prior Statement.*
>
> - The declarant <u>testifies</u> and
> - is subject to <u>cross-examination</u> about a prior statement . . . .

These gateway requirements enhance the prior statement's reliability. If the declarant appears as a witness, the jury can observe his demeanor in response to questions about the prior statement. In addition, adverse parties can cross-examine the witness about both his current testimony and prior statement. The ability to cross-examine may be limited with respect to the prior statement, but opposing counsel has some opportunity to test the declarant/witness's credibility. That cross-examination, finally, will occur in a formal courtroom setting with the declarant under oath.

If these conditions are met, the rule recognizes three types of prior witness statements that are admissible:

> (A) Statements that are inconsistent with the witness's courtroom testimony;
>
> (B) Statements that are consistent with that testimony; and
>
> (C) Pretrial identifications of a person.

Let's examine the rule's description of each of these subclasses of exemption. First, for prior inconsistent statements:

RULE 801. Definitions That Apply to This Article; Exclusions from Hearsay

(d) Statements That Are Not Hearsay. A statement that meets the following conditions is <u>not hearsay</u>:

(1) *A Declarant-Witness's Prior Statement.*

- The declarant <u>testifies</u> and
- is subject to <u>cross-examination</u> about a prior statement,
- and the statement:

  (A) is <u>inconsistent</u> with the declarant's testimony and was given under <u>penalty of perjury</u> at a trial, hearing, or other <u>proceeding or in a deposition</u> . . . .

Rule 801(d)(1)(A) thus exempts a witness's prior statement if the statement satisfies three conditions: (1) It is inconsistent with the witness's current testimony; (2) It was made under penalty of perjury; and (3) It occurred at a deposition or during a trial, hearing, or other proceeding.

These requirements further the policies that motivate the hearsay exceptions. The first requirement, that the prior statement was inconsistent, ensures that the admitted evidence is particularly useful. If a witness has made a prior statement at another proceeding that conflicts with one made at trial, the jury should know about that conflict and determine its meaning.

The other two requirements, that the prior statement be made under penalty of perjury and at a deposition or trial-like proceeding, help ensure the statement's reliability. The oath and formality of the prior proceeding offer some assurance that the witness made the statement seriously and truthfully. Equally important, the "proceeding" requirement ensures that the prior statement was recorded in some form. The existence of a transcript eliminates controversy about what the witness said on the prior occasion.

Rule 801(d)(1)(B) contains the second type of hearsay exemption for a witness's prior statements. This subsection applies to prior consistent statements:

RULE 801. Definitions That Apply to This Article; Exclusions from Hearsay

(d) Statements That Are Not Hearsay. A statement that meets the following conditions is <u>not hearsay</u>:

(1) *A Declarant-Witness's Prior Statement.*

- The declarant <u>testifies</u> and
- is subject to <u>cross-examination</u> about a prior statement,
- and the statement: . . .

(B) is <u>consistent</u> with the declarant's testimony and is offered:

i. to rebut an express or implied charge that the declarant recently fabricated it or acted from a recent improper influence or motive in so testifying; or

ii. to rehabilitate the declarant's credibility as a witness when attacked on another ground . . . .[1]

This exemption does not require that the witness's prior statement occurred under oath or at a proceeding. If the prior statement is consistent with the witness's court-

---

1   Subsection (ii) was added to Rule 801(d)(1)(B) on December 1, 2014. Note that cases decided before that time may refer to the prior version of 801(d)(1)(B), which included only the language in subsection (i).

room testimony, those guarantees of reliability are less important. The witness is willing to affirm the substance of the prior statement under oath in the courtroom, so the jury can assess credibility and responses to cross-examination at that time.

Instead, Rule 801(d)(1)(B) ties admissibility to rehabilitation of a witness's credibility. To introduce a statement under this subsection, a party must show (1) that the witness's credibility has been attacked, and (2) that the prior consistent statement has probative value in rehabilitating credibility. We will explore these requirements further in the Courtroom section.

For now, note that Rule 801(d)(1)(B) complements the process of witness rehabilitation we discussed in Chapter 18. In that chapter, we noted the use of prior consistent statements to buttress the believability of a witness whose credibility has been challenged. Rules 402 and 403 permit introduction of those statements for the purpose of showing the witness's consistency. Rule 801(d)(1)(B) makes clear that the jury may also consider the prior consistent statements for the truth of the matter asserted.

Rule 801(d)(1)(C) offers the final type of exemption for a witness's prior statements. This subsection allows introduction of any identification of a person, as long as the person who made the identification testifies at trial and is subject to cross-examination on the identification:

RULE 801. Definitions That Apply to This Article; Exclusions from Hearsay

(d) Statements That Are Not Hearsay. A statement that meets the following conditions is <u>not hearsay</u>:

   (1) *A Declarant-Witness's Prior Statement.*

- The declarant <u>testifies</u> and
- is subject to <u>cross-examination</u> about a prior statement, and the statement: . . .

   (C) <u>identifies</u> a person as someone the declarant perceived earlier.

Why does this provision admit prior identifications so generously, when the previous portions of the rule impose so many restrictions on admission of other types of prior statements? Out-of-court identifications have the unusual characteristic of being **more reliable** than in-court identifications.

A witness who identifies a person in court usually builds that testimony on an earlier identification. After a crime, for example, a victim or eyewitness may point out the perpetrator at the scene. Or these individuals may pick the defendant out of a properly conducted line-up or photo array. These identifications occur close in time to the event, and are more reliable than any occurring later. Indeed, the police act on these identifications to pursue the perpetrator.[2]

A courtroom identification that occurs months later looks persuasive to the jury, but is less reliable than the original identification. A trial witness does not choose the perpetrator from an array of similar-looking individuals. The trial witness simply points to the individual sitting at the defense table, next to the defense attorney, and announces "he's the one!" These courtroom identifications are dramatic, but they offer little test of the witness's accuracy.

The initial, out-of-court identification, moreover, can reshape a witness's recollection so that the witness "remembers" the person picked out of a line-up rather than the actual perpetrator. Psychology research shows that memory is fluid. Witnesses sometimes unconsciously substitute the image of a person seen in a line-up, or even in other contexts, for their hazy recollection of the actual perpetrator.[3] The courtroom identification may depend on these substitutions rather than on actual recognition of the person who committed the crime.

Rule 801(d)(1)(C) recognizes that, for all of these reasons, out-of-court identifications often are more important than in-court ones. By admitting evidence of the initial identification, Rule 801(d)(1)(C) allows parties to cross-examine the witness more effectively about that identification. Opposing counsel can ask about the circumstances of the identification and how certain the witness was. The witness must respond under oath and the jury can assess her credibility. Under the rather unusual circumstances of an identification, the out-of-court statement is more reliable and significant than the in-court one.

---

2   The identification provision applies in civil cases as well as criminal ones, but it is used most often to identify criminal defendants. That context is easy to understand, so we use it to illustrate the rule here. Similar dynamics affect identifications in other settings.

3   For discussions of this phenomenon, see Witness Testimony: Psychological, Investigative and Evidential Perspectives (Anthony Heaton-Armstrong et al. eds., 2006).

Counsel may also ask the witness to identify the defendant, or any other person in the courtroom, while seated on the stand. Rule 801 doesn't preclude that type of identification, and juries find it impressive. But the in-court identification often is a charade. Rule 801(d)(1)(C) recognizes that the "real action" occurred at the pretrial identification.

The exemption for prior identifications thus rests on both reliability and need. These identifications are more reliable than in-court ones for the reasons given above. The out-of-court statements are needed, moreover, precisely because—given the peculiar circumstances of identifications—they are more reliable than any testimony restricted to the courtroom.

C. In the Courtroom. Rule 801(d)(1) is a straightforward exemption from the hearsay rule, but it has multiple parts. Let's work our way through the issues arising under each part of this exemption.

1. "Subject to Cross-Examination." Rule 801(d)(1)'s first requirement, that the declarant testify at trial, raises few questions. But the related requirement, that the declarant be "subject to cross-examination about a prior statement," generates more controversy. Remember that parties usually try to introduce evidence of a witness's prior statement only when the witness cannot or will not testify live. If the witness claims loss of memory, privilege, or some other condition that prevents direct testimony, is the witness "subject to cross-examination" on the prior statement? Or will the same condition prevent effective cross-examination?

This problem has arisen in several contexts. The first involves witnesses who have suffered a memory loss. The Supreme Court addressed that issue in this rather extreme case:

Example: A prison inmate brutally beat John Foster, a correctional counselor, with a metal pipe. Foster's injuries included a fractured skull, and he was hospitalized for almost a month. When an FBI agent first interviewed Foster in the hospital, he was lethargic and unable to remember his attacker. Several weeks later, the agent interviewed Foster again; at that time, Foster was able to describe the attack, name James Owens as his attacker, and identify Owens from a photo array.

The government charged Owens with assault with intent to murder. But by the time of trial, Foster's memory had clouded again. He could remember what he was doing just before the attack, recall feeling blows on his head, and remember seeing blood on the floor. He could also remember talking to the FBI agent in the hospital and identifying Owens at that time, but he could no longer remember seeing the person who attacked him or why he thought it might have been Owens. Nor could Foster remember talking to any hospital visitors other than the FBI agent, although records showed that he had other visitors. He was unable to recall whether any of these visitors might have suggested that Owens was his attacker.

The prosecutor called Foster to the stand to testify about his hospital identification of Owens, arguing that it was admissible under Rule 801(d)(1)(C) as an identification. Owens conceded that the prior statement was an identification, but claimed that 801(d)(1) should not apply at all because Foster was not "subject to cross-examination" about his previous statement; although he was testifying in the courtroom as a witness, his memory was so impaired that counsel could not effectively cross-examine him.

Analysis: The Supreme Court upheld introduction of Foster's pretrial statement as a prior identification under Rule 801(d)(1)(C). The Court concluded that the "natural reading" of Rule 801(d)(1)'s cross-examination requirement was that the witness is "placed on the stand, under oath, and responds willingly to questions." Foster satisfied all of those criteria. The fact that he no longer remembered seeing his attacker and had forgotten other aspects of the intervening months did not make him unavailable for cross-examination. On the contrary, an essential purpose of cross-examination is to reveal defects in the witness's memory. Owens's counsel had ample opportunity to show through cross-examination the gaps in Foster's memory and the potential unreliability of his prior identification. Rule 801(d)(1)'s reference to cross-examination does not require more than that.[4]

Courts have reached the same result when a witness's memory failure appears feigned rather than physiological:

---

4   United States v. Owens, 484 U.S. 554, 561–64 (1988). In a separate part of the opinion, the Court held that Foster's loss of memory did not violate Owens's Sixth Amendment right to confront the witnesses against him. We will consider Sixth Amendment issues at greater length in Chapters 54 and 58.

Example: Darres Park, a federal inmate, participated in a scheme to smuggle amphetamines into the prison. Paul Long, another inmate, provided some information about the scheme to investigators and repeated that information to a grand jury. At Park's trial, however, Long claimed that he could not remember anything except his own name. He testified that he could not remember any information about Park or even that he had appeared before the grand jury. The prosecutor then moved to introduce Long's grand jury testimony under Rule 801(d)(1)(A) as a prior inconsistent statement made under oath in a proceeding.

Analysis: The trial judge admitted Long's grand jury statement, and the court of appeals affirmed. In addition to satisfying the other requirements of Rule 801(d)(1)(A), the court readily concluded that Long was "subject to cross-examination." Indeed, Long's behavior made him a particularly easy witness for defense counsel to discredit through cross. By making such extravagant claims of memory loss under oath in the courtroom, Long demonstrated that he was "a blatant liar—someone whose oath meant nothing to him. . . . That enabled counsel to ask the jury how reliable Long's out-of-court statement could be, given that Long was willing to lie to the jurors' faces."[5]

Notice that the reasoning in this example, involving witness Long, is somewhat at odds with the Supreme Court's decision in Owens. In Owens, the Court stressed that the witness "respond[ed] willingly to questions." Just the opposite was true with witness Long: By claiming that he couldn't remember anything but his own name, he appeared remarkably **unwilling** to respond to questions. Yet courts consistently follow the reasoning in the Long example, finding that witnesses who seem to be feigning lack of memory are "subject to cross-examination."

The key lies in distinguishing witnesses with real memory loss from those who pretend. In the latter case, as the court noted in the Long example, there is little difficulty concluding that the witness is subject to cross-examination. Indeed, a skilled attorney can destroy the credibility of a witness who feigns memory loss. The witness's refusal to respond willingly to questions does not prevent cross-examination of these witnesses.

Cases involving real memory loss are more challenging; effective cross-examination is difficult with a witness who cannot remember the incident, the identification,

---

5   United States v. Keeter, 130 F.3d 297, 301–02 (7th Cir. 1997).

or both. But the Supreme Court's decision in Owens establishes that, for these witnesses, appearance on the stand, taking an oath, and a willingness to answer questions are sufficient to satisfy the cross-examination requirement of Rule 801(d)(1).

A final area in which the cross-examination requirement raises questions involves witnesses who refuse to answer on the grounds of privilege. Here, the "willingness to respond" criterion plays a key role. Because of their refusal to answer, courts have found that these witnesses are **not** "subject to cross-examination." This is true even if the privilege claim is invalid because the government has granted immunity.[6]

Example: The United States prosecuted Anjel Torrez-Ortega for distribution of marijuana and cocaine. Armondo Valdez-Arieta had provided details of Torrez-Ortega's guilt to a grand jury. At trial, however, Valdez-Arieta asserted his Fifth Amendment privilege against self-incrimination and refused to answer questions. He continued to claim the privilege even after the government granted him immunity. The trial judge then allowed the prosecutor to introduce Valdez-Arieta's grand jury testimony.

Analysis: The court of appeals held that introduction of this prior testimony was erroneous. Quoting the Supreme Court's language in Owens, the court held that Valdez-Arieta's blanket assertion of privilege meant that he was not "subject to cross-examination." A witness's assertion of memory loss, the court noted, does not preclude cross-examination because it reveals one of the very aspects that cross-examination often seeks: that the witness's recollection, whenever expressed, is unreliable. An assertion of privilege has a very different effect; it may lead the jury to accept unquestioningly the witness's prior statement, without permitting any effective cross-examination. Rule 801(d)(1) does not allow the government to introduce a prior statement under these circumstances.[7]

---

6   We will see in Chapter 68 that the government can defeat the Fifth Amendment privilege against self-incrimination by offering a witness immunity from prosecution.

7   United States v. Torrez-Ortega, 184 F.3d 1128, 1132–35 (10th Cir. 1999).

These decisions suggest the current interpretation of "subject to cross-examination" in the federal courts: Witnesses who take the stand and claim lack of memory (whether real or feigned) are still subject to cross-examination, while those who completely refuse to testify by invoking the privilege against self-incrimination are not. A witness who invokes the Fifth Amendment more selectively might still be deemed subject to cross-examination.

 This entire question, however, remains somewhat volatile. The rationales supporting these results differ, and the Supreme Court recently has offered new interpretations of the defendant's Sixth Amendment right to confront witnesses, which we discuss in Chapter 58. Although those decisions do not explicitly address the susceptibility of a witness to cross-examination under Rule 801(d)(1), they may hold implications for this area. Keep your eyes open for possible developments in this area of law.

2. When Is a Statement "Inconsistent?" After passing 801(d)(1)'s "subject to cross-examination" hurdle, a party seeking to introduce a witness's prior statement must determine whether the statement is consistent, inconsistent, or an identification. What distinguishes consistent from inconsistent statements? Often the inconsistency is straightforward. Witnesses who initially cooperate with the government, for example, sometimes alter their testimony dramatically on the stand. In these cases, the prosecutor has no difficulty persuading the judge that the prior statement is inconsistent:

> **Example:** Leonard Comforth, a truck driver, was murdered while sleeping in his parked truck. Travis Friend confessed to shooting Comforth and made several sworn statements in which he implicated James Scruggs in the murder. The government prosecuted Scruggs and called Friend as a prosecution witness. Friend surprised the government by testifying at the Scruggs trial that he had no knowledge of Comforth's murder. The prosecutor then moved to introduce evidence of Friend's prior statements.

> **Analysis:** The court admitted Friend's prior statements under Rule 801(d)(1)(A). The prior statements flatly contradicted Friend's courtroom testimony and satisfied the other prerequisites for admission under the rule (discussed further below). Since Friend's prior statements were admissible under an

exemption from the hearsay rule, the jury could use the statements for the "truth of the matter" asserted by Friend. In other words, the jurors could rely upon Friend's prior sworn statements to conclude that Scruggs participated in the murder.[8]

More difficult issues arise when a witness offers evasive answers in court or testifies that she can no longer remember the underlying events. Government informants and cooperating witnesses have a particularly high rate of memory failure in the courtroom. Many courts, therefore, have confronted the question whether an evasive answer or claim of memory failure is "inconsistent" with a prior statement that gave detailed information about an event. Most courts have answered the question this way:

Example: The government charged John Milton, a staff attorney for the Equal Employment Opportunity Commission (EEOC), with stealing money from the United States. Milton had negotiated a settlement agreement on behalf of the EEOC with CW Transport, a company charged with employment discrimination. As part of the settlement, CW Transport deposited $1 million in an account that Milton managed for the EEOC. Money from the account was available to compensate minority job applicants who had been refused employment with CW Transport. The government claimed that Milton persuaded several acquaintances to submit false claims on this account and share the proceeds with him.

Anita Jones, one of Milton's acquaintances, testified to a grand jury that Milton helped her submit a fraudulent claim, that she received $5,913.07 from the EEOC account, that she gave Milton those funds, and that Milton gave her $1,100 in return. At trial, however, Jones claimed that she could remember almost nothing about her dealings with Milton or her testimony to the grand jury. The prosecutor moved to introduce Jones's grand jury testimony under Rule 801(d)(1)(A), but Milton objected that Jones's lack of memory was not "inconsistent" with her prior statement.

---

8   United States v. Scruggs, 356 F.3d 539, 547 n.4 (4th Cir. 2004).

Analysis: The trial court admitted Jones's testimony, finding that her lack of memory was "inconsistent" with her prior, detailed statement. The court of appeals agreed. The appellate court noted that Jones's current lack of memory did not impair defense counsel's ability to discredit her grand jury testimony. A witness who gives a detailed statement at one time and claims failed memory at another may appear inherently unreliable to the jury.

In addition, Jones stated on cross-examination that she was addicted to drugs when she appeared before the grand jury, was suffering from withdrawal, and was on the verge of a nervous breakdown. Thus, even though Jones claimed that she couldn't remember the content of her grand jury testimony, the jury received ample evidence from her demeanor and testimony about the context of the grand jury statement to assess the credibility of both that prior statement and her courtroom claims of failed memory.[9]

When a witness appears to be **feigning memory loss**, most courts agree with the disposition in Milton: The prior detailed statement is "inconsistent" with the current claims of lost memory. If the other requirements of 801(d)(1)(A) are satisfied, the prior statement is admissible under that hearsay exemption.

But what if the witness's memory lapse seems real? One court of appeals has suggested in dictum that a real memory loss is consistent with prior, more detailed statements, so the prior statements would not be admissible under Rule 801(d)(1)(A).[10] But this suggestion has not attracted a following.[11] Most courts treat memory loss, real or feigned, as inconsistent with a witness's prior detailed statements, paving the way for counsel to introduce those statements.

3. Proceeding. A witness's prior inconsistent statement is admissible only if it was made "under penalty of perjury" and at a "proceeding." These are two separate requirements. People make a surprising number of statements under penalty of perjury; tax returns, for example, satisfy that requirement. But Rule 801(d)(1)(A) requires more: The sworn statement must occur during a deposition, trial, hearing, or "other proceeding."

---

9   United States v. Milton, 8 F.3d 39, 46–47 (D.C. Cir. 1993). The criminal activity in *Milton* included John Milton's brother James. For simplicity in discussing the Rule 801(d)(1) issue, we have collapsed the two Miltons into one person.

10   United States v. Palumbo, 639 F.2d 123, 128 n.6 (3d Cir. 1981).

11   See, e.g., United States v. Gajo, 290 F.3d 922, 931 (7th Cir. 2002).

Statements from any trial, deposition, or courtroom hearing readily satisfy this requirement. But what other gatherings qualify as an "other proceeding"? Courts have held that grand jury hearings satisfy this requirement. If a witness tells one story to the grand jury and a different tale at trial, a litigant may introduce the inconsistent grand jury statement. Interrogations conducted by police and other investigators, on the other hand, are not proceedings. Even if a witness makes a formal statement under oath to the police, that statement is not admissible under Rule 801(d)(1)(A).

Courts have not articulated comprehensive criteria to distinguish these situations, but the combination of an audience and a transcript seem to mark a "proceeding." An audience, such as the grand jurors, enhances reliability by guarding against coercive interrogation techniques. Generation of a transcript increases reliability in a different way, by providing an accurate record of the witness's words.

4. Consistency, Credibility, and Rehabilitation. Prior consistent statements are admissible regardless of the context in which the witness made them: A witness's casual out-of-court comment to a friend may be admissible under Rule 801(d)(1)(B) if it is consistent with the witness's testimony in the courtroom. The statement need not have been made under oath or in a proceeding.

But Rule 801(d)(1)(B) imposes different restrictions on admission of a witness's prior consistent statement. These statements are admissible only if (1) the witness's credibility has been attacked, and (2) the prior consistent statement helps rehabilitate that credibility. These two requirements assure that the prior consistent statement adds value to the trial: Absent these circumstances, the prior statement would simply duplicate courtroom testimony.

Example: Jay Atwood sued Debt Collectors Inc. (DCI) under the Fair Debt Collection Practices Act. Among other practices, that statute prohibits debt collectors from using obscene language when they contact debtors. At trial, Atwood described several phone calls in which DCI employees peppered him with obscenities. On cross-examination, DCI's attorney questioned Atwood aggressively about his memory of those calls; her questions suggested that Atwood could not correctly recall the words used in calls placed three years earlier. In rebuttal, Atwood's attorney offered testimony from Jay's sister Lena. Lena testified that, shortly after each of the calls, Jay complained to her about the offensive words used by

DCI employees. The words he reported at the time of the calls matched the ones he testified to in court.

> **Analysis:** As you learned in Chapter 18, Lena's testimony is admissible to rehabilitate Jay's testimony. Her description of Jay's complaints bolsters his credibility by rebutting the cross-examiner's suggestion that Jay could not accurately remember the words by the time of trial. Now we can see that under Rule 801(d)(1)(B), Lena's testimony is also admissible for the truth of the matter asserted (to prove that Jay heard obscenities from DCI employees).

Remember that Rule 801(d)(1)(B) only applies if a party can demonstrate that the prior consistent statement actually helps rehabilitate the witness's credibility. Some prior statements, although consistent with the witness's courtroom testimony, do not effectively rebut the opponent's attack on credibility. For example, if Jay only told Lena about the calls the week before trial, Lena's testimony would not effectively rebut DCI's implication that Jay couldn't accurately remember those calls. Jay's memory at trial would be no stronger than his memory a week before trial, so the court would not admit his out-of-court statements for the truth of the matter asserted. Nor would the court be likely to admit those statements to bolster credibility—although judges have more discretion when admitting statements for that limited purpose.

Finally, note that Rule 801(d)(1)(B)(i) covers a specific type of rehabilitation: when the prior consistent statements are offered to disprove an allegation that the witness is lying. The timing of the prior consistent statements is especially important for this type of rehabilitation: the Supreme Court has held that the witness *must* have made the statements before the motive to lie or improper influence arose.

> **Example:** Matthew Tome and his ex-wife shared custody of their young daughter. The ex-wife alleged that Tome sexually assaulted the daughter when she was in his care. Police arrested Tome and charged him with sexual abuse of a child.
>
> In 1992, when she was six-and-a-half years old, the daughter testified at Tome's trial. The daughter's testimony was weak and halting; the prosecutor had to lead her through most of the story.

Tome claimed that his ex-wife had persuaded the daughter to fabricate the abuse. The two parents had bitterly disputed custody of their daughter; Tome argued that his ex-wife and daughter concocted the abuse allegations so that the wife could obtain sole custody.

To rebut the fabrication charge, the prosecutor called six witnesses who related statements that the daughter had made in 1990 describing Tome's abuse. The witnesses included the mother, a babysitter, a social worker, and several doctors. Tome objected to all of their testimony as hearsay.

Analysis: If the daughter fabricated the abuse to stay in her mother's custody, when did that motive arise? Families rarely keep records of their internal discussions, especially if the discussion involves pressuring a young child to lie about her father. But the mother in this case had petitioned the courts for sole custody in 1989, and the parents had bitterly disputed custody since that time. The judge didn't know if the mother and child had fabricated the abuse allegations; that was the very issue before the jury. But the motive to fabricate the allegations clearly existed as early as 1989. The statements made in 1990, therefore, arose after the motive to fabricate and were not admissible under Rule 801(d)(1)(B).[12]

In other cases, a court might determine the timing of a motive to lie through a witness's testimony, the content of the statements themselves, or other circumstantial evidence.

5. Out-of-Court Identifications. As explained above, identifications are an unusual type of statement: Early, out-of-court identifications often are more reliable than later, in-court ones. For that reason, Rule 801(d)(1)(C) admits any identification as long as the declarant is a witness and subject to cross-examination. This provision is most frequently used in criminal cases where the identity of the perpetrator is a disputed issue: The prosecutor will ask the witness to identify the individual in court and then elicit testimony about the witness's earlier identification to bolster the in-court identification.

However, the witness's prior identification is admissible even if the declarant cannot repeat the identification in court:

---

12   513 U.S. 150 (1995).

Example: An armed robber stole more than $600,000 from a New York City bank branch. One of the tellers, Patrick Crowl, identified Michael Anglin as the robber from a photo array held shortly after the crime. Crowl indicated that he was "very certain" Anglin was the robber, that the robber had stood directly in front of Crowl "putting the machine gun in [Crowl's] face for about 15 seconds or more," and that his recollection of the robber's face was "still fresh." Based on this and other evidence, the government prosecuted Anglin for the robbery.

At trial, Crowl could not identify Anglin as the armed robber. The court nonetheless allowed him to testify about his previous identification of Anglin from the photo array.

Analysis: The trial judge properly admitted Crowl's testimony about his prior identification of Anglin. Rule 801(d)(1)(C) allows such testimony regardless of whether the witness is able to repeat the identification in court. The jury was able to weigh the credibility of Crowl's identification, given his inability to repeat that identification, the circumstances of the prior identification, and other facts elicited on cross-examination.[13]

The declarant can testify about the identification, as Crowl did. But another person who witnessed the identification can also testify about that identification. The police officer who conducted the photo array, for example, could testify that Crowl picked Anglin from the array. The only requirement is that the person who made the identification (in this case Crowl) appear as a witness and be subject to cross-examination.[14]

---

13   United States v. Anglin, 169 F.3d 154, 157 (2d Cir. 1999).

14   Defendants and other parties sometimes challenge the fairness of the prior identification process. A defendant, for example, may claim that he differed markedly in appearance from other individuals in a line-up. Rule 801(d)(1)(C) does not preclude these arguments, but they operate separately from the rule. Challenges to the fairness of an identification procedure rest on constitutional and statutory grounds, rather than on the Rules of Evidence.

D. Rule 801(d)(1) and Rule 613. This is not the first time we have discussed use of a witness's prior statements; in Chapter 18, we examined the use of a witness's prior statements under **Rule 613**. How does the introduction of prior statements under Rule 613 differ from use of those statements under Rule 801(d)(1)?

The two rules allow introduction of prior statements for very different purposes. Rule 613 governs use of a witness's prior inconsistent statements to impeach the witness's credibility. Under some circumstances, parties also use that rule to introduce prior consistent statements rehabilitating a witness's credibility.[15] Parties who offer prior statements under Rule 613, therefore, do not offer them for the content of those statements. Instead, they introduce this evidence to illuminate the witness's credibility. If the statement conflicts with the witness's courtroom testimony, it casts doubt on the witness's ability to remember or tell the truth. And if the statement is consistent with the courtroom testimony, it bolsters the witness's credibility.

Statements introduced under Rule 613, in other words, are not offered "to prove the truth of the matter asserted." That is how these statements escape the hearsay prohibition, even though they clearly are out-of-court declarations. As noted in Chapter 18, all statements admitted under Rule 613 are subject to a limiting instruction by the judge directing the jury to only consider the statements as they relate to the witness's credibility and not for the truth of their contents.

Prior statements admitted under Rule 801(d)(1), conversely, are offered for their **content**. Parties introduce these statements because they want to give the jury the information contained in them. Out-of-court statements offered for this purpose are hearsay unless they fit within the bounds of 801(d)(1) or some other hearsay exception.

Given these different purposes, Rules 613 and 801(d)(1) impose different conditions on the introduction of a witness's prior statement. Rule 613 allows a party to offer evidence of any prior inconsistent statement, even a casual comment to a friend, as long as the inconsistency relates to a fact of consequence in the litigation. Because the party offers the statement for a limited purpose, to impeach the

---

15   As noted in Chapter 18, the introduction of prior statements to impeach or rehabilitate a witness's credibility really rests on Rules 401–403, the rules governing relevance and prejudice. Rule 613 simply outlines procedural requirements for using this evidence. But lawyers usually refer to introducing this evidence "under Rule 613," so we use the same phrase.

witness's credibility, reliability of the prior statement has little importance. The inconsistency itself, whatever its cause, is significant.

Under Rule 801(d)(1), on the other hand, a party offers a prior inconsistent statement for its substance. Under these circumstances, reliability is essential and the rule imposes strict requirements: The prior statement must have been made under penalty of perjury and at a proceeding.

Here, in sum, is how the two rules compare when a party offers a prior **inconsistent** statement:

Rule 613	Rule 801(d)(1)(A)
Any prior inconsistent statement related to a fact of consequence is admissible	Prior inconsistent statement must have been made under penalty of perjury and at a trial, hearing, other proceeding, or deposition
Statement is admissible only to impeach the witness's credibility	Party may rely upon the statement to prove the truth of the matters asserted
Judge will instruct the jury to use the prior statement only to assess credibility	No limiting instruction

For prior **consistent** statements, Rules 613 and 801(d)(1) merge in their requirements. Whether offered to rehabilitate a witness under Rule 613 or to prove the truth of the matter asserted under Rule 801(d)(1)(B), the prior consistent statement may take any form. Parties may only offer these statements, however, if the witness's credibility has been attacked and the prior statement will aid rehabilitation. The latter requirement often focuses on the timing of the prior statement. Indeed, if the statement fits within subsection 801(d)(1)(B)(i), then the prior consistent statement **must** have occurred before the motive to lie or improper influence arose.

Rules 613 and 801(d)(1)(B) converge in the case of prior consistent statements because it is impossible to separate the statement's content from its power to rehabilitate the witness. Since the statement is consistent with the witness's courtroom testimony, the content is already before the jury. The prior statement both reinforces that content and rebuts the attack on the witness's credibility.

Quick Summary

Out-of-court statements made by witnesses are hearsay when offered for the truth of the matter asserted; the witness's presence at trial does not negate the hearsay character of these prior statements. The witness's courtroom presence and availability for cross-examination, however, make these statements somewhat more reliable than other forms of hearsay. Rule 801(d)(1), therefore, exempts some prior statements by witnesses from the hearsay ban. The table on the next page summarizes the requirements for admitting a witness's prior statements under Rule 801(d)(1)'s three routes.

Test Your Understanding

To assess your understanding of the material in this chapter, click here to take a quiz, or go to the Quizzes module from the eBook on your eProducts bookshelf.

Admitting Prior Statements Under Rule 801(d)(1)

Prior statement must have been made by a witness at the current proceeding

Witness must be subject to cross-examination

- Witnesses with real or feigned memory loss are "subject to cross"
- Witnesses who assert a blanket privilege are **not** "subject to cross"
- Witnesses who claim privilege selectively may be "subject to cross"

Prior Inconsistent Statement: 801(d)(1)(A)	Prior Consistent Statement: 801(d)(1)(B)	Identification: 801(d)(1)(C)
• Memory failure constitutes inconsistency • Statement must have been given under penalty of perjury at a hearing, deposition, or other proceeding • Grand jury hearings count as proceedings; police interrogations do not	• Witness's credibility must be attacked • Statement must be probative for rehabilitation • If offered under 801(d)(1)(B)(i), prior statement *must* have been made before the motive to fabricate or improper influence began	• Must be an identification of a person

Statements are admitted for the truth of the matter asserted, not merely to impeach a witness

40

Hearsay Exceptions—Present Sense Impressions and Excited Utterances

---

Key Concepts

- **Rule 803(1):** Hearsay Statement Is Admissible if Declarant Makes the Statement While Perceiving the Event

- **Rule 803(2):** Hearsay Statement Is Admissible if Declarant Makes the Statement While Excited by the Event

- Both Exceptions Assume that Declarant Is Less Likely to Lie Under Certain Conditions

---

A. Introduction and Policy. In this chapter we turn to **Rule 803**, which collects twenty-three different exceptions to the hearsay rule. Those exceptions share a common characteristic: A litigant may invoke them even if the declarant is available to testify. Rule 804, in contrast, contains exceptions that apply only if the declarant is no longer available to testify.

Rule 803's first two exceptions are colorful ones. Rule 803(1) excepts "present sense impressions" from the hearsay ban, while 803(2) governs "excited utterances."

Present sense impressions are statements that describe an event as it unfolds. Sportscasters specialize in these statements: Whatever the sport, most of them note the athletes' movements as they occur. Generations of baseball fans have heard monologues like: "He's stepping up to the base, tapping his bat on the plate, and getting in position. The pitcher is winding up, and now here comes the pitch. . . ."

Excited utterances come from excited people responding to a startling event. These statements are as familiar to us as sports broadcasts. Common excited utterances are: "Touchdown!" "Watch out for the car!" and "Ouch!"

Present sense impressions and excited utterances arise frequently in litigation. When a crime or accident occurs, the victim and eyewitnesses make numerous statements about the event. Someone may call 911 to report the trauma, others may exclaim to one another about what they see. Victims and bystanders also talk about the incident to police, rescuers, and family members. Parties often offer these statements in court as present sense impressions or excited utterances. Witnesses who did not perceive the event may testify about what the victims and bystanders said: "She shouted that a man in a red shirt was pulling out a gun." "I heard him cry that the stairway was collapsing and crushing a young girl."

The Rules of Evidence permit parties to introduce present sense impressions and excited utterances because these statements have special indicia of reliability; as a class, each type of statement is more reliable than the usual out-of-court statement.[1] A person who describes an event as it unfolds before her lacks time to formulate a lie; the words match the events one by one. A present sense impression, therefore, is likely to offer the speaker's accurate report of what he saw.

Similarly, a person responding to a startling event has little opportunity to concoct falsehoods. In the words of the Advisory Committee, the "condition of excitement . . . temporarily stills the capacity for reflection and produces utterances free of conscious fabrication."[2]

Although present sense impressions and excited utterances carry these indicia of reliability, we know from everyday experience that these statements are not always reliable. A wrongdoer confronted with evidence of her guilt may be startled, but immediately protest "It wasn't me!" Under at least some circumstances, stress generates spontaneous reactions that are false rather than true. But the rationale behind hearsay exceptions does not assume that certain kinds of statements are always reliable, only that they are more reliable than most other hearsay statements, so that on balance it is better for the jurors to hear the statements than not to hear them. The jurors are free to reject the information if the circumstances persuade them that the declarant was lying or mistaken.

B. The Rule. Rule 803 opens with an introductory clause stating that all of its exceptions apply regardless of the declarant's availability. This provision, as noted above, relieves parties from proving that the declarant is unavailable. The rule

---

1   Remember that in Chapter 38 we discussed two rationales for hearsay exceptions: reliability and necessity. Present sense impressions and excited utterances rest particularly on the reliability rationale.

2   Fed. R. Evid. 803(2) advisory committee's note.

then articulates the straightforward exceptions for present sense impressions and excited utterances.

> ## RULE 803. Exceptions to the Rule Against Hearsay—Regardless of Whether the Declarant Is Available as a Witness
>
> The following are not excluded by the rule against hearsay, regardless of whether the declarant is available as a witness:
>
> (1) **Present Sense Impression.** A statement <u>describing or explaining</u> an event or condition, made <u>while or immediately after</u> the declarant <u>perceived</u> it.
>
> (2) **Excited Utterance.** A statement <u>relating to</u> a <u>startling</u> event or condition, made while the declarant was <u>under the stress of excitement</u> that it caused.

Rule 803(1) imposes two conditions that define present sense impressions. **First,** the exception applies only to descriptions or explanations of an event, not to more complex analyses or interpretations. The latter statements involve more complex mental processes that, because they incorporate reflection, also allow time for deception.

Second, for a statement to qualify as a present sense impression, the declarant must make it while perceiving the event or "immediately after" the event. We will explore the latter language further in the Courtroom section, but it usually provides no more than a few seconds of leeway. The time lapse must be short enough that the speaker has no time to create a lie.

Rule 803(2) contains a different set of prerequisites. **First,** the declarant must speak while excited by a startling event. The standard is subjective rather than objective: The particular declarant must have been excited by the event. The circumstances that support admission of an excited utterance, therefore, vary widely. Some people suffer extensive shock after witnessing a highway accident or homicide. Others, particularly professionals who respond to these incidents, are more controlled. The subjectivity of this standard relates to the rule's underlying rationale: The excitement must be great enough that the particular declarant would have had difficulty formulating a lie while speaking.

Second, an excited utterance must "relat[e] to" the startling event. This condition is easier to satisfy than Rule 803(1)'s requirement that the statement describe or explain an event. An excited utterance may move beyond description by analyzing or interpreting the event. But the utterance still must relate to the provoking event. Unrelated comments are not admissible under this exception, even if the declarant makes them while still excited. We will explore all of these requirements more fully in the next section. Meanwhile, note that some statements fall within both 803(1) and 803(2), some fall in just one category, and some—although occurring close in time to a startling event—fall in neither. Consider this example:

Example: Roger was juggling knives in the kitchen while his three young children played at his feet. His wife, Samantha, was on the phone in the same room talking to her sister Louise. Samantha, while eyeing her husband's antics, said to her sister, "Yes, he's practicing his juggling right now, using my best set of kitchen knives." Just at that moment, Roger dropped one of the knives on his four-year-old son Todd. Todd screamed, "Owwww, Daddy cut me!" Samantha shouted, "I warned you not to throw knives in the air with all those kids around!" And Todd's sister Megan yawned and commented, "Here we go again, Todd cries every day about something." Assume Louise overheard all of these statements and is called to testify about what she heard. Which of these statements would be admissible for the truth of the matter asserted?

Analysis: Samantha's initial comment to her sister is a present sense impression; she is describing Roger's actions as they occur. But she does not seem particularly excited by Roger's juggling practice, so the comment is not an excited utterance.

Todd's outcry is both an excited utterance and a present sense impression: He is describing the cut as it occurs and is responding to it in an excited way.

Samantha's second comment is an excited utterance; she is reacting in an excited way to the startling event of Roger dropping a knife on their son. But this is not a present sense impression because Samantha is referring to a previous action (warning Roger) and editorializing on the present scene.

Megan's comment, finally, is neither a present sense impression nor an excited utterance. She is analyzing the present moment in the context of Todd's ongoing behavior, so this comment goes beyond mere description. Nor does she seem particularly startled or excited by the injury to her brother. For her, it's just another day at home.

C. In the Courtroom. In this section, we'll first explore the prerequisites that parties must satisfy to introduce statements under 803(1) or 803(2). We'll then examine the question of how parties establish these foundational facts and who—judge or jury—decides if they have been met.

1. Description or Analysis? A present sense impression must describe or explain, rather than analyze, a contemporaneous event. Analysis invokes more complex mental processes that may provide an opportunity for deception; 803(1) excludes that type of observation. Here is a case that helps illustrate the distinction:

> **Example:** Cargill, a company that grows and processes "Honeysuckle White" turkeys, received consumer reports that some its turkeys had spoiled. To investigate the spoilage, Cargill sent Everett Fine to check the turkeys at several stores supplied by Cargill. Fine examined the turkeys at these stores and made contemporaneous notes of the production codes on the labels of any spoiled turkeys. Cargill ultimately determined that Boag Cold Storage, a warehouse that stored the turkeys before distribution, had allowed a batch of turkeys to thaw and spoil. In a lawsuit against Boag for damages, Cargill attempted to introduce Fine's notes to establish the distribution chain for the spoiled turkeys. Boag objected to the notes as hearsay.

> **Analysis:** Fine's notes were hearsay, but they fell within Rule 803(1)'s exception for present sense impressions. Fine recorded the production codes of the turkeys as he examined them in the store display cases. This contemporaneous recording of the notes described simply what Fine saw at the time he saw it.[3]

It is easy to imagine Fine including more than a simple list of production codes in his field notes. He might, for example, have jotted down his thoughts about why the turkeys had spoiled. A batch of spoiled turkeys with consecutive production codes might have prompted him to write: "Warehouse thaw? Check shipping dates & destinations." This type of comment is not admissible as a present sense impression. A judge would redact statements like this unless the proponent could find another hearsay exception supporting admission.

---

3   Cargill, Inc. v. Boag Cold Storage Warehouse, 71 F.3d 545, 554–55 (6th Cir. 1995).

The line between description and analysis can be blurry; it depends on the declarant's words and the context. To distinguish these two categories, think about the policy motivating that exception. Statements of present sense impression should stick closely to the unfolding facts; the absence of analysis suggests that the speaker is not engaging the mental processes that might support deception. Critical commentary, analysis, and other more complex observations all imply a degree of mental engagement that could include deception.

2. "Immediately After." The second prerequisite for statements admitted under Rule 803(1) is immediacy. The fact that these descriptions occur as an event unfolds enhances their reliability; the declarant has little time to reflect or fabricate.

Most present sense impressions occur contemporaneously with the events they describe. But Rule 803(1) grants a small amount of flexibility in timing: Descriptions made "immediately" after an event may also be admissible.

This window is always small: usually only a few seconds, and never more than a few minutes. Courts, however, seem to tie the permissible amount of time to what the declarant was doing during those intervening minutes or seconds. If the declarant spent that time searching for a way to communicate information to others, a judge is more likely to admit the statement as occurring "immediately" after an event.

This makes some psychological sense. A bystander who spends a few minutes searching for a pen to record a license plate number, or for a phone to notify police about an accident, may stay focused on the task of remembering the critical information. The event may stay fresh in the bystander's mind, and the effort to remember the event while finding a communication tool may keep the bystander too busy to fabricate. The jurors, moreover, can judge how the brief elapsed time might have affected the bystander's memory of details.

Here is a case in which the court stretched "immediately after" to eight minutes in order to accommodate an eyewitness's search for a phone. This seems near the upper limit of what courts will accept as a time gap under Rule 803(1):

Example: David Miller was helping a stranded motorist on the shoulder of Interstate 95 when a trailer truck sideswiped them and their vehicles. The truck killed the stranded motorist and injured Miller. The truck driver did not stop, and Miller did not see the truck that hit him. County police, however, received an anonymous 911 call about eight minutes after the accident. The caller said: "Good afternoon, I'm on Highway 95 South and I was in quite a bit of heavy traffic, when we noticed a truck which was pulling a trailer, but I couldn't get a license number because of the trailer and the heavy traffic, but it said 'Crown Amusements' on the side of the truck and as he went by a broken down truck . . . he sideswiped and hit one of the young men. He made no attempt to stop. This was in the area of mile marker 99 or 98, perhaps between the two. Ah, this is my first opportunity to reach a phone."

Miller sued the Crown Amusements Company for his injuries and moved to admit the recorded 911 statement to support his claim that the company's driver caused his injuries. Crown Amusements objected to the recording as hearsay.

Analysis: The trial judge noted that the 911 call came from a gas station located at the highway exit closest to the accident scene. The timing of the call fit perfectly with a driver witnessing the accident and driving immediately to the nearest exit to make a call. No closer rest stops or call boxes existed on that stretch of Interstate 95, and this accident occurred before cell phones became common. Finding that the content of the statement showed the caller's direct perception of the event and that the eight-minute gap stemmed entirely from the speaker's focused search for a phone, the court admitted the statement as a present sense impression.[4]

 Without the caller's search for a phone, the court would have rejected this eight-minute gap as too long to accommodate a present sense impression. Even with the search, the rationale in cases like this rests on somewhat shaky grounds. Some eyewitnesses may concentrate on remembering the details of an event while they locate a means of communication, but others could use that interval to modify their account. Depending on local precedent, a persuasive attorney might persuade the trial judge to reject delayed reports of present sense impressions like the one in Miller.

3. Startling Events and Excited Declarants. Why wasn't the 911 call in the previous example an excited utterance? Many motorists, after seeing a large truck

---

4   Miller v. Crown Amusements, Inc., 821 F. Supp. 703 (S.D. Ga. 1993).

hit a person standing on the side of the road, would be distressed and excited. Even after eight minutes, they most likely would convey a sense of panic, urgency, and distress.

The 911 caller who aided Miller, however, was not particularly excited. She spoke calmly and related the details she had seen. She concluded the call by checking with the dispatcher to make sure he had all of the necessary information and thanking him for his assistance. She spoke as a concerned citizen doing her civic duty, not as someone making an excited utterance.

To gain admission under Rule 803(2), the declarant must make a statement with genuine excitement or stress. The reliability of these statements rests on the spontaneity prompted by startling events and the difficulty most people would have lying while responding to them. It is not enough, therefore, that an event would have excited a reasonable person; the declarant must have been subjectively excited while making the statement.

Conversely, some events are startling to particular people under specific circumstances. Statements made under those circumstances may be admissible under Rule 803(2), even though most individuals would have found the occurrence routine:

> **Example:** Lois Marren, a secretary for the Metropolitan Sanitary District, suspected one of the District's purchasing agents, Thomas Moore, of rigging bids. Marren regularly searched Moore's office looking for evidence to support her suspicions. One day Marren called her colleague, Irene Marszalek, into Moore's office after Moore had left for the day. According to Marszalek, Marren was "just like jumping up and down" and talking "as if she had won a million dollars in a lottery." Marren told Marszalek, "I've found the evidence I've been waiting for for a long time." Marren had found some extra bid sheets, which demonstrated Moore's illegal behavior, in his wastebasket.
>
> The government prosecuted Moore for fraud, but Marren died before trial. To establish the connection between Moore and the incriminating bid sheets, the prosecutor called Marszalek to testify about Marren's statement. Moore objected to this testimony as hearsay.

Analysis: Searching a wastebasket rarely leads to excitement, but in this case it did. The trial court properly admitted Marren's statement as an excited utterance. The court of appeals affirmed this ruling, rejecting Moore's claim that Marren could not have been excited because she had been searching for evidence of Moore's wrongdoing for a long time. Although Marren had been looking for evidence of this nature, the successful conclusion of a search can still be exciting. "This is like panning for gold," the court concluded. "Discovery may to one degree or another be expected; but it is always exciting."[5]

4. "Relating to" the Event. Marren's statement in the previous example, that she had "found the evidence" she had been "waiting for for a long time," would not have been admissible as a present sense impression. Marren's words did not describe the scene before her, as the words "oh, here are some bid sheets in the wastebasket" might have done. Instead, Marren interpreted the significance of what she saw.

The exception for excited utterances, however, admits any statement "relating to" an event. This condition is more generous that Rule 803(1)'s requirement of description or explanation. The excited utterance exception relies upon the declarant's excitement, rather than on her descriptive focus, to enhance reliability.

5. How Long Does Excitement Last? Rule 803(2) does not limit excited utterances to statements that occur during the startling event or "immediately after." Instead, the declarant must speak while still in an excited state. The duration of this excited period depends on the characteristics of the declarant, as well as of the startling event. Criminal attacks, serious accidents, and similar events may generate stress that lasts for thirty minutes or longer:

Example: Xavier Giles was standing on a sidewalk near Earl Edwards. Giles watched as a van pulled up near Edwards, three men exited the van, and the men began speaking to Edwards. One of the men pulled out a gun and shot Edwards, killing him. Giles started to flee, and the gunman shot Giles in the hip. Giles continued to run until he collapsed a few blocks from the scene. An ambulance took Giles to the hospital, where police detective Jeremy Rosenberg interviewed him in the emergency room. When Rosenberg talked to Giles, about 40 minutes had elapsed since the shooting. Giles was lying on a bed in the emergency room, connected to

---

5   United States v. Moore, 791 F.2d 566, 571 (7th Cir. 1986).

both intravenous fluids and medical monitors; he was still bleeding from his gunshot wounds.

The government prosecuted Ricardo Delvi for the shooting and moved for permission to call Rosenberg as a witness. Rosenberg intended to testify about comments Giles made to him in the emergency room; these comments helped link Delvi to the crime.

Analysis: The trial judge admitted Giles's statement as an excited utterance. Although the statement occurred forty minutes after the shooting, Giles had suffered a series of traumatic events: He had witnessed a murder, suffered a serious wound, run several blocks from his assailants, and been transported to an emergency room. At the time he made his statement, he was still bleeding from his wounds and a witness described him as excited. Under these circumstances, Giles was not in a mental state where he was likely to fabricate a statement.[6]

In other cases, a similar amount of time may be enough to eliminate the declarant's excited condition:

Example: John McCrery, a hospital patient, suffered a cardiac arrest while in the hospital. His attending physician, Dr. Lucy Goodenday, resuscitated him, intubated him, and connected him to a respirator. Except for a few moments, McCrery remained conscious during these events. After McCrery stabilized, Goodenday left him to attend other patients. She returned two hours later and, after ascertaining that McCrery appeared calm and had a normal pulse, she asked him whether he had received any medications before the heart attack. McCrery nodded yes and, in response to further questions, indicated that he had received medication intravenously. When Goodenday asked who had given McCrery the medication, he wrote the first name of his nurse, "Pia," on a piece of paper.

---

6   United States v. Delvi, 275 F. Supp. 2d 412 (S.D.N.Y. 2003). The defendant in *Delvi* also objected that Giles had snorted heroin while he was running from his assailant. The district judge, however, found that this did not affect Giles's level of excitement. Giles was a heroin addict; his use of the drug shortly after the shooting was an automatic response to his stress and pain. Many victims of accidents or assaults make statements that count as excited utterances after receiving narcotics for pain. The fact that Giles had administered his own medication, the court concluded, did not affect the nature of his excited utterance.

The government prosecuted Pia Narciso for killing or attempting to kill McCrery and numerous other patients. McCrery died before trial, and the prosecutor attempted to introduce his handwritten note, arguing that it was an excited utterance.

Analysis: The trial judge properly rejected this argument. Although McCrery suffered a very stressful event—a heart attack and resuscitation—he appeared to have recovered from that event by the time Goodenday talked with him two hours later. He appeared calm and his pulse was normal. Under these circumstances, he had sufficient opportunity for reflection and his note did not bear the indicia of reliability that excited utterances convey.[7]

The existence of excitement sufficient to support an excited utterance, like most of the other predicates for admission of statements under 803(1) and (2), depends on the facts of each case. Thoughtful advocacy may sway the decision in close cases.

6. Can Written Statements Be Excited? In the prosecution of nurse Narcisco, described above, the government tried to admit a written statement as an excited utterance. The trial judge precluded that evidence because the hospital patient had calmed down by the time he wrote the note. But there is no absolute bar against admitting written statements as excited utterances. The judge will examine the facts that surround the writing, just as with oral statements.

The fact that a statement was written usually weighs against admission as an excited utterance; the act of writing implies that there was "time and opportunity for reflective thought."8 But other factors may persuade the judge that a declarant was sufficiently excited when she wrote a statement. Indeed, written excited utterances—as well as written present sense impressions—will probably become more common in the age of social media and texting. These media generate many more instances of real-time writing than occurred in the age of handwritten notes and typewritten letters.

---

7   United States v. Narciso, 446 F. Supp. 252 (E.D. Mich. 1977). The *Narciso* case, which included two nurses as defendants, was a notorious prosecution in the 1970s. The FBI investigated deaths at an Ann Arbor hospital when the number of fatalities jumped suspiciously in 1975. Their investigation led to prosecution of two Filipina nurses, Narciso and Leonora Perez. The case against the nurses was circumstantial and tainted by racist comments. A jury convicted Narciso and Perez of poisoning, although not of murder. After lengthy consideration, the trial judge set aside the verdicts and ordered a new trial in the interests of justice. The government then dropped the case.

8   State v. Hansen, 986 P.2d 346, 350 (Idaho Ct. App. 1999).

7. Foundation, Foundation, Foundation. The key to winning admission of an excited utterance or present sense impression is to lay the proper foundation. The judge will decide under Rule 104(a) whether the facts exist to support one of these exceptions.[9] How does a proponent persuade the judge that a statement conveys a present sense impression or constitutes an excited utterance? What types of evidence establish these facts?

Remember that the Rules of Evidence do not apply to preliminary determinations. The proponent, therefore, has considerable leeway in establishing foundation facts. In particular, the proponent may offer the statement itself as evidence that the declarant was excited or reciting a present sense impression. Indeed, the content of the statement alone may be sufficient to establish one of these foundation facts.

To show a present sense impression, proponents also commonly introduce:

- The declarant's in-court testimony, affirming that she made the statement as she perceived the event

- Testimony from other witnesses who can confirm that the declarant made the statement while the event unfolded

Establishing that the declarant was excited is somewhat harder, because excitement is a state of mind. Circumstantial evidence, however, can prove a declarant's state of mind. In addition to the content of the statement, proponents of excited utterances often introduce:

- The declarant's in-court testimony, affirming that he was excited when making the statement

- Testimony from witnesses who perceived the declarant when he made the statement. These witnesses could testify to:

  — The declarant's mannerisms and tone of voice when he made the statement (e.g., he was crying, he was speaking rapidly, he looked upset)

---

9   Refer to Chapter 34 on Preliminary Questions to review this concept.

— The time that elapsed between the provoking incident and the statement

— The declarant's relationship to the provocation (e.g., was she a bystander on the opposite side of the street or was she personally involved in the incident?)

• Evidence about the declarant's age, prior experiences, and other characteristics that might affect how excited the declarant would become in certain situations

• Evidence about how traumatic or exciting the event that provoked the declarant's statement was

Look back at the examples summarized in this chapter and consider what types of evidence the parties might have introduced to support or oppose admission of the hearsay statement in each case.

Quick Summary

Rule 803(1) excepts **present sense impressions** from the rule against hearsay. These impressions (a) must be limited to descriptions or explanation of an unfolding event, and (b) must occur contemporaneously with the event or "immediately after" the event.

Rule 803(2) excepts **excited utterances** from the hearsay ban. Statements are excited utterances if they (a) relate to a startling event, and (b) the declarant spoke while still feeling the stress of that event.

Statements that meet these conditions are admitted for the truth of the matters they assert. The exceptions rest on the assumption that declarants making these types of statements do not have the time or mental capacity to reflect on the situation and formulate a lie about what happened; thus, they are more reliable than other types of hearsay.

The judge determines whether the factual conditions for these exceptions are met. In making close factual calls, such as about the immediacy of a statement, the judge will refer to the policy underlying these exceptions. Statements made under circumstances that suggest little opportunity for fabrication are more likely to meet the factual predicates.

Test Your Understanding

To assess your understanding of the material in this chapter, click here to take a quiz, or go to the Quizzes module from the eBook on your eProducts bookshelf.

41

Hearsay Exception—State of Mind

Key Concepts

- **Rule 803(3):** Hearsay Exception for Statements Expressing the Declarant's Current State of Mind or a Mental or Physical Condition
- References to External Facts
- "I Think," "I Believe," "I Remember"
- Using State of Mind to Prove the Declarant's Previous or Subsequent Conduct
- The Mysterious *Hillmon* Case: Using the Declarant's State of Mind to Prove Another Person's Conduct

---

A. Introduction and Policy. In the last chapter we explored the rationale that supports admission of a hearsay statement conveying a present sense impression: A declarant who describes an event as it unfolds is unlikely to have the time or capacity to lie about the event. But what if the declarant describes an **internal** event rather than an external one? That is, what if the declarant describes her present state of mind? Does the rationale that supports admission of present sense impressions also justify admission of a declarant's expression of a state of mind?

The drafters of the Federal Rules concluded that the contemporaneous expression of an internal state is analogous to the immediate reporting of an external event.[1] Declarants who say "I'm hungry," "I'm so nervous that I'm dripping sweat," or "I plan to fly to Denver tomorrow" are reporting internal states that exist at the

---

1   The Advisory Committee, in fact, referred to Rule 803(3) as merely a "specialized application" of Rule 803(1), "presented separately to enhance its usefulness and accessibility." Fed. R. Evid. 803 advisory committee's note. As discussed in text, however, the rationales for 803(3) differ somewhat from those motivating 803(1). The possibilities of abuse under Rule 803(3) are also greater than under 803(1). See the Courtroom section infra.

moment they speak. When admitted to prove the declarant's state of mind at that moment, these statements are more reliable than most out-of-court declarations.

Remember the four flaws that can diminish the reliability of a declarant's statement: perception, memory, clarity, and sincerity. Expression of a declarant's current state of mind cannot suffer from the second of these problems, faulty memory. The declarant does not need to recall anything because he is voicing his immediate feelings.

Similarly, expressions of a current state of mind run few risks of misperception. People sometimes fool themselves about their deepest emotions, but no one else can perceive those feelings **more** accurately. A declarant's statement that she is sad, thirsty, in love, or planning to move to Montana is the most accurate perception we have of that individual's feelings at that moment.

Secondhand reports about a declarant's expressed state of mind also pose diminished risks of insincerity. As with present sense impressions, declarants usually offer comments about their current mental state without much reflection. People frequently voice these feelings in the moment, either spontaneously or in response to questions. Comments about a current state of mind thus give little opportunity to concoct a lie.

But this isn't always true; the risk of deception is greater when a declarant notes an internal state than when he describes an external one. People can control when they express states of mind, so they can formulate a deliberate lie before speaking. A child who wants to play a forbidden computer game, for example, may say "I'm sleepy," then close the door to her bedroom and turn on the game. More malicious wrongdoers may misstate their feelings and intentions even more egregiously.

The fourth threat to reliability, clarity, also poses risks when juries hear secondhand expressions about state of mind. Feelings of hunger, illness, joy, fatigue, and other mental states are highly subjective. The physical sensation that I describe as a "slight twinge" may be a "searing pain" to someone else. Without the opportunity for cross-examination, it may be difficult to pin down exactly what the declarant was feeling.

Rule 803(3) assumes that, on balance, a declarant's expression of his state of mind is sufficiently reliable to admit into evidence. Opposing counsel can note the power of speakers to lie about their present mental state, as well as the difficulty in ascertaining the meaning of some of these expressions. Juries can assess these risks based on their own life experience. Compared to other hearsay statements, a declarant's report of a current mental state still carries heightened indicia of reliability.

B. The Rule. The hearsay exception for state of mind appears in Rule 803, which governs exceptions that apply regardless of the declarant's availability. Read through the rule, and then we'll examine the different parts:

Rule 803. Exceptions to the Rule Against Hearsay — Regardless of Whether the Declarant Is Available as a Witness

The following are not excluded by the rule against hearsay, regardless of whether the declarant is available as a witness: . . .

(3) *Then-Existing Mental, Emotional, or Physical Condition.* A statement of the declarant's <u>then-existing</u>

- state of mind (such as motive, intent, or plan) or
- emotional, sensory, or physical condition (such as mental feeling, pain, or bodily health),

<u>but not</u> including a statement of memory or belief <u>to prove</u> the fact remembered or believed <u>unless</u> it relates to the validity or terms of the declarant's will.

The rule begins with a key point: The exception covers only statements about the declarant's "**then-existing**" state of mind. Comments like "My leg was hurting an hour ago," or "I was really miserable last night," are not admissible under this exception.

The rule then lists **four types** of internal states that a declarant might describe: an emotional, sensory, or physical condition, and the catch all "state of mind." These categories are broad; the rule seems to embrace every type of mental, emotional, or physical feeling that a declarant might describe about herself.

Section 803(3) drives this point home by offering two parentheticals that note **specific examples** of these categories: motive, intent, plan, mental feeling, pain, and bodily health. Once again, these examples signal the rule's broad application. It is hard to imagine any mental state that Rule 803(3) overlooks.

The rule then offers a very important exception to its broad sweep: **Statements of memory or belief** are not admissible under this exception when they are offered to prove the fact remembered or believed. The statement, "I remember how hot I felt yesterday," is admissible under this exception to show that at the moment the declarant spoke, she remembered her feelings of the previous day. But the statement is not admissible under this exception to prove that the declarant felt hot the previous day.

Similarly, the statement "I believe Diana is the person who pulled the trigger" is admissible under Rule 803(3) to show that at the moment the declarant spoke, he believed that Diana was the trigger person. This might be important if the declarant accused Diana at one time and Eliza on a different occasion; the case might turn on when the declarant held this belief about Diana. But this "I believe" statement is not admissible to prove that Diana was the person who pulled the trigger.

This clarification of Rule 803(3) is necessary to prevent semantic games that would largely destroy the ban against hearsay. A declarant could couch almost any out-of-court representation as a statement of memory or belief. Under these circumstances the speaker is not really conveying how she currently feels, but is using words about belief or memory to frame a factual representation. This distinction is essential to applying Rule 803(3), so we will look at more examples in the Courtroom section.

Finally, to complicate this complication, Rule 803(3) adds an exception to the caveat relating to statements of memory or belief: An out-of-court statement of memory or belief is admissible to prove the fact remembered or believed if that fact relates to the validity of the **declarant's will**. The unavailability of the testator, combined with a desire to further that person's intent, supports admission of these statements. In practice, this exception almost never arises.

C. In the Courtroom. Application of Rule 803(3) is straightforward in some cases, but harbors surprising complexities in others. In this section, we'll highlight some of the pitfalls that lurk within this rule.

1. What Is a State of Mind? Rule 803(3) sweeps broadly to include a large number of mental states. These include reports about physical sensations like hunger, thirst, and pain. The rule also includes all types of emotional states, such as fear, anger, happiness, and calm. And it includes cognitive schemes like intent, motive, or plan.

But be careful not to overapply Rule 803(3). People talk and write about their internal feelings, but they communicate much more often about external events. Most of the things people say are not reports about mental states.

The statement "I won the lottery," for example, is not a report about a mental state; it is a comment about something that happened to the declarant. The lucky winner might also say "I'm thrilled," "I'm excited," or "I'm delirious with joy." Those would all be statements of a mental state generated by winning the lottery, but the initial statement about winning the lottery is not.

The distinction is slippery, because people often intertwine comments about a mental state with other kinds of statements. An excited lottery winner, for example, might say: "I'm so excited—I just won the lottery! I have a million dollars, and I'm going to take a trip around the world!" These phrases express four distinct thoughts, but only two of them convey a state of mind.

The first and last of the winner's phrases express states of mind: She is excited and she has a current plan to take a trip around the world. But the middle two, "I just won the lottery" and "I have a million dollars," do not articulate states of mind. The first describes an event, winning the lottery, that the declarant experienced. And the second depicts an **external** condition about the declarant. The lottery winner is excited and she has a million dollars, but only the former is a mental state. Having a million dollars isn't just in her head, it's real.

Courts redact out-of-court statements like this to admit the phrases in which a declarant expresses a state of mind and exclude others falling outside any hearsay exception. In the above example, the court might admit evidence that the lottery winner said, "I'm so excited!" and "I'm going to take a trip around the world!" But the remaining words are inadmissible under 803(3); the proponent would have to identify another hearsay exception to admit them.

Here is a case further illustrating this distinction:

> **Example:** The United States prosecuted Melvin Joe for first degree murder of his wife, Julia Joe. Melvin admitted that he killed Julia, but claimed that he lacked the specific intent for first degree murder. He contended that he was drunk when he killed Julia and enraged because she had threatened to divorce him. To show Melvin's specific intent, the government called one of Julia's neighbors, Brett Smoker, to testify. Smoker testified that eight days before the crime, Julia told him that she was "afraid of Melvin" because "he's acting like he is going to kill me."

> **Analysis:** The first part of Julia's statement, that she was "afraid of Melvin," is admissible as an expression of Julia's state of mind. But the second portion, that Melvin was "acting like he is going to kill me," is inadmissible under that exception. Melvin's actions may have prompted Julia's fear, but they were not part of her mental state. Admitting that portion of Julia's statement for the truth of the matter asserted—that Melvin had, in fact, acted like he would kill Julia—violates the rule against hearsay.[2]

Parsing Julia's statement this way may seem odd. Why admit her statement of fear, but not the reasons for that emotion? Remember that all of Julia's words occurred outside the courtroom; when related by Smoker, they are subject to all of the flaws—perception, memory, sincerity, and clarity—that can mar secondhand testimony.

When Smoker testifies about what Julia said, opposing counsel has no opportunity to cross-examine Julia; nor can the jury assess her credibility. What did Julia mean when she said Melvin was "acting like he is going to kill me"? What specific actions did she perceive? Could she have been making the kind of rhetorical exaggeration people often make ("My wife will kill me if she finds out what I spent!")? If she planned to divorce Melvin, could Julia even have been lying about his actions?

The fact that Melvin did kill Julia makes us want to accept her complete out-of-court statement as true, but it might not be. Secondhand reports carry real risks of error.

---

2   This example is based upon United States v. Joe, 8 F.3d 1488 (10th Cir. 1993). On facts very similar to the ones described above, the court of appeals held that the first part of Julia Joe's out-of-court statement fell within 803(3), but that the second portion did not.

Against this background, Rule 803(3) grants a limited exception for statements voicing a state of mind. Julia's comment that she was "afraid of Melvin" has sufficient indicia of reliability, for the reasons discussed in the Introduction, that we are willing to admit that statement in court. But this special dispensation doesn't apply to the rest of her statement, which suffers from all of the potential defects identified above.

2. Circumstantial Evidence of Mental State. Statements about external facts or events don't qualify as expressions of a "state of mind" admissible under Rule 803(3). But those statements sometimes are admissible to **prove** state of mind. Here's why:

Out-of-court declarations are hearsay only when a party offers them to prove the truth of the matter asserted. If a party introduces a statement, instead, as circumstantial evidence of the declarant's mental condition, the statement isn't hearsay:

> **Example:** Marc, an enthusiastic hiker, died after eating poisonous mushrooms. Ginger, Marc's widow, attempted to claim the proceeds of Marc's million dollar life insurance policy. But the company denied payment, asserting that Marc committed suicide by intentionally eating the poisonous mushrooms. In a lawsuit over the insurance proceeds, Ginger attempts to prove that Marc was happy at the time of his death rather than suicidal. She offers the testimony of Marc's friend Charles who testifies that the day before his death, Marc told Charles: "I just got a great promotion at work" and "The country club is about to give me their 'Golfer of the Year' award."

> **Analysis:** Marc's statements were about external events, not his state of mind; they do not fall within Rule 803(3). But since Ginger offers these statements to prove that Marc was in a positive frame of mind at the time he ate the deadly mushrooms, she is not using the statements to prove the truth of the matters they assert. Neither Marc's promotion nor his golfing award is relevant to Ginger's dispute with the insurance company. Instead, Ginger is offering these statements as circumstantial evidence of Marc's mental state. The statements are not hearsay when offered for that purpose, and the trial judge should admit them.

It does not even matter whether Marc's statements were factually accurate; as long as he believed they were true, they are relevant to his mental state, which is the purpose for which they are being admitted under Rule 803(3). If the insurance company requests a limiting instruction, the court should tell the jury that these statements are not being offered to prove the truth of the matters asserted but only to prove Marc's state of mind at the time that he said them.

Many students and practicing lawyers confuse **expressions of** a state of mind with other statements that offer **circumstantial evidence about** the declarant's state of mind. The key to drawing the distinction, as always, is to focus on the purpose for which a party offers the statement in evidence.

3. I Think, I Believe, I Remember. Words like "I think," "I believe," or "I remember" sometimes fool students into concluding that a declarant's words are admissible under Rule 803(3). But these words usually are red herrings; most often they introduce statements about external facts or events. Those statements are not expressions of a state of mind.

Example: Orville Redden, a long-time worker for Happy Time Popcorn, developed a life-threatening lung disease from inhaling diacetyl, an ingredient used in microwave popcorn. In 2007, Redden filed a complaint against Happy Time, alleging that the company failed to adopt safety measures that would have protected him from the effects of diacetyl; the National Institute for Occupational Safety and Health had recommended those measures in 2000.

Happy Time moved for summary judgment on the ground that a three-year statute of limitations barred Redden's claim. The company argued that Redden developed clear symptoms of his lung disease before 2004, so that he knew or should have known of the claim before that time. Whatever the merits of his underlying claim, the company contended, he waited more than three years to file it.

To support its summary judgment motion, Happy Time offered a letter written by Orville's daughter, Marcia, to her sister in 2005. In that letter Marcia wrote: "I'm worried. Looking back, I remember that Dad has been wheezing, short of breath, and coughing for at least two years." Redden objected to these statements as hearsay.

Analysis: Remember that the Rules of Evidence apply to summary judgment motions; if a piece of evidence would not be admissible at trial, a party cannot rely upon it to obtain summary judgment. Marcia's letter is an out-of-court statement, so it is hearsay if offered to prove the truth of the matter asserted.

Marcia's first comment, "I'm worried," reflects her state of mind, so it is admissible under Rule 803(3). But her second statement describes her father's symptoms, rather than Marcia's mental state. The prefatory words "I remember" don't change the character of the second statement. Happy Time is not offering Marcia's letter to prove that, at the time she wrote it, Marcia had a mental state of thinking about her father; that fact is irrelevant to the lawsuit. Instead, Happy Time is relying upon the letter to show the truth of what Marcia remembered: that by 2005 her father had been showing symptoms of lung disease for at least two years. When offered for that purpose, Marcia's 2005 statement is hearsay and it does not fall within the state-of-mind exception.[3]

Even without the letter, Happy Time might be able to prove at trial that Orville's symptoms predated 2004. If called as a witness, for example, Marcia might concede that her father displayed symptoms of lung disease before that time. But those statements would be subject to cross-examination in the courtroom; Orville's attorney could probe just what Marcia noticed and how severe the symptoms were. The jury could also assess Marcia's manner: Is she the type of worrier who panics at every cough? The hearsay rule excludes out-of-court statements like Marcia's letter precisely because these safeguards aren't present.

On the other hand, memories and beliefs themselves are sometimes relevant to a legal dispute. Under those circumstances, Rule 803(3) may admit the full content of a memory or belief as a relevant "state of mind." In trademark litigation, for example, parties often introduce evidence of customer beliefs and memories to show confusion between two products:

Example: Leelanau Wine Cellars, Ltd. (LWC) has marketed wine under the trade name "Leelanau Cellars" for more than twenty-five years. A com-

---

3   More than 300 lawsuits have been filed challenging the use of diacetyl in popcorn and other products, although Orville's case is hypothetical. ConAgra, the largest supplier of microwave popcorn worldwide, has stopped adding diacetyl to its popcorn.

peting company, Black & Red, began selling a wine called "Chateau de Leelanau." LWC sued Black & Red for trademark infringement. To show actual confusion among customers, a fact that contributes to establishing infringement, LWC's manager testifies at trial that one buyer said to him, "I remember your Leelanau wine! I tried it at the Michigan State Fair." To accompany this testimony, LWC introduces independent proof that Black & Red sold its "Chateau de Leelanau" wine at the state fair, but LWC sold no wines there. Red and Black objects to the buyer's statement as hearsay.

Analysis: In this case, the buyer's memory is relevant to the legal dispute, and it is admissible under Rule 803(3). The reasoning is a bit tricky because there are two "truths" asserted in the buyer's statement. One is that a wine named "Leelanau" was sold at the state fair. LWC cannot offer the buyer's out-of-court statement to prove that truth. That would be using an expressed memory to prove the fact remembered; 803(3) does not allow that use.

But the buyer's statement also asserted the "truth" that, at the moment he spoke, he had a memory of trying a wine named Leelanau at the state fair. That is exactly what LWC wants to prove: that people believe that both Leelanau Cellars wine and Chateau de Leelanau wine as a single category of Leelanau wines. Because LWC wants to prove this truth of what the buyer said, the statement ordinarily would be excluded as hearsay. But Rule 803(3) admits out-of-court expressions of mental state under these circumstances. "I remember Leelanau wine from the state fair" is a mental state relevant to this lawsuit, admissible under 803(3), because it is evidence of the declarant's internal belief that the two wines are identical.[4]

Memories and beliefs are relevant to a relatively small number of issues. Most often, statements prefaced by "I remember" or "I believe" introduce factual assertions that are not states of mind admissible under Rule 803(3). But watch out for cases like the Leelanau one, in which the memory itself is relevant.

4. Looking Back. Rule 803(3) admits only expressions of a "then-existing" state of mind. An out-of-court statement that "my toe hurt yesterday" is not admissible under 803(3); it describes a past, rather than current, state of mind.

---

4   This example embellishes slightly on Leelanau Wine Cellars, Ltd. v. Black & Red, Inc., 452 F. Supp. 2d 772, 786–87 (W.D. Mich. 2006).

But a person's current mental state sometimes offers circumstantial evidence of their prior mental condition. If my toe hurts today, it might also have hurt yesterday.

Example: Edwards & Hanly, an investment banking firm, sued the Wells Fargo Securities Clearance Corporation for securities fraud. A key issue in the case was whether Wells Fargo's employees knew that a series of stock trades conducted over 13 months were short sales. At the end of the disputed period, Wells Fargo terminated an employee named Marianna Ianuzzi. Just after leaving the firm, Ianuzzi told her colleague Joseph Werba, "I know that the trades were short sales." Ianuzzi moved overseas and was not available to testify, so Edwards & Hanly called Werba to testify about Ianuzzi's statement. Wells Fargo objected that the statement was hearsay.

Analysis: Ianuzzi's statement is hearsay but it was an expression of her mental state, admissible under Rule 803(3). Technically, the statement establishes only that Ianuzzi knew on that day that the trades were short sales; she might have just discovered that fact. But Edwards & Hanly can use this statement to argue that Ianuzzi's knowledge on the day she spoke is some evidence that she knew the same facts earlier as well. Knowledge today is some evidence of knowledge yesterday, just as a leg that hurts today is some evidence that the leg also hurt yesterday. Wells Fargo, of course, can counter that this is rather weak evidence. The fact that Ianuzzi admitted knowing about the short sales after they ended does not offer much proof that she knew about them at an earlier point.[5]

Using expressions of a state of mind in this circumstantial way raises some risks of prejudice. If Ianuzzi had said, for example, "I knew for the last six months that the trades were short sales," Rule 803(3) would not admit that statement; that version of the statement focuses on Ianuzzi's prior mental state rather than her current one. Admitting her more ambiguous statement, "I know that the trades were short sales," raises some of the same risks. The jury might interpret Ianuzzi's statement to mean that she "had known" that the trades were short sales; that gives the statement considerably more weight than when it is used simply as circumstantial evidence that Ianuzzi might have known about the short sales at an earlier time.

---

5   This example is loosely based on Edwards & Hanly v. Wells Fargo Securities Clearance Corp., 458 F. Supp. 1110, 1118 & n.2 (S.D.N.Y. 1978), rev'd on other grounds, 602 F.2d 478 (2d Cir. 1979).

Judges address this issue under Rule 403. The length of time that has elapsed between the declarant's expression and the relevant time period is an important factor in the balance. In the Wells Fargo case, for example, Ianuzzi's statement occurred just as the critical time period ended; that increased its probative value and reduced its potential prejudice.

Remember that Ianuzzi's statement could not be used to prove that the trades actually **were** short sales, because that is a statement about the external world not covered by 803(3). The plaintiff used Ianuzzi's statement only to show that she knew about the sales. If the parties disputed whether short sales actually occurred, Edwards and Hanly would have to use other evidence to prove that fact.

5. Looking Forward. A declarant's expressed state of mind at one moment also offers circumstantial evidence about what the declarant did or thought at a later time. Rule 803(3) allows parties to introduce hearsay expressions about then-existing mental states to help prove subsequent thoughts or acts. Here is one case in which a defendant's mental state at one moment offered evidence of his mental state shortly thereafter:

> **Example:** The government prosecuted John Lea for assaulting Justin Babcock, a federal witness who had testified against Lea's friend Michael Yarbrough. Lea admitted the assault, but claimed that he attacked Babcock only because Babcock owed him money. Lea thus attempted to avoid the stiff penalties imposed on people who retaliate against federal witnesses by assaulting them.
>
> To raise this defense, Lea seeks to call another friend, Marcel Davis, to the stand. Davis will testify that he was sitting in a car with Lea just before the assault. According to Davis, Lea spotted Babcock and said: "Hold on a minute, there's Justin, he owes me some money, I want to go see if I can get it." The prosecutor objects to this testimony as hearsay.
>
> **Analysis:** Lea's statement "I want to go see if I can get it" is admissible under Rule 803(3) because it indicates Lea's then-existing plan to seek repayment of a debt from Babcock. Lea's stated intent is some evidence that his motive in

approaching Babcock, as well as his motive moments later in assaulting him, was related only to recovering the money Babcock owed him.[6]

In addition to using evidence of a declarant's state of mind to show motive, parties often offer this evidence as circumstantial proof that the declarant acted consistently with her expressed plans. A prosecutor, for example, might offer evidence that the defendant told a friend, "I plan to rob the First National Bank on Tuesday." This statement reflects the defendant's state of mind at the moment of speaking. And if the First National Bank was robbed the following Tuesday, the jury could infer that the defendant committed the robbery; her state of mind is circumstantial evidence that she acted in the manner she contemplated.

6. Looking Forward . . . with Someone Else. A declarant's expression of intent offers circumstantial evidence that the declarant acted on the intention. But what if the declarant voices a plan to do something with someone else? Is the declarant's out-of-court statement admissible to prove that the **other person** committed the intended act?

Suppose, for example, that Marilyn sends her brother an e-mail saying: "Bert and I plan on robbing the First National Bank on Tuesday." The e-mail expresses Marilyn's then-existing intention to rob the named bank on Tuesday; it is admissible as circumstantial evidence that Marilyn did rob the bank. But is it also admissible as circumstantial evidence that Bert robbed the bank?

The Supreme Court rendered a famous opinion on this issue in 1892. The case, *Mutual Life Insurance Co. v. Hillmon*,[7] arose out of a colorful nineteenth-century mystery:

On March 18, 1879, a man died at a campsite in Crooked Creek, Kansas. John H. Brown notified the closest authorities that the man was his friend, John Hillmon. Brown claimed that he and Hillmon had been traveling together to find a suitable site for a cattle ranch, and that he shot Hillmon accidentally while taking his gun from their wagon. After an inquest, the body was buried.

6   United States v. Lea, 131 F. Appx. 320, 321 (2d Cir. 2005).

7   145 U.S. 285 (1892).

Hillmon's widow Sallie filed claims under four life insurance policies held on Hillmon's life. The companies refused to pay the claims, contending that the body buried at Crooked Creek was not Hillmon. Instead, the companies argued that Brown, Hillmon, and others had concocted an elaborate plot to stage Hillmon's death and collect on his suspiciously numerous life insurance policies. The body in the Kansas grave, the insurance companies maintained, was that of Frederick Walters, a gullible young man whom Hillmon enticed to Southern Kansas with offers of employment and then killed to further the life insurance scam.

Sallie Hillmon sued the companies to force payment of the policies. As part of their defense, the companies introduced evidence that Walters left his home in Fort Madison, Iowa, in March 1878 and traveled about the Midwest seeking his fortune. Between March of 1878 and March of 1879, Walters wrote regularly to both his family and fiancée, Alvina Kasten, in Fort Madison. His last letters were mailed from Wichita, Kansas, during the first few days of March 1879. Family and friends in Iowa did not hear from Walters again after that time.

The companies also attempted to introduce the content of Walters's last letters. The one written to his sister sometime between March 3 and March 5 read in part: "I expect to leave Wichita on or about March the 5th with a certain Mr. Hillmon, a sheep trader, for Colorado, or parts unknown to me." Walters's letter to his fiancée, dated March 1, similarly stated: "I will stay here until the fore part of next week, and then will leave . . . with a man by the name of Hillmon, who intends to start a sheep ranch, and, as he promised me more wage[s] than I could make at anything else, I concluded to take it, for a while at least, until I strike something better."[8]

The trial court excluded the content of these letters, concluding that they were hearsay. With the letters excluded, the jury rejected the companies' claim of a scam and returned a verdict for Sallie Hillmon.

The Supreme Court reversed, holding that the content of Walters's letters was admissible to show his state of mind. The Court's decision was relatively uncontroversial with respect to **Walters's** intention. The letters showed that, at the time they were written, Walters intended to leave Wichita and travel toward Colorado

---

8   Id. at 288–89.

or "parts unknown." When Walters disappeared after writing these letters, his expressed intention offered some evidence that his body was the one discovered at Crooked Creek, located about 100 miles west of Wichita.

But if limited to this purpose, the letters offered only very weak evidence to support the insurance companies' claim. Walters was remarkably vague about where he intended to go and by what route. Someone leaving Wichita could travel in many directions toward "parts unknown," using several routes and adopting various speeds. If Walters left Wichita on March 5, as the letters suggested, he could have been in many places—dead or alive—by March 18.

Walters's expressed intent was much more helpful to the companies if it included his comment that he intended to **travel with Hillmon**. If Walters planned to travel with Hillmon, and if that was admissible as evidence that Walters did travel with Hillmon, then the chances that Walters died at Crooked Creek increased significantly. Brown conceded that Hillmon was at Crooked Creek; indeed, he claimed that Hillmon was the one who died there. But if so, then where was Walters?

The Supreme Court, controversially, held that the full content of Walters's letters was admissible to show his state of mind. The jury, in other words, could hear that Walters intended to travel to "Colorado or parts unknown" with Hillmon.

Admitting Walters's out-of-court reference to Hillmon is more dubious than may first appear. Think about how many times you have planned to do something with another person, but plans changed. An individual's expressed intent is only modest evidence of what that individual actually ended up doing; it is even weaker evidence of what another person has done.

The Walters letters, in fact, remind us why the rule against hearsay is important. Imagine that Walters was a witness, rather than a letter writer, on March 1, 1879. If Walters testified in court on that date that he planned to leave Wichita shortly and travel west with John Hillmon, an attorney could have cross-examined him about the extent and specificity of those plans. When and how had Walters met Hillmon? What exactly had Hillmon said about their destination and route? How many times had the two discussed the matter? Was this a single conversation that occurred late at night in a saloon after much whiskey? Or was it a matter they had considered carefully and soberly on several occasions?

Walters, of course, did not appear on a witness stand in March 1879, much less as a witness during the *Hillmon* litigation. But these questions are good reminders about the unreliability of secondhand reports. A secondhand report about someone else's plans, even when those plans intersect with those of the speaker, is very dubious indeed. Walters might have been lying to his sister and fiancée, Hillmon might have lied to Walters, or the parties might have left Wichita together but parted before reaching Crooked Creek; inferring from Walters's untested March 1 comment that he and Hillmon were together in Crooked Creek more than two weeks later requires overlooking several problems of reliability.

Indeed, the scammers in the *Hillmon* litigation might have been the insurance companies themselves. In 1899, during a retrial of the lawsuit, Sallie Hillmon produced a surprise witness. Henry Simmons, a cigar factory owner from Leavenworth, Kansas, testified that he had employed Walters in May of 1879—two months after the Crooked Creek shooting. Simmons produced personnel records supporting his testimony and persuasively identified Walters's photograph. After hearing this evidence, the jury returned a verdict for Sallie Hillmon.[9]

A legal scholar who has extensively researched the *Hillmon* case, moreover, offers a plausible argument that Walters never met Hillmon, and that the insurance companies used Walters, his family, and his fiancée to fabricate a defense to the Hillmon policy claims.[10] Many young men roamed the Kansas frontier during the late nineteenth century, and many had left families and fiancées behind. It would have been relatively easy for the insurance companies to identify a wanderer who resembled Hillmon; pay that adventurer to write and backdate letters fitting the *Hillmon* facts; and persuade the abandoned family and fiancée to go along with the scheme.

Walters's fiancée Alvina, notably, swore in just a single deposition that she received her letter in March 1879; she did not testify in any of the *Hillmon* trials.

No one knows for sure; both insurance fraud and forged court documents were well known to nineteenth-century America. But the dispute illustrates the unreliability of using one individual's out-of-court expression of intent to prove the actions of another person. The very mystery of the *Hillmon* case underscores the danger in its doctrine.

---

9 Marianne Wesson, The Hillmon Story, http://www.thehillmoncase.com/story.html (last visited July 14, 2017). The company appealed this verdict, as it had appealed the earlier one, and the Supreme Court once again reversed. The parties settled after that decision, with the companies paying the face amounts of the policies plus interest, and the litigation finally ended. Id.

10 Marianne Wesson, State of Mind: The Hillmon Case, the McGuffin, and the Supreme Court, http://www.thehillmoncase.com/research.html (last visited July 14, 2017).

Unfortunately, the current status of the *Hillmon* doctrine remains as murky as the facts of the original dispute. The text of Rule 803(3) does not expressly address the question of using one person's state of mind to prove the actions of another person; the rule does not appear to overrule or limit Hillmon. The Advisory Committee's note on the exception, moreover, offers surprisingly enthusiastic support of Hillmon's vitality. The Committee declared: "The rule of [*Hillmon*], allowing evidence of intention as tending to prove the doing of the act intended, is of course, left undisturbed."[11] These facts suggest that *Hillmon* is alive and well.

On the other hand, the House Report on Rule 803(3) noted that "the Committee intends that the Rule be construed to limit the doctrine of [*Hillmon*] so as to render statements of intent by a declarant admissible only to prove his future conduct, not the future conduct of another person."[12] And there is a plausible interpretation of both Rule 803(3)'s text and the Advisory Committee's note that is consistent with the House Committee's limited reading of *Hillmon*.

To see that interpretation, think again about a statement like "I plan to go to Topeka with Mary." This statement breaks into two parts: (1) the declarant's intention to go to Topeka, and (2) his belief that Mary will accompany him. Rule 803(3) admits the first part, but the rule's "memory or belief" proviso bars the second. That proviso prohibits admission of "statement[s] of memory or belief to prove the fact remembered or believed." So the declarant's belief that Mary will go to Topeka is not admissible to prove that Mary did go to Topeka.

In the view of many evidence scholars, this is the proper interpretation of Rule 803(3).[13] The exception, in other words, preserves *Hillmon*'s narrow ruling—that a declarant's expressed intention is admissible to prove the declarant's subsequent acts—while overturning the case's broader holding that a declarant's expressed intent is admissible to prove another person's actions.

But the issue is far from clear, and the temptation to follow *Hillmon*'s broader holding is strong. This is especially true in criminal cases in which a victim dies or disappears after saying that she plans to meet the defendant.

---

11   Fed. R. Evid. 803 advisory committee's note.

12   H.R. REP. No. 93–650 (1973) (citation omitted), reprinted in 1974 U.S.C.C.A.N. 7051, 7075, 7087.

13   See, e.g., Christopher B. Mueller & Laird C. Kirkpatrick, Evidence § 8.39, at 824–25 (3d ed. 2003).

Example: James Boyden, Jr., was drinking beer at the apartment of his sister, Marie Boyden Connors. Boyden left the apartment at about 8:00 p.m., telling his sister that he was going out "to meet Billy Herd." Several hours later, police found Boyden dead on a nearby street. The government prosecuted William "Billy" Herd for the murder, and filed a motion in limine seeking permission for Connors to testify about Boyden's final statement to her.

Analysis: After reviewing *Hillmon*, Rule 803(3), and appellate precedents, the trial judge allowed Connors to testify about Boyden's statement. This judge interpreted the plain meaning of Rule 803(3) to maintain the full scope of *Hillmon*, allowing use of a declarant's expressed state of mind to prove the actions of another person.[14]

Several Ninth Circuit decisions reach the same result, admitting a declarant's expressed state of mind to prove another person's actions.[15] The Second and Fourth Circuits, on the other hand, admit these statements only if some independent evidence corroborates the other person's actions.[16]

State courts, unburdened by the legislative history of the Federal Rules (and seemingly untroubled by the unreliability of statements like the one Boyden made), overwhelmingly favor *Hillmon*'s broad approach. The vast majority of states to address this issue have interpreted their own codes of evidence to admit statements of future plans in order to prove the subsequent actions of another.[17] But this is a volatile area of the law, and it is likely to evolve as parties urge alternate readings of Rule 803(3). The mystery of *Hillmon* lives on.

---

14   United States v. Houlihan, 871 F. Supp. 1495 (D. Mass. 1994).

15   See, e.g., United States v. Pheaster, 544 F.2d 353, 374–80 (9th Cir. 1976).

16   See, e.g., United States v. Best, 219 F.3d 192, 198–99 (2d Cir. 2000); United States v. Jenkins, 579 F.2d 840, 842–43 (4th Cir. 1978).

17   See People v. Chambers, 125 A.D.2d 88, 512 N.Y.S.2d 89 (N.Y. App. Div. 1987). By one count, at least 28 states had adopted the *Hillmon* doctrine and only three had rejected it. See Coy v. Renico, 414 F. Supp. 2d 744, 769–70 (E.D. Mich. 2006).

Quick Summary

Rule 803(3) allows a declarant's out-of-court statements about her current state of mind, mental condition, or physical condition to be admitted for the truth of the matter asserted. These statements are more reliable than most hearsay: They pose no risks of erroneous perception or memory, and raise limited credibility concerns. "State of mind," however, includes only the declarant's subjective feeling, not references to external facts that prompted those feelings.

Parties may use a declarant's state of mind as circumstantial evidence of the declarant's prior or subsequent actions. In the famous Hillmon case, the Supreme Court also allowed a party to use a declarant's state of mind to prove subsequent actions by another person. Some evidence scholars interpret Rule 803(3) to overrule this aspect of Hillmon, but at least some federal courts still follow the precedent. Others have adopted a compromise, admitting the statement only if independent evidence corroborates the third party's conduct.

Test Your Understanding

To assess your understanding of the material in this chapter, <u>click here</u> to take a quiz, or go to the Quizzes module from the eBook on your eProducts bookshelf.

42

Hearsay Exception—Medical Treatment

Key Concepts

- **Rule 803(4):** Hearsay Exception for Statements About Symptoms or Causes of Medical Conditions
- Made for the Purposes of Medical Diagnosis or Treatment
- Pertinent to Diagnosis or Treatment
- Statements by and to Family Members
- Diagnosis for Purposes of Litigation
- Statements Attributing Blame or Fault
- Psychological Conditions
- Domestic and Sexual Abuse

A. Introduction and Policy. Rule 803(3), which we examined in the last chapter, admits out-of-court statements about a declarant's physical condition. But that exception applies only to current conditions; it excludes out-of-court statements like "My head started hurting yesterday." 803(3) also precludes references to external events that might have caused the condition, such as "My head started hurting when I bumped into the wall."

Under most circumstances, secondhand reports that include references like these carry insufficient indicia of reliability. But what if the declarant made a statement like this while seeking medical diagnosis or treatment? Are people more likely to report accurately the history of physical symptoms, as well as any causes of them, when seeking medical care?

Rule 803(4) assumes that they are. That provision admits out-of-court statements made to obtain medical diagnosis or treatment. Other examples of statements admissible under this exception, when made to obtain medical diagnosis or treatment, are:

> "My stomach hurts and I feel like I'm going to throw up."
>
> "I fell off the roof and I heard my leg crack when I hit the ground."
>
> "The pain runs from my neck down my left arm to the wrist."

Under the hearsay exception recognized in 803(4), a party may introduce statements like these for the truth of the matter asserted. If the declarant made these statements to obtain medical diagnosis or treatment, in other words, a party may offer them to prove that the declarant's stomach really did hurt, that she fell off the roof, or that the pain runs from his neck down the left arm to the wrist.

But don't people lie to their doctors? Undoubtedly they do: They claim to drink less alcohol than they really consume, deny using illegal drugs, and pretend to eat carrots and broccoli with every meal. But the hearsay exception for statements made to obtain medical diagnosis and treatment rests on two grounds.

First, although patients do lie to their doctors, these statements as a class are more reliable than most out-of-court statements. This hearsay exception, like most of the others, does not guarantee that the declarant's statement was accurate; it merely assumes that the statement was **more likely** to be accurate than most other hearsay. An individual seeking medical diagnosis or treatment has a strong self-interest in reporting symptoms honestly and precisely: He is relying upon the listener to provide needed medical care.

Second, the exception serves a need for efficiency. Although any witness, including the declarant, may testify about statements fitting this exception, parties most often use Rule 803(4) to introduce medical records. Almost any statement made by a patient that appears in a medical record is admissible under 803(4). The exception thus reduces the need to call nurses, doctors, and other medical professionals to testify at the large number of trials involving an injury, disease, or other medical condition.[1]

---

1   The party seeking to introduce the medical records still must authenticate the records. But it is relatively easy to find a hospital administrator or other witness to authenticate the records, and the opposing party frequently stipulates to this fact. We discuss authentication further in Chapter 69.

B. The Rule.

> ## RULE 803. Exceptions to the Rule Against Hearsay — Regardless of Whether the Declarant Is Available as a Witness
>
> The following are not excluded by the rule against hearsay, regardless of whether the declarant is available as a witness: . . .
>
> **(4) *Statement Made for Medical Diagnosis or Treatment.*** A statement that:
>
> **(A)** is <u>made for</u>—and is <u>reasonably pertinent to</u>—<u>medical diagnosis or treatment</u>; and
>
> **(B)** describes
>
> - medical history;
> - past or present symptoms or sensations;
> - their inception; or their general cause.

Like the other exceptions we have studied in recent chapters, this exception applies whether the declarant is available or unavailable. The exception itself rests on three requirements.

First, the statement must be made for a medical diagnosis or treatment. This requirement is subjective; the patient must actually be seeking medical care.

Second, the statements must be reasonably pertinent to diagnosis or treatment. This is an objective counterpart to the first requirement. Courts construe this condition quite broadly, assuming that medical professionals guide consultations toward pertinent facts. If a doctor or other professional solicits information from a patient, the court will assume that the patient's responses are pertinent to diagnosis or treatment. We'll explore this requirement further in the Courtroom section.

Finally, the statements must fit within one of the three categories listed by the rule: (1) accounts of medical history; (2) descriptions of past or present symptoms or sensations; or (3) reports about the "inception" of the condition or its "general cause." All three of these categories are quite broad, and most statements made while seeking medical diagnosis or treatment fall within them. The categories, however, attempt to exclude statements that blame a particular person or organization for causing the condition. We'll examine this distinction further below.

Notice that this exception does not limit the declarant's statements to contemporaneous expressions. Unlike the hearsay exceptions in 803(1), 803(2), and 803(3), the "medical diagnosis or treatment" exception has no time limit. The declarant, moreover, may refer to external facts if those facts are pertinent to obtaining medical care. Thus, the following statements might be admissible under 803(4):

> "I twisted my ankle last week and it immediately swelled up and turned blue. It's not swollen anymore, but it's still tender when I touch it."
>
> "When I was a child I fell down and hit my head; ever since then I have suffered seizures in times of stress."

But these statements are only admissible under 803(4) if the declarant subjectively makes them for the purpose of getting medical diagnosis or treatment and if they are objectively pertinent to that medical care. If the above statements were made to a friend during a casual conversation or to an employer during a job interview, they would not be admissible under 803(4) for the truth of the matters asserted.

C. In the Courtroom.

1. Who Is the Declarant? Rule 803(4) does not refer to a particular type of speaker. The rationale behind the rule assumes that the declarant usually is the patient needing medical diagnosis or treatment; that person has the incentive to speak truthfully. But the rationale sometimes applies to family members who bring their children, spouses, parents, and other relatives for medical care—especially if the person needing treatment is too sick to speak for himself. Most of the time, these family members have the same incentive as the patient to speak carefully and truthfully. If the patient is very young or ill, the family member's perceptions may be more accurate than the patient's. Medical professionals often rely upon a family member's statement in giving medical care, affording further credibility to these statements.

 Family members, however, sometimes injure their loved ones— either accidentally or by design—and those cases disproportionately come to court. This situation creates a challenge for courts deciding whether to admit statements made by family

members under Rule 803(4). The question has generated surprisingly little discussion in the federal courts. Judges and scholars seem to assume that statements by family members are admissible as long as they meet the other requirements of Rule 803(4). The rule's open-ended language supports that result, although an advocate might challenge the assumption in an appropriate case.

One solution is to interpret Rule 803(4) to encompass statements made by any person seeking medical diagnosis for herself or another, but to exclude statements by family members and others under Rule 403 when the probative value of those statements is weak or their potential for prejudice is high.

2. Who Is the Audience? Just as Rule 803(4) fails to specify any particular type of declarant, it doesn't require that the person seeking medical treatment communicate with a physician or other medical professional. The exception's language embraces statements made to anyone, as long as the declarant made the statement for the purposes of medical diagnosis or treatment.

Example: Marjorie returned home from work to find her husband, Jayden, vomiting in the bathroom. "I've been sick as a dog for hours," Jayden told Marjorie, "and I have this odd headache. I need help getting to a doctor." Jayden then passed out on the bathroom floor; Marjorie called an ambulance and took Jayden to the hospital. Doctors determined that he was suffering from a bad case of food poisoning. Jayden later sued the Fried Fish Shack, where he'd eaten lunch. He called Marjorie to testify about his statement; the Fried Fish Shack objected to the statement as hearsay.

Analysis: Jayden's statement is admissible under 803(4). Although Marjorie is not a doctor, Jayden made his statement to enlist her help in securing medical care. Thus, the statement was "made for" medical treatment. The Advisory Committee's note to Rule 803(4) supports this result by observing: "Under the exception the statement need not have been made to a physician. Statements to hospital attendants, ambulance drivers, or even members of the family might be included."[2]

---

2   Fed. R. Evid. 803 advisory committee's note.

As a practical matter, however, most statements admitted under Rule 803(4) are statements to medical professionals.

3. Diagnosis OR Treatment. Rule 803(4) admits statements made for the purposes of medical diagnosis or treatment. In modern, specialized medicine, patients see some doctors exclusively for diagnosis—even though their ultimate aim is treatment. Rule 803(4)'s language admits a patient's statements to a radiologist or other specialist offering primarily diagnostic services without worrying about whether the doctor is "diagnosing" or "treating" the patient.

But the reference to diagnosis has a broader and more controversial implication. Rule 803(4) allows parties to admit statements made to doctors who they consulted purely to prepare for litigation. A doctor's expert opinion about a patient's condition is a type of diagnosis, even if the doctor renders that opinion only for purposes of pending litigation. A patient may even obtain this type of diagnosis after the condition has been treated and cured by other doctors:

Example: Kathleen O'Gee was a flight attendant for United Airlines. Shortly after take-off O'Gee noticed that the food buffet, a large 500–800 pound unit, had slid into the plane's aisle and was blocking an emergency exit. O'Gee attempted to push the buffet back into place, and felt a sharp pain in her back. O'Gee, another attendant, and the flight engineer finally succeeded in securing the food buffet, but O'Gee's problems were longer lasting. She spent much of the next year in bed receiving medical treatment for her back. Ultimately, O'Gee underwent surgery to remove a herniated disc from her back.

O'Gee sued Dobbs, the company that loaded the food buffet, claiming that Dobbs's employees improperly secured the heavy unit. But O'Gee did not call any of her treating physicians at trial. Instead, she called Dr. Koven, a doctor she saw after she had been treated medically and was preparing her case for trial. Koven sought to testify about the statements O'Gee made to him, describing both her symptoms and the manner in which they arose.

Analysis: Koven's testimony was admissible. Although he did not treat O'Gee, he diagnosed her condition. The fact that the diagnosis occurred for litigation rather than treatment is irrelevant under Rule 803(4). That exception allowed Koven to repeat O'Gee's statements, as long as her attorney laid a foundation establishing the pertinence of those statements to the doctor's diagnosis.[3]

This aspect of Rule 803(4) is essential in some cases. In medical malpractice cases, for example, a plaintiff almost always must obtain a non-treating physician's diagnosis to support the claim. Malpractice defendants may also have a medical expert, retained exclusively for litigation, examine the plaintiff. The plaintiff's statements to that doctor, as well as to any of her own, are admissible under Rule 803(4). Indeed, the defendant in the above example could have retained its own doctor to examine O'Gee; her statements to that doctor would have been admissible under 803(4).

Prosecutors also use 803(4) to introduce statements made by crime victims to a doctor who examines the victim to gather evidence for the prosecution. Even if the victim has been treated by his own doctor, the prosecution may need additional information about the victim's injuries. Under 803(4), the doctor can report to the jury any statement the victim made, as long as the statements were pertinent to diagnosis and fit the other conditions of the exception.

The difficulty with these applications of Rule 803(4) is that the statements a patient makes for purposes of obtaining a litigation-related diagnosis may be highly self-serving. O'Gee had a strong motive to exaggerate her injuries when she saw her special "litigation" doctor. Since O'Gee was no longer seeking medical treatment—just compensation through litigation—she had an incentive to tailor her comments in a way that would produce good compensation rather than good treatment. The underlying rationale of Rule 803(4) seems suspect in cases like this.

4. Cause and Source v. Fault and Blame. Rule 803(4) includes statements that a patient makes describing the "inception" or "general cause" of the condition when those statements are pertinent to medical care. This provision recognizes that proper diagnosis and treatment often require knowledge about how the condition arose. When a patient complains about a "sharp pain in the head," the doctor needs to know whether something recently hit the patient's head, whether the patient has been hiking in a tick-infested area, whether the patient has been exposed to

---

3   O'Gee v. Dobbs Houses, Inc., 570 F.2d 1084, 1088–89 (2d Cir. 1978).

a continuous loud noise, and numerous other facts that could each lead to very different diagnoses and treatment.

On the other hand, statements blaming specific individuals for the cause, or attributing a particular degree of fault to those individuals, usually are not relevant to medical care. The doctor needs to know that the patient was "hit above the eye with a heavy wrench" to offer the best treatment, but the doctor does not need to know that Steve was the one who hit the patient. Nor does the doctor need to know that Steve "did it on purpose because I won the poker game."

Statements admitted under 803(4) derive their reliability from the fact that the declarant made them while obtaining medical care. The patient's self-interest in getting good care makes these statements more reliable than most hearsay. But the indicia of reliability disappear when the patient makes statements unrelated to diagnosis or treatment. Rule 803(4)'s pertinence requirement, combined with the limited reference to the "general cause" of the condition, excludes most references to blame or fault.

 The line sometimes is hard to draw, particularly when long-term exposure to a workplace hazard has caused the medical condition. The trick is to follow the pertinence requirement while remembering the dangers of hearsay; courts redact statements to admit the narrowest declaration sufficient to obtain medical diagnosis and treatment. A patient's statement that "the factory I worked in for the past fifteen years had asbestos in the walls" probably is admissible when made to a doctor taking a case history. But a comment to the same doctor that "the owner of the factory refused to remove asbestos from our factory for fifteen years" almost certainly is not admissible.

Here is another example of the line between cause and fault:

Example: Radhica Ramrattan was severely injured when her car collided with a truck at an intersection. At the hospital, Ramrattan made numerous statements to the admitting nurse and treating physician about what happened. One of these, recorded in the medical records, was "patient indicates truck ran red light and smashed car; leg pinned against seat for 15 minutes before rescue." Ramrattan sued the truck driver and his employer for negligence; the defendants moved before trial to redact Ramrattan's medical records to exclude any reference to who was at fault in the collision.

Analysis: The court granted the defendants' motion, agreeing that Ramrattan's attributions of fault were not pertinent to her medical treatment. Ramrattan's statements that a truck smashed her car and that her leg was pinned against a seat for fifteen minutes were pertinent to treatment and admissible. But her comment that the truck ran a red light was not pertinent and would be redacted.[4]

5. Psychologists and Psychiatrists. Rule 803(4) applies broadly to statements made for "medical diagnosis or treatment," and most professionals agree that no defensible line exists between physical and psychological conditions. Indeed, many psychological illnesses stem from physiological causes and are treated with medication. But does Rule 803(4) include all statements made for purposes of obtaining medical treatment when the symptoms are psychological?

Most courts have assumed that it does. This colorful state case, decided before adoption of the Federal Rules, illustrates the assumption:

Example: Bonnie Ritter purchased a bottle of Coca-Cola from a vending machine and took a swallow. The drink tasted odd, so she examined the bottle more closely. Inside her Coke, Ritter found the torso and tail of a decomposed mouse. She consulted her physician, James Duncan, who conducted several tests and concluded that Ritter had suffered no physical injury from the contaminated drink.

But Ritter started to suffer severe emotional distress. She had trouble sleeping and, when she did sleep, she dreamed of mice. She was unable to drink translucent liquids and she developed an intense fear of mice. She consulted a psychiatrist, Dr. Glenn Bacon, and described her symptoms to him.

Ritter also sued Coca-Cola and called Bacon as a witness. Bacon described the symptoms that Ritter reported to him; Coca-Cola objected to the testimony as hearsay.

---

4   This example is based on Ramrattan v. Burger King Corp., 656 F. Supp. 522 (D. Md. 1987). The original opinion does not specify the exact statements made by the plaintiff at the hospital.

Analysis: Bacon's description of Ritter's statements was admissible under the common law doctrines predating Rule 803(4). Ritter consulted Bacon to obtain "psychotherapeutic relief for her symptoms." The same desire that motivates other patients to speak truthfully to doctors, the court concluded, prompted Ritter's statements. She wanted to recover from the psychological anguish she suffered and she described her experiences and symptoms for that reason.[5]

More recent cases reach the same result under the Federal Rules. In *Swinton v. Potomac Corp.*,[6] for example, plaintiff Swinton had suffered constant demeaning racist comments at work. After leaving the company due to this harassment, Swinton sought treatment from two psychologists. The psychologists recorded Swinton's description of the harassing incidents as part of the medical history needed to treat him, and Swinton offered these records during a race discrimination suit against his prior employer. The court approved admission of these statements under Rule 803(4), finding their admissibility well established.

Application of Rule 803(4) to medical treatment of psychological injuries can encompass a large number of statements. In many cases, however, these statements are just as reliable—and just as necessary for treatment—as descriptions of physical injuries. Just as a doctor cannot treat a bump on the head without knowing how the bump occurred, it would be difficult for a psychiatrist to address Ritter's fear of mice without knowing how that fear arose. In Swinton's case, adequate treatment probably required that the psychologist know that Swinton's exposure to insulting racist comments occurred at work; the occupational context creates a particular type of emotional injury. Swinton's recital of the racist slurs incriminated his employer, but so would descriptions of exposure to asbestos and other physical toxins in the workplace.

As the next section shows, however, statements about the "general cause" of a psychological injury sometimes are very difficult to separate from comments attributing blame.

---

5   Ritter v. The Coca-Cola Co., 128 N.W.2d 439 (Wis. 1964).

6   270 F.3d 794 (9th Cir. 2001).

6. Medical Treatment for Domestic or Sexual Abuse. Statements made to doctors play a particularly important role in prosecutions for domestic or sexual abuse. The victims of these crimes sometimes refuse to testify in court. The prosecutor, therefore, may use the victim's previous statement to a doctor to prove that the injury occurred. But can the prosecutor also use these statements to prove the identity of the perpetrator?

With most injuries, the identity of the person who caused the injury is irrelevant to medical treatment. As noted above, the doctor needs to know that the patient was hit on the head with a wrench, but not that Steve wielded the wrench. The line between cause and fault usually precludes evidence of identity, although in cases of occupational injury the employer's identity often is obvious.

In a series of child abuse cases, however, some courts have found the perpetrator's identity pertinent to treatment, and thus admissible under 803(4), on one of two grounds. **First**, some courts have held that treatment of a patient suffering regular, ongoing abuse may include separation of the patient from the abuser. Under this view, the identity of the abuser is pertinent to formulating the appropriate treatment.

Second, effective psychological treatment of an abuse victim may require the doctor to know who caused the abuse. An orthopedist may only need to know that someone broke the patient's arm, not who committed that act. But appropriate psychological treatment of that patient may depend on whether the attacker was a husband, boss, friend, or other person. Different psychological states both lead to and stem from these varying sources of abuse.

Courts have found these rationales especially persuasive in cases involving child sexual abuse: [7]

> **Example:** Gary Longie was accused of repeatedly sexually assaulting his daughter when she was between the ages of six and eleven years old. At trial, a pediatrician testified for the government that the daughter identified Longie as her abuser. The trial judge admitted these hearsay statements under Rule 803(4).

---

[7] Danaipour v. McLarey, 386 F.3d 289, 297–98 (1st Cir. 2004).

Analysis: The court of appeals affirmed, finding that statements identifying a family member as the abuser are "reasonably pertinent" to medical diagnosis or treatment. The court reiterated that the statements must meet the requirements of Rule 803(4): (1) the declarant's motive in making the statement must be consistent with the purpose of promoting treatment; and (2) the content of the statement must be the type that a doctor would reasonably rely upon in treatment or diagnosis. [8]

Other courts have observed that sexual abuse of a child by a family member generates emotional and psychological problems uniquely tied to the particular family relationship.[9] Identity of the abuser thus is pertinent to the patient's diagnosis and treatment.

 Two federal circuits and some state courts have used similar reasoning to admit statements made by adults who identify an alleged domestic abuser while seeking medical treatment.[10] These cases, as well as the ones involving child victims, are controversial. Those who support this application of Rule 803(4) note that health care workers cannot adequately treat child abuse or domestic violence without knowledge of the abuser's identity. Thus, they argue, the abuser's identity is "reasonably pertinent to" treatment and carries the same indicia of reliability as other statements made for the purpose of seeking medical treatment. Opponents of this interpretation point to the traditional line between "general cause" and attacker identity under Rule 803(4); they also stress the danger of relying upon any hearsay evidence to convict a criminal defendant.

---

8   United States v. Longie, 984 F.2d 955 (8th Cir. 1995).

9   United States v. Peneaux, 432 F.3d 882 (8th Cir. 2005).

10   United States v. John, 2017 WL 1046122 (9th Cir. 2017); United States v. Joe, 8 F.3d 1488 (10th Cir. 1993).

Quick Summary

Rule 803(4) creates an exception to the hearsay rule for statements made about the symptoms or cause of a medical condition, when the declarant makes those statements for the purpose of medical diagnosis or treatment. These statements are more reliable than other forms of hearsay because patients have a self-interest in reporting accurate information to obtain medical treatment. The exception also serves a pragmatic function by facilitating introduction of written medical records.

Rule 803(4) admits some statements made by family members helping a patient obtain medical care, as well as statements made by the patient to family members or other nonprofessionals in order to obtain that care. The touchstone is whether the statement was made by and to someone for "medical diagnosis or treatment." The rule also includes statements made to doctors who offer diagnoses in connection with litigation rather than treatment. Most courts have assumed that the rule also encompasses statements made to obtain treatment for psychological conditions.

The rule, however, does not include statements that assign fault or blame; courts redact those references from otherwise admissible statements. A growing number of courts have deviated from that practice by admitting statements that identify the alleged perpetrator of child sexual abuse; a few also admit identifications made by adult victims of domestic violence. These decisions remain controversial.

Test Your Understanding

To assess your understanding of the material in this chapter, <u>click here</u> to take a quiz, or go to the Quizzes module from the eBook on your eProducts bookshelf.

43

Hearsay Exception—Recorded Recollection

Key Concepts

- **Rule 803(5):** Allows Admission of Recorded Recollection
- Declarant Must Testify and Lack Current Memory
- Other Foundation Requirements
- Witness May Read Recorded Recollection; Only Adverse Party May Admit as Exhibit

---

A. Introduction and Policy. Rule 612, which we discussed in Chapter 16, anticipates that trial judges will allow witnesses to "refresh memory" from notes or other documents. To remain consistent with the hearsay rules, however, the witness may not testify from the written materials directly, but instead must speak from her own independent memory after it has been refreshed. For example:

> **Q:** What was the license plate number of the car that you saw driving away?
>
> **A:** I don't remember.
>
> **Q:** Did you write the number down anywhere?
>
> **A:** Yes, I wrote the number down on the back of my checkbook.
>
> **Q:** Would it refresh your memory to see the back of your checkbook where you wrote the number?
>
> **A:** Yes, it would.
>
> **Q:** Your honor, may I approach the witness?
>
> **Court:** You may.

[Counsel shows a checkbook to the witness. The witness looks at it and then gives it back to the attorney].

Q: Do you remember now what the license plate number was?

A: Yes. It was DFR-677.

Rule 612 allows this type of testimony, but in many cases it creates a legal fiction. In the above example, the odds are that the witness has completely forgotten the license plate number by the time of trial. When she looks at the back of her checkbook, she is not really refreshing an old memory but is creating a new short-term memory. After looking at the checkbook, the witness recites a number that she has just memorized by looking at the back of the checkbook—not one she genuinely remembers from seeing the actual license plate months or years earlier.

In a case like this, the witness's notation of the number, written immediately after the accident, is the best evidence of the license number. Pretending to refresh her memory by showing her the notation adds nothing to the probative value of the evidence. It is also disingenuous for the witness and her attorney to claim that she is "refreshing her memory" with the notation. Why not simply admit the notation itself?

Rule 803(5) allows admission of this type of evidence, called "recorded recollection," under specified circumstances. The rule is another exception to the hearsay bar. The witness's note about the license plate is hearsay: It is an assertion made outside the courtroom that a party wants to introduce to prove the truth of the matter asserted, the license plate number.

Rule 803(5) acknowledges that these recorded recollections are particularly reliable because (1) they were made when the declarant's memory was fresh, and (2) the declarant is available to testify in the courtroom, under oath, and subject to cross-examination about the circumstances under which she recorded the statement.

In addition to the fact that these statements are more reliable than most other hearsay, these statements are more needed than most other hearsay. The exception for recorded recollection applies only when the witness can no longer recall the information that was recorded. The only way to get those facts before the jury, therefore, is to allow the jury to hear the out-of-court statement. This combination of heightened reliability and a special need for the statement justifies Rule 803(5).

B. The Rule. Rule 803(5) has more prerequisites than the other hearsay exceptions we have studied:

RULE 803. Exceptions to the Rule Against Hearsay — Regardless of Whether the Declarant Is Available as a Witness

The following are not excluded by the rule against hearsay, regardless of whether the declarant is available as a witness: . . .

(5) *Recorded Recollection.* A <u>record</u> that:

    (A) is on a matter the <u>witness once knew</u> about <u>but now cannot recall</u> well enough to testify fully and accurately;

    (B) was <u>made or adopted</u> by the witness when the matter was <u>fresh</u> in the witness's memory; and

    (C) <u>accurately reflects</u> the witness's knowledge.

If admitted, the record <u>may be read into evidence</u> but may be received as an <u>exhibit only if offered by an adverse party</u>.

Rule 803(5) shares the same preamble as the other Rule 803 exceptions; this preamble excuses the proponent from showing that the declarant is unavailable. Unlike the other Rule 803 exceptions, however, Rule 803(5) requires that the declarant actually **be available**, because the rule applies only when the declarant testifies as a witness.

Rule 803(5) includes two parts. The first part, which contains three subsections, specifies when a recorded recollection is admissible. The second part, which consists of a single sentence, explains the manner of introducing the evidence. Let's look at each part of the rule.

1. Admissibility of Recorded Recollection. Embedded within the first part of **Rule 803(5)** are six requirements for admissibility. These requirements further the rationales for admission discussed in the Introduction.

First, the rule requires that the out-of-court statement appear in a "record." **Rule 101(b)(4)** makes clear that records include "a memorandum, report, or data compilation." The hearsay exception does not require an old-fashioned writing, but the declarant must have memorialized the recollection in some way.

Second, the witness testifying in court must either be the declarant who made the record or a person who saw the record and agreed that it was true. In the latter case, the person "adopted" the record as true, effectively making it her own statement. By requiring the witness to have either seen or confirmed the truth of the record, this requirement ensures that the opposing party can conduct an effective cross-examination about the record's accuracy.

Third, the declarant/witness must testify that she once knew about the information contained in the record, and that she made or adopted the record when she had that knowledge. This helps to satisfy **Rule 602**'s requirement that a witness have personal knowledge of an event.

Fourth, the witness must have made or adopted the record at a time when her knowledge was "fresh." This heightens reliability of the recorded information.

Fifth, the witness must testify that at the time she made or adopted the record, she knew that it accurately reflected the knowledge that she had. This further confirms the statement's reliability.

And **finally,** the witness must no longer recall the information contained in the record "well enough to testify fully and accurately." Satisfying this requirement demonstrates that the hearsay is necessary; direct testimony is not available.

2. Introducing Evidence. Although a recorded recollection is sufficiently reliable to present to the jury under the circumstances described above, Rule 803(5) recognizes a paradox in admitting the recorded statement into evidence: Because the statement is written, a jury may give it more weight than if the witness recalled the evidence and testified about it orally.

For that reason, the second part of Rule 803(5) prevents the party offering a recorded recollection from introducing the document directly into evidence as an exhibit. Instead, the party presenting the evidence must ask the witness to read the document into the record. This format gives the evidence an effect similar to the witness remembering the information and testifying about it orally.

An adverse party, however, may choose to introduce the document as an exhibit. A party might decide to do this if the document revealed some unreliability in its content. In the example involving the witness and the license plate, for example, imagine that the attorney laid a proper foundation for Rule 803(5) and then asked the witness to read the license number from her checkbook. If the numbers on the checkbook are smudged or difficult to read, opposing counsel might move to admit the checkbook as an exhibit. The checkbook's condition might suggest that the witness's recording of the plate number was unreliable.

C. In the Courtroom.

1. Insufficient Recollection. Rule 803(5) allows evidence of recorded recollections only when a witness lacks sufficient memory "to testify fully and accurately." Courts enforce this requirement to prevent parties from circumventing the hearsay rule and bolstering a witness's testimony with previous statements. The witness need not claim complete memory loss to invoke Rule 803(5), but the examining attorney must show that the witness forgot details important to the testimony. Without this foundation, the judge will exclude the recorded recollection:

> **Example:** The United States indicted Robert Craft and three colleagues for conspiracy to commit fraud through a bogus investment scheme known as "Wealth-Mart." As part of their scheme, Craft and his coconspirators hosted a series of investment seminars for their targets. At trial, the trial judge allowed several of these defrauded investors to read into the record notes they had taken at these seminars; the trial judge held that the notes were admissible under Rule 803(5).

> **Analysis:** The court of appeals disagreed with the trial court's ruling. Although the notes satisfied some of the prerequisites for admission under Rule 803(5), the prosecutor made no effort to establish that the investors lacked independent recall of events at the seminars. None of the investors declared on the stand that they lacked memory of the events; their responses to the prosecutor's questions, moreover, suggested that they continued to recall substantial detail from the seminars. Under these circumstances, the prosecutor failed to lay a proper foundation for the witnesses to read from the notes under 803(5).[1]

---

1   United States v. Dazey, 403 F.3d 1147, 1166–67 (10th Cir. 2005).

Here is a case in which counsel laid a proper 803(5) foundation:

Example: Garland and Bonnie Greger owned a house in central Missouri. The Discwasher Company built a factory next to the Gregers' home and began manufacturing disc-cleaning equipment. The company started emitting small sawdust particles onto the Gregers' land and the Gregers sued for nuisance. At trial, the district judge allowed Bonnie Greger to read aloud from a diary in which she recorded day-to-day problems with the factory. Bonnie testified that she made the entries as they occurred, that the entries were correct at the time, and that she could no longer remember specific details from the ongoing annoyances.

Analysis: The judge properly allowed Bonnie to read aloud from the diary. This is a classic example of details that a witness records as they occur but that are difficult to remember with particularity months or years later. Rule 803(5) allows a witness to read recorded recollection under these circumstances.[2]

The Greger example involved witnesses who genuinely forgot details of events that transpired months or years before trial. Rule 803(5) applies to these cases, but it also encompasses cases in which witnesses feign memory failure. Witnesses called by the prosecution, for example, sometimes "forget" details that would harm a friend or family member on trial. If the witness recorded his recollection at an earlier time, the prosecutor can attempt to lay a foundation for admitting that statement. Establishing that foundation is difficult with an uncooperative witness, but Rule 803(5) allows counsel to attempt this route.

2. Made or Adopted. Rule 803(5) recognizes that a witness need not memorialize a recollection himself, as our sample witness did in jotting a license number in her checkbook. Often, a witness makes a statement to a police investigator or other official. As long as the witness approved the content of the recording while his recollection was still fresh, and then affirms at trial that he believed the recording was accurate at the time, this combination will satisfy Rule 803(5).

Example: The government prosecuted Glen Williams for cashing government checks with forged signatures. Williams's friend, Gary Ball, testified for the prosecution. Ball recalled some details about Williams's

---

2   Greger v. International Jensen, Inc., 820 F.2d 937, 942–43 (8th Cir. 1987).

check-cashing activities, but could not remember others. The government then offered portions of a statement that Ball had made to an FBI agent before trial. The agent, rather than Ball, wrote the statement summarizing Ball's comments; the agent did not report Ball's words verbatim. The defense objected to the statement as hearsay.

Analysis: The trial judge allowed the prosecutor to read portions of Ball's statement into the record. Although the agent wrote the statement, Ball read the statement, agreed that it was accurate, and signed it. He thus adopted the statement. The prosecutor satisfied the other prerequisites of Rule 803(5), allowing Ball's recorded recollection to reach the jury.[3]

But if a witness refuses to adopt a statement, then Rule 803(5) does not allow its introduction into evidence:

Example: The government charged Sheldon Schoenborn, a prison inmate, with attacking another inmate. Shortly after the attack, an FBI agent interviewed a prisoner, Todd Coleman, who witnessed at least part of the attack. The agent compiled Coleman's comments into a report, but Coleman refused to sign the report. At trial, the prosecutor attempted to use Coleman as a witness. When Coleman claimed little memory of the events, the prosecutor attempted to have him read the FBI report under Rule 803(5). The defense objected on the ground that Coleman never adopted the report.

Analysis: The court of appeals agreed that Coleman never adopted the FBI agent's report. Therefore, the report was not admissible under Rule 803(5). Even if the agent accurately transcribed Coleman's words, as the agent claimed, the rule requires that the witness make or adopt the recorded recollection.[4]

3. Freshness. Rule 803(5)'s requirement that a witness record information "when the matter was fresh in the witness's memory" does not require contemporaneous notetaking. Courts, in fact, have allowed introduction of recorded recollections

---

3   United States v. Williams, 571 F.2d 344, 348 (6th Cir. 1978).

4   United States v. Schoenborn, 4 F.3d 1424, 1426–29 (7th Cir. 1993).

created as long as fifteen months after an event, as long as circumstances indicate that the witness genuinely remembered the information at the time it was recorded.

> **Example:** The government indicted Robert Smith and several of his relatives for conspiracy to defraud insurance companies. Over three years, the Smith family staged thirty different auto accidents and slip-and-fall cases, filing a variety of insurance claims based on the alleged injuries.
>
> Amy Payne, who took part in one of the staged accidents, provided testimony for the prosecution. At trial, Payne indicated that she could no longer recall who had parked the car and called the police during the staged accident she participated in. On cross-examination, the lawyer for one of Smith's co-defendants asked Payne to read from a statement she had given to a detective fifteen months after the accident. In that statement, Payne identified Robert Smith as the person responsible for those acts.
>
> Payne testified at trial that, although she could no longer remember who had done what during the staged accident, she did not intend to lie to the detective and she would not have lied in giving her statement. She affirmed that "if that's who I said it was, then that's who it was." Smith challenged this testimony as hearsay.

Analysis: Payne's prior statement was hearsay: Smith's codefendant offered this out-of-court statement to prove the truth of the matter asserted, that Smith (rather than any of his codefendants) was responsible for the staged accident. But the court allowed Payne to read the statement aloud under Rule 803(5). Payne testified at trial that she could no longer recall details of the staged event. At the same time, she stated that she would not have lied to the detective and that the details she gave him were true. Even though Payne's statement to the detective occurred fifteen months after the accident, these assurances were sufficient to invoke Rule 803(5).[5]

4. Beyond Writings. Most cases arising under Rule 803(5) involve written records of a witness's recollection. Judges, however, have construed the rule's reference to "record" broadly to include audiotapes and other media.

---

5   United States v. Smith, 197 F.3d 225, 230–31 (6th Cir. 1999).

Example: The government charged Donald Sollars with burning to the ground a drive-through convenience store called the "Milk Barn." Sollars's stepdaughter, Joleena Wade, told a federal investigator that she saw Sollars on the roof of the Milk Barn the night of the fire.

At trial, Wade claimed she could no longer remember seeing anyone on the roof; nor could she remember whether she had said anything to the investigator about seeing someone on the roof. She did, however, remember speaking to the investigator and acknowledged that she had a fresh recollection of the events at that time. Wade also testified that she answered the investigator's questions truthfully. The government then moved to play a tape recording of Wade's comments to the investigator.

Analysis: Rule 803(5) allowed the prosecutor to play the recording. It was an audio recording of Wade's recollection, created shortly after the disputed events. Since Wade could no longer remember the events themselves, Rule 803(5) allowed the government to "read" her recorded recollection into the record. In this case, the audiotape served as that reading.[6]

5. Recorded Recollection and Refreshment. Lawyers and judges sometimes confuse Rule 803(5) with the practice of refreshing memory under Rule 612. The table below outlines the difference between the two practices.

---

6   United States v. Sollars, 979 F.2d 1294, 1298 (8th Cir. 1992).

Refreshing Memory Compared to Recorded Recollection

Rule 612: Refreshing Memory	**Rule 803(5):** Recorded Recollection
• **Need Arises When:** Witness cannot recall details of an event or other matter of which she once had personal knowledge	• **Need Arises When:** Witness cannot recall details of an event or other matter of which she once had personal knowledge
• **What Witness Does:** Looks at evidence (usually a writing) to jog memory, then testifies orally without referring further to evidence	• **What Witness Does:** Reads into record information from a document or other record
• **What Type of Evidence:** Any writing or other evidence that will help witness remember; the witness need not have created or adopted the material	• **What Type of Document or Other Record:** One that the witness "made or adopted" when the matter was "fresh" in the witness's memory. Record must correctly reflect witness's personal knowledge at time it was recorded.
• **Who May Introduce Evidence Used to Refresh:** Only adverse party (i.e., party that did not call witness)	• **Who May Introduce Recorded Recollection:** Only adverse party (i.e., party that did not call witness)
• **Relationship to Hearsay:** Witness testifies directly from memory after refreshment, so there is no hearsay issue. If adverse party introduces writing into evidence, it is admissible only on the issue of credibility. For the jury to consider the writing for the truth of the matter asserted, it must fall within a hearsay exception.	• **Relationship to Hearsay:** Statements contained in the record are admitted as an exception to the hearsay rule. The jury may consider the content of the document or other record, as read into the trial record by the witness, for the truth of the matters asserted.

Evidence in Practice

To practice your knowledge of the hearsay exceptions you have learned so far, take the role of defense attorney in *State v. Hanley*. Click here or access the **Evidence in Practice** module from the eBook on your eProducts bookshelf.

Quick Summary

When a witness lacks current memory of an event, **Rule 803(5)** allows introduction of a recorded recollection. The recollection must appear in a "record" and the witness must be the declarant who made or adopted the recording. In addition, the witness must once have had personal knowledge of the details in the recording; must have made or adopted the record when the memory was still fresh; and must testify that she believed the record was accurate at the time it was made or adopted.

Most recorded recollections are written, but courts recognize records in other forms. To prevent the recorded recollection from disproportionately affecting jury deliberations, the witness may read the recorded information into the trial transcript, but the party offering the evidence may not introduce the document itself into evidence. An adverse party may choose to admit the record as an exhibit. In either case, the jury may consider information contained within the recorded recollection for any purpose; Rule 803(5) is an exception to the hearsay rule allowing an out-of-court statement to be considered for the truth of the matter asserted.

Test Your Understanding

To assess your understanding of the material in this chapter, click here to take a quiz, or go to the Quizzes module from the eBook on your eProducts bookshelf.

44

Rule 805—Hearsay Within Hearsay

Key Concepts

- **Rule 805:** Multiple Levels of Hearsay Are Admissible as Long as Each Layer Fits Within an Exception
- Challenges in Laying a Foundation

A. Introduction and Policy. When a witness repeats an out-of-court statement, that evidence is hearsay if offered to prove the truth of the matter asserted. For example, if a witness says, "Anderson told me the letters were mailed out on July 17th," that testimony is hearsay if offered to prove that the letters were, in fact, mailed on July 17th.

Similarly, any information in a document is hearsay if offered to prove the truth of the matter asserted. By definition, the statements in a document were made out of court. So statements in police reports, medical records, insurance claim forms, bank loan applications, and even widely distributed books are all hearsay.

The ubiquity of hearsay means that some testimony contains multiple levels of hearsay. Witnesses often try to testify about a chain of communications, such as:

> "Anderson told me that his secretary informed him the letters were mailed out on July 17th."

> "The nurse told me that the patient had been complaining about a headache and nausea."

> "My neighbor came by and said that she had just heard on the radio that a police officer had been shot downtown."

Written documents often contain statements made by third parties. A police officer, for example, may talk to several witnesses while investigating an accident. The officer will record the witnesses' statements, as well as her own observations, on a long written form. The form itself is hearsay, if offered in court to prove the truth of the matters asserted, because it consists of statements made outside the courtroom. But the form also contains secondhand statements: the officer's record of what other witnesses said. Even if the officer attempted to record the witnesses' statements verbatim, the form contains at least two levels of hearsay. It is an out-of-court report by a police officer containing out-of-court statements by witnesses.

These statements are called "hearsay within hearsay," otherwise known as "double hearsay" or "multiple hearsay." **Rule 805** allows hearsay within hearsay to be admitted as long as each out-of-court statement is admissible under an exception.

Example: Harry was stabbed by an intruder in his apartment. His roommate Dale came home to find Harry lying on the ground, weak but still lucid. "Call an ambulance," Harry said, "I was stabbed in the stomach with a switchblade knife." Dale became quite upset and dialed 911 in an excited state, exclaiming to the operator: "Please come quickly! My friend Harry says he was stabbed in the stomach with a switchblade!"

At trial, the prosecutor wishes to prove that Harry was stabbed in the stomach with a switchblade knife. She calls the 911 operator to the stand to testify about what Dale told her about Harry's statement. Is this admissible?

Analysis: Yes, the 911 operator's testimony is admissible to prove the truth of the matter asserted by Harry. The first step is to determine whether the operator can testify about what Dale told her. Dale's statement to the operator qualifies as an excited utterance, so Dale's statement is admissible for the truth of the matter asserted, even though it was an out-of-court statement.

But this only gets us halfway. Dale's statement was: "My friend Harry says he was stabbed in the stomach with a switchblade!" If we admit Dale's statement for the truth of the matter asserted, all we know for sure is that Harry **claimed he was stabbed** in the stomach. In order to admit Harry's statement to Dale, proving that he was **in fact stabbed** in the stomach, we must ensure that

Harry's statement fits some hearsay exception. In this case, Harry's statement was made for the purpose of medical diagnosis or treatment, so it is also admissible for the truth of the matter asserted.

The layers of hearsay in this example look like this:

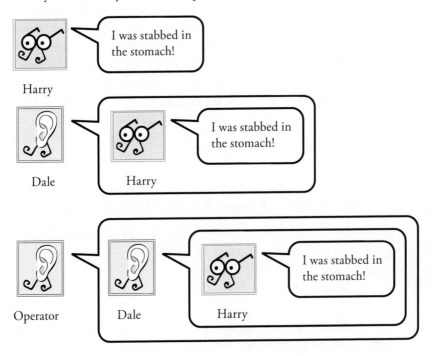

Because each layer of hearsay fits into its own exception, the operator's statement is admissible. The same analysis would apply if the prosecutor used a transcript or an audio recording of the 911 call instead of the 911 operator herself. Dale's voice on the recording would be a hearsay statement, admissible only because he was excited when he uttered it. And Harry's statement, reported by Dale, is only admissible because it was a statement made for the purpose of medical diagnosis or treatment.

If either of the layers fails to satisfy an exception, the entire statement is inadmissible to prove the truth of the matter asserted by the original declarant. For example, suppose Dale did not call 911 immediately; he first finished a phone call with his girlfriend. By the time Dale called 911 ten minutes later, he was quite calm and collected. Dale's statement, then, would not fit any hearsay exception and the operator could not testify about it. If Harry and Dale are unavailable to testify, the jury will never hear about Harry's statement to Dale.

Likewise, assume that part of Harry's statement was not made for the purpose of medical diagnosis or treatment. For example, if Harry calmly told Dale: "A man wearing a red shirt and black jeans attacked me a few minutes ago," Harry's description of the intruder's clothing would not fit any hearsay exception. Even if Dale was upset and excited when he relayed this information to the 911 operator, the operator would not be able to repeat Harry's description of the intruder's clothing as evidence of the intruder's appearance. Under these circumstances, Dale's statement to the operator fits the excited utterance exception to the hearsay rule, but Harry's calm description does not fit any exception.

B . The Rule. Rule 805's text is straightforward:

> ## RULE 805. Hearsay Within Hearsay
>
> Hearsay within hearsay is not excluded by the rule against hearsay if <u>each part</u> of the combined statements conforms with an exception to the rule.

The rule covers double hearsay, and even multiple levels of hearsay like triple hearsay, as long as each out-of-court statement is admissible under some hearsay exception.

C. In the Courtroom. Rule 805 does not raise many issues of interpretation. The difficulties lie primarily in recognizing the existence of multiple hearsay levels and, when they exist, coping with their presence.

1. Laying a Foundation. For the proponent of evidence that contains multiple hearsay, it can be difficult to lay a foundation for the first out-of-court statement in the chain. The facts needed to establish that foundation may be difficult to obtain.

In the example involving Harry and Dale, for example, assume that neither of these speakers is available at trial. For the operator to testify about Harry's statement, the prosecutor must establish a foundation for both that statement and for Dale's statement.

Laying a foundation for Dale's statement is similar to laying a foundation in an uncomplicated case of single hearsay. The operator spoke directly to Dale, so she can testify about his tone of voice, other exclamations he made, his coherency, and other matters that might show that he was in an excited state of mind. Those facts will establish the foundation to admit Dale's statement as an excited utterance.

But the operator did not speak directly to Harry, so it will be harder for the prosecutor to show that Harry spoke for purposes of obtaining medical diagnosis or treatment. If Harry asked explicitly for an ambulance, and if Dale mentioned that fact to the operator, then that is strong evidence that Harry was seeking medical care. But, as in the example given above, Dale would not necessarily repeat that statement to the operator. If Dale reports only that Harry said he was stabbed in the stomach with a switchblade knife, it may be difficult to establish that Harry made this statement to obtain medical assistance. The 911 operator won't know whether Harry asked explicitly for medical care, whether he was trying to get to the phone himself to summon an ambulance, or other facts that might establish the foundation for an 803(4) exception.

Similarly, even if Harry spoke under the stress of excitement when he made his statement to Dale, it may be difficult for the prosecutor to establish that fact. To admit Harry's statement as an excited utterance, the judge would want to know about Harry's tone of voice, what other statements or exclamations he made, how badly Harry was injured, how much time elapsed between the stabbing and Harry's statement, and many other factors. Since the 911 operator only spoke with Dale, she probably cannot answer these questions about Harry.

With multiple hearsay, in other words, the courtroom witness usually lacks information about early declarants in the communication chain. Without that information, it can be challenging to establish the foundation needed to admit those initial statements.

2. Truth of the Matter Asserted. Some testimony appears to contain multiple layers of hearsay, but closer examination reveals a simpler situation. Remember that out-of-court statements are hearsay only when a proponent offers them for the truth of the matter asserted. A statement offered for some other purpose, such as to show the existence of a warning, is not hearsay.

One out-of-court statement may include another statement that is offered to prove something other than the truth of its contents. The embedded statement, then, is

not hearsay. A party can introduce testimony like this by identifying an exception just for the layer that is hearsay:

> **Example:** Officer Ferguson responded to a report of a domestic dispute. When he arrived at the scene, he saw Tyler Kouris running out of the house yelling: "Help! My brother Xavier says he's got a gun and he's threatening to shoot his wife!" Ferguson ran into the house and saw Xavier Kouris in the kitchen with his back to the officer. When Xavier spun around to face the officer, Ferguson saw a black object in Xavier's hand. Ferguson immediately shot Kouris in the chest, killing him.
>
> It turned out that Xavier never had a gun; the object in his hand was a wallet with identification that he intended to show Officer Ferguson. Xavier's family sued Ferguson and the police department, claiming that Ferguson was unjustified in his use of deadly force against Xavier. At trial, Ferguson wants to take the stand and testify about what Tyler shouted when he arrived at the house. The plaintiff objects, arguing that although Tyler's statement to Ferguson was an excited utterance, Xavier's statement that he had a gun was inadmissible hearsay.

> **Analysis:** Ferguson's testimony, including Xavier's statement, is admissible. Although at first this appears to be hearsay within hearsay, it is really just a simple hearsay problem. Think the problem through this way:
>
> The first layer of this testimony is Tyler's statement to Ferguson. This statement qualifies as an excited utterance, so the statement: "My brother Xavier says he has a gun and he's threatening to shoot his wife!" is admissible for the truth of the matter asserted. In other words, the jury may consider this statement as evidence that Xavier really said that he had a gun and was going to shoot his wife.
>
> If we know that Xavier said this, do we also have to know whether Xavier really had a gun and really intended to shoot his wife? No, the truth of that matter is not relevant to the claim against Ferguson. In fact, we know that Xavier's statement was not true; he did not have a gun.
>
> In this case, only the fact that Xavier **claimed** to have a gun and threatened to shoot his wife is relevant; that statement by Xavier may have given Ferguson reasonable grounds to shoot him. Since we only care whether Xavier spoke

those words—not the truth of the words themselves—Xavier's statement is not hearsay.

After eliminating this possible layer of hearsay, we are left with Tyler's statement to Ferguson: a single layer of hearsay that is admissible as an excited utterance.

As we move through the other hearsay exceptions, watch for situations in which one out-of-court statement is embedded within another one. If a party offers both layers for the truth of the matter asserted, each layer must have its own hearsay exception in order for the statement to be admissible.

Quick Summary

 One out-of-court statement often is embedded in another out-of-court statement. A declarant, for example, will report on what someone else told him, or a document will contain a quote from a third party. Rule 805 provides that these double hearsay statements are admissible for the truth of the matter asserted as long as each level of the statement fits into an exception. However, it may be difficult to lay the foundation for the original out-of-court statement, because the witness testifying on the stand may not know much about the context of the original declarant's statement.

45

Hearsay Exception—Business Records

Key Concepts

- **Rule 803(6):** Admits Business Records
- Broad Definition of "Business"
- Record Must Be Kept in the Course of a Regularly Conducted Business Activity
- Must Be Regular Practice to Keep Record
- Trustworthiness Caveat Bars Records Made in Anticipation of Litigation
- Double Hearsay Issues

A. Introduction and Policy. Organizations generate hundreds, even thousands, of documents a day: payroll sheets, internal memoranda, shipping orders, employee evaluations, and much more. Many of these documents are relevant to litigation but, like any document, each one of them is hearsay if admitted for the truth of the matter asserted.

Although these records are hearsay, there are two reasons to believe that they are **more reliable** than other kinds of hearsay. First, organizations generate most of these documents according to well established, routine practices. The organization's procedures are likely to reduce mistakes in documentation and to detect those that do occur.

Second, organizations rely upon documents like these to make important decisions. Large businesses rely on routinely generated documents to make choices worth millions of dollars; smaller organizations like churches and public interest groups use their documents to make equally critical decisions. The individuals who create, verify, and maintain these documents know how essential they are to the organization's mission, so these individuals have strong incentives to exercise care and honesty about the information in these documents.

In addition to the extra indicia of reliability in organizational records, information in these documents is more needed than information contained in many other kinds of hearsay. Organizational records often document thousands of pieces of information, each one coming from a different employee. Some records may compile facts and figures gathered from hundreds of other employees. It would be nearly impossible to introduce this evidence in court if a party had to call each of the individual employees who contributed to a business record. Many of the employees would not even remember the information they previously had recorded.[1] Often, the only feasible way to give the fact finder information contained in a business document—which may be highly probative in litigation—is to introduce the document itself.

Recognizing both the extra indicia of reliability inherent in routine business records and the need for the information contained in those documents, courts created another exception to the hearsay rule, the "business records" exception. That exception now appears in Rule 803(6). The exception admits nearly every document that an organization generates in the ordinary course of "business." The rule, moreover, defines business to include any type of organization or association, whether or not conducted for profit.

B. The Rule. The business records exception is yet another hearsay exception appearing in Rule 803. Because of its placement in that rule, the exception applies whether or not the declarant is available to testify.

RULE 803. Exceptions to the Rule Against Hearsay— Regardless of Whether the Declarant Is Available as a Witness

The following are not excluded by the rule against hearsay, regardless of whether the declarant is available as a witness: . . .

(6) *Records of a Regularly Conducted Activity.* A <u>record</u> of an act, event, condition, opinion, or diagnosis if:

    (A) the record was made at or near the time by—or from information transmitted by—someone with <u>knowledge</u>;

---

[1] If the employee did not remember the information, Rule 803(5) would allow her to take the stand and read from a document in which she recorded the information, but this would still require every employee who recorded any relevant fact to testify live on the stand. As a practical matter, this would be very difficult.

(B) the record was kept in the <u>course of a regularly conducted</u> activity of a <u>business</u>, organization, occupation, or calling, <u>whether or not for profit</u>;

(C) making the record was a <u>regular practice</u> of that activity;

(D) all these conditions are shown by the testimony of the custodian or another <u>qualified witness</u>, or by a certification that complies with Rule 902(11) or (12) or with a statute permitting certification; and

(E) the opponent does not show that the source of information or the method or circumstances of preparation indicate a lack of <u>trustworthiness</u>.

Rule 803(6) has six key elements. **First**, the exception applies to any "record." **Rule 101(b)(4)** defines record expansively to include any "memorandum, report, or data compilation." Records admitted under Rule 803(6), moreover, may contain information about an "act, event, condition, opinion, or diagnosis." Taken together, this language is broad enough to include almost any kind of information that an organization documents, regardless of its format. For example, the information does not have to be a fact; it could be a conclusion, analysis, or opinion, as long as the document complies with the other conditions of 803(6).

Second, the exception builds upon **Rule 602**'s personal knowledge requirement. Information admitted under the business records exception must have been recorded by (a) a person with personal knowledge of the data, or (b) a person who received that information from someone else in the organization with personal knowledge. The manager of a Jolt Cola plant, for example, can record the number of products produced by the plant each month without personally counting each of the cans and bottles. She can rely upon the reports of other employees with personal knowledge of the plant's production.

The personal knowledge provision requires information to be recorded "at or near the time" that the data arose. This timing requirement, however, is not nearly as strict as the contemporaneousness condition of the exception for present sense impressions discussed in Chapter 40. Information contained in organizational records simply needs to be recorded within a reasonable time, as guided by the needs of the organization itself.

Third, the organization must have made the record in the course of a regularly conducted business activity, and the organization must have a regular practice of keeping such records. These requirements serve two purposes: (1) They ensure that the recordkeeping is a routine process, which will tend to make the recordkeepers more accurate; and (2) They ensure that those who keep the records know that the company will rely on the records to be accurate. We will examine these related requirements in more detail in the Courtroom section below.

Fourth, a qualified witness must introduce the record into evidence. This witness often is the document's "custodian," the person who maintains the record for the organization. But, as we'll see in the Courtroom section, courts have interpreted this provision very broadly. Any person with the necessary knowledge to lay a proper foundation for admission of a document is qualified to introduce the document.

Rules 902(11) and (12) provide an alternative to courtroom testimony by a qualified witness.[2] Rather than testifying live in court, the custodian or other qualified witness may submit a certificate giving the information required by 803(6). It does not matter whether a party uses a live witness or written certificate authored by that witness; the determination of who is a qualified witness remains the same.

Fifth, 803(6) provides a caveat that a business record is **not** admissible if "the source of information or the method or circumstances of preparation indicate a lack of trustworthiness." The caveat recognizes that some regular business records lack the indicia of reliability discussed in the Introduction. An organization that routinely investigates and documents the cause of any injury on its premises, for example, may conduct this regular business practice primarily to prepare for any litigation stemming out of the injury. Under these circumstances the reports, although satisfying the other requirements of Rule 803(6), may be more self-serving than reliable. We will explore this issue further in the Courtroom section.

Note that the **opponent** of evidence offered as a business record bears the burden of showing that the record lacks trustworthiness. The party offering the records must establish other elements of the exception, but the court will assume records are trustworthy unless the opponent argues otherwise.

Finally, Rule 803(6) defines "business" very broadly. Indeed, the sub-section does not even use the colloquial term "business records" in its title. Instead, the exception applies to records kept by any "business, organization, occupation, or

---

2   We examine these provisions further in Chapter 69, which discusses authentication of documents.

calling, whether or not for profit." Since this exception rests on the extra indicia of reliability provided by routine recordkeeping and organizational reliance, it makes sense to apply the exception to any organization fitting these requirements. Even this broad definition, however, requires courts to draw lines between personal records and business records. We turn to that issue in the next section.

C. In the Courtroom.

1. What Is a Business? Although lawyers refer to Rule 803(6) as the business records exception, the rule applies to any "business, organization, occupation, or calling, whether or not for profit." Courts have construed this language very broadly to include the records of prisons,[3] colleges,[4] hospitals,[5] and even an individual who collected guns for investment purposes.[6] Self-employed individuals qualify as "businesses" under Rule 803(6). Even personal records kept for business reasons can qualify for the exception as long as they meet all conditions of the rule:

Example: Howard Keogh worked as a blackjack dealer at the Dunes Hotel in Las Vegas. A significant portion of his income came from tips, which all the Dunes dealers pooled daily to share. The IRS claimed that Keogh underreported his tips on his tax returns. Since the Dunes Hotel did not keep track of its employees' tips, the IRS attempted to prove the amount that Keogh received in tips by using the entries kept in another blackjack dealer's diary. The other dealer, named Whitlock, kept meticulous notes of the amount of tips that he received from the pool every day. Keogh objected to the IRS's use of Whitlock's diary as hearsay.

Analysis: The diary entries were hearsay, but were admissible under Rule 803(6). Although the diary was Whitlock's personal record, the evidence showed that Whitlock made each entry immediately after receiving the tips each night, that he regularly and continuously kept the records, and that they

---

3   Wheeler v. Sims, 951 F.2d 796 (7th Cir. 1992).

4   United States v. Basey, 613 F.2d 198 (9th Cir. 1979).

5   United States v. Sackett, 598 F.2d 739 (2d Cir. 1979).

6   United States v. Huber, 772 F.2d 585 (9th Cir. 1985).

were kept in the course of his own business activity, or "calling," as a blackjack dealer.[7]

2. Who Is a Custodian or Other Qualified Witness? To introduce business records under Rule 803(6), the proponent must call a witness who can lay a foundation for the documents. This witness must be able to testify that:

(1) The record was kept in the course of a regularly conducted business activity;

(2) The record was kept as part of a regular practice; and

(3) The record was made by someone with personal knowledge of the recorded information or from information transmitted by a person with that personal knowledge.

The person who lays this foundation does not have to be the person who made the record, nor does the witness even need to know exactly who made the record, as long as the witness knows the organization's recordkeeping practices. The witness might have been hired after the records were made; as long as she can testify knowledgeably about the organization's recordkeeping practices at the earlier time, that is sufficient.

Occasionally, even a person from outside the organization can lay the appropriate foundation for business records:

Example: Antonio Franco was on trial for conspiring to distribute 1,000 kilograms of marijuana. The government's evidence against Franco included the fact that during the six months he allegedly participated in the conspiracy, Franco made fifteen deposits totaling over $5.5 million at a currency exchange called Oscar's.

To prove this large number of deposits, the government introduced ledgers from Oscar's that kept track of all customer accounts. No employee from Oscar's was able to testify at trial, so the government called Narcotics Agent Jose Garza to lay a foundation for the ledgers. Garza had reviewed

---

7   Keogh v. Commissioner, 713 F.2d 496 (9th Cir. 1983).

the records extensively and spoken with Oscar's employees about how they kept the ledgers. Based on these discussions, Garza was prepared to testify about all three foundational criteria identified above. The defendant objected, claiming that Garza was not qualified to lay the foundation for the business records.

Analysis: Garza was qualified to lay the foundation for admitting the ledgers. Courts interpret the "qualified witness" language of 803(6) very broadly to include anyone "with knowledge of the procedure governing the creation and maintenance of the type of records sought to be admitted." Through his examination of the records and discussions with Oscar's employees, Garza had acquired that knowledge.

In reaching this decision, the trial judge relied on hearsay statements from Oscar's employees to determine the extent of Garza's knowledge. But this was permissible because **Rule 104(a)** allows the judge to consider inadmissible evidence when making a preliminary determination.[8]

As noted in the Introduction, Rule 803(6) allows a custodian or other qualified witness to provide a written statement certifying the foundational requirements for a business record, rather than testifying live. The written certification must provide the same information that the witness would offer through live testimony.

3. Regularly Conducted Business Activities and Regular Practices. Rule 803(6) has two separate "regularity" requirements that sound similar. The first requirement, that the record was "kept in the course of a regularly conducted activity" ensures that the organization relies on the document as part of its regular business. This condition gives the document special indicia of reliability. If the organization relies upon the record as part of a regular business activity, then it has a strong incentive to keep the record honestly and accurately. In addition to the care that an individual recordkeeper would exercise with this type of record, the organization is likely to adopt procedures promoting accuracy and verification of these records.

The second requirement, that "making the record was a regular practice of that activity," means that the organization must make this type of record on a regu-

---

8   United States v. Franco, 874 F.2d 1136 (7th Cir. 1989). See Chapter 34 to review the rules governing preliminary determinations.

lar basis. The record need not be made daily or weekly, but there must be some regularity or routine. This requirement also enhances the reliability of business records; ad hoc documents don't have the type of reliability that Rule 803(6) seeks. Documents prepared on an irregular basis are more likely to contain unreliable comments or self-serving statements created for litigation.

A record that satisfies one of these regularity requirements usually satisfies the other as well. Courts that reject a record on one of these grounds, therefore, often do not distinguish between them. Here is an example of a record that did not satisfy either regularity requirement:

> **Example:** Ross Kraemer applied for a tenure-track position as a professor of Biblical Studies at Franklin and Marshall College, but the College rejected his application. The Chair of the Religious Studies department, Thomas Hopkins, wrote a letter to the College's Dean protesting the way in which Kraemer's application had been handled. Kraemer later sued the College for discrimination and sought to admit Hopkins's letter as evidence that the College had treated him unfairly. Although the letter was hearsay, Kraemer claimed it was admissible as a business record of the College.

> **Analysis:** The trial court held that the letter was inadmissible. Protesting the College's hiring process was not a "regularly conducted activity." Department chairs, moreover, did not make a regular practice of generating such letters; a letter protesting the hiring process was an unusual occurrence.[9]

Hopkins's letter might have been admissible if it had been part of the College's routine hiring process. Hiring professors is a "regularly conducted activity" that all colleges perform as part of their larger mission. And most colleges follow a "regular practice" to document their hiring. The college, for example, might keep a file on each applicant for a position; that file might include notes submitted by any member of the college who evaluated the candidate. If Hopkins's comments had appeared in that type of file, they might have been part of a regular practice of documentation related to a regularly conducted business activity.

Some business records fulfill one of the regularity requirements but not the other. A company, for example, might conduct a one-time retreat to discuss a change

---

9   Kraemer v. Franklin & Marshall College, No. CIV. A. 95–0020, 1995 WL 681122 (E.D. Pa. Nov. 14, 1995).

in its marketing plans. Formulating marketing plans almost certainly would be a regularly conducted business activity for the company, but notes kept during a one-time retreat probably would not constitute documents kept as a regular practice. Notes taken at the retreat, therefore, would not be admissible under 803(6).

Although disputes sometimes arise over the "regularly conducted activity" and "regular practice" requirements, these conditions usually impose no impediment to introduction of business records. In most lawsuits, the custodian or other witness presenting the business records simply answers "yes" to each of the foundation questions related to regularity. Opposing parties rarely challenge these assertions.

4. Lack of Trustworthiness. Even when a business record meets the other requirements of Rule 803(6), the rule excludes the record if the "source of information or the method or circumstances of preparation indicate a lack of trustworthiness." Courts most often apply this caveat to business records that were prepared in anticipation of litigation. Even if the organization regularly prepares those records, the organization's motives are suspect in the context of potential litigation.

The United States Supreme Court paved the way for Rule 803(6)'s trustworthiness caveat in the famous case of *Palmer v. Hoffman*.[10] In *Palmer*, a railroad company obtained a statement from one of its engineers, who had driven a train that collided with a car at a crossing. The company had a regular practice of obtaining statements from its employees after an accident.

When the injured motorist sued the railroad for negligence, the railroad attempted to introduce the engineer's statement as a business record. The engineer had died before trial, and the Court rejected admission of his statement. An employee's post-accident statement, the Court held, lacks the reliability of other business documents. This type of statement is "not for the systematic conduct of the enterprise as a railroad business. Unlike payrolls, accounts receivable, accounts payable, bills of lading and the like, these reports are calculated for use essentially in the court, not in the business. Their primary utility is in litigating, not in railroading."[11]

Courts continue to find that documents prepared in anticipation of litigation are too untrustworthy to qualify as business records. This may be true even when an interested party hires an outside consultant to investigate an accident and prepare a report:

---

10   318 U.S. 109 (1943).

11   Id. at 114.

Example: Thomas Sinkovitch was sailing his boat when it crashed into some submerged rocks, severely damaging the hull. His insurance company, Lloyd's of London, hired a marine investigator to examine the circumstances of the accident; that investigator produced a 343-page report. Based on the report, Lloyd's concluded that Sinkovitch failed to minimize damage to the boat after the initial crash. Lloyd's thus refused to pay the claim.

Sinkovitch sued to enforce payment of the claim. At trial, Lloyd's introduced the investigator's report to support its defense that Sinkovitch failed to minimize the damage to his boat.

Analysis: The trial court should not have admitted the investigator's report against Sinkovitch. Although the report satisfied most of Rule 803(6)'s requirements, Lloyd's commissioned it with an eye toward possible litigation with Sinkovitch. As soon as a claim is filed, an insurer has an economic incentive to develop information that would support denial of the claim. Even though Lloyd's hired an outside investigator to prepare the report, the motive to collect one-sided and biased information was too high to allow admission under 803(6).[12]

The trustworthiness caveat does not apply only to documents prepared in anticipation of litigation; courts sometimes apply the principle in other contexts. Here is one example:

Example: The SEC brought a civil action against Howard Ackerman and several coconspirators, seeking disgorgement of approximately $1.4 million of illegal profits earned from a stock fraud. The district court held all of the conspirators jointly and severally liable for disgorging the full amount of the ill-gotten gains.

Ackerman and two other defendants claimed they had derived only minor profit from the scheme, and that they should be responsible for disgorging only those amounts. To prove the limited extent of their individual profits, these defendants proffered photocopies of check stubs that Ackerman used to record the amount of disbursements to each participant in the

---

12   Certain Underwriters at Lloyd's v. Sinkovich, 232 F.3d 200 (4th Cir. 2000).

original fraud. Ackerman admitted, however, that he had altered some of the information on the check stubs before photocopying them, and he could not remember exactly what information he altered on each of the stubs.

Analysis: The check stubs were inadmissible hearsay. The stubs met most of the 803(6) requirements: The conspirators' scheme qualified as a "business" under that rule; Ackerman kept records of the disbursements in the course of the regularly conducted business activity; and it was the conspiracy's regular practice to keep those records. However, the fact that Ackerman admitted altering the check stubs indicated a lack of trustworthiness in the documents. The check stubs thus were not admissible under 803(6).[13]

Cases like this one are relatively rare; the vast majority of business records are sufficiently trustworthy to gain admission under 803(6) if they satisfy the other conditions of that rule. Most opponents fail to raise a trustworthiness objection. When they do, the questionable records usually are documents prepared in anticipation of litigation. But the case of Ackerman and his codefendants illustrates that trial courts retain discretion to exclude business records when other circumstances call their accuracy into question.

5. Insiders, Outsiders, and Double Hearsay. Rule 803(6) contemplates the possibility that business information will pass from one person to another; the rule admits records made by one person "from information transmitted by . . . someone with knowledge" of the business facts. This acceptance of transmitted information, however, is not as broad as it first appears.

Rule 803(6) encompasses only information transmitted from one organizational **insider to another**. If salespeople report their weekly sales to a manager who compiles a company-wide sales report, the report will qualify as a business record. The manager need not have firsthand knowledge of all the data in the report; she may obtain that information from other employees who have that information.

But the "transmitted by" language does not include customers or other third parties who provide information to an organization. Those statements do not fall within 803(6), even if the organization collects the information as part of a regularly conducted business activity. This distinction between insiders and outsiders

---

13   SEC v. Hughes Capital Corp., 124 F.3d 449 (3d Cir. 1997).

makes sense; the special indicia of reliability supporting Rule 803(6) derive from the organization's regular recordkeeping and its interest in keeping accurate and honest records. When an outsider provides information to the organization, that person lacks the same incentive to provide reliable information.

When a business record contains statements made by third parties, the record presents a double hearsay problem. Any information perceived directly by the organization's employees will fall within the business records exception. Those statements are hearsay, but they are admissible under Rule 803(6). Statements made by third parties constitute a separate level of hearsay; they do not fall within 803(6). The court must either redact these statements by organizational outsiders or identify a separate hearsay exception to support their admission.

Here is an example of business records containing inadmissible hearsay statements from third parties:

Example: In a class action against the Orange Computer company, the plaintiffs allege that Orange's new laptop model contains a faulty battery that fails to charge after only a few weeks. To support their claim, plaintiffs submit repair orders kept by CircuitWorld, a large laptop repair company unaffiliated with Orange. CircuitWorld keeps these orders in the course of its regularly conducted business, and the company has a regular practice of making these records.

CircuitWorld's repair orders contain the initial complaint from the laptop owner as well as notes made by any technician who worked on the machine. An order, for example, might include the comment, "customer says battery will not charge," followed by a technician's note, "tested battery and it fails to hold charge." Orange Computer challenges the records as hearsay.

Analysis: The repair orders are admissible as business records under 803(6), but the court will redact the customer statements before giving the orders to the jury. The CircuitWorld technicians who tested the laptops and noted their findings had a business duty to be accurate; they also routinely make notes of this type. The customer complaints, however, have no special indicia of reliability. The salesclerks who transcribed the complaints probably reported the customers' comments accurately, because they had a business incentive to do so. But there is no special reason to believe that the customers stated their dissatisfaction accurately; the truth of those statements does not fall within 803(6).

In this variation, a separate hearsay exception supports admission of the third-party statements as part of the business records:

Example: In another class action against Orange Computer, the plaintiffs claim that the keyboards and trackballs on their new laptops become unresponsive, so the computer no longer accepts input from the user. These plaintiffs offer evidence from CircuitWorld's call-in help line, which charges customers for live technical support provided by a CircuitWorld technician over the telephone.

The phone technicians keep meticulous records of everything the customer says. A typical call sheet reads: "9:54 p.m. Received call from Hilary, who says that she is using her Orange brand laptop right now tapping the keys on the keyboard and moving her finger on the trackpad, but the computer is not responding. I told her to reboot the laptop, and after she did so she told me that the problem persisted." Orange Computer objects to the call sheets as hearsay.

Analysis: As in the previous example, the technician's reports are business records: CircuitWorld keeps them in the ordinary course of business and the company has a regular practice of keeping these records. A CircuitWorld employee notes the time of the call as the call occurs, so Rule 803(6) admits the fact that a call came in at a certain time and that a certain phone technician handled the call.

The statements made by callers are, as in the previous example, hearsay within hearsay. The callers are not employees of CircuitWorld, so the extra indicia of reliability that attach to business records do not support admission of these statements. But in this case, the callers' statements qualify as present-sense impressions. The callers describe their actions and the computer's response as they occur. Thus, the content of these statements is admissible under **Rule 803(1).**

In this example, each hearsay level is admissible so the court does not need to redact the callers' statements from the call sheets. As we discussed in Chapter 44, **Rule 805** permits multiple levels of hearsay as long as each level fits within a hearsay exception. The full call sheets are admissible in this litigation for the truth of the matters asserted.

Examine business records carefully for the source of each statement contained in the record. If the information originated from a member of the organization, and if it traveled a route composed exclusively of organization insiders, then the information falls within 803(6). Information originating from outsiders, on the other hand, does not fall within 803(6). To admit that information for the truth of the matter asserted, a separate hearsay exception must support its admission.

Quick Summary

Rule 803(6) allows admission of records kept by an organization or institution. Although a business record is an out-of-court statement, it is admissible if:

(1) It was recorded by an individual with personal knowledge or transmitted to the recordkeeper by someone with personal knowledge, and the transmitter and recordkeeper were both members of the organization.

(2) It was kept in the course of a regularly conducted activity.

(3) It is the organization's regular practice to keep the record.

A custodian or other qualified witness must testify orally or through a written certificate about all three of these requirements to lay the foundation for admission of a business record. Even when a record meets all of these requirements, an opponent may challenge the document as too untrustworthy to admit. Courts usually exclude documents under this caveat when they were prepared in anticipation of litigation.

Watch out for double hearsay in connection with business records. Statements by customers and third parties are admissible only if they fall within another hearsay exception; they do not qualify under 803(6) even when they appear within a business record.

Test Your Understanding

To assess your understanding of the material in this chapter, click here to take a quiz, or go to the Quizzes module from the eBook on your eProducts bookshelf.

46

Hearsay Exception—Public Records

Key Concepts

- **Rule 803(8):** Admits Three Categories of Public Records
  - ∘ Activities of a Public Office
  - ∘ Observations of a Public Office
  - ∘ Results of Public Investigations
- Some Records Inadmissible Against Criminal Defendants
- Trustworthiness Requirement
- Opinions and Conclusions
- Third-Party Statements
- Intersection with Other Rules

A. Introduction and Policy. Just like private businesses and organizations, public agencies generate millions of documents a day. The information ranges from weather reports to tollbooth receipts to results of police investigations. The amount of information recorded by government agencies is staggering; inevitably, much of this information becomes relevant to litigation. **Rule 803(8)** allows parties to admit these public records into evidence for the truth of the matter asserted. There are two justifications for this rule.

First, these records are **more reliable** than most other hearsay statements. Courts assume that public officials perform their duties properly, knowing that they are under an obligation to the public to make accurate and honest observations. Judges also view public officials as neutral gatherers of information; a public agency usually has no incentive to exaggerate or alter the information that it records.

Second, public records are **more needed** than other kinds of hearsay. Because of the vast quantities of information recorded by public agencies, no individual official could recall all of that information and testify about it on the stand. Rule 803(8) recognizes that the only practical way of obtaining information contained within public records is to admit the records themselves.

One important category of public record, however, does not carry all of the indicia of reliability described above: reports made by police officers and other law-enforcement personnel. Although these individuals act in the public interest, they ally with the prosecution in criminal cases. Admitting reports by law-enforcement agents without the safeguards of live testimony and cross-examination poses too much risk of bias. This practice might also violate the defendant's Sixth Amendment right of confrontation.[1] Rule 803(8), therefore, includes an important exception for any "matter observed by law-enforcement personnel" in criminal cases.

B. The Rule. The public records exception appears in Rule 803, which admits evidence regardless of the declarant's availability.

> ## RULE 803. Exceptions to the Rule Against Hearsay — Regardless of Whether the Declarant Is Available as a Witness
>
> The following are not excluded by the rule against hearsay, regardless of whether the declarant is available as a witness: . . .
>
> **(8)** *Public Records.* A record or statement of a <u>public office</u> if:
>
> **(A)** it sets out:
>
> **(i)** the office's <u>activities</u>;
>
> **(ii)** a <u>matter observed</u> while under a legal <u>duty</u> to report, <u>but not including</u>, in a criminal case, a matter observed by law-enforcement personnel; or

---

[1]   As noted in Chapter 38, the Sixth Amendment restricts the use of some hearsay in criminal prosecutions. We return to that issue in Chapter 58.

> **(iii)** in a civil case or against the government in a criminal case, <u>factual findings</u> from a legally authorized investigation; and
>
> **(B)** the opponent does not show that the source of information or other circumstances indicate a lack of <u>trustworthiness</u>.

Rule 803(8) opens by referring to any "record or statement of a public office." The definitions in **Rule 101(b)(3)** and **(4)** explain that "record" includes any "memorandum, report, or data compilation," while a "public office" includes any "public agency." The exception thus applies broadly to any records of any government unit—state, local, or federal.

After this introduction, the public records exception divides into several parts:[2]

Subsection (A)(i) admits the "activities" of any public office. This subsection refers to documentation of all the activities engaged in by the public agency; for example, records of the money it has spent, the personnel it has hired, the meetings it has held, the votes it has taken, and the decisions it has made.

Subsection (A)(ii) admits records of "a matter observed" by any public agency. This subsection includes a wide range of concrete facts that a public agency might observe, ranging from inches of rainfall to the number of travelers passing a checkpoint. The subsection has two important caveats.

First, subsection (A)(ii) applies only to matters that the agency has a duty to report. Reports that exceed an agency's authority do not fall within the exception. This language, moreover, excludes information that third parties observe and report to agencies. This portion of the public records exception, like the business records one, excludes information reported by outsiders. Those outsiders lack the obligation that members of the agency feel to serve the public by reporting matters accurately and honestly.

---

2   The Advisory Committee changed the numbering of Rule 803(8)'s subsections as part of the 2011 restyling amendments. Before December 2011, subsection 803(8)(A)(i) was labeled 803(8)(A); 803(8)(A)(ii) was 803(8)(B); and 803(8)(A)(iii) was 803(8)(C). You will see references to 803(8)(A), (B), and (C) in many older opinions; these citations correspond to 803(8)(A)(i), (ii), and (iii).

Second, subsection (A)(ii) excludes all records of observations made by law-enforcement personnel when offered in a criminal case. This exclusion stems from the two concerns discussed in the Introduction: (1) law-enforcement personnel have a strong interest in ensuring that criminal defendants are convicted, so their observations may not be neutral; and (2) the Sixth Amendment guarantees criminal defendants the right to confront witnesses against them.

Subsection (A)(ii)'s criminal-case exclusion appears to bar evidence offered by both the prosecutor and the defense, but most courts have construed the exception to limit only the prosecutor. In most jurisdictions, therefore, the defendant may offer records fitting this subsection, even if they were made by law-enforcement personnel.[3] However, there are some district courts that consider themselves bound by the plain language of the rule and prohibit defendants from admitting police reports under this exception.[4]

Subsection (A)(iii) admits "factual findings from a legally authorized investigation." This is the most complex provision of Rule 803(8); there are three significant aspects to the subsection.

First, like police reports in subsection (A)(ii), results of a government investigation are not admissible against a defendant in a criminal case. The concerns described above support this result.

Second, although subsection (A)(iii) refers to "factual findings" of an investigation, courts have interpreted this phrase broadly to include the opinions and conclusions of the investigator, as well as the underlying facts. We'll discuss this issue further in the Courtroom section below.

Third, the investigation must have been "legally authorized." This requirement enhances reliability by ensuring that the investigator was performing an official function and therefore acting in the public interest in preparing the report.

---

3   Bailey v. Lafler, 209 F. Supp. 3d 955, 976 (W.D. Mich. 2016) ("[T]he language of [FRE 803(8)(A)(ii)] appears to prohibit the admission of all records of matters observed in criminal cases, which, if read literally, would exclude use by the defense as well as the prosecution. This meaning is not what Congress had in mind, and the cases have construed the provision to permit the defendant to introduce police reports under (A)(ii).").

4   United States v. Giovanelli, 747 F. Supp. 915 (S.D.N.Y. 1989).

Rule 803(8)(B), **finally,** allows an opponent to attack the admissibility of any public record on the ground that the record lacks "trustworthiness."[5] This is the same language used for the business records exception, although the Advisory Committee's note gives courts more guidance in applying the caveat in the public records context. We'll explore the trustworthiness requirement in further detail below.

C. In the Courtroom.

1. Law Enforcement and Criminal Defendants. As explained in the Introduction, the policies justifying the public records exception do not apply to many government reports offered against criminal defendants. Police and other law-enforcement personnel have a strong professional interest in convicting individuals who have committed crimes; their reports may not display the neutrality of other public records. The Sixth Amendment, moreover, limits the admissibility of secondhand statements against criminal defendants.

Subsections (A)(ii) and (A)(iii), therefore, both limit the use of public records against defendants in criminal prosecutions. A police report recording observations about the scene of a crime would be admissible in a civil lawsuit under subsection (A)(ii); it records "a matter observed while under a legal duty to report." But the prosecution cannot use this type of record against the defendant in a criminal case because police are "law-enforcement personnel."

Similarly, the report of a social worker who investigated a family's home after the father's arrest for child abuse would be admissible under subsection (A)(iii) in a child custody action. That report contains "factual findings from a legally authorized investigation." But the government could not introduce the report in its prosecution of the father.

These caveats to subsections (A)(ii) and (A)(iii) are based on the same principle: mistrust of law-enforcement records when used against a criminal defendant. However, subsection (A)(iii) provides much broader protection to the defendant: It prevents the prosecutor from using any public record that constitutes "factual findings from a legally authorized investigation," regardless of the agency generating

---

5   Before 2011, this language appeared at the end of section 803(8), without any separate letter designation. The 2011 restyling amendments labeled this provision subsection 803(8)(B). Be aware that before December 2011, citations to 803(8)(B) referred to the portion of the rule that is now labeled 803(A)(ii). In 2014, Congress amended the new 803(8)(B) to clarify the opponent's role in challenging trustworthiness.

the record. When offered against a criminal defendant, records of any government investigation remain inadmissible hearsay.

Subsection (A)(ii) offers somewhat narrower protection to the criminal defendant. That subsection denies the prosecutor evidentiary use only of records based on observations by "law-enforcement personnel." A prosecutor, therefore, may introduce records based on observations by other types of public officials, such as weather conditions recorded by the National Weather Service.

The courts have narrowed subsection (A)(ii) in another way, preventing prosecutors from introducing records of law-enforcement observations only when they were "made in an adversarial setting." Courts have allowed prosecutors to introduce law-enforcement records that include observations of "routine non-adversarial matters." As one appellate court put it: "[T]he purpose of the [803(8)(A)(ii)] exception was to exclude observations made by officials at the scene of the crime or apprehension, because observations made in an adversarial setting are less reliable than observations made by public officials in other situations. Congress, however, did not intend to exclude records of routine, non-adversarial matters."[6]

Here is an example of a court applying this distinction:

> **Example:** The government charged Francisco Hernandez-Rojas with illegally re-entering the country after having been deported. As part of its case, the prosecution had to establish that Hernandez-Rojas had, in fact, been deported. To satisfy this element, the prosecutor introduced a valid warrant of deportation with Hernandez-Rojas's name on it, which contained the dated notation "deported to Mexico, Calexico, California," and was signed by a United States Immigration Officer. Hernandez-Rojas objected to the deportation order as hearsay, and argued that 803(8)(A)(ii) did not apply because the deportation order was a record of a law enforcement officer's observations.

> **Analysis:** The Ninth Circuit held that the trial court properly admitted the warrant, because it was "a ministerial, objective observation," that had "inherent reliability because of the Government's need to keep accurate records of the movement of aliens." 803(8)(A)(ii), the court reasoned, bars only

---

6   United States v. Hernandez-Rojas, 617 F.2d 533, 535 (9th Cir. 1980).

"subjective report[s] made by a law enforcement official in an on-the-scene investigation, which . . . lack sufficient guarantees of trustworthiness because they are made in an adversary setting and likely to be used in litigation."[7]

Other examples of "ministerial" law-enforcement records admitted by courts include a Customs Inspector's document listing the license plate numbers of all cars that crossed the United States border,[8] and a police officer's report verifying that a breathalyzer was properly calibrated.[9]

 The plain language of Rule 803(8)(A)(ii) does not support this distinction between adversarial observations and ministerial ones. The Supreme Court, moreover, cast doubt on the distinction in *Melendez-Diaz v. Massachusetts*,[10] a Sixth Amendment case we will discuss further in Chapter 58. In light of *Melendez-Diaz*, some defense attorneys are pressing courts to abandon the ministerial-tasks distinction. The doctrine remains well established for now, but watch for possible changes.

2. Lack of Trustworthiness. The public records exception, like the exception for business records, gives judges discretion to exclude a record if the "source of information or other circumstances indicate a lack of trustworthiness." The Advisory Committee's note lists four factors that a court should consider in determining whether a public record of an investigation is trustworthy:

(1) The timeliness of the investigation;

(2) The special skill or experience of the official conducting the investigation;

(3) Whether a hearing was held by the public agency prior to the report being made; and

(4) Whether the motivation of the public agency is suspect—for example, whether the report was made in anticipation of litigation by a public agency that has a stake in the litigation.

---

7   Id.

8   United States v. Orozco, 590 F.2d 789 (9th Cir. 1979).

9   United States v. Wilmer, 799 F.2d 495, 501 (9th Cir. 1986).

10   557 U.S. 305 (2009).

The fourth factor, which mirrors the "anticipation of litigation" caveat from the business record exception, may be the most significant consideration in evaluating admissibility. But this factor alone does not necessarily preclude admission of a public record. Under some circumstances, courts will allow an agency to admit a public record that supports its own position in civil litigation:

Example: Terry Perrin was involved in an altercation with Troopers Von Schriltz and Anderson of the Oklahoma State Police, which ended with Trooper Anderson shooting and killing Perrin. As part of their normal internal procedures, the Oklahoma Department of Public Safety convened a Shooting Review Board to investigate the incident. The Board issued a report which concluded that there was "no doubt that [Anderson] acted within the guidelines set forth in the Policies and Procedures Manual."

Perrin's widow sued the Troopers for violating Perrin's civil rights. At trial, the Troopers introduced the Shooting Review Board report. The trial judge admitted the report under Rule 803(8).

Analysis: The court of appeals affirmed this result, finding no indication that the report was "untrustworthy." The report was prepared only five weeks after the shooting, so it was timely. The investigation was conducted by five members of the Oklahoma State Police who were well qualified to review the incident, and they convened a hearing in which they interviewed all the defendants and their supervisors. The only reason to suspect the trustworthiness of the report was that the State Police carried out the investigation internally. But this alone was not enough to preclude the report, because "an internal investigation is not necessarily biased." The agency's self-interest affected the weight of the evidence, not its admissibility.

The appellate court noted with approval that the trial judge specifically instructed the jury that this was "an agency hearing of its own personnel and for its own purpose" and that the report, though relevant, was to have no "determinative effect on any issue in the case." This instruction allowed the jury to decide for itself how much weight, if any, to give the internal review.[11]

---

11   Perrin v. Anderson, 784 F.2d 1040 (10th Cir. 1986).

The trustworthiness of public records offered under 803(8) thus turns on counsel's advocacy. Courts weigh the factors identified by the Advisory Committee, but do not find any of them determinative.

3. Factual Findings. Subsection (A)(iii) admits "factual findings from a legally authorized investigation" undertaken by a government office. This reference to "factual findings" is ambiguous. If a government investigator notes the length of skid marks from a car accident, that notation clearly is a factual finding. But what about the conclusion of the Shooting Review Board in the last example, that Trooper Anderson acted in accordance with State Police guidelines? Is that a factual finding? And what about a government accountant's calculation of the amount of money lost by stockholders due to insider trading? Any calculation of the amount in such a case will inevitably be the result of interpretations of the available evidence and estimations based on the accountant's expertise. Is that result still a factual finding? In any investigative report, facts quickly shade into interpretations and conclusions.

For more than a decade, judges struggled to interpret Rule 803(8)(A)(iii)'s reference to factual findings. Which parts of investigative reports fit that phrase and which did not? The Supreme Court settled the question in 1988 with a simple answer: The courts should interpret "factual findings" broadly to encompass all facts, opinions, and conclusions found in the report of an investigation. The following dispute generated the Supreme Court's ruling:

> **Example:** A naval plane crashed during a training exercise, killing the student pilot and instructor on board. The surviving spouses of the victims sued Beech Aircraft, the manufacturer of the airplane, claiming that the crash resulted from an equipment malfunction.
>
> At trial, Beech Aircraft sought to introduce the investigative report (the "JAG report") that was commissioned by the Navy immediately after the crash. The report made numerous findings, including:
>
> "13. At approximately 1020, while turning crosswind without proper interval, 3E955 crashed, immediately caught fire and burned.
>
> "7. The most probable cause of the accident was the pilots [sic] failure to maintain proper interval."

The plaintiffs conceded that the facts in the report, such as those reported in paragraph 13, were admissible under 803(8)(A)(iii), but they objected to the opinions in the report, such as those reported in paragraph 7.

Analysis: The Supreme Court held that all of the JAG report findings were admissible, whether they reported "straight facts" or relayed the opinions and conclusions of the investigator. After examining both the rule's plain meaning and the phrase's legislative history, the Court determined that there was no intention to limit 803(8)(A)(iii) to objective, tangible facts. The Court also noted that if any opinions or conclusions in a report are questionable, a trial court has discretion to exclude them under the "lack of trustworthiness" provision at the end of Rule 803(8). The Court, finally, noted the difficulty in drawing a sharp distinction between facts and conclusions; even seemingly objective facts derive from an investigator's inferences and judgments.[12]

Courts, therefore, no longer need to parse public records to determine which statements are facts and which are opinions. **All statements** contained in the report of a government investigation are "factual findings" under Rule 803(8)(A)(iii).

4. Hearsay Within Hearsay. As with business records, public records frequently contain statements by third parties. Those statements are hearsay within hearsay, governed by **Rule 805**. Police reports, for example, frequently obtain statements from witnesses. The report as a whole may be admissible under 803(8), but that provision does not include the third-party statements. Unless another hearsay exception admits those statements, the judge will redact them before giving the report to the jury.

Example: An EPA field officer investigated an oil spill on Crescent Beach. The officer wrote in her report: "At 9:15 a.m. I observed crude oil spread one inch thick for approximately three hundred yards along the beach. Local resident informed me that the oil first came ashore fifteen hours ago." Is the report admissible under 803(8) in a civil lawsuit?

---

12   Beech Aircraft Corp. v. Rainey, 488 U.S. 153 (1988).

Analysis: The first sentence of this report, containing the EPA investigator's direct observation, is admissible under 803(8)(A)(ii) and (A)(iii). But the second sentence, reporting the local resident's statement, does not fit within the public records exception. The judge will redact that sentence unless another hearsay exception supports admission of the resident's statement.

Investigators, however, may rely upon third-party statements to generate their own opinions and conclusions. The latter statements do not raise double hearsay issues. In the *Beech Aircraft* case, for example, the Navy investigators based their conclusions on interviews with eyewitnesses. Indeed, so little of the plane survived the crash that the investigation relied heavily on eyewitness reports.[13] The inferences and conclusions drawn from those reports represented the views of the investigators, so they were admissible under 803(8).

Here is another example of an investigative report that uses third-party statements in this manner:

Example: The EPA officer described above wrote in her final report: "At 9:15 a.m., I observed crude oil spread one inch thick for approximately three hundred yards along the beach. Based on these measurements, tidal and wind activity, and interviews with local residents, I conclude that the oil first came ashore fifteen hours before my initial observation." Is this report admissible in a civil lawsuit?

Analysis: This full paragraph is admissible under 803(8). Rather than simply parroting an unreliable hearsay statement, the public official has articulated her own conclusion about the timing of the oil spill. She conducted a thorough investigation, which included interviews with local residents, and then used her expertise to combine information from the interviews with other data. The fact that the officer's conclusion rests in part on a distillation of third-party statements does not make the conclusion inadmissible.

---

13   Id. at 157 n.2.

5. 803(8) and Other Rules. Most public records also qualify as business records; a public agency could qualify as an "organization" fitting within the broad bounds of Rule 803(6). The legislative history of Rule 803, however, makes clear that any document falling within both 803(6) and (8) must meet the latter section's requirements for admission. The prosecutor, for example, cannot evade the restrictions of Rule 803(8) by introducing an incriminating report under 803(6).

Public records satisfying Rule 803(8), meanwhile, must also comply with other evidentiary rules. A government report that describes a party's prior bad act, for example, might fulfill the conditions of 803(8) but violate Rule 404. Overly technical records, similarly, might produce the type of confusion excluded by Rule 403. When information in a public record violates another Rule of Evidence, the trial judge will redact inadmissible evidence and admit any remaining portion of the report.

 To review several of the hearsay exceptions you have studied so far, click here to see the video "Prosecution Dilemma 2.0" or go to the Videos module from the eBook on your eProducts bookshelf.

Quick Summary

Rule 803(8) allows parties to admit the records of any public office or agency, providing the record falls into one of three categories: (1) records of an agency's activities; (2) records of observations that the agency had a legal duty to report; or (3) reports of a legally authorized investigation.

Many records falling in the latter two categories, however, are not admissible against the defendant in a criminal case. The neutrality of these records is suspect and, at least under some circumstances, their admission would violate the criminal defendant's Sixth Amendment right to confront his accusers.

Conclusions, inferences, and opinions are admissible when contained in the report of a public investigation. These conclusions may rest on the statements of third parties without affecting admissibility under 803(8). But if a report simply repeats the statement of a third party, the third-party statement is hearsay within hearsay; it must satisfy another hearsay exception to be admissible.

The trial court may exclude a public record if circumstances indicate that the report lacks trustworthiness.

Test Your Understanding

To assess your understanding of the material in this chapter, click here to take a quiz, or go to the Quizzes module from the eBook on your eProducts bookshelf.

47

Hearsay Exceptions—Other 803 Exceptions

Key Concepts

- **Rule 803(7)** and **803(10):** Absence of Entries in Business Records and Public Records
- **Rule 803(16):** Ancient Documents
- **Rule 803(17):** Market Reports and Similar Commercial Publications
- **Rule 803(18):** Learned Treatises

A. Introduction and Policy. The prohibition against hearsay famously includes thirty-one exceptions; fortunately, you do not need to master all of them. You have already studied seven exceptions grouped within Rule 803; those are the most complex and frequently used exceptions in that Rule.

In this chapter, we will briefly discuss five other exceptions contained in Rule 803. These exceptions address very specific situations and are relatively easy to apply. The first two exceptions, as we'll see below, are not hearsay at all. To the extent they resemble hearsay, they rest on the rationales we have already explored: They have strong indicia of reliability and they are more needed than other types of hearsay. The other three exceptions similarly rest on these rationales.

B. The Rules.

1. 803(7) and 803(10): Absence of Business Records or Public Records.
These two exceptions complement the provisions for business and public records that we discussed in the last two chapters. Sometimes the **absence** of a record is as significant as the presence of one. If a garage attendant records the license plate of every car entering a garage, and the defendant's plate number does not appear in those records for a particular day, the missing entry is persuasive evidence that the defendant did not park in the garage that day.

No special hearsay exception is necessary to admit the absence of a business or public record, because silence usually does not constitute a statement. When declarants remain silent, they usually are not trying to communicate anything; instead, we infer some fact based on their silence. The defendant in the previous example was not making a "statement" when he failed to park his car in the garage; he just wasn't there.

Similarly, if individuals in a household do not call 911 on a certain night, they do not intend that absence of a call as an assertion. The residents might have been busy watching television that evening, or they might have taken other steps to address an emergency. The observation that they did not call 911 is a **fact** that a litigant could introduce as some evidence that the household encountered no emergency that evening, but it is not an **assertion** about anything.

Other examples of missing entries from business or public records that might relate to a lawsuit are:

- Sales records from the Buy-Right Pharmacy, showing that it sold no narcotic drugs on a particular day

- Records from the Pennsylvania Secretary of State's office, showing that it has no record of articles of incorporation for a certain company

- Records from the Securities and Exchange Commission, showing that a company did not file a required disclosure

- A list of cars towed by the local police department, showing no entry that an individual's car was towed on a particular day.

None of these examples, like the ones in the preceding paragraphs, are "statements." Absence of a record rarely, if ever, would constitute an assertion falling within the hearsay rules, so an exception for these absences is not necessary. But the Advisory Committee wanted to make the admissibility of "absent records" clear, so it provided rules **803(7)** and **803(10)**:

RULE 803. Exceptions to the Rule Against Hearsay — Regardless of Whether the Declarant Is Available as a Witness

The following are not excluded by the rule against hearsay, regardless of whether the declarant is available as a witness: . . .

(7) ***Absence of a Record of a Regularly Conducted Activity.*** Evidence that a matter is not included in a record described in <u>paragraph (6)</u> if:

    (A) the evidence is admitted to prove that the matter did not occur or exist;

    (B) a record was <u>regularly kept</u> for a matter of that kind; and

    (C) the opponent does not show that the possible source of the information or other circumstances indicate a lack of <u>trustworthiness</u>.

    . . . .

(10) ***Absence of a Public Record.*** Testimony—or a certification under Rule 902—that a <u>diligent search</u> failed to disclose a public record or statement if:

    (A) the <u>testimony</u> or <u>certification</u> is admitted to prove that

        (i) the record or statement does not exist; or

        (ii) a matter did not occur or exist, if a public office <u>regularly kept</u> a record or statement for a matter of that kind; and

    (B) in a criminal case, a prosecutor who intends to offer a certification provides written notice of that intent at least 14 days before trial, and the defendant does not object in writing within 7 days of receiving the notice—unless the court sets a different time for the notice or the objection.

These provisions flow from the rationales supporting most hearsay exceptions. If you keep those rationales in mind, the provisions are easier to remember. To admit the absence of a **business record** under **Rule 803(7)**, the party offering the evidence must address two points:

First, the proponent must show that the records containing the omission are kept in accordance with **Rule 803(6)**, the business record exception. A custodian or other qualified witness will testify that the records were kept in the course of a regularly conducted activity and that it was the regular practice of the business to keep the records.

Second, the party must show that the absence relates to a matter about which the business regularly kept records. A moving company, for example, probably could show that it keeps track of the addresses that its trucks visit each day. If the address "20 Creston Avenue" doesn't appear in the company's records, then the omission is some evidence that no truck from the company ever visited that address. But the company probably does not keep records of where its drivers stop for lunch each day. If the company claims that its drivers did not eat at Wendy's on May 13, it can't support that claim by pointing to a silence in the records. True, the company has no record that the drivers ate at Wendy's on May 13. But it does not keep regular records of where its drivers eat; the silence isn't meaningful.

Once a party meets these foundation requirements, the opponent has an opportunity to show that the record's absence offers unreliable evidence. Rule 803(7)'s "lack of trustworthiness" provision parallels the caveat in Rule 803(6)'s business records exception.[1] If circumstances suggest to the judge that particular business records—or their absence—are unreliable, the judge may exclude the evidence.

If the judge allows proof of a record's absence, Rule 803(7) specifies no particular manner of making that proof. Usually the witness who establishes the foundation elements will simply testify about the relevant record's absence.

The requirements for introducing evidence about the absence of a **public record** are just as straightforward. Under **Rule 803(10)**, the proponent must first show that the absent record relates to a matter for which the public office regularly kept records.[2] A party, for example, could show that a state's Department of Motor Vehicles regularly keeps records of all automobiles licensed in that state. The state's Department of Worker's Compensation, on the other hand, probably does not keep records of automobile licenses.

---

1   Congress amended Rule 803(7), like 803(6), in 2014 to clarify that the opponent carries the burden of showing a lack of trustworthiness.

2   As discussed in Chapter 46, Rule 101(b)(3) defines "public office" to include any "public agency."

Rule 803(10) then specifies two ways that the party can prove the record's non-existence. **First,** the party may call a witness to testify that a "diligent search" was made and no record was found. **Second,** the party may present a certified document from the agency, pursuant to **Rule 902**, attesting that a diligent search failed to yield the particular document. We discuss Rule 902, which governs authentication of documents, further in Chapter 69.

Rule 803(10) also states that in a criminal case, the prosecutor must provide notice to the defendant before offering certification of an absent record. This gives the defendant an opportunity to demand that the official who prepared the certificate testify in person. The Advisory Committee added this notice requirement to ensure compliance with the Sixth Amendment, which gives criminal defendants the right to cross-examine witnesses against them. We will discuss that constitutional requirement further in Chapter 58.

2. 803(16): Statements in Ancient Documents. Documents written many years before a dispute arises are more reliable than other writings because the author's motive is less open to suspicion. These documents are also more needed than other hearsay because the declarant who produced the document is unlikely to be available. Even if she could be found, she probably would not remember the information recorded many years ago.

Rule 803(16) recognizes these characteristics of "ancient" documents and creates a hearsay exception for documents that have been in existence since before the year 1998:

> ## RULE 803. Exceptions to the Rule Against Hearsay— Regardless of Whether the Declarant Is Available as a Witness
>
> The following are not excluded by the rule against hearsay, regardless of whether the declarant is available as a witness: . . .
>
> **(16) *Statements in Ancient Documents*.** A statement in a document that was prepared before January 1, 1998 and whose <u>authenticity</u> is established.

This exception imposes only two requirements. **First,** the document must have been created before January 1, 1998. The date is determined by the moment at which the information was originally recorded; if the hard copy of the document was later scanned or otherwise duplicated, the document's date of creation would still be the date that it was originally made.

The Advisory Committee chose this arbitrary date because of the proliferation of electronically stored information starting in the late 1990's. According to the Advisory Committee, electronically stored information is far less reliable than hard copies of documents, and admitting older documents that were created after this date would open the door for vast amounts of unreliable electronic documents. Thus, as the years go by, even very old documents will not qualify as "ancient documents" if they were originally created before this cut-off date.

Second, the party offering the document must establish its authenticity. We will study authenticity further in Chapter 69; the requirements are relatively easy to meet.

Watch out for hearsay within hearsay in ancient documents. Rule 803(16) admits the writing, but it does not encompass hearsay reported **within** the document; other exceptions are necessary to admit those statements for the truth of the matters they assert.

Example: Portia's Southern California ranch home burned to the ground in a wildfire. Her insurance company refused to pay the full amounts claimed by Portia, and she sued to recover those amounts. To prove the value of an antique chair destroyed in the fire, Portia offered a letter written by her mother in 1995. That letter describes the chair as "perfectly preserved, without a scratch on it." The letter also states: "My uncle tells me that the chair was owned by Abraham Lincoln." The insurance company objects to the letter as hearsay.

Analysis: Assuming that Portia can authenticate the letter, it is an ancient document fitting within Rule 803(16). The letter's firsthand description of the chair ("perfectly preserved, without a scratch on it") is admissible under that exception to prove the truth of the matter asserted. The letter, in other words, shows that the chair had no scratches or other defects in 1995.

The uncle's statement, however, is hearsay within hearsay. Rule 803(16) does not allow admission of that statement to show that Lincoln owned the chair. It would be admissible to show that Portia's mother, or Portia herself, believed that Lincoln owned the chair, but not to show the truth of the matter asserted. To do that, Portia would have to identify another hearsay exception covering the uncle's statement, and she is unlikely to find one.

3. 803(17): Market Reports and Similar Commercial Publications. Phone directories, whether published in hard copy or electronically, are hearsay: They contain thousands of assertions about how to reach particular people and organizations. The stock prices that appear in daily newspapers, websites, and television tickers are also hearsay; these sources make statements about the current price of publicly traded stocks.

Yet the general public relies upon these sources every day. Affected individuals quickly report any errors, such as an improperly listed phone number or a mistaken stock quote. To assure continued use, the producers of these documents work hard to maintain accuracy.

The reliability of market reports, directories, and some other commercial publications supports a hearsay exception for these sources. The need for information contained in them also supports admissibility. Many lawsuits include evidence of addresses, phone numbers, and prices. Calling individual witnesses to establish these facts would be expensive and time consuming.

Based on these factors, **Rule 803(17)** establishes a hearsay exception for market reports and similar commercial publications. The exception applies to directories and lists that the general public uses, as well as to more specialized tabulations that members of a particular occupation generally use and rely upon:

> **RULE 803. Exceptions to the Rule Against Hearsay — Regardless of Whether the Declarant Is Available as a Witness**
>
> The following are not excluded by the rule against hearsay, regardless of whether the declarant is available as a witness: . . .
>
> **(17) *Market Reports and Similar Commercial Publications.*** Market quotations, lists, directories, or other compilations that are generally relied on by the public or by persons in particular occupations.

This exception has two components. **First**, the document must be one of "[m]arket quotations, lists, directories, or other compilations." The exception encompasses only lists or compilations of data, not more discursive or evaluative material. A litigant, therefore, can use this exception to introduce a table of stock prices printed in the newspaper but not to introduce news articles about the market's performance from the same paper. Even if many people rely on that newspaper for information, and the paper has a strong commercial incentive to maintain high levels of accuracy, 803(17) includes only lists and similar compilations.

Second, a party offering evidence under Rule 803(17) must show that it is "generally relied on by the public or by persons in particular occupations." For some very widely used directories, such as a telephone directory, the judge may take judicial notice that the public generally uses and relies upon that document.[3]

In most cases, however, the judge will require the proponent to lay a foundation meeting the requirements of Rule 803(17). A good foundation is especially important to admit specialized documents relied upon within a particular occupation. To admit a directory of drug stores relied upon by pharmaceutical companies, for example, a member of the pharmaceutical industry would testify that members of the industry generally use the directory and rely upon it. An opposing party could cross-examine the foundation witness to dispute these assertions. The judge would resolve this question of fact under **Rule 104(a)** and would admit the evidence only if she is convinced that members of the public or a particular occupation use and rely upon the document.

4. 803(18): Learned Treatises. Some scientific or academic books and journals are so well respected that almost all practitioners in a field rely upon them. Usually these are reference books like *Gray's Anatomy* in medicine. The information in these books is more reliable than most other hearsay because experts consider it accurate and authoritative. This information is also more needed than other hearsay because it is a very convenient way to give the jury basic facts about art, history, architecture, biology, or any other field. Finding more satisfactory ways to instruct the jury about these fields would be difficult.

Rule 803(18), therefore, creates a hearsay exception for information contained in "learned treatises."

---

3   Rule 201 allows a judge to take judicial notice of facts that are "not subject to reasonable dispute." We discuss judicial notice further in Chapter 59.

RULE 803. Exceptions to the Rule Against Hearsay— Regardless of Whether the Declarant Is Available as a Witness

The following are not excluded by the rule against hearsay, regardless of whether the declarant is available as a witness: . . .

(18) *Statements in Learned Treatises, Periodicals, or Pamphlets.* A statement contained in a treatise, periodical, or pamphlet if:

(A) the statement is called to the attention of an <u>expert witness</u> on cross-examination or relied on by the expert on direct examination; and

(B) the publication is established as a <u>reliable authority</u> by the expert's admission or testimony, by another expert's testimony, or by judicial notice.

If admitted, the statement may be <u>read into evidence</u> but not received as an exhibit.

There are four significant points about this rule:

First, the rule allows parties to introduce learned treatises only in connection with an expert's testimony. The treatise must either be "called to the attention of an expert witness" during cross-examination or "relied on by the expert" during direct examination. A party, therefore, cannot simply introduce the treatise itself; a learned treatise is always connected to an expert witness in the courtroom.[4]

The drafters of Rule 803(18) imposed this requirement because they believed that lay jurors would have difficulty interpreting the meaning of a learned treatise on their own. An expert's testimony, they believed, is essential to guide the jury's understanding of the technical and specialized information in learned treatises. Therefore, Rule 803(18) begins with this unusual requirement that the treatise connect to expert testimony.

---

4   We discuss the process of qualifying expert witnesses in Chapter 62. For now, note that the presence of an expert witness is essential to introduce hearsay from a learned treatise.

Second, Rule 803(18) complements this requirement by providing in its final sentence that statements from a learned treatise "may be read into evidence but not received as an exhibit." To prevent the jury from examining portions of the treatise on their own, without an expert's guidance, the rule prohibits introduction of the treatise itself into evidence. Otherwise a lay jury may become confused or misled by the technical language or complicated concepts in the treatise.

Third, the rule requires the proponent of a learned treatise to establish that the treatise is a reliable authority. The rule offers three routes to lay that foundation: (a) The expert witness who relies upon or acknowledges the treatise may confirm that the treatise is a reliable authority in the field; (b) another expert witness may establish that fact; or (c) the judge may take judicial notice of the treatise's authoritativeness. Proponents usually follow one of the first two paths, asking an expert witness to testify that the treatise is a reliable authority. Judges take judicial notice of a treatise's status only when a publication is particularly well known and respected. *Gray's Anatomy* might elicit that treatment in the medical field.

Finally, Rule 803(18) encompasses learned treatises in almost any field of study. As long as an expert certifies a text as a "reliable authority" in a relevant field, the text fits within the exception.

C. In the Courtroom.

The hearsay exceptions for absence of business or public records, ancient documents, and market reports raise few questions in courtroom practice. The use of learned treatises is also straightforward, but introduction of these documents differs somewhat from that of other hearsay. This section examines in more detail the courtroom use of learned treatises.

1. Foundation and Testimony.

The process of introducing a learned treatise is unusual; the proponent must establish that the treatise is a reliable authority in a particular field and must also link the treatise to an expert's testimony. Here is an example illustrating how lawyers follow the requirements of Rule 803(18) in the courtroom.

For this example, assume that the plaintiff in a personal injury case suffered an epileptic seizure. As part of the lawsuit, the parties dispute the effects of that seizure. The plaintiff has called a witness, Dr. Ferguson, who has already been certified as an expert in the field of neurology. The plaintiff's attorney then lays a foundation for use of a neurology reference book in this way:

P's Attorney: Dr. Ferguson, I'd like to direct your attention to the book I'm holding. Do you recognize this book?

Witness: I certainly do.

P's Attorney: What is it?

Witness: It is titled "Neurologic Disorders: Diagnosis and Treatment," by Dr. Walter Harrison.

P's Attorney: And is this book relied on by practitioners in the field of neurology?

Witness: Yes it is. It is the foremost authority in this field.

P's Attorney: Your honor, I would like to certify Dr. Harrison's book as a learned treatise under Rule 803(18).

D's Attorney: No objection, your honor.

Judge: Very well, Dr. Harrison's book is accepted by this Court as a learned treatise.

With this foundation laid, the expert witness may rely upon the treatise during direct examination:

P's Attorney: Dr. Ferguson, is it possible for a woman who suffers from epileptic seizures to have no memory of her actions during her seizures?

Witness: Yes, not only is it possible, it is a frequent occurrence with epileptic patients.

P's Attorney: And what is the basis of your opinion on this matter?

Witness: I myself have treated dozens of epileptic patients who have reported memory loss during their seizures. And it is also a fact that I learned during my extensive training.

P's Attorney: Do you have any other support for this fact?

Witness: Yes, Dr. Harrison in his "Neurologic Disorders" treatise explains that this is true as well.

P's Attorney: Could you find that section of the treatise and read it to us?

Witness: Certainly. Here on page 625, Harrison writes "Once a seizure is completed, most patients will retain no memory of their actions during the seizure."

A party may also use a learned treatise to cross-examine an expert witness. Usually the cross-examiner will point out that the treatise differs from the expert's testimony on direct examination. The defendant in this hypothetical case, for example, might cross-examine Dr. Ferguson this way:

D's Attorney: Now Dr. Ferguson, in your direct testimony you testified that epileptic seizures almost never last more than two minutes, is that correct?

Witness: That is indeed what I said, and that is true.

D's Attorney: I'd like to direct your attention to Dr. Harrison's book "Neurologic Disorders." Do you still have a copy in front of you?

Witness: Yes I do.

D's Attorney: Could you please read what it says on page 615, the first line of the third full paragraph?

Witness: It says that "frequently seizures last between five and ten minutes."

Dr. Ferguson should now get a chance to explain the difference between his opinion and that of the learned treatise. If the judge does not give him this opportunity during cross-examination, the plaintiff's attorney will pursue the issue on redirect examination. But Dr. Ferguson's credibility will be somewhat impaired by this inconsistency.

In this example, Dr. Ferguson laid the foundation for a learned treatise that was used both on direct and cross-examination. But counsel does not have to follow this path. Any expert can lay the foundation for a learned treatise, or the judge may take judicial notice of the reliability of the treatise.

Notice that, whether a party uses the learned treatise on direct examination or cross-examination, the party cannot introduce the treatise itself into evidence. Instead, counsel allows the witness to rely upon the treatise on direct examination or calls the treatise to the witness's attention on cross-examination. Under the lawyer's direction, the witness will then read portions of the treatise into evidence but the book itself will not be admitted.

2. Purpose of Admission. Although learned treatises are not admitted into evidence in their entirety, the statements read aloud by witnesses are admitted as substantive evidence. Rule 803(18) is an exception to the hearsay rule, so it allows the jury to consider the information read aloud for the truth of the matter asserted. Even when an attorney confronts a witness with a learned treatise on cross-examination, the material read by the witness is substantive evidence.

In the example with Dr. Ferguson, therefore, the defense attorney accomplished two goals by cross-examining him with the learned treatise. First, the attorney impeached Ferguson's credibility by showing that his testimony differed from information given in a book that Ferguson himself touted as "the foremost authority in this field." But second, the cross-examination gave the jury substantive evidence that epileptic seizures frequently last between five and ten minutes.

Quick Summary

 **Rules 803(7)** and **803(10)** admit the absence of a business record or a public record to show that the event not recorded did not happen. The absence of a record is not hearsay, because silence rarely constitutes a statement. But Rules 803(7) and 803(10) eliminate any confusion over this issue by allowing parties to show the absence of a business or public record. The requirements of these rules assure the reliability of a record's absence.

Rule 803(16) admits "ancient documents," documents that were prepared before 1998 and have been properly authenticated. The exception, however, does not encompass hearsay contained within the documents; separate exceptions must support the admission of any hearsay within hearsay.

Rule 803(17) admits directories, lists, and other published compilations if they are generally relied on by the general public or by people in a specific occupation.

Finally, Rule **803(18)** admits "learned treatises," texts that are considered reliable and authoritative in a given field. Usually an expert witness certifies the text as reliable, although the judge sometimes takes judicial notice of that fact. A party cannot introduce the text itself into evidence. Instead, the party must use the treatise while examining or cross-examining an expert witness. In response to the lawyer's questions, the witness may read portions of the treatise into evidence.

48

Rule 804 Introduction—What Is Unavailability?

Key Concepts

- **Rule 804:** Hearsay Exceptions Apply Only if the Declarant Is Unavailable
- Five Types of Unavailability
  - Privilege
  - Refusal to Testify
  - Lack of Memory
  - Death or Illness
  - Cannot Be Found or Brought to Court
- Proponent Must Show Unavailability

A. Introduction and Policy. In the last eight chapters we examined the most important of the twenty-three hearsay exceptions listed in **Rule 803**. Those exceptions vary in their prerequisites: Some require the declarant to be available in court, others apply whether or not the declarant testifies. We turn now to a different category of exceptions, those governed by **Rule 804**. That rule establishes five exceptions that apply only if the declarant is "unavailable as a witness." Before the judge admits a statement under one of these exceptions, in other words, she must find that the declarant cannot or will not testify live.

The requirement of unavailability furthers one of the rationales motivating the hearsay exceptions: the policy of admitting statements that are **more needed** than other types of hearsay. If a declarant is unavailable to testify, the jury has much greater need for his former statement; there may be no other way to obtain that information.

At least in theory, each of the Rule 804 exceptions also has an extra indicator of reliability. Those indicia further the second rationale underlying the hearsay exceptions, the goal of admitting hearsay that is **more reliable** than other types of hearsay. We will examine the reliability indicators for each exception in upcoming chapters. In this chapter, we'll concentrate on the common question of how an advocate proves that a declarant is unavailable, thus qualifying the defendant's statements for one of the 804 exceptions.

B. The Rule. Rule 804(a) outlines five circumstances under which a declarant is considered "unavailable" to testify in court:

RULE 804. Exceptions to the Rule Against Hearsay — When the Declarant Is Unavailable as a Witness

(a) Criteria for Being Unavailable. A declarant is considered to be unavailable as a witness if the declarant:

(1) is exempted from testifying about the subject matter of the declarant's statement because the court rules that a <u>privilege</u> applies;

(2) <u>refuses</u> to testify about the subject matter despite a court order to do so;

(3) testifies to <u>not remembering</u> the subject matter;

(4) cannot be present or testify at the trial or hearing because of <u>death</u> or a then-existing <u>infirmity</u>, physical illness, or mental illness; or

(5) is <u>absent</u> from the trial or hearing and the statement's proponent has not been able, by process or other reasonable means, to procure:

(A) the declarant's attendance, in the case of a hearsay exception under Rule 804(b)(1) or (6); or

(B) the declarant's attendance or testimony, in the case of a hearsay exception under Rule 804(b)(2), (3), or (4).

But this subdivision (a) does not apply if the statement's proponent <u>procured or wrongfully caused</u> the declarant's unavailability as a witness in <u>order to prevent</u> the declarant from attending or testifying.

Let's examine each of these five types of unavailability.

1. Privilege. As we will discuss later in Chapters 66–68, courts recognize several evidentiary privileges that further social interests like the need to assure effective attorney–client relationships. If a witness invokes one of these privileges, and the court agrees that the privilege shields the witness's testimony, then subsection 804(a)(1) declares the witness unavailable.

2. Refusal to Testify. Some witnesses refuse to testify despite a court order to do so. The witness may claim a privilege, such as a journalist–source privilege, that the jurisdiction does not recognize. Or the witness may refuse to testify because, as in a domestic violence prosecution, she is protecting a family member. Or the witness may fear retaliation from the opposing party if she testifies. Under any of these circumstances, the judge may hold the witness in contempt and impose a penalty for her refusal to testify.

Meanwhile, the party who called the uncooperative witness should not suffer unfairly due to the witness's failure to testify. Subsection 804(a)(2) deems witnesses who refuse to testify despite a court order unavailable for the purposes of that rule.

3. Lack of Memory. A witness who claims that he lacks memory about the subject matter of a previous statement is unavailable under Rule 804(a)(3). The court need not find that the witness has **actually** lost his memory. Whether the witness's memory loss is real or feigned, the witness is unavailable to testify about the desired subject matter. As one court observed, the "crucial factor is not the unavailability of the witness but rather the unavailability of his testimony."[1]

Note that the language of 804(a)(3) says that a declarant is unavailable if he testifies to lack of memory of the subject matter of his statement. A witness could have excellent recall of many topics, and might testify about them in the courtroom. But if he has no memory of some relevant subject, then he is unavailable to testify about that matter. The witness, however, must testify that he has absolutely no recollection of the subject matter: Lack of memory of the details is not sufficient to show unavailability.[2]

---

1   Walden v. Sears, Roebuck & Co., 654 F.2d 443 (5th Cir. 1981).

2   See, e.g., North Miss. Communications, Inc. v. Jones, 792 F.2d 1330, 1336 (5th Cir. 1986).

4. Death, Physical Illness, Mental Illness. A declarant is unavailable if she is dead or so physically or mentally ill that she cannot testify at the proceeding. The physical or mental illness must be sufficiently disabling that (a) the declarant cannot come to court to testify, and (b) there is little likelihood of recovery within a reasonable time.

5. Absence. A declarant is unavailable under subsection 804(a)(5) if a party shows that she tried to find the declarant and bring him to the hearing, but was unable to do so. This type of unavailability most commonly arises when (a) the party cannot find the declarant after making a diligent search; or (b) the declarant refuses to come to court and is currently outside the court's jurisdiction. In the latter situation, the court lacks power to subpoena the absent declarant.

The fact that a declarant is outside the court's jurisdiction, however, is not sufficient by itself to make a declarant unavailable. Rule 804(a)(5) imposes two additional obligations on a party attempting to introduce the declarant's statement. **First,** the party must use any "reasonable means," in addition to serving a subpoena, to persuade the declarant to attend the trial. A civil litigant, for example, might offer to pay the declarant's travel expenses to testify at trial.

Second, for three of the hearsay exceptions contained in Rule 804, the proponent must use reasonable means to take the declarant's **deposition** if the declarant will not attend the trial. This is the meaning of the statement in subsection 804(a)(5) (B), that the proponent must have been unable to procure the declarant's "attendance **or testimony**" for three of the 804 exceptions. Courts sometimes refer to this requirement as the "deposition preference."

Wrongdoing Caveat. After reciting these five types of unavailability, Rule 804(a) ends with a provision meant to prevent improper behavior by parties. Although many circumstances may cause a witness to be "unavailable," a party offering that witness's out-of-court statement cannot cause that unavailability through wrongful means. A party, in other words, cannot obtain a favorable out-of-court statement from a witness, kill the witness to prevent recantation, and then introduce the favorable statement in court. The final sentence of Rule 804(a) attempts to prevent this type of chicanery.

C. In the Courtroom. The proponent of a hearsay statement offered under Rule 804 has the burden of proving that the declarant is unavailable. An uncorroborated statement by the proponent's attorney rarely suffices to prove unavailability. Instead, each type of unavailability requires a particular type of proof. We explore those methods in this section.

1. Privilege. To show unavailability on the basis of privilege, a party usually must call the declarant to the stand and question her. If the declarant asserts a privilege and the judge agrees that the privilege applies, then the declarant is unavailable under 804(a)(1).

In the case of the privilege against self-incrimination, however, it usually is obvious that a declarant will assert the privilege. Judges usually accept the unavailability of these declarants without requiring parties to call them to the stand:

> **Example:** Tyler is on trial for killing Maria. His defense is that Stuart killed Maria, and that Stuart admitted his guilt to Jeanette. Tyler wants to call Jeanette to the stand to testify about Stuart's hearsay statement under one of Rule 804(b)'s hearsay exceptions. The prosecution objects, arguing that Tyler has not shown Stuart's unavailability.

> **Analysis:** Parties usually must call a declarant to the stand to establish a claim of privilege constituting unavailability under Rule 804(a)(1). Under these circumstances, however, Stuart almost certainly will assert the privilege against self-incrimination. The context alone is enough for a court to determine that Stuart is unavailable, and most trial judges would declare him unavailable without proof.

2. Refusal to Testify and Lack of Memory. To establish either of these grounds for unavailability, a party must call the declarant to the stand. After the declarant refuses to testify or states her lack of memory, the judge will find the declarant unavailable. To prevent unfair prejudice, parties often make this showing outside the jury's presence.[3]

---

3   United States v. Bizzard, 674 F.2d 1382, 1387 (11th Cir. 1982).

3. Death or Illness. To establish a declarant's death, a party usually introduces a death certificate or other evidence of the declarant's demise. Sometimes, as when the declarant is a homicide victim, this fact has already been established.

If a declarant is alive, but physically or mentally unable to testify, the proponent of the evidence must introduce documentary evidence or live testimony to show the declarant's condition. A party, for example, might offer a written statement from the declarant's physician explaining the declarant's incapacity.[4]

If the declarant's illness is temporary, he is likely to recover within a reasonable time, and the trial can be continued until that time without undue prejudice to the parties, the trial judge has discretion to postpone the trial until the declarant's health improves. But if the incapacity will last longer, or any delay would prejudice the parties, then even a temporary disability may make a declarant unavailable.

4. Absence. To demonstrate that a declarant cannot be found or brought to court, a party must show a good faith, genuine effort to procure the declarant's attendance. A party could make this type of showing by documenting efforts made to contact the declarant, including registered letters or subpoenas sent to the declarant. If the declarant lives outside the court's jurisdiction, the party could introduce documentary evidence of that fact.

In addition, as explained above, the proponent must persuade the judge that he used other reasonable means to persuade the declarant to testify at trial. And, for three of the Rule 804 exceptions, the proponent must show that he used reasonable means to obtain the declarant's deposition when the declarant seemed unavailable for trial.

---

4   Remember that the Rules of Evidence do not apply to preliminary determinations, including the question whether a witness is unavailable. See Rule 104 and Chapter 34. The judge, therefore, may consider hearsay (like a doctor's letter) when deciding whether a witness is unavailable.

Quick Summary

 The five hearsay exceptions included in **Rule 804** apply only if the trial court rules that the declarant is "unavailable." There are five ways to prove unavailability:

1. The declarant claims a privilege that the judge accepts.

2. The declarant refuses to testify after the court orders him to do so.

3. The declarant testifies that she has no memory of the subject matter of the statement.

4. The declarant is dead or physically or mentally unable to testify.

5. The declarant cannot be found or compelled to come to court; nor could the proponent obtain a deposition.

The proponent of the hearsay statement has the burden of showing the declarant's unavailability. A declarant is not unavailable if the proponent wrongfully causes one of the above conditions.

49

Hearsay Exception—Former Testimony

Key Concepts

- **Rule 804(b)(1)**: Admissibility of Former Testimony
- Declarant Must Be Unavailable
- Testimony Under Oath at Prior Trial, Hearing, or Deposition
- Opportunity and Similar Motive to Develop Testimony
- Same Party or Predecessor in Interest
- Comparison to **Rule 801(d)(1)**

A. Introduction and Policy. Suppose that an appellate court reverses a verdict and the case is retried. Unfortunately, a key witness for the plaintiff died while the verdict was on appeal. Can the plaintiff introduce the witness's testimony from the first trial to support her claim in the second trial?

The witness's prior testimony is hearsay: It is a statement, made outside the current trial, offered for the truth of what the witness asserted. But this hearsay is very different from most hearsay statements; it poses very few of the risks usually associated with hearsay. Indeed, prior testimony is almost as reliable as firsthand testimony.

Recall that in Chapter 35 we identified four reasons why hearsay testimony is less reliable than firsthand courtroom testimony: (1) Hearsay compounds the risk that one of the speakers is mistaken or lying; (2) Opposing counsel can test firsthand testimony through cross-examination; (3) The fact finder can assess the credibility of a firsthand report by observing the witness; and (4) Firsthand testimony occurs under oath in a formal courtroom setting.

The prior testimony described above avoids three of these risks. The witness's testimony was recorded and preserved, so we don't have to worry about a secondhand report compounding errors. The prior testimony also occurred under oath in a formal courtroom setting, encouraging honesty. Perhaps most important, the opposing party had an opportunity to cross-examine the witness at the first trial.

The only difference between the prior testimony and live, firsthand testimony is that the fact finder will not have an opportunity to assess credibility by observing the witness. But the presence of the other three factors suggests that prior testimony is almost as likely to be accurate as live testimony. Thus, prior testimony is **more reliable** than other forms of hearsay.

This testimony, moreover, is particularly **needed** if the original witness has died or is otherwise unavailable, because the prior testimony may be the fact finder's only means of obtaining this evidence.

Based on these considerations, **Rule 804(b)(1)** creates a hearsay exception for prior testimony when a witness is unavailable to offer live testimony. In addition to the requirement of unavailability, which is common to all Rule 804 exceptions, 804(b)(1) imposes several conditions to enhance reliability of the former testimony. We explore those conditions further below.

B. The Rule. The hearsay exception for former testimony appears in Rule 804(b)(1):

RULE 804. Exceptions to the Rule Against Hearsay— When the Declarant Is Unavailable as a Witness

(b) **The Exceptions.** The following are not excluded by the rule against hearsay if the declarant is <u>unavailable</u> as a witness:

(1) *Former Testimony.* Testimony that:

(A) was given as a witness at a <u>trial, hearing</u>, or lawful <u>deposition</u>, whether given during the current proceeding or a different one; and

(B) is now offered against a <u>party</u> who had —or, in a <u>civil case</u>, <u>whose predecessor in interest</u> had—an

> opportunity and similar motive to develop it by direct, cross-, or redirect examination.

The exception starts with the foundation requirement that applies to all Rule 804 exceptions: The party offering the former testimony must show that the declarant is unavailable. Rule 804(a), which we examined in the previous chapter, defines unavailability.

Rule 804(b)(1) then outlines four additional requirements for admitting former testimony.

First, the prior testimony must have been given at a **trial, hearing, or deposition**. This requirement ensures that the declarant made the statement under oath and in a formal setting. The proceeding will also have produced a formal transcript recording the declarant's statement.

The prior testimony need not have occurred as part of the same lawsuit. If a party can satisfy the other requirements of Rule 804(b)(1), testimony from other lawsuits is admissible. Most often, however, parties introduce prior testimony from the same lawsuit.

Second, the opposing party must have had an **opportunity** to question the declarant in the prior trial or other proceeding. The opposing party need not actually have conducted an examination in the prior proceeding; this portion of the rule requires only that the party had an opportunity to do so. That opportunity, moreover, might have arisen on direct, cross, or redirect examination; the rule is not limited to opportunities to question through cross-examination.

Third, the opposing party's **motive** in questioning the declarant in the prior hearing must have been similar to the motive the opposing party would have in cross-examining the declarant in the current trial. We'll discuss this requirement in detail below; it ensures that the prior questioning substitutes adequately for the absent cross-examination in the current case.

Finally, in a criminal case, the party with the opportunity to question the declarant in the prior hearing must have been the **same** party as the opposing party in the current case.

In civil cases, the requirement is not as strict. Rule 804(b)(1) allows a party to introduce evidence as long as the opposing party or his **predecessor in interest** had an opportunity and similar motive to cross-examine the witness.

Some legislative history suggests that Congress intended the "predecessor in interest" phrase to incorporate the common-law doctrine of privity. If so, the language would expand the "same party" requirement only slightly. Courts, however, have not interpreted the language in the narrow common-law sense. In civil cases, the courts have been willing to admit prior testimony as long as a party in the prior proceeding had a motive to develop the declarant's testimony that is similar to the motives of the current opposing party.

> **Example:** Dan lost control of his car and plowed into Polly and Phoebe, who were walking on the sidewalk. Polly and Phoebe filed separate lawsuits against Dan. In Polly's trial, Dan called Mike the mechanic to testify that Dan's brakes suddenly failed so Dan lost control of the car through no fault of his own. Polly's attorney cross-examined Mike at length.
>
> Phoebe's trial begins several months after Polly's trial ended. Once again, Dan wants to call Mike as a witness, but Mike has moved away; Dan cannot locate him after a diligent search. Dan offers Mike's prior testimony, given during Polly's trial, but Phoebe objects to the testimony as hearsay.

> **Analysis:** A transcript of Mike's former testimony is admissible against Phoebe. Although Phoebe did not participate in Polly's trial, Polly had the same motive to cross-examine Mike as Phoebe would have. Even if Phoebe and Polly have no relationship to one another, Polly is Phoebe's "predecessor in interest" with respect to this testimony. Polly's cross-examination of Mike is enough to ensure that the statement is reliable, and the testimony fits the other requirements of Rule 804(b)(1).

C. In the Courtroom.

1. Similar Motives. Rule 804(b)(1) enhances the reliability of prior testimony by admitting these statements only when the opposing party had a "similar motive to develop" the declarant's testimony at the prior proceeding. If the stakes in the previous proceeding were different than in the current one, the opposing party might not have cross-examined the witness in the same manner that the party would employ at the current hearing.

Example: Thomas Bartelho and Gerald Van Bever were accused of committing several armed robberies. Van Bever pled guilty, but Bartelho proceeded to trial. At Bartelho's trial, the prosecutor introduced incriminating statements that Van Bever had made to FBI agents; these statements implicated Bartelho in the crime.[1] In response, Bartelho attempted to introduce possibly exonerating statements that Van Bever made during a pretrial suppression hearing.

At the suppression hearing, Van Bever had testified that he considered implicating innocent people when he spoke to the FBI agents and that he lied to the FBI about acquiring a gun. Bartelho wanted to introduce this testimony to suggest that Van Bever's statements incriminating Bartelho were lies. The government objected to admission of Van Bever's testimony from the suppression hearing as hearsay, arguing that it did not have a similar motive to cross-examine in the suppression hearing as it would have at trial.

Analysis: The evidence was inadmissible hearsay. The government conceded that Van Bever was unavailable for trial, because he would claim a Fifth Amendment privilege if called to testify in the case. Van Bever's testimony, moreover, was given under oath at a proceeding where the prosecution had an opportunity to cross-examine him. The prosecutor's motive at the pretrial suppression hearing, however, was substantially different from his motive at Bartelho's trial.

The suppression hearing focused on the voluntariness of Van Bever's statements to the FBI agents. The government's only interest on cross-examination, therefore, was to attack the credibility of Van Bever's assertions about the involuntary nature of his statements. At Bartelho's trial, the government had the opposite interest in cross-examining Van Bever; it was interested in developing Van Bever's credibility to support the statements in which he implicated Bartelho.[2]

---

1   The trial judge probably erred in admitting these statements; he took too broad a view of Rule 804(b)(3), the "statement against interest" exception we'll examine in Chapter 51. Bartelho, however, did not properly preserve his objection to admission of the original statements; he focused instead on attempting to introduce Van Bever's additional, possibly exonerating comments.

2   The fact pattern is based on United States v. Bartelho, 129 F.3d 663 (1st Cir. 1997). In the real case, the gov-

As this case suggests, a party's motive to cross-examine witnesses during a pretrial hearing may differ significantly from its motives at trial. Suppression hearings in criminal cases focus on narrow issues such as whether a confession was voluntary or the police had probable cause to support a search. Both prosecution and defense examine witnesses with these narrow purposes in mind; they have little motive to explore wider issues that will arise at trial.

Parties participating in pretrial hearings, moreover, often avoid revealing their trial strategies. Even if a party has an interest in cross-examining a pretrial witness, strategic considerations may counsel against a full-blown examination that would reveal the attorney's theory of the case. This is particularly true for the defense in criminal cases, where discovery is limited and the defense attorney can keep his strategy secret until the trial begins. At least in criminal cases, therefore, attorneys have a plausible argument that their motives during a pretrial hearing are not sufficiently similar to those at trial.

Testimony given in other proceedings, such as a prior trial, raises different issues. Whatever the context, many courts point to four factors when determining whether an opposing party had a similar motive to develop a witness's testimony in the prior proceeding: "(1) the type of proceeding in which the testimony [was] given, (2) trial strategy, (3) the potential penalties or financial stakes, and (4) the number of issues and parties."[3]

The fact-specific nature of this inquiry means that advocates play a significant role in persuading the judge whether to admit former testimony. To prevail on the "similar motive" issue, advocates must compare the prior proceeding carefully with the current one.

2. Against the Same Party in Criminal Cases. In criminal cases, Rule 804(b)(1) supports admission of prior testimony only if the opposing party's own counsel had an opportunity to cross-examine the witness at the prior proceeding. The rule recognizes no "predecessors in interest" or other substitute cross-examiners in criminal cases; the opposing party must have appeared in the prior proceeding and had an opportunity to develop the witness's testimony.

---

ernment conceded that Van Bever was unavailable, but the court never explained the basis of the unavailability.

3   United States v. Reed, 227 F.3d 763, 768 (7th Cir. 2000).

This restrictive principle makes sense in the criminal context. The criminal defendant should have the right to conduct his own cross-examination of any witnesses against him; it would be improper to force the defendant to rely upon someone else's cross-examination, even if that person had motives identical to the defendant's. And although the prosecution does not have the same constitutional rights to cross-examine the defendant's witnesses, it would be unfair to allow the defendant to admit former testimony when the prosecutor had no chance to examine the declarant if the prosecutor is forbidden from doing the reverse.

3. Predecessor in Interest. In civil cases, Rule 804(b)(1)'s requirement of party identity is more relaxed. A litigant may introduce former testimony as long as the opposing party or that party's "predecessor in interest" had an opportunity to develop the witness's testimony at the prior proceeding.

As noted above, courts have not interpreted Rule 804(b)(1)'s "predecessor in interest" language to incorporate the narrow, common-law meaning of privity. Instead, courts "look to the similarity of issues [between the prior case and the current one] and the purpose for which the [prior] testimony was given."[4] The test for identifying a predecessor in interest, in other words, is virtually the same as the standard for identifying a "similar motive" when the parties are identical. The test is harder to pass when the parties differ, because different parties are more likely to raise different issues and use testimony for different purposes. Here, however, is an example of a case in which a court identified a predecessor in interest:

> **Example:** The United States charged three officials of the Meadow Gold Dairies company of conspiring to fix milk prices. At the trial of these three individuals, the prosecutor relied on the testimony of Paul French, a former general manager of another dairy, who testified under a grant of immunity. Defense attorneys for the three Meadow Gold officials cross-examined French extensively. The trial ended in a hung jury, and the government dropped the charges.

---

4   Id.

A group of supermarkets then sued Meadow Gold and several other dairies, alleging that they violated the Sherman Antitrust Act by fixing prices. French did not testify at this trial, but the supermarkets offered French's prior testimony as evidence that a conspiracy existed among the dairies. The trial judge assumed that French was unavailable because he almost certainly would have invoked his right against self-incrimination. But Meadow Gold and the other dairies still objected to admission of French's prior testimony, arguing that they did not have an opportunity to cross-examine him during the criminal case against the three officials.

Analysis: The prior testimony was admissible, because the Meadow Gold officials in the prior criminal case were predecessors in interest for all of the dairy companies in the civil case. The legal issues in the two cases were not identical, but they were quite similar. In the criminal case, the defendant officials tried to prove that no conspiracy existed; in the civil case, the defendant companies had to prove either that no conspiracy existed or, if it did, that it occurred without any affirmative acts of concealment. These motives were similar enough to allow the individual defendants' cross-examination of French in the criminal case to substitute for the cross-examination that the companies would have conducted of him in the civil case.[5]

The predecessor in interest analysis, like that for similar motives, depends on the facts and issues in the two proceedings. Application of the predecessor in interest test is another area in which good advocacy may determine admissibility.

4. Opportunity to Develop Testimony. Rule 804(b)(1) admits prior testimony as long as the party or predecessor in interest (a) had an opportunity to develop the declarant's testimony at the prior proceeding, and (b) during the prior proceeding, had a motive for developing that testimony similar to the current opposing party's motive for cross-examination. The party or predecessor in interest need not have actually examined the declarant; it is only the opportunity and motive that matter.

---

5   The fact pattern is based on Supermarket of Marlinton v. Meadow Gold Dairies, 71 F.3d 119, 126 (4th Cir. 1995).

In practice, however, an absence of examination at the prior proceeding reduces the likelihood that a court will find a similar motive or predecessor in interest. The opposing party in the current litigation will almost always have a strong interest in cross-examining the unavailable declarant. If the opposing party or its predecessor in interest did not question the declarant at the prior proceeding, it is unlikely that a court will determine that the interests and motives were identical in the prior proceeding.

In the *Meadow Gold* case, for example, the vigorous cross-examination at the prior, criminal trial made it easier for the court to find that the defendants at that trial were predecessors in interest of the defendants at the civil trials. French's hearsay statements provided critical evidence at the civil trial; the civil defendants certainly would have cross-examined French if he had been available. If the criminal defendants had decided to forego cross-examination of French, that would have suggested motives very different from the civil defendants' interests.

Vigorous examination alone does not prove that the previous party was a predecessor in interest. But the absence of questioning can cut against such a finding.

5. 804(b)(1) and 801(d)(1)(A). Students often confuse the former testimony exception in Rule 804(b)(1) with the exemption for a witness's prior inconsistent statement contained in **Rule 801(d)(1)(A)** and discussed in Chapter 39. Comparing the two rules side-by-side illustrates the different indicia of reliability that they invoke:

	Prior Inconsistent Statements by Witness 801(d)(1)(A)	**Former Testimony 804(b)(1)**
Declarant:	• Must **testify** at current hearing or trial Must be subject to **cross-examination** concerning the statement	• Must be **unavailable**
Content of Statement:	• **Inconsistent** with current testimony	• **Any** content

	Prior Inconsistent Statements by Witness 801(d)(1)(A)	**Former Testimony 804(b)(1)**
Context of Prior Statement:	• Must have been given under **penalty of perjury** • Made at any prior trial, hearing, **other proceeding**, or deposition	• Must have been given as a witness, which implies that it was under **penalty of perjury** • Made during a trial, hearing, or deposition at which the current opponent (or, in a civil case, a predecessor in interest) had an **opportunity and similar motive** to develop the testimony

For prior inconsistent statements admitted under Rule 801(d)(1)(A), the declarant testifies at the current trial and is subject to cross-examination on the prior statement. There is no need, therefore, to require cross-examination with respect to the prior statement. The rule still requires that the prior statement occur at a proceeding and under penalty of perjury, two conditions that enhance reliability. The exception also furthers the goal of admitting hearsay statements that substantially aid the fact finder: Prior inconsistent statements play a special role in testing the witness's credibility.

In contrast, 804(b)(1) declarants are unavailable, so the opposing party has no chance to cross-examine the declarant during the current proceeding. The rule, therefore, requires the opportunity to develop testimony at the prior proceeding. The rule further enhances reliability by requiring that the former statement occurred during a trial, hearing, or deposition. Statements offered under 804(b)(1) are particularly needed, not for their impeachment value, but because the declarant is unavailable and cannot testify at trial about the information.

6. Depositions in Civil Cases. Rule 32 of the Federal Rules of Civil Procedure overlaps Rule 804(b)(1) of the Federal Rules of Evidence; both rules outline conditions under which parties may introduce depositions in civil cases. Under most circumstances, the rules reach the same result. But where they differ, a party may introduce a deposition by satisfying **either** rule. A deposition that is inadmissible under Rule 804(b)(1) in a civil suit occasionally is admissible under Rule 32. We will not examine Rule 32 further in this course, but you should note this possibility in practice.

Quick Summary

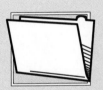 **Rule 804(b)(1)** allows admission of former testimony if the opposing party had an opportunity to develop the declarant's testimony during the prior proceeding, and if the opposing party had a similar motive to develop the declarant's testimony during that proceeding. This opportunity may have occurred on direct, cross, or redirect examination. The opposing party need not have actually conducted an examination; the opportunity suffices.

In civil cases, the prior testimony is admissible under 804(b)(1) if either the opposing party or that party's "predecessor in interest" had an opportunity to develop the testimony. Courts have defined this phrase, for purposes of admitting prior testimony, to include any party that had a similar motive and interest in developing the testimony in the prior proceeding as the current opposing party has. The predecessor in interest doctrine, however, does not apply in criminal cases.

Test Your Understanding

 To assess your understanding of the material in this chapter, <u>click here</u> to take a quiz, or go to the Quizzes module from the eBook on your eProducts bookshelf.

50

Hearsay Exception—Dying Declarations

Key Concepts

- **Rule 804(b)(2):** Dying Declarations
- Declarant Must Believe That Death is Imminent
- Statement Must Concern Circumstances of Death
- Admissible in Any Civil Case and in Homicide Prosecutions
- Declarant Need Not Die, but Must Be Unavailable

A. Introduction and Policy. Many people believe that a person's dying words carry special significance. In particular, we assume that individuals who are about to die will speak honestly. Judges have long shared this view, assuming that dying words are more reliable than other out-of-court statements. Dead declarants cannot testify at trial, so their words are also more needed than other hearsay. The hearsay exception for dying declarations is one of the oldest and best-known exceptions.

The assumption that dying declarations are truthful rests on three rationales. First, in a more religious era, judges assumed that a person would not want to meet her maker "with a lie upon her lips." A second, more secular justification is that dying people have little incentive to lie, because they cannot gain anything from deception. Finally, there is an intuitive appeal to heeding a dying person's last words, particularly if those words identify the person's killer.

All of these justifications are open to dispute. The dying declarations exception applies to any declarant, regardless of religious belief, so it is hard to defend on religious grounds. The secular justification also fails: There are many scenarios in which a dying person has incentives to lie. An individual might want to frame a life-long enemy or help heirs collect on a life insurance policy. And the intuitive appeal of these statements argues against their admissibility; an accusation from a dying victim may carry undue weight with jurors, who too readily believe those final words.

Even if dying declarations are sincere, they are likely to suffer from other flaws. Perception, memory, and clarity may be less reliable during the moments before death than at other times. Especially if the dying person has suffered a traumatic injury, he may feel great physical and emotional agony. These circumstances tend to reduce, rather than enhance, reliability.

Rule 804(b)(2) recognizes a hearsay exception for dying declarations but, perhaps because of the above concerns, it limits the exception in several ways. First, the rule admits dying declarations only in civil cases and homicide prosecutions; parties cannot rely on this exception in most criminal cases. Second, dying declarations are only admissible if they concern the cause or circumstances of the declarant's death; statements on that topic are less likely than others to be self-serving. Third, the declarant must believe that death is imminent. And, finally, the declarant must be unavailable to testify.

The final requirement of unavailability seems superfluous for a dying declaration. But the exception does not require that the declarant actually die; the exception requires only that the declarant believe death is imminent. If the declarant miraculously survives, but is unavailable at trial for other reasons, the "dying" declaration is admissible under this exception. The declarant's belief in death, rather than death itself, marks the statement as sufficiently reliable to admit under this exception.

The dying declaration is a staple of mystery novels and movies; it also appears with morbid regularity on the bar exam. The exception is less common in courtrooms: Real cases rarely turn on the final words uttered by a dying person.

B. The Rule. Rule 804(b)(2) recognizes a hearsay exception for dying declarations, although it uses a more ponderous title for the exception. Most judges and lawyers continue to refer to this exception as the one for "dying declarations."

> ## RULE 804. Exceptions to the Rule Against Hearsay—
> ## When the Declarant Is Unavailable as a Witness
>
> **(b) The Exceptions.** The following are not excluded by the rule
> against hearsay if the declarant is <u>unavailable</u> as a witness: . . .

> **(2)** ***Statement Under the Belief of Imminent Death.*** In a prosecution for <u>homicide</u> or in a <u>civil case</u>, a statement that the declarant, while <u>believing</u> the declarant's death to be <u>imminent</u>, made <u>about its cause or circumstances</u>.

As suggested in the Introduction, there are four important facets of this rule. **First**, like the other 804 exceptions, Rule 804(b)(2) applies only if the declarant is unavailable. In this context, death usually renders the declarant unavailable. But, as noted above, declarants occasionally recover after making a dying declaration. The declaration may still be admissible, but only if the declarant is unavailable for other reasons.

Second, this exception applies only in homicide prosecutions and civil proceedings; it does not apply to most criminal prosecutions. This limit recognizes the criminal defendant's constitutional right to confront witnesses, as well as policy concerns with convicting defendants based on secondhand statements. Courts are reluctant to infringe those interests by admitting dying declarations in most criminal trials. But in a homicide prosecution, it seems more fair to admit the victim's final statement about the cause of death.

Third, the declarant must believe that death is imminent when he makes the statement. This requirement is subjective; the declarant must actually hold this belief. And the declarant must believe both that death will happen very soon (within a few hours) and that it is inevitable. The assumptions of honesty motivating this exception require that the declarant believe that death is both close and certain.

This focus on the declarant's subjective belief permits the admission of dying declarations from declarants who experience miraculous recoveries. As long as the declarant subjectively believed that death was imminent, that belief satisfies this aspect of Rule 804(b)(2).

Finally, the content of the statement must concern the cause or circumstances of the declarant's death. People say many significant things while dying: They may confess to their own indiscretions, they may proclaim their love for their family, they may disclose where they have hidden valuable heirlooms. None of these statements, however, are admissible under 804(b)(2). Only a statement that describes the cause or circumstances of death counts as a "dying declaration" for hearsay purposes.

C. In the Courtroom.

1. When Is Death Imminent? Courts use poetic language when describing the imminence requirement of Rule 804(b)(2): The declarant must have "a settled hopeless expectation that death is near at hand," the statements must be "spoken in the hush of its impending presence," and the declarant "must have spoken with the consciousness of a swift and certain doom."[1] All of these judicial pronouncements, however poetic, focus on how long the declarant **believed** he would survive, not on how long the declarant actually survived. It is "the impression of almost immediate dissolution, and not the rapid succession of death, that renders the testimony admissible."[2]

The imminence requirement precludes many declarations by dying individuals. A patient with untreatable cancer, who has been given a prognosis of three to six months to live, does not believe his death is "imminent" during that period.[3] Conversely, some patients die unexpectedly from injuries that initially appear nonfatal. Statements by these patients are not dying declarations because the patients had no reason to expect death when they spoke.[4]

A declarant's sincere belief that death will occur swiftly and inevitably is more important than any specific time limit in determining whether a statement qualifies as a dying declaration:

> **Example:** David Stone, a prison inmate, was stabbed with a sharp metal shank. The wound was very deep; Stone bled profusely and turned gray from blood loss. He begged the medical personnel to save his life and repeatedly asked if he was going to die. Stone also told several people, "Mark Jordan struck me."
>
> Despite the doctors' best efforts, Stone died seven hours after he was stabbed. The government charged Jordan with murder and attempted to admit Stone's statements identifying Jordan as his attacker. Jordan objected to these statements as hearsay.

---

1   Shepard v. United States, 290 U.S. 96, 99 (1933).

2   Mattox v. United States, 146 U.S. 140, 151 (1892).

3   Sternhagen v. Dow Co., 108 F. Supp. 2d 1113 (1999).

4   United States v. Two Shields, 435 F. Supp. 2d 973 (2006).

Analysis: Stone's statements qualified as dying declarations. Stone clearly believed he was dying, because he begged the doctors to save his life. Even if he had not made those requests, a court could infer Stone's subjective expectation of imminent death from the severity if his wounds. The fact that death came seven hours after the stabbing did not disqualify the statement; throughout that period, Stone believed his death was "imminent" as defined by Rule 804(b)(2).[5]

2. Dying Declarations and Other Exceptions. Many dying declarations are also admissible under other hearsay exceptions, such as excited utterance, state of mind, statements to obtain medical treatment, and forfeiture (which we'll discuss in Chapter 52). In the previous example, for instance, Stone's statements about Jordan probably also qualified as excited utterances. When you see a fact pattern in which an individual makes statements just before dying, don't automatically jump to the dying declarations exception; there may be an easier way to admit the statement.

3. Proving State of Mind. The judge decides whether the conditions supporting admission of a dying declaration exist. Applying **Rule 104(a)**, the trial judge will determine whether the declarant sincerely believed death was imminent when the statement was made. The party offering the dying declaration must prove this belief by a preponderance of the evidence. The proponent can rely on any type of evidence to prove this belief, but courts most often consider:

- Statements by the declarant

- Statements made by medical personnel and others to the declarant

- The nature and extent of the wounds or illness

- The length of time between the statement and the declarant's death

- The opinion of medical personnel who treated the declarant about the declarant's health

---

5   This example draws upon United States v. Jordan, 66 Fed. R. Evid. Serv. 790 (D. Colo. Mar. 3, 2005). In Jordan, the victim made his statements to Bureau of Prison agents, which raised Sixth Amendment concerns that we discuss in Chapter 58. The facts, however, nicely illustrate the imminence requirement.

None of these factors are conclusive; a court will examine all of them, as well as any others noted by the parties, when deciding whether the declarant believed that death was imminent.

Quick Summary

Rule 804(b)(2) admits statements made by a declarant who believes that death is imminent, providing that (i) the statement concerns the circumstances or cause of death, and (ii) the case is a civil case or a homicide prosecution.

The declarant's subjective belief determines whether death is sufficiently imminent to create a dying declaration; if the declarant has a "settled, hopeless expectation that death is near at hand," the statement will qualify. The declarant does not actually have to die, but the declarant must be unavailable at trial or the statement is not admissible.

Test Your Understanding

To assess your understanding of the material in this chapter, click here to take a quiz, or go to the Quizzes module from the eBook on your eProducts bookshelf.

51

Hearsay Exception—Statement Against Interest

Key Concepts

- **Rule 804(b)(3)**: Hearsay Exception for Statement Against Declarant's Interest
- Declarant Must Be Unavailable
- Statements Offered in Criminal Cases Need Corroboration

A. Introduction and Policy. Individuals sometimes say or write things that are against their interest:

> "I owe Jim $550."
>
> "I robbed the Burger King on Main Street."
>
> "I cheated on the Contracts exam last week."

Even when made outside the courtroom, these statements are **more reliable** than most other hearsay. As the Supreme Court once noted, "reasonable people, even reasonable people who are not especially honest, tend not to make self-inculpatory statements unless they believe them to be true."[1]

This assumption, that self-inculpatory statements are true, underlies the hearsay exception in **Rule 804(b)(3).** That rule allows the judge to admit out-of-court statements that were against the declarant's interest at the time they were made. But Rule 804(b)(3), like the other 804 exceptions, admits these statements only if the declarant is unavailable at trial. Under the latter circumstances, these statements are **more needed** than other hearsay statements.

---

1   Williamson v. United States, 512 U.S. 594, 599 (1994).

In criminal trials, however, courts are suspicious of self-inculpatory statements made by unavailable witnesses. It is too easy for the defendant to claim that a third party committed the crime—and to arrange for a witness to testify that he overheard that third party confess. Conversely, the prosecutor may call a witness who claims to have heard a third party brag about committing the crime with the defendant. To prevent abuses by either the prosecution or defense, Rule 804(b)(3) requires corroboration in criminal trials for statements offered under that section. The party offering the statement must point to corroborating circumstances that demonstrate the trustworthiness of the third party's alleged confession.

B. The Rule.

> # RULE 804. Exceptions to the Rule Against Hearsay — When the Declarant Is Unavailable as a Witness
>
> **(b) The Exceptions.** The following are not excluded by the rule against hearsay if the declarant is <u>unavailable</u> as a witness: . . .
>
>   **(3)** *Statement Against Interest.* A statement that:
>
>   **(A)** a ~~reasonable person~~ in the declarant's position would have made only if the person believed it to be true be-cause, <u>when made</u>, it
>
>   • was so contrary to the declarant's <u>proprietary or pecuniary interest</u> or
>   • had so great a tendency to <u>invalidate the declarant's claim</u> against someone else or
>   • to expose the declarant <u>to civil or criminal liability</u>; and
>
>   **(B)** is supported by <u>corroborating</u> circumstances that clearly indicate its trustworthiness, if it is <u>offered in a criminal</u> case as one that tends to <u>expose the declarant to criminal liability</u>.

There are five important parts to this rule. **First,** as with all of the other 804 exceptions, the declarant must be unavailable for the exception to apply.

Second, the statement must be against the declarant's interest "when made." If the declarant believes a statement is against his interest at the time he makes it, the statement qualifies for the exception even if it ends up doing the declarant no harm. Conversely, if the declarant makes a statement that seems innocuous when made, the statement falls outside the exception even if later circumstances render the statement incriminating.

Third, the rule lists three ways that a statement can be against a declarant's interest: It could (a) be contrary to her proprietary or pecuniary interest; (b) render invalid a claim she has against another person; or (c) expose the declarant to civil or criminal liability.

Fourth, an objective standard governs the court's determination of whether a statement was sufficiently against the declarant's interest. The trial judge will ask whether a "reasonable person in the declarant's position" would have falsely made the incriminating statement. The judge will take the declarant's general circumstances into account, but not her personal idiosyncracies.

Finally, any statement that exposes the declarant to criminal liability is admissible in a criminal case only when corroborating circumstances clearly indicate the statement's trustworthiness. This requirement prevents the type of abuse noted in the Introduction; we explore it in greater detail below.

C. In the Courtroom.

1. What Is Against Interest? Rule 804(b)(3) defines several types of statements that may be against interest. For all of these, the rule explains that the statement must be "so contrary" to a declarant's interest that "a reasonable person in the declarant's position would have made [it] only if the person believed it to be true."

Finding that a statement meets this standard can be relatively straightforward when an individual makes an inculpatory statement to friends or family members:

> **Example:** Roberto Duran is a world-famous boxer from Panama who won more than 100 matches during his career. In 1993, Duran's championship belts—his most treasured possessions—disappeared from his home. Years later, Duran located the belts in the hands of a Miami businessman, Luis Gonzalez Baez, who was selling the belts for $200,000. Agents arrested

Baez for selling stolen property, but Baez claimed that the belts were not stolen. The United States confiscated the belts and filed an interpleader action to determine whether Baez or Duran owned the belts.

At trial, Duran introduced evidence from numerous family members that his brother-in-law, Bolivar Iglesias, stole the belts. Iglesias had gone into hiding in Panama, and even his close family members could not find him. In Iglesias's absence, Duran called as witnesses several family members who testified that they had heard Iglesias apologize to Duran for stealing his belts. Baez objected to these apologies as hearsay.

Analysis: Iglesias's out-of-court apologies were admissible. His statements ("I'm sorry that I stole your belts") subjected him to both civil and criminal liability, and no reasonable person would have confessed to that liability unless the statements were true. Iglesias was plainly unavailable, because he was beyond the court's jurisdiction and had eluded all reasonable attempts to locate him. The apologies thus satisfied Rule 804(b)(3).[2]

When a declarant speaks to a police officer, in court, or in other contexts related to law enforcement, it sometimes is more difficult to tell whether the declarant's statement is sufficiently against interest to satisfy Rule 804(b)(3); this is particularly true if the declarant received a grant of immunity from prosecution. Recall, for example, this price-fixing case from Chapter 49:

Example: The United States charged three officials from the Meadow Gold Dairies company of conspiring to fix milk prices. In the criminal case, the prosecutor relied on the testimony of Paul French, a former general manager of another dairy, who testified under a grant of immunity. A group of supermarkets then sued Meadow Gold and several other dairies, alleging that they violated the Sherman Antitrust Act by fixing prices.

French did not testify at the civil trial, but the supermarkets offered French's prior testimony as evidence that a conspiracy existed among the

---

2   United States v. Samaniego, 345 F.3d 1280 (11th Cir. 2003). The trial judge admitted evidence of Iglesias's apologies under Rule 803(3)'s "state of mind" exception. As the court of appeals pointed out, however, this exception reached only Iglesias's expressions of contemporaneous remorse ("I'm sorry"); it did not include his references to why he felt remorse ("because I stole your belts"). Rule 804(b)(3) covered the latter statements.

dairies. French was unavailable because he almost certainly would have invoked his privilege against self-incrimination. The civil plaintiffs claimed that French's testimony in the criminal case was against his interest, because he implicated himself in the scheme.

Analysis: The court rejected admission of French's prior testimony under Rule 804(b)(3), finding that his statements were not sufficiently against his own interest at the time he made them. French testified under a grant of immunity from the prosecutor, so his statements could not be used against him in any future criminal case. French, moreover, was aware of this protection.

The court conceded that French could be exposed to civil liability as a result of his statements, but found that possibility "remote" because plaintiffs rarely name individuals as defendants in civil antitrust suits. Thus, French's testimony during the criminal trial was not sufficiently against his interest to warrant admission in a subsequent trial under Rule 804(b)(3).[3]

2. Other Interests. In the *Duran* case discussed above, Iglesias's statements compromised more than just his criminal and civil interests; his apology to Duran might also have reduced his standing in the family or exposed him to physical retaliation. Confessing a wrong against a former boxing champ nicknamed the "Hands of Stone" is risky on numerous grounds.

Rule 804(b)(3) does not directly recognize these other types of interests; it admits only statements against pecuniary or proprietary interests, those that subject the speaker to civil or criminal liability, and those that extinguish a legal claim held by the speaker. The proponent of evidence under this exception must point to one of those interests. But other types of interests, including the family and physical ones present in the *Duran* case, may help persuade a court that no reasonable person would have made the statement unless it was true.

3. Minimizing Guilt. A declarant sometimes makes a statement that admits wrongdoing but minimizes her role while blaming others. Under these circumstances, the court must decide whether the statement was really against the declarant's interest. The declarant, forced into a corner by irrefutable evidence

---

3   The fact pattern is based on Supermarket of Marlinton v. Meadow Gold Dairies, Inc., 71 F.3d 119, 126 (4th Cir. 1995). In that case, the district court assumed that French was unavailable for the purposes of deciding the motion.

of wrongdoing, might have acknowledged some fault while attempting to spread the blame to others:

> **Example:** Nick Favia worked for Emalfarb Investment Corporation, a real estate developer. Favia embezzled almost $200,000 from the company by making out checks to fictitious payees. The Loyola "L" Currency Exchange cashed these checks for Favia, although the Exchange knew that the checks were not made out to him.
>
> Mark Emalfarb, president of the real estate company, discovered the embezzlement and confronted Favia. Favia admitted that he had written the checks and cashed them at Loyola "L." Favia told Emalfarb that Alan Fishman, the owner of Loyola "L," had agreed to pay checks made out to other parties "as long as there was money behind them."
>
> Emalfarb fired Favia; the two later executed a settlement agreement in which Favia ceded his house to Emalfarb and paid back some of the other embezzled funds. Emalfarb then sued Fishman, seeking civil damages under federal anti-racketeering laws. Favia claimed the privilege against self-incrimination and refused to testify at trial. Emalfarb then tried to introduce Favia's prior statements to show that Fishman cashed checks for Favia, knowing that Favia was not entitled to the proceeds.

> **Analysis:** The court refused to admit Favia's out-of-court statements in the civil trial against Fishman. Although Favia confessed to acts subjecting him to civil and criminal liability, he did so after Emalfarb confronted him with clear evidence of his wrongdoing. Favia had a strong interest in placating Emalfarb and shifting as much blame as possible to Fishman. Although the facts forced Favia to admit his own wrongdoing, the circumstances suggested that he might have been trying to "curry favor" with Emalfarb by minimizing his own guilt and highlighting Fishman's.[4]

Concerns about partially incriminating statements are even more prevalent when a declarant is in custody and offers to cooperate with law enforcement agents. As the Advisory Committee warned, "a statement admitting guilt and implicating

---

4   American Auto. Accessories, Inc. v. Fishman, 175 F.3d 534 (7th Cir. 1999).

another, made while in custody, may well be motivated by a desire to curry favor with the authorities and hence fail to qualify as against interest."[5]

4. Mixed Statements. Criminal suspects sometimes give police long narratives that include a mixture of statements. Some parts of the narrative may be inculpatory and against the declarant's interest; some may be neutral; and some may exculpate the declarant while shifting blame to others. The Supreme Court has held that courts must parse these statements, admitting only the portions of the narrative that were against the declarant's interest. Trial judges must redact the collateral statements, whether they are neutral or shift blame onto someone else.[6]

Applying this principle is straightforward in some cases. In the above case involving Nick Favia, for example, Favia's confession about his own wrongdoing could have been separated from his references to Alan Fishman and the Loyola "L" Currency Exchange. Favia's admission that he had embezzled money was against his own interest; his description of the company that assisted him by cashing checks was not. When a declarant admits guilt in a way that minimizes his role and blames others, it often is possible for the court to redact the latter statements. Once a court does that, of course, the remaining parts of the statement may no longer help the proponent.

 Under other circumstances, it is harder to separate aspects of the declarant's statement. If a declarant brags to a friend, "Bonnie and I robbed the bank together," the statement is difficult to parse. The entire sentence seems to be against the declarant's interest; she has not attempted to minimize her role by shifting blame to someone else. Surrounding circumstances, as well as the advocate's arguments, influence how closely judges parse statements like these.

5. Trustworthiness in Criminal Trials. As noted in the Introduction, courts are suspicious when either the prosecutor or a criminal defendant offers hearsay evidence that an unavailable third party confessed to the crime. To address this concern, a statement against interest is admissible in a criminal case only if "corroborating circumstances . . . clearly indicate its trustworthiness."

---

5   Fed. R. Evid. 804 advisory committee's note. These statements to law enforcement agents may also violate the Sixth Amendment if introduced to incriminate a third party at the third party's trial. We explore that issue in Chapters 55 and 58.

6   Williamson v. United States, 512 U.S. 594 (1994).

Most courts require corroboration both of the **declarant's** trustworthiness and of the **statement's** trustworthiness. The courts consider six factors in determining whether this type of statement is sufficiently trustworthy to admit under Rule 804(b)(3):

(1) Whether the declarant had pled guilty before making the statement or was still exposed to prosecution (that is, how far against the declarant's interest the statement was at the time);

(2) The declarant's motive in making the statement and whether there was a reason for the declarant to lie;

(3) Whether the declarant repeated the statement and did so consistently;

(4) The party or parties to whom the statement was made;

(5) The relationship of the declarant with the accused; and

(6) The nature and strength of independent evidence relevant to the conduct in question.[7]

The trial judge determines trustworthiness under Rule 104(a), so a party who offers an exculpatory statement under 804(b)(3) bears the burden of proving trustworthiness to the judge; the offering party must prove that fact by a preponderance of the evidence.

Example: Wallace Jones was shot in the leg during a six-person brawl at McDonald's. Jones told police that he clearly saw Timothy Bumpass shoot him, and most of the eyewitnesses backed him up. A few days after the shooting, however, Charlie Wilkinson walked into a police station and wrote out a statement confessing to the crime. Wilkinson was a friend of Bumpass and had been present at the shooting. The police did not believe Wilkinson's confession and arrested Bumpass. They believed that Bumpass had paid Wilkinson to confess because Bumpass, a convicted felon, faced a much longer sentence than Wilkinson did if convicted.

---

7   United States v. Bumpass, 60 F.3d 1099, 1102 (4th Cir. 1995).

At trial, Bumpass produced one eyewitness who testified that Wilkinson, rather than Bumpass, shot Jones. Bumpass then called Wilkinson to the stand, but Wilkinson claimed his Fifth Amendment right not to testify. Bumpass then offered Wilkinson's written statement as evidence under 804(b)(3).

Analysis: The court of appeals concluded that the trial court properly excluded Wilkinson's statement, because there were insufficient corroborating circumstances to indicate that the statement was trustworthy. The appellate court conceded that the statement was substantially against Wilkinson's interest, because he gave the statement before Bumpass was arrested and thus exposed himself to criminal liability. In addition, Wilkinson was present at the shooting and at least one witness said he had the gun, so there were circumstances to corroborate his statement.

The court ruled, however, that these facts were insufficient for the defendant to meet his burden of proof. Three other eyewitnesses contradicted Wilkinson's statement, including one who was a close friend of Bumpass; this friend swore under oath that Bumpass was the shooter. The fact that Wilkinson waited three days before making a voluntary confession also called his trustworthiness into question.[8]

 The *Bumpass* case was a close call; it is somewhat surprising that the trial judge and an appellate court believed that the defendant needed to produce more evidence than he did just to convince the judge to admit Wilkinson's statement. The jury, after all, could still have rejected that declaration. *Bumpass* demonstrates how suspicious courts are of third-party statements offered in a criminal case when the declarant admits criminal liability. Trustworthiness is a vague concept, and the circumstances of each case vary, so this is another area where good advocacy can make the difference.

---

8   Id.

658 • Learning Evidence: From the Federal Rules to the Courtroom •

Quick Summary

 **Rule 804(b)(3)** allows courts to admit hearsay statements that were against the declarant's interest at the time they were made. The rule rests on the common sense assumption that no reasonable person would make a statement against interest unless it was true. The hearsay exception includes a statement that (1) was against the declarant's proprietary or pecuniary interest, (2) rendered invalid a claim against another person; or (3) exposed the declarant to civil or criminal liability. Statements falling into any of these categories satisfy the exception if a reasonable person would not have made the statement unless it was true. If only part of a statement is against the declarant's interest, the court will redact other portions before admitting the "against interest" portion.

Statements that expose the declarant to criminal liability raise special concerns when offered by the prosecution or defense in a criminal case. These statements are admissible only if the proponent offers "corroborating circumstances that clearly indicate [the statement's] trustworthiness."

Test Your Understanding

 To assess your understanding of the material in this chapter, click here to take a quiz, or go to the Quizzes module from the eBook on your eProducts bookshelf.

52

Hearsay Exception—Forfeiture

Key Concepts

- **Rule 804(b)(6)**: Admits Hearsay Against Party That Intentionally and Wrongfully Procured Witness's Unavailability
- Wrongdoing
- Acquiescence
- Intent

A. Introduction and Policy. Declarants are unavailable to testify for many reasons. Some invoke privileges, some live in other jurisdictions, others are incapacitated or deceased.

But what if an opposing party causes a declarant's unavailability, intending to prevent her testimony? This type of malfeasance is relatively rare in our judicial system, but it is not unknown. There are celebrated examples of trials involving organized crime figures in which key witnesses "disappeared" at the last minute. More commonly, an abusive husband may threaten to beat his wife again if she testifies against him at trial.

In these situations, it seems unfair to give the opposing party the benefit of the hearsay exception. If a party uses physical threats or other wrongful behavior to prevent a witness from testifying, the least we can do is admit the witness's hearsay statements against that party.

The Advisory Committee drafted **Rule 804(b)(6)** for this very purpose. The exception admits out-of-court statements offered against a party who engaged or acquiesced in wrongdoing that intentionally caused a witness's unavailability. One could argue that this exception tracks the same rationales that support other hearsay exceptions. Parties may be more likely to silence truthful witnesses than lying ones; perhaps they are willing to rely on cross-examination and impeachment for the latter. In this sense, statements offered under Rule 804(b)(6) may be more reliable than other types of hearsay. These statements certainly are more needed than other hearsay because of the witness's unavailability.

Congress, the Advisory Committee, and the courts, however, relied on more direct policies of fairness and equity in adopting this exception. Rule 804(b)(6) aims to "prevent wrongdoers from profiting from their misconduct."[1] The exception rests on that rationale rather than on any assumptions about reliability.

The forfeiture exception also rests on a theory of implied waiver: By causing the unavailability of a witness, the opposing party waives the right to object to the witness's prior statements as hearsay. It is hard to imagine an attorney arguing, "admitting these statements against my client is unfair because I will have no chance to cross-examine the declarant," when the response would be: "It is hardly unfair when your client murdered the declarant to prevent her from being here!"

Rule 804(b)(6) is a relatively new exception: Congress codified the exception only in 1997, although it existed at common law before then. As a result, courts have not yet addressed some questions about how the rule applies in particular situations. We'll turn to those issues in the Courtroom section after examining the rule itself.

B. The Rule.

> ## RULE 804. Exceptions to the Rule Against Hearsay — When the Declarant Is Unavailable as a Witness
>
> **(b) The Exceptions.** The following are not excluded by the rule against hearsay if the declarant is <u>unavailable</u> as a witness: . . .
>
> **(6) *Statement Offered Against a Party That Wrongfully Caused the Declarant's Unavailability.*** A statement offered against a party that <u>wrongfully caused</u>—or <u>acquiesced</u> in wrongfully causing—the declarant's <u>unavailability</u> as a witness, and did so <u>intending</u> that result.

---

1   United States v. Gray, 405 F.3d 227, 242 (4th Cir. 2005).

Congress adopted the exception's lengthy title during its 2011 restyling of the Federal Rules. Many judges and lawyers continue to use the common-law shorthand, "forfeiture," to describe this exception. The exception itself rests on just three requirements:

First, the declarant must be unavailable. **Second**, the opposing party must have "wrongfully caused" or "acquiesced" in the declarant's unavailability. Rule 804(b)(6) does not apply to parties who use legitimate means, such as offering information about a privilege, to dissuade a witness from testifying. The rule's policy concerns arise only when an opposing party engages in wrongful behavior.

Finally, the opposing party must have intended to make the declarant unavailable. If the declarant's absence was an unintended consequence of the party's wrongdoing, the exception does not apply. This requirement also stems from the equitable concerns motivating the exception; if the party did not intend to prevent a witness from testifying, there is no reason to invoke the exception.

C. In the Courtroom.

1. What Is "Wrongfully Causing"? Attorneys and parties undertake many legitimate actions that may discourage a declarant from testifying. The defense attorney in a spousal abuse case may inform the alleged victim that she has a right to invoke the spousal privilege if she is reluctant to testify against her husband. A prosecutor may deter a defense witness from testifying by threatening to use the testimony against him in a future criminal prosecution. A large corporate defendant may transfer an employee with damaging knowledge to an overseas office, so that a plaintiff with scant resources would be unable to track her down or bring her back to testify. Would any of these actions constitute forfeiture under 804(b)(6)?

Probably not. The plain language of 804(b)(6) states that the opposing party must act "wrongfully." According to the Advisory Committee's notes, the wrongdoing does not have to be a criminal act, but it has to be improper in some way. Courts have interpreted the "wrongfully" language to mean "coercion, undue influence, or pressure to silence testimony and impede the truth-finding function of trials."[2] Merely persuading a witness to claim a privilege or forego testifying, therefore, does not fall within Rule 804(b)(6). But when persuasion becomes undue pressure, the party's actions trigger the forfeiture exception:

---

2   United States v. Scott, 284 F.3d 758, 762 (7th Cir. 2002).

Example: Robert Scott was on trial for conspiracy to distribute marijuana and cocaine. One of the government's key witnesses, Shawn Jones, refused to testify against Scott at trial. The government sought to introduce Jones's grand jury testimony under Rule 804(b)(6), arguing that Scott had intimidated Jones into refusing to testify.

The government presented the following evidence to prove that Scott had improperly influenced Jones: (1) Jones and Scott communicated regularly while in prison together; (2) Scott told a third party that he wanted to "make sure [Jones] doesn't testify against me again" and that "Jones better not testify if he knows what is good for him"; and (3) Jones looked "nervous and scared" whenever someone mentioned testifying against Scott.

Analysis: This evidence was sufficient to show that Scott threatened or intimidated Jones in order to prevent him from testifying. The trial court inferred the intimidation from Scott's statements to others, as well as from Jones's demeanor, rather than from any direct testimony that Scott coerced Jones. But it was reasonable under the circumstances to conclude that Jones refused to testify based on his conversations with Scott and that Scott improperly pressured Jones during those discussions.[3]

The definition of "wrongfully" remains an open issue under Rule 804(b)(6). Courts will continue to explore the line between permissible and wrongful conduct as the law develops in this area.

2. Acquiescing in Wrongful Acts. Rule 804(b)(6) does not require a proponent to show that the opposing party personally committed the wrongful act or even caused another to commit those acts. The proponent only needs to show that the opposing party "acquiesced" in the improper behavior. Evidence that the opposing party "tacitly agreed" to the wrongdoing is sufficient.

Courts have expanded the definition of acquiescence even further; one court held that "bare knowledge of a plot to kill [the victim] and a failure to give warning to appropriate authorities is sufficient to constitute" forfeiture under 804(b)(6).[4] In

---

3   Id.

4   United States v. Mastrangelo, 693 F.2d 269, 273–74 (2d Cir. 1982). Although this case pre-dated the codification of the forfeiture doctrine in 804(b)(6), it has been cited in more recent cases as an example of acquiescence

fact, if the opposing party is a member of a conspiracy, the opposing party need not even know about the wrongful act, as long as the court determines that the wrongdoing was part of the conspiracy:

Example: The government charged Michelle Cherry with participating in a drug conspiracy that included four other individuals. Ebon Sekou Lurks, a key witness against the defendants, was murdered before Cherry's trial. The government had ample evidence that one of Cherry's co-conspirators committed the murder, but no evidence suggested that Cherry participated in or even knew about the killing.

When the government offered Lurks's prior statements against Cherry in the drug conspiracy trial, Cherry objected on the ground that she had nothing to do with Lurks's murder.

Analysis: The appellate court ruled that if Cherry was participating in a conspiracy with another individual, and that individual killed Lurks as part of the conspiracy, then Lurks's statement was admissible against Cherry under the forfeiture exception. In other words, conspiracy liability is sufficient to constitute "acquiescence" under 804(b)(6).[5]

3. Intent. The forfeiture exception applies only if the opposing party committed a wrongful act with the intent of making the witness unavailable. In several respects, courts have interpreted this requirement broadly. The proponent, for example, need not prove that the opposing party's **only** motive was to prevent the witness from testifying. As long as the opposing party was "motivated in part by a desire to silence the witness," the forfeiture exception applies.[6]

Similarly, if a party acts wrongfully with the intent to silence a witness in one case, that intent "**carries over**" to other cases. The declarant's statements are

---

under the rule. United States v. Rivera, 412 F.3d 562, 567 (4th Cir. 2005).

5   United States v. Cherry, 217 F.3d 811, 821 (10th Cir. 2000). Under the law of conspiracy, the government had to prove that the killing of Lurks was within the "scope, furtherance, and reasonable foreseeability as a necessary or natural consequence" of the drug conspiracy in which Cherry knowingly participated. Id.

6   United States v. Houlihan, 92 F.3d 1271, 1279 (1st Cir. 1996). This case was decided before codification of Rule 804(b)(6), but has been quoted in at least one post-codification case. See United States v. Dhinsa, 243 F.3d 635, 654 (2d Cir. 2000).

admissible against the party in all future cases in which the wrongdoing makes the declarant unavailable.[7]

The forfeiture exception, finally, may apply when a party intimidates a **potential** witness. Even if a lawsuit has not yet been filed, a potential party who silences a potential witness triggers Rule 804(b)(6) if the wrongdoer has the requisite intent.[8] Wrongdoers who are more efficient than the opposition should not benefit from their acts.

Rule 804(b)(6), however, does not admit every statement by a murder or assault victim. The proponent must prove that the opposing party acted, at least in part, with the intent of making a potential witness unavailable. A husband who kills his wife to collect the proceeds of her life insurance also prevents her from testifying if he is caught and prosecuted. But the husband's intent is not to prevent testimony; his intent is to obtain life insurance proceeds. Many crimes have the incidental effect of silencing a witness, but the perpetrators do not act with that intent; in such cases 804(b)(6) does not apply.

The Supreme Court underscored this limit to Rule 804(b)(6) in a 2008 decision, *Giles v. California*.[9] That case explored Sixth Amendment limits to the forfeiture exception, a subject we'll discuss further in Chapter 58. In reaching its decision, the Court stressed that Rule 804(b)(6) "applies only if the defendant has in mind the particular purpose of making the witness unavailable."[10]

 An emerging issue under this case law centers on how readily prosecutors may rely upon the forfeiture exception in domestic violence and child abuse cases. The Supreme Court in *Giles* recognized that "[a]cts of domestic violence often are intended to dissuade a victim from resorting to outside help, and include conduct designed to prevent testimony to police officers or cooperation in criminal prosecutions."[11] As long as one of the abuser's intentions is to silence the victim, the victim's out-of-court statements may be admissible under the forfeiture exception. Parties are likely to litigate the contours of 804(b)(6)'s intent requirement vigorously in this context because victims of domestic violence and child abuse

---

7   United States v. Gray, 405 F.3d 227 (4th Cir. 2005).

8   United States v. Emery, 186 F.3d 921, 926 (8th Cir. 1999).

9   554 U.S. 353, 367 (2008).

10   Id. (quoting 5 C. Mueller & L. Kirkpatrick, Federal Evidence § 8:134, at 235 (3d ed. 2007)).

11   Id. at 377.

often become unavailable due to invocation of privilege, refusal to testify, disappearance, or death.

Quick Summary

Rule 804(b)(6) tries to ensure that parties do not benefit from intimidating, killing, or otherwise causing the unavailability of witnesses. If the proponent of a hearsay statement can prove that the opposing party intended to cause the declarant's unavailability through wrongdoing, and succeeded in making the declarant unavailable as a witness, then the declarant's prior out-of-court statements are admissible for the truth of the matters asserted. The opposing party need not commit the wrong, as long as he acquiesced in its commission. Current litigation focuses on examining the bounds of the rule's intent requirement.

Test Your Understanding

To assess your understanding of the material in this chapter, click here to take a quiz, or go to the Quizzes module from the eBook on your eProducts bookshelf.

53

Hearsay Exemption— Statements by an Opposing Party

Key Concepts

- **Rule 801(d)(2):** Every Statement by an Opposing Party Is Exempted from Hearsay Rule
- Adopted Statements
- Statements Made by Agents
- Statements Authorized by Party

A. Introduction and Policy. Rule 801(d)(2) allows a party to introduce any out-of-court statement made by an opposing party. The opposing party's statement need not have been against interest, made under oath, or have any other extra indicia of reliability. Because this exemption is so broad, and because an opponent's statements so frequently are relevant, this probably is the most commonly used exception to the hearsay rule. Many lawyers and judges refer to the exemption as the "party-opponent" one; the exemption carried this title before it was restyled in 2011.

The breadth of this exemption stems from the policy reasons that support it. Unlike almost all of the other hearsay exceptions, the party-opponent rule does not depend on reliability. There is no reason to think that everything an opposing party says is particularly reliable. Instead, the exemption derives from the concept of estoppel: The adversarial nature of the judicial system suggests that a party should be held accountable for any statement that she makes. In other words, a party should not be allowed to object to admission of her own statement on the grounds that the statement is unreliable.

This broad exemption for an opposing party's statements appears in Rule 801(d) (2), as part of the hearsay definitions. Like 801(d)(1)'s provision governing a witness's prior statements, 801(d)(2) defines statements by opposing parties as "not hearsay." Once again, this provision really creates an exception to the hearsay rules. Out-of-court statements by parties, just like other extrajudicial declarations, are hearsay when offered for the truth of their content. It is confusing to define these statements as "not hearsay," so as with 801(d)(1), we will refer to these statements as **exemptions** from the hearsay rule.

Note that the 801(d)(2) exemption includes any "statement" offered against a party. The statements may be inculpatory, exculpatory, or neutral; the rule imposes no restrictions on the content of these statements. **Any** statement by a party is exempt from the hearsay rule when offered against that party.[1]

Rule 801(d)(2) is an important and detailed rule, so we'll devote three chapters to examining its facets. This chapter explores the basics of Rule 801(d)(2) and statements by opposing parties. Chapter 54 examines special issues raised by the presence of multiple plaintiffs and defendants. And Chapter 55 addresses a particularly complex category of party-opponent statements: those made by coconspirators. But let's start with the basics.

B. The Rule. Rule 801(d)(2) describes five categories of statements by an opposing party. We will discuss the first four categories in this chapter and focus on the fifth category, involving statements by coconspirators, in a separate chapter.

RULE 801. Definitions That Apply to This Article; Exclusions from Hearsay

(d) Statements That Are Not Hearsay. A statement that meets the following conditions is <u>not hearsay</u>:

    (2) *An Opposing Party's Statement.* The statement is offered <u>against an opposing party</u> and:

        (A) was <u>made by the party</u> in an individual or representative capacity;

        (B) is one the party <u>manifested that it adopted</u> or believed to be true;

---

1   Rule 801(d)(2) was originally titled "Admission by party-opponent," and you may see that phrase in older decisions. But this hearsay exemption always encompassed all statements by an opposing party; it was never limited to "admissions." The Advisory Committee altered the confusing title during the 2011 restyling.

> **(C)** was made by a person whom the <u>party authorized</u> to make a statement on the subject;
>
> **(D)** was made by the party's <u>agent or employee</u> on a matter within the scope of that relationship and while it existed;
>
> . . . .

Rule 801(d)(2) imposes only one significant limit: To qualify for this exemption, a party's statement must be offered **against** that party. As we'll discuss further below, a party cannot introduce his own out-of-court statement under this hearsay exemption.

Apart from this limit, Rule 801(d)(2) is very broad. The rule admits every statement made directly by an opposing party, but it does even more than that: Subsection (B) admits any statement that the party has **adopted** as her own; subsection (C) admits any statement by a person that the party **authorized** to speak on that subject; and subsection (D) admits most statements made by the party's **agents or employees**. We will explore each of these specific provisions in more detail below.

C. In the Courtroom.

1. Opponents. Rule 801(d)(2) establishes a very broad exemption from the hearsay rule, allowing introduction of most out-of-court statements by parties. The rule, however, contains one very important limit: Parties cannot introduce evidence of their own statements under this rule—they can only offer evidence of an **opponent's** statements. This prevents parties from offering evidence of self-serving statements:

> **Example:** The United States prosecuted Scott McDaniel for stealing checks from the U.S. mail, changing the endorsements, and cashing the checks. The government called Patricia Locke, a postal inspector, to describe her investigation of McDaniel's wrongdoing. As part of her direct testimony, Locke recounted several out-of-court statements McDaniel had made to her.
>
> On cross-examination, McDaniel's counsel attempted to ask Locke about another statement that McDaniel had made to her; that statement includ-

ed exculpatory elements. The prosecutor objected to these questions as eliciting hearsay.

Analysis: The district judge properly stopped McDaniel's counsel from asking about statements that Locke did not describe during her direct examination. McDonald's out-of-court statements were hearsay when offered for the truth of the matters asserted. The government could ask Locke to describe those statements under Rule 801(d)(2)(A) because it was offering the statements against McDaniel. But when McDaniel's counsel asked Locke to describe other statements made by McDaniel, counsel was attempting to introduce his client's own statements. Rule 801(d)(2) does not allow a party to introduce his own statements, only those of his opponent.[2]

The ruling in *McDaniel* seems unfair at first: Doesn't it allow the prosecutor to distort McDaniel's out-of-court statements by introducing those that advanced the government's case and ignoring others? The solution to this, however, is for McDaniel (or any other party confronted with their out-of-court statements) to take the stand. McDaniel could explain or clarify the out-of-court statements that had been admitted against him. But he could not "testify" through the artifice of asking another witness to relay his statements.

As the court of appeals observed in *McDaniel*, allowing parties to introduce their own out-of-court statements would "effectuate an end-run around the adversarial process by, in effect, testifying without swearing an oath, facing cross-examination, or being subjected to firsthand scrutiny by the jury."[3] Rule 801(d)(2) avoids this self-serving strategy by allowing introduction of extrajudicial statements only **against** a party.

Rule 801(d)(2), in sum, is a single-edged sword: It allows parties to introduce out-of-court statements made by opposing parties, but not to introduce their own out-of-court statements. In this sense, Rule 801(d)(2) is similar to Rule 801(d)(1), which is more generous in allowing prior inconsistent statements than consistent ones.[4] The Rules of Evidence attempt to limit the use of cumulative or self-serving testimony in the courtroom.

---

2   This example is based on United States v. McDaniel, 398 F.3d 540, 544–45 (6th Cir. 2005).

3   Id. at 545.

4   See Chapter 39 for further discussion of Rule 801(d)(1), which admits some out-of-court statements by witnesses.

2. Statements. As noted in the Introduction, Rule 801(d)(2) admits **any** out-of-court statement made by an opposing party. The statement need not be incriminatory on its face; it may even seem exculpatory.

Example: The government prosecuted Emmy Bezler for stealing money from her employer. Several of Bezler's neighbors testified for the prosecutor, saying that they had heard Bezler say that she was having great difficulty paying off her student loans and could "really use" a little more money.

Analysis: Bezler's comments are admissible under Rule 801(d)(2) as an opposing party's statements. Even though the statements are not incriminating in themselves, they have some tendency to establish a motive for Bezler's alleged theft. Since Bezler is a party to the lawsuit, Rule 801(d)(2) allows the prosecutor to introduce any statements Bezler made outside the courtroom.

3. Personal Knowledge. The exemption for party-opponent statements is so broad that it allows introduction of an opposing party's statements even if the opposing party had no personal knowledge of what he was saying.

Example: Kenneth Poos was the director of a wolf research center, and he occasionally took tame wolves to schools to interact with children. One of these wolves was Sophie; she had been very gentle in thousands of contacts with children and Poos kept her in his backyard at home. Daniel Mahlandt, a three-year-old boy, saw Sophie and crawled under Poos's chain fence to get closer to her. Witnesses heard Daniel screaming and saw Sophie straddling Daniel, although they could not tell if Sophie was licking Daniel or biting him. Daniel had lacerations on his face and body, but they were injuries that could have been sustained from crawling under the fence.

Poos came home after the incident and talked with neighbors about what had happened. He then contacted the president of the wolf research center and told him: "Sophie bit a child."

Daniel's parents sued Poos and the research center; they claimed that Daniel suffered his injuries from Sophie rather than from crawling under the fence. At trial, the parents called the research center president to testify about Poos's statement. Poos objected to the testimony, claiming that he was mistaken when he contacted the research center president; he concluded later that Sophie had not caused the injury. Admitting his hasty initial statement, Poos argued, would violate Rule 602 because he lacked personal knowledge of the facts when he made that statement.

> **Analysis:** Poos's out-of-court statement is admissible for the truth of the matter asserted. Rule 801(d)(2) exempts every statement made by an opposing party; there is no requirement that the party had personal knowledge of the matter when speaking.[5]

This result seems counterintuitive. Poos's statement was based on the comments of neighbors who described the incident to him. Why does Rule 801(d)(2) admit this statement, simply because Poos is a party? Even more troubling is the fact that Poos himself cannot testify at trial about whether Sophie bit Daniel; he has no firsthand knowledge of that, so his testimony would violate **Rule 602**. Yet Rule 801(d)(2) allows Poos's opponent to introduce an identical out-of-court statement against him.

The explanation stems from the rationale motivating Rule 801(d)(2). Hearsay statements by opponents are not admitted because they are reliable or trustworthy; they are admitted on an estoppel theory. The exemption holds a party responsible for every statement that he makes, even if he made that statement without any personal knowledge, and even if there is evidence that he was mistaken or lying when he said it.

A party seeking to preclude his own statements still has one possible objection: **Rule 403**. If there is evidence that the statement is extremely unreliable—perhaps because the party-opponent was merely restating double or triple hearsay—a trial court may exclude the statement on grounds that it would cause unfair prejudice substantially outweighing any probative value. The Advisory Committee's note, however, states that the estoppel rationale behind 801(d)(2) "calls for generous treatment of this avenue to admissibility."[6] Any Rule 403 objection based on unreliability, therefore, faces an uphill battle.

---

5   Mahlandt v. Wild Canid Survival & Research Center, 588 F.2d 626 (8th Cir. 1978).

6   Fed. R. Evid. 801(d)(2) advisory committee's note.

4. Party's Availability Immaterial. As we have seen, some hearsay exceptions depend upon the availability of the out-of-court declarant to rebut or explain the extrajudicial statement. Rule 801(d)(1), for example, applies only if the declarant has testified as a witness.

Parties usually are present in the courtroom, but the hearsay exemption for party-opponent statements does not require availability. Even when a criminal defendant invokes the privilege against self-incrimination and declines to take the stand, the government may introduce evidence of the defendant's out-of-court statements. In the example given above, the prosecutor could present evidence of Emmy Bezler's out-of-court statements even if Bezler never testified.

5. Adoption by Signing a Document. Rule 801(d)(2)(B) provides that a party's "statement" need not consist of the party's own words. Instead, it is sufficient if the party "manifested that it adopted" a statement "or believed [the statement] to be true." One common way to adopt a statement is to sign a document prepared by others:

Example: In September 1993, a group of barges struck a bridge over a bayou near Mobile, Alabama. An Amtrak train, the "Sunset Limited," derailed while attempting to navigate the damaged bridge; several cars fell into the bayou and about fifty people died.

Gary Farmer, the train's assistant conductor, helped to rescue some of the passengers. Farmer later sued the companies responsible for the accident, claiming that he suffered post-traumatic stress disorder that left him incapable of working. Farmer claimed that he was in excellent health before the accident and had not suffered any emotional or mental disorders prior to that time.

The defendants then introduced evidence that Farmer had applied for disability benefits a few years before the accident, noting on his application form that he suffered from post-traumatic stress disorder. Farmer objected to introduction of the form as hearsay, claiming that a caseworker had filled it in erroneously.

Analysis: Farmer's disability application was admissible under 801(d)(2) as the statement of an opposing party. Even if Farmer did not fill out the form himself, he signed it. The signature showed that Farmer had adopted the statement, which suffices to establish an admission under 801(d)(2)(B).[7]

6. Adoption by Silence. An individual's silence can constitute an adoptive admission, but the circumstances must be such that a reasonable person would speak up rather than remain silent.

Example: Christina Weston-Smith sued the Cooley Dickinson Hospital, claiming that the hospital violated federal law by firing her because she had taken a maternity leave. The hospital moved for summary judgment, contending it had other reasons to fire Weston-Smith.

Weston-Smith defended against the summary judgment motion by offering deposition testimony in which she described a luncheon conversation she had with her supervisor, Donna Bowles. At the lunch, Weston-Smith asked Bowles whether she had been laid off because of the maternity leave. According to Weston-Smith, Bowles "clearly looked extremely uncomfortable and didn't answer. She sat there and turned color, you know, turned bright red and didn't answer the question, you know, he she [sic] evaded the issue, tried to talk about something different. I tried to bring her back to that question, I wanted to have the answer, but she clearly—her body language told me that she was well aware of what I was talking about, but she did not answer the question in words." The hospital objected to this testimony as hearsay.

Analysis: The court of appeals agreed with the hospital that the testimony was hearsay. Bowles's silence did not constitute an adoptive statement, because the lunch was a social occasion and Bowles might have decided that she did not want to discuss any aspect of Weston-Smith's termination. Others in Bowles's situation might have acted in the same manner; there was nothing unnatural in her silence. Weston-Smith, therefore, could not claim Bowles's silence as an opposing party's statement under Rule 801(d)(2)(B).[8]

---

7   In re Amtrak "Sunset Ltd" Train Crash, 136 F. Supp. 2d 1251, 1261–62 (S.D. Ala. 2001). The procedural context in the reported case was more complex than in this example, but the hearsay issue was the same.

8   Weston-Smith v. Cooley Dickinson Hosp., Inc., 282 F.3d 60, 66–68 (1st Cir. 2002).

Courts have articulated a variety of standards to determine whether silence constitutes an adoptive statement. The court in the Weston-Smith case asked "whether the circumstances as a whole show that the lack of a denial is so unnatural as to support an inference that the undenied statement was true."[9] The court in the next example used the somewhat more lenient sounding standard of whether "probable human behavior" would have produced a response rather than silence.[10]

Example: The United States charged Herman Hoosier with robbing a Clarksville, Tennessee, bank. Robert Rogers testified for the prosecutor that, before the Clarksville robbery, Hoosier bragged that he planned to rob a bank. Three weeks after the robbery, Rogers saw Hoosier and his girlfriend together, and noticed that Hoosier was wearing diamond rings and spending lots of money. When Rogers commented on Hoosier's wealth, Hoosier's girlfriend said, "That ain't nothing, you should have seen the money we had in the hotel room." Hoosier said nothing during the exchange.

The prosecutor called Rogers to the stand to testify about the statement made by Hoosier's girlfriend. Hoosier objected to Rogers's testimony as hearsay.

Analysis: The trial judge admitted Rogers's testimony, and the court of appeals affirmed. Hoosier's statement that he planned to rob a bank, related by Rogers in the courtroom, was the statement of an opposing party. Under the circumstances, moreover, Hoosier's silence in the face of his girlfriend's comment was an adoptive statement, admissible under 801(d)(2)(B). Since Rogers, Hoosier, and the girlfriend were alone at the time of this conversation, it seemed unlikely that Hoosier remained silent on the advice of counsel or because he feared that anything he said would be used against him. Hoosier had previously told Rogers that he planned to rob a bank. If his newfound money had stemmed from a more legal source, the "probable human behavior would have been for [Hoosier] promptly to deny his girlfriend's statement. . . ."[11]

---

9 Id. at 67.

10 United States v. Hoosier, 542 F.2d 687, 688 (6th Cir. 1976).

11 Id.

Note that Hoosier's girlfriend was not a party in this lawsuit; therefore, the prosecutor could not admit her statement directly under 801(d)(2)(A) as an opposing party's statement. Instead, the prosecutor had to argue that Hoosier adopted his girlfriend's statement as his own.

 Although courts use somewhat different formulas to describe when silence constitutes an adoptive statement, the formulas probably matter less than the facts of the case and the arguments of counsel. This is another area in which effective advocacy may persuade the court.

A criminal defendant's silence in the presence of police officers or other investigators, however, must be interpreted with care. Once a defendant has received, or should have received, Miranda warnings of the right to remain silent, the defendant's silence can no longer be held against him.[12] Even prior to the need for Miranda warnings, a reasonable person might choose to remain silent in the face of statements uttered in the presence of police officers. The constitutional dimensions of this issue are covered in courses on Criminal Procedure. For purposes of the Federal Rules of Evidence, it suffices to know that the presence of government authorities affects interpretation of a criminal defendant's silence.

7. Agents. Subsection (D) of Rule 801(d)(2) significantly expands the party-opponent exemption by including any statement "by the party's agent or employee on a matter within the scope of that relationship and while it existed." An agent is someone authorized to act for a party on a particular matter; attorneys, for example, are agents of their clients. Rule 801(d)(2) encompasses statements by agents like these, as well as statements by traditional employees.

The exemption includes statements than an employee or agent makes to **outsiders**, as well as those made within the agency or employment context. The exemption thus gives parties broad power to introduce damaging statements they find through discovery, interviews, or other means.

Example: A group of record companies, movie studios, and music publishers sued Grokster and Streamcast, claiming that the defendants' "file-sharing software contributed to massive infringement of copyrighted works owned by Plaintiffs." The district court initially granted sum-

---

12   *Miranda v. Arizona*, 384 U.S. 436 (1966).

mary judgment for the defendants, but the Supreme Court reversed and remanded for further consideration. The plaintiffs settled with Grokster after the Supreme Court decision, but continued their lawsuit against Streamcast. To support a motion for summary judgment against Streamcast, plaintiffs introduced numerous emails exchanged among Streamcast's employees. Streamcast objected that those emails were hearsay.

Analysis: The court held that emails sent by Streamcast's employees, as well as those sent by an independent graphic designer who worked with the in-house team, were all statements by agents or employees of Streamcast. The emails, which discussed Streamcast's business plan and other aspects of the file-sharing business, clearly fell within the scope of these workers' employment. Thus, the emails were admissible under 801(d)(2)(D). The court also held that attachments to the emails were admissible, even if created by others, because the employees had adopted those attachments within the meaning of 801(d)(2)(B). Having found these emails and other evidence admissible, the court held Streamcast liable for inducing copyright infringement through its MusicCity/OpenNap and Morpheus services.[13]

As the *Streamcast* decision indicates, the distinction between employees and independent contractors, which plays an important role in many legal contexts, is not as important under 801(d)(2)(D). Independent contractors, who perform discrete services for an employer without the same degree of supervision as an in-house employee, sometimes qualify as agents of the employer under the hearsay rules. An independent contractor's authority may be somewhat narrower than that granted a full-time, in-house employee, but statements by these agents are admissible against the person or company employing them as long as those statements are "within the scope" of their agency relationship.

8. Authorized Speakers. Rule 801(d)(2)(C) further expands the admissibility of an opposing party's statements by including any statement "by a person whom the party authorized to make a statement on the subject." This provision overlaps 801(d)(2)(D), which governs statements by agents, but it also embraces assertions by an individual that a party authorizes to speak outside the classic agency relationship. A party, for example, might authorize another person to speak on just a single subject or on a single occasion:

---

13   MGM Studios, Inc. v. Grokster, Ltd., 454 F. Supp. 2d 966, 973–74 (C.D. Cal. 2006).

Example: Mary Tipton sued her former employer, the Canadian Imperial Bank of Commerce, for sex discrimination and retaliatory discharge. Tipton complained that her supervisor treated her less favorably than he treated male managers and discharged her when she complained about this treatment. The Bank defended on the ground that Tipton was an abrasive and insubordinate employee.

At trial, the Bank introduced a letter of reference that Tipton had submitted to a business school in connection with her application to that program. The author of the letter, a business and social colleague of Tipton's, wrote that "because of her strong intelligence, [Tipton] sometimes works poorly with less skilled superiors." Tipton objected to introduction of the letter as hearsay.

Analysis: The trial judge admitted the letter offered by the Bank. Although the court of appeals did not reach this issue on appeal, the letter seems to fit the requirements of Rule 801(d)(2)(C). Tipton requested the letter from her colleague; in that way, she authorized the colleague to speak on her behalf about her credentials and workplace performance. Tipton did not see the letter before it was submitted, so she did not expressly adopt the statements contained in it. But one who authorizes another person to speak on a subject must live with the comments that the other person makes. Tipton's authorization of the letter of reference fits within this mold; the statements in the letter were statements authorized by an opposing party that the Bank could introduce against Tipton.[14]

9. Criminal Defendants. As the above examples make clear, Rule 801(d)(2) admits party statements in both civil and criminal cases. In fact, prosecutors commonly use 801(d)(2) to admit a criminal defendant's oral or written confessions. Using these out-of-court statements against a criminal defendant creates a dilemma for defendants with prior convictions. If the defendant takes the stand to rebut or explain the out-of-court statements, the prosecutor may be able to introduce evidence of the prior convictions to impeach the defendant as a witness.[15] Many defendants and their attorneys fear that evidence of prior convictions predisposes the jury to convict the defendant on the current charge. On the other hand, if

---

14   Tipton v. Canadian Imperial Bank of Commerce, 872 F.2d 1491, 1498 (11th Cir. 1989).

15   Recall Chapter 20, in which we examined the rules for impeaching a witness with evidence of prior convictions.

the defendant leaves the out-of-court statement unexplained, that statement may unfairly suggest guilt. Rule 801(d)(2) creates difficult strategic decisions for many criminal defendants.

 D. Relationship to Other Rules. Rule 801(d)(2) sheds new light on **Rule 407** (barring evidence of subsequent remedial measures); **Rule 408** (barring evidence of discussions during settlement negotiations); and **Rule 409** (barring evidence of a party's offer to pay medical expenses).[16] Without those special protections, parties could introduce an opposing party's statements about subsequent remedial measures, admissions during settlement discussions, and offers to pay medical expenses under Rule 801(d)(2). The "dance" of admission and exclusion for this type of evidence unwinds as follows:

- A party's concession of liability during a settlement negotiation, if offered to establish liability at trial, would be hearsay. The concession is a statement uttered outside the courtroom, offered for the truth of what it asserts.

- Rule 801(d)(2), however, would allow an opposing party to introduce this concession as an opposing party's statement.

- But Rule 408 will exclude the concession as a statement occurring during settlement negotiations, assuming that the requirements of Rule 408 are met.

What about **Rule 403**'s exclusion of evidence that is unfairly prejudicial? If a judge following the above path excludes the concession under Rule 408, then Rule 403 has no role to play. Rule 403 can exclude evidence that is admissible under other rules, but it cannot support admission of evidence that is otherwise excluded.

If, however, a judge concludes that one of the requirements of Rule 408 has not been met, so that the concession would be admissible under Rule 801(d)(2), then the opposing party could still argue for exclusion under Rule 403. Even if the concession fails to fall within the literal scope of Rule 408, the party might be able

---

16   See Chapters 9–11 to review these rules.

to persuade the judge that its admission would be unduly prejudicial. The judge's decision would depend on the facts of the case and the persuasiveness of counsel.

Quick Summary

Rule 801(d)(2) creates a very broad exemption from the rule against hearsay. This rule allows a party to admit any statement made by an opposing party outside the courtroom. The rule includes statements made directly by a party, those that a party adopts (including through silence construed as adoption), those made by agents or employees, and those made by a person authorized to speak for the party on that matter. The exemption even includes statements made by an opposing party who had no personal knowledge about the subject matter of the statement.

The exemption, however, is limited to statements introduced against a party; a party may not introduce his or her own out-of-court statement. And, as with any other hearsay statement, any statement that is admissible under a hearsay exception must also comply with Rule 403 and the other Rules of Evidence.

Test Your Understanding

To assess your understanding of the material in this chapter, click here to take a quiz, or go to the Quizzes module from the eBook on your eProducts bookshelf.

54

Statements by Opposing Parties in the Context of Multiple Parties

Key Concepts

- "Same Side" Issue: May One Party Offer Statement Against Another Party on the Same Side of the Litigation?
- "Spillover" Issue: Out-of-Court Statement by One Party Is Not Admissible Against Co-Plaintiffs or Codefendants
- Limiting Instruction to Prevent Spillover
- Confrontation Clause Limits Use of Statements with Spillover Effect Against Criminal Defendants

A. Introduction and Policy. Rule 801(d)(2), as we saw in the last chapter, allows litigants to introduce out-of-court statements made by another party. This liberal exemption from the hearsay rule raises two special problems when a case involves multiple plaintiffs or multiple defendants.

The first problem arises when a party attempts to introduce an out-of-court statement made by a party on the **same side of the litigation**. May one plaintiff introduce the out-of-court statements of another plaintiff? Similarly, may one defendant introduce extrajudicial statements made by other defendants? Here is an example of a case in which two defendants wished to introduce the out-of-court statements of a third codefendant:

Example: The government prosecuted Paul Alvarado, Robert Palow, and Evelyn Perez for distributing cocaine. All three were tried in a single trial. Palow and Perez both took the stand, testifying about various aspects of their criminal activities with Alvarado. These two defendants both described Alvarado as the leader of their criminal enterprise, quoting numerous statements Alvarado made while planning the crime and directing Palow and Perez in their roles. Alvarado objected to admission of these out-of-court statements attributed to him, arguing that they were hearsay and that Rule 801(d)(2) does not allow one defendant to introduce the out-of-court statements of another.[1]

As we'll discuss further below, courts split on this issue. Some allow one defendant (or plaintiff) to introduce out-of-court statements made by another party on the same side of the litigation; other courts do not. Rule 801(d)(2)'s language and policy do not offer a clear answer to this question.

The second question that arises with multiple parties is the spillover effect of out-of-court statements offered against one party: What effect do those statements have on other parties on the same side of the litigation? If one defendant makes an incriminating statement, is that statement admissible against all defendants or only against the defendant who made the statement? Similarly, if one plaintiff makes an unfortunate out-of-court admission, is that statement admissible against all plaintiffs? Here is a hypothetical variation on the last example:

> **Example:** At their joint trial for distributing cocaine, Alvarado, Palow, and Perez all invoke the Fifth Amendment and decline to testify. The prosecutor calls Officer Bly, who testifies that Palow confessed to him that "Paul, Evelyn and I were distributing cocaine." Alvarado, Palow, and Perez all object to this testimony as hearsay.

Bly's testimony clearly is admissible against Palow: He is recounting an out-of-court statement that Palow (a party) made to him, and the government has offered that statement against Palow. But what about Alvarado and Perez? Is the statement admissible against them?

As we'll discuss further below, Bly's testimony is not admissible against Alvarado and Perez; the jury may consider the statement only in assessing Palow's guilt.

But this result raises another, even more troubling question: Can a jury realistically separate the out-of-court admissions of one defendant from the guilt of other

---

1   United States v. Palow, 777 F.2d 52, 56 (1st Cir. 1985). For the court's ruling on this issue, see the Rule section below.

defendants? The question is particularly acute when the out-of-court statement, as in the example above, specifically names the other defendants. In criminal trials, this problem can raise constitutional issues. We'll explore below how the courts have addressed these issues.

B. The Rule. We don't need to learn any new provisions of the Federal Rules of Evidence in this chapter; the sections of Rule 801(d)(2) that we examined in the last chapter offer the Rules' only guidance on these multi-party issues. We examine in this section how Rule 801(d)(2) applies to each of the multi-party problems described above.

1. Same-Side Statements. On the first issue raised above, whether a litigant can introduce the out-of-court statement of another party on the same side of the lawsuit, Rule 801(d)(2)'s language is ambiguous. Until December 2011, the rule authorized any litigant to introduce a statement "against a party." Some courts, noting the unrestricted reference to any "party," allowed defendants to offer a codefendant's out-of-court statement against that codefendant. Similarly, a plaintiff could offer a co-plaintiff's declarations against that person.

This reading of Rule 801(d)(2) is consistent with the policies underlying that rule. As we discussed in the last chapter, parties cannot introduce their own statements under this hearsay exemption; that would allow them to circumvent the oath and cross-examination requirements of trial. But introducing a co-party's out-of-court statement does not generate this problem. Many co-plaintiffs or codefendants have adverse interests; this is particularly true in criminal cases, where codefendants may blame one another. As long as a party offers a statement against a co-plaintiff or co-defendant, Rule 801(d)(2) supports introduction of the statement.

The court in the first Alvarado example adopted this reasoning in allowing codefendants Perez and Palow to testify about Alvarado's extrajudicial statements:

> **Analysis:** The trial court allowed Perez and Palow to describe Alvarado's out-of-court statements, and the appellate court affirmed. Rule 801(d)(2), the court observed, requires only that a statement be introduced "against" a party, which courts have interpreted to mean "contrary to a party's position at trial." This requirement prevents "the introduction of self-serving statements by the party making them." Perez and Palow clearly were offering statements against Alvarado's position, not in a manner designed to serve his interests. Rule

801(d)(2) supported admission of those statements whether they came from a government witness or, as in the current case, from Alvarado's codefendants.[2]

 A few courts, however, have read Rule 801(d)(2) more narrowly. These courts focus on the fact that the subsection is captioned "An Opposing Party's Statement" (or, before December 2011, "Admission by Party-Opponent"). A codefendant or co-plaintiff, these courts have ruled, is not an "opposing party" or "party-opponent."[3]

2. Spillover Effects in Civil Cases. Rule 801(d)(2)(A) allows a litigant to introduce a party's statement against that party, but it does not authorize admission of the statement against anyone else. The party-opponent exemption from the hearsay rules is a generous one, but it only allows the statement to be used against the party who made the statement. Consider this example from a civil lawsuit:

Example: Patty Pratt, a passenger in a car driven by Saul Speed, suffered serious injuries when Speed collided with another car driven by Rhonda Wreck. Pratt sued both Speed and Wreck, claiming that the accident occurred because (1) Wreck ran a red light, and (2) Speed was driving so fast that he could not avoid the collision. At trial, Pratt calls Brian Bright as a witness. Bright testifies that he talked to Wreck the day after the accident and she told him: "I know I ran a red light before that collision, but the other guy was traveling at the speed of light. He was going so fast that I couldn't get out of his way." Both Speed and Wreck object to admission of this statement as hearsay.

Analysis: The statement is admissible against Wreck; she made the statement and Pratt is offering it against her as a party to the litigation. The statement, however, is not admissible against Speed. He did not make the statement, so it remains hearsay with respect to him.

How will a judge handle a statement that is admissible against one defendant but not another? In a civil case, the judge will handle this problem in the same way

---

2   Id. at 56.

3   See, e.g., U.S. v. Gossett, 877 F.2d 901, 906 (11th Cir. 1989).

that judges handle other instances in which evidence is admissible for one purpose but not another: The judge will give the jury a limiting instruction telling them that they may consider the content of Wreck's statement in assessing her liability, but not in evaluating Speed's behavior. The jury may have trouble using the out-of-court statement with regard to one of the defendants, while ignoring it with regard to the other, but that is a common problem with limiting instructions.[4]

When the portions of a statement are easily separable, as in this example, a judge may limit the witness's testimony to avoid unfair prejudice to another party. The judge, for example, might instruct Bright to testify only that Wreck said: "I know I ran a red light before that collision." If Bright stops his testimony there, the statement remains admissible against Wreck, but there is no chance that the jury will erroneously use the statement to assess Speed's liability; the statement no longer refers to Speed in any way. Speed's counsel might invoke **Rule 403** to persuade the judge to limit Bright's testimony in this way.[5]

In civil cases, in sum, Rule 801(d)(2) authorizes introduction of an out-of-court statement against the party who made the statement, but not against other parties. The judge will protect those other parties from any spillover effect of the statement by offering a limiting instruction, redacting the out-of-court statement, or excluding the statement under Rule 403, depending on the probative value of the out-of-court statement, the unfair prejudice to other parties, and other evidence in the case.

In a criminal case, Rule 801(d)(2) applies in exactly the same way. However, courts must also consider the criminal defendant's rights under the Confrontation Clause of the Constitution, which—as we will see—requires separate analysis.

C. The Confrontation Clause.
Courts face an additional challenge in criminal cases because of the constitutional protections that a criminal defendant receives. In light of those protections, the Supreme Court has held that a limiting instruction often is insufficient if a court admits an out-of-court statement against one defendant that also incriminates other codefendants. We explore the basis and implications of this ruling here.

---

4   For additional discussion of limiting instructions, see Chapter 5.

5   To make this argument successfully, Speed's counsel would have to anticipate the issue and file a preemptive motion. Once Bright testifies about Wreck's full statement, it is impossible to redact that information from the jury's memory. The process of civil discovery and depositions, however, often alerts attorneys to testimony that might be limited.

The Sixth Amendment to the Constitution gives criminal defendants a right to "confront" the witnesses against them:

Amendment VI: In all criminal prosecutions, the accused shall enjoy the right . . . to be confronted with the witnesses against him . . . .

Confronting witnesses, the Supreme Court has held, includes the right to cross-examine those witnesses. Only through cross-examination can the accused reveal inconsistencies, biases, or other flaws in an accuser's testimony. An out-of-court statement, repeated in the courtroom with no opportunity to examine the original speaker, poses the very danger that the Confrontation Clause aimed to avoid: conviction based on the untested claims of accusers who fail to speak publicly at trial.

We will discuss the Confrontation Clause at length in Chapter 58; for now we will focus on its application to out-of-court statements that a criminal codefendant makes to a law enforcement officer. Here are the facts from a case in which the Supreme Court addressed this issue:

Example: Evans and Bruton were accused of armed postal robbery. A postal inspector interrogated Evans and he confessed to the crime, saying that he and Bruton committed the robbery together.

The two were tried together, and the government called the postal inspector to the stand to testify about Evans's confession. The confession was hearsay, but it qualified as the statement of an opposing party when used against Evans. The government conceded that Evans's confession was not admissible against Bruton, so the trial judge gave the jurors a limiting instruction telling them that the statement was only admissible against Evans and that they should not consider it with respect to Bruton.[6]

Evans had no grounds to complain about this evidence. An opposing party offered his own statement against him, so the evidence was admissible under Rule 801(d)(2). Nor did Evans have a legitimate Sixth Amendment complaint about the evidence. Evans was his own accuser in the statement, admitting that he committed the robbery. If he wanted to do so, he could have "confronted" himself by taking

---

6   Bruton v. United States, 391 U.S. 123 (1968). Bruton was decided before adoption of the Federal Rules of Evidence, but the courts recognized a common law exception for statements of an opposing party that was similar to the provisions of Rule 801(d)(2).

the stand to explain or deny the statement. To the extent that the postal inspector accused Evans by reporting his out-of-court statement, Evans could confront the inspector; he was a live witness subject to cross-examination at trial.

For Bruton, however, admission of this statement raised both evidentiary and constitutional problems. Evans's confession was inadmissible hearsay with respect to Bruton; Bruton did not make the statement, so it did not qualify as an opposing party's statement when offered against him. The judge's limiting instruction attempted to cure this evidentiary problem; the trial judge instructed the jury not to consider Evans's statement when evaluating Bruton's guilt.

The Supreme Court, however, held that introduction of Evans's out-of-court statement also violated Bruton's Confrontation Clause rights. Bruton could confront the postal inspector—he was sitting on the witness stand, subject to cross-examination. But Bruton's real accuser in the statement relayed by the postal inspector was Evans; it was Evans who said that Bruton committed the robbery with him.

If Evans had taken the stand in his own defense, Bruton could have cross-examined him about that statement. In addition to examining Evans on his courtroom testimony, Bruton could have asked about this out-of-court statement. So if Evans had taken the stand, Bruton would have had no Sixth Amendment complaint. His only objection to Evans's out-of-court confession would have been the evidentiary one outlined above, and the judge addressed that objection with his limiting instruction.

But Evans did not take the stand in the joint trial with Bruton, and Bruton could not compel him to testify. The Supreme Court held that, under those circumstances, admission of Evans's confession to the postal inspector violated Bruton's Sixth Amendment rights. The violation, furthermore, was so severe that a limiting instruction could not cure the prejudice:

> [T]here are some contexts in which the risk that the jury will not, or cannot, follow instructions is so great, and the consequences of failure so vital to the defendant, that the practical and human limitations of the jury system cannot be ignored. Such a context is presented here, where the powerfully incriminating extrajudicial statements of a codefendant . . . are deliberately spread before the jury in a joint trial.[7]

---

7   391 U.S. at 135.

A codefendant's statement to law enforcement often provides particularly powerful evidence of guilt. As we will see in Chapter 58, moreover, these statements usually raise Sixth Amendment concerns when offered in a joint trial. *Bruton* holds that, under those circumstances, a limiting instruction cannot cure any Sixth Amendment violation; there is too much risk that the jury will misunderstand or disregard the instruction. Despite the judge's best efforts, the jury may use the extrajudicial statement against a defendant who did not make the statement and had no chance to cross-examine the defendant who did.

 *Bruton*'s full scope is somewhat uncertain. As we will see in Chapter 58, the Supreme Court has narrowed the category of out-of-court statements that raise Sixth Amendment concerns. A suspect's statement to law enforcement agents, however, almost certainly implicates the Sixth Amendment. When one defendant makes that type of statement, while others do not, *Bruton* gives the prosecutor these options:

1. The prosecutor can **redact** the defendant's admission so that it does not implicate any other defendants. The redacted statement will be admissible under Rule 801(d)(2) against the defendant who made it, and will not infringe the Confrontation Clause rights of other defendants. We discuss redaction further in the Courtroom section.

2. The prosecutor can sever the trial and try each of the defendants **separately**, introducing the out-of-court admission against the defendant who made the statement at that defendant's trial.

3. The prosecutor can **forego** use of the statement, relying on other evidence instead.

If the defendant who made the out-of-court admission takes the stand, the prosecutor may also be able to use that statement to impeach the testifying defendant. The judge will give the jury a limiting instruction, because the statement still is admissible only against the defendant who made it. If the prosecutor uses the statement solely for impeachment, moreover, it is admissible only to assess the credibility of that defendant. But using the statement under these conditions causes no *Bruton* problem because the defendant who made the statement takes the stand. Other defendants, therefore, have the opportunity to cross-examine him.

As we'll see in the next chapter, the final subsection of Rule 801(d)(2) gives prosecutors another avenue for avoiding *Bruton* problems; that subsection governs admission of statements by coconspirators. For now, however, let's focus on the first four subsections of that hearsay exemption.

D. In the Courtroom. Admitting statements of opposing parties in the context of multiple parties is a complex area. We explore below some of the complications that arise.

1. Adoptions, Agents, and Authorized Speakers. Rule 801(d)(2) offers several paths for admitting out-of-court statements against a party. Subsection 801(d)(2)(A) describes the simplest situation, admission of a statement made directly by a party. But 801(d)(2)(B) allows introduction of statements adopted by a party, including statements endorsed through silence; 801(d)(2)(C) permits introduction of statements made by a person that the party authorized to speak on that subject; and 801(d)(2)(D) admits statements made by a party's agent or employee. In some cases involving multiple defendants, these provisions allow the plaintiff to introduce one defendant's statement against **all** of the defendants. Similarly, a defendant sometimes can introduce one plaintiff's out-of-court statement against all of the plaintiffs. The trick is to find an adoption, authorization, or agency relationship linking the multiple parties:

Example: The government charged Lonnie Wickliffe and Edmund Powell with first degree murder of Joe Knight. At the joint trial of Wickliffe and Powell, Richard Carter testified that he saw the two defendants shortly after the alleged homicide. According to Carter, Powell told Wickliffe that he "love[d] how cold hearted Wickliffe was" and that he "dug the shit" out of how Wickliffe "cut, stabbed, and beat" Joe while Powell "pulled Joe's hair and shot him in the head." Carter also testified that, although Wickliffe said nothing in response to Powell, he nodded his head, grinned, and clapped Powell's hands in a "high five." Powell and Wickliffe both objected to this testimony as hearsay.

Analysis: Powell's statements, as recounted by Carter, are admissible against **both** Wickliffe and Powell. Powell spoke the words, so they are admissible against him under 801(d)(2)(A) as his own statement. But Wickliffe manifested his agreement with and adoption of the statement by nodding, grinning, and clapping hands with Powell. Thus, Powell's words are admissible against Wickliffe under 801(d)(2)(B).

Since the statement is separately admissible against both defendants, the jury may consider the statement in assessing the guilt of both Powell and Wickliffe. The judge will not give the jury a limiting instruction. Nor is there any *Bruton* issue in this case, even assuming Powell declines to testify, because Wickliffe adopted Powell's words. In that sense, he became his own accuser and has no Confrontation Clause complaint.[8]

2. Redacted Statements. Numerous cases consider how to redact a defendant's out-of-court admission to comply with *Bruton*. Two Supreme Court opinions supply the most important guidelines on this issue.

In *Richardson v. Marsh*,[9] the Court held that a defendant's out-of-court statement raises *Bruton* issues only if the defendant fails to take the stand and the out-of-court statement expressly implicates a codefendant. If the statement only implicates the codefendant after being linked with other evidence, introduction of the statement does not violate *Bruton*. This hypothetical illustrates the distinction:

Example: The government charged Clara Anderson and Ben Williams with stealing artworks from a museum. No one saw the robbers, but other evidence implicated these two defendants. The government tried Anderson and Williams jointly; neither defendant took the stand at trial. A police officer, however, testified that Williams admitted during a stationhouse interrogation: "Yeah, I robbed the museum. I didn't think you'd catch me—I dressed as a vampire so no one would know it was me." The government also introduced evidence that detectives found a vampire costume in Anderson's car.

Analysis: Williams's out-of-court statement is admissible against him under Rule 801(d)(2). The statement is not admissible against Anderson, because it was not her statement. To cure that hearsay problem, the judge will instruct the jury to consider the statement only with respect to Williams's guilt.

8   Wickliffe v. Duckworth, 574 F. Supp. 979, 983–84 (N.D. Ind. 1983).

9   481 U.S. 200 (1987).

Even if the jury limits its consideration in this manner, Williams's statement enhances the probability that Anderson is also guilty. The jury can legitimately reason that the vampire costume in Anderson's car belonged to Williams and that she helped him rob the museum. Or the jury might decide that, if Williams wore a vampire costume, any accomplice might have dressed the same way. Again, the vampire costume in Anderson's car then offers circumstantial evidence of her guilt.

This use of Williams's statement, however, does not violate *Bruton*. The statement, when combined with other evidence in the case, **implicitly** links Anderson to the crime. The Sixth Amendment, however, creates concerns only when the out-of-court statement **explicitly** refers to a codefendant.

Eleven years after *Richardson*, the Supreme Court recognized a significant caveat to this distinction between explicit and implicit references to a codefendant. In *Gray v. Maryland*,[10] the Court held that a redacted confession that simply "blanks out" a codefendant's name may violate *Bruton*. When a confession simply substitutes blanks for names, it is too easy for the jury to fill in those blanks with a codefendant's name. This raises the same Sixth Amendment concerns that were present in *Bruton*.

In the hypothetical described above, for example, Williams might have said, "I robbed the museum with Clara Anderson. We both dressed up as vampires so no one would recognize us." The police officer might redact this statement and report that Williams said: "I robbed the museum with _____. We both dressed up as vampires so no one would recognize us." This version of Williams's statement does not **explicitly** refer to Anderson.

As the Court realized in *Gray*, however, the blank speaks loudly when a codefendant is seated in the courtroom. The jurors will assume that the police arrested the right accomplice; they almost inevitably will assume that Williams identified Anderson in his statement. If Williams doesn't testify, Anderson has no opportunity to cross-examine him on that statement.

Bruton, *Richardson*, and *Gray* together create these guidelines governing the redaction of out-of-court statements to law enforcement officers that implicate a codefendant:

---

10   523 U.S. 185 (1998).

1. A statement that explicitly names a codefendant and implicates that codefendant on its face violates *Bruton*. The statement cannot be admitted in this form.

2. A statement that simply replaces the codefendant's name with blanks or other obvious marks of deletion also violates *Bruton*. A statement in this form inevitably will tempt the jury to fill in the blanks with the codefendant's name.

3. A statement that does not refer explicitly to a codefendant, and that contains no obvious omissions tempting the jury to fill in the gaps, satisfies *Bruton*. The prosecutor can admit statements that satisfy this condition in their initial form or that can be redacted to reach this form. These statements still are admissible only against the defendant who made the out-of-court statement, and the judge will instruct the jury not to consider these statements in connection with any codefendants. The form of the statement makes it plausible that the jury will follow those instructions, resolving the Sixth Amendment concerns raised by *Bruton*.

These guidelines, of course, apply only when the government tries the defendants jointly and the defendant who made the out-of-court statement fails to take the stand at trial. Most prosecutions raise no *Bruton* issues.

Quick Summary

 The presence of multiple plaintiffs or defendants raises several challenging issues under **Rule 801(d)(2)**. Sometimes one party attempts to introduce the out-of-court statement of a party on the same side of the lawsuit. Courts have divided over whether 801(d)(2) permits litigants to do this.

Even greater difficulties arise when one party makes an out-of-court statement that affects the interests of other parties on the same side of the litigation. An opponent may offer this statement against the party who made it, but the statement is not admissible against other parties. The judge will attempt to avoid this spillover effect by instructing the jury to consider this statement only with respect to the party who made it.

In criminal prosecutions, introduction of one defendant's out-of-court statement to law enforcement officers may violate the Sixth Amendment rights of a codefendant. If the statement expressly implicates the codefendant, or if a redaction leaves obvious blanks referring to another person, then the statement is admissible at a joint trial only if the declarant testifies in court. If the declarant invokes the privilege against self-incrimination, or is unavailable for other reasons, the prosecutor cannot introduce this type of extrajudicial statement. Instead, the prosecutor must sever the trials or rely upon other evidence.

The flow chart on the next page summarizes the steps necessary to introduce the out-of-court statement of one defendant in the presence of other defendants. These steps illustrate some of the Sixth Amendment's impact on criminal cases.

Admitting a Defendant's Out-of-Court Statement in the Presence of Codefendants

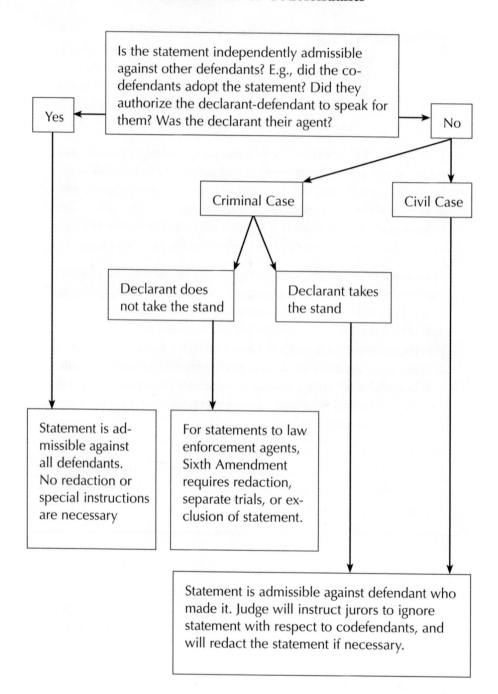

55

Hearsay Exemption—
Statements of Coconspirators

Key Concepts

- **Rule 801(d)(2)(E):** Admits Conspirator's Out-of-Court Statement Against All Coconspirators
- Course of Conspiracy
- Concealment
- "In Furtherance of" the Conspiracy
- Preliminary Determinations

A. Introduction and Policy. In the previous chapter, we examined some of the complex issues generated by statements of opposing parties that are offered in trials with multiple parties. In this chapter, we explore one final variation on that problem: extrajudicial statements by one member of a conspiracy.

Many crimes result from the combined efforts of two or more people. The illegal drug trade depends upon complex networks of distributors; even prosecution of a low-level courier may rely upon communications between that individual and others in the chain. Much white collar crime requires collaboration among two or more individuals. Even the teenager who robs a convenience store may have a friend driving the getaway car.

These criminal activities, like any joint enterprise, frequently advance through verbal or written statements. The drug courier will call a contact higher-up in the network for instructions; a doctor and physical therapist submitting bogus Medicare claims will write sham prescriptions for patients; the convenience store thief may tell his driver to "keep the engine running."

To prosecute these crimes effectively, prosecutors need to introduce statements like the ones above against **all** participants in the illegal scheme. Introducing an incriminating statement against only the perpetrator who made the statement would divide a single criminal enterprise into a confusing array of fragmented pieces.

Criminal ventures, however, do not fit comfortably within the opposing-party exemptions we have already examined. Courts developed the concepts of agency, employment, and authorization to handle legitimate businesses and commercial enterprises, which use formal employment contracts and job descriptions. Criminal collaborators operate in more ambiguous and shadowy ways; some of their statements might qualify as statements by an agent, but others would not.

To accommodate the realities of criminal enterprises, Rule 801(d)(2)(E) allows a litigant to introduce the statement of one coconspirator against any other member of the conspiracy, as long as the statement was made during the course of the conspiracy and to further the joint enterprise.

This provision, like the other portions of Rule 801(d)(2), rests on principles of estoppel. A conspirator who speaks in furtherance of a conspiracy communicates on behalf of all members of the enterprise, just as an agent speaks on behalf of her principal. Rule 801(d)(2)(E) holds coconspirators accountable for statements made by any member of the conspiracy; one coconspirator cannot claim that another coconspirator's statement is unreliable.

B. The Rule. Subsection (E) of **Rule 801(d)(2)** contains the hearsay exemption for statements of coconspirators. Like the exemptions for other out-of-court statements by parties, the rule defines these statements as "not hearsay." But it is less confusing to acknowledge that this is another **exemption** from the hearsay rule.

RULE 801. Definitions That Apply to This Article; Exclusions from Hearsay

(d) **Statements That Are Not Hearsay.** A statement that meets the following conditions is <u>not hearsay</u>:

   (2) *An Opposing Party's Statement.* The statement is offered <u>against an opposing party</u> and: . . .

      (E) was made by the party's <u>coconspirator</u> <u>during</u> and <u>in furtherance of</u> the conspiracy. . . .

The value of this provision, as explained above, lies in the fact that it allows a party to introduce one conspirator's out-of-court statement against all other conspirators. The conspirator who made the statement need not even be present at the trial. If a coconspirator makes an incriminating statement that falls within Rule 801(d)(2)(E), then skips town and evades arrest, the prosecutor can introduce that statement against the coconspirators who stand trial.

Rule 801(d)(2)(E) identifies just three elements that a proponent must establish to introduce a statement under that section. We'll discuss each of these elements in more detail in the Courtroom section:

First, the statement must be made by a "coconspirator." The references to "conspiracy" and "coconspirator" in this rule are broader than the technical definitions used in the substantive law of conspiracy. A prosecutor can invoke Rule 801(d)(2)(E) in most cases of criminal activity involving more than one individual.

Second, the statement must occur "in furtherance of the conspiracy." This requirement implements the basic rationale for the exemption: A statement that advances the underlying joint enterprise speaks for all of the participants and should be admissible against them.

Finally, the statement must also occur "during" the conspiracy. Statements made before the conspiracy begins or after it ends are not admissible under this exemption. This requirement largely overlaps the previous one, but it can be helpful in confirming the line between admissible and inadmissible statements.

C. In the Courtroom.

1. The Meaning of Conspiracy. The meaning of "conspiracy" in Rule 801(d)(2)(E) is quite different from the definition of that concept in statutes punishing conspiracies as criminal offenses. Statutes punishing conspiracy as a crime require the government to prove elements like a meeting of the coconspirators' minds, a particular type of intent, and an overt act. Rule 801(d)(2)(E) does not incorporate any of those elements. Instead, a party invoking the coconspirator exemption to the hearsay rule only has to prove that the declarant and the party against whom the statement is offered were members of a common venture. In other words, the declarant and defendant must have agreed to use their joint efforts in some way to reach a common goal.

Because the definition of conspiracy under Rule 801(d)(2)(E) is much broader than in other contexts, the government may introduce the statements of a coconspirator even when it lacks sufficient evidence to convict the individuals of criminal conspiracy. Indeed, a prosecutor relying upon Rule 801(d)(2)(E) for evidentiary purposes does not even have to charge the defendant with conspiracy. The meaning of conspiracy in Rule 801(d)(2) is entirely separate from the definition of conspiracy in statutes punishing that crime.

Example: A government informant repeatedly asked Oscar Villegas to get him some heroin. Villegas finally agreed and told the purported purchaser to meet him at a designated corner. The corner was near the home of Villegas's brother-in-law, Guillermo Gil. Villegas met the informant/purchaser on the corner and they began to negotiate the sale.

When the informant asked about the price, Villegas said he would have to ask his "partner." Villegas then walked over to talk to Gil, who was outside his home working on a truck that he owned. Villegas had told the informant that the "heroin was in the truck." While the informant left, ostensibly to obtain cash for the purchase, surveillance agents saw Gil pull a brown paper bag from his truck and give it to Villegas. Shortly thereafter, the informant returned and Villegas gave him a bag that resembled the one Gil had taken from the truck. The bag contained heroin.

The government tried Villegas and Gil jointly for distribution of heroin. In a bench trial, the district judge found that Villegas had been entrapped and acquitted him of the charge. But the judge convicted Gil, relying in part on Villegas's statements to the informant. Gil objected to reliance on these statements, claiming that since Villegas had been acquitted, there was no conspiracy to support admission of the statements.

Analysis: The court of appeals rejected Gil's argument, stressing that the "conspiracy" needed to admit a statement under Rule 801(d)(2)(E) differs from a conspiracy punished by criminal law. Villegas's acquittal based on entrapment might have defeated a substantive conspiracy charge, but the two men still worked together on a common venture with the illegal goal of selling heroin. The hearsay exemption rests on the existence of that common venture, not on other characteristics (like the absence of entrapment) that might affect punishment for conspiracy.

The court noted, as several courts have, that the "conspiracy" exemption is really a "joint venture" exemption, a "concert of action" exemption, or a "partnership in crime" exemption. These phrases better connote the kind of relationship underlying the exemption.[1]

2. Course of Conspiracy. The hearsay exemption for coconspirator statements is narrower than the other exemptions for party statements, because it includes only statements that occur "during" the conspiracy. Courts rarely have to decide when an 801(d)(2)(E) conspiracy starts; by the time statements occur, the venture usually is under way. A conspiracy sufficient to satisfy 801(d)(2)(E) begins as soon as two or more people agree to pursue a common goal.

Judges much more frequently must determine when a conspiracy ended. Parties often make incriminating statements at the time of arrest or during station house interrogations. A crucial question under Rule 801(d)(2)(E) is whether the prosecutor can admit one coconspirator's post-arrest confession against other members of the conspiracy. If these confessions fall within 801(d)(2)(E), the confession of a single coconspirator could greatly aid prosecutors in convicting all members of a criminal enterprise.

The courts, however, have held that an arrest almost always ends a conspiracy. Post-arrest statements, therefore, usually are not admissible against coconspirators under Rule 801(d)(2)(E).

Example: Police arrested Gary Martin and Otis Fuson for breaking into an apartment. Officers transported the two suspects to the station, advised them of their rights, and questioned them. Martin almost immediately confessed to the crime, telling Officer Jerry Lee that he entered the apartment alone but that Fuson helped him break in. Fuson did not confess to any illegal acts. Martin committed suicide before trial, and the government attempted to introduce his confession against Fuson as a coconspirator's statement under 801(d)(2)(E).

---

1   United States v. Gil, 604 F.2d 546, 548–50 (7th Cir. 1979).

> **Analysis:** Martin's statement was not admissible against Fuson. At the time Martin made the statement, the two alleged conspirators had been arrested and were in custody. The conspiracy thus had ended.[2]

The inadmissibility of Martin's statement seems to frustrate legitimate law enforcement efforts. If one coconspirator confesses to a crime after arrest, why isn't that confession admissible against other members of the conspiracy?

Although these confessions are tempting evidence, the rationale supporting admission of coconspirator statements ends with arrest. The exemption rests on the assumption that one member of a conspiracy speaks for the others, because they are all pursuing a common goal. But police put an end to the common project once they arrest members of the conspiracy. Isolated in separate interrogation rooms, the individual conspirators may each attempt to escape prosecution, but they are no longer working together to sell drugs, rob a convenience store, or pursue their former goal.

Post-arrest statements by former coconspirators, moreover, suffer from the same flaws that affect other statements against interest made in the criminal context.[3] Each member of the former conspiracy may downplay his own guilt, shifting the blame to others. Indeed, coconspirators may vie for favorable police treatment by offering extravagant indictments of the other conspirators' guilt.

Police and prosecutors may still use one conspirator's words to convict others; this is a staple of law enforcement. But the turncoat conspirator must come into the courtroom and testify under oath against other members of the conspiracy, giving those other conspirators an opportunity to cross-examine their former colleague's accusations. Out-of-court, post-arrest statements by a coconspirator fall outside the estoppel rationale supporting Rule 801(d)(2), and they are often unreliable.

Under some circumstances, courts find that a conspiracy has survived arrest. The arrest of one or two conspirators, for example, may not terminate the rest of the conspiracy. Here is an unusual case in which a court found that a conspiracy survived the arrest of all but one member:

---

2   Fuson v. Jago, 773 F.2d 55, 59–60 (6th Cir. 1985) (habeas challenge by prisoner convicted under Ohio law).

3   See Chapter 51 for further discussion of statements against interest.

Example: Fadi Haddad agreed to supply cocaine to Charles Unger, an undercover government agent. After several discussions, Haddad told Unger that he could obtain a kilogram of cocaine from a supplier in Chicago but he needed $28,000 up front. Unger agreed to supply the cash and met Haddad in a local Denny's parking lot. Haddad arrived at the meeting with a friend, Ali Charri. Unger gave Haddad a box, which he said contained the cash for the cocaine. After Haddad accepted the money, police arrested him and Charri.

At the station house, Haddad's pager rang continuously; the Chicago supplier, John Leydon, was trying to reach him. Charri agreed to place a police-monitored call to Leydon; he called Leydon and, without revealing the arrest, said that he and Haddad could not make the trip to Chicago to pick up the cocaine. Leydon replied that the suppliers in Chicago were angry about the delay and the deal would be cancelled. The government attempted to introduce Leydon's statements against Haddad at Haddad's trial for attempting to distribute cocaine.

Analysis: Leydon's statement was admissible under the exemption for a coconspirator's statements. Although Haddad and Charri had been arrested at the time Leydon spoke, Leydon was still attempting to carry out the goals of the conspiracy. His comments to Charri clearly indicated his desire to complete their criminal plan. Thus, the conspiracy was still alive and Leydon's statements occurred during its "course."[4]

The court's decision in the *Haddad* case pushes the endpoint of a conspiracy about as far as it logically can stretch. The reasoning, however, is persuasive and other courts may reach similar results. Note that Leydon's statements appear particularly reliable in context. Because he believed that the conspiracy was ongoing, he had no incentive to lie when he spoke to Charri or to shift blame to other members of the group.

3. Concealment. Prosecutors sometimes argue that a conspiracy is ongoing because the participants are engaged in continued efforts to conceal the crime. If the participants are, in fact, working together to conceal the crime—as Richard Nixon and his advisors famously worked to cover up the Watergate burglary—then

---

4   United States v. Haddad, 976 F.2d 1088, 1093 (7th Cir. 1992).

the conspiracy is still active and statements made by one conspirator during the cover-up are admissible against all members of the conspiracy.

But when the members of a conspiracy disband and go their separate ways, concealing the wrongdoing only in the sense that they keep quiet about it, the conspiracy does not continue. A former conspirator who brags about a completed crime to a friend may have that statement admitted against him later in court, but the statement is inadmissible against other members of the former conspiracy.

Similarly, unilateral steps by one conspirator to cover up a crime do not signal an ongoing conspiracy. Here is a particularly dramatic example of that principle:

Example: The government charged Dustin Honken with murdering several witnesses scheduled to testify against him in a drug trafficking trial. The government also charged Angela Johnson with conspiring with Honken by helping him dispose of the victims' bodies.

While Johnson was in jail awaiting trial, she concocted a plan with Robert McNeese (another inmate) to persuade a prisoner already serving a life sentence to confess to the murders charged against her and Honken. To make the other prisoner's perjured confession more realistic, Johnson gave McNeese a map showing where the five bodies were buried as well as some details about how the victims were killed. McNeese promised to convey these items to the prisoner who had agreed to "take the rap" for Johnson and Honken.

Unfortunately for Johnson, McNeese was a jailhouse informant who turned the map and other information over to the government. Police followed Johnson's map, finding the bodies just where she indicated they would be buried. The prosecutor filed a pretrial motion in the pending murder prosecution of Honken, seeking permission under Rule 801(d)(2)(E) to introduce Johnson's map against Honken as a co-conspirator's statement.

Analysis: The trial judge held that Johnson's map did not qualify as a co-conspirator statement because her conspiracy with Honken ended before she drew it. Johnson and Honken conspired to kill the witnesses and to conceal the bodies, but that project ended with the witnesses' burial. There was no evidence that Johnson and Honken agreed to adopt any and all stratagems to cover up the murders; nor was there evidence that they had discussed Johnson's specific plan with McNeese. Indeed, Honken and Johnson were separately incarcerated at the time Johnson hatched this ill-conceived plan. Thus, Johnson's oral and written statements to McNeese were not admissible against Honken under Rule 801(d)(2)(E).[5]

The Honken case implements the language and rationale of Rule 801(d)(2)(E): There is no evidence that Johnson's conspiracy with Honken was still active at the time she struck her deal with McNeese. The theory that Johnson was speaking for Honken rings hollow when the two were separately incarcerated.

Some types of concealment do occur as part of the initial conspiracy; these statements are admissible against coconspirators.

Example: Marcus Franklin, a Detroit police officer, planned to rob several cash machines and an armored truck. Franklin, who had previously worked for the company operating the machines and truck, recruited two current employees named Clarke and Stinson to aid in the robbery. The employees gave Franklin keys to open the cash machines and truck; in return, Franklin promised them a share of the proceeds.

Franklin, Clarke, and Stinson were arrested. Stinson pled guilty and testified against Franklin and Clarke at trial. As part of his testimony, Stinson said that he had received a call from Franklin the morning after the robbery. Franklin told him to "stop by" and, when he did, gave Stinson a bag containing $100,000. Franklin also shared some of the details of the robbery. Finally, he told Stinson "not to get caught with [the bag of money] and to stash it." The statements were clearly admissible against Franklin as those of an opposing party. However, Clarke objected to the introduction of these statements on the ground that they occurred after the conspiracy had achieved its goal and ended, and therefore were inadmissible against him.

---

5   United States v. Honken, 378 F. Supp. 2d 928, 946–47, 959–61 (N.D. Iowa 2004).

> **Analysis:** The evidence is admissible against Clarke under 801(d)(2)(E). Franklin made the statement just hours after the robbery and while he was "dispersing the ill-gotten proceeds" to Stinson. Statements that occur at this stage, including his warning to Stinson "not to get caught" are part of the joint criminal venture itself rather than unilateral attempts to conceal it.[6]

4. In Furtherance of the Conspiracy. Rule 801(d)(2)(E) admits a coconspirator's out-of-court statements against other members of the conspiracy only if the statements were made "in furtherance of the conspiracy." This requirement overlaps the one that statements occur "during" the conspiracy. A conspirator's confession to police officers usually means that the conspiracy—or at least that conspirator's role in it—has ended. It would also be difficult to argue that the confession is "in furtherance of" any conspiracy that remains.

Rule 801(d)(2)(E) does not require a coconspirator's statement to **further** the conspiracy; the statement need only be "**in furtherance of** the conspiracy." A statement may be admissible even if it does not successfully secure some objective or otherwise advance the criminal enterprise. The rule supports introduction of the statement as long as it bears some positive relationship to the conspiracy's goals.

The two most common categories of statements that fall outside the furtherance requirement are confessions, discussed above, and boasts to people outside the conspiracy. Criminals, like other humans, seem to enjoy bragging about their accomplishments. Their boasts may lead to arrest, but courts usually hold that these bragging statements are not "in furtherance of the conspiracy." Thus, they are not admissible against their coconspirators under Rule 801(d)(2)(E).

 To review the coconspirator's exception, as well as several other evidence rules, click here to see the video "Joint Action" or access the Video module via the eBook on your eproducts bookshelf.

5. Civil Cases. The coconspirator exemption to the hearsay rule plays a prominent role in criminal cases; prosecutors frequently invoke the exemption against

---

defendants. The exemption, however, is also available in civil cases. Parties in civil antitrust cases, for example, have used Rule 801(d)(2)(E) to urge the admission of an opponent's out-of-court statements against all members of an antitrust conspiracy.[7]

6. Preliminary Determinations. Under Rule 104(a), the judge decides whether the factual conditions necessary to support admission of a statement under Rule 801(d)(2)(E) exist. The judge, in other words, decides whether a conspiracy exists, whether the out-of-court statement was made during the conspiracy, and whether the statement was "in furtherance of the conspiracy." The proponent of the statement must prove these facts, as with any other evidentiary question, by a preponderance of the evidence.

When making these preliminary determinations, the judge does not have to follow the Rules of Evidence. The judge, therefore, may consider the challenged statement itself, other hearsay, and any other evidence when deciding whether a coconspirator's statement is admissible.[8]

But the final sentence of Rule 801(d)(2) places a special restraint on preliminary determinations involving statements of coconspirators, agents or employees, and people authorized to speak for someone else. When admitting those statements under subsections 801(d)(2)(C)–(E), the content of the challenged statement is not alone sufficient to support admissibility:

RULE 801. Definitions That Apply to This Article; Exclusions from Hearsay

(d) Statements That Are Not Hearsay. . . .

  (2) *An Opposing Party's Statement*. . . .

  The statement must be considered but does not by itself establish

- the declarant's <u>authority</u> under (C);
- the existence or scope of the <u>relationship</u> under (D);
- or the existence of the <u>conspiracy</u> or participation in it under (E).

---

7   See, e.g., Re/Max Int'l, Inc. v. Realty One, Inc., 173 F.3d 995, 1012 (6th Cir. 1999).

8   To review these principles, which govern all preliminary determinations on the admissibility of evidence, see Chapter 34.

In other contexts, a judge sometimes decides that a piece of evidence is admissible or inadmissible simply by examining the challenged evidence. The Advisory Committee and Congress, however, rejected the notion of relying exclusively on the statement of an alleged coconspirator, agent, or authorized person to establish the existence of the relationship. The judge will consider that statement in determining whether the requisite relationship exists, but some other evidence must also help establish the relationship.

Here is an example of a case in which the proponent of an alleged agent's statement failed to win admission of the statement because no evidence—other than the statement itself—demonstrated the agency relationship:

Example: In 1992, riots erupted in Los Angeles after a jury acquitted four police officers of wrongdoing in the beating of black motorist Rodney King. During the riots, a mob pulled Reginald Denny, a white truck driver, from his truck and beat him nearly to death. Marika Tur, an independent journalist, captured the Denny beating on videotape and copyrighted her video. Numerous television stations broadcast Tur's tape without obtaining her permission; she sued CBS Broadcasting, which operated several of those stations.

To support her claims, Tur testified that after she saw the video broadcast on a local television station, she called the station and spoke to a man who identified himself as an editor. The "editor" admitted that the station had not purchased the video from Tur, but had obtained it from another source. CBS objected to this testimony as hearsay; Tur argued that it was admissible because the local station was a subsidiary of CBS and the editor was an agent or employee of those companies.

Analysis: The "editor's" statements were inadmissible hearsay. Tur introduced no evidence, other than her own allegation, that the local station was owned by CBS. Nor did she offer any evidence to establish the unnamed "editor's" position at the station or the scope of his responsibilities. The anonymous speaker's identification of himself as an "editor" was not sufficient to demonstrate either agency or the scope of that relationship. Without some independent evidence to establish the factual prerequisites of Rule 801(d)(2)(D), Tur could not rely on that exemption to introduce the statement.[9]

 D. Relationship to Other Rules. Rule 801(d)(2)(E) exists within a complex web of exceptions to the hearsay rule and other evidentiary constraints. The provision's relationship to other parts of Rule 801(d)(2) are especially important to keep in mind. Remember that:

1. Reliance upon subsection (E), the coconspirator exemption, is not necessary to introduce a statement against the party who made the statement. Subsection (A) of Rule 801(d)(2) readily supports admission of a statement against the speaker, without any need to prove that the statement was made during and in furtherance of a conspiracy.

2. Subsection (E)'s value is that it allows a party to admit one conspirator's out-of-court statement against all other members of the conspiracy. If the party offering the statement can prove the elements of subsection (E), this greatly enhances the value of the statement.

3. Admission of a conspirator's statement does not raise any *Bruton* Sixth Amendment issues with respect to coconspirators. Since the conspirator speaks for all members of the conspiracy, the statement is admissible against all of those members. The prosecutor, therefore, does **not** need to redact references to other members of the conspiracy, and the judge need not give the jury a limiting instruction.

4. Prosecutors facing a *Bruton* issue, therefore, often argue that the defendants were engaged in a conspiracy and that the statement is admissible against all of them as coconspirators. To make this argument, of course, the statement must have been made during the conspiracy and in furtherance of it. Post-arrest confessions, which often raise *Bruton* issues, don't satisfy those requirements.

---

9   This example is based on L.A. News Serv. v. CBS Broad., Inc., 305 F.3d 924, 934 (9th Cir. 2002), reported as amended in other respects, 313 F.3d 1093 (9th Cir. 2002).

5. Even if a statement does not satisfy the coconspirator exemption of 801(d)(2)(E), it may satisfy one of the other "opposing party" exemptions. The other provisions of Rule 801(d)(2) sometimes support the admission of statements by one defendant against several others, even if the statement was made after the criminal enterprise had ended.

In addition to recalling the different parts of Rule 801(d)(2), remember that an out-of-court statement by a party—including one by a coconspirator—may be admissible under one of the many **other** exceptions to the hearsay rule. Rule 801(d)(2) is so broad that students often focus too heavily on that rule, forgetting that a statement falling outside the opposing-party provision may satisfy a different exception to the hearsay rule.

In the homicide prosecution of Angela Johnson and Dustin Honken, for example, the trial judge ruled that Johnson's gruesome map and jailhouse statements were not admissible against Honken as coconspirator statements; the conspiracy had ended before Johnson spoke. Johnson's statements, however, **were** admissible against Honken under Rule 804(b)(3), the "against interest" provision we examined in Chapter 51. Johnson's statements were contrary to her penal interest when she made them, and she was unavailable at Honken's trial because she claimed her Fifth Amendment privilege. After hearing Johnson's statements and other evidence, juries convicted both Honken and Johnson of homicide.[10]

---

10   See United States v. Honken, 381 F. Supp. 2d 936, 997–98 (N.D. Iowa 2005). Both defendants were sentenced to death for their crimes; Johnson's death sentence was later overturned and she was re-sentenced to life without parole.

Quick Summary

The coconspirator exemption from the hearsay rule is a valuable evidentiary tool for prosecutors. The exemption allows the prosecutor to introduce an out-of-court statement by one member of a conspiracy against all other members of the conspiracy. Courts have interpreted "conspiracy" broadly to include any joint venture; the enterprise need not satisfy the criminal law definition of conspiracy. The statement, however, must have been made "during" the conspiracy and "in furtherance of" the venture.

If a statement does not satisfy these conditions, the prosecutor may be able to admit the statement against other defendants under other exceptions to the hearsay rule, including the other opposing-party provisions of 801(d)(2).

Rule 801(d)(2) establishes a special standard governing the judge's preliminary determination of whether a conspiracy exists. Although the judge must consider the out-of-court statement when making that determination, the statement alone is not sufficient to establish a conspiracy. Some other evidence suggesting conspiracy must support the determination. The same limit applies to determinations of authority or agency under Rule 801(d)(2)(C) and 801(d)(2)(D). To admit statements under these exemptions, some evidence of the authorization or agency must exist other than the out-of-court statement.

Test Your Understanding

To assess your understanding of the material in this chapter, click here to take a quiz, or go to the Quizzes module from the eBook on your eProducts bookshelf.

56

Residual Exception

Key Concepts

- **Rule 807:** Admits Some Hearsay Falling Outside Enumerated Exceptions
- Must Have Equivalent Circumstantial Guarantees of Trustworthiness
- Proponent Must Have No Other Reasonable Way to Prove Facts
- Proponent Must Give Notice
- Courts Use Exception Very Rarely

A. Introduction and Policy. Although the Rules of Evidence define thirty different hearsay exceptions, the drafters wanted to give judges flexibility to handle statements not covered by those exceptions. The Advisory Committee concluded: "It would . . . be presumptuous to assume that all possible desirable exceptions to the hearsay rule have been catalogued and to pass the hearsay rule on to oncoming generations as a closed system."[1]

Rule 807 gives judges that flexibility by allowing them to admit hearsay that falls outside the standing exceptions, as long as the evidence has sufficient "guarantees of trustworthiness" and is the best available way to prove a needed fact. In practice, judges use Rule 807 sparingly; they share the view of the Advisory Committee that "the residual hearsay exceptions will be used very rarely, and only in exceptional circumstances."[2] Judges are reluctant to second-guess the existing exceptions by finding that other statements are sufficiently reliable to give to a jury.

---

1   Fed. R. Evid. 803(24) advisory committee's note (now codified as Rule 807).

2   Id.

When Congress first adopted the Rules of Evidence, the "residual exception" appeared in Rules 803(24) and 804(b)(5). In 1997, the Advisory Committee combined these two exceptions into a new Rule 807. This consolidation did not make any substantive changes, so judges still consult cases decided under 803(24) and 804(b)(5) when construing Rule 807.

B. The Rule.

> ### RULE 807. Residual Exception
>
> **(a) In General.** Under the following circumstances, a hearsay statement is not excluded by the rule against hearsay even if the statement is <u>not specifically covered by a hearsay exception in Rule 803 or 804</u>:
>
> **(1)** the statement has <u>equivalent circumstantial guarantees of trustworthiness</u>;
>
> **(2)** it is offered as evidence of a <u>material fact</u>;
>
> **(3)** it is <u>more probative</u> on the point for which it is offered than any other evidence that the proponent can obtain through reasonable efforts; and
>
> **(4)** admitting it will <u>best serve the purposes of these rules and the interests of justice</u>.
>
> **(b) Notice.** The statement is admissible only if, before the trial or hearing, the proponent gives an adverse party <u>reasonable notice</u> of the intent to offer the statement and its particulars, including the declarant's name and address, so that the party has a fair opportunity to meet it.

As the underlined phrases suggest, hearsay must satisfy six conditions to gain admission under Rule 807. **First**, the statement must **not be** "specifically covered by a hearsay exception in Rule 803 or 804." Courts have adopted two different approaches to this language, which we explore more fully in the Courtroom section. For now, note that this language rarely excludes evidence that satisfies the other five requirements of Rule 807.

Second, a statement admitted under Rule 807 must have "circumstantial guarantees of trustworthiness" that are "equivalent" to those found in the enumerated exceptions of Rules 803 and 804. This condition reflects the policy justifying most of the hearsay exceptions, that some out-of-court statements are more reliable than others. Under Rule 807, the trial judge decides whether a statement meets the trustworthiness requirement. In the Courtroom section, we will examine some of the factors judges consider.

Third, a statement must offer evidence of a "material fact." This condition adds little to a judge's assessment because it duplicates **Rule 402**'s relevance requirement. A few courts have suggested that Rule 807 imposes a slightly tougher relevance standard than 402, but no court has based a ruling on that ground.

Fourth, the proffered hearsay must be "more probative" of the information it conveys "than any other evidence that the proponent can obtain through reasonable efforts." If the declarant is available, the judge will force the party to call that declarant rather than rely upon Rule 807. Similarly, if the party can reasonably obtain other, equally probative evidence of the information contained in the hearsay, the judge will require the party to present that other evidence. The residual exception is a rule of last resort.

Fifth, the trial judge must find that admitting the statement "will best serve the purposes of these rules and the interests of justice." Like the requirement of materiality, this requirement means very little in practice. It reiterates **Rule 102**'s lofty proclamation that the Rules of Evidence as a whole "should be construed so as to administer every proceeding fairly, . . . to the end of ascertaining the truth and securing a just determination."

Finally0 Rule 807 contains a notice requirement: The proponent of a statement must inform the opposing party of her intent to use the statement, the details of the statement, and the name and address of the declarant. The proponent must give "reasonable notice" so that the opposing party may prepare a response.

These six conditions reduce to just three key requirements:

* The judge must determine that the proffered statement has sufficient guarantees of trustworthiness;

- The statement must be the most effective way to prove a fact in consequence, despite reasonable efforts to find otherwise admissible evidence; and

- The proponent of the evidence must give notice of her intent to use the statement at trial.

C. In the Courtroom.

1. The "Near Miss" Problem. What happens if a hearsay statement narrowly misses admission under an existing exception? The exception for present sense impressions, for example, admits statements that are "made while or immediately after" perceiving an event.[3] Suppose Jenna texts a friend: "Malik left 5 minutes ago." Five minutes is a little long to qualify as "immediately after" an event, especially if Jenna had her phone available throughout that time. But if Jenna's text seems trustworthy and contains vital information unavailable from any other source, should the judge admit the text under Rule 807's residual exception?

The federal courts have held that Rule 807 gives judges discretion to admit "near miss" statements like Jenna's text. The text must satisfy Rule 807's trustworthiness, probative value, and notice requirements, but most judges believe that a statement's near-miss status poses no independent bar to admission.

A dissenting view focuses on the introductory words of Rule 807, which say that the residual exception applies only to statements that are "not specifically covered by a hearsay exception in Rule 803 or 804." This alternative view, sometimes called the near-miss interpretation, argues that a statement falling just outside an existing exception is "covered" by that exception.[4] This interpretation of Rule 807 reads the rule as if it began: "A statement [arising from a situation] not specifically covered by a hearsay exception in Rule 803 or 804 . . . ."

---

3   To review the exception for present sense impressions, see Chapter 40.

4   See United States v. Clarke, 2 F.3d 81, 84 (4th Cir. 1993). Conversely, one judge has characterized the current approach as the "close-enough" view. United States v. Laster, 258 F.3d 525, 534 (6th Cir. 2001) (Moore, J., dissenting). This phrase is somewhat misleading, however, because the current view does not admit statements that are "close enough" to existing exceptions; it simply allows judges to assess those statements under Rule 807's stringent standards.

This is a plausible interpretation of Rule 807's wording; in fact, some commentators argue that it is the most natural reading. The near-miss interpretation of Rule 807 also has a policy rationale: It prevents parties from using the residual exception to undermine the specific limits imposed by other exceptions. If the drafters thought that present sense admissions are reliable only if made immediately after an event, why should a single judge have power to admit a statement that was delayed by several minutes?[5]

 Parties press this near-miss perspective to resist admission of statements proffered by opponents, and some judges have voiced support for the interpretation.[6] It would restrict Rule 807 to statements arising in novel situations, ones not foreseen by the other hearsay exceptions.

So far, however, the courts have rejected the near-miss approach to Rule 807. Instead, courts read the rule's opening words as referring to whether a **particular proffered statement** is "specifically covered by a hearsay exception in Rule 803 or 804." If a hearsay statement is admissible under an existing exception, the statement should be admitted under that exception rather than under Rule 807. But if the statement falls outside any of the established exceptions, then it is not "covered" by those rules and the court may consider it for admission under Rule 807.

This perspective preserves the judge's discretion to apply Rule 807's trustworthiness and probative value standards to the circumstances of each case. Those requirements still bar most statements proffered under Rule 807. The only difference between the near-miss interpretation and the current approach to Rule 807 is that the former automatically bars any near-miss statement from admission while the latter allows the judge to evaluate those statements under Rule 807's remaining conditions.

This example illustrates the current approach to Rule 807:

---

5   Some language in the Advisory Committee notes further supports the near-miss view. See Fed. R. Evid. 803(24) advisory committee's notes (now codified as Rule 807) (the purpose of the residual exception was to "provide for treating new and presently unanticipated situations").

6   See, e.g., United States v. Laster, 258 F.3d 525 (6th Cir. 2001) (Moore, J., dissenting); United States ex rel. Miller v. Bill Harbert Int'l Construction, Inc., No. 95–1231, 2007 WL 842079 (D.D.C. Mar. 16, 2007).

Example: Donovan, the former CEO of a major chemical company, was dying of cancer. On his deathbed he called for his wife. "I have something I need to tell you," he said. "My company illegally dumped thousands of gallons of toxic waste into the town watershed over the last ten years." The wife reported the statement to the proper authorities after Donovan's death. When the information became public, town residents sued the chemical company, claiming that the dumped chemicals caused an unusually high level of birth defects. At trial, the plaintiffs call Donovan's widow to report Donovan's deathbed statement.

Analysis: Donovan's statement is hearsay, and it does not quite fit any existing exception. The statement was not a dying declaration, because it did not concern the cause of Donovan's own death. A court might also reject application of the "against interest" exception, because Donovan knew he was about to die. Therefore, he would not suffer any pecuniary loss or liability from his statement.

The policy rationales behind both of these established exceptions, however, support admission of Donovan's statement. The plaintiffs, moreover, have no other way to introduce this evidence because Donovan is dead. Under the current approach to Rule 807, the trial judge has discretion to admit Donovan's statement if she finds the statement sufficiently trustworthy.

The near-miss approach, on the other hand, would automatically exclude Donovan's statement because it is the type of statement covered by the dying declaration and against-interest exceptions.

2. Trustworthiness. A statement's admissibility under Rule 807 often turns on its trustworthiness. Courts consider numerous factors when determining whether a statement has sufficient guarantees of trustworthiness. These include:

1. Whether the statement was made under oath.

2. Whether the declarant had firsthand knowledge of facts in the statement.

3. Whether the declarant ever recanted the statement.

4. Whether other evidence corroborates the statement.

5. Whether that corroborating evidence is subject to cross-examination.

6. Whether other evidence undermines or contradicts the statement.

7. Whether the declarant had any incentive to lie when making the statement.[7]

Here is one example of a case in which factors like these supported admission of hearsay statements under the residual exception:

Example: Amy Travel Services used aggressive telemarketing techniques to sell thousands of "vacation passports" to consumers. The buyers each paid about $300 for the passports, believing that the single payment would cover the full vacation cost. In fact, many buyers had to pay over a thousand dollars more in order to take the vacation. The Federal Trade Commission ("FTC") sued Amy Travel after receiving numerous complaints. As part of its case, the FTC submitted several affidavits from dissatisfied customers who described their experiences with the travel agency. Amy Travel objected to these affidavits as hearsay.

Analysis: The appellate court ruled that the affidavits were properly admitted under the residual exception to the hearsay rule. The affidavits contained sufficient guarantees of trustworthiness because "each was made under oath subject to perjury penalties and the affiants describe[d] facts about which they ha[d] personal knowledge—their contacts with defendants." The appellate court also pointed out that because Amy Travel ran a nationwide telemarketing program, they deceived hundreds if not thousands of customers throughout the country, and it would have been "cumbersome and unnecessarily expensive" for the FTC to bring all of those customers to the courthouse for live testimony.[8]

Decisions admitting evidence under the residual hearsay exception, however, remain rare. When courts compare the guarantees of trustworthiness urged under Rule 807 to those associated with established hearsay exceptions, they usually find the proffered statements lacking in trustworthiness.

---

7   See United States v. Carlson, 547 F.2d 1346 (8th Cir. 1976); United States v. West, 574 F.2d 1131 (4th Cir. 1978); United States v. Barlow, 693 F.2d 954, 962 (6th Cir. 1982); United States v. Donlon, 909 F.2d 650, 654 (1st Cir. 1990).

8   FTC v. Amy Travel Service, Inc., 875 F.2d 564, 576 (7th Cir. 1989).

Example: Conoco, a large oil drilling company, operated a number of oil fields on behalf of several "working interest" owners. Conoco extracted oil from the field and delivered it to the working interest owners, who resold the oil. The Department of Energy ("DOE") sued Conoco, claiming that some of its working interest owners were violating Department price controls when they resold the oil on the open market.

The DOE attempted to prove some of these overcharges by submitting purchase summaries prepared by the crude oil buyers. The buyers prepared these summaries, long after the actual sales, in response to Conoco's request for information during a DOE audit. Because the buyers did not complete the summaries as part of their regular course of business, the summaries did not qualify as business records under **Rule 803(6)**. Nor did the summaries qualify as market reports under **Rule 803(17)** because members of the industry did not generally rely upon them. The DOE, however, argued that the summaries had sufficient indicia of reliability to be admitted under the residual exception.

Analysis: The appellate court rejected the purchase summaries under the residual exception. The court acknowledged that the summaries had some indicia of reliability because (1) Conoco relied on them in the course of its own business dealings; and (2) the buyers had no incentive to lie or exaggerate when they compiled the summaries.

The court, however, concluded that the summaries were less trustworthy than hearsay admitted under other exceptions. Unlike business records, the summaries were not prepared contemporaneously with the events being recorded. The buyers who prepared the summaries, moreover, did not rely on them for their own business dealings, so they had no special incentives to be accurate.

The court also pointed out that DOE made no showing that equally probative evidence was unavailable through other means. The buyers undoubtedly had their own business records of the prices they paid, and DOE could have subpoenaed those records directly instead of relying upon the summaries transmitted to Conoco.[9]

3. Probative Value. In addition to showing that a statement is sufficiently trustworthy, advocates urging the admission of hearsay under Rule 807 must persuade

---

9   Conoco, Inc. v. Department of Energy, 99 F.3d 387, 392–93 (Fed. Cir. 1997).

the judge that it is "more probative . . . than any other evidence that the proponent can obtain through reasonable efforts." In Conoco, the proffered statement failed this condition as well as the trustworthiness one; the court stressed that Conoco could have obtained readily admissible evidence from the buyers.

Conversely, the following case illustrates a hearsay statement that carried special indicia of trustworthiness and also offered information unavailable from any other source. Although decided before codification of the Federal Rules, this case remains a leading decision on application of the residual exception:

Example: The clock tower of the Dallas County courthouse collapsed on July 7, 1957, causing $100,000 worth of damage. The county claimed that the collapse stemmed from a lightning strike on July 2 and sought reimbursement from its insurance company. The company refused to pay, claiming that lightning had not struck the tower. The company claimed that improper construction, not covered by the insurance policy, caused the collapse. The parties took their dispute to court.

At trial, several town residents testified for the county that they saw lightning strike the tower. The county also produced charred timbers from the roof of the courthouse building, claiming these resulted from the lightning strike.

The insurance company contested the county's claims about the lightning strike. It also argued that the charred timbers originated from a fire on the courthouse roof more than 50 years earlier. To support this argument, the company offered an article printed in the local newspaper on June 9, 1901. The article reported that the county's new courthouse roof had caught fire early that morning. Dallas County objected to the article as hearsay.

Analysis: The newspaper article was admissible as an ancient document, but the reporter had not witnessed the fire himself. His report incorporated statements from other sources, and those statements were hearsay that did not qualify for any known hearsay exception.

The appellate court, however, held that it was proper to admit the article. The information reported by the article had sufficient guarantees of trustworthiness, because it was "inconceivable . . . that a newspaper reporter in a small town would report there was a fire in the [roof] of the new courthouse—if there had been no fire." The reporter had no motive to falsify; indeed, the newspaper would have been subject to ridicule if it had falsely reported such a dramatic event. Furthermore, since the alleged fire occurred so long ago, the insurance company had no other reasonable means to prove the event. By the time of the trial, eyewitnesses to the fire had died or the passage of 58 years had dimmed their memories.[10]

 The concepts of trustworthiness and probative value are fluid ones, so good advocacy may convince a judge to admit a hearsay statement under Rule 807. Even given the best advocacy, however, judges are reluctant to expand the hearsay exceptions. Courts admit statements under Rule 807 only rarely, when both trustworthiness and probative value are clear.

Evidence in Practice

To practice your knowledge of the hearsay exceptions, take the role of a defense attorney in *Ashton v. Apex Financial*. Click here or access the **Evidence in Practice** module from the eBook on your eProducts bookshelf.

Quick Summary

 **Rule 807** gives trial judges some flexibility to admit hearsay statements that are sufficiently reliable but do not fit any of the enumerated hearsay exceptions. The trial judge (1) must find that the statement has guarantees of trustworthiness equivalent to those offered by one of the established exceptions, and (2) must determine that there is no other reasonable way for the proponent to get the information to the jury with the same probative effect. The party offering the statement must also (3) give advance notice to the opposing party. Although Rule 807 allows judges to admit hearsay that falls outside the 30 enumerated exceptions, judges exercise this discretion only under extraordinary circumstances.

---

10   Dallas County v. Commercial Union Assurance Co., 286 F.2d 388 (5th Cir. 1961).

57

Attacking a Declarant's Credibility

Key Concepts

- **Rule 806:** Parties Can Impeach Declarants with Article VI Tools
- Rule Does Not Apply to Most Statements That Are "Not Hearsay"
- Extrinsic Evidence of Declarant's Dishonest Acts

A. Introduction and Policy. When a trial judge uses a hearsay exception to admit an out-of-court statement, parties face special hurdles in challenging that evidence. Under most circumstances, the out-of-court statement was not made under oath; the jury has no chance to observe the declarant's demeanor; and the parties have no opportunity to cross-examine the declarant. Without further information, jurors may form a false impression of the declarant's credibility, picturing him as an honest, disinterested, upstanding citizen. How can a party hurt by the declarant's statement reveal that the declarant has a widespread reputation for lying, strong biases favoring the other party, and three felony convictions?

Rule 806 gives parties a way to attack a declarant's credibility, whether or not the declarant appears as a witness. That rule allows parties to impeach declarants in the same manner that they impeach witnesses, using any of the tools recognized by Article VI of the rules. The attacker, in other words, may show the declarant's bias or incapacity, offer character witnesses to prove the declarant's reputation for dishonesty, or show that the declarant has been convicted of crimes admissible under Rule 609.[1]

Without Rule 806, a party could not invoke any of the Article VI impeachment rules against a declarant, because those rules apply only to witnesses. But Rule

---

1   See Chapters 17–23 for further discussion of these tools.

806 allows parties to impeach declarants as if they were witnesses. Similarly, once the declarant's credibility has been attacked, a party may rehabilitate the declarant using Article VI's tools. With a few modifications, Rule 806 simply applies all of the Article VI rules to hearsay declarants.

B. The Rule.

RULE 806. Attacking and Supporting the Declarant's Credibility

When a <u>hearsay</u> statement—<u>or a statement described in Rule 801(d)(2)(C), (D), or (E)</u>—has been admitted in evidence,

- the declarant's credibility may be attacked,
- and then supported,

by <u>any evidence</u> that would be admissible for those purposes <u>if the declarant had testified as a witness</u>.

The court may admit evidence of the declarant's inconsistent statement or conduct, <u>regardless of</u> when it occurred or whether the declarant had an <u>opportunity to explain or deny it</u>.

If the party against whom the statement was admitted calls the declarant as a witness, the party may examine the declarant on the statement <u>as if on cross-examination</u>.

There are six points to note about this rule. **First,** it applies to all hearsay statements admitted under an exception, as well as to statements governed by Rule 801(d)(2) (C), (D), or (E). We discussed the latter statements in Chapters 53–55; they are declarations made by an opposing party's agent, spokesperson, or coconspirator. The rules define these statements as "not hearsay," but they are out-of-court statements offered for the truth of the matter asserted, so Rule 806 includes them.

Rule 806 does not apply to other out-of-court statements that fail to qualify as hearsay. These include statements offered for a purpose other than to prove the truth of the matter asserted, prior statements by witnesses, and statements made or adopted by the opponent.[2] As we'll see in the Courtroom section, Rule 806 isn't necessary in these contexts.

Second, as discussed in the Introduction, Rule 806 allows a party to attack a declarant's credibility by introducing any evidence that would be admissible if the declarant had testified as a witness. This evidence includes:

- Evidence of the declarant's bias, prejudice, or interest in the case

- Statements made by the declarant that are inconsistent with the hearsay statements (**Rule 613**)

- Evidence that the declarant lacks personal knowledge (**Rule 602**) or the capacity to testify truthfully (**Rule 603**)

- Reputation or opinion evidence, given by a character witness, that the declarant is untruthful (**Rule 608(a)**)

- Any criminal convictions allowed by **Rule 609**

This list omits one type of evidence that parties often use to impeach witnesses: questions about dishonest acts, which Rule **608(b)** allows on cross-examination to show a witness's untruthful character. If the declarant testifies, then Rule 608(b) allows the opponent to pose those questions on cross-examination. But if the declarant does not testify, courts have struggled with how to apply Rule 608(b) to declarants, since it is not possible to cross-examine someone who doesn't testify. We explore the courts' conflicting answers to this problem in the Courtroom section.

Third, once a declarant's credibility has been attacked, the other party may rehabilitate the declarant in any way that is allowed with witnesses. The party, therefore, may offer evidence rebutting allegations of bias, prejudice, incapacity, or interest; introduce consistent statements; and call positive character witnesses.

Fourth, Rule 806 allows a party to present a declarant's inconsistent statements without giving the declarant an opportunity to "explain or deny" those inconsistencies. Rule 613 imposes the latter requirement when a party impeaches a witness

---

2   To review these concepts, see Chapters 36 (truth of the matter asserted), 39 (prior statements by witnesses), and 53 (statements made or adopted by an opposing party).

with prior inconsistent statements. The requirement is fair enough when a witness testifies, but it may be impossible to fulfill in the hearsay context. Many declarants never appear in the courtroom at all, giving the opposing party no way to provide an opportunity for denial or explanation of inconsistent statements.

Fifth, Rule 806 allows any party to impeach a hearsay declarant, just as **Rule 607** permits any party to impeach a witness.[3] Parties who present hearsay evidence usually do not impeach their own declarants, but Rules 607 and 806 allow them to do so. A witness may surprise a party by offering damaging statements by an out-of-court declarant; or a party may want to "draw the sting" of an opponent's impeachment of a declarant by raising any negative information preemptively.

Finally, Rule 806 recognizes that parties sometimes use a hearsay exception to avoid cross-examination of a witness. If a declarant's out-of-court statement is admissible, then a party can introduce that statement without subjecting the declarant to cross-examination. Under these circumstances, the opposing party should be allowed to call the declarant as a witness and cross-examine the declarant about the statement. Rule 806 allows the opposing party to do this, overriding **Rule 611**'s provision that the party who calls a witness usually must ask nonleading questions on direct examination.

C. In the Courtroom.

1. Statements That Are Not Hearsay. Rule 806 allows impeachment of a declarant only when the declarant's statement was (a) hearsay or (b) an assertion by the opposing party's agent, spokesperson, or coconspirator. The rule does not apply to other out-of-court statements. Rule 806, therefore, does not allow impeachment of a declarant when a party offers the declarant's statement for a purpose other than to prove the truth of the matter asserted.

> **Example:** Samantha Jones slipped on the dance floor at Studio 94, an exclusive New York nightclub. Jones sued Studio 94, claiming that she slipped on a spilled drink and that the club was negligent in allowing spills to accumulate on the dance floor. At trial, Studio 94 offered evidence from one of its waitresses, who testified that another dancer shouted "Watch

---

3   We discussed Rule 607 in Chapter 17.

out for that spilled drink!" just before Jones fell. The club argued that Jones was contributorily negligent in ignoring this warning.

Citing Rules 806 and 609, Jones offered evidence that the other dancer (Darren Star) had been convicted for using an underage ID. Studio 94 objected to this impeachment of its Star declarant.

Analysis: Evidence of Star's conviction is not admissible. Studio 94 did not introduce Star's words to prove that a drink really did spill on the dance floor; it offered the words to show that someone shouted a warning at Jones. Since Studio 94 didn't offer Star's words for the truth of the matter asserted, his statement isn't hearsay and Rule 806 doesn't apply.

This result makes sense because Star's credibility is irrelevant to Jones's dispute with the nightclub. Even if Star lied about seeing a spilled drink on the floor, he happened to shout a timely warning. The existence of the warning is all that matters to the club's defense, and Star's credibility doesn't affect that fact.

Similarly, Rule 806 does not apply when the court admits prior statements by a witness that fall within Rule 801(d)(1)'s "not hearsay" category. For these statements, the declarant also appears as a witness, so Rule 806 is unnecessary; parties may impeach these witnesses/declarants by using the usual Article VI rules.

Rule 806, finally, does not apply to out-of-court statements made or adopted by an opposing party. As we saw in Chapter 53, a party may introduce any out-of-court statement made or adopted by an opponent; Rule 801(d)(2)(A) and (B) define these statements as "not hearsay." The opponent may regret these statements and dispute them in court, but he is unlikely to attack his own credibility. Rule 806 thus is unnecessary in this context.

Rule 806, however, does apply to statements of an opponent's agent, spokesperson, or coconspirator that are admitted as "not hearsay" under Rule 801(d)(2)(C), (D), or (E). Although an opponent wouldn't want to impeach his own credibility, he often does want to impeach the credibility of these declarants:

Facts: The government charged Oswald Cobblepot (the "Penguin") with laundering money for Max Shreck, a notorious drug lord. Selina Kyle, an undercover agent who posed as Shreck's accountant, testified for the prosecution that Shreck told her how to funnel proceeds from drug sales to Cobblepot; he also told her how to compensate Cobblepot for his services. The trial judge admitted Shreck's out-of-court statements under Rule 801(d)(2)(E), finding that they were admissible statements by a coconspirator. Cobblepot then called a character witness to testify that Shreck had a reputation for dishonesty. The prosecutor objected to appearance of the character witness.

> **Analysis:** The character witness's testimony is admissible. Although Rule 801(d)(2)(E) defines a coconspirator's statement as "not hearsay," Rule 806 specifically allows a party to impeach those declarants. Through character witnesses and other means, Cobblepot may attempt to show that Shreck is untrustworthy and that his statements to Kyle were unreliable.

2. Evidence of Specific Acts. As we saw in Chapter 19, parties may impeach witnesses by cross-examining them about specific dishonest actions. If Max Shreck testified live against Cobblepot in the previous example, Cobblepot's lawyer could ask Shreck on cross-examination: "You lied on your most recent credit card application, didn't you?" But if Shreck stays outside the courtroom, appearing only as a declarant in Kyle's testimony, Cobblepot can't use this strategy to impeach Shreck: There is no opportunity for cross-examination.

At least one federal court has responded to this problem by suggesting in dictum that a party in Cobblepot's position should be able to impeach the declarant by introducing **extrinsic evidence** of the declarant's dishonest acts.[4] Cobblepot, in other words, could call an employee of the credit card company to testify about Shreck's false statements. **Rule 608(b)** prohibits that type of evidence when offered against a live witness,[5] but extrinsic evidence may be the only way to reveal a non-testifying declarant's dishonest acts. Stressing Rule 806's goal of allowing parties to impeach declarants as freely as they discredit witnesses, the Second Circuit suggested that Rule 806 might allow extrinsic evidence of a declarant's dishonest acts.

Other courts, however, have rejected this approach:

---

4   United States v. Friedman, 854 F.2d 535, 570 n.8 (2d Cir. 1988).

5   See Chapter 19 to review this point.

Example: The government accused Neil and Isaac Saada, owners of Scrimshaw Handicrafts, with intentionally flooding their warehouse and filing a fraudulent insurance claim. The prosecutor's evidence suggested that Neil and an associate intentionally broke a sprinkler head in the warehouse, causing dirty water to spray all over the merchandise. The Saadas claimed that Neil broke the sprinkler head accidentally, so the insurance claim was legitimate.

Linda Chewning, a Scrimshaw employee, testified for the defendants. Chewning testified that on the night of the warehouse flood she heard Tom Yaccarino, the company's vice president, scream: "Oh my God, Neil did something stupid, [threw] something, now he has got a mess. . . . I can't believe it. He is so stupid. He threw it. He is stupid, he is dumb." Yaccarino died before trial, but the court admitted this statement as an excited utterance. The trial court then allowed the prosecutor to impeach Yaccarino by introducing evidence that he was a former judge who had been removed from the bench and disbarred due to unethical conduct.

Analysis: The court of appeals held that extrinsic evidence of Yaccarino's misconduct was inadmissible. Although the government was unable to impeach Yaccarino by asking questions about this misconduct on cross-examination, strict adherence to the extrinsic evidence ban was necessary "to avoid minitrials on wholly collateral matters which tend to distract and confuse the jury . . . and to prevent unfair surprise arising from false allegations of improper conduct." The court thus interpreted Rule 806 as incorporating Rule 608(b)'s ban on extrinsic evidence of specific acts used to impeach a witness's credibility.

The court noted that its ruling did not leave the government or similarly situated parties helpless. If the witness relating the declarant's statement knows the declarant, then the opponent may cross-examine the witness about the declarant's dishonest acts. The government, in other words, could have asked Chewning: "Isn't it true that Yaccarino was disbarred after acting unethically as a state court judge?" The government could also have called character witnesses to testify about Yaccarino's dishonesty. And if a declarant has been convicted of crimes admissible under Rule 609, then Rule 806 allows introduction of that evidence.[6]

---

6   United States v. Saada, 212 F.3d 210, 221–22 (3d Cir. 2000) (internal quotations and citations omitted).

 This issue remains unsettled in the federal courts, with some judges expressing sympathy for the Second Circuit's expansive reading of Rule 806 and others following the Third Circuit's more restrictive interpretation in the Saada case.

Quick Summary

 Rule 806 allows parties to attack a declarant's credibility in the same ways they impeach witnesses. The rule attempts to even the playing field for parties hurt by the admission of hearsay. These parties frequently lack the chance to cross-examine the declarant directly, but Rule 806 gives them most of the impeachment tools they could have used if the declarant had taken the stand.

Rule 806 makes a few adjustments to the impeachment rules found in Article VI. First, the impeaching party need not give the declarant an opportunity to deny or explain an inconsistent statement, as otherwise required by Rule 613. Second, if an opposing party calls the declarant as a witness, the party can question her as though on cross-examination—that is, using leading questions. Courts, finally, differ on whether parties may impeach declarants by admitting extrinsic evidence of dishonest acts other than criminal convictions allowed by **Rule 609**. At least one court has suggested that extrinsic evidence should be admissible, because parties cannot cross-examine non-testifying declarants about their dishonest acts. Other courts have enforced Rule 608(b)'s bar on extrinsic evidence in this context.

Test Your Understanding

 To assess your understanding of the material in this chapter, click here to take a quiz, or go to the Quizzes module from the eBook on your eProducts bookshelf.

58

The Sixth Amendment and Hearsay

Key Concepts

- Confrontation Clause Protects Criminal Defendants, Not Other Parties
- Confrontation Means Cross-Examination
- The Clause Applies Only to "Testimonial Statements"
- Testimonial Is Hard to Define
- Availability, Cross-Examination, and Exceptions

A. Introduction and Policy. The Sixth Amendment guarantees each criminal defendant the right "to be confronted with the witnesses against him." Read literally, that clause could bar the use of many types of hearsay against criminal defendants: A defendant usually cannot "confront" an out-of-court declarant.

The Sixth Amendment's framers plainly intended to bar the use of some hearsay in criminal cases. They drafted the Confrontation Clause to prevent abuses like those that marked the seventeenth-century trial of Sir Walter Raleigh. In that case, an English jury convicted Raleigh of treason based solely on two out-of-court statements. One of the statements came from a prisoner in England's notorious Tower of London; the prosecutor introduced this statement even though the prisoner had attempted to recant it. Raleigh repeatedly asked the prosecutor to produce this prisoner for cross-examination, but the Crown refused.

For a humorous introduction to the Raleigh trial, click here to see a video: "The Trial of Sir Walter Raleigh" or access the Video module via the eBook on your eproducts bookshelf. For a transcript of the actual trial, see 1 D. Jardine, Criminal Trials 400 (1832).

By giving a defendant the right to confront "witnesses against him," the Sixth Amendment prevents this type of prosecutorial abuse. But the amendment does not forbid all hearsay. Ordinary business records, for example, raise none of the concerns that marred Raleigh's trial. Business owners create these records to serve their commercial purposes, not to bear "witness" against potential defendants. If a store records the sale of rat poison to the defendant's credit card, the Sixth Amendment allows the prosecutor to use that record to suggest that the defendant had access to poison.

The Supreme Court has struggled for more than thirty years to articulate the line dividing these examples. Why do some hearsay statements require cross-examination, while others do not? In addressing that question, the Court has offered two different formulas for testing the constitutionality of hearsay under the Sixth Amendment.

Initially the Court focused on the **reliability** of hearsay statements offered against a defendant. In *Ohio v. Roberts*, the Court ruled that the Sixth Amendment permitted hearsay statements if they carried sufficient "indicia of reliability."[1] The Roberts opinion also identified two paths for proving reliability: The prosecutor could show that the statement fell "within a firmly rooted hearsay exception" or that it bore "particularized guarantees of trustworthiness."[2] Because of the first path, constitutionality under *Roberts* closely tracked the Federal Rules of Evidence. Hearsay that satisfied one of the specific exceptions usually passed constitutional muster; statements falling outside those bounds usually did not.

In 2004, the Court dramatically changed course. The Court declared in *Crawford v. Washington* that the concept of reliability was too "amorphous," and that the Confrontation Clause established "a procedural rather than a substantive guarantee."[3] That procedural guarantee, the Court declared, is **cross-examination**. Under *Crawford*, a criminal defendant has the right to cross-examine any person who makes a "testimonial" statement against him.

 As we'll see below, the concept of "testimonial" has proved as amorphous as the principle of reliability. The Supreme Court Justices have divided sharply while attempting to mold that key distinction; some have suggested abandoning or modifying

---

1   448 U.S. 56, 66 (1980).

2   Id.

3   541 U.S. 36, 61 (2004).

Crawford. Sixth Amendment interpretation remains volatile in the Supreme Court and lower courts.

But at least for now, *Crawford* governs the constitutionality of hearsay offered against criminal defendants. Despite the disagreement among the Justices, the Court has produced a series of majority opinions applying *Crawford.* We'll examine those decisions in this chapter and then note some of the open issues.

B. Confrontation and *Crawford* Basics. The first point to remember about *Crawford* is this: Out-of-court statements must satisfy **both** the hearsay rule and the Confrontation Clause. Before worrying about the constitutional analysis, check whether an out-of-court statement is admissible under the hearsay rule. If the statement doesn't satisfy the Federal Rules, then there is no need to conduct a Confrontation Clause analysis.

Second, remember that the Confrontation Clause limits only evidence offered in criminal cases against a defendant. The clause has no impact in civil cases, nor does it restrict the evidence that a defendant introduces against the state. *Crawford* applies only to hearsay offered against a criminal defendant.

Despite these limits, *Crawford* recognizes that the Sixth Amendment confers a key right on every criminal defendant: "to be confronted with the witnesses against him." That guarantee limits the type of evidence that prosecutors can offer in the courtroom. As we saw in Chapter 54, when discussing the Bruton case, the Supreme Court has long equated confrontation with cross-examination. *Crawford* confirms that concept by declaring that the Sixth Amendment gives criminal defendants the right to test all evidence against them "in the crucible of cross-examination."[4]

Since confrontation means cross-examination, an expansive reading of the Sixth Amendment would prevent prosecutors from admitting **any** out-of-court statement against a criminal defendant unless the declarant was subject to cross-examination. The Court avoided that result in *Crawford* by focusing on the critical word "witnesses" in the Confrontation Clause. Witnesses, the Court ruled, are people who make "testimonial" statements against a criminal defendant.

Under *Crawford,* therefore, a criminal defendant's Sixth Amendment right to "be confronted with the witnesses against him" is a right to "cross-examine people who

---

4   Id.

make testimonial statements against him." Courtroom testimony by live witnesses is inherently testimonial, and the defendant has a right to cross-examine those witnesses at trial. But only some out-of-court statements are testimonial; the Sixth Amendment limits admission of just those statements.

We can summarize these principles in three simple rules that describe a prosecutor's Sixth Amendment obligations:

> 1.   The prosecutor may introduce **nontestimonial hearsay** as long as those statements comply with the hearsay rules. The Sixth Amendment does not limit the admission of nontestimonial hearsay.[5]
>
> 2.   The prosecutor may introduce **testimonial hearsay** if the statements comply with the hearsay rules, and the **declarant is available** as a witness. Under those circumstances, the defendant has a chance to cross-examine the declarant about the prior testimonial statement.
>
> 3.   If the hearsay statement is **testimonial** and the declarant is **unavailable** at trial, the prosecutor may offer the statement only if the defendant had a **prior opportunity to cross-examine** the declarant.

These rules, in turn, focus Confrontation Clause litigation on three questions:

> •   Is the proffered statement testimonial?
>
> •   If so, is the declarant available for cross-examination?
>
> •   If the statement is testimonial and the declarant is not currently available for cross-examination, can the prosecutor establish both that the declarant is unavailable and that the defendant had a prior opportunity to cross-examine that declarant?

C. What Statements Are Testimonial? Focusing on the Sixth Amendment's reference to "witnesses," *Crawford* attempts to divide hearsay into two categories.

---

5   Other constitutional provisions, such as the Fourth Amendment or Due Process Clauses, may bar these statements in unusual cases. We focus in this chapter only on the distinctive limits imposed by the Sixth Amendment.

The first category includes statements that resemble a witness's in-court testimony. These statements "bear testimony" against the accused and require confrontation.[6] A crime victim, for example, may visit the police station and give the police a sworn statement describing the perpetrator and details of the crime. This statement resembles testimony that the same victim might give in court: It is designed to identify the perpetrator and convict him of the crime. The prosecutor should not be able to insulate the victim's statement from cross-examination by asking a police officer to read the statement in court. Instead, the Sixth Amendment guarantees the defendant the right to confront the victim—who is the true "witness against him."

The second category comprises statements that do not share these features of in-court testimony. The business records described in the Introduction, for example, do not "bear testimony" against an accused in the same way that a crime report does. A store maintains credit card receipts to collect payment—not to prove that a perpetrator has purchased tools for a crime. The prosecutor may use the business records in court without triggering the defendant's right to confront the person who made them.

Crawford defines the first type of statement as "testimonial" and the second as "nontestimonial." To further explain this distinction, the Court has offered several verbal formulas:

> A testimonial statement is a "solemn declaration or affirmation made for the purpose of establishing or proving some fact."[7]
>
> Testimonial statements are "made under circumstances which would lead an objective witness reasonably to believe that the statement would be available for use at a later trial."[8]
>
> Testimonial statements have "a primary purpose of creating an out-of-court substitute for trial testimony."[9]

---

6   541 U.S. at 51 (quoting 2 N. Webster, An American Dictionary of the English Language (1828)).

7   Michigan v. Bryant, 562 U.S. 344, 353–543 (2011); Crawford, 541 U.S. at 51 (quoting 2 N. Webster, An American Dictionary of the English Language (1828)).

8   Crawford, 541 U.S. at 52 (quoting Brief for National Association of Criminal Defense Lawyers et al. as Amici Curiae 3).

9   Bryant, 562 U.S. at 358.

> The "primary purpose" of testimonial statements "is to establish or prove past events potentially relevant to later criminal prosecution."[10]

 These formulas, like many legal standards, do not define precise categories. Lower court judges struggle to apply the standards to particular statements, and thoughtful advocacy may sway a judge's decision. The formulas, unfortunately, may also be in flux. As we'll see in section C.2.b below, several Justices have proposed significant variations to these standards. None of those proposals have won support from a majority of the Court, but some advocates and lower courts cite them.

Applying the Supreme Court's Confrontation Clause jurisprudence, therefore, involves a great deal of uncertainty. Within that cloud of uncertainty, however, the Court's decisions dictate fairly clear results for several types of statements. We turn next to those categories.

1. Straightforward Cases. Although the concept of testimonial remains elusive, six types of hearsay have proved relatively easy to categorize under the Supreme Court's precedents.

a. Testimonial: Formal Statements During Litigation. Sworn statements that occur before grand juries, at pretrial hearings, during trial, and at post-trial proceedings are all testimonial. Speakers make these statements under oath, as part of a formal proceeding, and in the presence of a judge or prosecutor; these speakers are "witnesses" in every sense of the word. The Constitution guarantees a criminal defendant the right to confront these witnesses—either at the original proceeding or when the statements are offered against him later.

b. Testimonial: Statements Responding to Conventional Police Interrogation. The police obtain many statements that are not affidavits, depositions, or confessions. Victims and witnesses provide details about a crime; suspects offer alibis and denials. *Crawford* declared that when these statements are made in response to "interrogations by law enforcement officers," they "fall squarely within" the category of testimonial statements.[11] Victims, suspects, and witnesses realize

---

10   Bryant, 562 U.S. at 356 (quoting Davis v. Washington, 547 U.S. 813, 822 (2006)).

11   541 U.S. at 53.

that police interrogations have a prosecutorial purpose; the police want to solve and prosecute crimes. These statements, like those in the previous section, also resemble trial testimony in their structure and purpose. The disputed statement in *Crawford* itself fell in this category:

> **Example:** Michael Crawford stabbed Kenneth Lee in the torso. The state charged Crawford with attempted murder, and he claimed self defense. Crawford's wife Sylvia witnessed the stabbing but she did not testify at trial; Michael invoked the state's marital privilege to prevent Sylvia from testifying. To rebut Michael's claim of self defense, the prosecutor offered a taped statement that Sylvia gave police during a stationhouse interrogation several hours after the fight. At one point in her statement, Sylvia admitted seeing no weapon in the victim's hands; this undermined Michael's claim of self defense.

> **Analysis:** The Supreme Court held that Sylvia's statement was testimonial. She spoke at the police station, in custody, while herself under suspicion, and "[i]n response to often leading questions from police detectives." Sylvia's "recorded statement, knowingly given in response to structured police questioning" easily qualified as testimonial. Since Michael had no opportunity to cross-examine Sylvia on her statement, the Sixth Amendment barred its admission.[12]

Less formal police questioning may produce nontestimonial statements; we turn to that problem when we address "hard cases" below. But statements that respond to classic stationhouse interrogation, like the one in *Crawford*, fall firmly in the testimonial category.

c. Not Testimonial: Business Records. The Supreme Court has noted repeatedly in dictum that many business records are not testimonial.[13] Like the store receipts described in the Introduction, most business records are "created for the administration of an entity's affairs and not for the purpose of establishing or proving some fact at trial."[14] For that reason, they are not testimonial.

---

12   Id. at 65, 53 n.4.

13   Bullcoming v. New Mexico, 564 U.S. 647, 668, 670 (2011) (Sotomayor, J., concurring in part); Bryant, 562 U.S. at 362 n.9 (2011); Melendez-Diaz v. Massachusetts, 557 U.S. 305, 321–24; Crawford, 541 U.S. at 56.

14   Melendez-Diaz, 557 U.S. at 324.

Example: The United States charged Cynthia Yeley-Davis with conspiring to distribute methamphetamine. Police obtained records of Yeley-Davis's cell phone calls from her phone provider. The prosecutor offered these records at trial to show that Yeley-Davis spoke frequently to methamphetamine suppliers. Following the procedures outlined in Rule 803(6), the prosecutor used a written certificate to show that the records satisfied the business records exception. Yeley-Davis objected that admission of the records violated her Sixth Amendment rights.

Analysis: The cell phone records were not testimonial. The phone company maintained these records to bill Yeley-Davis for her calls, not to create evidence for use at trial. The prosecutor, therefore, could introduce the records accompanied by a simple certificate. The Sixth Amendment gave Yeley-Davis no right to cross-examine any live witness about these nontestimonial records.[15]

The Supreme Court has warned, however, that some business records are created for use at trial. A store, for example, may routinely document shoplifting offenses to report those crimes and aid prosecution. The Federal Rules of Evidence already exclude this type of business record because documents created for litigation "lack . . . trustworthiness."[16] The Sixth Amendment dictates the same result: An organizational record made "for the purpose of establishing or proving some fact at trial" is testimonial.[17] As long as courts rigorously enforce Rule 803(6)'s trustworthiness caveat, business records admitted in federal court will not be deemed testimonial.[18]

d. Not Testimonial: Statements in Furtherance of a Conspiracy. Supreme Court dicta also declare that statements made in furtherance of a conspiracy are nontestimonial.[19] The very purpose of these statements, to advance a criminal endeavor, suggests that they are not "made under circumstances which would lead an objective witness reasonably to believe that the statement would be available for use at a later trial."[20] The Sixth Amendment therefore allows introduction of

---

15   United States v. Yeley-Davis, 632 F.3d 673, 679 (10th Cir. 2011).

16   See Chapter 45 and Rule 803(6) to review this caveat to the business records exception.

17   Melendez-Diaz, 557 U.S. at 324.

18   Remember that records maintained by public agencies must satisfy the even more stringent standards of Rule 803(8), the hearsay exception for public records, before gaining admission. We discussed that principle in Chapter 46. Rules 803(6) and 803(8) thus work together to exclude the testimonial records of organizations from criminal trials.

19   Bryant, 562 U.S. at 362 n.9; Melendez-Diaz, 557 U.S. at 324; Giles v. California, 554 U.S. 353, 374 n.6 (2008); Crawford, 541 U.S. at 56.

20   Crawford, 541 U.S. at 52 (quoting Brief for National Association of Criminal Defense Lawyers et al. as Amici

coconspirator statements against all members of the conspiracy, even if the speaker is not available for cross-examination.

But remember that this reasoning—like the coconspirator exception itself—applies only to statements made in furtherance of a conspiracy. A conspirator's stationhouse confession does not further any conspiracy. That confession is not admissible against fellow conspirators under Rule 801(d)(2)(E), and it would be considered testimonial.

e. Not Testimonial: The Defendants' Own Statements. The courts uniformly assume that a defendant's own statements are not testimonial. It is difficult to argue that a defendant has a Sixth Amendment right to confront himself. If there is such a right, the defendant can satisfy it by choosing to take the stand at trial. The Confrontation Clause thus imposes no restrictions on a very important type of prosecution evidence—the defendant's confession or other incriminating statements.

f. Not Testimonial: Statements Admitted to Prove a Point Other than the Truth of the Matter Asserted. The Supreme Court has observed in dicta that the Confrontation Clause "does not bar the use of testimonial statements for purposes other than establishing the truth of the matter asserted."[21] If a statement is not offered for its truth, then it does not "testify" to anything and the defendant has no constitutional right to cross-examine the declarant. Numerous lower court opinions apply this principle.

> **Example:** Thomas Henderson robbed a bank in 1981. Henderson's friend, Earl Bass, knew about the robbery. After a falling out with Henderson, Bass called the FBI and offered to provide information about the robbery. Bass did not testify at Henderson's robbery trial, but his information helped the FBI build their case against Henderson. Henderson served 15 years in prison for the robbery. Six months after his release, Bass was shot to death. The United States charged Henderson with retaliatory murder for shooting Bass.
>
> At trial, an FBI agent recounted Bass's 1981 telephone call offering to provide information about the robbery. The prosecutor used this phone call to

Curiae 3).

21   Bryant, 562 U.S. at 367 n.11; Crawford, 541 U.S. at 59 n.9.

help show retaliation, an element of the crime charged against Henderson. Henderson objected to the hearsay as violating the Sixth Amendment.

Analysis: If the prosecutor had offered Bass's 1981 statement to show that Henderson robbed a bank, it would have been testimonial; Bass contacted law enforcement agents and expressly accused Henderson of bank robbery. But the prosecutor in the murder trial did not offer Bass's statement for the truth of the matter asserted. Instead, the prosecutor introduced the statement only to show that—whether or not Bass's accusation was true—Henderson had a motive to retaliate against Bass. On that issue, the FBI agent was the "witness" against Henderson. Henderson had ample opportunity to cross-examine the agent when he testified about Bass's call.[22]

2. Hard Cases. The statements discussed above are relatively easy to categorize under *Crawford*. But other hearsay is harder to characterize as testimonial or non-testimonial. This section discusses two types of statements that have particularly challenged the courts, as well as a third category that courts are just beginning to explore.

a. Statements to Law Enforcement Outside Traditional Interrogation. Stationhouse interrogations like the one in *Crawford* fall within a core category of testimonial statements. But citizens talk to law enforcement officers under many other circumstances. If a wife dials 911 and cries, "help—my husband is hitting me," is that statement testimonial? What if a robbery victim points to a fleeing man and tells a passing police officer, "that crook just grabbed my wallet"? The Supreme Court has concluded that at least some of these statements are not testimonial.

To draw this line, the Court has focused on the "primary purpose" of the speaker's interaction with law enforcement. If the primary purpose of the exchange is "to establish or prove past events potentially relevant to later criminal prosecution," then the statement is testimonial.[23] If the interaction has another primary purpose, such as "to enable police assistance to meet an ongoing emergency," then the statement is nontestimonial.[24]

---

22   This example represents a simplified version of the facts in United States v. Henderson, 626 F.3d 326 (6th Cir. 2010).

23   Davis v. Washington, 547 U.S. 813, 822 (2006).

24   Bryant, 562 U.S. at 349; Davis, 547 U.S. at 822.

This "primary purpose" test is an objective one: The trial judge asks what a reasonable person would have believed under the circumstances. To apply that standard, the judge must evaluate all of the circumstances surrounding the statement. The judge, furthermore, must consider the perspectives of both the declarant and any other participant in the exchange; each of these may affect how a reasonable person would have viewed the statement's purpose.

The Supreme Court has decided three cases applying this primary purpose test to statements that crime victims made to law enforcement agents. These decisions, together with *Crawford* itself, set rough guideposts for dividing testimonial statements to law enforcement officers from nontestimonial ones. In the first of these cases, as in *Crawford*, the Court ruled that a statement to police was testimonial:

Example: Police responded to the report of a domestic disturbance at Amy and Hershel Hammon's home. The officers found Amy alone on the front porch; she appeared frightened but there was no fight in progress. One officer took Amy into the living room, excluded Hershel from their discussion, and asked Amy "what had occurred." After giving an oral account, Amy handwrote and signed a battery affidavit against Hershel.

The state prosecuted Hershel for battery, but Amy did not respond to a trial subpoena. In her absence, the prosecutor introduced Amy's affidavit and asked the officer to recount her oral statements. Hershel objected to this evidence under the Sixth Amendment.

Analysis: The Court held that Amy's statements, like those of Sylvia Crawford, were testimonial. Although Amy spoke shortly after Hershel's attack, in her own living room, and near the crime scene, her "statements deliberately recounted, in response to police questioning, how potentially criminal past events began and progressed." Amy understood that she was assisting the officers with a criminal investigation. "Objectively viewed," the Court concluded, "the primary, if not indeed the sole, purpose of the interrogation was to investigate a possible crime."[25]

---

25   Davis, 547 U.S. at 819, 829–30. The Hammon case was consolidated with Davis and decided under that name in the Supreme Court.

Hammon demonstrates that testimonial statements may occur at a crime scene, shortly after the crime occurs. A crime victim does not need to visit the police station or wait a designated period of time to "bear testimony" against the accused. The key elements that made Amy Hammon's statement testimonial were her focus on past events, her deliberate recounting of those events, and the absence of any other purpose for her statement.

But in a second case, decided as a companion to *Hammon*, the Court established that some statements to law enforcement agents are not testimonial. Even a statement directly identifying the perpetrator and describing his actions may qualify as nontestimonial:

Example: Adrian Davis was accused of assaulting his girlfriend Michelle McCottry. During the assault, McCottry called 911 and had this conversation with the operator:

Operator: What's going on?

McCottry: He's here jumpin' on me again.

Operator: Okay. Listen to me carefully. Are you in a house or an apartment?

McCottry: I'm in a house.

Operator: Are there any weapons?

McCottry: No. He's usin' his fists.

Operator: Okay. Has he been drinking?

McCottry: No.

Operator: Okay, sweetie. I've got help started. Stay on the line with me, okay?

McCottry: I'm on the line.

Operator:	Listen to me carefully. Do you know his last name?
McCottry:	It's Davis.
Operator:	Davis? Okay, what's his first name?
McCottry:	Adrian.
Operator:	What is it?
McCottry:	Adrian.
Operator:	Adrian?
McCottry:	Yeah.
Operator:	Okay. What's his middle initial?
McCottry:	Martell. He's runnin' now.

Police arrested Davis, and the state prosecuted him for felony violation of a domestic no-contact order. McCottry did not appear at trial, and the prosecutor offered the 911 tape to prove Davis's guilt. Davis objected to the admission of the tape, claiming that McCottry's statements were testimonial and therefore their admission violated the Confrontation Clause.

Analysis: The Supreme Court held that McCottry's words were not testimonial. The Court assumed that the 911 operator was a law enforcement agent. The operator, moreover, questioned McCottry about both her assailant's acts and identity. But the Court noted four key differences between McCottry's statements and those made by Sylvia Crawford and Amy Hammon. First, McCottry "was speaking about events as they were actually happening," while Crawford and Hammon described acts that had already occurred. Second, McCottry was "facing an ongoing emergency" and her statements to the operator were "plainly a call for help against bona fide physical threat." Crawford, on the other hand, spoke in the safety of the police station and faced no threat from anyone. Hammon, similarly, was safe from her husband's threats by the time she spoke to police.

Third, the questions the operator asked McCottry were "necessary to be able to resolve the present emergency." Even establishing the perpetrator's identity was urgent, because officers arriving on the scene needed to know "whether they would be encountering a violent felon." Police questioned Crawford and Hammon, in contrast, only "to learn . . . what had happened in the past." In both of those cases, any immediate threat had ended.

Finally, Crawford and Hammon made more formal, considered statements than those made by McCottry. Crawford "was responding calmly, at the station house, to a series of questions." Hammon, similarly, "deliberately recounted" her husband's acts and signed a written affidavit. McCottry, on the other hand, offered "frantic answers . . . over the phone, in an environment that was not tranquil, or even . . . safe."

These four factors persuaded the Court that the "primary purpose" of McCottry's statement "was to enable police assistance to meet an ongoing emergency," rather than to create evidence for trial. Thus, the statement was not testimonial.[26]

The Court's final case in this series, *Michigan v. Bryant*, presented facts that fell between those raised in *Hammon* and *Davis*.

Example: Detroit police received a call that a man had been shot and was lying in a gas station parking lot. Officers arriving at the scene found the victim, Anthony Covington, bleeding from an abdominal gunshot wound. Covington had trouble speaking and appeared to be in severe pain. As the officers arrived, they each asked Covington "what had happened, who had shot him, and where the shooting had occurred." Covington fielded these questions while asking when medics would arrive.

When responding to the officers, Covington explained that "Rick" had shot him about twenty-five minutes earlier through the door of a house located several blocks away. After the shooting, Covington used his car to drive to the gas station. Once there, he collapsed on the ground just outside the car.

---

26   Davis, 547 U.S. at 826–29.

Ambulance workers arrived five to ten minutes after the police, cutting off further questions. Covington died several hours later from his gunshot wound. The police went to the house Covington described and gathered circumstantial evidence tying its resident, Richard Bryant, to the murder. But Covington's statements remained crucial evidence against Bryant; the prosecutor relied upon this hearsay at Bryant's trial. Bryant objected that the statements were testimonial hearsay violating the Sixth Amendment.

Analysis: The circumstances in *Bryant* shared some of the testimonial characteristics of the statements in *Crawford* and *Hammon*. The shooting was over when the police questioned Bryant, and the conversation occurred several blocks from the crime scene. Police repeatedly questioned Covington to confirm his identification of Bryant; they also pressed him to provide more details of the crime. These factors suggested that the questioning focused on establishing "past events potentially relevant to later criminal prosecution."

But other facts resembled those in *Davis*. When the police arrived at the scene, they did not know when or where Covington had been shot; they questioned Covington in part to determine whether the shooter was nearby and whether the crime was ongoing. Covington was seriously wounded, impairing any attempts to make the type of "deliberately recounted" statements offered by Sylvia Crawford and Amy Hammon. And, although Covington responded to a series of police questions, those questions were "disorganized" and the entire "situation was fluid and somewhat confused." Each of the responding officers briefly questioned a bleeding, badly injured victim lying in a parking lot; this differed from the more "structured interrogation" conducted in *Crawford* and *Hammon*.[27]

Focusing on the latter facts, a majority of the Supreme Court held that Covington's statements were nontestimonial. Justices Scalia and Ginsburg, stressing the former facts, determined that the statements were testimonial. Justice Scalia, who had authored *Crawford*, delivered a particularly stinging dissent in which he denounced the Court as the "obfuscator of last resort" and declared that the majority opinion "distorts our Confrontation Clause jurisprudence and leaves it in a shambles."[28]

---

27   Bryant, 562 U.S. at 357, 366, 377.

28   Id. at 379, 380 (Scalia, J., dissenting).

 *Bryant* expands the circle of statements admissible under the Sixth Amendment; it gives the police significant freedom to stabilize a crime scene while also gathering evidence for trial. But *Crawford* and *Hammon* recognize the testimonial nature of many statements made to law enforcement officers in the wake of a crime. Lower courts continue to explore the line between testimonial and nontestimonial statements made in the immediate aftermath of a crime.

b. Laboratory Reports. The Supreme Court Justices have also divided sharply over the testimonial character of laboratory reports prepared as part of a criminal investigation. Lab reports play a pivotal role in many prosecutions. In drug cases, for example, they often establish both the presence of an illegal drug and the quantity seized from the defendant. For other crimes, lab reports may document facts like blood alcohol content or cause of death.

The trial exhibit on the next page illustrates a simple laboratory report. That report prompted the following Supreme Court decision:

> **Example:** The state charged Luis Melendez-Diaz with cocaine trafficking. At trial, the prosecutor introduced several bags of white powder seized from Melendez-Diaz. The state also presented three certificates from a state laboratory; each of these certificates declared that the white powder was cocaine and noted the weight of that cocaine. The technicians who tested the samples swore to the truth of these certificates before a notary, but they did not appear at trial. Melendez-Diaz complained that this absence violated his Sixth Amendment right to confrontation.

> **Analysis:** In a 5–4 opinion, the Supreme Court agreed that the laboratory certificates were testimonial statements requiring cross-examination. The majority noted that the certificates were "quite plainly affidavits," which fell within the "core class of testimonial statements" identified by *Crawford*. Each affidavit, furthermore, was a "solemn declaration or affirmation made for the purpose of establishing or proving some fact" relevant to the defendant's crime. The affidavits, finally, were "made under circumstances which would lead an objective witness reasonably to believe that the statement would be available for use at a later trial." Indeed, that was the state laboratory's only purpose in preparing the affidavits disputed by Melendez-Diaz. The lab reports thus matched the criteria marking testimonial statements.[29]

---

29   Melendez-Diaz v. Massachusetts, 557 U.S. 305, 310–11 (2009) (quoting Crawford, 541 U.S. at 51–52).

[State's Exhibit 13]

The Commonwealth of Massachusetts
Executive Office of Health and Human Services
Department of Public Health
State Laboratory Institute
305 South Street   Boston, MA 02130-3597
617-983-6622

DATE RECEIVED: 11/19/2001
DATE ANALYZED: 11/28/2001

NO. 615741
I hereby certify that the powder **CONTAINED** in 19 plastic bags
MARKED: 615741 **Submitted by** P.O. FRANK MCDONOUGH
of the BOSTON POLICE DEPT.

Has been examined with the following results:
The powder was found to contain: Cocaine, a derivative of Coca
leaves, as defined in Chapter 94 C, Controlled Substance Act,
Section 31, Class B.

NET WEIGHT: 22.16 grams
DEFENDANT: MONTERO, ELIS A. ET AL

_____/s/_____/s/_____
Assistant Analysts Della Saunders Michael Lawler

Sworn and subscribed to before me on this day, 12-04-01. I know the
subscribers to be assistant analysts of the Massachusetts Department
of Public Health.

My Commission Expires 8-25-06 _____/s/____
NOTARY PUBLIC

Chapter 111, Section 13 of the General Laws
This certificate shall be sworn to before a justice of the Peace or Notary Public, and
the jurat shall contain a statement that the subscriber is an analyst or assistant analyst
of the department. When properly executed, it shall be prima facie evidence of the
composition, quality, and the net weight of the narcotic or other drug, poison, medicine,
or chemical analyzed, and the court shall take judicial notice of the signature of the
analyst or the assistant analyst, and of the fact that he/she is such.

The Court confirmed this result two years later in *Bullcoming v. New Mexico.*[30] The report in that case documented the defendant's high blood alcohol content, supporting his conviction for aggravated driving while intoxicated. This report was not notarized, but the analyst had signed a "Certificate of Analyst" affirming (1) that the blood sample was properly sealed when he received it, (2) that he followed the procedures outlined in the report, and (3) that the reported results were correct.

In another 5–4 decision, the *Bullcoming* Court ruled that the blood alcohol report was testimonial. Although the certificate was not notarized, the majority concluded that it resembled the *Melendez-Diaz* reports in "all material respects." The majority also rebuffed the state's attempt to send a surrogate technician—someone with no connection to the original analysis—to testify in court. The Supreme Court held that testimony from "an analyst who did not sign the certification or personally perform or observe the performance of the [reported] test" could not satisfy the defendant's confrontation rights.[31]

Despite the sharp divisions in these two cases, *Melendez-Diaz* and *Bullcoming* offered some guidelines to police, prosecutors, defense attorneys, and lower court judges. A majority of the Supreme Court agreed in both cases that laboratory reports are testimonial if "made under circumstances which would lead an objective witness reasonably to believe that the statement would be available for use at a later trial." Unfortunately, the Court's June 2012 decision in *Williams v. Illinois*[32] disrupts that guidance:

> **Example:** L.J. was raped and robbed. Hospital attendants examined her, took a vaginal swab, and sent the swab to the Illinois State Police. After finding semen in the swab, the police sent the sample to a laboratory for DNA analysis.
>
> At that time, the police had no suspect for the rape. Once the lab's DNA report was in hand, however, a forensic specialist searched the state's DNA database for a matching profile. The search yielded a match with Sandy Williams, whose blood had been profiled in connection with an unrelated arrest.

---

30   564 U.S. 647 (2011).

31   Id. at 664, 657.

32   567 U.S. 50 (2012).

The state then charged Williams with the crimes against L.J. Karen Abbinanti, the analyst who created the DNA profile from Williams's blood, testified live about how she generated that profile. But the state did not call any of the analysts who produced the DNA profile from the rape swab; those analysts worked in a different state. The defendant challenged the introduction of the swab profile under the Sixth Amendment, noting that he had no opportunity to cross-examine the analysts who generated that report.

Analysis: Five Justices concluded that the swab DNA report was **not** testimonial, but they rested their decision on two different grounds. A plurality of four Justices offered a new definition of testimonial. These Justices declared that evidence is testimonial only when it has "the primary purpose of accusing a targeted individual of engaging in criminal conduct." The plurality narrowed the *Crawford* language, in other words, to include the concept of "accusing a targeted individual." Using this definition, the plurality concluded that the DNA profile generated from the rape swab was not testimonial: Analysts created that profile when no "targeted individual" was accused. Indeed, for all the analysts knew, the profile might have been used to exclude a suspect from further investigation. In *Melendez-Diaz* and *Bullcoming*, on the other hand, analysts tested specimens obtained from particular suspects. The resulting reports, under the plurality's test, qualified as testimonial.[33]

Justice Thomas concurred in the judgment, but emphatically rejected the plurality's standard. Instead, Thomas decided that the DNA report was non-testimonial because it was not "formalized." The laboratory reports in *Melendez-Diaz* and *Bullcoming* were testimonial, Thomas explained, because of their formality: The first was a notarized affidavit, while the second included a "Certificate of Analyst" attesting that the contents were true. The Williams report, in contrast, was a bare report that "certifie[d] nothing." Using this route, Justice Thomas joined the four members of the plurality to rule the DNA report non-testimonial.[34]

The four dissenting Justices roundly rejected both the plurality's test and the line drawn by Justice Thomas. The dissenters adhered to the now-familiar language from *Crawford*, *Melendez-Diaz*, and *Bullcoming*, which defines testimonial evidence as a statement created "to establish 'some fact' in a criminal

---

33   Id. at 81–86 (plurality opinion).

34   Id. at 103, 111–12 (Thomas, J., concurring in the judgment).

proceeding" and "under circumstances which would lead an objective witness reasonably to believe that [it] would be available for use at a later trial."[35] Using this standard, the four dissenters concluded that the DNA report in *Williams* was testimonial, just like the laboratory reports in *Melendez-Diaz* and *Bullcoming*.

 The fractured *Williams* decision has been widely criticized by academics, and it has frustrated prosecutors, defense attorneys, and judges. Five Justices rejected the plurality's standard, and five rejected the dissent's position. Justice Thomas held the deciding vote, but no Justice supported his reasoning—and no Justice had ever joined his earlier opinions proposing a similar standard. How should lower-court judges and advocates proceed under these circumstances?

Lower courts have adopted different approaches, but here is one way to synthesize the Supreme Court's decisions. First, a laboratory report is **not testimonial** if it fails both the *Williams* plurality's "targeted individual" standard and Justice Thomas's formality line. Those were the circumstances in *Williams* itself. Conversely, if a report satisfies both the plurality standard and the Thomas line, it is **testimonial**. Those were the circumstances in both *Melendez-Diaz* and *Bullcoming*.

What if a laboratory report is highly formalized but does not accuse a targeted individual? Suppose, for example, that the DNA swab report in *Williams* had been notarized: Would the report then have counted as testimonial? The Court's opinions, stretching from *Crawford* to *Bullcoming*, hold that it would. The *Williams* plurality, which represented only four Justices, could not overrule those precedents—and Thomas supported them. A highly formalized report prepared "under circumstances which would lead an objective witness reasonably to believe that [it] would be available for use at a later trial" is **testimonial**, even if it does not accuse a targeted individual.

What, finally, about a laboratory report that accuses a targeted individual but fails Thomas's formality test? Suppose, for example, that Massachusetts amended the laboratory report on page 717 by changing the opening phrase "I hereby certify" to "I hereby report," and eliminating all of the material below the analysts' signa-

---

35   Id. at 118, 121 (Kagan, J., dissenting) (quoting Melendez-Diaz and Crawford).

tures. Is an unsworn "report" about a substance seized from a targeted individual testimonial?

Once again, the Court's confrontation opinions place this type of report on the **testimonial** side of *Crawford*'s line. Even without a sworn statement, any laboratory report prepared as part of a criminal investigation probably meets *Crawford*'s standard: These reports are "solemn" and prepared "under circumstances which would lead an objective witness reasonably to believe that the statement would be available for use at a later trial." The Court's majority opinions repeatedly endorse these definitions; neither the *Williams* plurality nor Justice Thomas's concurrence had the power to overrule precedents joined by five members of the Court.

These guidelines offer one way to determine whether a lab report is testimonial after *Williams*. Advocates and lower courts may adopt different readings, but this one seems to apply the Court's fragmented opinions most faithfully.

 The confusion generated by *Williams*, unfortunately, doesn't stop with laboratory reports. Should lower courts apply the plurality's "targeted individual" standard to other types of statements, such as eyewitness reports or autopsy results? What about Justice Thomas's focus on formality? Should that perspective affect decisions about whether other statements are testimonial?

Most lower courts consider these standards dicta; five Justices have never endorsed either the "targeted individual" limit or the formality requirement. The sharp disagreements in *Williams*, however, suggest that the Court's *Crawford* consensus is fraying. In response, advocates and lower courts may begin offering their own interpretations of the Confrontation Clause.

3. Statements Among Private Parties. Statements made from one private party to another are less likely to be deemed testimonial, but they can still be testimonial if the "primary purpose" of the statement is to create information that could be used in court. The Supreme Court has set out six factors to consider in making this determination:

> **Example:** One morning a preschool teacher noted a suspicious bruise on the face of one of her students, a three-year-old known as L.P. When she asked him how he got the bruise, he said "Dee, Dee." When asked whether Dee was big or little, L.P. said "Dee is big." The teacher immediately

called a child abuse hotline. L.P.'s mother's boyfriend, who was caring for L.P., was named Darius Clark, and his nickname was Dee.

The day after the teacher noticed the bruise, a social worker removed L.P. and his sister, eighteen-month-old A.T. The children were taken to a hospital, where doctors found numerous injuries consistent with child abuse. Darius Clark was ultimately indicted on five counts of felonious assault. At Clark's trial, L.P. was found incompetent to testify because of his young age. The prosecutor sought to admit L.P.'s out-of-court statements to the teacher, invoking a state evidence hearsay exception that allowed for the admission of "reliable statements" by child abuse victims.

The trial judge ruled that the child's statements were reliable and therefore admissible under the state hearsay rules. Clark's attorney objected, arguing that the statements violated the Confrontation Clause because they were testimonial. The trial judge overruled the objection and admitted the statements. Clark was convicted on almost all charges and sentenced to 28 years in prison. He appealed the Confrontation Clause issue all the way to the United States Supreme Court.

Analysis: The Supreme Court unanimously upheld the conviction, holding that L.P.'s statements were not testimonial. The majority opinion, authored by Justice Alito, invoked a familiar and relatively straightforward test: a statement is testimonial if the "primary purpose" of the conversation was to create an out-of-court substitute for trial testimony. The Court applied this test to Clark's case by looking to six different factors:

(1) Whether the interrogator was a law enforcement official. The Court held that statements to private parties are less likely to be made with the primary purpose of creating a substitute for in-court testimony. In this case, the teachers had a duty to report suspected child abuse under Ohio's mandatory reporting law, but the Court concluded that "mandatory reporting statutes alone cannot convert a conversation between a concerned teacher and her student into a law enforcement mission aimed primarily at gathering evidence for a prosecution." The teacher's reporting duty did not render L.P.'s statements testimonial because the teachers "undoubtedly would have acted with the same purpose whether or not they had a state-law duty to report abuse."

(2) The presence or absence of an "ongoing emergency" (as in *Davis* and *Bryant*). In this case, the Court held that the teachers were attempting to protect L.P. and prevent additional harm, and thus were acting out of "an immediate concern . . . to protect a vulnerable child who needed help."

(3) The "informality of the situation." This was not a formal interrogation, but a conversation between a teacher and a young child in a classroom.

(4) Whether similar evidence was regularly admitted "at the time of the founding." The Court noted that eighteenth century English courts admitted hearsay statements from rape victims who were too young to offer competent testimony.

(5) The age of the declarant. Here, L.P. was three years old, and "statements by very young children will rarely, if ever, implicate the confrontation clause" because those children almost never intend their statements to substitute for trial testimony.

(6) Absence of other indications that "the primary purpose of the conversation was to gather evidence for . . . prosecution." The teachers did not tell L.P. that his answers "would be used to arrest or punish his abuser." Similarly, "L.P. never hinted that he intended his statements to be used by the police or prosecutors." [36]

Clark displays a welcome consensus after the jumbled opinions in *Williams v. Illinois*. Six Justices joined the *Clark* majority, and two more agreed that the "primary purpose" test was appropriate for identifying testimonial statements. Only Justice Thomas applied a different standard; he adhered to his narrower, formalistic definition of testimonial.

The *Clark* opinions, however, continue to reflect some tension over *Crawford*'s future. The majority injected two new areas of uncertainty:

(1) The Court quoted *Bryant* and noted that when "determining whether a statement is testimonial, 'standard rules of hearsay, designed to

---

36   Ohio v. Clark, 135 S.Ct. 2173 (2015).

identify some statements as reliable, will be relevant.' "[37] This could be seen as a sign that at least some members of the Court are laying the groundwork for a return to "reliability" being a prominent factor in the Confrontation Clause test.

(2) The Court stated that ". . . the primary purpose test is a necessary, but not always sufficient, condition for the exclusion of out-of-court statements under the Confrontation Clause."[38] The majority gave no examples of what other conditions must exist, and cited no authority for this particular statement. However, this dictum implies that there are some statements that are made with the primary purpose of substituting for in-court testimony but are nevertheless admissible under the Confrontation Clause. This leaves the door open for admission of such statements under the *Williams* "targeted individual" test, for a return to the Roberts "reliability" test, for a more expansive reading of the "founding era" exceptions, or for some yet unknown distinction.

These statements prompted Justice Scalia's concurrence, which Justice Ginsburg joined. The two worried that the majority might "attempt to smuggle longstanding hearsay exceptions back into the Confrontation Clause" and "return to *Ohio v. Roberts*."[39] For that reason, they declined to join the majority opinion.

 In addition to the majority's cryptic dicta, *Clark* did not involve any laboratory reports—the type of extrajudicial statements that divided the Justices so contentiously in *Melendez-Diaz, Bullcoming,* and *Williams.* Despite the apparent consensus in *Clark,* the Justices may continue to struggle with the appropriate status of laboratory reports.

In short, although *Clark* came a long way to restoring predictability and consistency after the *Williams* case, this area of law is almost certain to remain in flux for the foreseeable future.

---

37   Id. at 2180.

38   Id. at 2180–81.

39   Id. at 2185 (Scalia, J., concurring in the opinion).

D. Availability and Cross-Examination. Most of the post-*Crawford* litigation has focused on the critical line between testimonial and nontestimonial statements. But the availability of a speaker for cross-examination is just as important; that presence satisfies the confrontation guarantee. In this section, we explore how availability and cross-examination affect the prosecutor's use of hearsay.

1. Currently Subject to Cross-Examination. If a witness is subject to cross-examination in the courtroom, then the Sixth Amendment allows the prosecutor to introduce any hearsay statements by that witness—even if the statements were testimonial. The Sixth Amendment does not mandate cross-examination that occurs at the same time as a testimonial statement; it requires only some opportunity to confront the witness.

The hearsay exemption contained in Rule 801(d)(1), for example, poses no Sixth Amendment problems. That exemption, for a witness's prior statements and identifications, requires the declarant to testify and be "subject to cross-examination" at trial. Even if the prior statement was testimonial, it is admissible under these conditions.

Similar reasoning applies to testimonial hearsay admitted as a recorded recollection under Rule 803(5). The exception itself requires the declarant's courtroom testimony, so the recorded hearsay raises no Sixth Amendment issues. The same result occurs under other exceptions whenever the declarant testifies live. The prosecutor, for example, may offer a victim's excited utterance from the crime scene to complement her courtroom testimony. Even if the crime-scene statements were testimonial, the victim's trial presence eliminates any Sixth Amendment objection to admitting the prior statement.

One question that arises in these cases is whether any witness who testifies live in the courtroom is also available for cross-examination. We explored that issue in Chapter 39, when we first discussed the hearsay exemption for a witness's prior statements. In *United States v. Owens*,[40] one of the cases examined in that chapter, the Supreme Court held that a defendant may have sufficient opportunity to confront a witness even if the witness remembers neither his prior statement nor the facts underlying that statement. The Sixth Amendment is satisfied as long as the witness testifies under oath and responds to cross-examination. Those conditions allow the defendant to probe the witness's credibility and expose his memory loss to the jury.

---

40   484 U.S. 554 (1988).

Following *Owens*, lower courts have held that witnesses who suffer real or feigned memory loss—but who respond willingly to questions on the stand—are available for cross-examination. On the other hand, a witness who invokes a privilege in response to cross-examination usually is not available. Under the latter circumstances, the defendant has no way to test the witness's prior statements or to probe the witness's credibility before the jury.

2. Unavailability and Prior Cross-Examination. If a declarant is not subject to cross-examination in the current trial, the prosecutor must surmount two hurdles before introducing testimonial hearsay. First, the prosecutor must prove that the declarant is, in fact, unavailable. Second, the prosecutor must demonstrate that the defendant had a prior opportunity to cross-examine the declarant.

The state usually has little trouble proving a declarant's unavailability. Courts have assumed that the five categories of unavailability listed in Rule 804(a) all satisfy the Sixth Amendment requirement. But the state must make a good faith effort to secure a witness's testimony; the prosecutor cannot simply assume that a witness is unavailable.[41]

The second test, establishing prior cross-examination, is much harder for the state to pass. Often the defendant had no opportunity to cross-examine the declarant. The defense, for example, has no chance to question witnesses who testify before a grand jury; nor can defense lawyers cross-examine witnesses when they talk to the police. As a practical matter, the requirement of prior cross-examination excludes most testimonial hearsay—unless the declarant also appears at trial to testify.

If defense counsel did have an opportunity to question the declarant, the court must still determine whether that opportunity was sufficient to satisfy the Sixth Amendment. This question is analogous to the one that arises under Rule 804(b)(1), the hearsay exception for prior testimony, and the courts have relied upon that standard for guidance. For the prior opportunity to suffice, the defendant must have had a similar **motive** to cross-examine the witness at the prior proceeding.

> **Example:** Colin Taplin was driving his car, with Preston Tillman Bailey as a passenger. Police stopped the car, searched it, and discovered cocaine. The government charged both Taplin and Bailey with conspiracy to transport cocaine. Taplin moved to suppress evidence seized from the car,

---

41   See Barber v. Page, 390 U.S. 719 (1968).

claiming that the search violated his Fourth Amendment rights. Bailey joined that motion and, at the suppression hearing, testified about his own expectation of privacy in the car. Bailey's testimony included statements incriminating Taplin in drug trafficking.

The judge granted Taplin's suppression motion, but the government proceeded to trial with other evidence of Taplin's cocaine dealing. Bailey refused to testify at Taplin's trial, claiming the Fifth Amendment privilege against self-incrimination. The prosecutor then sought to introduce portions of Bailey's testimony from the suppression hearing. Taplin objected under the Sixth Amendment.

Analysis: The prior testimony is inadmissible under the Sixth Amendment. Bailey's testimony at the suppression hearing undoubtedly was testimonial, allowing Taplin to raise a Sixth Amendment claim. Bailey's privilege claim made him unavailable at trial, and Taplin's attorney had a chance to cross-examine Bailey at the suppression hearing.

Taplin's motive for cross-examining Bailey at that hearing, however, was quite different from his motive for questioning the out-of-court statements at trial. The suppression hearing focused on whether Taplin and Bailey had expectations of privacy that the police violated through their search. As Bailey attempted to establish his privacy interest, Taplin had no motive to cross-examine him on other aspects of his testimony. Those aspects, which incriminated Taplin, were vital at trial. Admission of Bailey's statement, therefore, violated Taplin's right to confront witnesses against him.[42]

3. Exceptions to Confrontation. Eighteenth century courts accepted two types of testimonial hearsay, even when the defendant had no prior opportunity to cross-examine the declarant: (a) statements that satisfied the forfeiture exception, and (b) dying declarations. Based on this history, the Supreme Court has suggested that the Sixth Amendment may recognize "founding-era exceptions" for hearsay falling into either of these categories.[43] A prosecutor, in other words, could introduce a statement qualifying for one of these exceptions without showing that the defendant had any chance to cross-examine the declarant.

---

42   This example is based on United States v. Taplin, 954 F.2d 1256 (6th Cir. 1992). Taplin arose before Crawford, and the court decided the case under 804(b)(1). The situation, however, illustrates the "prior opportunity" issues that now arise under the Sixth Amendment.

43   Giles, 554 U.S. at 358; Crawford, 541 U.S. at 54.

a. Forfeiture by Wrongdoing. Special treatment for the forfeiture exception rests on policy grounds as well as founding-era practices. This hearsay exception, as the Supreme Court has observed, "extinguishes confrontation clause claims on essentially equitable grounds."[44] If the defendant kills a witness to prevent him from testifying in court, then she implicitly waives her right to confront that witness.

Based on this reasoning, as well as the founding-era history, the Supreme Court has strongly intimated that hearsay satisfying Rule 804(b)(6)'s forfeiture exception requires no confrontation. The lower courts assume that even testimonial statements are admissible against the defendant if they fall within this exception.

But to qualify for this treatment, the defendant must have acted with the **specific purpose** of preventing a witness from testifying.[45] The federal forfeiture rule imposes this condition, as we saw in Chapter 52, but some state rules do not. In other words, even if a statement is admissible under a state's forfeiture exception, it will not be admissible under the Confrontation Clause unless the defendant made the declarant unavailable for the specific purpose of preventing his courtroom testimony.

b. Dying Declarations. The Supreme Court has suggested several times in dicta that founding-era practices exempt dying declarations from the Sixth Amendment.[46] Following this lead, state courts have held that dying declarations require no confrontation—even when the statements were testimonial accusations to police officers.

> **Example:** Police Captain Bryan McGee responded to a radio call about a shooting. When he arrived at the scene, McGee found several officers already attending to the victim, Igol Isaacs. McGee knelt down beside Isaacs, who lay bleeding on the sidewalk, and asked: "Who shot you?" Isaacs, who was struggling to breathe, did not respond. McGee then said: "I don't think you're going to make it. Who shot you?" After another exchange, Isaacs identified his shooter as "Tom." McGee pressed Isaacs for Tom's last name, but he was not able to respond further. Isaacs died later that night at the hospital, and the state prosecuted Thomas Clay for his murder. The

---

44   Davis, 547 U.S. at 833 (quoting Crawford, 541 U.S. at 62).

45   Giles v. California, 554 U.S. 353 (2008).

46   Crawford, 541 U.S. at 56 n.6; Giles, 554 U.S. at 358–59; Bryant, 562 U.S. at 3511 n.1; id. at 395, 395–96 (Ginsburg, J., dissenting).

prosecutor called McGee to testify at trial about Isaacs's identification. Clay objected to this testimony under the Sixth Amendment.

Analysis: A New York appellate court reviewed these facts shortly after the Supreme Court decided *Michigan v. Bryant.* The state court concluded that Isaacs's statement, unlike the one in *Bryant*, was testimonial. McGee arrived after other officers had taken control of both the scene and Isaacs. He did not check with those officers, but immediately approached the only eyewitness to the crime and pointedly asked "Who shot you?" Most important, when Isaacs failed to respond to this initial inquiry, McGee advised him, "I don't think you're going to make it." The "evident purpose" of this question was "to give Isaacs what might have been—and, in fact, turned out to be—his final opportunity to bear witness against his assailants."[47]

The court nonetheless admitted Isaacs's statement, finding that it was a dying declaration. Eighteenth-century admission of those statements, the court concluded, established a "Sixth Amendment . . . exception for testimonial dying declarations."[48]

History may support special treatment for dying declarations, but policy does not. Dying witnesses are as susceptible to police pressure and leading questions as healthy ones. Police officers, in fact, may be particularly anxious to give dying victims a chance to "testify" against the person they believe committed the crime; that was the path Captain McGee pursued in the above case. Defendants have the same Sixth Amendment interest in cross-examining these declarants as they have in probing the truth of other testimonial statements. Supreme Court dicta and lower court decisions, however, suggest that dying declarations are free of Sixth Amendment constraints.

E. Putting It All Together: Combining the Rules and the Constitution.
Out-of-court statements are admissible only if they satisfy **both** the Confrontation Clause and the hearsay rule. The Confrontation Clause, however, affects a relatively small number of statements; it does not apply to civil cases or to evidence offered by the accused against the government in a criminal case. When analyzing the admissibility of most statements, therefore, you should apply the

---

47   People v. Clay, 926 N.Y.S.2d 598, 603, 606 (N.Y. App. Div. 2011).

48   Id. at 609 (quoting Crawford, 541 U.S. at 56).

evidentiary rules first and then consider the Confrontation Clause. If an out-of-court statement fails to satisfy Rules 801–807, it is not admissible—regardless of the Sixth Amendment—and your analysis can stop there. If a statement is admissible under the Federal Rules of Evidence, then turn to the Confrontation Clause as the last step of your analysis. The flow chart on the next page outlines the basic steps of that analysis.

As this flow chart suggests, the Sixth Amendment gives the prosecutor several avenues to admit out-of-court statements against a criminal defendant. Indeed, many hearsay exceptions impose conditions that serve to satisfy the Confrontation Clause. In a criminal case, for example, Rule 804(b)(1) admits prior testimony only if the opponent had an opportunity and similar motive to cross-examine the witness at the prior proceeding. Testimony that fulfills these conditions will also satisfy the Confrontation Clause.

Many other hearsay exceptions have Sixth Amendment protections built into their definition. The Confrontation Clause, therefore, limits admission of relatively few categories of evidence. Indeed, we can divide the hearsay exceptions into three categories: (1) Those that never raise Confrontation Clause issues because the exception itself satisfies the clause; (2) Those that usually do not generate Confrontation Clause issues but might occasionally admit evidence violating the clause; and (3) Those that often raise Confrontation Clause issues when a prosecutor relies upon the exception to admit evidence against a criminal defendant.

The federal hearsay exceptions we have studied that, under current law, **never** raise Confrontation Clause issues are:

- **801(d)(1)**—A Declarant-Witness's Prior Statement. These statements are admissible under the hearsay rule only if the declarant is on the stand and subject to cross-examination, which satisfies the Confrontation Clause.

- **801(d)(2)**—An Opposing Party's Statement. The courts have held that these statements raise no Confrontation Clause issues. The defendant may not complain about confronting himself or others speaking on his behalf.

Confrontation Clause Analysis

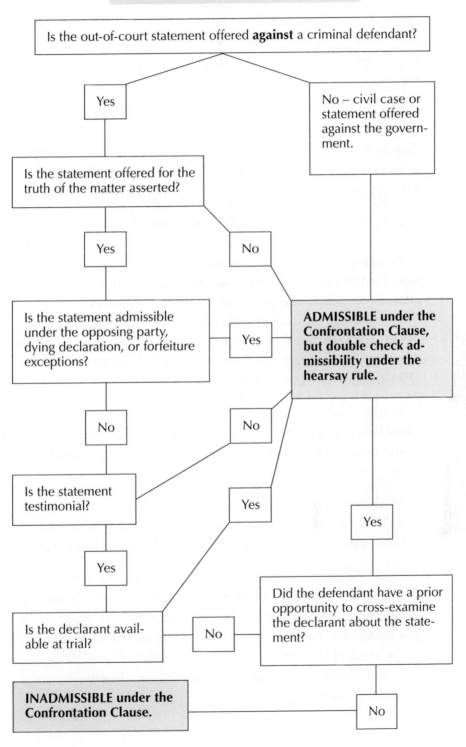

Is the out-of-court statement offered **against** a criminal defendant?

Yes

No – civil case or statement offered against the government.

Is the statement offered for the truth of the matter asserted?

Yes

No

Is the statement admissible under the opposing party, dying declaration, or forfeiture exceptions?

Yes

ADMISSIBLE under the Confrontation Clause, but double check admissibility under the hearsay rule.

No

No

Is the statement testimonial?

Yes

Yes

Yes

Yes

Did the defendant have a prior opportunity to cross-examine the declarant about the statement?

Is the declarant available at trial?

No

INADMISSIBLE under the Confrontation Clause.

No

- **803(5)**—Recorded Recollection. These statements are admissible only if the declarant is on the stand and subject to cross-examination, which satisfies the Confrontation Clause.

- **803(6)**—Records of a Regularly Conducted Activity (Business Records). These records rarely are testimonial, and courts should use the exception's "trustworthiness" clause to exclude any that cross the testimonial line. Records generated by public agencies, moreover, must satisfy Rule 803(8)'s more stringent standard; they are not admissible as business records.

- **803(10)**—Absence of a Public Record. The absence of an entry is not a statement, so the absence itself is not testimonial. A witness who testifies about a missing record is subject to cross-examination, satisfying the Confrontation Clause. A prosecutor may offer written "certification" under this rule only after following the specified "notice-and-demand" procedure. That procedure, according to the *Melendez-Diaz* Court, satisfies the Confrontation Clause. If a criminal defendant objects in a timely fashion to written certification, both Rule 803(10) and the Confrontation Clause would require the prosecutor to offer live testimony about the record's absence.

- **804(b)(1)**—Former Testimony. This testimony is admissible in criminal cases only if the defendant had an opportunity and similar motive to cross-examine the declarant on the prior occasion, which satisfies the Confrontation Clause.

- **804(b)(2)**—Statement Under the Belief of Imminent Death (Dying Declarations). This is a founding-era exception that the Supreme Court appears to have grandfathered into the Confrontation Clause.

- **804(b)(6)**—Statement Offered Against a Party That Wrongfully Caused the Declarant's Unavailability (Forfeiture). This is a founding-era exception and it rests on the assumption that the defendant waived his confrontation rights by making the witness unavailable. Under federal law, and to satisfy the Confrontation Clause, the defendant must have specifically intended to prevent the witness from providing evidence against him.

Four other federal exceptions we studied **usually do not** raise Confrontation Clause issues but occasionally do so:

- **803(4)**—Statement Made for Medical Diagnosis or Treatment. In most situations, these statements are nontestimonial because speakers make them to private parties and/or for the purpose of obtaining medical care; thus, the patient would not expect them to be used in court. The exception, however, includes statements made for the purpose of obtaining diagnoses related to litigation; and a few courts have also held that the identity of abusers is pertinent to treating victims of sexual or domestic abuse. In these unusual cases, a statement admitted under this exception could qualify as testimonial.

- **803(7)**—Absence of a Record of a Regularly Conducted Activity. The absence of an entry is not a statement, so the absence itself is not testimonial. But if a witness searches business records to provide evidence for the prosecutor, a statement declaring the absence of those records most likely is testimonial. A witness participating in the search must testify live about the absence of the records.

- **803(17)**—Market Reports and Similar Commercial Publications. The lists and tabulations commonly admitted under this exception contain no testimonial statements; they are telephone directories, stock market reports, and similar compilations. Law enforcement agencies, however, may publish and rely upon some lists that include testimonial evidence. In those rare cases, a list might satisfy this exception but not the Confrontation Clause.

- **803(18)**—Statements in Learned Treatises, Periodicals, or Pamphlets. Most learned treatises address general subjects rather than gathering evidence to convict a particular defendant. In unusual cases, however, a law enforcement agency might publish a book documenting the crimes of a notorious criminal. In rare situations like this, admission of a learned treatise might violate the Confrontation Clause.

These exceptions to the federal hearsay rule, finally, raise Confrontation Clause issues in a **significant** subset of cases:

- **803(1) and (2)**—Present Sense Impression and Excited Utterance. When made to private parties, these statements probably present no Confrontation Clause problems. Similarly, they satisfy the Sixth Amendment when made to law enforcement agents for the primary purpose of obtaining immediate aid. But when made to law enforcement agents for the primary purpose of creating prosecution evidence, they trigger the defendant's confrontation rights.

- **803(3)**—Then-Existing Mental, Emotional, or Physical Condition. Under some circumstances, such as when made to law enforcement agents gathering evidence for prosecution, these statements are testimonial and raise Confrontation Clause problems. Under other circumstances, such as when made to private parties, they are not testimonial.

- **803(8)**—Public Records. Many public records are testimonial, but the exception already restricts admission of those records against criminal defendants. In most cases, prosecutors who comply with the exception probably satisfy the Confrontation Clause as well. But the exception may allow some statements—such as ministerial law enforcement records and observations by government employees—that would qualify as testimonial.

- **803(16)**—Statements in Ancient Documents. Confessions, police reports, and other testimonial statements do not lose their testimonial character with time. Even if a document was prepared before January 1, 1998, it may be testimonial.

- **804(b)(3)**—Statement Against Interest. Statements against interest made to private parties probably are not testimonial, but those to government agents often are. Many of these statements trigger Sixth Amendment concerns, especially when the prosecutor attempts to introduce one perpetrator's confession against another participant in the crime.

- **807**—Residual Exception. Before *Crawford*, courts often used this rule to admit grand jury testimony, but those statements clearly are testimonial after *Crawford*. Other statements admitted under this exception similarly could raise confrontation issues.

F. The Future of *Crawford*. Although *Crawford* attempted to establish a bright-line test for enforcing the Confrontation Clause, the concept of "testimonial" has proved difficult to administer. The Justices differ on how to define this key concept; those disagreements have prompted a series of uneasy alliances supporting the Court's opinions. As the Court continues to address the constitutional limits on hearsay, it may depart from *Crawford*'s analysis. Even if the Court adheres to *Crawford*, lower courts face many open issues in identifying testimonial statements, determining a declarant's availability, and measuring the defendant's prior opportunities for cross-examination. These issues promise lively developments in Confrontation Clause jurisprudence for many years to come.

Quick Summary

The Confrontation Clause of the Sixth Amendment restricts admission of hearsay when (1) the statement is offered against a criminal defendant, and (2) that statement is testimonial. Although the Supreme Court has not fully defined "testimonial," it has characterized testimonial statements as ones "made under circumstances which would lead an objective witness reasonably to believe that the statement would be available for use at a later trial." Statements made solemnly, to government agents, and to establish facts related to a crime are most likely to be testimonial.

Testimonial statements certainly include all formal statements made during litigation, such as testimony given at pretrial hearings or in pretrial depositions. They also include most statements made to law enforcement personnel. Statements made to law enforcement agents in emergency situations, however, are not testimonial if they are made for the primary purpose of aiding the victim, securing the agents' safety, or otherwise ending the emergency.

Prosecutors may admit out-of-court statements offered for a purpose other than to prove the truth of the matter asserted; these uses are not testimonial. Prosecutors may also admit statements that satisfy the party-opponent exemption to the hearsay rule; defendants do not have a right to confront themselves or others who spoke for them. Most statements made among private parties are not testimonial, but the courts have not closely examined the Sixth Amendment's impact on these statements. Some of these private declarations, especially those carrying formal markings, may be testimonial.

Even if a statement is testimonial, it is still admissible if the defendant (a) has a chance to cross-examine the declarant at trial, or (b) the declarant is unavailable but the defendant had a prior opportunity to cross-examine the declarant on the statement. Statements that satisfy the dying-declaration or forfeiture exceptions, finally, are admissible as founding-era exceptions to the defendant's right to confront witnesses.

Test Your Understanding

 To assess your understanding of the material in this chapter, click here to take a quiz, or go to the Quizzes module from the eBook on your eProducts bookshelf.

59

Judicial Notice

Key Concepts

- **Rule 201:** Judicial Notice Allowed
- Adjudicative and Legislative Facts
- Two-Part Standard
- Instructions to Jury in Civil and Criminal Cases
- Judicial Notice Allowed at Any Time
- Stipulations and Judicial Notice

A. Introduction and Policy. Some facts are so well accepted that it seems unnecessary to prove them in court. Heavy objects thrown out a window will fall to the ground. Water flows downhill. Memorial Day was celebrated on May 29 in 2017.

Rule 201 allows the judge to take judicial notice of facts like these. The rule eases litigation for parties, jurors, and the court by allowing the judge to recognize facts that are "not subject to reasonable dispute."

B. The Rule. Rule 201, which governs judicial notice, contains six sections. The easiest way to master the rule is to examine the sections one by one; we'll do that in this section. The rule opens by noting that it applies only to a particular type of fact:

> ## RULE 201. Judicial Notice of Adjudicative Facts
>
> **(a) Scope.** This rule governs judicial notice of an <u>adjudicative</u> fact only, not a legislative fact.

What is an adjudicative fact? It is one that helps prove the elements of a specific case. Most of the issues that parties dispute at trial are adjudicative facts: Was the traffic light red when the car went through the intersection? How fast was the car traveling? What injuries did the plaintiff suffer in the collision? In a personal injury suit arising from a car collision, all of these are adjudicative facts.

Courts distinguish adjudicative facts from legislative facts; the latter inform a court's ruling on a legal issue. When weighing the constitutionality of campaign finance laws, for example, courts may take judicial notice of facts such as the financial cost of political campaigns, the existence of political corruption, and citizen perceptions of fairness. All of these are legislative facts; they inform the court's decision on a legal principle, whether the challenged campaign finance law violates First Amendment principles.

Rule 201 applies only to adjudicative facts. Neither Rule 201 nor any other rule restricts a judge's discretion to take judicial notice of legislative facts. Thus, under the Federal Rules of Evidence, judges may **always** take judicial notice of legislative facts and they may do so without following any prescribed procedures.

Rule 201(a) makes clear that the remainder of the rule applies only when a judge takes judicial notice of an **adjudicative fact**. For those facts, judges and parties must follow the guidelines prescribed by the remainder of Rule 201. That rule continues:

RULE 201. Judicial Notice of Adjudicative Facts

(b) Kinds of Facts That May Be Judicially Noticed. The court may judicially notice a fact that is <u>not subject to reasonable dispute</u> because it:

(1) is <u>generally known</u> within the trial court's territorial jurisdiction; or

(2) can be <u>accurately and readily determined</u> from sources whose accuracy cannot reasonably be questioned.

This section is the heart of Rule 201. It establishes a two-part test that adjudicative facts must pass to secure judicial notice. **First**, a fact must satisfy section (b)'s general standard. The fact must be one that is "not subject to reasonable dispute."

Second, the fact must also fall within one of section (b)'s two specific categories. The fact must either be "generally known" within the court's jurisdiction or it must be "accurately and readily determined from sources whose accuracy cannot reasonably be questioned."

We will explore these requirements further in the Courtroom section. For now, note the two categories of facts subject to judicial notice. Some facts, like the fact that Canada is a nation, are generally known; almost anyone in the courtroom would know that fact. Other facts, like the name of Canada's national anthem, may not be known by anyone in the courtroom, but can be easily ascertained. After checking a reliable source, such as the Canadian government's website, no one would reasonably dispute the name of Canada's national anthem (which is "O Canada").

The next section of Rule 201 clarifies that a court may take judicial notice on its motion or at a party's request.

Rule 201. Judicial Notice of Adjudicative Facts

(c) Taking Notice. The court:

 (1) <u>may</u> take judicial notice on its own; or

 (2) <u>must</u> take judicial notice if a party <u>requests</u> it and the court is <u>supplied</u> with the necessary information.

Note that, although subsection 201(c)(2) uses the word "must," it does not force a court to take judicial notice of every fact offered by a party. The party must specifically request judicial notice and proffer information supporting that request. The judge will examine the information and decide whether the fact fits the requirements of section 201(b) outlined above. If the fact satisfies those requirements, the judge must take judicial notice of the fact; failing to do so is an abuse of discretion that an appellate court may reverse.

On the other hand, the judge may refuse to take judicial notice, even when requested to do so by a party, if the judge finds that the fact fails the test outlined in Rule 201(b). In other words, the judge will refuse to take judicial notice if:

- The fact is subject to reasonable dispute **OR**

- The fact is neither generally known within the territorial jurisdiction of the court nor readily verifiable from reliable sources.

A fourth section of Rule 201 empowers courts to take judicial notice at any stage of a proceeding:

RULE 201. Judicial Notice of Adjudicative Facts

(d) Timing. The court may take judicial notice at <u>any stage</u> of the proceeding.

This provision allows judges to take notice of suitable facts even in response to post-verdict motions. Appellate courts likewise may take judicial notice of adjudicative facts.

Section (e) complements this provision by guaranteeing a party the right to be heard on the issue of judicial notice, no matter when the court takes that notice:

RULE 201. Judicial Notice of Adjudicative Facts

(e) Opportunity to Be Heard. On timely request, a party is <u>entitled to be heard</u> on the propriety of taking judicial notice and the nature of the fact to be noticed. If the court takes judicial notice <u>before notifying a party</u>, the party, <u>on request, is still entitled to be heard</u>.

This opportunity to be heard, however, is limited. The judge does not have to conduct a formal hearing on the propriety of taking judicial notice; she only has to offer **some opportunity** to be heard. The section, moreover, does not guarantee a right to be heard before a judge takes judicial notice of a relevant fact. The judge has discretion to take judicial notice without giving any prior notice to the parties. If a party contests judicial notice of that fact, the judge will then hear the party's argument. If the party persuades the judge that judicial notice was inappropriate, the judge will withdraw her judicial notice of that fact.

Section (f), finally, articulates the relationship between the judge and jury when a judge takes judicial notice of a fact:

RULE 201. Judicial Notice of Adjudicative Facts

(f) **Instructing the Jury.** In a <u>civil case</u>, the court must instruct the jury to accept the noticed fact as <u>conclusive</u>. In a <u>criminal case</u>, the court must instruct the jury that it <u>may or may not</u> accept the noticed fact as conclusive.

This section declares that judicially noticed facts bind the jury in civil cases, but not in criminal ones. In a civil case, the judge instructs the jury to accept any judicially noticed fact as conclusive. This outcome accords with the principle that judicially noticed facts are beyond reasonable dispute. If a fact is not subject to reasonable dispute, a jury cannot reasonably find contrary to that fact.

In criminal cases, however, judicially noticed facts do not bind the jury. The judge will instruct the jury that it may accept a judicially noticed fact as conclusive, but it does not have to do so. To protect the rights of a criminal defendant, the jury is the final arbiter of all facts in criminal cases. The jury in a criminal case has the right to reject even indisputable facts.

C. In the Courtroom.

1. Subject to Reasonable Dispute. The first part of Rule 201(b)'s two-part test raises few issues in practice. Courts have held that a wide range of facts are not subject to reasonable dispute. Facts that have been judicially noticed include:

- The fact that credit cards play a vital role in American society[1]

- The fact that bingo is a senior citizen pastime[2]

---

1   First Nat'l Bank of South Carolina v. United States, 413 F. Supp. 1107, 1110 (D.S.C. 1976), aff'd, 558 F.2d 721 (4th Cir. 1977).

2   Seminole Tribe of Fla. v. Butterworth, 491 F. Supp. 1015, 1019 (S.D. Fla. 1980), aff'd, 658 F.2d 310 (5th Cir. 1981).

> • The fact that the Ku Klux Klan has a history of violence against African Americans[3]

Whether a fact is subject to reasonable dispute, however, may change depending on the era and circumstances. In 1967, a judge took judicial notice of the fact that most establishments that sell beer also sell cigarettes;[4] that fact is less clear today, after widespread adoption of anti-smoking ordinances.

2. Generally Known. Indisputability alone does not render a fact suitable for judicial notice. The fact must also fall within one of Rule 201(b)'s specific categories: The fact must be either "generally known within the trial court's territorial jurisdiction" or "accurately and readily determined from sources whose accuracy cannot reasonably be questioned."

To fit within the first category, a fact must be generally known to the public. Facts that are known by members of a particular religion, occupation, or other group do not qualify as generally known. The fact that impairment of a particular portion of the liver reduces life expectancy, for example, may be generally known among physicians, but one court held that it is not generally known to the public.[5]

On the other hand, Rule 201(b) allows a court to take judicial notice of facts that are generally known within the court's jurisdiction, even though they may not be well known in other parts of the country. Facts about riptides, hurricanes, and floods, for example, may be generally known in South Carolina but not Kansas. A Kansas court, conversely, might more readily find that facts about tornados and dust storms are generally known in that jurisdiction.

3. Capable of Determination. Even if a fact is not generally known, Rule 201(b) allows the court to take judicial notice of the fact if it is both indisputable and "can be accurately and readily determined from sources whose accuracy cannot reasonably be questioned." This provision relieves parties from proving a large number of facts that are easy to verify but cumbersome to prove.

---

3   Marshall v. Bramer, 828 F.2d 355, 357 (6th Cir. 1987).

4   Carling Brewing Co. v. Philip Morris, Inc., 277 F. Supp. 326, 330 (N.D. Ga. 1967).

5   Fielder v. Bosshard, 590 F.2d 105, 110–11 (5th Cir. 1979).

Courts, for example, have taken judicial notice of prices, interest rates, distances between cities, and many other facts of this nature. Parties could prove many of these facts by introducing documents under the business records or public records exceptions to the hearsay rule,[6] but judicial notice offers a quicker route when the opposing party does not dispute the fact.

This prong of Rule 201(b) also allows parties to prove facts that are well known only within a particular occupation or other subgroup. Although those facts do not qualify as generally known, a reliable source often documents them. One court, for example, took judicial notice of the history and beliefs of the Mennonite church from sources documenting those facts.[7] Another judicially noticed the impact of Graves' disease on patients when a party supplied reliable sources reporting those data.[8]

4. Other Situations. Occasionally, a fact seems indisputable although it is neither generally known nor readily verifiable from accurate sources. Rule 201 does not allow a judge to take judicial notice of facts like this; the fact must fall within one of the rule's specific categories. Here is an unusual case illustrating this possibility:

> **Example:** Duane Switzer sued the judges, magistrates, law clerks, and staff attorneys associated with federal courts in the Tenth Circuit. Switzer claimed these individuals had committed fraud by issuing opinions that purported to be written by Article III judges but were really authored by law clerks or staff attorneys. Switzer also maintained that the judges issued these opinions without reading them. A district judge dismissed Switzer's complaint, taking judicial notice that the "judges of the Tenth Circuit first review, approve and sign all Orders and Rulings before they are entered in their respective cases."

> **Analysis:** The court of appeals concluded that this fact was not appropriate for judicial notice. Although the judges of the Tenth Circuit may know that they review and approve their opinions before issuing them, that is not a fact that is generally known. Nor is it a fact that "can be accurately and readily

---

6   See Chapters 45–46 for discussion of these exceptions.

7   Bethel Conservative Mennonite Church v. Commissioner, 746 F.2d 388, 392 (7th Cir. 1984).

8   Harris v. H&W Contracting Co., 102 F.3d 516, 522 (11th Cir. 1996).

determined from sources whose accuracy cannot reasonably be questioned." The court, however, affirmed dismissal of the complaint on other grounds.[9]

5. Judicial and Agency Decisions. The Switzer example illustrates that internal judicial routines usually do not satisfy the requirements for judicial notice. Court and agency **decisions**, on the other hand, easily fit within Rule 201. Courts frequently take judicial notice of judgments rendered by other courts or by administrative agencies. These decisions are readily verifiable from reliable sources and are not subject to reasonable dispute.

Judicial notice of a judgment, however, extends only to the terms of the judgment, not to facts underlying the decision. A judge cannot judicially notice a fact proven in one lawsuit and impose that finding on the parties in another case, unless the fact independently satisfies the requirements of Rule 201.

6. Supporting Sources. When a party offers a source to show that it is easily verifiable under Rule 201(b)(2), the source does not have to be admissible. Parties, therefore, may rely upon books, public records, business records, and other types of hearsay without showing that the source fits within one of the hearsay exceptions. Rule 201(b)(2) requires only that the source be one "whose accuracy cannot reasonably be questioned." The judge decides whether a source satisfies that standard, subject only to appellate review for an abuse of discretion.

7. Instructing the Jury. Rule 201(f) draws a key distinction between instructing the jury in civil cases and instructing the jury in criminal prosecutions. When the judge takes judicial notice of a fact in a civil trial, the judge will instruct the jury to accept that fact as conclusive. In criminal cases, however, the judge instructs the jury that it **may** accept a judicially noticed fact as conclusive. The jurors in a criminal case retain the right to reject facts that the judge considers indisputable:

> **Example:** The government charged Jesús Bello with assaulting a fellow prisoner at the Metropolitan Detention Center in Guaynabo, Puerto Rica. As one element of the crime, the statute required the government to prove that the assault occurred on land "under the exclusive or concurrent jurisdiction" of the United States. After reviewing government maps, letters from government officials, and various legislative acts, the judge took ju-

9   Switzer v. Coan, 261 F.3d 985, 989 (10th Cir. 2001).

dicial notice that the Guaynabo detention center fit that description. The judge then instructed the jury in this manner:

"Even though no evidence has been introduced about it in your presence, I believe that the fact that the Metropolitan Detention Center is within a land reserved for the use of the United States and under its exclusive jurisdiction . . . is of such common knowledge and can be so accurately and readily determined from the Metropolitan Detention Center officials that it cannot reasonably be disputed. You may, therefore, reasonably treat this fact as proven even though no evidence has been presented on this point before you. As with any fact presented in the case, however, the final decision whether or not to accept it is for you to make and you are not required to agree with me."

Analysis: The court of appeals approved both the taking of judicial notice and the use of this instruction. The fact that the Detention Center fell within federal jurisdiction was not subject to reasonable dispute, and the judge properly verified this fact by reference to reliable sources. In criminal cases, however, the jury does not have to accept judicially noticed facts. Rule 201(f) directs the judge to instruct the jury that it "may or may not" accept these facts. The judge properly complied with that mandate in this case.[10]

Although the jury may disregard judicially noticed facts in criminal cases, the doctrine still plays an important role: It eliminates the need to prove particular facts in the courtroom. In Bello, for example, authenticating the maps and other documents showing federal ownership of the Detention Center was somewhat cumbersome for the government. Yet without some evidence of this element of the crime, the judge would have directed a verdict of acquittal for the defendant. Judicial notice allowed the government to offer evidence of the jurisdictional element in an expeditious manner.

8. Judicial Notice on Appeal. Rule 201(d) allows a court to take judicial notice "at any stage of the proceeding." This provision permits judicial notice even while a case is on appeal.

---

10   United States v. Bello, 194 F.3d 18, 23 (1st Cir. 1999).

Example: Stanislaw Opoka and his wife, both Polish citizens, remained in the United States after their temporary travel visas expired. The Board of Immigration Appeals (BIA) entered an order deporting Mr. Opoka, and Opoka appealed. While Opoka's appeal was pending before the Court of Appeals, BIA granted his wife status as a lawful permanent resident of the United States. Opoka urged the Court of Appeals to take judicial notice of this change in his wife's status.

Analysis: The court of appeals took judicial notice of Mrs. Opoka's changed status. BIA's order granting her permanent residence was an agency record appropriate for that treatment. The agency's decision, moreover, did not exist at the time BIA entered its order deposing Mr. Opoka. By taking judicial notice of the later decision, the court of appeals did not interfere with BIA's discretion; the agency might adhere to its decision deporting Mr. Opoka. But in light of the agency's later decision involving Mrs. Opoka, the court of appeals vacated the deportation order and remanded for further consideration of Mr. Opoka's case.[11]

9. Judicial Notice and Stipulations. Judicial notice is not the only way to admit undisputed facts. If both parties agree on a fact, they can make a **stipulation** that the fact is true. Usually the party who proposes the stipulation will write out the exact language for the jury; if the other side agrees, the proponent or the judge will read the stipulation to the jury.[12]

Stipulations, unlike judicial notice, do not have to satisfy the "not subject to reasonable dispute" standard. A stipulation only means that these two parties, for the purposes of this litigation, agree to the fact. Judicially noticed facts thus are indisputable, while stipulated facts are simply undisputed.

Stipulated facts usually are very specific. A criminal defense attorney, for example, may stipulate that the substance purchased by an undercover officer is cocaine, or that the victim died as a result of a stab wound to the chest. In a contracts action, the parties may stipulate that the plaintiff gave the defendant appropriate notice of breach. As with judicial notice, the jury must accept stipulated facts as true in a civil case, but is not required to do so in a criminal case.

---

11   Opoka v. INS, 94 F.3d 392, 395 (7th Cir. 1996).

12   We also discussed stipulations in Chapters 6 and 7, when we discussed their effect on relevance and minimizing undue prejudice.

There are many reasons why parties propose and agree to stipulations. **First,** especially in civil lawsuits, judges press parties to save trial time by stipulating to undisputed or easily proven facts. Judges are impatient with parties who waste courtroom time by proving the obvious.

Second, contesting every element of a claim or crime may damage a party's credibility. If a defendant charged with selling drugs claims mistaken identity, the jury will find it odd if the defendant also argues that the delivered substance was sugar rather than cocaine. If the defendant wasn't there, why would he contest that element?

Third, some stipulations avoid detailed proof of facts that will engender sympathy or create powerful emotions on the part of the jury. Defendants in personal injury lawsuits sometimes offer to stipulate to the extent of the plaintiff's injuries, hoping to foreclose extensive proof of those injuries. Similarly, the defendant in a homicide prosecution may prefer to stipulate to the fact that the victim is dead rather than to have a coroner testify in great detail about the cause of death.

Finally, some facts honestly are beyond dispute, and the parties realize that it would be a waste of time to contest those facts. Jurors have limited attention; parties fare better by focusing their trial strategy on central, disputed facts rather than marginal, undisputed ones. Many attorneys seek stipulations for indisputable facts before asking the judge to take judicial notice of them.

Although these factors encourage litigants to stipulate facts, parties may also refuse to make stipulations. A litigant may choose to prove even an undisputable fact with direct, courtroom evidence. Personal injury plaintiffs often opt to prove the extent of their injuries, just as prosecutors often choose to prove the manner of a homicide victim's death.[13]

When an opposing party refuses to stipulate to a fact that is beyond reasonable dispute, the party who sought the stipulation can ask the judge to take judicial notice of the fact. If the fact is generally known within the jurisdiction or can be readily determined from an unimpeachable source, the judge will take judicial notice.

---

13   Very occasionally, as in the Old Chief case we studied in Chapters 6–7, a court will hold that these direct methods of proof create unfair prejudice that substantially outweighs probative value, violating Rule 403. Under these limited circumstances, a court may hold that a stipulation is the best way to present evidence to the jury. Trial judges, however, have been reluctant to extend Old Chief beyond the specific statute at issue there.

Quick Summary

Rule 201 allows a court to take judicial notice of adjudicative facts that are not subject to reasonable dispute. In addition to meeting this standard, the fact must be (1) one that is generally known in the court's territorial jurisdiction or (2) readily ascertainable from a reliable source. A judge may take judicial notice of an appropriate fact without a party requesting that treatment. The court must take judicial notice of a fact if a party requests that notice and supplies the necessary information.

Sources supporting judicial notice need not themselves be admissible; indeed, judicial notice often takes the place of more cumbersome methods of proof. If a party contests judicial notice of a fact, however, the court must give the party an opportunity to be heard.

In civil cases, the judge instructs the jury to accept as conclusive any facts that have been judicially noticed. In criminal cases, the judge instructs the jury that it may, but is not required to, accept judicially noticed facts.

A court may take judicial notice of a fact at any time, even when a case is on appeal.

In addition to seeking judicial notice, parties may use stipulations to present undisputed facts to the jury. A stipulation need not satisfy the requirements of Rule 201; the parties only need to agree that, for purposes of the lawsuit, they will accept a particular fact as true. Stipulations, like judicially noticed facts, bind the jury in a civil trial; in a criminal trial, a jury is free to disregard stipulated facts.

Test Your Understanding

To assess your understanding of the material in this chapter, click here to take a quiz, or go to the Quizzes module from the eBook on your eProducts bookshelf.

60

Lay Opinions

Key Concepts

- **Rule 701:** Allows Non-Experts to Testify as to Opinions Under Three Conditions
- Lay Opinion Must Be Based on Personal Observation
- Must Be Helpful to Jury
- May Not Rest on Scientific, Technical, or Specialized Knowledge

---

A. Introduction and Policy. Most courtroom witnesses stick to the facts. They do not explain legal rules to the jury, make arguments, speculate about what might have happened, or offer advice. **Rule 602** requires all witnesses to testify based on their "personal knowledge."[1] For most witnesses, that personal knowledge centers on facts related to the case.

Article VII of the Federal Rules of Evidence, however, recognizes that litigants often seek opinions from witnesses. Under some circumstances, those opinions are both relevant to the dispute and helpful to the fact finder. **Rules 701 through 706** describe when opinion testimony is admissible.

These rules divide witnesses into two categories: lay witnesses and expert witnesses. Parties must take special steps to qualify a witness as an expert but, once qualified, the expert has significant power to offer opinions. Other witnesses, known as lay witnesses, may offer opinions under some circumstances, but the rules impose greater constraints on them. We will explore opinions from lay witnesses in this chapter, then turn to expert witnesses in Chapters 61–64.

---

1   To review the requirements of Rule 602 and personal knowledge, see Chapter 14.

Why do the rules allow lay witnesses—ordinary eyewitnesses, victims, or other participants in a controversy—to offer any opinions at all? Shouldn't these witnesses simply state the facts and leave opinions to the lawyers and jury?

Evidentiary rules originally tried to make just this distinction, confining lay witnesses to factual recitations. The attempt failed because the line between fact and opinion is too blurry, even in everyday speech. Suppose, for example, that a witness testifies that it was "sunny" at the time of an accident, that the defendant's speech was "slurred," or that a box was "heavy." These statements sound like facts, but each conveys the witness's opinion about a phenomenon experienced in the natural world.

Reasonable people may differ on whether a day was sunny or hazy, whether the defendant's speech was slurred or accented, and whether a box was heavy or manageable. A good attorney might force a witness to paint a more precise picture for the jury by asking follow up questions. The attorney, for example, might ask the witness to give examples of the slurred speech or to compare the weight of the box to other objects.

But the witness's testimony would be awkward and difficult to follow if she could not also testify that the day was sunny, the defendant's speech was slurred, and the box was heavy. The Federal Rules recognize this difficulty by giving lay witnesses limited authority to offer opinions.

B. The Rule. **Rule 701** governs the admissibility of opinion testimony by lay witnesses:

RULE 701. Opinion Testimony by Lay Witnesses

If a witness is not testifying as an expert, testimony in the form of an opinion is limited to one that is:

(a) rationally based on the witness's <u>perception</u>;

(b) <u>helpful</u> to clearly understanding the witness's testimony or to determining a fact in issue; and

(c) <u>not</u> based <u>on scientific, technical, or other specialized knowledge</u> within the scope of Rule 702.

This rule first acknowledges the two types of opinion witnesses: lay witnesses and expert witnesses. Rule 701 then outlines **three requirements** that lay witnesses must satisfy when offering an opinion.

First, the opinion must be **"rationally based on the witness's perception."** This perception requirement resembles the personal knowledge condition of Rule 602. Rule 701 repeats the obligation to underscore a key distinction between lay witnesses and experts: Lay witnesses testify only about matters they have directly perceived, while experts may offer opinions based on a broader range of facts.

Second, the lay opinion must **help** the fact finder. This requirement tracks the reason we allow lay witnesses to offer opinions: Opinions often help a lay witness convey his factual impression. As explained in the Introduction, we do this so naturally in everyday speech that we hardly notice when facts shade into opinions. An eyewitness can convey a more helpful impression to the jury by noting that the defendant "looked tired," rather than simply testifying that "he moved more slowly than usual, and his eyelids drooped." The witness's conclusion that the defendant "looked tired" helps the jury imagine the defendant's appearance.

Finally, lay opinions must be **non-technical**. In the language of Rule 701, they may not draw upon "scientific, technical, or other specialized knowledge." Congress and the Advisory Committee added this provision in 2000 to prevent litigants from "proffering an expert in lay witness clothing."[2] Before the rule changed, parties sometimes attempted to escape the restrictions on expert witnesses by questioning them as if they were lay witnesses. Rule 701(c) now draws a firmer line between expert and lay opinions.

C. In the Courtroom. Rule 701's first requirement, that a lay witness's opinion be "rationally based on the witness's perception," raises few problems in the courtroom. This prong of Rule 701 requires simply that a lay witness base her opinion on personal knowledge and that the opinion be one that a reasonable person could reach. Judges most often use this portion of Rule 701 to exclude lay opinions that are speculative or that rest upon hearsay rather than personal knowledge. We explore the other facets of Rule 701, which generate more debate, below.

1. Helpfulness. Lay opinions are admissible only if they "help" the fact finder. A lay witness's opinion may fulfill this role by capturing nuances that purely factual

---

2   Fed. R. Evid. 701 advisory committee's note.

details lack. The whole of a witness's observation, in other words, may give the jury more information than a simple sum of the parts. Judges, for example, routinely allow lay witnesses to describe individuals as happy, sad, angry, or drunk. These opinions help the jurors picture the individual's state. Here is an example of a case in which the court of appeals ruled that a lay opinion could have helped the jurors understand a critical fact:

Example: The government prosecuted Johnny Yazzie, Jr., for statutory rape. Yazzie, who was 20, had sexual intercourse with a minor who was fifteen and a half years old. Yazzie claimed that the encounter was consensual and that he reasonably believed the minor was at least sixteen years old. The governing statute recognized such belief as an affirmative defense.

Yazzie called several witnesses who testified about the minor's appearance and behavior. The judge allowed these defense witnesses to testify that the minor smoked cigarettes and drank beer, drove a car, used make-up, was tall, and had a "fully developed" body. The judge, however, refused to allow the witnesses to express their opinions that, based on the minor's appearance and behavior, they believed she was at least sixteen years old. The jury convicted Yazzie and he appealed.

Analysis: The court of appeals reversed, holding that the trial judge should have allowed the lay witnesses to give opinions about the minor's age. These opinions would have helped the jury because "one's reasons for concluding that a person is a particular age are both too complex and too indefinable to set out fully." The jurors, moreover, could not easily draw their own conclusions on this issue because more than a year had passed between the incident and trial. The minor looked and acted differently at trial than she had at the time of the sexual encounter.[3]

Notice that the *Yazzie* court mentioned both (1) the additional information conveyed by the lay opinion, and (2) the jurors' inability to view the underlying facts and form their own opinions. These two factors are important elements in persuading a judge that a lay witness's testimony will assist the fact finder. Yazzie included a third element as well: (3) The opinion related to a central aspect of the

---

3   United States v. Yazzie, 976 F.2d 1252, 1255–56 (9th Cir. 1992).

case. Judges are more likely to admit lay opinions that illuminate a key issue than ones related to a more tangential matter.

If a lay opinion does not meet these criteria, courts may exclude it as unhelpful:

> **Example:** Robert Kostelecky injured his hand while working on an oil rig for the Noble Drilling Corporation. Kostelecky sued Noble for negligence; Noble claimed that Kostelecky's own carelessness caused the accident. Jester Beck, a coworker who witnessed the accident, testified for the company at trial. Beck described Kostelecky's work on the rig and the equipment he was handling the day of the accident. Beck also testified that he warned Kostelecky, shortly before the accident, to move away from the equipment and allow it to fall to the floor. If Kostelecky had moved, he would not have been injured. Beck concluded by testifying that, in his opinion, Kostelecky's conduct caused his own injury. Kostelecky objected to Beck's lay opinion.
>
> **Analysis:** The court of appeals agreed that Beck's concluding statement was improper. The opinion added nothing to Beck's more specific testimony; the jurors could decide themselves, based on testimony from Beck and others, whether Kostelecky's conduct caused the accident. Beck's lay opinion, therefore, was not helpful to the jury.[4]

The helpfulness of lay opinions sometimes is subject to debate. In these cases, effective advocacy may sway the judge's ruling.

2. Lay Opinion and Expert Opinion. Rule 701's final requirement, distinguishing lay and expert opinions, causes the most difficulty in court. Lay witnesses may not offer opinions based on "scientific, technical, or other specialized knowledge." Only experts may give opinions based on one of those grounds.

In many cases, lay opinions are easy to distinguish from expert ones. Opinions based on everyday observations and experience, such as the slipperiness of a sidewalk or the color of a getaway car, are lay opinions. A radiologist's diagnosis of

---

4   These facts are based on Kostelecky v. NL Acme Tool/NL Industries, Inc., 837 F.2d 828 (8th Cir. 1988).

cancer, an antique dealer's valuation of rare coins, and a pathologist's matching of DNA, on the other hand, are all expert opinions.

As always, however, there is a middle ground between these two extremes. People gain knowledge from a large variety of everyday experiences. A lay person who has smoked marijuana, for example, almost certainly would recognize the smell of that drug; people who have never smoked marijuana might not recognize its distinctive odor.

Judges allow lay witnesses to give opinions based upon their distinctive experiences, as long as those events don't reflect specialized training. The reference to "specialized knowledge" in Rule 701 does not prevent lay witnesses from using unusual, unique, or distinctive experiences to support their opinions. Instead, Rule 701's restrictive language excludes know-how gained through specialized training, education, or professional experience; only properly qualified experts may voice opinions based on that type of knowledge.

In addition to drawing upon a wide range of life experiences, lay witnesses may draw reasonable inferences from their experience; Rule 701 doesn't limit their testimony to simplistic conclusions. But lay witnesses must use a "process of reasoning familiar in everyday life." They cannot invoke "a process of reasoning which can be mastered only by specialists."[5]

Following these principles, courts have readily allowed lay opinions from homeowners testifying about the value of their own land;[6] franchise managers estimating the amount of profits lost from breach of the franchise agreement;[7] and eyewitnesses who observed that a defendant was drunk.[8] Here are two cases that raised closer questions about the admissibility of lay opinions:

Example: Isaac Huddleston was on trial for distributing cocaine. The government's star witness was Lawrence Moore, who had sold Huddleston cocaine for five months. After Moore was arrested, he agreed to cooperate with the government in the prosecution against Huddleston. At tri-

---

5   Fed. R. Evid. 701 advisory committee's note.

6   Kestenbaum v. Falstaff Brewing Corp., 514 F.2d 690, 698–99 (5th Cir. 1975).

7   Diesel Machinery, Inc. v B.R. Lee Industries, Inc., 328 F. Supp. 2d 1029, 1039 (D.S.D. 2003), aff'd, 418 F.3d 820 (8th Cir. 2005).

8   See Singletary v. Secretary of Health, Education & Welfare, 623 F.2d 217 (2d Cir. 1980).

al, Moore testified that he personally sold Huddleston narcotics and that Huddleston talked to him about buying drugs from other suppliers. The government also asked Moore to testify about the quality of the cocaine Huddleston purchased. Huddleston objected to this last piece of evidence, claiming that since Moore was not an expert, he could not give an opinion about the quality of the cocaine.

Analysis: The trial judge admitted Moore's lay opinion, and the court of appeals affirmed. Although an opinion about the quality of cocaine usually requires scientific expertise and specialized analysis, Moore's opinion was "rationally based on his perception." For an experienced narcotics trafficker, assessing the quality of cocaine requires neither scientific expertise nor specialized analysis.[9]

Example: In 1980, Darrell Lawson attempted to blackmail International Harvester Company. The company immediately called the FBI, then arranged a meeting with Lawson.

At the arranged meeting time, three undercover FBI agents met with Lawson, spoke with him for a few minutes, and gave him a briefcase full of money in exchange for some typewritten pages of information. At the end of the meeting, Lawson saw that one of the agents was carrying a gun; he pulled out his own gun and tried to shoot the FBI agents. The agents quickly subdued Lawson, and the government prosecuted him for his crimes.

At trial, Lawson presented an insanity defense. Both the government and the defense called expert witnesses to testify about whether or not Lawson was sane. In rebuttal, the government also asked the three FBI agents to testify that in their opinion, Lawson was sane at the time of the meeting. Lawson objected to the agents offering a lay opinion on his sanity.

Analysis: The trial court properly admitted the lay opinions of the FBI agents, even though they had only met the defendant once for a few minutes. Previous cases had allowed witnesses to offer lay opinions about a defendant's

---

9   This example is based on *United States v. Huddleston*, 810 F.2d 751, 754 (8th Cir. 1987).

sanity. Although cases decided before the codification of Rule 701 limited that testimony to witnesses who had known the defendant for a long time, the Federal Rules generally loosened the rules on admissibility. Under the circumstances of this case, the jury could decide what weight, if any, to give to the FBI agents' testimony.[10]

 The line between expert and lay opinions, like that between helpful and unhelpful opinions, is a fuzzy one. Advocacy that focuses on how the witness gained her knowledge may persuade the judge that the knowledge is either "specialized" or merely unusual.

3. Laying a Foundation. Before a lay witness gives an opinion based on particular knowledge, he must lay a foundation establishing that he has the information required to form the opinion. A lay witness who testifies that he smelled marijuana emanating from a car, for example, would first have to testify that he had smelled marijuana in the past and could recognize its smell. Similarly, a franchise manager estimating the lost profits to her company would first have to describe her familiarity with the business's financial records.

In this sense, lay opinion testimony is no different from any other testimony; under **Rule 602,** a witness may testify only about what she knows personally. When offering a lay opinion, a trial lawyer must establish that the witness has personal knowledge of both the opinion **and** of the facts it draws upon.

Example: Meraldo Lizardo, a Deputy Sherriff in Essex County, Massachusetts, was on trial for selling cocaine. Government agents had recorded numerous phone conversations between Lizardo and others involved in the drug trade. During these conversations, Lizardo frequently used code words and phrases, such as: "You know that's a federal" and "Have you talked to the tiger?"

One of Lizardo's primary purchasers, Tilson Yturrino, agreed to testify for the prosecution. As part of his testimony, Yturrino interpreted Lizardo's phone conversations for the jury. Lizardo, for example, explained that when Lizardo said, "You know that's a federal," he meant that federal

---

10   United States v. Lawson, 653 F.2d 299, 303–04 (7th Cir. 1981).

agents might investigate a transaction, leading to a broader, more aggressive inquiry. Lizardo's attorney objected to this testimony.

Analysis: Yturrino's opinion about the meaning of Lizardo's code words was proper lay opinion: It was "helpful to the jury," and it was not based on scientific or technical knowledge. While most lay witnesses would not know what Lizardo meant when he used these phrases, Yturrino's "first-hand familiarity with the surrounding events and conduct" demonstrated that he had sufficient personal knowledge to form a basis for this opinion. As the court noted: "Yturrino, as a co-conspirator, was present at or a participant in many conversations between [the cocaine supplier] and Lizardo. He was thus in a position to understand even the . . . conversations in which he was not a part."[11]

4. Experts Giving Lay Opinions. How firm is the line between lay witnesses and experts? Is it possible for a person with specialized training, who could appear as an expert, to give a lay opinion? Yes, the rules allow **any** witness with personal knowledge of an event to give a lay opinion related to that event. Experts may give lay opinions just like any other witness.

Litigants sometimes ask a highly qualified witness to give a lay opinion, rather than follow the special rules for qualifying that witness as an expert. In particular, a party may want to avoid disclosing the expert testimony before trial, as the Rules of Civil and Criminal Procedure require.[12] If the expert's testimony is sufficiently nontechnical, the party may choose to have the expert testify as a lay witness offering a lay opinion:

Example: Police stopped William LeCroy for driving a car with bald tires. While searching the car, police discovered a bloody knife and other evidence linking LeCroy to the murder of Joann Tiesler.

At LeCroy's homicide trial, Jeff Branyon testified for the government. Branyon was a police crime scene specialist who investigated Tiesler's murder. To help link the bloody knife found in LeCroy's car with the murder, Branyon testified that blood stains found on the victim's shirt "appeared

---

11   United States v. Lizardo, 445 F.3d 73, 83–84 (1st Cir. 2006).

12   Fed. R. Civ. P. 26; Fed. R. Crim. P. 16.

to have been made by someone wiping a bloody knife off on the shirt." LeCroy objected that Branyon's testimony was expert opinion that failed to comply with the required discovery rules for experts.

Analysis: The appellate court upheld admission of Branyon's testimony about the blood stain, concluding that it was based on Branyon's ordinary perception rather than scientific or technical knowledge. "Just because Agent Branyon's position and experience could have qualified him for expert witness status," the court concluded, "does not mean that any testimony he gives at trial is considered 'expert testimony.' In this case, Branyon made layperson observations about the shirt and knife."[13]

A witness offering a lay opinion, however, cannot stray into giving an expert opinion until she is first qualified as an expert.

Example: The United States prosecuted Raul Figueroa-Lopez for possession of cocaine with the intent to distribute. As part of its case, the government called both drug and immigration agents who had investigated Lopez. All of the agents were experienced narcotics officers who had the experience and training to testify as experts. The government, however, did not qualify any of the agents as experts. Instead, the agents offered lay opinions that:

(1) Lopez's car moved in a "suspicious" manner;

(2) Lopez engaged in "countersurveillance" driving;

(3) Lopez used code words for drug deals during his conversations;

(4) Lopez's use of a rental car and the way he hid the cocaine (in the car's door panels) were consistent with the practices of experienced drug dealers; and

(5) The quantity and purity of Lopez's cocaine indicated that he was "close to the source of the cocaine."

---

13   United States v. LeCroy, 441 F.3d 914, 927 (11th Cir. 2006).

The defense objected to all of the statements as improper lay opinions.

Analysis: The court of appeals agreed that most of the agents' testimony was improper as lay opinion. The statement about Lopez's "suspicious" driving was permissible lay opinion because it "related to matters 'common enough' to qualify" for Rule 701. Any bystander watching Lopez's car might have labeled his driving suspicious. But all of the other opinions voiced by the witnesses required specialized knowledge. A lay person, for example, would not know that driving a rental car or hiding cocaine in the car's door panels was evidence of an "experienced drug dealer."

The distinction was important because the government had not followed the required disclosure procedures for expert witnesses. Those procedures, the court noted, are critical to ensure that the opposing party has "a fair opportunity to test the merit of the expert's testimony through focused cross-examination." Thus, the trial judge improperly admitted the statements as lay opinions.[14]

Note that the decision in Figueroa-Lopez differs from two of the examples described above. The court in Figueroa-Lopez found that deciphering code words was an expert matter, while the court in Lizardo permitted a lay opinion on that issue. Similarly, the Figueroa-Lopez court held that an opinion about cocaine quality drew on expert knowledge, while the Huddleston court allowed a lay witness to testify on the same matter.

In part, these differences represent the leeway trial judges have when applying the Rules of Evidence. The meaning of code words and the quality of cocaine are both opinions that fall in a gray area between lay and expert opinion.

More important, the judicial decisions differ because of **who offered** the testimony and **how they reached** their opinion. The agents in Figueroa-Lopez were trained as experts, while the witnesses in Lizardo and Huddleston were drug dealers who gained their insights in the field. Allowing government trained experts to offer lay opinions belied the nature of their knowledge and permitted the government to escape the procedural rules governing expert opinion. When an expert attempts

---

14   United States v. Figueroa-Lopez, 125 F.3d 1241, 1246 (9th Cir. 1997).

to testify as a lay witness, judges may draw a stricter line between expert and lay opinions.

Quick Summary

Lay witnesses may voice opinions about what they perceived, especially when their opinions are the most helpful way to convey information to the jury. Examples include qualitative descriptions of distance, size, or brightness, as well as the expressions on people's faces. Lay opinions must be based on personal observation, and the witness must use ordinary reasoning in order to form the opinion. The lay opinion must also be helpful to the jury.

Lay opinions cannot draw upon technical, scientific, or specialized knowledge; to offer these opinions, a witness must qualify as an expert. Lay witnesses, however, may base their opinions on unusual life experiences, as long as the knowledge is non-technical and the attorney lays a foundation demonstrating the witness's particular experience.

Even experts have "lay" opinions and may testify as lay witnesses rather than qualifying as experts. Under those circumstances, however, the witness may not volunteer opinions based on her professional expertise.

Test Your Understanding

To assess your understanding of the material in this chapter, click here to take a quiz, or go to the Quizzes module from the eBook on your eProducts bookshelf.

61

What Subjects Are Appropriate
for Expert Testimony?

Key Concepts

- **Rule 702:** Admission of Expert Testimony
- Judge Serves as Gatekeeper
- Flexible Inquiry Into Reliability, Fit, and Unfair Prejudice
- ***Daubert*** Factors: Non-Exclusive Criteria for Assessing Reliability
- Rule Applies to All Types of Expertise
- ***Daubert*** Hearings

A. Introduction and Policy. Lay witnesses offer opinions rooted in their personal experience and perceptions. Expert witnesses, on the other hand, give testimony based on their "scientific, technical, or other specialized knowledge." That phrase encompasses a wide range of fields, from acrobatics to zoonosis, that may produce courtroom evidence.[1]

The very breadth of expert knowledge, however, poses a problem for courts. Jurors usually lack training in the technical field supporting an expert opinion. How, then, can jurors weigh the value of the expert's testimony? If a party presents a witness claiming expertise in "xanthomorphology," how does the jury know if such a field even exists? Is the witness the only xanthomorphologist in the world? How do xanthomorphologists arrive at their conclusions?[2]

---

1   Zoonosis is the process of transmitting infectious disease from animals to humans.

2   As far as we know, xanthomorphology is an imaginary field that we invented for illustration.

Judges could admit the testimony of all purported experts, allowing opposing counsel to expose any charlatans on cross-examination. But jurors tend to trust "expert" witnesses, especially if the expert sports a lengthy resume and uses sophisticated jargon. The Federal Rules of Evidence, therefore, impose a gatekeeping function on trial judges. Before allowing the expert to testify, the judge must determine that both the field of expertise and the expert's application of that knowledge are reliable.

Reliable, of course, is an amorphous term. How does a trial judge know that a scientific, technical, or other specialized field is reliable? For much of the twentieth century, judges measured reliability by asking whether the principle underlying an expert's opinion was "sufficiently established to have gained general acceptance in the particular field in which it belongs." This "general acceptance" test stemmed from *Frye v. United States*,[3] a 1923 case in which the Court of Appeals for the District of Columbia Circuit rejected a polygraph test as unreliable.

The *Frye* test established a bright line and was relatively simple for courts to apply; a judge merely looked to the members of a scientific or technical field to determine whether a witness's approach was generally accepted within that field, and then followed their lead. It also seemed sensible for judges to defer to experts in a given field to determine whether a scientific principle or method was sound.

The *Frye* test came under some criticism, however. Although it is true that scientists are well qualified to determine whether a certain principle is generally accepted in scientific fields, this is not the only criterion that should matter when deciding whether to admit scientific testimony. **Rules 401** and **403** set out specific tests for balancing relevance with undue prejudice or confusion, and it is the trial judge, not a community of scientists, that is best able to determine whether any type of evidence is admissible under these tests.

With this in mind, in 1993 the Supreme Court announced a new test for determining the reliability of expert testimony. In *Daubert v. Merrell Dow Pharmaceuticals*,[4] the Court stressed that judges, not a closed circle of experts, determine the reliability of expert testimony. To decide whether testimony is reliable, the Court suggested, judges should consider factors such as:

---

3   293 F. 1013, 1013 (D.C. Cir. 1923).

4   509 U.S. 579 (1993).

- Whether the theory or technique has been tested

- Whether it has been subject to peer review and publication

- The technique's error rate

- The existence of standards controlling the technique's application

- Whether the theory or technique has been generally accepted in the relevant scientific community

We discuss these factors further below. For now, note that the final *Daubert* factor incorporates Frye's general acceptance test. *Daubert* differs from *Frye* because the Court ruled that general acceptance no longer controls admissibility; it is merely one factor that the trial judge may consider. The Court, moreover, stressed that even these enumerated factors are not exhaustive; judges may consider any factor useful in determining "the scientific validity—and thus the evidentiary relevance and reliability—of the principles that underlie" proposed expert testimony.[5]

The Supreme Court based its *Daubert* decision on its interpretation of Rule 702, the primary rule governing expert testimony. Congress, the Court held, intended to loosen the *Frye* standard when it adopted the Federal Rules of Evidence. Congress confirmed that interpretation in 2000 by amending Rule 702 to conform further with the Supreme Court's *Daubert* ruling. The federal courts, therefore, all follow *Daubert*'s approach to judging the reliability of expert testimony.

Most state courts have also switched from the *Frye* test to *Daubert*. But some states continue to apply the *Frye* test, so you may hear about that test in practice. Remember that the difference between *Frye* (the old federal rule) and *Daubert* (the current federal approach) is this:

The ***Frye* rule** allowed scientists and other experts to set the bounds of reliability within their fields. Courts admitted expert testimony based on whether the expert's approach had gained "general acceptance" within the field.

Daubert shifts this gatekeeping role to judges. The trial judge now decides whether an expert's approach is sufficiently reliable to present to the jury. In

---

5   Id. at 594–95.

making that decision, the judge relies upon a variety of factors that include—but are not limited to—general acceptance.

 For a further explanation of the shift from *Frye* to *Daubert*, click here to see the video "Expert Testimony—Frye and Daubert" or access the Video module via the eBook on your eproducts bookshelf.

B. The Rule. Rule 702 packs half a dozen concepts into a relatively brief text. We will devote several chapters to exploring fully the implications of this rule. But first, let's look at the complete rule:

RULE 702. Testimony by Expert Witnesses

A witness who is <u>qualified as an expert</u> by knowledge, skill, experience, training, or education may testify in the form of an opinion or otherwise if:

(a) the expert's <u>scientific, technical, or other specialized knowledge</u> will <u>help</u> the trier of fact to understand the evidence or to determine a fact in issue;

(b) the testimony is based on <u>sufficient facts or data</u>;

(c) the testimony is the product of <u>reliable principles and methods</u>; and

(d) the expert has <u>reliably applied the principles and methods</u> to the facts of the case.

The underlined text refers to **six different principles** related to expert testimony. First, the court must find that the **witness qualifies** as an expert before the witness offers an opinion on technical or scientific matters. We will examine the process of qualifying an expert in the next chapter.

Second, Rule 702 repeats **Rule 701**'s **definition of expert** testimony. An expert is a witness who offers "scientific, technical, or other specialized knowledge."

As we saw in the last chapter, the distinction between this type of expert knowledge and lay opinions sometimes is elusive. The important point for interpreting
Rule 702 is that, if the judge rules that a witness's testimony invokes scientific,
technical, or other specialized knowledge, then the requirements of Rule 702 apply.

Third, expert testimony must "**help the trier of fact**." This language is similar
to Rule 701's requirement that lay opinions be "helpful" to the fact finder, but the
language has additional implications when applied to experts. A party may not
offer an expert opinion, no matter how valid the underlying science, if the expert's
perspective doesn't fit the facts of the case. Testimony that asbestos causes lung
disease, for example, won't help the fact finder if the plaintiff can't prove that she
was exposed to asbestos.

This "fit" requirement is stricter than mere relevance. Courts don't want parties
to distract the jury with complex scientific testimony that relates to a tangential
issue. Nor will they allow parties to present expert evidence to support one premise
of an argument when another premise lacks scientific support. Astronomers, for
example, understand many facets of the moon's phases. But, as the Supreme Court
colorfully suggested in *Daubert*, a defendant could not present detailed testimony
about lunar phases in order to argue that he acted irrationally when the moon
was full. We will explore other, more common applications of the fit requirement
in the Courtroom section.

Fourth, the expert's testimony must rest on "**sufficient facts or data.**" We will
discuss this condition in Chapter 63 when we explore the bases of expert opinion.

Finally, Rule 702 imposes two reliability hurdles that all expert testimony must
surmount: (1) The testimony must be "the product of **reliable principles and
methods**," and (2) The witness must have "**reliably** applied the principles and
methods **to the facts** of the case." We will discuss these two reliability requirements at length in the next section.

C. In the Courtroom.
In the remainder of this chapter, we explore three
key restrictions on expert testimony: reliable principles, reliable application, and
fit. We also examine the diversity of fields governed by these restrictions and the
interplay of the restrictions with **Rule 403**'s balancing test. All of these considerations affect the admission of expert testimony, especially when that testimony
adopts controversial positions.

1. Reliable Principles. Rule 702 demands that an expert base her testimony on "reliable principles and methods." A party, in other words, must be able to point to the principles and methods underlying an expert's testimony, and those principles and methods must satisfy *Daubert*'s reliability test.

Many types of expert testimony readily satisfy this first requirement. A radiologist, for example, might have diagnosed a plaintiff's lung cancer. The radiologist's opinion rests on scientific knowledge; a lay person could not recognize the signs of lung cancer on an x-ray. The scientific knowledge supporting the radiologist's diagnosis, moreover, easily satisfies all of the criteria mentioned by the Supreme Court in *Daubert*:

> • The technique of using x-rays to diagnose lung cancer has been tested repeatedly by comparing x-ray diagnoses to surgical results.
>
> • The technique has been discussed in countless peer reviewed publications.
>
> • When a tumor is visible on a lung x-ray, it almost always is cancerous; researchers have determined the false-negative and false-positive rates of x-ray diagnosis.
>
> • Radiologists follow recognized standards in distinguishing lung tumors from other images on an x-ray.
>
> • Radiologists and treating physicians generally accept x-ray identification as the first step in diagnosing lung cancer.

The principles underlying an expert's testimony do not have to satisfy all of the factors listed in *Daubert*. But many types of testimony, like this one, easily satisfy all of the indicia of reliability.

The *Daubert* test was designed to address more difficult cases. Many medical and scientific controversies affect litigation. Do cell phones cause brain tumors? Do polygraph machines accurately detect lies? How do trial judges assess the reliability of principles underlying expert testimony on issues like this? The facts in *Daubert* itself illustrate Rule 702's approach to reliability:

Example: Joyce Daubert took Bendectin, an anti-nausea drug manufactured by Merrell Dow Pharmaceuticals, while she was pregnant. After her son was born with severe birth defects, Joyce claimed that Bendectin caused the injuries; she and her family sued Merrell Dow. At trial, Merrell Dow showed that all of the published research on Bendectin—involving more than 130,000 patients in over 30 studies—found no link between the drug and birth defects.

In response, the Dauberts offered testimony from eight experts who had reanalyzed the data in the published studies. Based on these reanalyses, the plaintiffs' experts contended that Bendectin could cause birth defects. The trial judge, however, excluded this testimony because it did not reflect generally accepted principles. On the contrary, as the defendant's expert had testified, published studies on Bendectin unanimously rejected a possible link between the drug and human birth defects.

Analysis: By discarding exclusive reliance on the "general acceptance" test, the Supreme Court gave the Dauberts an opportunity to demonstrate the reliability of their experts' reanalysis of the published data. The Court's more flexible test allowed the Dauberts to try to convince the lower court that other factors, such as the existence of standards controlling their experts' approach, rendered their expert testimony reliable. Sometimes the established wisdom about a drug is wrong; Rule 702 and the *Daubert* opinion allowed the plaintiffs to try to identify sufficiently reliable testimony to make that case.[6]

Daubert, however, does not require trial judges to admit all proffered evidence on a scientific issue; the opinion did not write a blank check for any witness claiming to be an expert. Instead, when parties offer novel or controversial scientific perspectives, *Daubert* and Rule 702 charge trial judges with the difficult task of probing those perspectives to determine whether they have sufficient indicia of reliability to reach the jury.[7]

---

6   Daubert, 509 U.S. 579.

7   Judge Kozynski, writing on remand in Daubert, described this role with some incredulity: "Our responsibility . . . is to resolve disputes among respected, well-credentialed scientists about matters squarely within their expertise, in areas where there is no scientific consensus as to what is and what is not 'good science,' and occasionally to reject such expert testimony because it was not 'derived by the scientific method.' " Daubert v. Merrell Dow Pharms., 43 F.3d 1311, 1316 (9th Cir. 1995). Despite this skepticism, judges have taken on the task.

Despite *Daubert*'s flexible test, trial judges reject many types of expert testimony as unreliable. Courts, for example, have continued to exclude evidence purporting to find a connection between Bendectin and birth defects.[8] Here is another example of testimony that failed to satisfy *Daubert*'s standard:

Example: James O'Conner was a pipefitter who worked at a Commonwealth Edison nuclear power plant. O'Conner claimed that he was exposed to excessive doses of radiation at work and that the radiation caused cataracts in his eyes. He sued Commonwealth Edison for his injuries.

Commonwealth Edison moved for summary judgment, arguing that there was no evidence that radiation caused O'Conner's cataracts. In response, O'Conner submitted affidavits from Dr. Karl Scheribel, the physician who diagnosed his cataracts. Scheribel claimed that he was able to identify cataracts caused by radiation simply by inspecting the cataracts. The medical articles Scheribel cited to support his method, however, showed just the opposite: Those authors concluded that visual inspection alone could not distinguish radiation-induced cataracts from other cataracts. Nor was Scheribel able to cite any other evidence supporting his approach. He had treated only 5 patients with radiation-induced cataracts during his 20 years of practice, and he had conducted no studies demonstrating the reliability of his method.

Analysis: The trial court rejected Scheribel's affidavits and granted summary judgment for Commonwealth Edison. The appellate court affirmed, agreeing that Scheribel's method "had no basis in scientific fact." Scheribel had conducted no tests to prove his method; nor did any published studies support it. And Scheribel appeared to be the only doctor applying his method; no scientific community had accepted his technique. Under *Daubert*, Scheribel's method lacked reliability.[9]

Conversely, courts admit many types of evidence that researchers question. A 2009 report by the National Research Council of the National Academies, *Strengthening Forensic Science in the United States: A Path Forward*, challenges the validity of some

---

8   See, e.g., Wilson v. Merrell Dow Pharms., 160 F.3d 625 (10th Cir. 1998); Daubert v. Merrell Dow Pharms., 43 F.3d 1311 (9th Cir. 1995) (on remand from the Supreme Court's decision).

9   O'Conner v. Commonwealth Edison Co., 13 F.3d 1090, 1106 (7th Cir. 1994).

traditional forensic techniques like fingerprint analysis. Many of these techniques, the report notes, have developed without controlled studies validating them. The report recommends that scientists build a stronger foundation supporting these techniques; it also cautions that expert witnesses should more clearly acknowledge the limits of their techniques when testifying. Only limited progress has been made: A 2016 report from the President's Council of Advisors on Science and Technology, *Forensic Science in Criminal Courts*, reiterates many of the same concerns.

2. Reliable Application. Rule 702 requires two types of reliability: (a) reliable principles underlying the expert's approach, and (b) reliable application of those principles to the facts of the case. Most appellate opinions focus on the first type of reliability, but the second type is equally important in practice. If a pathologist fails to follow established protocols for testing a sample, the trial judge may reject the pathologist's testimony as unreliable. Courtroom attorneys, therefore, must pay as much attention to the manner in which their experts apply scientific principles as to the principles themselves.

Example: Eduarda Alves was injured in a low-speed collision while driving a Mazda automobile. The Mazda's airbag deployed and hit Alves in the eyes, blinding her. Alves sued Mazda, claiming that the airbag should not have deployed at low speeds. In response to Mazda's motion for summary judgment, Alves offered affidavits from two engineers, Ralph Ridgeway and Thomas Lacek. Ridgeway and Lacek both examined photos of Alves's accident and, based on a published method developed by Kenneth Campbell, concluded that Alves was traveling slower than 10 miles per hour when the crash occurred. Mazda argued that the expert opinions were unreliable.

Analysis: The district judge concluded that Ridgeway and Lacek had sufficient experience to offer opinions on accident reconstruction. Campbell's model for estimating speeds, moreover, appeared to be reliable under *Daubert*. In his publications, however, Campbell explicitly noted that the model was valid only for cars traveling 15–60 miles per hour and that the model's accuracy decreased as speed declined from 30 miles per hour to 15. Since Alves's experts applied this model to a car they claimed was traveling at less than 10 miles per hour, they did not apply the model reliably to the facts of the case. The judge excluded the affidavits and granted summary judgment for the defendant.[10]

3. Supplementing the *Daubert* Factors. In *Daubert*, the Supreme Court listed five factors that courts might consider when assessing the reliability of expert evidence. The Court, however, stressed that these factors were not exclusive; judges should consider **any** factor illuminating the reliability of expert testimony.

Lower courts have taken the Court at its word, weighing numerous other criteria to determine reliability. One factor cited by several courts is whether the expert developed an idiosyncratic approach specifically for the litigated controversy or as part of a broader program of research. On remand in *Daubert*, for example, the court of appeals noted that none of the plaintiffs' experts had engaged in independent research on Bendectin and birth defects. Nor had any of the experts attempted to publish their innovative analyses of the Bendectin data. These facts contributed to the court's perception that "what's going on here is not science at all, but litigation."[11]

Conversely, the fact that an expert's courtroom testimony parallels opinions offered in other contexts may weigh in favor of reliability:

Example: The Ambrosini family sued the Upjohn Company, claiming that a drug Mrs. Ambrosini had used caused birth defects in their daughter Teresa. In response to Upjohn's motion for summary judgment, the Ambrosinis offered an affidavit from Dr. Goldman, an expert in the biology of birth defects. Goldman stated his opinion that the drug taken by Teresa's mother caused the child's birth defects. The trial judge rejected this affidavit, ruling that Goldman's testimony derived from unreliable scientific principles.

Analysis: The court of appeals reversed, finding that Goldman's opinion was sufficiently reliable. In addition to discussing the factors outlined in *Daubert*, the court noted that the Food and Drug Administration had invited Dr. Goldman to testify at a public hearing about the risk of birth defects

---

10   Alves v. Mazda Motor of America, Inc., 448 F. Supp. 2d 285, 298–99 (D. Mass. 2006).

11   Daubert v. Merrell Dow Pharms., 43 F.3d 1311, 1318 (9th Cir. 1995).

associated with the same drug taken by Mrs. Ambrosini. The fact that Goldman testified about this risk "in a public hearing, without any connection to the Ambrosinis' litigation," the court suggested, "reduces concerns that Dr. Goldman is simply 'a gun for hire.' "[12]

 The factors listed in *Daubert* remain central. If an attorney can make his case for reliability based on those factors, that is the safest avenue toward admitting expert testimony. On the other hand, a party need not satisfy all of the *Daubert* criteria to show that evidence is reliable, and courts remain open to considering new factors. Successful trial lawyers try to understand as much as possible about the science supporting an expert's testimony, so that they can make the best case for admitting that evidence.

4. Does the Expert Evidence Fit? Even if expert evidence passes *Daubert*'s two reliability tests, the evidence may fail another test articulated in Rule 702. The evidence must "help the trier of fact" or, as the Court declared in *Daubert*, must "fit" the facts of the case.

Judges often allow parties to present lay evidence that bears only tangentially on a dispute. **Rule 401**'s relevance standard is quite low, allowing parties to introduce evidence that has "any tendency to make a fact more or less probable."[13] If the jury finds lay evidence unhelpful, they can simply disregard it.

Greater risks arise if the minimally relevant evidence comes from experts. The jury may believe that a complex professional opinion resolves a key factual dispute, when the opinion relates only to a minor subpoint. Or the jurors may have difficulty understanding that an expert opinion is relevant only if they first find that a predicate fact exists.[14] For these reasons, judges exercise more control over the "fit" between expert evidence and the facts in a case. In the words of Rule 702, a judge will admit expert evidence only if it will "help the trier of fact to understand

---

12   Ambrosini v. Labarraque, 101 F.3d 129, 139 (D.C. Cir. 1996). The contested drug in Ambrosini was De-po-Provera. During the 1960s, when Mrs. Ambrosini used the drug, it was prescribed to prevent miscarriages. The FDA revoked approval of the drug for those purposes in 1970, in part because of concerns about birth defects. In 1992, the FDA approved Depo-Provera for use as a contraceptive, its primary use today.

13   See Chapter 6 to review application of this standard.

14   See Chapter 34 for further discussion of this concept.

the evidence or to determine a fact in issue." Unless the expert testimony fits the case well, it may not help the jury.

The fit requirement sometimes leads courts to reject expert evidence related to causation. On remand from the Supreme Court's decision in *Daubert*, for example, the court of appeals held that the *Dauberts'* proffered testimony did not fit the legal principles of their case. The court interpreted controlling tort law to require the plaintiffs to show that Bendectin more than doubled the risk of birth defects. Even assuming that the plaintiffs' expert testimony was reliable, the experts did not claim this great a risk from Bendectin. Thus, the court concluded that the *Dauberts'* expert testimony would not help the jury in determining any relevant facts.[15]

Sometimes the parties lack sufficient information to support a confident expert opinion. This often happens in medical malpractice cases, in which the patient's continued deterioration or death prevents the parties from identifying earlier states of a disease or injury. If an expert lacks essential information to reach an accurate conclusion, the court may exclude the expert's testimony as unhelpful:

Example: Manual Porter fractured his big toe at work. His doctors prescribed ibuprofen, a common pain reliever, while Porter awaited surgery to reset the bone in his toe. Shortly after his course of ibuprofen and toe surgery, Porter developed kidney failure. The rapidity of his kidney failure required a transplant. Even with a transplant, however, Porter died within a few years. Porter (and then his estate) sued the drug companies that manufactured ibuprofen, claiming the drug caused his kidney failure.

To show that the ibuprofen caused his kidney failure, Porter submitted affidavits from several experts. The trial judge, however, excluded these affidavits under *Daubert* and granted summary judgment for the drug companies.

Analysis: The court of appeals affirmed, finding several defects in the experts' testimony. Dr. Benjamin's testimony, for example, did not satisfy *Daubert*'s fit requirement. Benjamin, a pharmacologist, admitted that he could determine whether ibuprofen caused Porter's kidney failure only if he knew whether Porter was taking any other medications at the time, if he knew more about

---

15   Daubert v. Merrell Dow Pharms., 43 F.3d 1311, 1319 (9th Cir. 1995). One of the plaintiffs' experts was willing to estimate a higher risk from Bendectin, but the court found that expert unreliable.

Porter's overall health, and if he was able to rule out various environmental factors that contribute to kidney failure. Since the parties were unable to supply this information, the court concluded that Benjamin's testimony did not fit the facts of the case.[16]

With lay testimony, the evidentiary rules allow jurors to decide how well a witness's testimony fits the controversy. Unless lay testimony lacks any basis in personal knowledge, courts allow the jury to determine the helpfulness of that evidence. With expert witnesses, Rule 702 requires the judge to exercise greater control over this decision. If the testimony draws upon scientific or technical principles, the jury may not be able to see gaps between those principles and the facts of the case.

5. Rule 403. In *Daubert*, the Supreme Court pointed to yet another barrier shielding the jury from potentially misleading evidence: **Rule 403**. That rule requires the trial judge to exclude any evidence when the danger of unfair prejudice, confusion of the issues, or misleading the jury substantially outweighs the evidence's probative value.[17] Quoting Judge Weinstein, a well-regarded authority on evidence, the *Daubert* Court observed: "Expert evidence can be both powerful and quite misleading because of the difficulty in evaluating it. Because of this risk, the judge in weighing possible prejudice against probative force under Rule 403 of the present rules exercises more control over experts than over lay witnesses."[18]

Rule 403, therefore, forms the third step in a three-part analysis that many courts undertake when assessing expert evidence:

(1)   Is the evidence reliable, both in its underlying principles and its application to the case?

(2)   Does the evidence fit the case and help the trier of fact?

(3)   Even if the evidence satisfies these requirements, does the danger of unfair prejudice, confusion, or misleading the jury substantially outweigh the probative value?

---

16   Porter v. Whitehall Lab., 9 F.3d 607, 613–17 (7th Cir. 1993).

17   See Chapter 7 for a general discussion of Rule 403.

18   Daubert, 509 U.S. at 595 (quoting Jack B. Weinstein, Rule 702 of the Federal Rules of Evidence Is Sound; It Should Not Be Amended, 138 F.R.D. 631, 632 (1991)).

These three questions do not exhaust a court's evaluation of expert evidence. As we will see in Chapters 62–64, parties may also raise questions about a particular expert's qualifications, the basis of the expert's testimony, and whether the expert has offered an opinion that is too conclusive. We will explore those issues separately. For now, focus on these three questions as the heart of a court's *"Daubert"* inquiry.

6. Technical and Other Specialized Knowledge. The *Daubert* case focused on scientific testimony from medicine and the biological sciences. Much of the Court's discussion seemed to envision expert testimony from other natural sciences. During the years after *Daubert*, lower courts questioned whether *Daubert's* approach governed evaluation of other types of expert witnesses, such as accountants testifying about business practices, auto mechanics explaining car repairs, or farmers describing crop cultivation. Witnesses like these draw upon "technical or other specialized knowledge," but they often develop their insights without publication, peer review, or controlled studies.

Today, it is clear that *Daubert's* gatekeeping approach applies to **all types** of expert testimony. The Supreme Court announced this decision in *Kumho Tire Company v. Carmichael,*[19] and Congress amended Rule 702 in 2000 to codify that result. The criteria that a court considers when assessing reliability, however, may vary depending on the type of expert evidence at issue. The facts and decision in *Kumho Tire* illustrate this:

> **Example:** Patrick Carmichael was driving a minivan when its right rear tire blew out, causing an accident that killed one of his passengers. Carmichael sued Kumho Tire, the tire manufacturer, claiming its product was defective.
>
> Carmichael relied upon the testimony of an engineer, Dennis Carlson, Jr., as an expert in "tire failure analysis." Carlson testified that a blowout occurs when the outer tread of a tire separates from the inner steel-belted carcass of the tire. Carlson claimed that this separation could occur for only one of two reasons: underinflation of the tire by the user or a manufacturing defect. Carlson then testified that he had inspected the remains

---

19   526 U.S. 137 (1999).

of Carmichael's tire and found no significant signs of underinflation. Therefore, he concluded, the tire must have blown out because of a defect.

Kumho Tire disputed both Carlson's claim that a blowout occurs for only one of two reasons and his method of determining underinflation from the tire's remains. The trial court agreed with these critiques and excluded Carlson's testimony as unreliable. Applying the *Daubert* factors, the trial judge concluded that Carlson's method had not been subject to peer review or publication, had no known rate of error, and was not generally accepted in the relevant scientific community. Carmichael appealed, arguing that the judge had been too "inflexible" in applying *Daubert*.

Analysis: The Supreme Court confirmed that *Daubert* applies to every type of expert testimony, not just scientific testimony. Judges, therefore, must act as gatekeepers examining technical evidence like Carlson's testimony. The factors set out in *Daubert*, however, were flexible guidelines rather than a rigid test. The trial judge, the Court concluded, has considerable discretion in deciding how to test an expert's reliability. This is particularly true for technical or other specialized knowledge that falls outside traditional scientific fields.

In some cases, the Court suggested, it may be appropriate to apply one or two of the *Daubert* factors to a non-scientific expert. For example, if an engineer uses a method that she developed from her own experience, a judge could ask how often the method produces an erroneous conclusion. Or, if a court evaluates a perfume tester purporting to identify perfume aromas, the court might inquire whether the witness's method is generally accepted by other perfume testers. For some experts, the Court acknowledged, the *Daubert* factors may offer no help at all. Under those circumstances, the trial judge must determine other methods of assessing reliability, looking to the particular field of expertise.

The Court, finally, concluded that the trial judge applied a sufficiently flexible standard in evaluating Carlson's testimony and that the judge did not abuse his discretion when excluding the testimony. In addition to failing all of the criteria set out in *Daubert*, Carlson's method demanded more signs of underinflation than methods used by other tire failure analysts; his testimony was internally inconsistent; and his conclusions stemmed from a somewhat cursory examination of the tire. Carlson's method, in sum, failed to satisfy either *Daubert*'s factors or any other set of reasonable reliability criteria.[20]

 Introducing or challenging expert testimony under Rule 702 requires very fact specific arguments. Trial attorneys must probe the methods used by their experts, as well as those of the opponent. Understanding the expert's method, its relation to methods used by other experts in the field, and application of the technique to the disputed facts allows the attorney to craft arguments that will persuade the trial judge.

7. *Daubert* Hearings. A judge's evaluation of scientific or technical evidence can be time consuming; the parties, moreover, may present witnesses supporting or attacking the proposed evidence. Judges, therefore, frequently evaluate the reliability, fit, and potential prejudice of expert testimony in a pretrial proceeding known as a *Daubert* hearing. *Daubert* hearings sometimes dispose of a case. In many medical malpractice or product liability actions, for example, the plaintiff relies upon expert testimony to show breach of duty or causation. If an expert's testimony does not survive the *Daubert* hearing, the plaintiff may lack sufficient evidence to go to trial. Similarly, a negative *Daubert* ruling may substantially weaken a prosecution case built on disputed laboratory evidence or a criminal defense based on a novel psychiatric syndrome. As with other rules of evidence, application of Rule 702 may make or break a party's case.

8. Was There a Revolution? Many attorneys and judges viewed *Daubert* as a revolution in the rules governing expert testimony. Practitioners feared that *Daubert* might open courtrooms to junk science and untested theories. Judges worried that they would have to master endless scientific details to apply a more open-ended test than the *Frye* "general acceptance" standard.

But *Daubert*'s revolution was not as dramatic as it first seemed. Lawyers and judges have had to learn more about some scientific and technical evidence presented in court, but that change stems both from *Daubert* and from the rapid proliferation of scientific knowledge. For well established scientific and technical methods, *Daubert* poses few problems; if a method is generally accepted, as *Frye* required, opponents may not even challenge the testimony's reliability.

---

20   Id. at 158.

For more controversial techniques, there is some evidence that *Daubert* **diminished** admissibility rather than enhancing it. Many judges tend to be conservative, and so perhaps less likely than scientists to approve of new scientific principles or methods. By stressing the trial judge's gatekeeper function, and encouraging judges to identify factors defining reliability, *Daubert* made some judges more skeptical of expert claims.

Quick Summary

 Rule 702 determines what types of "scientific, technical, or other specialized knowledge" will support expert testimony. That rule, together with the Supreme Court's pivotal decision in *Daubert v. Merrell Dow Pharmaceuticals*, requires courts to serve as gatekeepers for all types of expert testimony. Before admitting any challenged expert testimony, the trial judge must make several determinations. The three discussed in this chapter are:

1. That the proffered testimony is **reliable**.

2. That the testimony will assist the fact finder by **fitting** the facts of the case.

3. That the possibility of **unfair prejudice, confusion, or misleading** the jury does not substantially outweigh the testimony's probative value.

The first condition, reliability, includes two different requirements: (a) The testimony must rest on reliable scientific principles or methods, and (b) The expert must have applied those principles and methods reliably to the facts.

When assessing reliability, the trial judge may apply some or all of the criteria articulated in *Daubert*:

1. Whether the theory or technique has been tested.

2. Whether it has been subject to peer review and publication.

3. Whether the technique has a recognized error rate and, if so, what that rate is.

4. Whether standards control use of the technique.

5. Whether the theory or technique has been generally accepted in the relevant professional community.

Courts, however, may expand upon these criteria. Varying types of expert evidence require different factors to assess reliability. *Daubert* promotes a flexible approach in which the judge serves as a buffer between the jury and dubious technical or scientific methods. To implement that approach, judges sometimes hold a pretrial *Daubert* hearing to determine the admissibility of scientific testimony.

The flow chart on the next page summarizes these aspects of Rule 702.

Test Your Understanding

 To assess your understanding of the material in this chapter, click here to take a quiz, or go to the Quizzes module from the eBook on your eProducts bookshelf.

Rule 702: The Pathway Through the Expert Evidence Gate

Is the evidence based on **scientific, technical, or other specialized** knowledge? If so, **Rule 702** applies.

↓

The trial judge serves as a **gatekeeper**, shielding the jury from potentially misleading or prejudicial evidence. This purpose controls the flexible inquiry outlined below.

↓

Are the principles and methods supporting the evidence **reliable**? Use the following *Daubert* criteria as guidelines, but look to other factors if appropriate for the field:
- Prior testing of the technique or theory
- Peer review and publication
- Error rate
- Controlling standards
- General acceptance

↓

Has the technique been **reliably applied**?

↓

Does the evidence **fit the facts** of the case? Will it help the fact finder?

↓

Is the evidence excludable under **Rule 403**? Do unfair prejudice, confusion, or potential to mislead jury substantially outweigh probative value?

↓

Proffered evidence that clears these hurdles is an **appropriate subject** for expert testimony.

62

Qualifying Experts

A. Introduction and Policy. Rule 702 and *Daubert* instruct trial judges to act as gatekeepers for expert testimony. That task, as we saw in the last chapter, can be a difficult one. But even if the judge approves an expert technique, or the technique is so well established that an opponent doesn't challenge it, a party must still find a witness to bring that information to court. Your Uncle Bob can't just read books on knee surgery and discuss the matter with the jury; a witness presenting expert evidence must be "qualified" as an expert in the field. This chapter explores the process of qualifying an expert witness to testify in court.

B. The Rule. The rules of evidence provide few details about how to qualify expert witnesses. **Rule 702**, which we examined in the previous chapter, offers the only guidance on this point:

> ## RULE 702. Testimony by Expert Witnesses
>
> A witness who is <u>qualified as an expert</u> by <u>knowledge, skill, experience, training, or education</u> may testify in the form of an opinion or otherwise if . . . .

This rule clarifies two points about expert witnesses. **First,** a witness must in fact be qualified before offering evidence about "scientific, technical, or other specialized knowledge."

Second, the witness may establish her qualifications by pointing to a number of different factors: her knowledge, skill, experience, training, or education. The Federal Rules allow witnesses to demonstrate their expertise on any of these grounds. Many experts possess formal degrees in their field, but education is not essential to qualify as a witness. Other forms of training, experience, skill, or knowledge may suffice.

C. In the Courtroom.

1. How to Qualify an Expert. The process of qualifying an expert has three stages. First, the attorney who called the expert lays a foundation for the witness's expertise by asking questions about the witness's credentials and qualifications. The attorney may use leading questions to do this, even though the questions occur during direct examination, because the attorney is eliciting uncontested background information about pedigree. After the attorney has laid the foundation, she will move that the judge certify the witness as an expert.

Here is an example of an attorney laying a foundation for an expert witness. The attorney represents a train conductor who was assaulted by a passenger at Union Station in Chicago and who has sued the railroad company, alleging that it provided inadequate security. To prove that the security was inadequate, the attorney calls John Kandish, a witness she hopes to qualify as an expert in the field of industrial and premises security:

Q: Mr. Kandish, what is your educational background?

A: I have earned bachelors' degrees in criminal justice and sociology, and masters' degrees in industrial safety and industrial security.

Q: And you also received training at the Chicago Police Academy, is that correct?

A: Yes, I took two courses in crowd security and industrial security at the Chicago Police Academy.

Q: And have you worked in the security industry?

A: Yes, I served as a private security guard for five years for various banks in the city of Chicago, and I then worked for ten years as a security specialist for the Federal Reserve Bank. After that, I was the Corporate Director of Security and Vice President of First National Bank in Chicago for seven years.

Q: And now you run your own security consulting company, is that right?

A: Yes, after I left First National Bank, I founded Kandish Security, which provides security consultation services for companies and public agencies. Over the past twelve years my company has advised hundreds of different companies and organizations about issues ranging from employee theft, ATM security, loss prevention, guarding against premise security claims, violence and crime prevention.

Q: And how many individuals does Kandish Security currently employ?

A: I oversee twelve different consultants who work for my company.

Q: Mr. Kandish, have you ever been certified in court as an expert in industrial and premises security?

A: Yes, I have testified over a dozen times in federal court as an expert, in cases involving the security of banks, service stations, night clubs, health care facilities, shopping malls, apartment buildings, theaters, and restaurants.

Q: Thank you Mr. Kandish. Your honor, we would like to move that Mr. Kandish be certified as an expert in industrial and premises security.[1]

After an attorney finishes laying this foundation and moves for expert certification, most judges allow opposing counsel to "voir dire" the witness. This is the **second** stage of qualifying an expert. In this stage, the opposing counsel has a chance to ask the witness questions in order to test his credentials.

Officially, these questions allow opposing counsel to probe the witness's credentials in order to establish that the witness lacks sufficient qualifications to testify as an expert. In practice, however, it is extremely difficult to persuade a judge that a witness fails to qualify as an expert. Although judges carefully supervise the

---

1   This testimony is loosely based on the expert who testified in Maguire v. National R.R. Passenger Corp., No. 99 C 3240, 2002 WL 472275 (N.D. Ill. Mar. 28, 2002). The witness in that case had somewhat stronger credentials than the ones given here.

admissibility of expert **fields** under Rule 702 and *Daubert*, they are much more lenient when qualifying a particular witness within the field. Once *Daubert*'s reliability, fit, and Rule 403 requirements have been met, the judge will certify almost any witness with specialized training or experience in the field.

Why, then, do attorneys bother to voir dire a potential expert before the court rules on the witness's qualifications? Voir dire gives opposing counsel an opportunity to make a preemptive cross-examination of the witness's credentials. Rather than allowing the witness to proceed directly from a recitation of her credentials to her substantive testimony, opposing counsel will show the jury the gaps in the witness's expertise. Even if the judge certifies the witness as an expert, the jury may view the expert's testimony more skeptically.

This is the very reason that judges apply a lenient standard when certifying individual witnesses as experts. Although jurors may have difficulty judging the reliability of an entire scientific field, they can more readily determine the extent of an individual's expertise in that field. And cross-examination can more readily expose the flaws in an individual's training than it can reveal problems in the theoretical underpinnings of an entire scientific field.

Here is how opposing counsel might voir dire the expert witness examined above:

Q: Mr. Kandish, you testified that you completed two courses at the Chicago Police Academy?

A: That's right.

Q: But these were two-week classes for a few hours at night, am I right? They were not the same as the full-time six-month training program that actual police officers receive.

A: Correct.

Q: In fact, Mr. Kandish, you've never been a police officer, is that correct?

A: That's correct, I have not.

Q: Mr. Kandish, have you ever written any scholarly articles or books on the subject of premises security?

A: No, I have not.

> **Q:** Now, you testified that your company has provided security consulting services for a wide variety of different companies and agencies, is that correct?
>
> **A:** Yes, as I said, we have evaluated the security situation for hundreds of different companies.
>
> **Q:** As you know, this litigation involves an attack in a railroad terminal. Have you ever provided consulting services or worked as a security guard in a railroad terminal?
>
> **A:** No, I have not.

This examination won't prevent Mr. Kandish from qualifying as an expert; he has sufficient credentials to offer expert testimony. But by posing these questions, opposing counsel exposed the blemishes on Kandish's resume before he began to testify about his opinions.

After the voir dire, opposing counsel decides whether to object to the witness's certification as an expert. Opposing counsel often accepts the witness, stating on the record that he has no objection to certifying the witness to be an expert. Occasionally, if the witness's credentials seem particularly thin, opposing counsel may decide to object.

In the **third** stage of qualifying an expert, the judge rules on the motion to certify the witness. Usually, for the reasons given above, the judge grants the motion to certify the witness as an expert.

The parties may shorten this three-step process by stipulating that the witness is an expert.[2] The party opposing the expert witness, in fact, often offers to stipulate to expert status. The opponent knows that the judge ultimately will certify the witness as an expert and, by stipulating to the witness's qualifications, the opponent can avoid a lengthy demonstration of the witness's qualifications to the jury.

For the same reason, the party offering an expert witness usually refuses to stipulate to expert status.[3] As with many other aspects of evidence, expert status is

---

2 For discussion of stipulations, see Chapters 2 and 59.

3 Remember that a party is almost never required to accept a stipulation offered by the opponent: See the dis-

not just a question of admissibility but also of advocacy. The party offering the witness wants the jury to trust the witness's expertise on critical issues. This is especially important because parties usually call opposing experts. When a battle of the experts occurs, the jury often relies on the qualifications of the competing experts to decide which opinion to believe. Thus, most trial lawyers believe it is imperative for the jury to hear the full qualifications of their experts.

2. Expertise Includes Experience or Informal Training. Most lay people think that "expert witnesses" are doctors or engineers with many years of formal education. But parties present experts in a wide range of fields. Judges have certified experts on anti-cult movements,[4] cultural attitudes of Hmong refugees,[5] the organizational structure of mafia crime families,[6] and many other subjects. Many of these fields do not lend themselves to formal schooling or training. Witnesses, however, may qualify as experts in these areas because of their independently developed knowledge, skills, or experience.

Expert witnesses on business practices, for example, often obtain specialized knowledge through their work in the field:

> **Example:** Kent Dyer, a wildlife photographer, took a well composed photo of a mother mountain lion protectively holding a baby mountain lion in her mouth. Jason Napier, a sculptor, saw Dyer's photo and later created a bronze sculpture of the same subject. Dyer sued Napier for copyright infringement. Napier offered Jane Kinne as an expert witness who could identify copyrightable elements in Dyer's photo and offer an opinion about whether the two works contained more similarities or differences. Dyer objected to Kinne's qualification as an expert.

> **Analysis:** Kinne's testimony was admissible. The trial judge acknowledged that Kinne was not a professional photographer or sculptor, but noted that she had worked for almost 60 years in the business of licensing photography rights. During this time she participated in numerous professional organizations related to licensing those rights; and she had "represented every major

---

cussion of Old Chief in Chapter 7.

4   Scott v. Ross, 140 F.3d 1275, 1285–86 (9th Cir. 1998).

5   Dang Vang v. Vang Xiong X. Toyed, 944 F.2d 476, 480–81 (9th Cir. 1991).

6   United States v. Amuso, 21 F.3d 1251, 1263–64 (2d Cir. 1994).

wildlife photographer and many of the lesser known" photographers at least once. She had also served as an expert witness and consultant in more than 500 cases. Based on this background, the judge found that Kinne easily qualified as an expert on the copyrightable elements of photos and the differences between works on similar subjects.[7]

Similarly, police officers often develop specialized knowledge of criminal practices through their field work or job training:

Example: The government charged Cesear Garcia with drug trafficking. As part of its case, the government presented expert testimony from Special Agent Keith Cromer. Cromer testified about the organization of Mexican drug trafficking organizations, the use of code language in those organizations, and the manufacture, packaging, and distribution of narcotics. Garcia objected to Cromer's qualifications as an expert witness.

Analysis: The trial judge certified Cromer as an expert and the court of appeals affirmed. Cromer had worked as a DEA agent for several years. He had attended a 16-week training course at the DEA Academy that included instruction on the structure of drug trafficking organizations and the process of illegal distribution of narcotics. Cromer had taken part in at least 50 drug investigations; 85–90% of those investigations involved Mexican drug trafficking organizations. Cromer also had participated in numerous wiretap investigations and was familiar with the coded language that some drug traffickers use. Based on this training, experience, and knowledge, Cromer qualified as an expert in narcotics organizations.[8]

Experts who possess practical skills, such as auto mechanics, plumbers, and electricians, also develop their knowledge through apprenticeships, hands-on training, and years on the job. These experiences suffice to qualify experts in many fields.

With experts who base their knowledge on experience or informal training, however, Rule 702's fit requirement assumes special importance.[9] Jane Kinne, the

---

7   Dyer v. Napier, 81 U.S.P.Q. 2d 1035 (N.D. Ariz. 2006).

8   United States v. Garcia, 447 F.3d 1327, 1335 (11th Cir. 2006).

9   We discussed this requirement in Chapter 61.

expert who developed an extensive knowledge of photo licensing, probably could not testify about the laboratory process of developing photos; she might not have experience in that field. Similarly, an auto mechanic with on-the-job training may be qualified to explain the process of replacing an oil filter. If asked to testify about the chemical reactions inside the internal combustion engine, however, the witness probably would need to have more formal training. An expert witness's qualifications must match the testimony she offers.

Quick Summary

To qualify a witness as an expert, the attorney offering the expert must demonstrate that the witness has specialized knowledge, skill, experience, training or education. The attorney does this by eliciting testimony from the witness about the basis of her expertise. Formal education is not necessary to qualify an expert; many experts develop specialized knowledge in other ways. **Rule 702** applies a flexible standard embracing many paths to expertise.

After the attorney offering the witness elicits her qualifications, the opposing party has a chance to voir dire the expert, ostensibly to test her expertise. In practice, opponents frequently use this voir dire to demonstrate the limits of the witness's qualifications to the jury. When voir dire concludes, the judge decides whether to certify the witness as an expert. Even if the judge certifies the witness, the witness's qualifications may limit the extent of her testimony.

Test Your Understanding

To assess your understanding of the material in this chapter, click here to take a quiz, or go to the Quizzes module from the eBook on your eProducts bookshelf.

63

Bases of Expert Opinion

Key Concepts

- Expert Opinions Are More Complex than Lay Ones
- **Rules 703** and **705**: Expert Testimony Need Not Rest on Personal Observation
- Data Supporting Expert Opinion Need Not Be Admissible
- Conditions for Expert to Disclose Inadmissible Supporting Evidence

A. Introduction and Policy. In the last two chapters, we discussed the appropriate subjects for expert testimony and the process of qualifying an expert. Parties sometimes struggle to persuade the judge that an expert's method is reliable and that his testimony fits the facts of the case. The payoff for qualifying a witness, however, is substantial. Experts impress jurors, especially if they appear knowledgeable and explain concepts in a way that engages the jury. And for many controversies, expert testimony is essential to establish the elements of the case.

In addition to these practical advantages, the evidentiary rules confer at least four special powers on expert witnesses compared to lay witnesses. The first two powers are relatively minor, but the second two are substantial.

First, if the expert's testimony requires knowledge of other trial testimony, the expert may remain in the courtroom even if the judge excludes other witnesses under **Rule 615**.[1] **Second,** experts are the only witnesses who can certify documents as learned treatises under **Rule 803(18)**. These treatises may then be read to the jury and considered for the truth of the matter asserted even though they are hearsay.[2]

---

1   Refer to Chapter 14 to refresh your recollection of motions to exclude witnesses under Rule 615.

2   Chapter 47 discusses this hearsay exception.

Third, experts may do more than give commonsense opinions; they may state conclusions based on their special training or experience. An expert's opinions are more complex than those of most lay witnesses. A lay witness, for example, could testify that a defendant "looked drunk." A properly qualified expert could testify that, based on the defendant's blood alcohol content, the defendant was incapable of safely operating workplace machinery. Similarly, a lay witness could testify that a red stain on the defendant's shirt "looked like blood." An expert could testify that the stain was human blood and that DNA testing matched the blood to that of a murder victim.

Trial attorneys use expert witnesses primarily because of their power to offer opinions like these. Without testimony interpreting blood alcohol content, the extent of the employee's drunkenness might be less clear. Without a DNA expert, the link between the defendant and the victim might be much more tenuous. Many cases stand or fall on the existence of expert opinions.

But expert witnesses have a **fourth** power that is equally important. Experts, unlike lay witnesses, do not have to base their opinions exclusively on personal observations. Instead, experts may rely on a wide range of data, including information—such as hearsay evidence—that is not admissible in court. Under some circumstances, the expert may even reveal inadmissible evidence to the jury.

In this chapter, we focus primarily on this final attribute of expert witnesses. **Rules 703** and **705** codify the special relationship between an expert's opinion and the underlying data.

B. The Rules. Rule 702, which we studied in the last two chapters, requires all experts to base their testimony on "sufficient facts or data." **Rule 703** supplements this rule by describing the kinds of data that experts may use:

RULE 703. Bases of an Expert's Opinion Testimony

An expert may base an opinion on facts or data in the case that the expert has been <u>made aware of</u> or <u>personally observed</u>. . . .

This rule describes a key power that experts possess: The expert need not confine his testimony to matters he personally observed. Instead, experts may base opinions on facts they have "been made aware of." The expert may learn these facts by reviewing data before trial or by listening to other witnesses during the trial itself.

If the expert relies upon facts gathered before trial, those facts may include inadmissible hearsay. The next sentence of Rule 703 acknowledges that experts sometimes rely upon data that is not admissible in court. An expert witness may offer an opinion based on inadmissible evidence, but only if experts in that field **reasonably rely** upon that type of information:

RULE 703. Bases of an Expert's Opinion Testimony

. . . If <u>experts</u> in the particular field would <u>reasonably rely</u> on those kinds of facts or data in forming an opinion on the subject, they <u>need not be admissible</u> for the opinion to be admitted. . . .

As we'll see in the Courtroom section, this portion of Rule 703 allows experts to rely upon a wide variety of inadmissible evidence, as long as experts in the field reasonably rely upon that data.

Rule 705 complements Rule 703 by discussing the manner in which experts convey the data supporting their opinions. Before enactment of the Federal Rules, courts required experts to recite the full basis of an opinion before giving the opinion. This requirement produced tedious testimony in which the jurors often lost the point of the expert's opinion while the witness or examining attorney recited all of the factual predicates. Rule 705 changed this practice by allowing the expert to offer an opinion **without first** recounting all of the underlying data:

RULE 705. Disclosing the Facts or Data Underlying an Expert's Opinion

Unless the court orders otherwise, an expert may state an opinion—and give the reasons for it—<u>without first testifying to the underlying facts or data</u>. . . .

This language allows an expert to eliminate any reference to the facts supporting an opinion. This power gives experts two significant advantages. Under Rule 705, an expert may state a bare conclusion, such as that the plaintiff "will never walk again," or that a confiscated substance is "high quality cocaine." In practice, attorneys rarely examine an expert by eliciting just the bottom line; a curt conclusion carries less weight than one backed by explanation. The primary value of Rule 705 is that an expert may state a conclusion **first**, capturing and focusing the jury's attention. The witness may then explain the data that produced this conclusion.

A second advantage of Rule 705 is that it allows an expert to offer an opinion, even if the evidence supporting the opinion is inadmissible. Since Rule 703 allows experts to base their opinions on inadmissible evidence, it is essential to allow them to voice those opinions. Thus, Rule 703 and Rule 705 work together—Rule 703 allows experts to base their opinions on inadmissible evidence, and Rule 705 allows experts to testify about those opinions without having to state the basis for them.

But as noted above, an expert's opinion carries little weight unless she explains the basis for that opinion. Courts, therefore, frequently confront this problem: An expert bases her conclusions on inadmissible facts, and the attorney wants to back up the expert's conclusions by asking the expert to explain the facts underlying her opinion. What happens then? The concluding portions of Rule 703 and Rule 705 address this situation. Rule 703 provides:

> ## RULE 703. Bases of an Expert's Opinion Testimony
>
> . . . But if the facts or data would otherwise be inadmissible, the proponent of the opinion may <u>disclose them</u> to the jury <u>only if</u> their <u>probative value</u> in helping the jury evaluate the opinion <u>substantially outweighs their prejudicial effect</u>.

The default rule, in other words, is that an expert may **not** disclose inadmissible information to the jury. This ban furthers the policies of other evidentiary rules, which prevent the jury from hearing information that may be prejudicial, misleading, or violate public policy. The court, however, may allow the expert to disclose the otherwise inadmissible evidence if the probative value of that evidence would substantially outweigh its prejudicial effect. This standard is the **reverse of Rule 403**; it requires a strong showing of probative value (or of minimal prejudice) to support disclosure. And unlike Rule 403, which looks to the general probative value for any relevant fact, Rule 703 only takes into consideration the probative value of the evidence "in helping the jury evaluate the [expert's] opinion."

Rule 705, finally, recognizes that an **opposing party** may want to reveal otherwise inadmissible evidence supporting an expert's testimony. The expert's underlying facts may be unreliable or speculative; if so, the party calling the expert may not want to reveal the underlying facts. In such a case, the opposing party may want to force the expert to reveal the data. Even if the underlying facts are solid and trustworthy, the opposing party might not be able to cross-examine the expert effectively without delving into this information:

RULE 705. Disclosing the Facts or Data Underlying an Expert's Opinion

. . . But the expert may <u>be required</u> to disclose those facts or data on cross-examination.

In sum, Rules 703 and 705 answer two critical questions about expert testimony. First, these rules explain **what kind** of information experts may rely upon to support their opinions. And, second, the rules identify **when** an expert may disclose supporting data that would not otherwise be admissible.

C. In the Courtroom. Experts sometimes base their opinions on personal observations, just as lay witnesses do. An art historian will personally examine a portrait to decide if it is a forgery, while a chemist will personally test a substance to determine if it is cocaine. But, as the rules discussed above make clear, experts need not limit their opinions to facts obtained from personal perception. In this section, we explore further an expert witness's power to use and disclose other types of information.

1. Attendance at Trial. Rule 703 allows expert witnesses to base their opinions on facts they have "been made aware of." An expert may learn these facts by attending trial and listening to the testimony of other witnesses. A party may then call the expert to the stand and ask him to give an opinion based on that other testimony:

Example: The United States charged Douglas Crabtree and Patrick Cray with misapplying funds obtained from the State Bank of Farmersville. One of the government's witnesses, FBI Agent John Turner, listened to all of the defense testimony. The government then called Turner in rebuttal to offer an expert opinion about the defendants' use of bank funds.

Analysis: Turner properly based his opinion on facts gleaned from testimony by the defense witnesses. The trial judge, moreover, properly allowed Turner to remain in the courtroom after excluding all other witnesses under **Rule 615**. Turner's continued presence was necessary to provide the foundation for his testimony.[3]

Trial attendance sometimes is the most efficient way for an expert to obtain necessary facts. Indeed, if a prosecution expert will respond to the defense witness's assertions, as in Crabtree, trial attendance may be the **only** way for the expert to obtain critical information. In most cases, however, trial attendance is an expensive way to brief an expert witness. If the expert charges an hourly professional fee, few parties want to cover the cost of an expert attending days or weeks of trial.

When an expert does base an opinion on trial testimony, the expert must clarify what parts of the testimony support her opinion. If witnesses offered conflicting testimony, the expert must identify the version of the facts she is using as the basis of her opinion. Similarly, if an expert discounts the testimony of a witness, she should reveal that fact. Otherwise, the factual basis of an opinion based on trial testimony may be unclear.

2. Hypothetical Questions. Another way for an expert to base an opinion on facts learned at trial is for the expert to testify in response to a hypothetical question. The examining attorney will formulate a hypothetical that summarizes the relevant evidence offered in the case. The attorney will then ask the expert to give an opinion assuming that all of those facts are true.

Example: A Los Angeles overpass collapsed during an earthquake, killing five motorists. The city sued the company that built the overpass, claiming that it failed to meet industry standards when constructing the overpass. At trial, the city concludes its case by calling Dr. Anselm, a professor

---

3   This example expands upon United States v. Crabtree, 979 F.2d 1261, 1270 (7th Cir. 1992).

of structural engineering at the University of Southern California. After qualifying Dr. Anselm as an expert, the city's attorney asks the following question:

Q: Dr. Anselm, assume the following facts: First, assume that a highway overpass was constructed using standard materials, including six-inch steel supports and concrete panels three feet thick. Also assume the overpass had three concrete supports along its span, each composed of the same steel supports and concrete.

Also assume the overpass was twenty-seven feet off the ground at its highest point, where the center support was connected, and twenty-two feet off the ground where it connected with each of the side supports. And also assume the overpass was one hundred twenty feet long.

Now assume that a 6.5 magnitude earthquake occurred with an epicenter 2.2 miles from the overpass, and lasted approximately twenty-seven seconds. There were two aftershocks, with the same epicenter, the first measuring 3.2 and lasting eleven seconds, and the second measuring 3.0 and lasting seven seconds.

Dr. Anselm, in your expert opinion, would such a structure survive the earthquake if it were constructed in a method consistent with industry construction standards?

Dr. Anselm could then give her opinion, based on the assumed facts she was "made aware of" while listening to the hypothetical. The attorney eliciting this opinion, moreover, may include contested facts in the hypothetical. In the collapsing overpass case, for example, the city's witnesses might claim that the earthquake measured 6.5 on the Richter scale, while defense witnesses estimated a more powerful quake of 7.0. The city attorney is free to assume the more favorable 6.5 magnitude on direct examination, although the defense may ask the witness to assume a 7.0 quake on cross-examination.

Although hypothetical questions are permissible, they are subject to at least two forms of abuse. **First**, attorneys sometimes insert facts into the hypothetical that have not been proven. By linking an unproven fact with a series of proven ones, the attorney might mislead the jury into thinking that all of the assumed facts have been proven. To avoid this problem, hypothetical questions may not assume facts that are not in evidence.

Second, attorneys sometimes use a long hypothetical as an opportunity to sum up the case; rather than presenting facts to an expert, these advocates are previewing their closing argument. There are famous examples of hypothetical questions that asked an expert to assume hundreds of facts. Judges may preclude these questions as argumentative, confusing to the jury, or failing to elicit testimony "helping the trier of fact."

3. Reasonably Relied upon by Experts in the Field. Experts frequently rely upon data that would not be admissible in court. Rule 703 allows expert witnesses to base opinions on this information, as long as experts in the field reasonably rely upon those data. The rule assumes that, if data are good enough for experts to rely upon, then courts should not second-guess that judgment.

Here is a case illustrating the wide variety of sources, including inadmissible hearsay, that may inform an expert's opinion:

> **Example:** Clear Channel Communications contracted with the Outrigger Wailea Resort, located in Hawaii, for the resort to host a music industry conference in February 2002. In January 2002, Clear Channel cancelled the conference, noting that the September 11 attacks had discouraged international travel. Outrigger sued Clear Channel for breach of contract. In defense, Clear Channel asserted the contract's "Force Majeure" clause, which excused performance if terrorism or other events made it "inadvisable, illegal, or impossible" for a party to perform.
>
> Both parties moved for summary judgment. To support its Force Majeure defense, Clear Channel offered affidavits from several experts. Dr. Lawrence Boyd, an economist, concluded in his affidavit that holding an international conference in Hawaii in February 2002 would have been "inadvisable" given the state of Hawaiian tourism, international travel, and other factors. Outrigger objected to Boyd's conclusion, claiming that it lacked an adequate factual foundation.

> **Analysis:** The trial judge overruled Outrigger's objection, ruling that Boyd based his conclusions on evidence reasonably relied upon by economists when constructing economic models. Boyd applied his model using facts gathered from news reports, data obtained from the State of Hawaii Department of Business and Economic Development, statistics from the Center for Labor

Education and Research, and facts provided by employees of both Clear Channel and Outrigger. Although much of this evidence was hearsay, the statements were the type of data reasonably relied upon by economists who conduct this sort of work. Boyd's affidavit satisfied the requirements of Rules 702 and 703.[4]

Experts in many other cases similarly base their opinions on information provided by third parties. A chemist might review another chemist's laboratory analyses to reach a conclusion;[5] a real estate appraiser might rely upon the findings of other appraisers;[6] a Drug Enforcement Agent might use information from field agents to deduce the current market value of heroin;[7] or a medical specialist might rely upon the diagnoses and tests of other doctors to identify the cause of a patient's illness.[8]

Like the economist in the Outrigger case, experts may also rely on information from lay people. Many experts use statements provided by the parties, while others rely upon eyewitnesses to an event. To diagnose a patient's condition and estimate the extent of her disability, a doctor may obtain information from the patient, family members, and nursing aides, as well as from other doctors, nurses, and laboratory technicians. As long as medical experts reasonably rely upon these sources, the testifying doctor may do so.

The reasonable reliance standard, however, includes two different components: Experts in the witness's field must in fact rely upon the type of evidence that the expert used, and that reliance must be reasonable. The reasonable reliance standard gives judges another opportunity to serve as gatekeepers for technical and scientific testimony. If the judge decides that experts in a field unreasonably rely upon particular facts, the judge may exclude the witness's testimony.

---

4   OWBR LLC v. Clear Channel Communications, Inc., 266 F. Supp. 2d 1214, 1230–31 (D. Haw. 2003). Although the court admitted Boyd's affidavit, it rejected Clear Channel's interpretation of the Force Majeure clause and granted summary judgment for Outrigger on that issue.

5   United States v. Posey, 647 F.2d 1048, 1051 (10th Cir. 1981).

6   United States v. 1014.16 Acres of Land, 558 F. Supp. 1238, 1242 (W.D. Mo. 1983), aff'd 739 F.2d 1371 (8th Cir. 1984).

7   United States v. Golden, 532 F.2d 1244, 1247–48 (9th Cir. 1976).

8   Asad v. Continental Airlines, Inc., 314 F. Supp. 2d 726, 741–46 (N.D. Ohio 2004).

Some rulings combine both elements of the standard. A judge may reject an expert's opinion because it relies upon data that seem untrustworthy and because the data fail to comply with standards observed by other experts:

Example: The Canarsie Kiddie Shop opened a children's clothing store and called it "Kids 'r' Us." The well known Toys "R" Us Company sued Canarsie, claiming trademark infringement. One element of the plaintiff's claim was whether an ordinary consumer was likely to confuse the two brand names.

To support its claim of actual confusion, Toys "R" Us called an expert witness, Dr. Sorenson, who ran a marketing consulting firm. Sorenson testified that, in his opinion, the average consumer did confuse the two brand names. He based his conclusion on a survey of 450 consumers conducted by his company. Canarsie objected to Sorenson's testimony, claiming that the survey was flawed in many respects; thus, it was not the type of information that marketing professionals reasonably relied upon.

Analysis: The trial judge sustained the objection, refusing to admit the expert's opinion. Although some aspects of Sorenson's study were well designed, others introduced fatal flaws. One of the interviewers guessed the purpose of the study and shared that speculation with others; this violated the study protocol. Interviewers also conducted many of their interviews in a bowling alley, which did not offer the general "purchasing environment" targeted by the study's design. And the interviewers frequently questioned subjects who had overheard their discussion with previous subjects; this tainted the independent recall of the subjects.

The trial judge allowed the plaintiff to call another marketing expert to attempt to defend the data generated by Sorenson's survey. Although chosen by the plaintiff, this expert agreed that the survey was flawed in the ways identified above. Based on this testimony and his own evaluation, the trial judge determined that it was unreasonable for Sorenson to rely on the survey data; the judge, therefore, precluded the expert testimony altogether.[9]

---

9   Toys "R" Us, Inc. v. Canarsie Kiddie Shop, Inc., 559 F. Supp. 1189, 1205 (E.D.N.Y. 1983).

The flaws in Sorenson's survey were not unusual; limited time and resources often constrain the quality of marketing surveys. But even if the second expert had testified that Sorenson's data fell within the range of data commonly relied upon by marketing experts, Rule 703 would have allowed the judge to reject the testimony. Under Rule 703, the judge may independently assess the reasonableness of data informing an expert opinion.

4. Admitting Underlying Facts That Are Otherwise Inadmissible. Experts may base their opinions on inadmissible evidence; the opinion is admissible even when the underlying facts are not. Rules 703 and 705, moreover, recognize two ways in which the parties may introduce otherwise inadmissible facts supporting an expert opinion.

First, the party **opposing** an expert always has the right to ask the expert to divulge the basis of her opinion during cross-examination. Opposing counsel may pursue this option if she wants to attack an expert opinion as based on flimsy data. Assume, for example, that the defendant in a car collision case calls an accident reconstruction expert to testify in his favor. The expert states that, based on his investigation, the defendant was driving only 30–35 miles per hour and that he braked two seconds before the impact. These facts suggest that the defendant was not negligent.

Based on discovery, the plaintiff's attorney may know that a severe storm washed away all forensic evidence of the collision shortly after the accident, and that the expert based his opinion solely on interviews with the plaintiff, defendant, and other eyewitnesses. Accident reconstruction experts reasonably rely upon interviews like this, so the expert's testimony satisfies Rule 703. But an opinion based solely on interviews is less persuasive than one that incorporates other evidence. By questioning the expert about the facts supporting his opinion, the plaintiff's attorney casts doubt on the value of that testimony.

The **second**, and far more common, route for introducing inadmissible, underlying facts is for the party sponsoring the expert to try to admit the facts during direct examination. The party will argue that knowledge of the underlying facts is essential for the jury to understand and evaluate the expert's opinion. Rule 703 directs the judge to apply a **reverse-403 balancing test** in this situation. In other words, the judge will allow the expert to reveal the inadmissible facts supporting his opinion only if the probative value of admitting those facts substantially outweighs any prejudice caused by their admission.

Example: Wendell sued his employer, Dragon Industries, claiming that prolonged exposure to asbestos at his workplace caused him to develop mesothelioma (a form of cancer). At trial, Wendell calls Dr. Farnsworth, who testifies that, in his expert opinion, Wendell's mesothelioma was caused by exposure to asbestos over a number of years. Wendell's attorney then asks Dr. Farnsworth how he reached that conclusion. If allowed to answer, Dr. Farnsworth will testify that he formed his opinion after examining Wendell's x-rays and reading a written medical history prepared by Wendell's family doctor, Dr. Goode. Dr. Goode's written history notes the presence of exposed asbestos at Dragon's workplace, as well as the number of years Wendell worked at the company.

Dragon's attorney concedes that doctors routinely rely upon medical histories prepared by other doctors to form their opinions, so he has no objection to Dr. Farnsworth giving his opinion. Dragon, however, objects to Dr. Farnsworth revealing the facts that form the basis of his opinion because Dr. Goode's written history is inadmissible hearsay.

Analysis: The trial judge must decide whether the underlying facts will help the jury evaluate Dr. Farnsworth's opinion and, if so, whether the probative value of those facts admitted for that purpose substantially outweighs any prejudicial effect. In this case, it would be nearly impossible for the jury to evaluate Dr. Farnsworth's opinion unless he testifies about the extent of asbestos exposure he believed that Wendell received. Probative value, therefore, is high. And disclosing the information will cause little prejudice; Wendell is likely to offer other evidence about the extent of his asbestos exposure at Dragon Industries. Applying Rule 703's reverse-403 balancing test, the court probably will allow Dr. Farnsworth to explain the basis of his opinion.

But even if the judge allows Farnsworth to testify about the information he gleaned from Dr. Goode's written history, the jury may use this testimony only to evaluate Farnsworth's opinion. The jury may not use information from Goode's written report to establish the truth of those matters. If Goode's medical history states that Wendell worked at Dragon Industries for 20 years, for example, the jury may not use that information to conclude that Wendell actually worked at Dragon for that period. The jury may use the information only to judge whether Farnsworth's opinion makes sense, given that he **believed** Wendell worked at Dragon Industries for 20 years.

Rule 703, in other words, does not create a new hearsay exception; it allows introduction of an out-of-court statement for a purpose other than to prove the truth of the matter asserted. The judge will give the jury a limiting instruction to clarify this. In the example given above, the judge would tell the jury to consider information from Dr. Goode's report only for the purpose of evaluating Dr. Farnsworth's testimony.

If the facts underlying an expert's opinion are themselves admissible, then the parties may freely introduce them. The judge need not apply Rule 703's strict balancing test or give the jury a limiting instruction.

Example: Wendell sues Dragon Industries, asserting the facts outlined above. Dr. Farnsworth, however, diagnoses the cause of Wendell's mesothelomia after personally examining Wendell and asking him questions about any asbestos exposure. Wendell tells Dr. Farnsworth directly about the exposed asbestos at Dragon Industries and about how long he worked at the company.

As in the previous example, Dragon objects to Dr. Farnsworth revealing the facts supporting his opinion, claiming that they are inadmissible hearsay.

Analysis: Wendell's statement to Farnsworth is hearsay, because it occurred out of court. The statement, however, is admissible under Rule 803(4) because Wendell made the statement for the purpose of medical diagnosis and treatment. The information about Wendell's exposure to asbestos, including the number of years he had worked at Dragon Industries, was necessary for Dr. Farnsworth to diagnose Wendell's disease and its cause. Farnsworth may testify about Wendell's statement without satisfying Rule 703's balancing test, and the judge will not give any limiting instruction. The jury may consider Wendell's statement to Farnsworth both to evaluate the reliability of Farnsworth's testimony and as substantive evidence of the workplace conditions at Dragon and how long Wendell worked there.

5. The Confrontation Clause and Expert Opinions. As we saw in Chapter 58, the *Crawford* case holds that the Sixth Amendment usually bars the prosecution from admitting "testimonial" hearsay against a criminal defendant.[10] But Rule 703 allows an expert witness to base an opinion on inadmissible evidence—as long as "experts in the particular field would reasonably rely on those kinds of facts." Under Rule 703, may prosecutors ask their expert witnesses to offer opinions based on inadmissible, testimonial hearsay? Or does that practice violate the Sixth Amendment?

The Supreme Court is still struggling to resolve this issue, but a few points are (relatively) certain. First, if the expert relies upon an out-of-court statement that is non-testimonial, there is no Sixth Amendment conflict. For example, if a state psychologist bases her expert opinion on the defendant's own statements, or if an accountant offers an opinion based upon business records, there is no *Crawford* violation: Neither a party's own statement nor business records are testimonial.

Second, if the prosecutor asks the expert a hypothetical question, and the expert bases her opinion solely on facts stated in the hypothetical, there is no Sixth Amendment problem. Suppose, for example, that the prosecutor calls an accident reconstruction expert in a reckless driving case. The expert has no first-hand knowledge of the accident scene. The prosecutor could ask: "Assume that the car was traveling at fifty miles per hour and the skid marks made by the car were ten and a half feet long. How long before impact did the defendant hit the brakes?" The expert could then give her opinion based on an assumption that the information in the question was true. The expert, for example, might reply: "Based on those assumptions, the defendant applied the brakes one and a half seconds before impact."

The key to this second approach is that the prosecutor must introduce evidence about all of the facts assumed in the hypothetical question; otherwise, the expert's opinion will be irrelevant and inadmissible. When introducing evidence about those assumed facts, the prosecutor will have to comply with the Sixth Amendment. The defendant, therefore, will have a chance to cross-examine both the expert and the witnesses testifying about the underlying facts.

But what if the expert relies on out-of-court, testimonial statements to reach her conclusion? Suppose, for example, that the prosecutor offers no evidence about the length of the skid marks in the reckless driving case; instead, the accident reconstruction expert reviews a police report to obtain that information. Based on

---

10   Crawford v. Washington, 541 U.S. 36 (2004).

that out-of-court evidence, the expert testifies that "in my opinion, the defendant applied the brakes one and a half seconds before impact."

Rule 703 appears to allow this testimony. Accident reconstruction experts routinely rely upon police reports for information, and that reliance seems quite reasonable. As explained in the previous section, the party calling the expert could even reveal the skid measurements in the underlying police report—as long as the judge found that the report's probative value in helping the jury assess the expert's opinion substantially outweighed its prejudicial effect. The judge would instruct the jury to use the report only to assess the expert's opinion, but Rule 703 allows the report's admission for that limited purpose.

This result raises no Sixth Amendment issues in civil cases or when a criminal defendant calls an expert witness. If a prosecutor offers this type of expert testimony, however, the expert's opinion seems to make an end run around *Crawford*. The police officer who measured the skid marks and noted them in the report almost certainly made a testimonial statement: The prosecutor could not introduce that report without allowing the defendant to cross-examine the officer. If the expert bases her opinion on this testimonial evidence, the defendant has no opportunity to test the underlying data. Rule 703 would not admit the underlying report for the truth of the matters asserted there, but the expert uses those facts to reach a conclusion that is offered for the truth of the matter asserted.

The Supreme Court addressed this tension in the 2012 decision *Williams v. Illinois*,[11] which we discussed in Chapter 58. Here is a recap of the *Williams* case, together with additional facts related to the expert opinion:

---

11   567 U.S. 50 (2012).

Example: L.J. was robbed and raped. After the assault, a rape kit was prepared and sent to the Illinois State Police. The police forwarded the kit to a private company, Cellmark, which created a DNA profile of the man who produced the semen recovered from L.J. Cellmark sent their report, detailing the DNA profile, back to the Illinois police. Sandra Lambatos, a forensic specialist at the police lab, compared Cellmark's DNA profile with all known profiles in the Illinois DNA database. She found a match with the DNA of Sandy Williams, who had provided a blood sample to the police when he was previously arrested on unrelated charges. Based largely on this evidence, the state charged Williams with the rape.

At trial, the prosecutor called two expert witnesses in connection with the DNA match. Karen Abbinanti testified that she personally created a DNA profile from the defendant's blood sample and entered that profile into the Illinois DNA database. Abbinanti had personal knowledge of the test she performed, and was subject to cross-examination, so Williams raised no Sixth Amendment challenge to her testimony.

Then Lambatos took the stand. Lambatos testified that she received the DNA profile from Cellmark and compared it to all profiles in the Illinois database. She further testified that, after obtaining an initial match, she personally compared the two profiles. Based on this comparison, Lambatos offered her expert opinion that "the semen identified in the vaginal swabs of [L. J. was] consistent with having originated from Sandy Williams."

Williams acknowledged that Lambatos could offer an expert opinion about whether the two profiles matched. But, he argued, Lambatos could not testify that the Cellmark profile derived from "the semen identified in the vaginal swabs of [L.J.]" The state had not introduced the Cellmark report, which made this link; nor, under *Crawford*, could it introduce that report without supplying testimony from a technician who had participated in the analyses. Allowing Lambatos to make this link as part of her expert testimony, Williams claimed, violated his Sixth Amendment right to confront the witnesses against him.

The prosecutor responded that Rule 703 permitted Lambatos's testimony, because forensic experts routinely rely on the work of other laboratories. The trial judge accepted this argument and Williams was convicted.

Analysis: As explained in Chapter 58, five Justices concluded that the Cellmark report was not testimonial. On that ground, they approved Lambatos's testimony and upheld Williams's conviction. But all nine Justices also addressed the Rule 703 issue at length.

In the opening plurality opinion, Justice Alito and three other Justices concluded that Lambotos's statement satisfied both Rule 703 and the Confrontation Clause. Her reference to the vaginal swabs, they argued, was not offered to prove the truth of the matter asserted (that the Cellmark profile came from L.J.). Instead, the plurality found that Lambatos was simply assuming a fact posited by the prosecutor. Using hypothetical questions to cross-examine an expert witness, these four Justices noted, was a well established practice. At least in a bench trial, like the *Williams* one, there was no chance that the judge would confuse assumed facts with proven ones.

The other five Justices, however, emphatically rejected this analysis. Justice Thomas and the four dissenters declared that an expert witness may **not** use Rule 703 to introduce testimonial evidence unless the defendant has a chance to cross-examine the maker of the testimonial statement. If the Cellmark report had been testimonial, these Justices agreed that Lambatos could not have testified that the profile in that report came from L.J. The most she could have said was that she received a DNA profile from Cellmark and that the Cellmark profile matched Williams's profile. The prosecutor would have had to call a laboratory analyst (or analysts) from Cellmark to establish that their profile derived from the semen taken from L.J.'s body.

 *Williams*, therefore, offered no binding precedent on the Rule 703 issue. The fractured opinions, combined with the complexity of the underlying issues, have provoked widespread confusion in the lower courts. Some courts have followed the plurality's "not for the truth of the matter" approach, even though a majority of the Justices rejected that rationale. Others have invoked the principles articulated by Justice Thomas and the four dissenters, which prohibit prosecution experts from offering opinions that depend solely on out-of-court testimonial statements.

The Supreme Court almost certainly will return to the issue over the next few years; hopefully the Court's next decision will provide more guidance than *Williams* does.

Meanwhile, the ongoing tension between Rule 703 and the Sixth Amendment illustrates the difference between **reliability** and **cross-examination**, two bedrock principles governing hearsay. Rule 703 rests heavily on reliability: The expert must testify that other experts reasonably rely on the type of evidence supporting her opinion, and the judge must agree that the reliance is reasonable. But *Crawford* shifted the focus of the Confrontation Clause from substantive reliability to the procedural right of cross-examination. In both *Crawford* and *Melendez-Diaz*, the Court stressed that the Sixth Amendment gives criminal defendants "a procedural rather than a substantive guarantee."[12] For a judge to decide that an expert has used "reliable" data, and that therefore it is unnecessary to cross-examine the individuals who provided that data, contradicts *Crawford*'s holding.

The *Williams* case, unfortunately, has muddied these waters as well. The *Williams* plurality held that Cellmark's report was non-testimonial partly because they believed the report was reliable. Since Cellmark generated a DNA profile without attempting to link it to a particular defendant, the plurality found the result was particularly reliable, and "reliability is a salient characteristic of a statement that falls outside the reach of the Confrontation Clause."[13] The dissent, for its part, stuck to the procedural guarantee of cross-examination as the guiding principle behind *Crawford*.[14] This debate, so visible in the context of expert reports, marks an ongoing division on the Supreme Court over *Crawford*'s viability. The Court continues to uphold *Crawford*'s procedural guarantee of cross-examination, but at least four of the Justices repeatedly urge a return to reliability as the governing principle. It remains to be seen how this division affects further development of Confrontation Clause doctrine.

---

12   Crawford, 541 U.S. at 61 (2004); Melendez-Diaz v. Massachusetts, 557 U.S. 305, 317 (2009).

13   Williams, 567 U.S. at 83 (plurality opinion).

14   Id. at 118–25 (dissenting opinion).

Quick Summary

Expert witnesses have powers that lay witnesses lack. First and foremost, the expert may offer opinions that apply her technical or scientific expertise to the facts of the case. This power allows experts to generate more sophisticated conclusions than a lay witness could. This is the primary reason that parties call expert witnesses: to help the jury draw conclusions that are beyond the knowledge of most jurors.

Second, experts may base their opinions on facts other than ones they personally observed outside the courtroom. Some experts rest their opinions on facts learned by watching other witnesses testify at trial. Other experts respond to facts in a hypothetical question posed by the examining attorney. Experts, finally, may even rely upon otherwise inadmissible evidence—such as hearsay—as long as experts in their field reasonably rely upon that type of information.

If the facts supporting an expert's opinion are inadmissible, the expert may not disclose those facts unless (1) the court determines that the probative value of admitting the facts to help the jury evaluate the expert's opinion substantially outweighs the prejudice of admitting the facts; or (2) opposing counsel asks about the underlying facts on cross-examination.

In criminal cases, some applications of Rule 703 raise difficult Sixth Amendment issues. The Supreme Court and lower courts are struggling to reconcile those provisions.

Test Your Understanding

To assess your understanding of the material in this chapter, click here to take a quiz, or go to the Quizzes module from the eBook on your eProducts bookshelf.

64

Limits on Opinion and Expert Testimony

Key Concepts

- **Rule 704:** No Automatic Prohibition of Testimony on Ultimate Issues
- Courts Continue to Protect the Province of the Jury Under **Rules 701, 702,** and **403**
- Mental State of Criminal Defendant
- Opinions on Other Legal Conclusions
- Probability Evidence
- Polygraphs
- Expert Testimony About Eyewitness Reliability

A. Introduction and Policy. The rules we studied in the last four chapters allow both lay and expert witnesses to voice opinions on a wide range of matters. This testimony, however, must comply with several important constraints. Lay opinions, for example, must be helpful to the fact finder. Expert testimony must be both helpful and reliable; judges play a special gatekeeping role when parties offer expert testimony in the courtroom.

The common law imposed another significant limit on both lay and expert testimony: No witness could offer an opinion about an "ultimate issue" that would resolve the case. A witness, for example, could not testify that in her opinion the defendant was negligent or that the plaintiff lacked mental capacity. The common law held that resolving these issues fell within the "province of the jury," and no witness could invade that territory.

This prohibition sometimes triggered heated battles over whether a witness's statement embraced an ultimate issue or merely established a fact related to one of those issues. The Federal Rules of Evidence attempted to end those disputes by sweeping away the rigid bar against ultimate-issue testimony. **Rule 704(a)** declares that testimony "is not objectionable just because it embraces an ultimate issue."

This change made it easier for parties to present some types of evidence in court. In slip-and-fall cases, for example, courts now allow eyewitnesses to offer an opinion that the place where the plaintiff fell was "safe," even though the floor's condition is one of the dispositive issues that the jury will resolve.[1] And in drug distribution prosecutions, some courts allow experts to testify that circumstances like the quantity of narcotics in the defendant's possession suggest that the narcotics were "intended for distribution."[2] Although intent is an element of the crime, which the jury must find beyond a reasonable doubt, some judges allow witnesses to frame their opinions using that word.

Courts, however, remain wary of witnesses who intrude too far into the realm of the jury—or of the court itself. Although Rule 704 removed the strict rule against testimony on ultimate issues, courts continue to patrol a more fuzzy boundary. Judges still reject testimony that threatens to supplant the judge's power to declare the law, the jury's authority to apply the law to the facts, or the jury's task of resolving credibility.

In this chapter, we look first at the language of Rule 704. We then examine the rules that judges invoke in their continued struggle to protect the domains of judge and jury. Finally, we turn to a series of issues affected by these constraints. These include testimony expressing probabilities, reporting polygraph results, and critiquing the reliability of eyewitnesses.

B. The Rules. The first portion of **Rule 704** discards the common-law rule that strictly barred testimony about an ultimate issue:

> ## RULE 704. Opinion on an Ultimate Issue
>
> **(a) In General—Not Automatically Objectionable.** An opinion is not objectionable just because it embraces an <u>ultimate issue</u>.

---

1   See, e.g., Getter v. Wal-Mart Stores, Inc., 66 F.3d 1119, 1124 (10th Cir. 1995).

2   See, e.g., United States v. Brown, 7 F.3d 648, 651 (7th Cir. 1993).

This provision relaxes the common-law prohibition against witnesses discussing ultimate issues, but it does not permit every opinion on an ultimate issue. Judges retain significant authority, especially under **Rules 403** and **701–702**, to restrict testimony that treads too far on the fact finder's role.

Rule 701(b), for example, requires that a lay opinion be "helpful to clearly understanding the witness's testimony or to determining a fact in issue." Rule 702 similarly requires that expert testimony "help the trier of fact." A judge may conclude that a witness is not being "helpful" if the witness tries too emphatically to steer the jury's finding on an ultimate issue.

Rule 403 similarly restrains testimony that intrudes too far into judicial or jury decision making. If a witness attempts to testify directly about how the jury should decide an ultimate issue in the case, the judge may conclude that the unfair prejudice resulting from that testimony substantially outweighs its probative value. We will explore these limits further in the Courtroom section.

In 1984, Congress further complicated the problem of ultimate opinions by adding section (b) to Rule 704. This amendment stemmed from public outrage over a jury's determination that John Hinckley, who attempted to assassinate President Reagan, was not guilty by reason of insanity.[3] In response to outcries about the insanity defense, Congress changed federal substantive law on that issue and added section (b) to Rule 704. The latter section prevents expert witnesses from offering opinions, as they did in the *Hinckley* case, about the defendant's mental state:

RULE 704. Opinion on an Ultimate Issue

(b) Exception. In a <u>criminal case</u>, an <u>expert witness</u> must not state an opinion about whether the defendant <u>did or did not have a mental state or condition that constitutes an element</u> of the crime charged or of a defense. Those matters are for the trier of fact alone.

---

3   Insanity Defense Reform Act of 1984 (Chapter IV of Title II of the Comprehensive Crime Control Act of 1984, Pub. L. No. 98–473, 98 Stat. 1837, 2057–68 (codified at Fed. R. Evid. 704(b) and in scattered sections of 18 U.S.C. (Supp. III 1985)). For discussion of the amendment's background, see Reform of the Federal Insanity Defense: Hearings Before the Subcomm. on Criminal Justice of the House Comm. on the Judiciary, 98th Cong. 150–93 (1983).

As drafted, Rule 704(b) is very broad; it would prevent any expert from offering an opinion about whether a criminal defendant possessed a mental state constituting an element of any crime or defense. As we'll see in the Courtroom section, however, the courts have read this section quite narrowly. As construed by the courts, this section primarily restricts the type of words experts use rather than the content of their opinions.

C. In the Courtroom. Rule 704 attempted to eliminate lengthy disputes about whether a witness expressed an opinion on an ultimate issue. Instead, the judge focuses on whether the opinion will help the fact finder (Rules 701–702) and whether the testimony is unduly prejudicial (Rule 403). Helpfulness and prejudice, however, are in the eye of the beholder; some judges are more tolerant than others of testimony that addresses ultimate issues. We examine below some common tendencies in the federal courts; trial attorneys, however, find significant differences among judges in practice.[4]

1. Legal Conclusions. Although Rule 704 allows witnesses to testify about ultimate issues, most judges prefer witnesses to avoid legal terms like "negligent" or "guilty beyond a reasonable doubt." These phrases threaten to usurp the judge's authority to articulate the legal standards governing the case, exceed the witness's expertise, and confuse the jury. Most judges, therefore, rule that testimony expressing legal conclusions either is not helpful to the jury or violates Rule 403.

The distinction between a helpful opinion and a forbidden legal conclusion often seems like a matter of semantics. For a juror, testimony that the defendant "drove safely" may convey the same meaning as the conclusion that he "exercised reasonable care." Most judges, however, would allow a witness to use the first phrase but not the second.[5]

This line between helpful testimony and legal conclusions is so thin that even a verb form can make a difference:

---

4   Some of this discussion relies on Ric Simmons, Conquering the Province of the Jury: Expert Testimony and the Professionalization of Fact-Finding, 74 U. Cin. L. Rev. 1013 (2006).

5   See, e.g., Owen v. Kerr-McGee Corp., 698 F.2d 236, 239–40 (5th Cir. 1983).

Example: Police found a plastic bottle containing 25 "rocks" of crack cocaine in Thyrus Brown's pocket. Brown was also carrying a semi-automatic pistol, extra rounds of live ammunition, and $82 in cash. A grand jury indicted Brown for possession of cocaine with intent to distribute. Brown admitted that he possessed the cocaine but claimed that he was an addict and that the drug was for his personal use.

At trial, the government qualified Special Agent John Schaefer as an expert on cocaine distribution. Schaefer described the quantity of cocaine that distributors and users typically possess, the fact that distributors usually carry handguns, and the fact that addicts usually carry paraphernalia that Brown lacked. During this testimony, the prosecutor and Schaefer had the following exchange:

Q: Now, Agent Schaefer, can you tell the ladies and gentle-men of the jury what this information that you have described that you familiarized yourself with, concerning the defendant and his activities, what that indicates to you?

A: That this crack cocaine was intended for distribution.

Defense counsel objected to Schaefer's response as conveying a legal conclusion. Since Brown was indicted for "intent to distribute" cocaine, this testimony directly embraced a legal standard governing the case.

Analysis: The trial judge permitted the testimony, and the court of appeals affirmed. The appellate judges admitted that they "would have preferred that the agent use a word other than 'intended' to indicate his analysis." Nonetheless, the court found the testimony helpful to the jury. The court noted that lay jurors probably do not know the quantities of cocaine typically carried by addicts and distributors. Nor are they familiar with the paraphernalia that users carry. The agent's explanation, therefore, helped the jury understand how these facts related to the defendant's alleged intent to distribute.

The court, moreover, stressed that Schaefer testified that "the cocaine was intended for distribution," rather than that the defendant "intended to distribute the cocaine." In context, this statement reiterated Schaefer's explanation that the circumstances surrounding this cocaine suggested that it probably would be distributed. The circumstantial evidence supported a conclusion that Brown intended to distribute the cocaine, and that is what

> the jury found, but Schaefer's testimony stopped short of that ultimate legal determination.[6]

Although the distinction between the phrases "was intended" and "intended" seems unbearably slight, note that the court also considered the content of Schaefer's remaining testimony. In the context of that testimony, Schaefer's conclusion was helpful to the jury. Schaefer didn't simply announce his opinion that Brown intended to distribute cocaine; he explained in detail the circumstances that typically accompany drug dealing and those that mark an individual user. He also expressed his expert opinion that the overall pattern of circumstances in Brown's case resembled cocaine distribution rather than personal drug use.

In many cases, good advocacy reinforces the line between forbidden legal conclusions and helpful testimony. Lay jurors are more likely to understand everyday words like "drove safely" and "wanted to sell" than legal standards like "exercised reasonable care" or "intended to distribute." The best trial lawyers encourage their witnesses to testify in vivid, comprehensible words that engage the jury's sense of fairness. These words hold the jury's attention while also avoiding evidentiary challenges.

2. Rule 704(b) and Mental States. Rule 704(b) seems to adopt a strict bar against expert conclusions about a criminal defendant's mental state when that mental state is an element of the crime or a defense. Read literally, Rule 704(b) would restrict expert testimony offered by either the prosecution or the defense in a wide range of criminal cases.

The courts, however, have construed Rule 704(b) narrowly, turning the section into surplusage that prevents testimony about legal conclusions. Courts restrain experts from testifying explicitly that the defendant possessed a particular mental state, but they allow experts to testify that circumstances were **consistent with** that state. Since juries usually deduce a person's mental state from circumstantial evidence, the latter evidence comes very close to testimony about "whether the defendant did or did not have the mental state." The distinction, however, follows the same line we traced in the previous section: It prevents witnesses from uttering legal conclusions, while allowing them to come as close as possible to that line.

---

6   United States v. Brown, 7 F.3d 648, 650–54 (7th Cir. 1993).

Special Agent Schaefer's testimony in the above example illustrates how narrowly the courts have interpreted Rule 704(b); the court in that case upheld an expert opinion that cocaine seized from the defendant's pocket "was intended for distribution." The court in another drug trafficking case similarly allowed the prosecutor to ask a drug trafficking expert: "Now, in your opinion, Special Agent Pace, would an individual in possession of approximately $200,000 worth of cocaine, would that be an amount consistent with personal use or use for possession for distribution?" The expert, rather predictably, responded: "Possession with intent to distribute."[7]

Even in cases involving the insanity defense, where Congress intended Rule 704(b) to have its greatest impact, courts have allowed experts to offer substantial testimony about the defendant's mental state:

> **Example:** The government charged Edward Brown with attempted bank robbery. Brown claimed insanity as a defense. Federal law requires a defendant claiming insanity to prove by clear and convincing evidence that "as a result of a severe mental disease or defect," he "was unable to appreciate the nature and quality or the wrongfulness of his acts" at the time of the crime.[8]
>
> The government's expert, Dr. Scheftner, testified at trial that Brown suffered from a major depressive disorder, as well as drug and alcohol abuse disorders. Scheftner described common symptoms of these disorders, some of which Brown exhibited. Scheftner, for example, acknowledged that Brown might have experienced major depressive episodes with psychotic features. He offered his opinion, however, that Brown's disorders were not severe.
>
> At the conclusion of this testimony, the prosecutor asked Scheftner: "Dr. Scheftner, does a finding that a person suffers from a major depressive episode with psychotic features in and of itself indicate that a person is unable to understand the wrongfulness of his acts?" The prosecutor followed this question with one substituting the phrase "nature or quality" for the word "wrongfulness." Brown's lawyer objected to both questions under Rule 704(b).

---

7   United States v. Gomez-Norena, 908 F.2d 497, 502 (9th Cir. 1990).

8   18 U.S.C. § 17(a).

Analysis: The trial judge allowed Scheftner to respond to the questions, and the court of appeals affirmed. Scheftner's diagnosis of Brown's disorder did not express any opinion about Brown's mental state at the time of the attempted robbery. Nor did Scheftner's testimony that Brown might have suffered major depressive episodes with psychotic features touch on that issue.

Instead, the challenged questions simply asked Scheftner to offer general observations about whether the latter symptoms inevitably affect the sufferer's ability to understand the wrongfulness of his acts or their nature and quality. Although these questions incorporated the legal language of the insanity defense, they did not ask whether Brown himself met that standard. Thus, the questions did not violate Rule 704(b).[9]

These restrictive readings of Rule 704(b) represent the majority of federal court rulings on the subject. In some cases, however, courts have read Rule 704(b) more expansively to preclude expert testimony related to a criminal defendant's state of mind:

Example: A grand jury indicted Aaron Shaffer for possession and distribution of child pornography. The government's trial evidence showed that Shaffer had stored more than two dozen child pornography videos on his computer and that he had distributed these videos to others through Kazaa, an internet-based file-sharing program. Shaffer claimed that he did not knowingly obtain or distribute child pornography, as the charged crimes require. Instead, he contended that he unknowingly obtained and stored these videos as part of his more general quest for sexually explicit materials.

To support his defense, Shaffer proffered the testimony of a computer expert who had examined the hard drive of his computer. The expert was prepared to testify that, based on the file structure of Shaffer's hard drive, Shaffer was on a "porn fishing expedition with no particular calculation toward any particular type of material, other than generally sexually explicit material." The government objected to this testimony under Rule 704(b).

---

9   United States v. Brown, 32 F.3d 236, 240 (7th Cir. 1994).

Analysis: The trial judge sustained the objection, rejecting the expert's testimony, and the court of appeals affirmed. The appellate court concluded that the expert "sought to suggest to the jury, at the very least by inference, that Mr. Shaffer did not knowingly possess or distribute unlawful child pornography as opposed to simple adult pornography." The court also noted that Rule 704(b) prohibits expert "inference[s]" about a defendant's mental state, as well as more explicit opinions. Thus, the rule gave the trial judge discretion to bar the testimony.[10]

 The expert inference in *Shaffer*, that the file structure on a defendant's computer was more compatible with a "porn fishing expedition" than with knowing collection of child pornography, is strikingly similar to the inference in drug trafficking cases that a particular quantity of cocaine is more consistent with distribution of narcotics than individual use. The conflicting results in these cases may reflect different judicial approaches to Rule 704(b). Alternatively, the variation may display appellate deference to trial court decisions or sympathy for the prosecution's case. Whatever their origin, the fine distinctions drawn under Rule 704(b) allow room for persuasive advocacy.

3. Probabilities. Witnesses sometimes quantify the likelihood of an occurrence by citing probabilities. A lay witness may comment, "I was 99% sure that the oncoming car was going to turn." Expert witnesses are even more likely to use probabilities. A medical expert in a product liability case, for example, may estimate a 40% probability that the defendant's drug caused the plaintiff's injury.

Expert testimony about probabilities often is quite valuable. Some scientific techniques allow precise calibration of probabilities, and those calculations directly inform a jury's fact finding. Many modern trials include testimony that explicitly recites probabilities.

Some testimony referring to probabilities, however, crosses the line discussed above: It introduces conclusions that courts find unhelpful or prejudicial. An early case in this area illustrates some of the most important concerns that arise with probability evidence:

---

10 United States v. Shaffer, 472 F.3d 1219, 1225 (10th Cir. 2007).

Example: The state charged Malcolm and Janet Collins, a married couple, with robbing an elderly woman. At trial, the eyewitnesses had some trouble identifying Malcolm and Janet as the robbers. The eyewitness, however, suggested that (1) a white woman with a blonde ponytail grabbed the victim's purse; (2) the woman then jumped into a partly yellow car; and (3) a black man with a mustache and a beard drove the car away. The prosecutor's evidence also showed that Malcolm Collins was a black man with a mustache who sometimes wore a beard; Janet Collins was a white woman with a blonde ponytail; and the couple owned a partly yellow car.

To build on this evidence, the prosecutor introduced testimony from a college mathematics instructor. The witness described how to calculate the probability that a series of discrete characteristics (such as blonde hair or a black beard) will occur in combination. The prosecutor then gave the instructor assumed probabilities for each of the identifying characteristics described by the eyewitnesses, and asked the mathematician to calculate the probability that a random couple would include a white woman with a blonde ponytail, a black man with a mustache and beard, and a partly yellow automobile. The witness calculated this probability as one chance in twelve million.

The jury convicted Malcolm and Janet, and Malcolm appealed.

Analysis: The California Supreme Court reversed the conviction, holding the probability evidence improper. The court identified four separate defects in the testimony:

First, the expert's calculation lacked a proper factual **foundation**. The prosecutor simply directed the expert to assume that one out of every ten automobiles is partly yellow, one out of every four men has a mustache, etc. The state introduced no evidence to support these factual predicates.

Second, the calculation was **technically flawed**. The expert's approach assumed that each of the individual probabilities was independent of the other. But the probabilities assumed by the prosecutor lacked that independence. The prosecutor, for example, listed the presence of a bearded black man as one factor and the presence of a man with a mustache as a second factor. Men with beards, however, are more likely than men without beards to sport mustaches; the two factors are not independent.

Third, the calculation distracted the jury from assessing **conflicts in the eyewitnesses' testimony**. The witnesses' memories, for example, differed on the shade of the blonde woman's hair. By ignoring these differences, the probability calculation encouraged the jury to overlook its crucial role in resolving testimonial conflicts.

Finally, the prosecutor's use of the testimony confused the rarity of an event with the **probability of the defendants' guilt**. A combination that occurs in just one out of twelve million couples sounds very rare. But a surprisingly small number of people—just 4900—will generate twelve million potential couples, because every person in the population may pair with every other person. From a statistical perspective, the question in a case like Collins is: How many couples matching the eyewitnesses' descriptions could have committed the crime?

In a large metropolitan area like Los Angeles, where this crime occurred, at least one other couple might well have matched the eyewitnesses' testimony. The prosecutor's mathematical evidence erroneously suggested that there was only one chance in twelve million that the Collinses were innocent. Instead, based simply on the mathematical calculations, the probability of the defendants' innocence was far greater.[11]

Most testimony about probabilities stands on firmer ground than the evidence in Collins. The concerns noted by the Collins court, however, parallel those that courts weigh today. Courts will reject probability evidence if it lacks a sufficient factual foundation, contains technical flaws, distracts the jury from important credibility issues, or confuses the rarity of an event with the probability of the defendant's guilt. Under any of these circumstances, a court may hold that the testimony is unhelpful or unfairly prejudicial.

Several recent cases consider the appropriate uses of probability testimony when describing DNA matches. Scientists assume that every individual (except an identical twin) has a unique DNA profile. Much of that profile, however, overlaps with the DNA of other humans; it creates our distinctively human features like two

---

11   People v. Collins, 68 Cal. 2d 319, 438 P.2d 33 (1968). Collins has generated extensive scholarly commentary. Although the points summarized above all originate in the court's opinion, they reflect refinements offered by scholars over the years. We calculated the population size needed to produce twelve million distinct couples with the help of Dr. John Jones, Professor of Mathematics at the Arizona State University.

eyes, ten fingers, and ten toes. These portions of the DNA profile are not useful in linking suspects to blood, semen, or other body tissue left at the scene of a crime.

When investigating crime-scene tissue, DNA scientists instead examine portions of the DNA chain that tend to vary greatly among individuals. The pathologist compares several of these DNA fragments, called alleles, taken from the crime-scene tissue and the suspect's tissue. If the samples are well preserved, this type of comparison is very effective at **ruling out** the possibility that crime-scene tissue came from a particular suspect. Once the pathologist identifies several inconsistencies between the two samples, it is safe to conclude that the crime-scene tissue does not match the suspect.

Using DNA **to link** a suspect to a crime scene is somewhat less certain. By comparing several alleles that vary significantly among humans, and finding matches on those alleles, laboratory scientists can estimate the probability that a particular individual supplied tissue left at a crime scene. The scientists, however, do not profile the entire DNA of either the crime-scene sample or the suspect; that would be unduly time consuming and expensive. The match rests on comparing a limited number of alleles. As a result, the pathologist cannot rule out the possibility that the crime-scene tissue came from a different person; the researcher can only state the probability that another person would have a similar set of matching alleles.

This recent decision illustrates the difficult issues that arise when a party attempts to explain the probability basis of DNA testing to the jury:

> **Example:** A man entered the Doe family home at night and sexually assaulted nine-year-old Jane Doe. Some of Jane's statements pointed to Trent Brown, a family friend, as the perpetrator. But some of her other statements, as well as some circumstantial evidence, pointed toward Trent's brother Troy. Police recovered semen from Jane's underwear and subjected the sample to DNA testing. The state then charged Troy with the crime.
>
> At trial, the state pathologist testified that Troy's DNA matched the DNA in the semen taken from Jane's underwear, and that only one in three million people randomly selected from the population would also match that semen. Pressed to explain the probabilities differently, the pathologist testified that there was a 99.99967% chance that the DNA in Jane's underwear came from Troy. The jury convicted Troy and the state courts

affirmed. Troy then filed a federal habeas corpus claim, challenging the DNA testimony at his trial.

Analysis: The district court granted Troy's habeas petition and the court of appeals affirmed. The court noted several problems with the pathologist's testimony. First, the pathologist improperly accounted for the DNA similarities among close family members. Troy had four brothers who lived close enough to the Does to have committed the crime; indeed, some of the evidence pointed to Troy's brother Trent as the perpetrator. The probability that one of Troy's brothers would match both Troy and the crime-scene sample on the tested alleles was 1/66.

Second, even focusing on the chance that the sample would match a person randomly drawn from the population, the pathologist improperly translated this probability (one in three million) to the conclusion that there was a 99.99967% chance that the tissue in Jane's underwear came from Troy. This error duplicated one of the mistakes in Collins: The frequency of a combination in the population is not the inverse of the likelihood that a person matching that combination is guilty.[12]

 The Supreme Court reversed the grant of Troy's habeas petition, but only because he had forfeited his DNA claim procedurally. The Court acknowledged that, "[g]iven the persuasiveness" of DNA evidence, it is essential to present that evidence "in a fair and reliable manner."[13] Watch, therefore, for further developments on the admissibility of testimony related to DNA testing. This is a complex area in which parties and judges are struggling to understand the science and properly convey probabilities to juries.

4. Polygraphs. Polygraph machines measure a subject's physiological reactions to questions. The machines operate on the assumption that people who lie or speak with a guilty conscience produce different physiological responses than people who speak the truth with a clean conscience. Law enforcement agents use polygraphs to investigate crimes, and some government agencies use them to screen job applicants. Scientific studies, moreover, suggest that polygraphs are at least as accurate

---

12   Brown v. Farwell, 525 F.3d 787 (9th Cir. 2008), rev'd sub nom. McDaniel v. Brown, 558 U.S. 120 (2010).

13   McDaniel, 558 U.S. at 136.

as other forensic techniques like fingerprint comparisons; indeed, polygraphs are more reliable than eyewitness testimony.[14]

Judges, however, remain reluctant to admit polygraph evidence in court. Some of that reluctance is historical. *Frye v. United States*, the case that governed reliability of expert testimony before *Daubert*, declared in 1923 that polygraphs were unreliable.[15] For more than 50 years, courts uniformly followed that holding.

Another part of the reluctance, however, stems from the polygraph's intrusion on the jury's right to assess a witness's credibility. As the Tenth Circuit observed in one case, "[w]hen polygraph evidence is offered in evidence at trial, it is likely to be shrouded with an aura of near infallibility, akin to the ancient oracle of Delphi."[16] Rather than measuring the credibility of witnesses based on their collective judgment, jurors might defer to the findings of a single expert.

The polygraph's relationship to assessing credibility, a core jury function, has thus impeded its acceptance in court. But the improved science of polygraphy, combined with *Daubert*'s changed standard for assessing reliability, has prompted courts to revisit the admissibility of polygraphs. Half a dozen circuits now allow trial judges to admit polygraph evidence under at least some circumstances.[17]

Even in these jurisdictions, judges rarely admit polygraph results unless all parties stipulate to its admission. But the admissibility of polygraph results continues to evolve; persuasive attorneys may convince judges that this evidence can help jurors without creating unfair prejudice.

5. Testimony About Eyewitnesses. Psychology studies have shown that eyewitness testimony is much less reliable than people commonly believe. One study, for example, found that 43% of subjects were unable to pick an individual out of

14   See, e.g., J. Widackl & F. Horvath, An Experimental Investigation of the Relative Validity and Utility of the Polygraph Technique and Three Other Common Methods of Criminal Identification, 23 Forensic Sci. 596, 596–600 (1978).

15   Frye v. United States, 293 F. 1013, 1014 (D.C. Cir. 1923). See Chapter 61 for further discussion of the Frye test.

16   United States v. Alexander, 526 F.2d 161, 168 (8th Cir. 1975).

17   See, e.g., United States v. Posado, 57 F.3d 428, 434 (5th Cir. 1995); United States v. Beyer, 106 F.3d 175, 179 (7th Cir. 1997); United States v. Williams, 95 F.3d 723, 728–30 (8th Cir. 1996); United States v. Cordoba, 104 F.3d 225, 227 (9th Cir. 1996); United States v. Call, 129 F.3d 1402, 1404–05 (10th Cir. 1997); United States v. Gilliard, 133 F.3d 809, 812 (11th Cir. 1998).

a photo array just eight minutes after viewing the individual under highly favorable conditions.[18] Other studies have identified a range of factors that affect the reliability of a particular witness's testimony.

To help jurors understand these limits on eyewitness testimony, criminal defense lawyers began during the 1970s to offer expert testimony about witness perception and memory. At first, courts uniformly rejected this testimony.[19] Some courts asserted that the testimony was not helpful to the jury; others complained that the testimony impermissibly infringed the jury's traditional task of determining credibility.

During the last twenty-five years, federal courts have grown more tolerant of expert testimony discussing the reliability of eyewitnesses. Appellate courts now leave admission of this testimony to the trial judge's discretion, and many judges permit the testimony. The courts, however, continue to limit this expert testimony in two ways.

First, the expert may only describe general findings about eyewitness testimony; the expert may not offer an opinion about whether a particular eyewitness is reliable. This limit parallels the restriction that many courts place on testimony about legal conclusions, which we discussed above.

Second, most courts allow expert testimony about eyewitness reliability only when circumstances suggest that an eyewitness identification is less reliable than usual. Courts, for example, have permitted expert testimony when eyewitness identifications were cross-racial, occurred a long time after the event, stemmed from an incident that caused the witness great stress, or happened after a suggestive photo-spread identification.[20] Jurors may find expert testimony helpful to understand the impact of these factors on a witness's reliability. In more routine cases, courts hold that the jurors' "common sense" and the adversary's "skillful cross-examination" are sufficient to expose any weaknesses in the testimony.[21]

---

18   K.R. Laughery, J.E. Alexander, & A.B. Lane, Recognition of Human Faces: Effects of Target Exposure Time, Target Position, Pose Position, and Type of Photograph, 55 J. Applied Psychol. 477, 477–83 (1971). The subjects in this experiment viewed four pictures of the same individual for a total of 32 seconds, in adequate light, and without any accompanying stress. The photo array from which they subsequently attempted to identify the individual included 150 pictures.

19   See, e.g., United States v. Fosher, 590 F.2d 381, 382–84 (1st Cir. 1979); United States v. Watson, 587 F.2d 365, 368–69 (7th Cir. 1978). See generally Elizabeth F. Loftus, Eyewitness Testimony 198 (Harvard University Press 1996).

20   See, e.g., United States v. Smith, 736 F.2d 1103, 1106 (6th Cir. 1984); United States v. Sebetich, 776 F.2d 412, 418–19 (3d Cir. 1985).

21   See, e.g., United States v. Harris, 995 F.2d 532, 535 (4th Cir. 1993).

Quick Summary

The common law prohibited witnesses from testifying about the ultimate issues in a case. **Rule 704** abolished that rigid approach, but courts continue to protect the provinces of the judge and jury. Under **Rules 701** and **702**, courts may exclude testimony that expresses a legal conclusion as unhelpful. Alternatively, judges may exclude this evidence as unduly prejudicial under Rule 403. These constraints, however, usually affect the form of a witness's testimony rather than its substance.

Rule 704(b) appears to impose a more substantial limit on experts who testify about a criminal defendant's mental state. But judges have read that section narrowly to conform with other rulings about testimony reflecting legal conclusions.

Judicial concern about testimony that invades the jury's province continues to restrict expert testimony expressing probabilities, reporting polygraph results, and describing research on the reliability of eyewitness testimony. Judges admit all three forms of evidence, but they scrutinize it closely to determine whether it is sufficiently helpful to the jury and avoids unfair prejudice. Results in these areas continue to evolve.

Test Your Understanding

To assess your understanding of the material in this chapter, click here to take a quiz, or go to the Quizzes module from the eBook on your eProducts bookshelf.

65

Court-Appointed Experts

Key Concepts

- Judges Have Inherent Power to Appoint Their Own Experts
- **Rule 706:** Creates Process for These Appointments

A. Introduction and Policy. When one party calls an expert witness, the opponent may respond in kind. The two experts, both claiming to draw upon the same specialized knowledge, often present completely opposite opinions. These competing perspectives may confuse the jury rather than illuminate the issues. How can lay jurors choose between witnesses who rest their claims on specialized knowledge that the jury lacks?

At one time, idealistic reformers hoped that court-appointed experts could replace these confusing courtroom battles. A neutral expert, commentators thought, could advise the jury on scientific and technical issues while parties stuck to the facts.

Experience has proven these hopes unrealistic. Within almost every field, experts disagree as much as they agree. Indeed, science and technology achieve some of their greatest advances when experts dispute previously held beliefs. Even when experts endorse the same scientific principles, they may differ in how to apply those principles to the facts of a particular case. The prospect of neutral, court-appointed experts instructing jurors on science proved illusory.

When the Advisory Committee drafted the Federal Rules of Evidence, its members recognized that the use of court-appointed experts was "a relatively infrequent occurrence." The committee, however, suggested a new role for these appointments: The very possibility that a judge might appoint a neutral expert would "exert a sobering effect" on party-appointed experts, inducing those experts to testify more responsibly.[1]

Rule 706, therefore, establishes a procedure for court-appointed experts. Although the rule remains underutilized, judges have started to identify new uses for its process. Court-appointed experts may grow in importance as judges grapple with increasingly technical and international issues.

B. The Rule. Judges have inherent authority to appoint experts; the Federal Rules don't create that power. **Rule 706**, however, codifies this power and outlines procedures for its implementation. The first section of the rule establishes the process of appointment, as well as the parties' rights to examine and cross-examine the expert:

RULE 706. Court-Appointed Expert Witnesses

(a) Appointment Process. On a <u>party's motion or on its own</u>, the court may order the parties to show cause why expert witnesses should not be appointed and may ask the parties to <u>submit nominations</u>.

The court may appoint any expert that the <u>parties agree on</u> and any of its <u>own choosing</u>.

But the court may only appoint <u>someone who consents</u> to act.

(b) Expert's Role. The court must inform the expert of the <u>expert's duties</u>. The court may do so in writing and have a copy filed with the clerk or may do so orally at a conference in which the parties have an opportunity to participate. The expert:

(1) must <u>advise the parties</u> of any findings the expert makes;

(2) may be <u>deposed</u> by any party;

(3) may be <u>called to testify</u> by the court or any party; and

(4) may be <u>cross-examined</u> by any party, including the party that called the expert.

---

1   Federal R. Evid. 706 advisory committee's note.

The underlined phrases signal the key portions of the process for appointing and using a court-appointed expert. One of the parties may petition the judge to appoint an expert, or the judge may decide to appoint one herself. Having decided to appoint an expert, the judge may ask each of the parties for nominations, urge the parties to agree on an expert, or simply find her own expert.

Once appointed, the expert must report his findings to all parties. Each of the parties may also depose the expert and call the expert to testify at trial. If none of the parties call the expert at trial, the judge may call the expert herself. Finally, regardless of who calls the expert, each party may cross-examine the witness during trial.

Section (c) of the rule describes how court-appointed witnesses are compensated:

RULE 706. Court-Appointed Expert Witnesses

(c) Compensation. The expert is entitled to a <u>reasonable compensation</u>, as <u>set by the court</u>. The compensation is payable as follows:

(1) in a <u>criminal case</u> or in a <u>civil case involving just compensation</u> under the Fifth Amendment, from any funds that are provided by law; and

(2) in any <u>other civil case</u>, by the parties in the proportion and at the time that the court directs—and the compensation is then charged like other costs.

In short, the trial judge decides what compensation is reasonable for the expert. In criminal cases and eminent domain proceedings, the judge may use public funds to pay the expert. In all other civil cases, the parties pay the expert's cost in whatever proportion the judge deems to be fair.

Section (d) allows the trial judge to decide whether to tell the jury that the expert was court-appointed:

RULE 706. Court-Appointed Expert Witnesses

(d) Disclosing the Appointment to the Jury. The court may authorize disclosure to the jury that the court appointed the expert.

Judges usually reveal the expert's status. Indeed, the prospect of a neutral expert testifying as the "court's witness" at trial may encourage parties to settle after receiving the expert's report. Under some circumstances, however, a judge may conclude that disclosing the expert's court-appointed status would give the expert **too much** influence over the jury's decision. For that reason, judges sometimes withhold information about the expert's status.

Section (e) of Rule 706, finally, clarifies that even when a court does call its own expert witness, parties may still call their own experts:

RULE 706. Court-Appointed Expert Witnesses

(e) Parties' Choice of Their Own Experts. This rule does not limit a party in calling its own experts.

C. In the Courtroom. Court-appointed experts remain rare in litigation. Some judges, however, use court-appointed experts to advise them on provisions of foreign law. As domestic disputes increasingly raise foreign legal issues, Rule 706's importance may grow.

Example: In 1973, President Nixon gave the government of Honduras a plaque containing a small piece of moon rock encased in a lucite ball. Twenty-five years later, the plaque surfaced in the United States. Honduras requested return of the plaque, claiming it had been taken illegally from the country. The United States filed a civil forfeiture action to determine ownership. To resolve the dispute, the judge had to consult Honduran law and trace the effects of two military coups on the plaque's status.

Analysis: With the parties' agreement, the district judge appointed an expert in Honduran law to research the relevant issues. The expert issued a preliminary report, was deposed by both parties, and submitted a final report. Based on the court-appointed expert's report, as well as other evidence provided by the parties, the judge determined after a bench trial that the plaque had been stolen from the Honduran government.[2]

Litigants and judges sometimes identify new uses for court-appointed experts. In this case, for example, the plaintiffs proposed using a court-appointed expert to resolve confidentiality issues:

Example: Dr. Daniel Bortnick, a plastic surgeon, placed a used computer on the curb outside his home to await trash pickup. A scavenger took the computer to a repair shop, fixed it, and found confidential medical files on the hard drive. The scavenger gave the computer to a local news station, which aired a story about how Bortnick had left medical records on the discarded computer. Several patients sued Bortnick for wrongfully disclosing their private medical information. During discovery, the patients wanted to examine the computer and all of its files. The defendant resisted this request, claiming that unfettered examination would violate the privacy rights of other patients, as well as of his employees.

Analysis: Following a suggestion from the plaintiffs, the court appointed an expert to examine the computer and identify information discoverable by the plaintiffs. By using an expert for this purpose, the court accommodated both the plaintiffs' needs and the privacy rights of others.[3]

---

2   United States v. One Lucite Ball Containing Lunar Material, 252 F. Supp. 2d 1367 (S.D. Fla. 2003).

3   G.D. v. Monarch Plastic Surgery, P.A., 239 F.R.D. 641, 648–50 (D. Kan. 2007).

Quick Summary

Courts have inherent power to appoint their own expert witnesses. **Rule 706** recognizes this power and outlines procedures for its implementation. Judges rarely exercise this power, but new uses for court-appointed experts may be emerging.

Test Your Understanding

To assess your understanding of the material in this chapter, click here to take a quiz, or go to the Quizzes module from the eBook on your eProducts bookshelf.

66

Introduction to Privileges

Key Concepts

- Purposes of Evidentiary Privileges
- **Rule 501:** Federal Rules of Privilege Develop Through Common Law
- State Privilege Rules Apply in Diversity Cases
- Overview of Privileges
- Common Privilege Issues

A. Introduction and Policy. In every trial, lawyers give the jury numerous pieces of evidence, including oral testimony, documents, and physical objects. Based on these inputs, the judge directs the jurors to decide what happened and to render a verdict. This task would be challenging enough if lawyers gave jurors all of the available information. But as we have seen, juries do not get all of that information; the Rules of Evidence exclude some information because it is unfairly prejudicial, unreliable, or capable of misuse.

Occasionally the evidentiary rules exclude information to further a policy interest outside the courtroom. **Rule 407**, for example, encourages defendants to undertake subsequent remedial measures, while **Rule 410** facilitates plea bargaining.[1] But most of the rules we have studied so far withhold evidence to improve the fact finder's ability to determine the truth. By censoring misleading, unreliable, or inflammatory evidence, these rules attempt to further a trial's central truth-finding function.

Privileges impose a much different brand of censorship on trial evidence. Privileged information usually is extremely probative. Quite often, privileged information is also reliable and non-prejudicial. In short, privileged evidence is exactly the

---

1   See Chapter 9 to review Rule 407 and Chapter 12 to review Rule 410.

kind of information we want to give the jury to help them determine the truth. Yet a series of privileges, such as the attorney-client privilege or privilege against self-incrimination, withhold this crucial information from the jury. Why does the law recognize privileges?

Two kinds of justifications support the evidentiary privileges. The first is utilitarian: It argues that privileges are essential to protect certain socially beneficial relationships. Privileges that draw upon this justification must meet three criteria:

1. The relationship must be one that society wants to foster.

2. Confidential communications must be essential to maintaining the relationship.

3. The injury to the relationship from disclosure must be greater than the benefit to the truth-seeking process from that disclosure.[2]

All three of these criteria are subjective: Which relationships does society want to foster? How essential is confidentiality to those relationships? And how does a court or legislature balance the injury to a relationship against the benefit to truth-seeking—especially for entire categories of relationships and cases?

Nevertheless, these criteria provide useful guidelines for creating and explaining privileges. Most people agree that (1) the attorney-client relationship is critical to the justice system; (2) clients would not tell their attorneys the truth if attorneys could be forced to disclose those confidences; and (3) disclosure would injure the attorney-client relationship so severely that the loss to the truth-seeking process is a reasonable price to pay. These considerations explain why every jurisdiction recognizes an attorney-client privilege. Conversely, no judicial system recognizes a privilege that shields communications to drug dealers or car mechanics. The first relationship is not socially desirable, and the second does not require confidentiality.

The second justification for privileges rests on the inherent value of privacy. These privileges protect privacy as an end in itself, not just as a means for promoting

---

2   Dean Wigmore first proposed these criteria, together with a fourth, self-evident requirement that the communication originate in a confidence. 8 Wigmore on Evidence § 2285 (Arthur Best ed., Aspen Books 4th ed. 2008). The federal courts still rely upon these criteria when determining whether to recognize a new privilege. See, e.g., In re Grand Jury Investigation, 918 F.2d 374, 383–84 (3d Cir. 1990) (using the test to determine whether to recognize a clergy-communicant privilege).

a relationship. The privilege against self-incrimination draws primarily on this justification. To preserve human dignity and personal autonomy, our society has a deeply held belief that the state should never be able to compel an individual to testify against himself.

Some privileges draw upon both of these justifications. The privilege shielding spousal communications, for example, exists partly to foster strong marital relationships. But the privilege also rests on a belief that individuals should be able to keep intimate communications absolutely private. Dual justifications also support the privilege between a clergy member and a communicant.

Keep these justifications in mind as we examine particular privileges in this chapter and the next two. Knowing the policies that support privileges will help you understand which privileges exist, as well as the scope and qualifications of those privileges.

B. The Rule. Until September 2008, the Federal Rules of Evidence contained only one, rather uninformative rule governing privileges.[3] The first part of that rule directs courts to apply "common law" to most privilege claims:

RULE 501. Privilege in General

The common law—as interpreted by United States courts in the light of reason and experience—governs a claim of privilege unless any of the following provides otherwise:

- the United States Constitution;
- a federal statute; or
- rules prescribed by the Supreme Court. . . .

The Federal Rules of Evidence, in other words, do not codify any privileges; they leave privileges to common-law development in the courts. Why do the rules adopt such an unusual approach to the law of privileges? The subject simply proved too controversial for Congress.

---

3   In September 2008, Congress approved Federal Rule of Evidence 502, which governs inadvertent waivers of the attorney–client privilege. We explore the impact of that rule further in Chapter 67. The rule, however, addresses only one aspect of the attorney–client privilege. Like Rule 501, it leaves the bulk of that privilege to common-law development.

When the Advisory Committee first proposed the Federal Rules of Evidence, it included thirteen rules in Article V governing privileges. But those proposals unleashed a storm of controversy: Professions that did not receive privileges, like medicine and journalism, protested their omission; politicians weary of Watergate criticized proposed changes in the privilege for state secrets; and some legislators feared that federal privileges would override state privileges in diversity suits. Proponents of codifying the evidentiary rules worried that the controversy would delay or scuttle the entire Federal Rules project, so they deleted the detailed rules on privilege and substituted the current Rule 501.[4]

Since that time, the courts have continued to develop and apply privileges as a matter of federal common law; we list those privileges in the next section. As Rule 501 recognizes, the Constitution, federal statutes, and other federal rules create some privileges.

At the same time that it left the federal law of privileges to judicial development, Congress addressed the problem of privileges in federal diversity actions. The second part of Rule 501 directs courts to apply state-law privileges whenever a claim or defense rests on state law. This language includes almost all issues in diversity actions:

> ## RULE 501. Privilege in General
>
> . . . But in a civil case, <u>state law</u> governs privilege regarding a claim or defense for which state law supplies the rule of decision.

This provision parallels **Rule 601**, which directs courts to determine a witness's competence under state law whenever a witness testifies with respect to a matter based on that law.[5]

C. Overview of Privileges.
We will discuss the most important privileges in the next two chapters. In this section, however, we offer an overview of the privileges recognized by federal law, as well as some developed under state law.

---

4   The thirteen proposed rules now appear separately in most copies of the Federal Rules of Evidence, accompanied by the label "not enacted." We include them in our appendix.

5   See Chapter 14 for further discussion of Rule 601.

1. Federal Privileges. Federal law recognizes three major privileges, as well as several others that arise less frequently. Under Rule 501, these privileges apply to all claims and defenses resting on federal law. Most states recognize privileges quite similar to the ones described in this section, so these privileges generally are available in diversity cases as well.

The most commonly invoked privilege in federal court is the **right against self-incrimination**, which is guaranteed by the Fifth Amendment of the Constitution. This privilege is very broad: It applies in both civil and criminal cases; it protects an individual against coercive interrogation; and it shields the privilege holder during pretrial discovery as well as at trial. The privilege, however, applies only to testimony that might subject the individual to criminal liability. An individual cannot invoke the Fifth Amendment to avoid disclosure of information that simply raises the prospect of embarrassment or civil liability.

Courses on Criminal Procedure and Constitutional Law discuss the Fifth Amendment right against self-incrimination in detail, but we will examine the privilege briefly in Chapter 68.

The **attorney-client privilege** also arises frequently in federal court. This privilege protects all confidential communications between a client and her attorney that are made for the purpose of legal advice or representation. The client may be an individual, an organization, or a corporation. Protected communications, moreover, include those made to any individual working with the attorney to provide legal services. A related **work product privilege** complements the traditional attorney-client privilege. We will discuss both of these privileges in Chapter 67.

The third most common privilege invoked in the federal court is the **spousal privilege**. Under federal law, as well as the law of most states, this privilege encompasses two overlapping privileges. The spousal **testimonial privilege** allows one spouse to refuse to testify against the other in a criminal proceeding or grand jury investigation. The privilege shields almost any information that the spouse might offer; it is not restricted to confidential communications. This privilege, however, persists only during the life of the marriage; if the marriage ends, the ex-spouses may not invoke this privilege.

The spousal privilege for **confidential communications** applies in both civil and criminal cases, and it survives the end of a marriage; in these ways, it is broader than the testimonial privilege. This second spousal privilege, however, protects only confidential communications that the spouses share during the marriage. This privilege does not protect discussions that occurred before marriage, non-confidential statements made during the marriage, or conduct that the spouse observed during the marriage.

We will discuss the overlapping spousal privileges further in Chapter 68. In addition to the limits noted above, both of these privileges recognize exceptions for cases involving intra-family disputes like child abuse, domestic violence, or tort actions by one spouse against another.

Federal law also recognizes several privileges that protect important interests but arise less frequently. In 1996, for example, the Supreme Court recognized a **psychotherapist-patient privilege**.[6] This relatively new privilege protects all confidential communications between a patient and a psychologist, psychiatrist, or social worker, as long as those communications were made to obtain psychological diagnosis or treatment. Most courts hold that the privilege contains a narrow exception for cases in which the patient poses a serious risk of harm that can be avoided only if the therapist discloses confidential information.

Other privileges available under federal law include the **executive privilege**, which protects certain advice given to high-level government decision-makers; and the **clergy-communicant privilege**, which applies to confidential communications with members of the clergy for the purpose of obtaining spiritual advice.

2. Privileges That Are Not Fully Recognized Under Federal Law. In 1972, the Supreme Court held that there was no **reporter's privilege** in the federal courts. The case, *Branzburg v. Hayes*,[7] considered whether a reporter's privilege could be derived from the First Amendment of the Constitution, and held that no such privilege existed.

Branzburg was decided before the promulgation of the Federal Rules of Evidence, and specifically before Rule 501, which explicitly affirmed that courts had the power to create privileges through common law. In the decades since Branzburg, a number of federal circuits have used Rule 501 to recognize a reporter's privilege within their jurisdiction.[8] Other circuit courts have found that *Branzburg* foreclosed any such possibility and have refused to recognize a common-law privilege.[9] The

---

6   Jaffee v. Redmond, 518 U.S. 1 (1996).

7   408 U.S. 665 (1972).

8   See, e.g., Zerilli v. Smith, 656 F.2d 705 (D.C. Cir. 1981).

9   See, e.g., McKevitt v. Pallasch, 339 F.3d 530 (7th Cir. 2003).

scope of any federal journalism privilege, therefore, remains unclear. Members of Congress have tried to create a statutory privilege for journalists, but those proposals have never won full congressional approval.

Federal law provides even less protection for the **physician-patient** relationship: There is no federal common-law or constitutional privilege shielding that relationship. Some federal statutes protect the confidentiality of medical information in selected contexts, but none of these offer the full protection of a privilege.

Most states, in contrast, recognize both a reporter's privilege and a physician–patient one. The privileges are statutory in some states and common-law in others. A few states also recognize **intra-family privileges** that are more expansive than the federal spousal privileges. A few, for example, recognize privileges between parents and children.

The elements of these state-based privileges vary widely from state to state. Where they exist, however, they govern state claims and defenses litigated in federal court—even if federal law recognizes no similar privilege.

D. Common Privilege Issues.

Before turning to specific privileges in the next two chapters, we note four issues that arise with respect to every privilege. You should examine each of these issues when assessing the application of any privilege

- **Who holds** the privilege? In other words, who may assert the privilege and who may waive the privilege?

- **When** does the privilege apply? Does it apply in all proceedings or just under certain circumstances?

- **What** does the privilege cover? Does it shield only certain communications or information between certain people? Does it only apply to communications on a certain topic or made under certain conditions? This is also known as the **scope** of the privilege.

- **How strong** is the privilege? Some privileges are **absolute**; an opponent cannot overcome them. But other privileges are **qualified**; the opponent can pierce the privilege by making a specific showing. Even if the privilege is absolute, it may have **exceptions**.

In proceedings governed by the Federal Rules of Evidence, the judge resolves issues like these as part of a preliminary determination governed by **Rule 104**. Remember, however, that **Rule 1101(c)** recognizes privileges in "all stages of a case or proceeding."[10] The rules of privilege, therefore, apply even during preliminary determinations. When a party asserts an absolute privilege, which includes most of the privileges recognized by federal law, the judge does not hear the privileged information during the preliminary determination. Instead, the judge determines whether the privilege exists by looking at the facts of the asserted relationship, any claims of waiver, and similar matters.

If a party asserts a qualified privilege, such as the journalist–source privilege recognized under many state laws, then the judge often reviews the privileged information in camera (without disclosure to other parties) to determine whether to pierce the privilege.

Quick Summary

 Evidentiary privileges preserve human dignity and protect valuable relationships. To further these concerns, courts preclude information protected by privileges—even though that information is probative, reliable, and non-prejudicial. The Federal Rules of Evidence do not codify any privileges. Instead, federal courts develop federal privileges as a matter of common law. These courts apply state rules of privilege when state law controls a claim or defense. The privileges most frequently applied in federal court are the privilege against self-incrimination, the attorney-client privilege, and two overlapping spousal privileges.

For every privilege, you should know (1) who holds the privilege and has the power to waive it; (2) when the privilege applies; (3) what information the privilege covers; and (4) whether the privilege is absolute or qualified.

---

10   We discussed Rule 1101(c) in Chapter 3. For further discussion of Rule 104 and preliminary determinations, see Chapter 34.

67

Attorney-Client Privilege

Key Concepts

- Protects Confidential Legal Communications Between Client and Attorney Related to Legal Services
- Crime-Fraud Exception
- Waiver
- Corporate Context
- Work Product Privilege

A. Introduction and Policy. The attorney-client privilege is the oldest of all the evidentiary privileges. The privilege is rooted in two related policy concerns, reflecting the two theories behind privileges that we discussed in Chapter 66. First, the attorney-client relationship is critically important to society; indeed, the Sixth Amendment recognizes the right of criminal defendants to "the Assistance of Counsel." Effective legal representation, moreover, requires open, honest communication between the lawyer and client; an attorney can ably represent the client only if she knows as many facts as possible about the case. Obtaining that information, in turn, demands confidentiality: A client will not share incriminating facts if he believes that the attorney will disclose the information in court.

Second, the privilege promotes privacy and confidentiality as ends in themselves. An attorney and her client share a special relationship of trust; they are one legal unit during the course of representation. To break the unit apart by forcing the lawyer to testify against her client would violate the deep-seated principle that the attorney is the client's legal representative.

Attorneys honor two overlapping commitments to maintain the confidences of their clients. The first is a **professional obligation** to keep client information confidential; the rules of professional responsibility prohibit an attorney from disclosing to any person information that a client wants to keep confidential.[1] If a criminal defense attorney learns embarrassing information about a client when interviewing a third-party witness, the lawyer should not recount that information to friends and family members. Similarly, if a corporate attorney discovers damaging information about a company while reviewing documents, the attorney should not share those details with the press. Confidentiality is a professional obligation that attorneys owe their clients.

The second type of attorney-client commitment is an **evidentiary privilege**. This privilege, recognized in all state and federal courts, prevents an attorney from offering testimony or other evidence about confidential client communications. The evidentiary privilege is stronger than the professional obligation; it protects attorney-client communications even if the attorney is subpoenaed to testify in court. But the evidentiary privilege is also narrower than the professional obligation; it covers only confidential communications made to obtain legal services.

In this book we focus on the evidentiary privilege that protects the attorney-client relationship. Courses in Professional Responsibility discuss the related, but distinct, professional obligation.

B. The Rule. Congress has not codified the attorney-client privilege, just as it has not codified any other federal rules of privilege. The proposed rule that the Advisory Committee sent to Congress in 1972, however, provides a useful foundation for examining the attorney-client privilege as developed under federal common law. We will use the proposed rule to answer the four key questions identified in the last chapter: Who holds the privilege? When does the privilege apply? What does the privilege cover? How strong is the privilege?[2]

1. Who Holds the Privilege? As proposed Rule 503 made clear, the client holds the attorney-client privilege. This makes sense because the privilege protects the client, not the lawyer:

---

1   Model Rules of Prof'l Conduct R. 1.6 (2002).

2   The 1972 proposed rules on privilege appear in the appendix, immediately following the current rules of evidence.

RULE 503 (Not Enacted). Lawyer-Client Privilege

(b) General rule of privilege. A <u>client</u> has a privilege to refuse to disclose and to prevent any other person from disclosing confidential communications made for the purpose of facilitating the rendition of professional legal services to the client . . . .

Although the client holds the privilege, his attorney often asserts the privilege on his behalf. The proposed rule also recognized this process:

RULE 503 (Not Enacted). Lawyer-Client Privilege

(c) Who may claim the privilege. The privilege may be claimed by the <u>client</u> . . . . The person who was the <u>lawyer</u> at the time of the communication may claim the privilege but <u>only on behalf</u> of the client. His authority to do so is <u>presumed</u> in the absence of evidence to the contrary. . . .

If an attorney receives a discovery request, subpoena to testify, or other inquiry that would violate the attorney-client privilege, the lawyer will zealously assert the privilege on the client's behalf. The law assumes both that the client wants to claim the privilege and that the attorney has authority to assert that claim. Clients, therefore, rarely file a formal evidentiary motion to prevent a lawyer from providing evidence protected by the privilege; the attorney usually asserts the privilege on her own.

As we will see in the Courtroom section, ownership of the privilege matters because it determines who has the power to **waive** the privilege. Waiver of the attorney-client privilege presents several thorny issues that we discuss further below.

2. When Does the Privilege Apply? The attorney-client privilege prevents disclosure of privileged information **in any context**. The privilege applies at trial, but it also applies to grand jury proceedings, pretrial hearings, and every other stage of litigation.

Most notably, the attorney-client privilege applies during discovery. Lawyers often assert the privilege to withhold privileged documents from the opponent. Indeed, attorneys must assert the privilege during discovery; otherwise, disclosure of the communication would waive the privilege and prevent the client from asserting it later.

This prospect, however, creates an enormous challenge for litigators. Discovery in some civil cases encompasses extensive electronic files; it may also include truck-loads or warehouses of paper documents. How do lawyers or their clients screen all of this material before disclosure to assure that they don't inadvertently reveal privileged communications?

To address this growing problem, the Advisory Committee drafted **Rule 502**. You will discuss the details of that rule in Complex Litigation or Trial Practice classes, so we explore it only briefly here. There are two important sections of the rule for Evidence students.

First, if a client or attorney **inadvertently** discloses information covered by the attorney-client privilege during a federal proceeding, the disclosure does not waive the privilege if the holder of the privilege both (a) "took reasonable steps to prevent disclosure," and (b) then "took reasonable steps to rectify the error."

Second, if an attorney or client **intentionally** discloses some privileged informa-tion in a federal proceeding, other privileged communications remain protected unless (a) they "concern the same subject matter," and (b) the communications "ought in fairness to be considered together."

These provisions have reduced some of the anxiety and cost of civil discovery. Note, however, that Rule 502 does not address other aspects of the attorney-client privi-lege. That privilege remains largely a creature of common law in the federal courts.

3. What Does the Privilege Cover? Rule 503(b), proposed by the Advisory Committee during the 1970s and quoted above, summarizes the scope of the attorney-client privilege: The privilege encompasses "confidential communications made for the purpose of facilitating the rendition of professional legal services to the client." The rule continues by explaining that these communications usually must occur between the client "or his representative and his lawyer or his lawyer's representative."

Existence of the attorney-client privilege, therefore, depends on the presence of five factors:

- A **client** or the client's representative

- An **attorney** or her representative

- A **communication** between those two parties

- **Confidentiality** of the communication, and

- A **purpose** of facilitating professional legal services to the client

Each of these requirements raises issues in application, so we will explore each one further in the Courtroom section.

4. How Strong Is the Privilege? The attorney-client privilege is absolute, rather than qualified. A party, in other words, may not overcome the privilege by proving a strong need for the protected information. The privilege, however, does recognize several exceptions. Only three of these, all recognized by proposed Rule 503, arise with any frequency. The first is the crime-fraud exception:

RULE 503 (Not Enacted). Lawyer-Client Privilege

(d) Exceptions. There is no privilege under this rule:

    (1) Furtherance of crime or fraud. If the services of the lawyer were sought or obtained to enable or aid anyone <u>to commit or plan to commit</u> what the <u>client knew or reasonably should have known</u> to be <u>a crime or fraud</u>; . . . .

If a client asks an attorney to help him perpetuate a crime or a fraud, then the request itself is illegal, and there is no policy justification for shielding such communications. A client needs to be able to disclose **prior** illegal acts to further his legal representation, but society has no reason to facilitate **new** crimes. This crime-fraud exception generates some difficult line-drawing issues in practice, so we explore it further in the Courtroom section.

The second common exception to the attorney-client privilege applies when either the lawyer or client claims a breach of their own relationship:

Rule 503 (Not Enacted). Lawyer-Client Privilege

(d) Exceptions. There is no privilege under this rule: . . .

    (3) Breach of duty by lawyer or client. As to a communication relevant to an issue of <u>breach of duty by the lawyer to his client or by the client to his lawyer</u>; . . . .

This exception allows an attorney to disclose privileged information if necessary to defend against a malpractice action. Similarly, if a criminal defendant attacks his conviction on the ground that his trial attorney provided ineffective assistance, the court can inquire into relevant aspects of that representation. In these situations, the former client implicitly waives the attorney-client privilege for all communications related to the alleged breach of duty.

The final significant exception to the attorney-client privilege arises when an attorney represents two or more clients jointly. If the joint representation breaks down, and one client sues another, then any client may disclose the confidential communications that occurred during the representation:

Rule 503 (Not Enacted). Lawyer-Client Privilege

(d) Exceptions. There is no privilege under this rule: . . .

    (5) Joint clients. As to a communication relevant to a matter of common interest between two or more clients if the communication was made by any of them to a lawyer retained or consulted in common, when offered <u>in an action between any of the clients</u>.

This exception often arises in divorce cases. If the spouses believe the divorce will be amicable, they may try to save money by hiring a single attorney to execute the divorce, draw up papers dividing the property, and establish any child custody arrangements. If the divorce then turns contentious, the original attorney must withdraw from representing either spouse. At that point, both spouses lose the privilege; either one may force the attorney to testify about any relevant communications with either spouse.

Attorneys who represent multiple clients on a common matter must explain this possible loss of privilege at the start of representation. The attorney, in other words, should explain that any party may disclose confidential communications if the joint representation breaks down; the other parties will not be able to prevent disclosure under those circumstances.

C. In the Courtroom. In this section, we explore the five factors that define the scope of the attorney-client privilege: a client, an attorney, a communication, confidentiality, and a purpose of facilitating legal advice. We also examine the crime-fraud exception to the privilege and rules governing waiver of the privilege.

1. Who Is a Client? A client is any individual or entity who obtains legal services from a lawyer or consults a lawyer about obtaining those services. Government agencies, corporations, and nonprofit organizations may all become clients.

Complex issues arise when a corporation or other organization invokes the attorney-client privilege. Which employees represent the corporation? Does a communication between any worker and a company lawyer evoke the privilege? Or do only some workers count as clients?

No court would consider every corporate employee a client for the purpose of applying the attorney-client privilege. Construing the privilege that broadly would shield an enormous amount of information without furthering the policies that underlie the privilege.

Federal common law uses a functional, multi-factor test to identify employees who qualify as the "client" in a corporate setting. The test derives from a Supreme Court decision addressing these facts:

> **Example:** The Upjohn Corporation was a large, multinational corporation that produced and sold pharmaceuticals around the world. In 1976, an independent audit of one of the company's foreign subsidiaries indicated that the subsidiary had been paying bribes to local government officials to further the company's business.
>
> Upjohn's general counsel and board chair realized that these bribes might not be isolated incidents. The chair sent a letter to the managers of all foreign offices, asking them to complete a questionnaire prepared by the

company's lawyers. The questionnaire sought detailed information about the "nature and magnitude of any payments made . . . to any employee or official of a foreign government." The letter made clear that the company sought this information for legal purposes, that the managers should respond directly to the company's general counsel, and that the managers should treat the matter as "highly confidential."

After receiving responses from its overseas managers, Upjohn filed a voluntary disclosure with the SEC and the IRS, describing some of the questionable payments. The IRS immediately began an investigation of Upjohn and sent the company a summons demanding all of the completed questionnaires submitted by foreign managers. Upjohn refused, claiming the information was privileged.

Analysis: The Supreme Court upheld Upjohn's privilege claim. The Court refused to articulate a "broad rule . . . to govern all conceivable future questions in this area." Instead, the Court focused on multiple factors that allowed the foreign office managers to communicate as clients in this case:

- The managers provided information directly to the company's counsel to help the company secure legal advice

- The managers knew this was the purpose of supplying the information

- They provided this information in response to a superior's request

- The communications related to matters within the scope of the managers' duties

- Other employees could not provide this information to counsel

- All parties treated the communications as highly confidential

Under these circumstances, the Court concluded, the Upjohn managers were clients, and their communications qualified for the attorney-client privilege.[3]

When federal law governs a corporation's assertion of privilege, courts use the *Upjohn* factors to determine whether a particular employee was a "client" entitled to protection of the attorney-client privilege. A corporation need not prove all of

---

3   Upjohn v. United States, 449 U.S. 383, 396–97 (1981).

the *Upjohn* factors to prevail, although several of them are necessary for any claim of attorney-client privilege; no client may assert the privilege without showing both confidentiality and a purpose of obtaining legal advice.

The key *Upjohn* factor seems to be the requirement that an employee speak about matters within the scope of her duties. This factor coincides with the privilege's rationale. As the Court observed in *Upjohn*, the privilege exists so that parties may give their lawyers the information necessary to produce "sound and informed advice."[4] To render that advice, lawyers must speak to corporate employees who have responsibility for the disputed matter.

Some states apply a test like the *Upjohn* one to identify corporate employees who speak as clients. Others recognize only members of a corporation's "control group" as clients protected by the attorney-client privilege. The control-group test is much narrower than the *Upjohn* one; it includes only corporate officers authorized to act on advice given by the company's attorney.

2. Who Is an Attorney? The client stands on one side of a protected attorney-client privilege, and the lawyer stands on the other. A "lawyer" is any person who is authorized to practice law or who the client **reasonably believes** is authorized to practice law. The privilege does not depend upon authority to practice law in a particular jurisdiction. A client who consults in Iowa with a lawyer licensed to practice law in Louisiana (or even in Liechtenstein) may claim the privilege.

The privilege, moreover, recognizes that attorneys accomplish their work with the help of numerous "representatives," including secretaries, paralegals, accountants, translators, and a host of others. These representatives fall within the scope of the attorney-client privilege as long as their services are necessary to further the legal representation. The representatives need not be permanently on the attorney's payroll. If an attorney hires an accident reconstruction expert to help prepare a client's case, for example, that consultant becomes a representative of the attorney. Both the client's and the attorney's confidential communications with the consultant will fall within the attorney-client privilege.

3. What Is a Communication? The attorney-client privilege shields **communications** between an attorney and client. The communications may be written or oral; as with hearsay, communications also include assertive acts like pointing

---

4   Id. at 390.

a finger or nodding the head.[5] The privilege, moreover, protects both communications by the client to the lawyer and those flowing from the lawyer to the client.

The privilege, however, protects only these communications; it does not protect the **underlying information**. If a third party discovers the underlying information without relying on the attorney-client communication, the privilege imposes no bar on admitting that information in court. We discussed this type of distinction in Chapter 10, when we discussed the admissibility of statements made during settlement negotiations. **Rule 408** precludes admission of those statements, but allows independent evidence of information discussed during the settlement. The attorney-client privilege includes a similar limit.

In the *Upjohn* case, for example, the IRS could not explore the possibility that Upjohn paid foreign bribes by obtaining the questionnaires that the foreign managers completed for the company counsel. Those questionnaires were communications between a client and attorney. The government, however, could have interviewed the Upjohn managers itself, asking directly about payments to foreign governments. The managers might have refused to cooperate or invoked the privilege against self-incrimination, but the attorney-client privilege would not have sheltered those direct inquiries.

Here is another example of the difference between a client's communication to her attorney and the facts that were communicated:

> **Example:** Kathy is accused of armed robbery. She admits to her attorney in confidence that she purchased a gun from her brother the day before the robbery. Two days later, as part of their regular investigation, police interview Kathy's brother. The brother admits that he sold Kathy a gun the day before the robbery. At trial, the prosecutor calls Kathy's brother to the stand to testify about the gun he sold Kathy. Kathy's attorney objects, claiming that the information is privileged.

> **Analysis:** The privilege does not bar the brother's testimony. Kathy's communication to her attorney is privileged because she made the statement in confidence to her lawyer for the purpose of soliciting legal services. But Kathy's brother is not testifying about that communication. Most likely, nei-

---

5   See Chapter 37 for further discussion of assertive acts in the hearsay context.

ther the brother nor the prosecutor knows what Kathy told her lawyer. The brother is offering his personal knowledge about the gun. The fact that Kathy disclosed that information to her attorney is irrelevant to the admissibility of her brother's testimony.

This principle means that a client cannot hide information, documents, or objects by communicating them to an attorney. For example, if the client has possession of a preexisting letter or a document that is incriminating, h2 cannot give the document to the attorney and claim that it is now privileged. Any writings which came into existence independent of the attorney-client interactions are **not** privileged.

Example: Robert Rhea was charged with a series of rapes and sexual assaults of his 13-year-old stepdaughter. At trial, the stepdaughter testified that Rhea sometimes gave her gifts in exchange for the sexual encounters. She noted that Rhea once bought her a stereo in return for her promise to give him six "lovings." To be sure Rhea did not demand additional "lovings," the stepdaughter recorded these six acts on a calendar in her room at Rhea's apartment.

Based on this testimony, the government obtained a warrant and searched Rhea's apartment. They did not, however, find a calendar. The defense attorneys, meanwhile, looked through materials that Rhea had given them from his apartment to aid their trial preparation. Among those materials, they found a calendar with the notation "Bought stereo—6" on one date, and the numbers 1 through 6 on six subsequent dates.

The defense attorneys informed the trial judge ex parte that they had the calendar in their possession, and the judge ordered the attorneys to turn over the calendar to the prosecution. After the attorneys complied, the defendant successfully moved to remove both attorneys and the judge from the case. At a new trial before a different judge, the prosecutor offered both the stepdaughter's testimony and the calendar as evidence. Rhea claimed that the calendar was privileged.

Analysis: Both the trial and appellate courts rejected Rhea's claim that the calendar was privileged. The calendar was a physical object, rather than a communication between Rhea and his attorneys. Giving the calendar to the attorneys did not transform the calendar itself into a privileged communication.

The fact that Rhea gave his attorneys the calendar in response to their request for any items from his apartment relevant to his defense, however, **was** privileged. Rhea's response to that request was equivalent to him saying to his lawyers: "This calendar was in my apartment and it is related to my stepdaughter's charges." The prosecutor, therefore, could not ask the attorney how he obtained the calendar; nor could the prosecutor ask Rhea whether he gave the calendar to his attorney. The prosecutor avoided these issues, however, by having the stepdaughter identify the calendar; he did not rely on any privileged communications to admit the item.[6]

The *Rhea* case confirms that an object given to an attorney does not itself become privileged. The facts of this case, moreover, show that attorneys have an **affirmative duty** as officers of the court to disclose any contraband or physical evidence of a crime that comes into their possession. Thus, Rhea's lawyers had an obligation to give the calendar to the trial judge. They did not, however, have to disclose how they obtained the calendar.

4. When Is a Communication Confidential? The fourth limit on the scope of the attorney-client privilege is confidentiality: The privilege protects only communications that the client and attorney make in confidence. Communications lose their confidentiality if they occur in the presence of people who fall outside the privilege. Representatives of the client or lawyer do not destroy confidentiality if they are privy to a communication. Both the lawyer and client, for example, could bring an assistant to a meeting in order to record notes. But other third parties do affect the privilege: If a client blurts information to his lawyer in front of the lawyer's friend, the communication is not confidential.

If an eavesdropper overhears a communication, existence of the privilege depends on whether the client took reasonable precautions to ensure confidentiality. If the client acted reasonably, then the communication remains subject to the privilege. If not, then the privilege does not apply:

---

6   United States v. Rhea, 33 M.J. 413, 419 (C.M.A. 1991).

Example: Jay Lentz was convicted of kidnapping and murdering his wife. An appellate court overturned the conviction and remanded to the District Court for a new trial. While waiting in prison for that trial, Lentz called his attorney and made incriminating statements about his case. This conversation, like all phone conversations between inmates and others, was recorded by the government. The prison administrators had made clear to inmates that all phone conversations were monitored.

Analysis: Lentz's communication with his attorney was not privileged. Lentz was on notice that all phone conversations in prison were monitored, and therefore he did not reasonably believe that the conversation was confidential.[7]

A lawyer sometimes asserts that the mere fact she represents a particular client is confidential. Under most circumstances, however, courts reject this claim; the mere **identity** of a client is not sufficiently confidential to warrant protection by the attorney-client privilege. In unusual cases, however, disclosure of the client's identity "would implicate the client in the very matter for which legal advice [had been] sought in the first case."[8] Under these circumstances, the client's identity is confidential and falls within the privilege:

Example: Late at night, Andy runs a red light and kills a pedestrian. He leaves the scene of the accident and does not call the police. The next day, he visits an attorney's office, tells her what happened, and asks what liability he would face if he came forward. With Andy's permission, the attorney contacts the investigating officer and prosecutor assigned to the case; she discusses resolution of the case but does not name her client. One week later, the prosecutor subpoenas the attorney to appear at a grand jury and reveal the name of her client. He also asks her to turn over all her billing records for the past week so that he can see who visited the attorney's office the day after the incident.

---

7   This example is based on the facts of United States v. Lentz, 524 F.3d 501 (4th Cir. 2008). Note that the prison, like all prisons, provided confidential avenues for inmates to consult with their lawyers. Lentz opted to use this non-confidential route.

8   In re Grand Jury Proceedings (Pavlick), 680 F.2d 1026, 1027 (5th Cir. Unit A 1982) (en banc).

Analysis: The attorney can refuse to answer any question about her client's identity and can refuse to turn over her billing records. In this case, the client's identity was part of the confidential communication that Andy conveyed to the attorney. Disclosing Andy's identity, either by responding to the prosecutor's question or by turning over the billing records, would implicate him in the very matter for which he sought legal advice.

5. Purpose. The attorney-client privilege only protects communications that a lawyer or client makes for the purpose of receiving legal services. The privilege protects initial consultations with a lawyer, even if the parties do not pursue the representation. It also shields communications made to further any type of legal representation; the privilege is not limited to legal advice related to litigation.

The services, however, must relate to law rather than business, accounting, politics, policy, or other matters. Lawyers often provide a range of overlapping professional services to their clients; as a result, courts sometimes must draw difficult lines separating communications related to legal services from other professional communications:

Example: Randolph and Karin Louis retained Richard Frederick, a lawyer and accountant, to represent them on legal matters and file their tax returns. The IRS began investigating the Louises and requested hundreds of documents from Frederick. Frederick refused to comply, invoking the attorney-client privilege.

Analysis: The court of appeals held that any communications related to Frederick's preparation of tax returns did not fall within the attorney-client privilege. Allowing lawyers to invoke the privilege for preparing tax returns, the court ruled, would "impede tax investigations, reward lawyers for doing nonlawyers' work, and create a privileged position for lawyers in competition with other tax preparers." On the other hand, communications made in connection with a tax audit might involve lawyerly work such as statutory interpretation or application of judicial precedent. None of the disputed communications involved this type of legal work, so the court did not elaborate further on means for identifying those communications.[9]

---

9   This example is based on United States v. Frederick, 182 F.3d 496, 500 (7th Cir. 1999).

6. Crime-Fraud Exception. Clients often discuss prior crimes with their attorneys; the attorney-client privilege exists to facilitate those confidences. But if a client seeks help in carrying out an ongoing crime or seeks advice about how to commit future crimes, the attorney-client privilege does not protect those communications. Clients cannot use the privilege as a cloak to hide the perpetration of a crime or fraud.[10]

The crime-fraud exception to the attorney-client privilege applies if (1) the client is committing or intending to commit a fraud or crime, and (2) the attorney-client communications are in furtherance of that alleged crime or fraud. In the *Lentz* case described above, for example, the incarcerated defendant asked his attorney for advice that would help him hire a hit man to kill the potential witnesses against him. The attorney properly refused to provide this help; he also persuaded Lentz to give up the plan. The crime-fraud exception, however, provided a second ground for admitting Lentz's statements at trial.

In *Lentz*, the attorney understood the client's illegal purpose. But the crime-fraud exception applies even if the lawyer is ignorant of the client's intent or illegal plans:

> **Example:** Eugene Cleckler owned two businesses, Ezy-Rider and Gene's Marine. In an attempt to defraud the I.R.S., Cleckler claimed that some sales made by Gene's Marine were actually made by Ezy-Rider. Cleckler's attorney, Edward Selfe, did not know that Cleckler was falsely attributing sales to Gene's Marine; he suggested that Cleckler produce additional documentation, such as invoices and deposit slips, to support his case. Cleckler gave Selfe falsified documents, and Selfe passed the false documents to the IRS.
>
> At trial, the IRS attorney called Selfe to the stand and asked him about his suggestion that Cleckler provide additional documentation. Cleckler objected, claiming that this testimony violated his attorney-client privilege.

Analysis: This communication was not privileged because it related to an ongoing crime that Cleckler was perpetrating. Cleckler obtained his attorney's assistance to further his criminal activity. Although Selfe did not realize

---

10   United States v. Gordon-Nikkar, 518 F.2d 972, 975 (5th Cir. 1975).

his role in the scheme, Cleckler used his attorney's advice to support his false claims and to provide fabricated documents to the IRS.[11]

Finally, as implied by its name, the crime-fraud exception applies to either crimes or frauds. Many crimes, such as Lentz's plan to hire a hit man, do not include fraud. Conversely, many frauds are simply private torts rather the crimes. The crime-fraud exception, however, applies to both of these categories.

7. Waiver. An attorney may not waive the attorney-client privilege without the client's permission. Since the client holds the privilege, only the client may decide to waive the privilege.

Sometimes a client expressly waives the attorney-client privilege; the client may not care about sharing the privileged information with others. More often, a client inadvertently waives the privilege by sharing a significant part of a confidential communication with a third party. Once a client reveals the communication to someone outside the privilege, he waives the privilege in other contexts as well. An opponent may then introduce the privileged communication in court.

To waive the privilege, however, a client must reveal the content of her **communications** with a lawyer, not merely the same **facts** she told the lawyer:

> **Example:** Remember Kathy, the armed robber who purchased a gun from her brother the day before the robbery. As explained above, Kathy confided the fact of her gun purchase to her attorney. She also told her best friend, Thelma, that she had purchased a gun before the robbery. Thelma notified the prosecutor about Kathy's admission. Thelma and Kathy's brother then ran away to Sierra Leone and disappeared. The prosecutor summoned Kathy's lawyer before a grand jury and asked the lawyer whether Kathy had admitted purchasing a gun from her brother.
>
> **Analysis:** Kathy's lawyer should refuse to answer this question; Kathy's communication still benefits from the attorney-client privilege. Kathy disclosed similar facts to both Thelma and the lawyer, but she did not tell Thelma about her discussions with the lawyer. The attorney-client privilege protects

---

11   This example is based on United States v. Cleckler, 265 F. App'x 850 (11th Cir. 2008). In the reported case, it is not clear whether the attorney was aware of his client's fraudulent behavior.

communications, not facts. Just as the prosecutor could compel Thelma or Kathy's brother to discuss the fact of Kathy's gun purchase without violating the attorney-client privilege, Kathy can discuss those facts with third parties without waiving the privilege.

On the other hand, assume Kathy had said to Thelma: "So I told my lawyer about buying the gun from my brother. I mean, what should I do about that? I asked the lawyer, 'Can they force my brother to testify against me?' " This would constitute a waiver of the privilege because Kathy is revealing the content of her confidential attorney-client discussions to a third party.

If a client waives the privilege with respect to one portion of her communications with an attorney, then the court may force the attorney to testify about any related communications that "ought in fairness to be considered" with the disclosed material. Courts developed this requirement as a matter of common law, and new Rule 502 (discussed above) codifies it.[12]

Rule 502 also governs the difficult problem of inadvertent waivers of the attorney-client privilege. As we discussed in the Rules section, complex lawsuits and voluminous document productions sometimes inadvertently disclose privileged communications. Either the client or the lawyer might cause this type of mistaken disclosure. The new rule, building on common-law decisions, prevents waiver of the privilege as long as the privilege holder used reasonable measures to prevent the disclosure and takes reasonable steps to rectify it.

Waiver, finally, presents special issues in the context of corporate or organizational clients. The *Upjohn* case, discussed above, recognizes that multiple employees may speak for the corporation when providing confidential information to counsel. The corporation as an entity, however, decides whether to waive the privilege. Members of its "control group," such as the executive officers, decide whether to waive the attorney-client privilege.

This distinction can produce troubling ethical issues. The managers in the *Upjohn* case, for example, responded to the board chair's request to provide confidential information to the company's counsel. Some of the managers probably made

---

12   The requirement is analogous to the rule of completeness that Rule 106 establishes for documents and recordings. See Chapter 24 for full discussion of Rule 106. The court's common-law approach to partial waiver of the attorney–client privilege, however, also applies to oral statements.

incriminating statements, admitting the payment of bribes, in those confidential responses. Those managers, however, could not control whether the company decided to assert the attorney-client privilege. If Upjohn's board of directors decided that the corporation would best be served by scapegoating the mid-level managers, they could have waived the attorney-client privilege and turned the managers' admissions over to the government. The corporation could even have brokered a deal with the government, offering to waive the privilege in exchange for lenient treatment of the corporation.

When an attorney for a corporation seeks information from corporate employees, therefore, the attorney must make clear that the employee will have no say over whether the corporation releases the information to others. An employee who has information that incriminates both himself and the corporation should retain his own private attorney and discuss the situation with her before disclosing information to the corporation's attorney.

D. Work Product. An attorney preparing for trial will create many different kinds of documents: She will interview non-client witnesses and take notes on those interviews; she will conduct her own investigations and write down her observations; and she will write down her thoughts about the strengths and weaknesses of her case. None of these documents are covered by the attorney-client privilege because none of them constitute communications between the attorney and the client. Yet it seems important to provide some protection for these documents; otherwise the opposing party could make discovery demands to see all of the opposing party's pretrial work.

To protect this information, courts created the **work product** privilege, which protects all work that either the attorney or client does independently to prepare for trial.[13] Congress later codified the privilege in Federal Rule of Civil Procedure 26(b)(3) and Federal Rule of Criminal Procedure 16(a)(2) and (b)(2).

The work product privilege is easily confused with the attorney-client privilege, but the two privileges are distinct. Most important, the work product privilege is much **broader** than the attorney-client privilege: It protects any documents or other materials prepared by an attorney or client, rather than just communications

---

13   In 1947, the Supreme Court recognized the need to shield "work product" from discovery in civil litigation; in 1975 the Court extended that shield to criminal cases. Hickman v. Taylor, 329 U.S. 495 (1947); United States v. Nobles, 422 U.S. 225 (1975).

between the two. Additional facts from the *Upjohn* case, discussed above, illustrate the scope of this protection:

Example: While exploring the possibility that some of its offices had paid bribes to foreign countries, Upjohn's general counsel interviewed the managers of those offices. The counsel's notes of these interviews reflected the most important questions he asked and the "substance of the responses" to those questions. But counsel indicated that his notes also contained "my beliefs as to the importance of these [responses], my beliefs as to how they related to the inquiry, [and] my thoughts as to how they related to other questions. In some instances they might even suggest other questions that I would have to ask or things that I needed to find elsewhere."

The IRS sought access to these notes as part of its investigation of Upjohn.

Analysis: Notes of the general counsel's questions and the employees' responses fell within the attorney-client privilege. All of the questioned employees qualified as clients under the test described above, and they responded to counsel's questions to further the company's legal representation. The counsel's notes about his own reactions and plans, however, were not communications; thus, they did not fall within the attorney-client privilege.

Instead, these notes constituted the general counsel's work product. To represent a client effectively, the Court noted, "it is essential that a lawyer work with a certain degree of privacy." Litigants cannot simply demand disclosure of an opponent's research and strategies. The counsel's notes about his reactions and plans fell within the work product privilege.[14]

The work product doctrine thus complements the attorney-client privilege by shielding the attorney's own observations, reflections, and plans. The work product privilege also protects work that the client does in anticipation of litigation. Upjohn's managers, for example, might have compiled summaries of their contacts with foreign governments to prepare for their meetings with the IRS investigators. These summaries would also qualify as work product sheltered by that doctrine.

---

14   Upjohn, 449 U.S. at 400 n.8; id. at 397 (quoting Hickman v. Taylor, 329 U.S. 495, 511 (1947)).

1. Limits on Work Product Protection. The work product privilege has two important limitations: First, the privilege only protects documents or objects prepared **in anticipation of litigation**. Work done for clients who seek legal advice for other purposes—such as drafting a will or incorporating a business—is not covered by the work product doctrine. This limit grows out of the doctrine's origin as a limit on pretrial discovery. Courts, however, have construed this limit narrowly. "Litigation" includes administrative inquiries, and a party may "anticipate litigation" long before that process formally begins. Upjohn, for example, received protection for documents that its general counsel created before the IRS even knew of the foreign payments; the counsel's notes stemmed from his internal investigation of the payments, an investigation he began because he assumed the matter would be litigated at some point in the future.

Second, when work product consists solely of **facts about the dispute**, the privilege is **qualified**. An opposing party may obtain access to this type of work product by demonstrating that it has "substantial need for the materials to prepare its case and cannot, without undue hardship, obtain their substantial equivalent by other means."[15] For example, if an earthquake demolished one of Upjohn's foreign offices and destroyed all records related to that office, the IRS might be able to obtain copies of in-house summaries that the corporation had prepared about the office in anticipation of litigation.

However, when the work product consists of "mental impressions, conclusions, opinions, or legal theories of a party's attorney or other representative concerning the litigation," the privilege is nearly absolute.[16] The Supreme Court addressed this distinction in the *Upjohn* case, described above:

> **Example:** When Upjohn's general counsel resisted producing the notes described above, the IRS claimed that it had an overwhelming need for access to those notes. The employees interviewed by the general counsel were "scattered across the globe," and Upjohn had "forbidden its employees to answer questions it considers irrelevant." Thus, the government claimed it had a substantial need for the materials and would suffer undue hardship if it attempted to obtain equivalent information through other means.

---

15   Fed. R. Civ. P. 26(b)(3).

16   Id.

> **Analysis:** The Supreme Court held that the "substantial need" and "undue hardship" test does not apply to materials reflecting an attorney's mental processes. The Court refused to decide whether a stronger showing could compel disclosure of an attorney's mental processes or legal strategies. It signaled, however, that only extraordinary circumstances could justify such disclosure.[17]

The Supreme Court has not returned to this issue, but lower courts assume that the work product privilege extends absolute protection to an attorney's mental processes and legal strategies.

2. Waiver. Lawyers hold an independent interest in their work product, so they usually control waiver of the work product privilege. But attorneys exercise this control in their clients' interest and, under some circumstances, a client may control the privilege. Courts, for example, have held that a client may demand disclosure of work product that the attorney created on the client's behalf.

Rule 502 protects work product materials, as well as those shielded by the attorney-client privilege, from inadvertent disclosure during discovery. If an attorney took reasonable steps to prevent disclosure of protected work product, as well as reasonable steps to rectify an inadvertent disclosure, then the disclosure does not waive the work product privilege. This protection, like the one for waiver of attorney-client privilege, reduces litigation costs.

On the other hand, if a party intentionally waives work product protection, Rule 502 extends that waiver to other materials that "concern the same subject matter" and "ought in fairness" be considered with the disclosed materials. This provision prevents strategic disclosures that would unfairly distort litigation.

---

17   Upjohn, 449 U.S. at 399–402.

Quick Summary

 The attorney-client privilege has five components: a client, an attorney, a communication, confidentiality, and a purpose of facilitating professional legal services to the client. The privilege includes representatives of the attorney, such as paralegals or accountants working for the lawyer. But the privilege only protects the communication itself, not the underlying facts communicated. Clients cannot use the privilege to hide documents or other items that exist independently of the attorney-client relationship.

The client, rather than the attorney, controls the privilege and decides whether to waive it. The attorney, however, usually asserts the privilege on behalf of the client. Disclosing the confidential communication to a third party waives the privilege; revealing part of the communication may waive the privilege with respect to related portions.

Corporate employees who satisfy the *Upjohn* test count as "clients" whose communications with counsel may qualify for the attorney-client privilege. The corporation itself, however, controls the privilege; its corporate officers decide whether to waive the privilege.

If a client seeks legal assistance to commit a crime or fraud, the privilege does not protect any communications.

A work product privilege complements the attorney-client privilege by protecting documents and other materials prepared in anticipation of litigation. An attorney's mental impressions and legal theories receive protection that courts assume is absolute; no showing of need can compel disclosure of this information. Litigants may gain access to more factual work product by showing a substantial need for the information and an inability to obtain the information in any other way without undue hardship. This type of work product, in other words, receives only qualified protection.

Rule 502 prevents inadvertent waiver of both the attorney-client privilege and work product doctrine, as long as an attorney takes reasonable steps to avoid and rectify any inadvertent disclosures.

Test Your Understanding

 To assess your understanding of the material in this chapter, <u>click here</u> to take a quiz, or go to the Quizzes module from the eBook on your eProducts bookshelf.

68

Other Privileges

Key Concepts

- Two Types of Spousal Privilege:
  - **Spousal Testimonial** Privilege
  - **Marital Communications** Privilege
- **Psychotherapist-Patient** Privilege
- **Executive** Privilege
- **Clergy-Communicant** Privilege
- Privilege Against **Self-Incrimination**

A. Introduction. Although the attorney-client privilege is the oldest and most well known evidentiary privilege, federal courts recognize a number of other evidentiary privileges, five of which we discuss here: two different spousal privileges, a Psychotherapist-Patient privilege, an executive privilege, and a clergy-communicant privilege.[1] As discussed in Chapter 66, Congress has not codified any of these privileges in the Federal Rules. But the Supreme Court has formally approved four of these privileges and has recognized the fifth, the clergy-communicant privilege, in dictum.

All state and federal courts also recognize a privilege against self-incrimination based on the Fifth Amendment of the Constitution. That amendment prevents the government from compelling an individual to produce information that could be used against her in a criminal trial. The constitutional guarantee is broader than a mere evidentiary privilege; it protects the individual against coerced confessions outside the courtroom as well as during judicial proceedings.

---

1   The federal courts have also recognized privileges for trade secrets, Fed R. Civ. P. 26(c)(1)(G); Fed. Open Market Comm. of Fed. Reserve Sys. v. Merrill, 443 U.S. 340, 355–56 (1979); and for the identity of a government informer, Roviaro v. United States, 353 U.S. 53 (1957).

Each of these privileges includes a complex web of rules; we provide just an over-view of the major federal privileges here. Although we focus on federal law, we indicate the scope of some of these privileges under state law. Remember that, as noted in Chapter 66, many states recognize privileges that federal law does not embody. Most states, for example, apply both a physician–patient privilege and a journalist–source privilege. State laws establish privileges for a wide variety of other communications, including those with school guidance counselors, mediators, telephone operators, and chiropractors.[2] When a claim or defense rests on state law, federal courts apply these state laws of privilege under Rule 501.

B. Spousal Privileges. The federal courts recognize two different, but over-lapping, spousal privileges. Distinguishing and applying these two privileges can be confusing. We explore each one separately below, then compare their features in a table. A majority of states recognize both of these privileges, but the contours of the privileges vary among the states.

1. The Spousal Testimonial Privilege. The first spousal privilege applies under relatively narrow circumstances. This privilege arises only when a spouse is a **criminal defendant** or the target of a grand jury investigation. Under these circumstances, the other spouse may refuse to testify against the defendant or target spouse. The privilege, however, does not apply in civil proceedings.

This privilege rests on both of the policies we identified in Chapter 66. It aims to promote marriages; if the government could compel one spouse to testify against the other, that pressure almost certainly would undermine the marriage. But the privilege also furthers privacy interests that society values for their own sake. Compelling one spouse to testify against the other violates our notions of privacy, decency, and dignity.

Because this privilege focuses on the act of testifying, it applies only during the **life of the marriage**. Once a marriage ends, the testimonial privilege offers no protection to either spouse. Unless another privilege applies, the government can compel either spouse to testify against the other at a criminal trial—and to spill the beans about anything that happened during the marriage.

On the other hand, while the spouses remain married, this privilege applies even to information that one of the spouses **obtained before the marriage**. Again,

---

2   See, e.g., Ohio Rev. Code Ann. § 2317.02 (West 2011) (recognizing these and other privileges).

since the privilege focuses on the act of testifying, the government cannot force one spouse to describe acts that the other engaged in before the wedding. This facet of the privilege makes it a favorite for books and movies: A wrongdoer may try to silence an eyewitness by marrying him or her. Once the marriage takes effect, the government cannot compel the spouse to testify against the other.

The testimonial privilege, moreover, shields **any information** that one spouse might offer against the other. Unlike the attorney-client privilege, which protects only communications, the spousal testimonial privilege shelters all information that the government might attempt to obtain from a spouse. The spouse may simply claim the privilege and remain silent.

The testimonial privilege, however, has one very important limit: The **witness spouse** controls the privilege. This means that the witness spouse may waive the privilege, choosing to testify against the spouse who is the subject of a grand jury investigation or is defending against criminal charges. The Supreme Court recognized this limit in *Trammel v. United States*,[3] reasoning that if one spouse is willing to testify against the other, then the marriage must not hold much vitality. The policies supporting the privilege, therefore, no longer apply.[4]

In addition, the federal courts recognize several exceptions to the spousal testimonial privilege. The privilege does not arise if the government suspects one spouse of committing a crime against the other spouse or against a child in their custody; nor does the privilege exist if the government suspects both spouses of jointly committing a crime. Under any of these circumstances, the government can compel the spouses to testify against each other before a grand jury or at trial.

2. The Marital Communications Privilege. The second spousal privilege protects confidential communications between two spouses. This privilege, like the testimonial one, rests on both utilitarian and intrinsic grounds. It fosters strong marriages by allowing spouses to communicate freely with one another. The privilege also creates a valued zone of privacy for every individual who marries.

---

3   445 U.S. 40 (1980).

4   This limit, sadly, undermines the plot of many books and movies relying upon the testimonial privilege. A wrongdoer may silence an eyewitness through marriage, but only for as long as the eyewitness is willing to remain silent.

The marital communications privilege is broader than the testimonial privilege in several ways. First, it applies at all stages of **all judicial proceedings**, both civil and criminal. The privilege applies, moreover, regardless of whether either spouse is a party to the litigation. No litigant may force a spouse to reveal information protected by this privilege.

Second, the marital communications privilege protects marital confidences even **after the marriage ends**. The privilege assumes that spouses will communicate freely only if they know that their confidences can never be used against them. Communications protected by this privilege, therefore, retain their protection even after the marriage ends.

Finally, and most important, **both spouses control** the communication privilege. This means that neither spouse may waive the privilege without the other's consent. Neither the government nor any civil litigant may persuade one spouse to testify against the other, unless the other spouse also consents.

On the other hand, the marital communications privilege is narrower than the testimonial privilege in three ways. First, the privilege protects only communications that occur **during the life of the marriage**. Even if the spouses have been married for fifty years, a litigant may compel one spouse to divulge confidences that the other spouse shared before the wedding.

Second, the privilege protects only communications that one spouse makes to the other in **confidence**. The presence of a third party almost always defeats the marital communications privilege because spouses, unlike lawyers, do not need secretaries or other assistants to aid their conversations. The essence of the marital communications privilege lies in the private communication between two spouses. Courts recognize a small exception for statements made in the presence of very young children, on the ground that these children are unlikely to understand the communication and are omnipresent, but otherwise the communication must be private to elicit the privilege.

Finally, and most important, this second spousal privilege only protects **communications** between the spouses. The privilege does not protect matters that the testifying spouse observed during the marriage:

Example: Ronald Lofton was on trial for using the mail to distribute narcotics. The government called Lofton's wife to the stand to testify that (1) she had seen a package of cocaine delivered to their home; and (2) her husband had told her not to be "nosy" about the packages he was receiving, saying "the less you know, the better off you are." The wife was willing to testify, but Lofton objected and cited both spousal privileges.

Analysis: The marital communications privilege precluded admission of the wife's testimony about the husband's statements. The husband clearly intended those statements as communications and they occurred during the marriage. No third parties were present and, without any evidence to the contrary, a court would assume that the husband intended the statements to be confidential. The wife could not waive this privilege on her own, so the privilege prevented the wife's testimony even though she was willing to take the stand.

The communications privilege, however, did not shelter the wife's observation of the packages. These observations were not communications between the spouses. The testimonial privilege applied to these observations, but the wife had power to waive that privilege without the husband's consent. If she was willing to testify about her observations at trial, Lofton could not prevent her from doing so.[5]

As in the context of hearsay, however, some actions are assertive conduct and are protected by the marital communications privilege:

Example: In November 2015, Diana Arnold overheard her wife Janet talking on the telephone. During the course of the conversation Janet made incriminating statements about setting fire to a house. A few days later, Janet drove Diana to a house that had just burned down. The couple looked at the house without speaking, then drove away.

During the following months, Diana and Janet separated and divorced. The state later charged Janet with conspiracy to commit arson. At trial, the prosecutor attempts to call Diana to the stand to testify about (1) the

---

5   The facts of this example are loosely based on United States v. Lofton, 957 F.2d 476 (7th Cir. 1992). The wife in that case resisted testifying at trial, but she had been willing to testify at a suppression hearing.

phone conversation she overheard and (2) the fact that Janet drove with her to the burned house. Diana refuses to testify, claiming spousal privilege. Janet also objects to her testimony based on spousal privilege.

Analysis: A court would first consider whether the testimonial privilege applies, but that privilege has lapsed with the marriage. Neither Diana (the testifying spouse) nor Janet (the target spouse) can claim that privilege.

The marital communications privilege, on the other hand, survives the dissolution of the marriage; if either spouse invokes it, Diana cannot be forced to testify. The telephone conversation was a communication, but it was not a confidential one between spouses. Janet had that conversation with a third party, and Diana happened to overhear it. The government can compel Diana to testify about that conversation, even though both she and Janet object to the testimony.

The drive to the burned house presents a closer question; a court would need more information to decide whether this was a communication. If Janet drove Diana to the house in response to a prior question, the drive might constitute a type of response. Assume, for example, that Diana had said to Janet "I heard you on the phone the other day; you'd better tell me what that was all about," and Janet had responded: "I'll do better than that; I'll show you." If the silent drive-by followed that exchange, it clearly would be an assertive act covered by the communications privilege. On the other hand, if Janet simply drove by the house without any prior conversation, a court probably would find that this was simply an act rather than a privileged communication.[6]

Courts recognize similar exceptions to the marital communications privilege as to the testimonial privilege. Neither spouse, in other words, may assert the communications privilege if (1) one spouse commits a crime against the other spouse or against a child that is in their custody; or (2) the spouses jointly commit a crime.

The intra-family crime exception rests on the ground that crimes against family members are unlikely to further marital harmony. In addition, admitting this testimony often is essential to prosecuting the crime; spouses frequently are the

---

6   The facts of this example derive from Arnold v. State, 353 So. 2d 524 (Ala. 1977). In that case, the court held that the drive-by was an assertive act but failed to explain why.

only witnesses to intra-family crimes, especially crimes of violence like domestic or child abuse.

Example: Jayne White's husband Joseph cared for Jayne's children while Jayne served in the army. Joseph told Jayne that he was tired of taking care of her children; he threatened to kill Jayne and her daughter Jasmine unless other arrangements were made. One week later, Jasmine suffered a massive subdural hematoma from a blow to the head while in Joseph's care. Jayne came home and the couple rushed the girl to the hospital, but she died two days later.

Joseph was charged with involuntary manslaughter. During the trial, the prosecutor called Jayne to the stand to testify about Joseph's threat the week before Jasmine died. Joseph objected, claiming that the marital communications privilege protected his statements to Jayne.

Analysis: Jayne's testimony was admissible. Because this was an intra-family crime, the marital communications privilege did not apply. The appellate court noted that "protecting threats against a spouse or the spouse's children is inconsistent with the purposes of the marital communications privilege: promoting confidential communications between spouses in order to foster marital harmony."[7]

Note that even if a witness spouse like Jayne invokes one of the spousal privileges, the intra-family crime exception allows the prosecutor to issue a subpoena compelling the testimony. Victims of domestic violence often are reluctant to testify, so simply giving control of the privilege to the witness spouse (as the testimonial privilege does) may not be sufficient to allow prosecution. The intra-family crime exception eliminates both privileges, allowing the prosecutor to obtain needed evidence.[8]

Some courts have interpreted this exception broadly to include intra-family crimes against property as well as people:

---

7   United States v. White, 974 F.2d 1135, 1138 (9th Cir. 1992).

8   Some spouses refuse to comply even when ordered to testify, giving rise to some of the hearsay issues we studied in previous chapters. States also vary in their recognition of the intra-family crimes exception, generating situations in which a prosecutor attempts to rely upon hearsay in the face of a spouse's privilege assertion.

> **Example:** James Peters and his wife got into a heated argument, during which he threatened to burn down the house. After the argument was over, James allegedly took a gas can from the garage, poured gasoline around the interior of the house that he owned jointly with his wife, and set the house on fire. During his subsequent trial for arson, James's wife testified about what he had said during the argument. James objected, citing spousal privilege.

> **Analysis:** The testimony, like the testimony in the previous example, is admissible. James committed a crime against property that was co-owned by his wife; therefore the intra-family crime exception applies to her testimony.[9]

Finally, when two spouses jointly commit a crime, neither of the spousal privileges applies. This is true even if the government prosecutes just one of the spouses. Consider this hypothetical variation on the previous arson case:

> **Example:** James Peters and his wife Anita were no longer able to keep up with their mortgage payments and owed thousands of dollars to other creditors. Together they came up with a scheme to burn down their house and claim the insurance proceeds. One night they poured gasoline around the interior of the house, set the house on fire, and filed an insurance claim. The prosecutor offered Anita immunity from prosecution in response for her testimony against James. At trial, James objected to Anita's testimony under the marital privileges.

> **Analysis:** James and Anita committed this crime together, so neither spousal privilege applies. The prosecutor may compel Anita to testify.

3. Comparing the Privileges. The table on the next page summarizes the major features of the two spousal privileges. Note that both privileges apply to some situations, while only one privilege applies in others.

---

9   The facts of this example draw from Peters v. District Court of Iowa, 183 N.W.2d 209 (Iowa 1971), although the court in that case limited its holding to the spousal testimonial privilege.

Two Spousal Privileges: Federal Law

	Spousal Testimonial Privilege	Marital Communications Privilege
Does the privilege apply in civil proceedings?	No, just in grand jury investigations or criminal prosecutions of the spouse	Yes
Does the privilege protect actions and observations?	Yes	No, just confidential communications
Does the privilege apply to communications or events that occurred before the marriage?	Yes	No
Does the privilege survive end of the marriage?	No	Yes
Who may waive the privilege?	Only the witness spouse; the target spouse may not prevent testimony	Both spouses must consent to waiver
Are there exceptions?	Yes, for intra-family crimes and jointly committed crimes	Yes, for intra-family crimes and jointly committed crimes

C. Psychotherapist-Patient Privilege.

In 1996 the Supreme Court recognized a Psychotherapist-Patient privilege under federal common law.[10] The Court stressed that psychotherapy benefits society as a whole because it facilitates treatment of mental health problems. Successful therapy, moreover, "depends upon an atmosphere of confidence and trust in which the patient is willing to make a frank and complete disclosure of facts, emotions, memories, and fears," many of which would cause "embarrassment or disgrace" if disclosed.[11] In this sense, psychotherapy differs from other types of medical treatment, which may proceed based on physical examination and objective tests.

The Court, finally, observed that recognizing a Psychotherapist-Patient privilege has little impact on the truth-seeking process. If courts did not recognize the privilege, then many patients would withhold incriminating information from their therapists and no evidence would be available to compel. Creation of a Psychotherapist-Patient privilege, therefore, met all of the criteria listed in Chapter 66.

The federal Psychotherapist-Patient privilege is a broad one. It applies to licensed **social workers**, as well as to psychiatrists and psychologists. The Supreme Court included social workers because they charge less than most psychologists and psychiatrists; for many individuals, a licensed social worker is the only realistic option for mental health treatment.

The Supreme Court, moreover, refused to qualify the privilege with the general balancing test adopted by some lower courts. Allowing a litigant to overcome the privilege by balancing a need for the evidence against the particular patient's privacy interest would eviscerate the privilege; uncertainty about the privilege's application would deter too many patients from confiding freely in their therapists. The Court, however, stopped short of declaring the privilege absolute, and a few lower courts have qualified the privilege modestly by allowing criminal defendants to pierce the privilege when necessary to support their defense.[12]

The privilege, however, applies only to communications that a patient makes to a licensed therapist for the purpose **of diagnosis or treatment of a mental or**

---

10   Jaffee v. Redmond, 518 U.S. 1 (1996). The Advisory Committee had included a Psychotherapist-Patient privilege among the rules it proposed to Congress in 1975. Over the next twenty years, the circuits split over recognition of the privilege. By the time the Supreme Court resolved that split in favor of the privilege, all fifty states and the District of Columbia recognized some form of the psychotherapist privilege.

11   Id. at 10.

12   See, e.g., United States v. Mazzola, 217 F.R.D. 84 (D. Mass. 2003).

emotional problem. Psychologists and social workers sometimes confer with individuals for other purposes, such as to offer vocational counseling. The privilege does not cover communications made for purposes like these.

 The circuits currently split over whether a **"dangerous patient" exception** applies to the psychotherapist privilege. This exception is analogous to the crime fraud exception in the attorney—client context. That exception is easy to justify because society has no interest in allowing individuals to seek legal advice about how to commit a future crime or fraud. In contrast, if an individual shares her violent urges with a therapist, the therapist may help the patient overcome those tendencies, thereby preventing the crime altogether. Society has an interest in encouraging this type of confidential communication rather than punishing it through disclosure.

On the other hand, if a patient confides a clear intent to commit a violent crime, a therapist should not simply let the violence unfold; most states require a therapist to notify the authorities under these circumstances. If the crime nonetheless occurs, should the government be able to compel testimony from the psychotherapist?

One court offered an elegant solution to this problem by affirming the therapist's duty to warn, but precluding the therapist's testimony in any future proceeding:

Example: Roy Lee Hayes, a postal worker, began experiencing bouts of extreme depression and erratic behavior. Over the next thirteen months, he sought treatment from several psychologists and psychiatrists, and received psychotropic medications to help control his condition. During these counseling sessions, Hayes frequently told his therapists that he had a strong urge to kill Veda Odle, his supervisor at work. During a few sessions, Hayes described in some detail how he planned to commit the crime.

One of the therapists ultimately determined that Hayes posed a serious threat to Odle. That therapist warned Odle of the danger, and she contacted the authorities. The government obtained Hayes's records from the therapists and charged Hayes with threatening to murder a federal official. Before trial, Hayes moved to suppress his medical records on the grounds that they were privileged.

Analysis: The court granted Hayes's motion, finding that the communications to his therapists were privileged. Although the therapist acted appropriately in warning Odle about Hayes's statements, the Psychotherapist-Patient privilege still protected the statements from admission in any court proceeding. The court thus distinguished the evidentiary privilege from the therapist's professional, ethical, and legal duty to warn innocent third parties. The therapist could fulfill that duty to warn without compromising the evidentiary privilege.[13]

The Supreme Court has not yet ruled on whether a dangerous patient exception exists, but the Justices gave a hint in dictum in the *Jaffee* case when they stated that the exception may not apply if there is "a serious threat of harm to the patient or to others [which] can be averted only by means of a disclosure by the therapist."[14]

A patient, on the other hand, may waive the psychotherapist privilege if he puts his **mental condition in issue** during trial. Courts are divided as to the scope of this waiver:

Under the **broader view**, courts have held that a party waives the psychotherapist privilege anytime he puts his mental or emotional condition at issue in the trial. For example, if a criminal defendant pleads insanity as a defense, he cannot object to the prosecutor examining his therapist about communications related to his alleged sanity. Likewise, if a plaintiff claims emotional distress, she cannot object if the defendant calls her therapist to the stand to testify about their communications.[15]

Under the **narrower view** of the waiver, a party does not waive the privilege unless she places the privileged communication at issue, for example by calling her psychotherapist to the stand to testify about her mental or emotional condition.[16]

---

13   United States v. Hayes, 227 F.3d 578, 581–82 (6th Cir. 2000).

14   Jaffee, 518 U.S. at 18 n.19.

15   See, e.g., Doe v. City of Chula Vista, 196 F.R.D. 562 (S.D. Cal. 1999).

16   See, e.g.,Vanderbilt v. Town of Chilmark, 174 F.R.D. 225 (D. Mass. 1997).

D. Executive Privilege. The executive privilege protects confidential communications between the President of the United States and his or her close advisors. Few cases raise this privilege, but the ones that do make headlines. The executive privilege, for example, lay at the center of President Nixon's failed attempt to withhold the Watergate tapes from public scrutiny.[17]

There are two levels of executive privilege. The **first**, most protected level of the privilege shelters military, diplomatic, and national security secrets. This privilege is absolute; to protect these vital interests, courts will not compel disclosure of this information even for an in camera review. To invoke this highest level of protection, however, the President must specifically claim the existence of a national security interest and must point to circumstances suggesting the presence of such concerns.[18]

The **second**, more common level of executive privilege protects the President's "more generalized interest in confidentiality."[19] This level of the privilege shields the President's conversations with top advisors so that these leaders can feel "free to explore alternatives . . . in a way many would be unwilling to express except privately."[20] These discussions are "presumptively privileged," but an opponent can overcome the privilege by making a sufficient showing of need. This level of the privilege, in other words, is a qualified one.

 Because executive privilege cases are rarely litigated, it is unclear what kind of showing is necessary to pierce this privilege. In the landmark Nixon case, the Supreme Court held that a narrowly tailored subpoena seeking specific facts needed to adjudicate a criminal case was sufficient to overcome the privilege.[21] Conversely, in a case involving a civil plaintiff's attempt to obtain information about Vice President Cheney's energy task force, the Court implied that the plaintiff's broad request for information to further a civil claim would not defeat the privilege.[22] The second level of executive privilege, therefore, probably requires the party seeking disclosure to a show a significant need—like the interests at stake in criminal adjudication—for specific, particularized information.

---

17   United States v. Nixon, 418 U.S. 683 (1974).

18   Id. at 710–11.

19   Id. at 711.

20   Id. at 708.

21   Id. at 712–13. The Court emphasized that the requested tapes were "precisely identified" and "specifically enumerated" in the subpoena. Id. at 668.

22   Cheney v. United States District Court, 542 U.S. 367, 387–88 (2004).

Judicial decisions on executive privilege remain scarce because the President often invokes the privilege before a Congressional committee rather than in court. When this happens, the executive and legislative branches usually resolve the conflict through compromise: A Congressional committee subpoenas an executive branch official to testify, the President claims the privilege, and the parties work out a deal in which the President waives the privilege in exchange for the committee closing its session or restricting the scope of its inquiry.

E. Clergy-Communicant Privilege.

The clergy-communicant privilege does not arise very often, but it has been recognized by every federal court to consider the question.[23] The scope of this privilege tracks the attorney-client privilege and the Psychotherapist-Patient one: The clergy-communicant privilege covers (1) communications (2) made in confidence (3) by a person seeking spiritual counseling (4) to a member of the clergy. The privilege applies to communications with clergy members of any religion, as long as the communicant legitimately seeks spiritual counseling.

Although the Supreme Court has never explicitly held that a clergy-communicant privilege exists, the Court has approved the privilege several times in dicta, stating that it is a privilege "rooted in the imperative need for confidence and trust," and that it "recognizes the need to disclose to a spiritual counselor, in total and absolute confidence, what are believed to be flawed acts or thoughts and to receive priestly consolation and guidance in return."[24]

The communicant controls this privilege, just as the client controls the attorney-client privilege. As with the latter privilege, however, the clergy member usually asserts the privilege on the communicant's behalf.

To qualify for the privilege, a communicant must reasonably believe that her statement to a clergy member will remain confidential. Usually the presence of a third party, other than an agent of the clergy member, will defeat the privilege. Courts, however, have recognized that group counseling sessions should qualify for the privilege, as long as the presence of each group member was essential to the communication and furthered its spiritual purpose:

---

23   The Advisory Committee also included a clergy-communicant privilege, proposed Rule 506, in the package of privileges presented to Congress in 1975. Congress rejected that privilege along with the other proposed privilege rules.

24   Trammel v. United States, 445 U.S. 40, 45 (1980).

Example: On November 18, 1985, an arsonist burned down a house that a black family had purchased in an all-white neighborhood of Pittsburgh. A few days later, the four family members who lived next door had a joint counseling session with Reverend Ernest Knoche, a pastor in the Lutheran Church. Two of the individuals were members of Reverend Knoche's church; the others were not.

Four years later, the federal government convened a grand jury to investigate the arson. The prosecutor subpoenaed Reverend Knoche and asked him what the four neighbors had told him during the counseling session. Reverend Knoche refused to answer, citing the clergy-communicant privilege.

Analysis: The appellate court held that, although the traditional clergy-communicant privilege shielded only a private confession, the more modern privilege applies in some group contexts. For the privilege to shield those group communications, the presence of each group member has to be essential to the spiritual counseling. The court remanded to the district court to determine whether the facts in this case satisfied that standard. Some of the factors that the court might consider, the appellate court suggested, were: (1) the nature of the communicants' relationship with each other; (2) the pastoral counseling practices at this particular church; (3) whether the four parties shared a commonality of interest at the time of the communication; and (4) whether all the members of the group reasonably expected that their counseling session with Reverend Knoche would remain confidential.[25]

The clergy-communicant privilege does not include an exception for crime/fraud or dangerous acts. Several states, however, have expanded their mandatory reporting laws to abrogate the privilege in cases of child sex abuse. In those states, clergy members must report instances of child abuse even if they receive that information during spiritual counseling.[26]

F. Right Against Self-Incrimination.

The Fifth Amendment states that "no person . . . shall be compelled in a criminal case to be a witness against himself." The Supreme Court has interpreted this clause quite broadly, so that it prevents

---

25   In re Grand Jury Investigation, 918 F.2d 374, 385–87 (3d Cir. 1990).

26   See Rachel Goldenberg, Note, Unholy Clergy: Amending State Child Abuse Reporting Statutes to Include Clergy Members as Mandatory Reporters in Child Sexual Abuse Cases, 51 Fam. Ct. Rev. 298 (2013).

the government from extracting incriminating information from individuals at any time, whether or not they are testifying.[27] Courses in Constitutional Law and Criminal Procedure explore that case law more thoroughly; for our purposes, it is enough to know that an individual can invoke the Fifth Amendment privilege at any stage during a civil or criminal proceeding if she believes her answer could be used against her in a criminal trial.

Courts protect Fifth Amendment rights carefully. A prosecutor, in fact, may not even call a witness to the stand if he knows that the witness will invoke her right against self-incrimination; the jury might be prejudiced by hearing the witness "take the Fifth." But if the defendant chooses to testify, she waives her Fifth Amendment right and the prosecutor may attempt to elicit incriminating information on cross-examination.

When invoked, the Fifth Amendment privilege is absolute. Prosecutors, however, can overcome the privilege by granting a witness **immunity** for her testimony. Immunity is a guarantee that information learned from the testimony will not be used against the witness in any future criminal proceeding. If a witness receives immunity, she cannot rely on the privilege to avoid testifying because the testimony can no longer be used against her. In a sense, the immunity grant creates a new evidentiary privilege that replaces the Fifth Amendment one; if the prosecutor tries to use the witness's immunized testimony against her, she can object on the ground that she made the statements under a grant of immunity.

Prosecutors usually offer witnesses **use immunity**. This type of immunity guarantees the witness that the prosecutor will not use anything she says—or any information derived from those statements—in any future prosecution. Prosecutors may also offer witnesses a broader type of immunity known as **transactional immunity**. Under this type of immunity, the prosecutor guarantees that he will not prosecute the witness for any wrongdoing that she mentions in her testimony, even if the prosecutor obtains independent evidence of that wrongdoing. Prosecutors rarely offer transactional immunity, because a more limited grant of use immunity is sufficient to defeat the Fifth Amendment privilege.

---

27   A complex body of case law, beginning with Miranda v. Arizona, 384 U.S. 436 (1966), describes when a person is being "compelled" by the government to give a statement outside the courtroom. The Fifth Amendment binds the federal government directly, id. at 479–80; the Fourteenth Amendment applies that restraint to state and local governments. Pennsylvania v. Muniz, 496 U.S. 582, 589–90 (1990).

The right against self-incrimination only applies to **testimony**, not to items from the witness's body. The privilege, therefore, doesn't prevent the prosecutor from compelling an individual to give fingerprints or blood samples. Nor does the privilege prevent the prosecutor from putting an individual in a line-up for identification.

The Fifth Amendment, finally, only applies to people. Unlike the attorney-client privilege, the right against self-incrimination does not protect corporations. Corporate employees may claim the privilege on their own behalf, but not to protect the corporation.

Quick Summary

Federal courts recognize two kinds of **spousal privilege**: (1) the testimonial privilege, which prevents the government from compelling one spouse to testify against the other in a criminal proceeding, unless the testifying spouse waives the privilege; and (2) the marital communications privilege, which prevents a spouse from testifying about confidential marital communications unless both spouses waive the privilege. Both privileges contain exceptions for intra-family crimes, as well as crimes committed jointly by the spouses.

The **psychotherapist-patient privilege** has been broadly defined by the Supreme Court: It protects any confidential communications between a patient and a psychologist, psychiatrist, therapist, or social worker who provides mental or emotional counseling.

The **executive privilege** includes both an absolute privilege for secrets affecting national security and a qualified privilege for other confidential communications between the President and his or her close advisors. The **clergy-communicant** privilege protects confidential communications made to a religious advisor for the purpose of receiving spiritual guidance or counseling. Finally, the Fifth Amendment **right against self-incrimination** protects a witness from being forced to disclose information that could be used against him in a criminal prosecution.

Test Your Understanding

 To assess your understanding of the material in this chapter, click here to take a quiz, or go to the Quizzes module from the eBook on your eProducts bookshelf.

69

Authentication

Key Concepts

- Parties Must Authenticate All Evidence Except Live Testimony
- Evidence "Sufficient to Support a Finding" That the Evidence "Is What the Proponent Claims"
- **Rule 901:** Nonexhaustive List of Ways to Authenticate Evidence
- **Rule 902:** Documents That Are Self-Authenticating
- Authentication Doesn't Trump Other Evidentiary Objections

A. Introduction and Policy. Trial witnesses introduce themselves to the jury and swear to tell the truth. Other types of evidence, however, cannot identify themselves or swear to truthfulness. How does the jury know that the gun in the prosecutor's hand was the murder weapon? Or that the document on the table is the contract that the plaintiff signed?

Before introducing evidence other than live testimony, parties must establish the identity of the evidence. The Federal Rules of Evidence call this process "identification" or "authentication," using those terms interchangeably. More colloquially, judges and lawyers refer to this process as "laying a foundation" for admission of documentary, real, or demonstrative evidence.

Authentication serves three important functions. First, authentication is necessary to establish **relevance**. By itself, a wallet is not relevant to a theft prosecution. The wallet becomes relevant when the victim identifies it as the one taken from his pocket, or when a police officer identifies the wallet as the one found in the defendant's house. A piece of evidence becomes relevant only when a party provides information linking it to the controversy.

Second, authentication offers the jury some assurance that a piece of evidence is **genuine**. By identifying a bag of white powder as one seized from the defendant, a police witness swears that the defendant had this particular bag—not some other bag containing a different substance—in her pocket. Verification like this is critical in cases that depend on the composition or condition of an item.

Finally, authentication places the evidence in proper **context**. At trial, jurors listen to a series of witnesses offering testimony that seems stilted and disjointed. Technical objections and sidebars often interrupt the testimony, making the story even harder for jurors to piece together. Authentication of evidence gives attorneys an opportunity to remind jurors why a piece of evidence is important and how it relates to other parts of the case. Handled perfunctorily, authentication is yet another dry, technical process that jurors must observe. Handled well, authentication helps jurors focus on key pieces of evidence.

Although authentication serves these three functions, there are two objectives that it does **not** serve. As an evidence student and trial attorney, it is important to know both what authentication does and what it does **not do**.

First, authentication does not **guarantee** the identity or genuineness of any evidence. Through authentication, a party provides some information that an item is what the party claims it is. Even after an item has been authenticated and admitted into evidence, however, an opponent can challenge that item's identity. The accused in a pick-pocket case may swear that the wallet was his own, even if the alleged victim has already identified the wallet as his. The defense lawyer in a narcotics prosecution can show that the police left an authenticated bag of cocaine unattended on a desk for two days, so that any person could have tampered with the contents. Just as parties challenge testimony given by live witnesses, they may contest the validity of evidence that has been authenticated.

Second, authentication does not establish **compliance with other evidentiary rules**. Authentication only offers some assurance that the evidence is what the proponent claims. The proponent must also satisfy any other Rules of Evidence. Documents, for example, contain out-of-court statements. To admit a document into evidence, a party must both authenticate the document **and** satisfy any hearsay objections. Authentication likewise does not satisfy Rule 403's balancing test or any other provision limiting introduction of evidence.

Authentication Does . . .	Authentication Does Not . . .
• Help establish relevance	• Foreclose challenges to relevance or genuineness
• Help show genuineness	• Satisfy other Rules of Evidence
• Place evidence in context	

B. The Rules. Article IX of the Federal Rules governs authentication; it contains just three rules. The first, **Rule 901**, begins by offering a general standard for authentication:

RULE 901. Authenticating or Identifying Evidence

(a) **In General.** To satisfy the requirement of authenticating or identifying an item of evidence, the proponent must produce evidence sufficient to <u>support a finding</u> that the item is <u>what the proponent claims</u> it is.

This section includes two important concepts. **First**, the threshold for establishing authenticity is very low. A party does not have to prove beyond a reasonable doubt, or even by a preponderance of the evidence, that a document is authentic. The party only needs to introduce evidence "sufficient to support a finding" of authenticity. As long as some reasonable jury could find the document or object authentic, the evidence is admissible. The opponent, after all, can contest the bona fides of the evidence on cross-examination.

Second, Rule 901(a) provides a common-sense definition of authenticity: The rule requires a party to show that an object or document "is what the proponent claims it is."

Article IX next divides evidence into two categories: (1) evidence that requires some kind of **extrinsic** information to be authenticated and (2) evidence that is **self-authenticating**, so it needs no extrinsic information to establish its authenticity.

For the first category of evidence, Rule 901(b) offers ten examples of ways to authenticate common documents or objects. The rule, however, makes clear that these examples are merely illustrations; parties may authenticate evidence in any manner that satisfies the general principles of Rule 901(a).

RULE 901. Authenticating or Identifying Evidence

(b) **Examples.** The following are <u>examples only</u>—not a complete list—of evidence that satisfies the requirement: . . . .

All of the methods listed in Rule 901(b) require some type of **extrinsic** information to authenticate the proffered evidence. That is, the proffered evidence does not simply announce its own authenticity. The most common type of extrinsic evidence offered under Rule 901(b) is testimony from a witness who provides information to authenticate the evidence. We will explore some of the specific examples listed in Rule 901(b) further in the Courtroom section.

The second category of evidence consists of documents that display their identity in an obvious and trustworthy manner; these documents do not need extrinsic proof of identity. For example, an original public document from a government agency, bearing both the official seal of the agency and a signature from the appropriate government official, contains sufficient information on its face to prove the identity and genuineness of the document.

As **Rule 902** explains, these documents are known as **self-authenticating** documents:

RULE 902. Evidence That Is Self-Authenticating

The following items of evidence are self-authenticating; they require no extrinsic evidence of authenticity in order to be admitted: . . . .

Rule 902 goes on to list fourteen categories of documents that are self-authenticating; we will examine some of these categories in the Courtroom section. Unlike Rule 901, these categories are not simply illustrative; they are comprehensive. A document that does not fall within one of Rule 902's categories is not self-authenticating; instead, it must be authenticated in a manner that satisfies Rule 901.

Rule 903 rounds out the authentication rules by declaring:

RULE 903. Subscribing Witness's Testimony

A subscribing witness's testimony is necessary to authenticate a writing <u>only if</u> required by the law of the jurisdiction that governs its validity.

This rule, like several others we have studied, overturns an outdated common-law rule. A "subscribing witness" is a person who signs a document to indicate that she saw another person execute the document. At common law, subscribing witnesses often had to appear in court to confirm the identity of documents they signed. Rule 903 eliminates this cumbersome requirement in federal trials unless the law of another jurisdiction governs a dispute and that jurisdiction requires testimony from subscribing witnesses. This exceptional situation rarely arises.

C. In the Courtroom. Rules 901 and 902 outline numerous ways to establish the authenticity of different types of evidence. You will explore many of these provisions in a trial practice class or if you work as a trial lawyer. In this section, we explore just some of the most common situations that arise under these rules. These examples will help you understand the general principles governing authentication.

1. Distinctive Features. If a piece of evidence has distinctive characteristics, a witness familiar with the item can identify it in court. Rule 901(b)(1) explicitly recognizes this avenue of authentication; this type of identification is "Testimony of a Witness With Knowledge" that "an item is what it is claimed to be."

Parties frequently authenticate evidence this way. A robbery victim, for example, may easily identify the wristwatch taken from him; a monogram, broken catch, or scratch may make the watch distinctive. A product liability plaintiff who gathered the charred pieces of a burned microwave similarly could identify those pieces later in court. Here is how an attorney might authenticate evidence with distinctive features:

Example: A flight from Colombia to Spain stopped in Puerto Rico. Customs officials noticed two odd-looking suitcases that were unusually heavy. The suitcases also had a strong chemical odor and unusual, hand-made rivets. Agent Ruiz performed a scratch test on the side of the suit-cases and discovered that the cases were made of cocaine bonded chemi-cally with acrylic suitcase material. Luggage tags on the suitcases matched claim checks held by passenger Luis Mahecha-Onofre. Ruiz arrested Ma-hecha-Onofre, and the United States prosecuted him for possession of cocaine with intent to distribute.

The prosecutor offered the suitcases into evidence at trial. Before asking the judge to admit the suitcases, the prosecutor asked Ruiz to identify them:

Q: Agent Ruiz, I'd like you to look at the items marked Government Ex-hibits 22-A and 22-B. Do you recognize these items?

A: Yes, these are the suitcases I noticed at the airport on July 27, 1989.

Q: How do you know these are the same suitcases you saw at that time?

A: The suitcases have an unusual shape and color. That attracted my atten-tion at the airport, and you can see it here. They are unusually heavy and hard. These handmade rivets are quite distinctive—I've never seen another suitcase with rivets or screws like this. I can also see on the sides of each case the scratches I made to test for cocaine. The scratches turned blue, indicating cocaine, and you can see those blue scratches here. Finally, these cases have the same baggage tag numbers—004501 and 004502—that were on the bags we tested and seized.

Q: Thank you Agent Ruiz. At this point, your honor, the United States offers into evidence Government Exhibits 22-A and 22-B, which have been identified as the suitcases seized from Iberia Airlines flight 910 on July 27, 1989.[1]

---

1   This fictional transcript is based on the facts in United States v. Mahecha-Onofre, 936 F.2d 623 (1st Cir. 1991).

 Judges vary in how many distinguishing features they require before accepting an item as authenticated. The party offering the evidence, however, usually benefits from noting as many distinctive features as possible. In addition to securing a positive ruling from the judge, detailed authentication focuses the jury's attention on the evidence and establishes its genuineness with the jurors. As with many other aspects of Evidence, laying the proper foundation is not just a matter of proving the bare minimum to **admit** the evidence, but also of providing sufficient information to **persuade** the jury that the evidence is what the lawyer claims it to be.

Law enforcement officers usually ensure the distinctiveness of evidence by marking or tagging potentially incriminating items as soon as they take custody of those items. Agent Ruiz, for example, also scratched his initials on the cocaine-alloy suitcases seized at the Puerto Rico airport. This step made the suitcases even more readily identifiable in court.

2. Chain of Custody. Critical pieces of evidence sometimes lack distinctive features that allow easy identification by a witness; one rock of cocaine looks much like another. Evidence also may change hands before a party has the chance to tag it with a unique identifier. Under these circumstances, parties often rely upon a "chain of custody" to authenticate evidence. To demonstrate a chain of custody, the party calls a series of witnesses, each of whom describes how they obtained the item and passed it to the next person in the chain:

Example: Danny Zink left his car with the Dashboard Company to have a music system installed. Mark Lawless, a Dashboard employee, removed a paper sack from the car's glove compartment so that he could install the system more easily; Lawless tossed the sack in a trash can. When Zink picked up the car, he noticed that the sack was missing and complained. Lawless retrieved the sack from the trash and gave it to his foreman, Gerald Robinson. Robinson opened the sack and found a stack of $20 bills that appeared odd; some were double printed and others had unusual colors. Robinson gave the sack of bills to his manager, Lester Howell, and Howell called the police. The police arrived, identified the bills as counterfeit, marked the sack and bills with identifying numbers, and arrested Zink.

Analysis: The United States prosecuted Zink for possession of counterfeit money with intent to defraud. At trial, the arresting police officer identified the marked sack and bills, testifying that he obtained them from Howell. Howell swore that he received the bag from Robinson; Robinson described obtaining the bag from Lawless; and Lawless explained finding the sack in the glove compartment, throwing it in the trash, retrieving it from the trash, and giving it to Robinson. The court held that this testimony adequately authenticated the sack and bills presented in court as the ones found in Zink's car. A witness testified about every link in this extensive chain.[2]

Note that the chain in Zink was not ironclad; Zink's attorney could have argued that the sack Lawless retrieved from the trash was not the same one Zink left in his glove compartment. Zink could also have claimed that the sack originally contained his lunch and that one of the Dashboard employees substituted counterfeit bills to frame him. Authentication does not **prove** that an item is what its proponent claims; it merely offers enough evidence for the jury to make that finding. The opponent may always contest the evidence after it has been admitted.

Parties also use chain-of-custody testimony to establish that the condition of evidence has not changed in a way that would affect the case. In a drug prosecution, for example, the arresting officer may testify that she seized a substance from the defendant, sealed it in a tamper-proof bag, marked the bag, and delivered the bag to a laboratory for testing. A laboratory technician then will testify that he opened the bag, removed the substance, and immediately tested its composition. This testimony establishes that the substance tested by the technician (which proved to be heroin) was the same substance as the one seized from the defendant.

3. Handwriting. Trials sometimes require proof that a person signed a document or authored a handwritten note. Rules 901 and 902 offer at least five avenues for authenticating handwriting. **First**, the person who authored the note or signature may identify the writing as her own. **Second**, someone who saw the act of writing may identify the person who wrote or signed the document. Both of these methods are types of testimony by a "witness with knowledge," approved by Rule 901(b)(1).

Third, Rule 901(b)(3) provides that an expert witness may identify handwriting by comparing the disputed writing with a sample that has been verified by other

---

2   This example is a slightly modified version of United States v. Zink, 612 F.2d 511 (10th Cir. 1980).

means. To prove that a defendant signed a check, for example, the plaintiff may obtain letters, court papers, or other documents that the defendant admits signing. The plaintiff may even compel the defendant to provide a handwriting sample before trial. The expert will compare these samples to the disputed check.

Fourth, Rule 901(b)(3) allows the trier of fact to compare signatures in the same manner that an expert does. A party, in other words, may introduce both the disputed writing and the admitted samples into evidence. The jurors will compare the writings and draw their own conclusion.

Finally, Rule 901(b)(2) allows a lay person who is familiar with another person's handwriting to identify that handwriting in court. Family members, coworkers, and long-time friends often can authenticate handwriting in this manner. Familiarity with the handwriting, however, must develop outside the litigation; a lay witness cannot authenticate another person's handwriting after studying that handwriting to prepare for trial.

Example: Janette Smith was a salesperson at a store in the Fred Meyer Jewelry chain. Smith claimed that Ricardo Salas, her store manager, sexually harassed her and treated her unfairly in other ways. The company's employee relations administrator investigated the claim and told Smith that the results of the investigation were "inconclusive." Smith failed to report back to work and the company terminated her. Five months later, Smith committed suicide. Her estate sued Fred Meyer Jewelry for sex discrimination, wrongful discharge, and wrongful death. To support its claim, Smith's estate attempted to introduce twelve pages of her handwritten diary. Fred Meyer Jewelry objected that the diary had not been properly authenticated.

Analysis: The district judge sustained Fred Meyer Jewelry's objection. The plaintiff presented a witness who identified Smith's handwriting, but he offered no evidence that he was familiar with that handwriting before the suit was filed. Under Rule 901(2), a lay witness may identify another person's handwriting only if that familiarity is acquired outside the context of the litigation.[3]

---

3   Thomas v. Fred Meyer Jewelry, Inc., No. Civ. 02–3090-CO, 2005 WL 1502644, *2 (D. Or. June 23, 2005).

Authentication failed in this case because the attorney did not use the right technique. The witness who attempted to authenticate the diary lacked sufficient familiarity with Smith's handwriting to do so, but friends or family members surely would have been able to perform that role. Alternatively, the attorney might have obtained known samples of Smith's handwriting and asked an expert or the fact finder to compare those samples to the original. The example demonstrates the need to plan ahead for authentication.

4. Voice Identification. Voice identification plays a key role in some disputes. If a relevant transaction occurred by phone, a witness who participated in the transaction may have to identify the other speaker by voice. Both police and private parties sometimes record conversations; before playing a lawfully obtained recording in the courtroom, the proponent must identify the speakers and provide other authenticating information.

Rule 901(b)(5) makes voice identification relatively easy. Any witness who is familiar with a person's voice may identify that voice in court. The witness may develop that familiarity "at any time," so a witness who meets a telephone caller after the call may use the subsequent meeting to identify the voice on the call.

Unlike the provision governing handwriting, Rule 901(b)(5) allows a witness to develop voice recognition solely in connection with litigation. Police officers who listen to wiretaps or talk to perpetrators by phone, therefore, may identify the speakers' voices in court, even if they have never heard those voices outside of the investigation:

Example: Officer Zinselmeier, an undercover police officer, talked to Juanita Vitale twice by phone. Vitale agreed to sell Zinselmeier narcotics, and the two arranged a place to meet. The two met at 1:00 a.m. in a well-lit parking lot, where Vitale entered Zinselmeier's car and exchanged the drugs for cash. Police then arrested Vitale and charged her with drug trafficking.

At trial, Vitale objected to Zinselmeier identifying her as the woman he spoke with by phone. Vitale argued that Zinselmeier did not know her at the time of the phone calls and that all of their contacts arose out of the criminal investigation.

Analysis: The court allowed Zinselmeier to identify Vitale as the woman he talked to by phone. The order of the phone call and in-person meeting did not affect Zinselmeier's ability to recognize Vitale's voice. And the fact that Zinselmeier knew Vitale only through the investigation did not bar his voice identification under Rule 901(b)(5).[4]

5. Photographs and Videos. Parties often offer photos and videos to illustrate the scenes depicted in them. When offered for these purposes, a party must authenticate the visual aid as a **fair and accurate** representation of the underlying scene at the relevant time. Sometimes the photographer or videographer will authenticate the image; a crime scene technician, for example, may identify a photo as the one he took of the victim's corpse. But testimony from the photographer or videographer is not necessary. Instead, a litigant may call any person familiar with the underlying scene to testify that the photo or video accurately portrays the scene as it appeared at the relevant time.

Example: The Saturn Manufacturing Company patented an industrial shredder used to pulverize refuse. The Williams Patent Crusher & Pulverizer Company began marketing a similar shredder, and Saturn sued for patent infringement. At trial, Saturn offered videos showing operation of both its shredder and the Williams one. Dan Burda, a witness who watched the filming of both videos, testified that the videos accurately and fairly depicted the two shredders.

Analysis: Burda's testimony was sufficient to authenticate the videos. He had observed the actual operation of each shredder during the filming process, and therefore he could state that the videos fairly and accurately represented how the machines operated when the videos were made. If Williams wanted to offer additional views of the shredders or focus on different features, it could offer—and authenticate—its own videos, photos, or other evidence.[5]

6. Emails, Texts, and Social Media. The author of an email can easily authenticate the email by testifying that she wrote the message. Similarly, someone who watched the author compose the email can establish its authenticity.

---

4   United States v. Vitale, 549 F.2d 71, 73 (8th Cir. 1977).

5   Saturn Mfg., Inc. v. Williams Patent Crusher & Pulverizer Co., 713 F.2d 1347, 1356–57 (8th Cir. 1983).

But what if the author is unavailable—or denies that she wrote the electronic message? Litigants still have several tools for authenticating emails and text messages. Most often they turn to Rule 901(b)(4), which allows authentication through "appearance, contents, substance, internal patterns, or other distinctive characteristics of the item, taken together with all the circumstances." This commonsense approach allows parties to use distinguishing features of an email to show that the message is what the proponent claims. Courts, for example, have considered the following factors from the content of an e-mail or text:

- the author's known e-mail address or phone number;

- the author's electronic signature;

- the author's name, nickname, or screen name;

- the author's customary use of emoji or emoticons;

- a writing style similar to the author's known style of writing;

- facts that only a small set of individuals (including the author) know;

- facts or attachments that are uniquely tied to the author, such as personal information, photos of pets or loved ones, or contact information of close friends.

Rule 901(b)(4) also allows courts to consider factors outside the content of the message, such as:

- a witness testifying that the author told her to expect the message prior to its arrival;

- the author acting in accordance with an exchange with the witness;

- the author orally repeating the content of the message soon after it was sent.

Forensic information (such as a message's hashtag value), finally, may tie the message to a particular phone or computer.[6]

Note that a proponent does not have to introduce evidence on all of these factors to authenticate an email or text message. The standard for authenticating electronic messages is the same low bar that applies to authenticating paper ones: The proponent only needs to offer "evidence sufficient to support a finding that the item is what the proponent claims it is." Evidence of just a few distinguishing features should suffice to authenticate an email or text message.

Example: The United States prosecuted Mohamed Siddiqui, a professor, for submitting false statements to the National Science Foundation. The government alleged that Siddiqui forged letters supporting his nomination for a prestigious award. One of those letters purported to come from Dr. von Guten. Von Guten testified that he did not write a letter supporting Siddiqui for this award. The government also offered an email, produced by von Guten, in which a person named "Mo" wrote: "Please tell the NSF that I had permission to use your name." Siddiqui challenged the government's ability to authenticate this email.

Analysis: The trial judge admitted the email, holding that the government had properly authenticated it. The email came from an address that von Guten had previously used to correspond with Siddiqui. The email also referred to previous contacts between Siddiqui and von Guten that only the two of them knew about. And Siddiqui frequently used the nickname "Mo" when talking to others. These facts, the judge held, offered sufficient circumstantial evidence to authenticate the email.[7]

Parties follow the same general approach to authenticate posts on social media sites. An admission by the alleged author will authenticate a post; so will testimony from a witness who saw the author make the post. If that type of evidence is not available, parties turn to forensic and circumstantial evidence. Some

---

6   The factors in both of these lists are drawn, with only minor edits, from Paul W. Grimm, Gregory P. Joseph, & Daniel J. Capra, Best Practices for Authenticating Digital Evidence 9–13 (West Academic 2016).

7   This example expands slightly on United States v. Siddiqui, 235 F.3d 1318, 1322–23 (11th Cir. 2000).

judges require more evidence to authenticate social media posts than email messages or texts; they remain wary of the "general lack of security of the medium." As one trial judge observed:

> [A]ccount holders frequently remain logged in to their accounts while leaving their computers and cell phones unattended. Additionally, passwords and website security are subject to compromise by hackers. Consequently, proving only that a message came from a particular account, without further authenticating evidence, has been held to be inadequate proof of authorship.[8]

Judges, however, differ on this point. Some rely heavily on internet protocol addresses to authenticate social media posts.[9]

All judges will consider distinctive characteristics of a post to link it to the alleged author. These characteristics are similar to the ones listed above for emails and text messages. Judges, however, may demand somewhat more linking characteristics than they do with emails or text messages. They may also want to know how secure the account holder keeps the account. For example, if the account holder regularly gives out her password to others and allows others to post under her name, a trial judge may hesitate to authenticate any material posted on the site.[10]

7. Public Records. Under **Rule 902**, some documents authenticate themselves; a party offering these documents does not need to lay any foundation other than the documents. Public records constitute one important category of self-authenticating documents. Under section 902(1), a party may introduce an original public document from any federal, state, or local government unit if that document bears both a signature attesting to the document's authenticity and the official seal of the government unit. The signature and seal substitute for live testimony authenticating the document.

Section 902(2) offers a similar avenue for authenticating public records produced by government units that lack their own seals. And section 902(4) allows a party to introduce a certified copy of any "official record." The certificate must provide

---

8   State v. Eleck, 130 Conn. App. 632, 639, 23 A.3d 818, 822 (2011), aff'd on other grounds, 302 Conn. 945, 30 A.3d 2 (2014).

9   See Grimm, Joseph & Capra, supra note 61, at 19.

10   See, e.g., Sublet v. State, 442 Md. 632, 113 A.3d 695 (2015).

the same information given by the signature and seal, or it must comply with other federal rules.

Similarly, section 902(3) establishes avenues for authenticating public documents from foreign countries. In most cases, the foreign document must carry both (1) the signature of a foreign official responsible for verifying the document and (2) a diplomatic or consular certification.

Finally, section 902(5) recognizes a "book, pamphlet, or other publication purporting to be issued by a public authority" as self-authenticating. Here is just one example of how parties may rely upon Rule 902 to authenticate public documents:

> **Example:** Louisiana property owners filed a class action against the United States, claiming that the Army Corps of Engineers had widened a navigation channel in a manner that made their property vulnerable to destruction by Hurricane Katrina. To support its motion to dismiss, the United States submitted the National Weather Center's "Tropical Cyclone Report on Hurricane Katrina." The plaintiffs objected that the report had not been authenticated.

> **Analysis:** The report was issued by a "public authority" so it was self-authenticating under Rule 902(5). Although the court considered the document when weighing the motion to dismiss, it ultimately denied the motion as to most of the plaintiffs' claims.[11]

8. Newspapers and Periodicals. Newspapers and periodicals are self-authenticating under Rule 902(6). This means that a party may introduce a relevant newspaper or periodical without offering extrinsic evidence that the periodical is what it purports to be. Remember, however, that authentication does not establish admissibility; many newspaper articles and periodicals constitute inadmissible hearsay.

---

11   Tommaseo v. United States, 75 Fed. Cl. 799, 806–07 (Ct. Cl. 2007).

Example: The Procter & Gamble Company sued Randy Haugen, claiming that he disseminated false rumors linking P&G to Satanism. Haugen defended in part on the ground that the Satanism rumors were so widespread that his few acts did not harm the company's reputation. To support that defense, Haugen offered numerous newspaper articles discussing P&G's alleged link to Satanism. P&G submitted a motion in limine to exclude this evidence, arguing that Haugen could not authenticate it.

Analysis: The court denied P&G's motion. The newspaper articles were self-authenticating under Rule 902(6). The court noted, however, that P&G could object to introduction of these publications at trial if Haugen's use of the documents constituted hearsay. If Haugen used the documents as examples of publications that disseminated the Satanism rumors, he would be using the documents simply to show that those statements were made, not to prove the truth of the matters asserted. On the other hand, if Haugen relied on these publications as reports of rumors spread by **others**, that would be an impermissible hearsay use.[12]

9. Business Records. Rule 902 complements the business records exception to the hearsay rule by allowing self-authentication of those records. Section 902(11) governs domestic records, while 902(12) applies to foreign records. A certificate satisfying the requirements of the business records exception (Rule 803(6)) also authenticates the document. The proponent of the records must give the opposing party reasonable notice and an opportunity to inspect the records and certificate before trial; that allows the opposing party a chance to challenge authenticity. Parties rarely challenge the authenticity of business records, so the Advisory Committee concluded that it was wasteful to require parties to produce a witness for every record.

Rule 902(12), the section governing foreign records, permits self-authentication only in civil cases. A federal statute, however, separately authorizes self-authentication of foreign business records in criminal cases. Under 18 U.S.C. § 3505, the government can readily authenticate records of illegal business dealings even when those transactions cross national boundaries.

---

12 Procter & Gamble Co. v. Haugen, No. 1:95-CV-94 TS, 2007 WL 701812 (D. Utah Mar. 2, 2007). Haugen and his codefendants were distributors who worked for Amway, a company that competes with Procter & Gamble. Two weeks after the judge ruled on the motion in limine, a jury awarded Procter & Gamble $19.25 million in their suit against the former Amway distributors.

10. Electronically Generated Records. Rule 902(13) allows authentication of electronically generated records by certificate rather than live courtroom testimony. A "qualified person" must certify that the electronic process "produces an accurate result." A certificate, for example, could authenticate a spreadsheet generated by software that calculates data based on an algorithm. A party might also use a certificate to authenticate a page printed from a website. As long as a person familiar with the electronic process certifies authenticity using evidence that would be sufficient to establish authenticity at trial, the court will accept the certificate in lieu of live testimony.

As with self-authenticating business records, a party who plans to use a certificate must provide the opposing party with reasonable notice in case the opposing party wants to challenge the accuracy of the electronic process. Remember, too, that authentication of electronically generated records does not prevent a party from objecting to those records on other grounds. An authentic spreadsheet or webpage may contain inadmissible hearsay, unfairly prejudicial information, or other objectionable evidence.

11. Websites. Three types of webpages are self-authenticating: government-owned pages, pages that purport to be newspapers or periodicals, and pages that constitute business records.[13] Techniques for authenticating other webpages vary—and depend on what the proponent wants to prove. It is straightforward to authenticate an existing webpage; the judge and parties can view the page online. If the alleged author denies authoring the page, the proponent can rely upon forensic evidence, eyewitness testimony, or distinguishing characteristics to link the author to the page.

If a party wants to introduce a page that no longer exists (or has been altered), the party will draw upon the techniques discussed throughout this chapter. A witness, for example, may testify that she accessed a particular URL on a specific date and time; that she printed the page offered in evidence; and that the printed page fairly and accurately reflects the content of the online page. Rule 902(13), discussed above, allows the witness to offer the same evidence by affidavit. If an opposing party disputes authenticity, the proponent may point to forensic evidence, distinguishing characteristics, and other supporting evidence.[14]

---

13   Under Rule 101(b)(6), "a reference to any kind of written material or any other medium includes electronically stored information." The sections of Rule 902 allowing self-authentication of government publications, newspapers or periodicals, and business records, therefore, include internet versions of those materials.

14   For further discussion of approaches to authenticating websites, see Grimm, Joseph & Capra, supra note 61, at 15–19; Jonathan L. Moore, Time for an Upgrade: Amending the Federal Rules of Evidence to Address the Challenges of Electronically Stored Information in Civil Litigation, 50 Jurimetrics J. 147 (2010).

12. Evidence to Support a Finding. Remember that a party does not have to provide absolute proof of identity to authenticate evidence. The proponent only needs to offer enough information for a reasonable jury to conclude that the evidence is genuine.

Example: The Drug Enforcement Agency installed video cameras in an apartment rented by William Redman, a drug informant. The cameras recorded Sharon Jackson, one of Redman's neighbors, selling him a substance that looked like rocks of crack cocaine. After Jackson returned to her own apartment, Redman left the building and met the agents who had been watching the video. Redman handed a substance to the agents, who put it in a sealed container and transported it to a laboratory. Lab testing demonstrated that the substance was crack cocaine, and the government prosecuted Jackson for distributing crack.

Redman died of natural causes before trial. A DEA agent testified that he watched the interaction between Redman and Jackson on videotape, received the substance from Redman shortly thereafter, and marked the substance for transport to the lab. Jackson argued this testimony was insufficient to authenticate the cocaine as the substance she gave Redman because of the gap in time between the video transaction and Redman's meeting with the agents.

Analysis: The court of appeals upheld the government's authentication of the substance purchased from Jackson. Redman's unavailability "cast some doubt on the chain of custody" because of his "brief absence from the video camera's field of view." But the government offered sufficient evidence for the jury to conclude that the substance Redman gave to the agents was the same one he obtained from Jackson. The break in the chain of custody affected the weight of the government's case, but did not constitute plain error in its authentication.[15]

Jackson's attorney, of course, was able to argue to the jury that Redman might have substituted crack for a more innocuous substance while he was out of the surveilling agents' sight; authentication did not block attacks on the government's

---

15   United States v. Jackson, 345 F.3d 59, 65 (2d Cir. 2003).

case. By authenticating the substance, the government simply passed a threshold test of admissibility.

13. Admissions and Stipulations. In federal civil trials, parties authenticate most pieces of evidence before trial. The Federal Rules of Civil Procedure require parties to disclose the evidence they plan to present at trial at least 30 days before the trial. An opponent must then raise most evidentiary objections, including authentication, within 14 days of the disclosure or the objection is waived.[16] Civil parties may also authenticate evidence through pretrial admissions or stipulations.[17] Civil litigants must know the rules of authentication, but they usually raise those objections before trial.

Pretrial authentication is less common in criminal trials. The government often prefers to demonstrate the genuineness of its evidence directly to the jury. Conversely, if there is any defect in a government chain of custody or other evidence, the defendant wants the opportunity to reveal that fact. Sometimes, however, the parties stipulate authenticity to avoid tedious and unproductive testimony.

 To review some of the concepts discussed in this chapter, click here to see the video "Authentication" or access the Video module via the eBook on your eproducts bookshelf.

---

16   Fed. R. Civ. P. 26(a)(3)(B). The court may adjust either of these timeframes, but the basic framework of pretrial disclosure and waiver of objections governs most civil trials.

17   Federal Rule of Civil Procedure 36 governs admissions in civil cases. To review stipulations, see Chapters 2 and 59.

Quick Summary

The Federal Rules of Evidence require parties to authenticate evidence before introducing it into evidence. Authentication usually is straightforward: A party simply offers information that would allow a reasonable juror to conclude that the evidence is what the party claims it to be. **Rule 901** provides a non-exhaustive list of methods that parties may use to authenticate different types of evidence. **Rule 902** complements that list by noting types of documents that authenticate themselves.

Civil litigants often authenticate evidence through pretrial disclosure, admissions, or stipulations. Criminal parties sometimes stipulate the authenticity of evidence, but this is less common. Even after evidence has been authenticated, an opponent may contest the relevance or genuineness of the evidence. An opposing party may also object to authenticated evidence on other grounds; authentication does not satisfy any of the other Rules of Evidence.

Test Your Understanding

To assess your understanding of the material in this chapter, click here to take a quiz, or go to the Quizzes module from the eBook on your eProducts bookshelf.

70

Best Evidence

Key Concepts

- **Article X:** Party Must Offer Original Writing, Recording, or Photograph to Prove Content
- Duplicates Frequently Allowed
- Exceptions, Proof by Admission, and Public Records
- Relationship to Other Rules

A. Introduction and Policy. The Federal Rules of Evidence allow litigants to use many kinds of evidence in the courtroom. A plaintiff injured in an automobile collision may try to prove the defendant's fault through her own testimony, eyewitness testimony, fragments of glass or other debris collected at the accident site, the defendant's blood alcohol level, and expert opinion. The evidentiary rules allow the plaintiff to choose which types of evidence best support her claim.

The rules do constrain some choices that parties make about evidence. The hearsay rule, for example, requires parties to provide live testimony in court rather than secondhand reports about statements made outside the courtroom. Similarly, **Rule 404** prevents the victim of an auto accident from proving the defendant's fault by arguing that the defendant had a propensity to drive recklessly. Most evidentiary rules, however, forbid a party to use one type of evidence while leaving the party free to choose any other type.

The "best evidence" rule, contained in **Article X** of the Federal Rules, is an exception to this approach. When a party relies upon a writing, recording, or photograph to **prove the content** of that document, Article X requires the party to introduce the original document. The rule recognizes numerous exceptions to this requirement, including widespread allowance of accurate copies; we will explore those exceptions below. But the core principle of the best evidence rule is: If a party wants to prove the content of a document, then the party should produce the document itself.

Why do the Rules of Evidence impose this special requirement on writings, recordings, and photographs? The rules do not require accident victims to produce testimony from the eyewitness who stood closest to the scene. Nor do they require prosecutors in homicide cases to introduce the actual gun that killed the decedent. What is so special about writings, recordings, and photographs?

The best evidence rules rests on three policies. First, the content of a writing, recording, or photograph is **more detailed and difficult to describe** than most events or objects that witnesses relate in the courtroom. A stabbing victim can more readily describe the defendant's use of a knife than a fraud victim can relate the provisions of a three-page deceptive contract.

Second, writings, recordings, and photographs are relatively **easy to produce**, especially since modern rules allow for liberal use of duplicates. Rigid requirements that parties produce particular witnesses or pieces of physical evidence might artificially impede litigation. A default rule requiring writings, recordings, or photographs under some circumstances entails fewer costs.

Finally, the rule reduces opportunities for **fraud and distortion**. If parties could prove the content of writings, recordings, or photographs through oral testimony, they might mischaracterize complex documents. The best evidence rule helps avoid both intentional and inadvertent deceptions.

As this Introduction suggests, the best evidence rule is poorly named. The rule does not require parties to introduce the "best" evidence under all circumstances. Instead, the rule is a relatively narrow provision imposing modest constraints on parties who attempt to prove the content of a writing, recording, or photograph.

The Advisory Committee recognized that the common-law phrase "best evidence rule" overstates this rule's scope; the committee adopted the title "Contents of Writings, Recordings, and Photographs." But most lawyers continue to use the simpler "best evidence" phrase. We follow that convention here. Once you have mastered the rule, you will be comfortable recognizing the evidence needed to prove the content of writings, recordings, and photographs.

B. The Rules. The best evidence rule appears in Article X of the Federal Rules of Evidence. That article contains eight separate rules, many with several sections; all of these sections combine to create the best evidence rule. Before we examine the individual sections, let's take a bird's eye view of the best evidence rule. The flow chart on the next page illustrates the portions of the best evidence rule.

With that overview in mind, let's examine each element of the best evidence rule. Although the rule has many pieces, it imposes fewer constraints than its detail suggests. Under most circumstances, parties comply naturally with the best evidence rule by introducing evidence that is appropriate for their case.

1. Writings, Recordings, and Photographs. The best evidence rule applies only to writings, recordings, and photographs. **Rule 1001** defines those categories broadly, using the following language:

RULE 1001. Definitions That Apply to This Article

In this article:

(a) A "writing" consists of letters, words, numbers, or their equivalent set down in any form.

(b) A "recording" consists of letters, words, numbers, or their equivalent recorded in any manner.

(c) A "photograph" means a photographic image or its equivalent stored in any form. . . .

When applying the best evidence rule, therefore, think very broadly about the categories of evidence it encompasses. Any type of document, data compilation, recording, still photograph, or motion picture will fall within the rule. Here are two contemporary examples of items that qualified as writings, recordings, or photographs:

> **Example:** Lee Seiler, a graphic artist, claimed that he drew a series of creatures called Garthian Striders during the 1970s. In 1980, Lucasfilm released the blockbuster movie titled "The Empire Strikes Back." That movie included a memorable sequence with giant machines known as Imperial Walkers. Seiler sued Lucasfilm for copyright infringement, claiming that the Imperial Walkers copied his own Garthian Striders.

The Best Evidence Rule

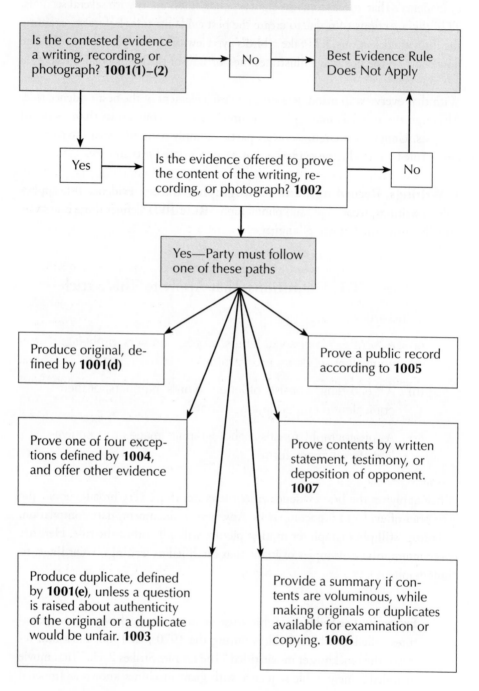

Analysis: Seiler's drawings of the Garthian Striders were "writings" as defined by Rule 1001(a). The court of appeals concluded that an artistic drawing is the "equivalent" of "letters, words, [or] numbers . . . set down in any form." The best evidence rule focuses on symbolic representations and data compilations, types of evidence that a witness cannot readily reproduce in oral testimony. Seiler's drawings fit this concept.[1]

Example: The government charged Vincent Bennett with importing marijuana from Mexico. Police officers spotted Bennett's boat just north of the Mexican border, traveling north along the California coastline. After government agents detained the boat, x-ray examination revealed more than 1500 pounds of marijuana concealed in its hull.

To prove that Bennett imported this marijuana from Mexico into the United States, the prosecutor offered testimony from Customs Officer Malcolm Chandler. Chandler testified that he discovered a global positioning system (GPS) while searching Bennett's boat, and that the GPS had a "backtrack" feature that revealed the boat's previous voyage. Chandler testified that he examined the backtrack feature and it showed that Bennett had navigated the boat from Mexican waters into U.S. waters just before the boat was seized. Bennett objected that the GPS display was a writing or recording that should have been introduced in accordance with the best evidence rule.

Analysis: The court of appeals agreed with Bennett and reversed his conviction for importing marijuana, finding that the GPS display was a writing or recording subject to the best evidence rule. The display was a symbolic representation of Bennett's journey, similar to a logbook or written record of the trip. The government, therefore, could not simply describe the display through oral testimony; it had to comply with the best evidence rule.[2]

---

1   Seiler v. Lucasfilm, Ltd., 808 F.2d 1316, 1318–19 (9th Cir. 1986).

2   United States v. Bennett, 363 F.3d 947, 952–54 (9th Cir. 2004).

2. Offered to Prove the Content. The most important provision of the best evidence rule is the phrase that limits its application to situations in which a party wants to prove the content of a writing, recording, or photograph. This element appears in **Rule 1002**, which states the core principle of the best evidence rule:

Rule 1002. Requirement of the Original

An original writing, recording, or photograph is required in order to <u>prove its content</u> unless these rules or a federal statute provides otherwise.

What does it mean to "prove [the] content" of a writing, recording, or photograph? We can decipher that critical phrase by recognizing **two categories** of cases in which parties prove the content of a writing, recording, or photograph.

In the first category, the writing, recording, or photograph **has independent legal significance**: The content of the document itself controls some facet of the litigation. If the parties dispute the meaning of a written contract, for example, the contract itself shows the words that were used. The parties may still differ over how to interpret those words, but the contract documents the words.

Similarly, if a party complains that a photograph is libelous, the photograph shows what the defendant published. The parties may dispute whether the representation was true or false, complimentary or defamatory, but the photograph provides the point of departure.

In cases like these, a party plainly seeks to prove the content of a writing, recording, or photograph. The contract claimant needs to show what the contract **says** before he offers his interpretation. And the libel plaintiff needs to prove what the photograph **shows** before complaining about the implications. These uses readily fall within Rule 1002's reference to proving the content of a document.

In the Imperial Walker case, Lee Seiler's copyright claim fell in this first category. Seiler's drawings of Garthian Striders had independent legal significance; Seiler claimed that Lucasfilm had copied these particular drawings. It didn't matter whether the drawings were good, bad, realistic, or deceptive; Seiler contended that Lucasfilm copied his particular drawings, so the drawings were at issue.

In the second category of cases in which a party seeks to prove the content of a writing, recording, or photograph, the party chooses an item falling in one of those categories as a **convenient option** for proving some fact. In these cases, the party could have chosen some other means of proof, but settled on a writing, recording, or photograph.

In the Bennett prosecution, for example, the government might have had other ways to prove that Bennett transported marijuana from Mexico into the United States. An eyewitness might have seen Bennett's boat cross the international border; a police officer might have obtained a confession from Bennett; or a jailhouse informant might have reported an incriminating statement. There are many ways to prove that a boat has crossed an international boundary.

The prosecutor chose the GPS backtrack recording as one convenient means of establishing the international passage. To do so, the prosecutor had to prove the content of the recording—not because the recording had independent legal significance, but because the prosecutor chose that means to establish the fact of importation. The prosecutor in Bennett, therefore, also sought to "prove [the] content" of a writing, recording, or photograph.

The best evidence rule applies equally to both categories of evidence; separating them simply helps explain the different ways in which parties "prove [the] content" of a writing, recording, or photograph. The only difference between the categories is that parties who offer evidence falling in the first category **must** introduce a writing, recording, or photograph. They cannot escape the best evidence rule by introducing a different type of evidence. Parties offering evidence that falls in the second category have a choice. They may avoid the best evidence rule, if they find it onerous, by choosing a different type of evidence.

3. Requirement of an Original. When the best evidence rule applies, its default principle requires the party to produce the original writing, recording, or photograph. For some documents, there is only one original. A handwritten note passed by an eighth grader in study hall, for example, is a unique original. In other cases, however, several versions of a document might count as originals. If the eighth grader sends her friend an email, for example, what is the original of that writing? Is it the version stored on the sender's computer? The one that the recipient opens? Print-outs of either version?

Rule 1001(d) answers these questions by defining "original" quite broadly:

> ## RULE 1001. Definitions That Apply to This Article
>
> In this article: . . .
>
> **(d)** An "original" of a writing or recording means
>
> - the writing or recording <u>itself</u> or
> - any <u>counterpart intended to have the same effect</u> by the person who executed or issued it.
> - For electronically stored information, "original" means any <u>printout—or other output readable by sight—if it accurately reflects</u> the information.
> - An "original" of a photograph includes the <u>negative or a print</u> from it. . . .

This definition answers our question about the email: For any "electronically stored information," an original includes "any printout—or other output readable by sight—if it accurately reflects the information." A screenshot of the email stored on the sender's computer, a screenshot of the copy on the recipient's computer, and printouts of either version, therefore, all may qualify as originals of the email.

Section 1001(d) adopts a similarly inclusive definition of photographic originals. These originals include any prints, as well as the negative. Remember that "photographs" include motion pictures and videos, so every DVD at a store may be an "original" of that recording.

Section 1001(d), finally, deals with the common commercial situation in which parties to the transaction intend several copies of a document to have the same effect. If the parties sign a contract in triplicate, for example, then there are three originals. Similarly, both the "merchant copy" and the "customer copy" of a credit card receipt are originals of that receipt.

Identification of an original, however, sometimes depends on what the party offering the document **is trying to prove**. If the parties dispute how much the plaintiff paid for dinner at the defendant's restaurant, then both copies of the credit card receipt are originals that may be used to prove the total bill. But if the parties dispute whether the plaintiff signed the receipt or a waiter forged the signature, then only the copy bearing the plaintiff's purported signature is the original.

4. Duplicates. In addition to defining original broadly, Article X recognizes that mechanically produced copies often are as reliable as an original. **Rule 1001(e)** identifies the types of duplicates that are particularly reliable:

> ## RULE 1001. Definitions That Apply to This Article
>
> In this article: . . .
>
> **(e)** A "duplicate" means a counterpart produced by a <u>mechanical</u>, <u>photographic</u>, <u>chemical</u>, <u>electronic</u>, or <u>other equivalent process</u> or technique that <u>accurately reproduces</u> the original.

Thus, any duplicate must be a copy generated by a method that "accurately reproduces the original." In addition, the rule specifies that the duplication process must follow one of four processes or an "equivalent" technique. Section 1001(e) precludes handwritten or other personally crafted copies, no matter how carefully they are made. Even a manuscript copied by the most meticulous monk does not count as a duplicate under section 1001(e).

For duplicates meeting section 1001(e)'s standard, the best evidence rule allows relatively free substitution of duplicates for originals:

> ## RULE 1003. Admissibility of Duplicates
>
> A duplicate is admissible to the <u>same extent</u> as the original unless
>
> - a genuine question is raised about the original's <u>authenticity</u> or
> - the circumstances make it <u>unfair</u> to admit the duplicate.

This rule eases trial practice in many respects. For example, if a party possesses multiple, identical copies of a memo, the party does not have to worry which—if any—of those copies is the "original." As long as the copies were made by mechanical means recognized in Rule 1001(e), and the opposing party raises neither of the special concerns noted in Rule 1003, any of these copies are admissible.

Similarly, if only a small portion of a transcript or other lengthy document is relevant, a party may copy the relevant pages and introduce them, rather than tearing the pages out of the original or burdening the jury with the entire document.

Rules 1001(e) and 1003 also allow parties to enhance writings, recordings, or photographs by enlarging them, using electronic means to eliminate background noise, and adjusting the brightness and contrast in images.

Rule 1003 imposes just two limits on the use of duplicates. **First**, the court will reject a duplicate if its use would be **unfair**. Admission of an enhanced video image that altered the scene portrayed, for example, would be unfair. **Second**, Rule 1003 requires use of an original writing, recording, or photograph if a party challenges the authenticity of the original. Under those circumstances, the fact finder must examine the original to resolve the controversy.

Example: William P. Boswell filed a lawsuit to establish his ownership of a piece of property known as the "Feed Yard." The parties agreed that Marsden and Melva Larsen signed a deed transferring this property to Boswell's father in 1974. Boswell claimed that his father later altered the deed to transfer the Feed Yard to him. To support this claim, Boswell produced a copy of the altered deed. He did not produce the deed itself, either in its original or altered form. The defendant, who also claimed ownership of the Feed Yard, disputed the authenticity of the deed offered by Boswell.

Analysis: Since the defendant disputed authenticity of the altered deed, Boswell had to produce the original or account for its loss under other provisions of the best evidence rule. Boswell did neither, so the court granted summary judgment for the defendant.[3]

5. Exceptions. The Federal Rules of Evidence recognize that parties sometimes cannot produce an original or reliable duplicate of a writing, recording, or photograph. Under four circumstances, **Rule 1004** excuses this failure and allows the party to introduce other evidence of the document's contents:

---

3   Boswell v. Jasperson, 109 F. App'x 270 (10th Cir. 2004). This type of action to establish ownership of property is called an action to quiet title.

RULE 1004. Admissibility of Other Evidence of Content

An original is not required and other evidence of the content of a writing, recording, or photograph is admissible if:

(a)   all the originals are <u>lost or destroyed</u>, and not by the proponent acting in bad faith;

(b)   an original <u>cannot be obtained</u> by any available <u>judicial process</u>;

(c)   the <u>party against whom</u> the original would be offered had control of the original; was at that time put on notice, by pleadings or otherwise, that the original would be a subject of proof at the trial or hearing; and <u>fails to produce</u> it at the trial or hearing; or

(d)   the writing, recording, or photograph is <u>not closely related to a controlling issue</u>.

If a party claims that the originals were **lost or destroyed**, then the party may introduce other evidence to prove the content of a writing, recording, or photograph. This exception does not apply, however, if the party's own bad faith caused loss or destruction of the originals.

Example: In Lee Seiler's copyright claim against Lucasfilm, described above, Seiler claimed that his original drawings of "Garthian Striders" had been lost. In their place, Seiler produced "reconstructions" of the drawings that he made after Lucasfilm's movie was released.

Analysis: The trial judge held that Seiler's own bad faith was responsible for any loss or destruction of his originals. After holding a 7-day evidentiary hearing on the matter, the judge concluded that "Seiler testified falsely, purposefully destroyed or withheld in bad faith [his] originals, and fabricated and misrepresented the nature of his reconstructions." Since Seiler could not establish an exception to the best evidence rule and he failed to introduce his original drawings, the judge granted summary judgment for Lucasfilm. The court recognized no Return of the Garthian Striders.[4]

In addition to the exception for loss or destruction, Rule 1004 excuses production of an original if a party **cannot obtain** that original through judicial process or procedure. This circumstance usually arises when a third party possesses the original and refuses to produce it.

Similarly, if an **opponent controls** the original, then the party proving the content of that original need not produce it. As long as the pleadings or some other circumstance notifies the opponent that the content of the original will be the subject of proof, the opponent must produce the original.

Finally, if the writing, recording, or photograph is **not closely related** to a controlling issue, then the parties need not produce an original. Just as the judge protects the jury from hearing burdensome proof about collateral matters,[5] Rule 1004(d) shields the parties from the burden of producing original documents related to collateral issues.

6. Proof by Admission. Rule 1007 establishes another avenue for parties to comply with the best evidence rule: If an opponent admits the contents of a writing, recording, or photograph, then the party does not have to produce the original document or account for its absence.

RULE 1007. Testimony or Statement of a Party to Prove Content

The proponent may prove the content of a writing, recording, or photograph by the testimony, deposition, or written statement of the party against whom the evidence is offered. The proponent need not account for the original.

Note, however, that Rule 1007 does not allow every statement of an opposing party to establish the content of a writing, recording, or photograph. The statement must

---

4   Seiler, 808 F.2d at 1318.

5   See Chapter 18 for further discussion of this issue.

occur in writing, in testimony, or in a deposition. Unsworn oral statements, in other words, do not satisfy Rule 1007.

7. Public Records. If a party needs to prove the content of a public record, **Rule 1005** eases the burden of doing so. Parties ordinarily cannot produce original public records in court because those records remain with the public agency. Rule 1005 reduces disputes over the authenticity of public-record duplicates by specifying how to prove the content of these records:

RULE 1005. Copies of Public Records to Prove Content

The proponent may use a copy to prove the content of an official record—or of a document that was recorded or filed in a public office as authorized by law—if these conditions are met:

- the record or document is otherwise admissible; and
- the copy is certified as correct in accordance with <u>Rule 902(4)</u> or is testified to be correct by a <u>witness who has compared it with the original</u>.

If no such copy can be obtained by <u>reasonable diligence</u>, then the proponent may use <u>other evidence</u> to prove the content.

The rule thus offers three avenues for proving the content of a public record: (1) introduction of a copy that has been certified under Rule 902(4);[6] (2) testimony by a witness who has compared a copy with the original; or (3) other evidence, when one of the first two methods is not obtainable by reasonable diligence.

8. Summaries. Modern disputes can involve voluminous records. Producing all of these documents in court would overwhelm the patience of the parties, the storage capacity of the courthouse, and the attention of the jury. Rule 1006 recognizes this reality by allowing the parties to introduce summaries of writings, recordings, or photographs "that cannot be conveniently examined in court."

---

6   We examined Rule 902, which provides for self-authentication of public documents, in Chapter 69.

RULE 1006. Summaries to Prove Content

The proponent may use a <u>summary, chart, or calculation</u> to prove the content of voluminous writings, recordings, or photographs that <u>cannot be conveniently examined in court</u>.

- The proponent must make the originals or duplicates <u>available for examination or copying</u>, or both, by other parties at a reasonable time and place.
- And the <u>court may order</u> the proponent to produce them in court.

As the underlined phrases show, Rule 1006 allows summaries in any form, including a "chart" or "calculation." The rule prevents deception by requiring the party offering the summary to make the originals or duplicates available for examination and copying. The court, moreover, may direct the party to produce the originals or duplicates in court.

9. Who Decides? Applying the best evidence rule often requires preliminary determinations about factual issues. **Rule 104**, which we studied in Chapter 34, governs preliminary decisions on the admissibility of evidence. **Rule 1008** supplements Rule 104 with several guidelines that apply particularly to preliminary factual decisions underlying the best evidence rule.

The first sentence of Rule 1008 declares that the judge usually resolves these preliminary factual questions:

RULE 1008. Functions of the Court and Jury

<u>Ordinarily, the court determines</u> whether the proponent has fulfilled the factual conditions for admitting other evidence of the content of a writing, recording, or photograph under Rule 1004 or 1005. . . .

The second sentence of Rule 1008, however, assigns resolution of three types of preliminary facts to the jury:

RULE 1008. Functions of the Court and Jury

. . . But in a jury trial, the jury determines—in accordance with Rule 104(b)—any issue about whether:

(a) an asserted writing, recording, or photograph <u>ever existed</u>;

(b) <u>another one</u> produced at the trial or hearing is the <u>original</u>; or

(c) <u>other evidence</u> of content <u>accurately reflects</u> the content.

These three factual issues arise relatively rarely; the judge determines most factual issues related to the best evidence rule. The judge, for example, decides whether evidence is a writing, recording or photograph; whether that evidence is an original or duplicate; and whether all originals have been lost or destroyed. Despite Rule 1008, most preliminary determinations related to the best evidence rule follow Rule 104(a).

C. In the Courtroom. The most perplexing issues that arise under the best evidence rule occur when a party attempts to prove a fact without reference to a writing, recording, or photograph, and the opponent claims that the party **should have followed** the best evidence rule.

Resolution of these objections turns on what the party offering the evidence **is trying to prove**. If a party tries to prove the content of a writing, recording, or photograph, then the best evidence rule applies. But if the party tries to prove a fact that could be shown with multiple types of evidence, then the party has no obligation to use a writing, recording, or photograph to prove the fact—even if one is available.

In all of the examples previously discussed in this chapter, parties attempted to prove the content of a writing, recording, or photograph; thus they were bound by the best evidence rule. In some of these cases, a writing was integral to the case. William Boswell, for example, had to rely upon a property deed to assert his ownership of the Feed Yard; he could not escape the best evidence rule.

In other cases, a party chose to rely upon evidence falling within the best evidence rule, although other proof might have been available. When prosecuting Vincent

Bennett for importing marijuana, for example, the government opted to introduce testimony describing the records on Bennett's GPS. Having chosen to rely upon the content of a recording, the government had to produce the recording itself; the best evidence rule forbid it from simply describing the contents of that recording.

But what if a party chooses to rely upon evidence other than a writing, recording, or photograph? Under what circumstances can the opponent raise a best evidence objection to proof that does not use documents like these?

If the writing, recording, or photograph has independent legal significance, then the best evidence rule compels production of that document. A party cannot simply describe a document when the content of that document is essential to the litigation.

Example: Visual Scene, a manufacturer of sunglasses, agreed to supply sunglasses to R & R Associates. The parties signed a four-page contract governing their long-term relationship. After several years, the sunglasses declined in quality; R & R sued Visual Scene to force compliance with the contract. At trial, R & R's only evidence of the contract's terms came from its president, who testified: "We have a detailed agreement with these sunglass dudes and they're just not living up to it. Their sunglasses fail every specification in the contract." Visual Scene moved for judgment as a matter of law, arguing that R & R had failed to prove the terms of the contract.

Analysis: The judge granted Visual Scene's motion because R & R did not provide sufficient evidence of the terms of its contract with Visual Scene. To prevail on its claim, R & R had to prove the content of that writing; thus the best evidence rule applied. To comply with that rule, R & R had to produce an original of the contract, provide an acceptable duplicate, show that Visual Scene had admitted the content of the contract, or establish one of the exceptions.[7]

---

7   This example creates a hypothetical extension of the facts in R & R Associates, Inc. v. Visual Scene, Inc., 726 F.2d 36 (1st Cir. 1984).

On the other hand, if a party attempts to prove a fact that exists independently of any documents, then the party does not have to use a document to prove that fact. The party may introduce oral testimony or other types of evidence.

Example: In the contract dispute described above, R & R also offered evidence of its damages. R & R's president testified that, based on his personal knowledge, the company had paid $31,850.19 to Visual Scene for the defective sunglasses. Visual Scene objected to this testimony under the best evidence rule.

Analysis: This testimony did not violate the best evidence rule. R & R could have proven the amount it paid Visual Scene by introducing a receipt or cancelled check. If it had chosen to rely on writings of that nature, the best evidence rule would have applied. But the company's president had personal knowledge of the amount paid and could testify directly about that amount. R & R was trying to prove the amount paid to Visual Scene, not the content of a particular writing, so it could choose any type of admissible evidence to accomplish that goal.[8]

The Advisory Committee's note to Rule 1002 supports this result, declaring that "payment may be proved without producing the written receipt."[9] When a party testifies in greater detail about the terms of a business transaction, however, the party probably is trying to prove the content of a written contract and the best evidence rule applies. Drawing the line between testimony that attempts to prove the content of a document and testimony that attempts to prove facts that just happen to appear in a document can be difficult. Persuasive advocacy affects resolution of these issues. But if the document is readily available, prudent trial lawyers simply produce the document rather than risk losing the case due to the best evidence rule.

D. Best Evidence and Other Rules. Remember that evidence must pass through every evidentiary net to gain admission. Compliance with the best evidence rule does not guarantee

---

8   Id. This is the issue that the court resolved in the R & R Associates case.

9   Fed. R. Evid. 1002 advisory committee's note.

admissibility under other rules. The rules governing authentication, for example, are distinct from the best evidence rule. The two sets of rules sometimes overlap, particularly for public records, but they impose independent requirements.

Watch particularly for hearsay issues intertwined with best evidence ones. When a party introduces a document that has independent legal significance, the party usually does not offer the document to prove the truth of any matter asserted in the document. Proving the "content" of a document under these circumstances differs from proving the "truth of the matter asserted" in the document.

But when a party chooses a document to prove a fact reflected in the document, the second category of cases discussed above, the evidence often is hearsay. In these cases, the party uses the content of a document to prove the truth of the matter asserted there. Thus, the evidence must comply with the best evidence rule and must fit within an exception to the hearsay doctrine.

Example: Spartan Grain & Mill Co. sued Boyce Blackmon to recover payment for a flock of chickens it sold Blackmon. Blackmon claimed that the chickens were diseased, and he refused to pay. To support this defense, Blackmon testified that a veterinarian gave him a lab report that confirmed infection in the chickens. Spartan Grain objected to Blackmon's testimony.

Analyis: Blackmon's testimony violated the best evidence rule. Blackmon could have chosen several routes to prove that the chickens were diseased. He could, for example, have offered his own observations of the chickens' symptoms. Or he could have called the veterinarian to testify in court. By relying on the lab report, Blackmon sought to prove the fact of disease through the content of a document; this invoked the best evidence rule.

In addition, Blackmon's testimony was hearsay; he recounted an out-of-court statement, the lab report, to prove the truth of the matter asserted in that report. If Blackmon had offered the lab report itself, it might have qualified for admission under the business records exception to the hearsay rule. But his oral description of the document did not satisfy any hearsay exception.[10]

---

10   This example draws on Spartan Grain & Mill Co. v. Ayers, 517 F.2d 214 (5th Cir. 1975).

To review some of the concepts discussed in this chapter, click here to see the video "Best Evidence" or access the Video module via the eBook on your eproducts bookshelf.

Quick Summary

When litigants attempt to prove the content of a writing, recording, or photograph, the best evidence rule requires introduction of an original. **Rule 1002.** The Federal Rules of Evidence, however, define "original" broadly **(Rule 1001(d))**, and allow liberal substitution of duplicates. **Rules 1001(e)** & **1003.** A party may also avoid the requirement of an original by proving one of four exceptions to the best evidence rule, described in **Rule 1004**, or by showing that the opponent has admitted the content of the writing, recording, or photograph as provided in **Rule 1007.** If a party wants to prove the content of a public record, **Rule 1005** offers special guidance. And if the documents are voluminous, **Rule 1006** allows the party to introduce a summary, while giving the opponent an opportunity to examine or copy the originals or duplicates. **Rule 1008**, finally, governs preliminary determinations of factual questions underlying application of the best evidence rule. The rule reserves a few questions for the jury, but the judge decides most of these issues under the general standards of **Rule 104(a).**

Remember that compliance with the best evidence rule does not relieve a party's obligation to comply with other Rules of Evidence. Documents must also satisfy the rules governing authentication, hearsay, and other matters.

Test Your Understanding

To assess your understanding of the material in this chapter, click here to take a quiz, or go to the Quizzes module from the eBook on your eProducts bookshelf.

71

Presumptions

Key Concepts

- Four Categories of Presumptions
- **Rule 302:** State Law Governs Presumptions in Diversity Suits
- **Rule 301:** Bubble-Bursting Presumptions Are the Default Rule In Other Federal Civil Cases
- Constitutional Law Governs Presumptions in Criminal Cases

A. Introduction and Policy. We have almost finished our examination of the Federal Rules of Evidence. Those rules determine the admissibility of each piece of trial evidence, from live testimony to smoking guns. Trial attorneys, however, must do more than simply introduce these pieces of evidence; they must weave the individual items into a tapestry that tells a compelling story.

To tell that story, lawyers often urge the jury to draw inferences from the evidence. If a criminal defendant fled town shortly after the crime, the prosecutor will ask the jury to infer that the defendant realized he was guilty. If the plaintiff in an age discrimination case received excellent annual evaluations before she was fired, the plaintiff's lawyer will ask the jury to infer that the plaintiff was a good worker. Inferences are common, both in the courtroom and in daily life.

The law channels some of these inferences through procedural devices known as **presumptions**. Presumptions arise in almost every substantive field of law; you probably have encountered them in Torts, Criminal Law, and many other courses. Although substantive law determines the operation of most presumptions, the Federal Rules of Evidence provide some guidelines for applying these devices in federal court.

Presumptions reflect a range of policies. Some offer predictable resolutions of common issues, such as the presumption that a letter placed in the mail has been delivered. Others attempt to place the burden of producing evidence on the party who has access to that evidence, such as a presumption that the driver of a car had the owner's permission to operate the vehicle.

Just as presumptions further different policies, they play different roles in the courtroom. Some are conclusive, while others are just suggestive. Some shift the burden of proof, while others shift only the burden of producing evidence. Most presumptions, however, fall into one of four categories. We will explore those categories in the next section, before turning to the evidentiary rules governing presumptions. To apply any presumption, you must first know what **type** of presumption it is.

B. Four Types of Presumptions.

Presumptions can assume many forms. It is easiest to master this area, however, if you divide presumptions into the four categories described below. Some presumptions adopt variations on these categories, but most fall into one of these basic groups.

1. Permissive Inferences. The first type of presumption is the permissive inference. With this type of presumption, the judge simply instructs the jury that it may infer one fact from another. If a litigant intentionally destroyed evidence after a claim was filed, for example, the judge may tell the jurors: "You may infer that the evidence would have been unfavorable to that litigant." The jury may disregard this suggestion; a permissive inference merely gives the jury an option.

Some scholars maintain that permissive inferences are not true presumptions, because they have no binding effect. In effect, the judge is merely telling the jurors that they are allowed to make an inference that they probably would have made on their own anyway. Courts, however, often refer to these inferences as presumptions, so it is easiest to think of them as a separate category within the field of presumptions. Permissive inferences, moreover, can be very helpful to the party benefiting from the inference. The instruction reassures jurors that the law allows them to infer one fact from another and often nudges them in that direction.

2. Presumptions That Shift the Burden of Production. A second type of presumption shifts the burden of producing evidence from one party to another. Students, lawyers, and judges find this category of presumptions the hardest to understand, but the category is essential to master because many presumptions fall in this category.

Remember that the plaintiff in any civil lawsuit has two different burdens: the burden of proof and the burden of producing evidence. The first burden requires a civil plaintiff to persuade the jury that each element of her claim is more likely true than false. If the plaintiff and defendant offer competing stories and the jury can't decide which one is true, then the defendant wins. A civil plaintiff must establish her case by a preponderance of the evidence; that is her **burden of proof**.

But a civil plaintiff also has a **burden of producing evidence**. During her case-in-chief, she must produce enough evidence on each element of the claim that a reasonable jury could find in her favor. Otherwise, the judge will direct a verdict for the defendant. The plaintiff cannot simply sit back and hope that the defendant will introduce such damaging evidence that he proves the plaintiff's case; the plaintiff must carry the burden of producing evidence to support her claim.

The prosecutor in a criminal case, similarly, must meet both a burden of proof and a burden of production. The prosecutor's burden of proof is a higher one of proving guilt beyond a reasonable doubt. Similarly, the prosecutor's burden of producing evidence requires the prosecutor to introduce enough evidence of guilt that a reasonable jury could find the defendant guilty beyond a reasonable doubt. Like the civil plaintiff, a prosecutor cannot hope that the defendant will provide evidence of his own guilt.

This second category of presumptions incorporates this distinction: Presumptions in this group satisfy the burden of producing evidence, but not the burden of proof. If a party successfully invokes one of these presumptions, the opponent must respond by producing some contrary evidence. But once the opponent responds, the original party retains the burden of proof on the issue. Here is an example of a presumption falling in this category:

> **Example:** Melvin Hicks, an African American man, worked for the Missouri Department of Corrections and Human Resources. The Department fired Hicks, and he filed a Title VII suit claiming race discrimination. Hicks proved during his case-in-chief that (1) he was African American, (2) he was qualified for his position, (3) the Department discharged him, and (4) a white man replaced him.

Analysis: Under Title VII law, these facts created a presumption of racial discrimination that shifted the burden of producing evidence to the defendant employer. Hicks's proof, in other words, was sufficient to withstand the defendant's motion for a directed verdict. The employer had to counter Hicks's case by producing its own evidence.[1]

Once the plaintiff establishes the facts to invoke a presumption that shifts the burden of production, how does the opposing party respond? What type of evidence, in other words, meets the shifted burden of production? Most often, the opponent offers evidence to contradict the presumed fact. The plaintiff's evidence in *Hicks*, for example, created a presumption that he was fired because of his race. The employer responded to this presumption by offering evidence that Hicks had committed repeated workplace infractions. This evidence, if believed by the jury, suggested that Hicks was fired because of his misconduct—not because of his race.

When a party responds to a burden-of-production-shifting presumption by offering evidence that disputes the presumed fact, the new evidence destroys the presumption and eliminates it from the case. For this reason, many courts call this type of presumption a **bursting-bubble presumption.** The presumption creates a bubble that buoys the proponent's case and forces the opponent to respond. But once the opponent replies, that response "bursts the bubble" and removes the presumption from the case. [2]

The employer's evidence of workplace misconduct in *Hicks* destroyed Hicks's presumption and removed it from the case. Hicks could still argue that the basic facts he proved (such as the fact that the Department replaced him with a white worker) showed race discrimination. He could also attack the Department's evidence of workplace infractions as false. But Hicks would have to persuade the jury, based on the whole record, that the Department more likely than not fired him because of his race. And he would have to make that showing without the aid of any presumption or instruction from the judge.

A bursting-bubble presumption, in other words, requires an opponent to produce evidence rebutting the presumption, but it does not shift the burden of proof to the opponent. We will explore this concept further in the Courtroom section. For

---

1   St. Mary's Honor Center v. Hicks, 509 U.S. 502 (1993).

2   Courts also sometimes call these presumptions "Thayer-type presumptions," since the scholar James Thayer favored presumptions of this type.

now, remember that a bursting-bubble presumption has a limited effect: It shifts the burden of producing evidence, but not the burden of proof.

3. Presumptions That Shift the Burden of Proof. A third type of presumption shifts the burden of **proof** to an opposing party. Like presumptions in the second category, these presumptions arise once a party introduces sufficient evidence of facts needed to invoke the presumption. And like presumptions in the second category, these presumptions require the opponent to respond to the presumed fact by producing evidence in response. These presumptions, however, go one step further: They require the opposing party to carry the burden of proof in overcoming the presumed fact. In a civil case, the opposing party usually must persuade the jury that the presumed fact more likely than not is false.

Some courts refer to these presumptions as "strong presumptions" to distinguish them from the "weak presumptions" in the second category. Others call them Morgan-type presumptions because the evidence scholar Edmund Morgan championed them. Still others designate them the "reformist approach" because they gained favor during the second half of the twentieth century. Whatever their name, presumptions in this category shift the burden of proof to an opposing party. Here is an example:

> **Example:** Shortly before declaring bankruptcy, David and Hannah Armstrong transferred several pieces of property, including their house, their vehicles, and their interest in the Maverick Land and Cattle Company, to relatives and institutions controlled by their friends. Phillip Kelly, the trustee of the Armstrongs' bankruptcy estate, filed an action to set aside these transfers as fraudulent.
>
> At trial, Kelly established several "badges of fraud." These are indicators, such as transfer of most of the debtor's property or transfers to relatives, that suggest fraud. The trial judge instructed the jury that it could infer fraud from those badges, but had no obligation to do so. Kelly objected, arguing that these badges of fraud did more than merely create a permissive inference; they shifted the burden of proof to the Armstrongs.

> **Analysis:** The court of appeals agreed with Kelly. Under controlling law, establishment of several badges of fraud shifts the burden of proof to the debtor. The trial judge, therefore, should have instructed the jurors that, if

they found multiple badges of fraud in the Armstrongs' transactions, then the Armstrongs had the burden of proving by a preponderance of the evidence that they did not act fraudulently. If the Armstrongs could not meet this burden of proof, then the jury should find for Kelly. The court remanded for a new trial on the fraud claims.[3]

Note that, even if a presumption shifts the burden of proof, the jury must find the facts supporting the presumption before the burden shifts. If the jury in the new Kelly trial fails to find the existence of any badges of fraud, then no burden of proof will shift to the debtors and the trustee's claim most likely will fail.

4. Conclusive Presumptions. Conclusive presumptions, sometimes called irrebuttable presumptions, **require** the fact finder to draw a particular inference. These presumptions don't merely shift the burden of production or burden of proof, they conclusively establish a fact relevant to the litigation. Here is an example of a conclusive presumption:

Example: Margarita Alvarado suffered severe burns when her nightgown and robe caught fire. Alvarado sued J. C. Penney, the store that sold the products, claiming that the nightgown and robe were defectively designed. One design defect, Alvarado argued, was the use of flammable cloth in the sleepwear.

J. C. Penney moved for summary judgment on this claim, citing a statute that shielded retailers from liability if the product complied with applicable legislative or regulatory safety standards. This statute, J. C. Penney argued, created a conclusive presumption of care.

Analysis: The trial court agreed with J. C. Penney's interpretation of the statute. If J. C. Penney could show that the cloth used in the sleepwear complied with applicable safety standards, then it would be entitled to judgment on that claim. J. C. Penney, however, did not introduce sufficient evidence of compliance as part of its summary judgment motion; the court denied the motion and set the case for trial.[4]

---

3   Kelly v. Armstrong, 141 F.3d 799, 802–03 (8th Cir. 1998).

4   Alvarado v. J.C. Penney Co., 713 F. Supp. 1389, 1390–92 (D. Kan. 1989) (applying Kansas law).

As the *Alvarado* case suggests, a conclusive presumption does not necessarily eliminate the jury's role; the party invoking the presumption still must establish the facts giving rise to the presumption. At trial, therefore, J. C. Penney must offer evidence showing that its clothing contained the type of cloth prescribed by government regulations. If no reasonable jury could dispute the type of cloth in J. C. Penney's sleepwear, and if that cloth satisfied the regulations, then the judge will grant J. C. Penney judgment as a matter of law on that claim.

On the other hand, if reasonable people could differ over the type of cloth in J. C. Penney's sleepwear, the jury will resolve that issue. The judge will give the presumption its conclusive effect by instructing the jurors that if they find that the sleepwear contained a certain type of cloth, then they must find that J. C. Penney is not liable for any design defect related to flammability. The jury, in other words, will decide whether facts underlying the presumption exist.

C. The Rules. The Federal Rules of Evidence contain two provisions related to presumptions. **Rule 302** declares that, when state law governs a civil claim or defense, state law also determines the effect of any presumption on that issue:

> ## RULE 302. Applying State Law to Presumptions in Civil Cases
>
> In a civil case, <u>state law</u> governs the effect of a presumption regarding a claim or defense for which state law supplies the rule of decision.

This rule is similar to **Rule 501**, which requires federal courts to apply state rules of privilege in diversity cases, and to **Rule 601**, which adopts the same approach for determining witness competence.[5]

Rule 301 offers an important complement to Rule 302's federalism provision. Rule 301 establishes a default principle governing presumptions in civil cases that are not governed by state law or other federal laws:

---

5   See Chapter 66 for further discussion of Rule 501 and Chapter 14 on Rule 601.

RULE 301. Presumptions in Civil Cases Generally

In a civil case, <u>unless a federal statute or these rules provide otherwise</u>, the party against whom a presumption is directed has the <u>burden of producing evidence</u> to <u>rebut the presumption</u>. But this rule does not shift the burden of persuasion, which remains on the party who had it originally.

Note three points about Rule 301. **First**, the rule applies only to civil proceedings. The Advisory Committee proposed a separate rule, Rule 303, which would have governed presumptions in federal criminal cases. Congress deleted that rule because it planned to enact separate legislation governing presumptions in criminal cases, but it never completed that task. The Federal Rules of Evidence, therefore, do not affect presumptions in criminal cases.

The Supreme Court, meanwhile, has issued a series of constitutional decisions governing presumptions in criminal cases. Those constitutional issues lie outside the bounds of the evidentiary rules, so we leave them to courses in Criminal Procedure and Constitutional Law. This chapter, like Rules 301 and 302, focuses on presumptions in civil actions.

Second, Rule 301 creates a default principle that applies only when some other provision does not. We already know from Rule 302 that state law controls the effect of presumptions for claims and defenses governed by state law. Rule 301 also acknowledges that Congress may give presumptions particular effect under specific statutes. Congress, in fact, frequently enacts presumptions as part of the substantive law in a field. Rule 301 applies only when no other state or federal rule does.

Finally, when Rule 301 applies, most courts agree that it creates the second type of presumption we discussed above: a presumption that shifts the burden of producing evidence, but not the burden of proof. As we discuss further below, Rule 301 presumptions are bursting-bubble presumptions.

D. In the Courtroom.

1. Bursting Bubbles in Federal Court. Rule 301 declares that a presumption shifts "the burden of producing evidence" to an opposing party, but it "does not shift the burden of persuasion." Most courts have interpreted this rule, as well as the legislative history supporting it, to embrace the bursting-bubble approach to presumptions.[6]

Rule 301, however, controls only when no other state or federal rule defines the operation of a presumption. In diversity cases, judges look to state law to determine the effect of a presumption. And Congress often sets the contours of a presumption as part of a statute creating the presumption. The bursting-bubble approach is the default rule in federal court, but advocates should research the law of any case carefully to determine whether a different type of presumption applies.

2. Bursting Bubbles in Operation. The bursting-bubble approach mystifies many students and lawyers, so it is worth examining in closer detail. Under this approach, a presumption disappears once the opposing party offers some evidence disputing the presumed fact. The opposing party need not persuade the fact finder that she is right; she only needs to offer evidence that a reasonable jury **could** accept.

In the Hicks case described above, for example, the plaintiff introduced enough evidence to create a presumption of race discrimination. The defendant responded to this presumption by offering evidence that it fired the plaintiff because of workplace misconduct. This evidence, if believed by the fact finder, was sufficient to refute any inference of discrimination; thus, it was enough to burst the bubble of the plaintiff's presumption.

Destroying the presumption, however, doesn't end the case: After weighing all of the evidence, the fact finder may still find in favor of the party who originally benefited from the presumption. In the Hicks case, for example, the fact finder might not have believed the employer's claims. After reviewing all of the evidence, the jury might have concluded that misconduct was merely a pretext for firing Hicks. Despite the employer's evidence, and without relying on any presumption, the fact finder might have found that Hicks proved race discrimination by a preponderance of the evidence.

---

6   See, e.g., In re Yoder Co., 758 F.2d 1114, 1118–20 (6th Cir. 1985) (discussing rule language, legislative history, scholarly responses, and other judicial rulings); Nunley v. City of Los Angeles, 52 F.3d 792, 796 (9th Cir. 1995).

Alternatively, the jury could have accepted the defendant's evidence and ruled for the defendant. The jury in Hicks might have agreed that Hicks committed several serious workplace infractions and that the employer terminated him for that reason. Once a bursting-bubble presumption drops out of the case, a jury may reach any conclusion supported by the evidence. In fact, the jury can even reject the evidence offered to rebut the presumption and still find for the party who offered that rejected evidence.

The fact finder in Hicks came to the latter type of conclusion. The trial judge, sitting as the fact finder, concluded that the defendant's claimed reasons for discharging Hicks were pretextual. Other employees, the judge found, had not been fired after committing similar or more serious acts; the employer's explanation for Hicks's termination was not credible. On the other hand, the judge also rejected Hicks's interpretation of the facts. After weighing all of the evidence, the judge decided that Hicks had "proven the existence of a crusade to terminate him" but he had "not proven that the crusade was racially rather than personally motivated."[7]

The result in Hicks puzzles many students: If the fact finder doesn't believe the evidence offered to rebut a presumption, then how can that evidence burst the presumption's bubble? The answer lies in understanding the difference between producing evidence and meeting a burden of proof. A bursting-bubble presumption only shifts the first burden, one of producing evidence. Once the opposing party offers some evidence that is plausible enough that a reasonable jury **could** believe it, the presumption disappears from the case. The fact finder then weighs the evidence supplied by both parties without any regard for the presumption.

This means that in a jury trial, the jury never even hears about a bursting-bubble presumption. This type of presumption is merely a procedural device that structures the order of proof and determines the availability of judgments as a matter of law. When one party introduces evidence that creates a bursting-bubble presumption, the opponent must offer evidence to counter that presumption. If the opponent does not offer evidence that a reasonable jury could find sufficient to defeat the presumption, then the party creating the presumption is entitled to judgment as a matter of law. If the opponent does introduce the necessary evidence, then the jury decides the case without reference to any presumption.

3. Presumption Variations. Although most presumptions fit into one of the four categories described above, courts recognize many variations. A presumption that

---

7   Hicks, 509 U.S. at 508.

shifts the burden of proof, for example, may require the opposing party to meet that burden with a preponderance of the evidence or with clear and convincing evidence. Similarly, a presumption that shifts the burden of producing evidence may require a particular type of evidence from the opposing party.

One common variation combines a bursting-bubble presumption with a permissive inference. In this variation, the judge substitutes a permissive inference for a presumption whose bubble has burst. Even after the opposing party introduces evidence to destroy the presumption, in other words, the judge instructs the jury that it may infer the presumed fact from the original evidence. Availability of this residual inference depends on the substantive law governing the case.

 For humorous review of the concepts discussed in this chapter, click here to see the video "Shall We Dance?" or access the Video module via the eBook on your eproducts bookshelf.

As these variations suggest, presumptions are members of a family; there is no single type of presumption. Whenever you encounter a presumption, study its features carefully using the guidelines given above. Don't assume that one presumption will behave just like another one; research the law governing the presumption that applies to your case. Presumptions channel the fact finder's inferences, but they do so in different ways.

Quick Summary

Presumptions are procedural devices that establish rules for making inferences. Most presumptions fall into one of four categories: (1) permissive inferences, (2) presumptions that shift the burden of producing evidence, (3) presumptions that shift the burden of proof, and (4) conclusive presumptions. Courts and legislatures, however, have created many variations on these categories; examine every presumption carefully to determine how it functions.

Rule 302 directs federal courts to follow state law when applying presumptions in diversity cases. **Rule 301** establishes presumptions that shift the burden of production (bursting-bubble presumptions) as the default rule in other civil cases. The Federal Rules contain no provision governing presumptions in criminal cases. Constitutional doctrine shapes the burden of proof and operation of presumptions in those cases.

Test Your Understanding

To assess your understanding of the material in this chapter, click here to take a quiz, or go to the Quizzes module from the eBook on your eProducts bookshelf.

72

The Role of the Jury

A. Introduction and Policy. Our judicial system relies on trials to settle factual disputes. A trial is a heroic enterprise: The lawyers try to reconstruct a past event and the jury determines the truth about what happened. Did the defendant shoot the victim? Did the company know about the defect at the time of the accident? Were the products defective when they were delivered? The primary purpose of a courtroom trial is to uncover the truth about past events; this is a courageous mission.

But discovering the truth is not the only goal of litigation. The legal system wants to determine the truth, but it also seeks to protect valuable rights and policy interests: We attempt to protect privileged communications, encourage settlements, protect the rights of rape victims, safeguard judicial economy—the list goes on.

Most important, we commit the truth-finding process in most cases to a jury, a group of lay individuals from all walks of life who know nothing about the law or the facts of the particular case. This mandate complicates the trial process in dozens of different ways. Judges must determine whether evidence is unduly prejudicial; give arcane limiting instructions that may do more harm than good; and screen scientific testimony to prevent experts from dazzling lay listeners.

Why do we give the impossible task of truth-finding to jurors? Because in our society, jurors give the judicial process **legitimacy.** We want trial verdicts to be correct, but we care as much about society accepting those verdicts. The jury process, despite all its flaws, confers that legitimacy: It is the truth-finding method we have chosen to support capital punishment and billion dollar awards.

The final Rule of Evidence that we will study, **Rule 606(b)**, helps maintain this legitimacy. Rule 606(b) forbids jurors from testifying about most things that were said, done, or even thought about during the jury deliberations. The rule turns the jury into a black box whose internal workings cannot be examined, much less challenged. Thanks to Rule 606(b), the jury is a mysterious—perhaps even mystical—truth machine. Judges and lawyers enter thousands of data points into this machine: days of testimony, piles of documents, opening and closing arguments, and hours of incomprehensible instructions. In return, the jury produces one priceless output: the verdict. The civil defendant is either liable or not liable; the accused is either guilty or not guilty.

In almost every case, this result disappoints at least one party. The party's first instinct will be to open the black box and make sure the truth machine was operating properly. What did the jury talk about during deliberations? Did the jurors consider the criminal defendant's prior convictions only for the purpose of assessing credibility? Did they assume that the civil defendant was insured, so awarding damages wouldn't "hurt" anybody? Even worse, perhaps one of the jurors slept through most of the deliberations. Or perhaps a group of jurors bullied or threatened a holdout juror. Surely it would make sense to interview the jurors to determine whether there were any improprieties. And if there were any missteps, the disappointed party will argue, it is critical to depose the jurors, get them to sign affidavits, and call them to testify at a post-trial hearing about flaws in the verdict.

But procedures like this would destroy the justice system. If parties and lawyers could attack verdicts by calling jurors to testify about what happened in the jury room, the losing party would launch this type of attack in **every** case. No verdict would ever be final, and no juror would ever be safe from persistent phone calls from losing attorneys. Most important, our faith in the legitimacy of jury verdicts would quickly evaporate as disappointed parties clamored to expose the incompetence of the juries deciding their cases.

To protect the **finality** and **legitimacy** of jury verdicts, Rule 606(b) greatly restricts the power of judges to admit testimony, affidavits, or other statements from jurors that reflect the jury's decision making process.

B. The Rule. We studied the first half of Rule 606 in Chapter 14, when we discussed the competence of witnesses. **Rule 606(a)** prohibits a juror from testifying as a witness in the same case in which the juror serves. **Rule 606(b)** addresses a juror's competence to testify about the jury's decision making after the verdict or indictment has been rendered. 606(b) thus has a very different purpose than 606(a):

RULE 606. Juror's Competency as a Witness

(b) During an Inquiry into the Validity of a Verdict or Indictment.

(1) *Prohibited Testimony or Other Evidence.* During an inquiry into the <u>validity of a verdict or indictment</u>, a juror <u>may not testify about</u>

- any <u>statement made or incident that occurred</u> during the jury's deliberations;
- the <u>effect of anything</u> on that juror's or another juror's vote; or
- any juror's <u>mental processes</u> concerning the verdict or indictment.

The court may not receive a <u>juror's affidavit or evidence</u> of a juror's statement on these matters.

(2) *Exceptions.* A juror may testify about whether:

(A) <u>extraneous prejudicial information</u> was improperly brought to the jury's attention;

(B) an <u>outside influence</u> was improperly brought to bear on any juror; or

(C) a mistake was made in <u>entering the verdict</u> on the verdict form.

Rule 606(b) throws a blanket of secrecy over jury deliberations by declaring jurors **incompetent** to testify about that process. The Federal Rules of Evidence do not prevent jurors from **talking** about the deliberations; after a trial verdict, most jurisdictions allow the juror to discuss the details of deliberation with friends, lawyers, and even reporters.[1] But Rule 606(b) assures that none of these comments will matter in a legal sense. None of the juror's statements—whether made casually to friends, on the record to a newspaper reporter, under oath in an affidavit, or on the witness stand—are competent evidence. Rule 606(b) uses the concept of competence to prevent both sworn statements and idle gossip from tainting jury verdicts.

The rule, moreover, protects many types of statements made by jurors. It includes a juror's report about "any statement" that occurred during the course of deliberations. It also includes identification of "the effect of anything" that influenced the juror's decision or the decision of any other juror. And, finally, it encompasses even a juror's description of her own "mental processes concerning the verdict." We will examine the scope of this protection in greater detail below; for now, note that Rule 606(b) attempts to include any type of juror comment that might taint the legitimacy or finality of a verdict.

However, there are four important limits on this protection. **First**, the rule does not come into play until **after** the jury reaches a verdict. If a juror reports inappropriate behavior by another juror while the trial or deliberations are still under way, the judge can receive those reports and decide whether to take action. If necessary, the judge will admonish the jurors, dismiss the juror who committed the impropriety, or (in an extreme case) declare a mistrial. This limit reflects Rule 606(b)'s focus on the finality and legitimacy of verdicts. If a problem comes to light before the jury issues a verdict, the judge should be allowed to try to correct the problem.

Second, Rule 606(b) allows a juror to testify about "extraneous prejudicial information" that was "improperly brought to the jury's attention." A juror may also describe any "outside influence . . . improperly brought to bear on any juror." Jurors, in other words, may testify about any attempts to bribe, coerce, or otherwise influence a jury improperly. Despite our need to ensure the finality of verdicts, we do not want to countenance blatant jury tampering. Rule 606(b) allows courts to obtain evidence that such **external interference** occurred. As we'll see in the Courtroom section, this exception forces courts to draw difficult lines between evidence of a jury's internal discussions, which Rule 606(b) bars, and testimony about external influences on the jury, which the rule allows.

---

1   This openness applies only to trial jury deliberations, not to grand jury ones. Federal law forbids grand jury members to discuss any matter that comes before them, including their deliberations. See Fed. R. Crim. P. 6(e)(2). Furthermore, although few states restrict comments by trial jurors, many prohibit lawyers from contacting those jurors to discuss the details of the case or deliberations.

Third, 606(b) allows jurors to testify about whether they made a clerical error when transferring the verdict onto the verdict form. Frequently the judge polls the jury after reading the verdict form, asking each individual juror whether he or she voted for the verdict on the form. This practice usually detects any clerical mistake. But if the judge did not poll the jury, Rule 606(b) allows a juror to tell the judge—and then testify, if necessary—that the verdict entered on the form was not the proper one.

Finally, the Supreme Court has ruled that in a criminal case in which the defendant was found guilty, the Sixth Amendment's guarantee of a fair and impartial jury will override Rule 606(b) in one specific circumstance: when a juror's statement indicates she acted out of racial stereotypes or animus. We will discuss this in more detail in Section C.4. below.

C. In the Courtroom.

1. Extraneous Information and Outside Influences. The most important question that courts face under Rule 606(b) is determining whether a juror's testimony relates to an internal matter of deliberation, which the rule bars, or to external influences, which the rule permits. The Supreme Court addressed this issue in a particularly colorful case:

> **Example:** A jury convicted William Conover and Anthony Tanner of mail fraud. A few days before sentencing, the defendants moved for a new trial due to juror misconduct. Tanner's attorney claimed that one of the jurors, Vera Asbul, called him and reported that several jurors drank large quantities of alcohol during lunch breaks in the trial; as a result, they slept through the afternoon sessions. Another juror subsequently reported that he and three other jurors smoked marijuana "quite regularly" throughout the trial, while two others ingested cocaine.
>
> The lower courts rejected these juror statements under Rule 606(b) and denied the defendants' motion for a new trial.

Analysis: The Supreme Court affirmed the lower court decisions, agreeing that Rule 606(b) barred the jurors' statements about sleeping, alcohol abuse, and use of illegal drugs. All of these allegations referred to the jury's internal behavior and decision making processes; they resembled "allegations of the physical or mental incompetence of a juror," which the courts historically had treated as "'internal' rather than 'external' matters."[2]

The Court acknowledged that "postverdict investigation into juror misconduct would in some instances lead to the invalidation of verdicts reached after irresponsible or improper juror behavior." Allowing these investigations, however, would result in a "barrage of postverdict scrutiny." Although the quality of some verdicts might improve through scrutiny, the Court wryly concluded that "[i]t is not at all clear . . . that the jury system could survive such efforts to perfect it."[3]

The *Tanner* Court brushed aside arguments that the alcohol and drugs consumed by the jurors were external influences. Instead, the Court characterized the jurors' testimony as referring to their "intoxicated nature." That intoxication was an internal matter, analogous to testimony about whether a juror was asleep or mentally incompetent.

Tanner confirms that an influence is external only if it comes from **outside** the jury room rather than originating with the jurors themselves. The decision also suggests, however, that courts will stretch to label ambiguous processes as internal rather than external.

Lower court decisions have resolved the status of some common challenges to jury decision making. Rule 606(b), for example, prohibits inquiries into allegations that one or more jurors coerced a holdout juror; this conduct is internal to the jury process. In fact, a judge may not even ask about internal jury coercion when she polls the jury to confirm a verdict.[4] Internal factors also include evidence that jurors misunderstood jury instructions[5] or improperly calculated the damage award.[6]

---

2   To support this point, the Court cited a case in which a juror wrote to the judge a few days after the verdict to explain that "she had 'eyes and ears that . . . see things before [they] happen,' but that her eyes 'are only partly open' because 'a curse was put upon them some years ago.'" Despite this and other evidence of the juror's insanity, the circuit court ruled that Rule 606(b) prohibited consideration of the juror's testimony. United States v. Dioguardi, 492 F.2d 70, 75 (2d Cir. 1974).

3   Tanner v. United States, 483 U.S. 107, 116, 118, 120–21 (1987).

4   United States v. Freedson, 608 F.2d 739 (9th Cir. 1979).

5   Karl v. Burlington Northern R.R., 880 F.2d 68, 73–74 (8th Cir. 1989).

6   Michaels v. Michaels, 767 F.2d 1185, 1205–06 (7th Cir. 1985).

Rule 606(b), on the other hand, allows inquiry into external influences on a verdict such as a juror conducting outside research or investigation;[7] jurors reading media accounts about the case;[8] one of the jurors possessing prior knowledge about a party or a witness that was not disclosed;[9] jurors reviewing documents or items that had not been admitted into evidence,[10] and any kind of contact between jurors and outsiders regarding the case.

2. Testimony by Non-Jurors. Rule 606(b) only restricts the competence of **jurors** to offer evidence about their decision making. Bailiffs, attorneys, and any other person who obtains personal knowledge related to a jury deliberation may testify about that information. These individuals may testify about both internal jury processes and external influences, as long as their information stems from personal knowledge rather than secondhand juror reports.

> **Example:** After deliberating all day, a jury was deadlocked. The judge allowed the jurors to go out to dinner and continue deliberating over their meal as long as no one else was in the room at the time. After dinner, the jury returned to the courthouse and reached a verdict within fifteen minutes.
>
> The defense attorney moved for a new trial, claiming that the jurors drank excessive alcohol during their deliberations over dinner. The trial judge held a hearing to investigate this claim. At the hearing, the judge reviewed records from the restaurant, which showed that the 12-member jury ordered ten alcoholic beverages and two soft drinks. The judge also heard testimony from the federal marshal who accompanied the jurors to the restaurant; the marshal stated that the jurors ordered just one round of drinks and that none of the jurors appeared intoxicated after dinner.
>
> **Analysis:** The trial court acted properly in conducting this post-trial hearing. The judge could not hear testimony from any juror on the challenge, because intoxication is a matter of internal jury deliberation. But the judge properly

---

7   Anderson v. Ford Motor Co., 186 F.3d 918, 920–21 (8th Cir. 1999).

8   United States v. Boylan, 898 F.2d 230, 258–59 (1st Cir. 1990).

9   United States v. Humphrey, 208 F.3d 1190, 1198–99 (10th Cir. 2000).

10   Government of Virgin Islands v. Joseph, 685 F.2d 857, 863–64 (3d Cir. 1982).

examined restaurant records and heard testimony from the marshal. Evidence from these third parties did not violate Rule 606(b).

After considering this evidence, the judge dismissed the defendant's motion; there was no evidence that any juror had more than one alcoholic beverage and no evidence that the deliberations were unfair.[11]

The Supreme Court made a similar point in Tanner, noting in dictum that a judge could consider evidence of juror intoxication if it came from sources other than the jurors.[12] The testimony of third parties, therefore, provides a check on extreme cases of jury misconduct.

3. Mental Processes of Jurors. In addition to barring jury testimony about internal statements and conduct, Rule 606(b) precludes a juror from testifying about her thoughts and feelings during deliberations. A juror, therefore, cannot testify that she felt threatened or pressured by other jurors. Nor can the juror testify about what she believes she **would have decided** if other evidence had been presented at trial:

> **Example:** Michael Burns was convicted of conspiring to distribute over 500 grams of methamphetamine. Police chemist Matthew Barb testified about the quantity of the illegal drug seized from Burns. After trial, investigators discovered that Barb was a drug addict who had stolen drugs from samples in his police laboratory. Burns then moved for a new trial, suggesting that Barb might have tampered with evidence in his case and that the improprieties tainted his verdict.
>
> To support his motion, Burns offered an affidavit from Patricia Kassab, one of the jurors who convicted Burns. Kassab wrote in her affidavit that if she had known about Barb's drug addiction and lab thefts, she would have had reasonable doubts about the quantity of methamphetamine admitted against Burns.

---

11   This example is based on United States v. Taliaferro, 558 F.2d 724 (4th Cir. 1977).

12   483 U.S. at 127.

Analysis: The appellate court held that Rule 606(b) barred Kassab's affidavit. The court observed that the rule "generally prohibits a juror from testifying about her or other jurors' mental processes during jury deliberations." The court then readily concluded that "the principle behind this prohibition extends to testimony about what those mental processes would have been had the evidence at trial been different."[13]

Even when a juror offers testimony about improper external influences, the judge will redact any description of how the outside influences affected the juror's mental processes or the jury's deliberations. Rule 606(b) admits only statements about the outside influences themselves:

Example: Timothy Lloyd was accused of computer sabotage. The government alleged that Lloyd placed a crippling virus on his employer's server and activated the program after he was fired. Lloyd claimed that another employee must have caused the damage because he had no access to the company's computer after he was fired. The jury rejected this defense and convicted Lloyd after twelve hours of deliberations.

Three days after the verdict, one of the jurors contacted the judge and reported that over the weekend during deliberations, she watched a television news report about the "Love Bug" virus, which was "sent by e-mail all over the world" and caused many computer systems to crash. In response to the judge's questions about how this information might have affected her decision, the juror explained that the news report convinced her that it was possible for Lloyd to activate a program on his employer's server even if he did not have physical access to the computer. She thought this realization might have influenced her vote on the case. The judge ruled that this extraneous information caused substantial prejudice to Lloyd and ordered a new trial.

Analysis: The appellate court overturned the trial court's decision. Rule 606(b) allowed the juror to describe the news report to the judge because this was an "extraneous" influence on a member of the jury. But the judge should not have asked the juror how the news report affected her thoughts or vote.

---

13   United States v. Burns, 495 F.3d 873, 875 (8th Cir. 2007).

> The court should "only inquire into the existence of extraneous information," not "into the subjective effect of such information on the particular jurors."[14]

If a court can only probe the **existence** of external information, rather than the **effect** of that information on a juror, how does the judge determine whether the extraneous information tainted the verdict? The court in *Lloyd* explained that the law applies an objective standard to this question. The judge need not ask how the external information subjectively affected a particular juror. Instead, the question is whether the "probable effect of the . . . information on a hypothetical average juror" would have created substantial prejudice.[15]

4. Racial Bias Against Criminal Defendants. Although Rule 606(b) strictly forbids jurors to testify about internal deliberations, the Supreme Court has held that the Sixth Amendment removes that bar when a juror offers evidence in a criminal case that "racial animus was a significant motivating factor in [a] juror's vote to convict."[16]

Example: Miguel Peña-Rodriguez was charged with sexually assaulting two teenage girls in a public restroom. A jury convicted him on two of the counts against him. After the jury was discharged, two jurors approached Peña-Rodriguez's lawyer and said that during deliberations, a juror named H.C. had made racist statements about the defendant and one of the defendant's witnesses. H.C. allegedly told other jurors: "in [his] experience . . . , Mexican men had a bravado that caused them to believe they could do whatever they wanted with women," "nine times out of ten Mexican men were guilty of being aggressive toward women and young girls," and "I think he did it because he's Mexican and Mexican men take whatever they want." H.C. also allegedly said that he did not believe the defendant's alibi witness because he was an "illegal."[17]

The attorney moved for a new trial based on this evidence, arguing that his client had been denied his Sixth Amendment right to a fair trial. The trial

---

14   United States v. Lloyd, 269 F.3d 228, 237 (3d Cir. 2001).

15   Id. at 238 (quoting United States v. Gilsenan, 949 F.2d 90, 95 (3d Cir. 1991)).

16   Peña-Rodriguez v. Colorado, 137 S.Ct. 855, 869 (2017).

17   Id. at 862. In fact, the alibi witness was a legal resident of the United States. Id.

court and both state appellate courts rejected the motion, finding that the state's version of Rule 606(b) precluded this evidence from consideration.

Analysis: The Supreme Court reversed the lower courts, holding that the trial judge had discretion to consider the jurors' statements despite Rule 606(b). In so doing, the Court created a narrow exception to Rule 606(b) based on the Sixth Amendment. The Court noted that an "offhand comment" would not trigger this constitutional exception. Instead, a convicted defendant must show "that one or more jurors made statements exhibiting overt racial bias that cast serious doubt on the fairness and impartiality of the jury's deliberations and resulting verdict." In addition, those statements "must tend to show that racial animus was a significant motivating factor in the juror's vote to convict." Trial judges, the Court stressed, retain "substantial discretion" to determine whether a defendant has made these showings. Rule 606(b), however, does not automatically bar the inquiry.[18]

 In deciding *Peña-Rodriguez*, the Court emphasized the "unique historical, constitutional, and institutional concerns about racial bias in the judicial system."[19] The Court also relied on "the experiences of the 17 jurisdictions that have recognized a racial-bias exception to the no-impeachment rule."[20] These statements suggest that the Court will limit the Sixth Amendment exception to racial bias rather than broadening it to include sexism, religious bias, or other forms of discrimination. Defense attorneys, however, undoubtedly will press to expand the exception; consider the policy arguments that you would make on both sides of that issue.

---

18   Id. at 869. Peña-Rodriguez involved a state rule modelled on Federal Rule of Evidence 606(b). The holding clearly applies to the federal rule, as well as other state rules following the same format.

19   Id. at 868.

20   Id. at 870.

Quick Summary

 **Rule 606(b)** prevents a court from considering a juror's statements about what any juror said, thought, or did during deliberations. The rule forbids statements about any **internal** matters, including juror intoxication, a juror's mental or physical incompetence, and coercion by some jurors against others. The rule does not prevent jurors from testifying about **external** influences, such as threats stemming from non-jurors, exposure to media reports about the trial, or independent research conducted by the jurors. Nor does the rule prevent testimony from non-jurors; bailiffs, lawyers, and other individuals may testify about their personal observations of the jurors.

Rule 606(b) protects the finality and legitimacy of verdicts. Without the rule, losing parties might contact jurors after every trial, seeking information about improprieties. The parties would complain about even minor missteps, magnifying their extent and effect. Finality would suffer, and the jury system as a whole would lose legitimacy.

The Supreme Court, however, has held that the Sixth Amendment right to a fair trial overrides these weighty concerns under at least one circumstance: when jurors offer evidence "that racial animus was a significant motivating factor in [a] juror's vote to convict."

Test Your Understanding

 To assess your understanding of the material in this chapter, click here to take a quiz, or go to the Quizzes module from the eBook on your eProducts bookshelf.

* * *

Jury decision making is a black box, but the Federal Rules of Evidence are not. The rules are a complex sophisticated machine with hundreds of moving, but visible, parts. The Advisory Committee, members of Congress, federal judges, and trial lawyers all contribute to the evolution of those rules. We hope this book has persuaded you that Evidence is a vibrant, growing area of the law—and that you will contribute to its growth as a practicing lawyer.

The Federal Rules of Evidence

In effect December 1, 2017
(Effective July 1, 1975, as amended to December 1, 2017)

ARTICLE I. GENERAL PROVISIONS

ARTICLE II. JUDICIAL NOTICE

ARTICLE III. PRESUMPTIONS IN CIVIL CASES

ARTICLE IV. RELEVANCE AND ITS LIMITS

ARTICLE VII. OPINIONS AND EXPERT TESTIMONY

ARTICLE VIII. HEARSAY

ARTICLE IX. AUTHENTICATION AND IDENTIFICATION

ARTICLE X. CONTENTS OF WRITINGS, RECORDINGS, AND PHOTOGRAPHS

ARTICLE XI. MISCELLANEOUS RULES

The Federal Rules of Evidence

In effect December 1, 2017
(Effective July 1, 1975, as amended to December 1, 2017)

ARTICLE I. GENERAL PROVISIONS

Rule 101.   Scope; Definitions

(a) Scope. These rules apply to proceedings in United States courts. The specific courts and proceedings to which the rules apply, along with exceptions, are set out in Rule 1101.

(b) Definitions. In these rules:

(1) "civil case" means a civil action or proceeding;

(2) "criminal case" includes a criminal proceeding;

(3) "public office" includes a public agency;

(4) "record" includes a memorandum, report, or data compilation;

(5) a "rule prescribed by the Supreme Court" means a rule adopted by the Supreme Court under statutory authority; and

(6) a reference to any kind of written material or any other medium includes electronically stored information.

Rule 102.   Purpose

These rules should be construed so as to administer every proceeding fairly, eliminate unjustifiable expense and delay, and promote the development of evidence law, to the end of ascertaining the truth and securing a just determination.

Rule 103. Rulings on Evidence

(a) Preserving a Claim of Error. A party may claim error in a ruling to admit or exclude evidence only if the error affects a substantial right of the party and:

    (1) if the ruling admits evidence, a party, on the record:

        (A) timely objects or moves to strike; and

        (B) states the specific ground, unless it was apparent from the context; or

    (2) if the ruling excludes evidence, a party informs the court of its substance by an offer of proof, unless the substance was apparent from the context.

(b) Not Needing to Renew an Objection or Offer of Proof. Once the court rules definitively on the record—either before or at trial—a party need not renew an objection or offer of proof to preserve a claim of error for appeal.

(c) Court's Statement About the Ruling; Directing an Offer of Proof. The court may make any statement about the character or form of the evidence, the objection made, and the ruling. The court may direct that an offer of proof be made in question-and-answer form.

(d) Preventing the Jury from Hearing Inadmissible Evidence. To the extent practicable, the court must conduct a jury trial so that inadmissible evidence is not suggested to the jury by any means.

(e) Taking Notice of Plain Error. A court may take notice of a plain error affecting a substantial right, even if the claim of error was not properly preserved.

Rule 104. Preliminary Questions

(a) In General. The court must decide any preliminary question about whether a witness is qualified, a privilege exists, or evidence is admissible. In so deciding, the court is not bound by evidence rules, except those on privilege.

(b) Relevance That Depends on a Fact. When the relevance of evidence depends on whether a fact exists, proof must be introduced sufficient to support a finding that the fact does exist. The court may admit the proposed evidence on the condition that the proof be introduced later.

(c) Conducting a Hearing So That the Jury Cannot Hear It. The court must conduct any hearing on a preliminary question so that the jury cannot hear it if:

(1) the hearing involves the admissibility of a confession;

(2) a defendant in a criminal case is a witness and so requests; or

(3) justice so requires.

(d) Cross-Examining a Defendant in a Criminal Case. By testifying on a preliminary question, a defendant in a criminal case does not become subject to cross-examination on other issues in the case.

(e) Evidence Relevant to Weight and Credibility. This rule does not limit a party's right to introduce before the jury evidence that is relevant to the weight or credibility of other evidence.

Rule 105. Limiting Evidence That Is Not Admissible Against Other Parties or for Other Purposes

If the court admits evidence that is admissible against a party or for a purpose—but not against another party or for another purpose—the court, on timely request, must restrict the evidence to its proper scope and instruct the jury accordingly.

Rule 106. Remainder of or Related Writings or Recorded Statements

If a party introduces all or part of a writing or recorded statement, an adverse party may require the introduction, at that time, of any other part—or any other writing or recorded statement—that in fairness ought to be considered at the same time.

ARTICLE II. JUDICIAL NOTICE

Rule 201.   Judicial Notice of Adjudicative Facts

(a) Scope. This rule governs judicial notice of an adjudicative fact only, not a legislative fact.

(b) Kinds of Facts That May Be Judicially Noticed. The court may judicially notice a fact that is not subject to reasonable dispute because it:

    (1)   is generally known within the trial court's territorial jurisdiction; or

    (2)   can be accurately and readily determined from sources whose accuracy cannot reasonably be questioned.

(c) Taking Notice. The court:

    (1)   may take judicial notice on its own; or

    (2)   must take judicial notice if a party requests it and the court is supplied with the necessary information.

(d) Timing. The court may take judicial notice at any stage of the proceeding.

(e) Opportunity to Be Heard. On timely request, a party is entitled to be heard on the propriety of taking judicial notice and the nature of the fact to be noticed. If the court takes judicial notice before notifying a party, the party, on request, is still entitled to be heard.

(f) Instructing the Jury. In a civil case, the court must instruct the jury to accept the noticed fact as conclusive. In a criminal case, the court must instruct the jury that it may or may not accept the noticed fact as conclusive.

ARTICLE III. PRESUMPTIONS IN CIVIL CASES

Rule 301. Presumptions in Civil Cases Generally

In a civil case, unless a federal statute or these rules provide otherwise, the party against whom a presumption is directed has the burden of producing evidence to rebut the presumption. But this rule does not shift the burden of persuasion, which remains on the party who had it originally.

Rule 302. Applying State Law to Presumptions in Civil Cases

In a civil case, state law governs the effect of a presumption regarding a claim or defense for which state law supplies the rule of decision.

ARTICLE IV. RELEVANCE AND ITS LIMITS

Rule 401. Test for Relevant Evidence

Evidence is relevant if:

(a) it has any tendency to make a fact more or less probable than it would be without the evidence; and

(b) the fact is of consequence in determining the action.

Rule 402. General Admissibility of Relevant Evidence

Relevant evidence is admissible unless any of the following provides otherwise:

- the United States Constitution;
- a federal statute;
- these rules; or
- other rules prescribed by the Supreme Court.

Irrelevant evidence is not admissible.

Rule 403. Excluding Relevant Evidence for Prejudice, Confusion, Waste of Time, or Other Reasons

The court may exclude relevant evidence if its probative value is substantially outweighed by a danger of one or more of the following: unfair prejudice, confusing the issues, misleading the jury, undue delay, wasting time, or needlessly presenting cumulative evidence.

Rule 404. Character Evidence; Crimes or Other Acts

(a) Character Evidence.

    (1) Prohibited Uses. Evidence of a person's character or character trait is not admissible to prove that on a particular occasion the person acted in accordance with the character or trait.

    (2) Exceptions for a Defendant or Victim in a Criminal Case. The following exceptions apply in a criminal case:

        (A) a defendant may offer evidence of the defendant's pertinent trait, and if the evidence is admitted, the prosecutor may offer evidence to rebut it;

        (B) subject to the limitations in Rule 412, a defendant may offer evidence of an alleged victim's pertinent trait, and if the evidence is admitted, the prosecutor may:

            (i) offer evidence to rebut it; and

            (ii) offer evidence of the defendant's same trait; and

        (C) in a homicide case, the prosecutor may offer evidence of the alleged victim's trait of peacefulness to rebut evidence that the victim was the first aggressor.

    (3) *Exceptions for a Witness.* Evidence of a witness's character may be admitted under Rules 607, 608, and 609.

(b) Crimes, Wrongs, or Other Acts.

    (1) Prohibited Uses. Evidence of a crime, wrong, or other act is not admissible to prove a person's character in order to show that on a particular occasion the person acted in accordance with the character.

(2) Permitted Uses; Notice in a Criminal Case. This evidence may be admissible for another purpose, such as proving motive, opportunity, intent, preparation, plan, knowledge, identity, absence of mistake, or lack of accident. On request by a defendant in a criminal case, the prosecutor must:

(A) provide reasonable notice of the general nature of any such evidence that the prosecutor intends to offer at trial; and

(B) do so before trial—or during trial if the court, for good cause, excuses lack of pretrial notice.

Rule 405. Methods of Proving Character

(a) **By Reputation or Opinion.** When evidence of a person's character or character trait is admissible, it may be proved by testimony about the person's reputation or by testimony in the form of an opinion. On cross-examination of the character witness, the court may allow an inquiry into relevant specific instances of the person's conduct.

(b) **By Specific Instances of Conduct.** When a person's character or character trait is an essential element of a charge, claim, or defense, the character or trait may also be proved by relevant specific instances of the person's conduct.

Rule 406. Habit; Routine Practice

Evidence of a person's habit or an organization's routine practice may be admitted to prove that on a particular occasion the person or organization acted in accordance with the habit or routine practice. The court may admit this evidence regardless of whether it is corroborated or whether there was an eyewitness.

Rule 407. Subsequent Remedial Measures

When measures are taken that would have made an earlier injury or harm less likely to occur, evidence of the subsequent measures is not admissible to prove:

- negligence;

- culpable conduct;

- a defect in a product or its design; or

- a need for a warning or instruction.

But the court may admit this evidence for another purpose, such as impeachment or—if disputed—proving ownership, control, or the feasibility of precautionary measures.

Rule 408.   Compromise Offers and Negotiations

(a) **Prohibited Uses.** Evidence of the following is not admissible—on behalf of any party—either to prove or disprove the validity or amount of a disputed claim or to impeach by a prior inconsistent statement or a contradiction:

   (1)   furnishing, promising, or offering—or accepting, promising to accept, or offering to accept—a valuable consideration in compromising or attempting to compromise the claim; and

   (2)   conduct or a statement made during compromise negotiations about the claim—except when offered in a criminal case and when the negotiations related to a claim by a public office in the exercise of its regulatory, investigative, or enforcement authority.

(b) **Exceptions.** The court may admit this evidence for another purpose, such as proving a witness's bias or prejudice, negating a contention of undue delay, or proving an effort to obstruct a criminal investigation or prosecution.

Rule 409.   Offers to Pay Medical and Similar Expenses

Evidence of furnishing, promising to pay, or offering to pay medical, hospital, or similar expenses resulting from an injury is not admissible to prove liability for the injury.

Rule 410.   Pleas, Plea Discussions, and Related Statements

(a) **Prohibited Uses.** In a civil or criminal case, evidence of the following is not admissible against the defendant who made the plea or participated in the plea discussions:

   (1)   a guilty plea that was later withdrawn;

   (2)   a nolo contendere plea;

   (3)   a statement made during a proceeding on either of those pleas under Federal Rule of Criminal Procedure 11 or a comparable state procedure; or

(4) a statement made during plea discussions with an attorney for the prosecuting authority if the discussions did not result in a guilty plea or they resulted in a later-withdrawn guilty plea.

(b) Exceptions. The court may admit a statement described in Rule 410(a)(3) or (4):

(1) in any proceeding in which another statement made during the same plea or plea discussions has been introduced, if in fairness the statements ought to be considered together; or

(2) in a criminal proceeding for perjury or false statement, if the defendant made the statement under oath, on the record, and with counsel present.

Rule 411.   Liability Insurance

Evidence that a person was or was not insured against liability is not admissible to prove whether the person acted negligently or otherwise wrongfully. But the court may admit this evidence for another purpose, such as proving a witness's bias or prejudice or proving agency, ownership, or control.

Rule 412.   Sex-Offense Cases: The Victim's Sexual Behavior or Predisposition

(a) Prohibited Uses. The following evidence is not admissible in a civil or criminal proceeding involving alleged sexual misconduct:

(1) evidence offered to prove that a victim engaged in other sexual behavior; or

(2) evidence offered to prove a victim's sexual predisposition.

(b) Exceptions.

(1) *Criminal Cases.* The court may admit the following evidence in a criminal case:

(A) evidence of specific instances of a victim's sexual behavior, if offered to prove that someone other than the defendant was the source of semen, injury, or other physical evidence;

(B) evidence of specific instances of a victim's sexual behavior with respect to the person accused of the sexual misconduct, if offered by the defendant to prove consent or if offered by the prosecutor; and

(C) evidence whose exclusion would violate the defendant's constitutional rights.

(2) *Civil Cases.* In a civil case, the court may admit evidence offered to prove a victim's sexual behavior or sexual predisposition if its probative value substantially outweighs the danger of harm to any victim and of unfair prejudice to any party. The court may admit evidence of a victim's reputation only if the victim has placed it in controversy.

(c) Procedure to Determine Admissibility.

(1) *Motion.* If a party intends to offer evidence under Rule 412(b), the party must:

(A) file a motion that specifically describes the evidence and states the purpose for which it is to be offered;

(B) do so at least 14 days before trial unless the court, for good cause, sets a different time;

(C) serve the motion on all parties; and

(D) notify the victim or, when appropriate, the victim's guardian or representative.

(2) *Hearing.* Before admitting evidence under this rule, the court must conduct an in camera hearing and give the victim and parties a right to attend and be heard. Unless the court orders otherwise, the motion, related materials, and the record of the hearing must be and remain sealed.

(d) Definition of "Victim." In this rule, "victim" includes an alleged victim.

Rule 413. Similar Crimes in Sexual-Assault Cases

(a) Permitted Uses. In a criminal case in which a defendant is accused of a sexual assault, the court may admit evidence that the defendant committed any other sexual assault. The evidence may be considered on any matter to which it is relevant.

(b) Disclosure to the Defendant. If the prosecutor intends to offer this evidence, the prosecutor must disclose it to the defendant, including witnesses' statements or a summary of the expected testimony. The prosecutor must do so at least 15 days before trial or at a later time that the court allows for good cause.

(c) Effect on Other Rules. This rule does not limit the admission or consideration of evidence under any other rule.

(d) Definition of "Sexual Assault." In this rule and Rule 415, "sexual assault" means a crime under federal law or under state law (as "state" is defined in 18 U.S.C. § 513) involving:

(1) any conduct prohibited by 18 U.S.C. chapter 109A;

(2) contact, without consent, between any part of the defendant's body—or an object—and another person's genitals or anus;

(3) contact, without consent, between the defendant's genitals or anus and any part of another person's body;

(4) deriving sexual pleasure or gratification from inflicting death, bodily injury, or physical pain on another person; or

(5) an attempt or conspiracy to engage in conduct described in subparagraphs (1)–(4).

Rule 414.   Similar Crimes in Child-Molestation Cases

(a) Permitted Uses. In a criminal case in which a defendant is accused of child molestation, the court may admit evidence that the defendant committed any other child molestation. The evidence may be considered on any matter to which it is relevant.

(b) Disclosure to the Defendant. If the prosecutor intends to offer this evidence, the prosecutor must disclose it to the defendant, including witnesses' statements or a summary of the expected testimony. The prosecutor must do so at least 15 days before trial or at a later time that the court allows for good cause.

(c) Effect on Other Rules. This rule does not limit the admission or consideration of evidence under any other rule.

(d) Definition of "Child" and "Child Molestation." In this rule and Rule 415:

   (1) "child" means a person below the age of 14; and

   (2) "child molestation" means a crime under federal law or under state law (as "state" is defined in 18 U.S.C. § 513) involving:

      (A) any conduct prohibited by 18 U.S.C. chapter 109A and committed with a child;

      (B) any conduct prohibited by 18 U.S.C. chapter 110;

      (C) contact between any part of the defendant's body—or an object—and a child's genitals or anus;

      (D) contact between the defendant's genitals or anus and any part of a child's body;

      (E) deriving sexual pleasure or gratification from inflicting death, bodily injury, or physical pain on a child; or

      (F) an attempt or conspiracy to engage in conduct described in subparagraphs (A)–(E).

Rule 415. Similar Acts in Civil Cases Involving Sexual Assault or Child Molestation

(a) Permitted Uses. In a civil case involving a claim for relief based on a party's alleged sexual assault or child molestation, the court may admit evidence that the party committed any other sexual assault or child molestation. The evidence may be considered as provided in Rules 413 and 414.

(b) Disclosure to the Opponent. If a party intends to offer this evidence, the party must disclose it to the party against whom it will be offered, including witnesses' statements or a summary of the expected testimony. The party must do so at least 15 days before trial or at a later time that the court allows for good cause.

(c) Effect on Other Rules. This rule does not limit the admission or consideration of evidence under any other rule.

ARTICLE V. PRIVILEGES

Rule 501. Privilege in General

The common law—as interpreted by United States courts in the light of reason and experience—governs a claim of privilege unless any of the following provides otherwise:

- the United States Constitution;
- a federal statute; or
- rules prescribed by the Supreme Court.

But in a civil case, state law governs privilege regarding a claim or defense for which state law supplies the rule of decision.

Rule 502. Attorney-Client Privilege and Work Product; Limitations on Waiver

The following provisions apply, in the circumstances set out, to disclosure of a communication or information covered by the attorney-client privilege or work-product protection.

(a) **Disclosure Made in a Federal Proceeding or to a Federal Office or Agency; Scope of a Waiver.** When the disclosure is made in a federal proceeding or to a federal office or agency and waives the attorney-client privilege or work-product protection, the waiver extends to an undisclosed communication or information in a federal or state proceeding only if:

  (1) the waiver is intentional;

  (2) the disclosed and undisclosed communications or information concern the same subject matter; and

  (3) they ought in fairness to be considered together.

(b) **Inadvertent Disclosure.** When made in a federal proceeding or to a federal office or agency, the disclosure does not operate as a waiver in a federal or state proceeding if:

  (1) the disclosure is inadvertent;

  (2) the holder of the privilege or protection took reasonable steps to prevent disclosure; and

  (3) the holder promptly took reasonable steps to rectify the error, including (if applicable) following Federal Rule of Civil Procedure 26(b)(5)(B).

(c) **Disclosure Made in a State Proceeding.** When the disclosure is made in a state proceeding and is not the subject of a state-court order concerning waiver, the disclosure does not operate as a waiver in a federal proceeding if the disclosure:

  (1) would not be a waiver under this rule if it had been made in a federal proceeding; or

  (2) is not a waiver under the law of the state where the disclosure occurred.

(d) Controlling Effect of a Court Order. A federal court may order that the privilege or protection is not waived by disclosure connected with the litigation pending before the court—in which event the disclosure is also not a waiver in any other federal or state proceeding.

(e) Controlling Effect of a Party Agreement. An agreement on the effect of disclosure in a federal proceeding is binding only on the parties to the agreement, unless it is incorporated into a court order.

(f) Controlling Effect of this Rule. Notwithstanding Rules 101 and 1101, this rule applies to state proceedings and to federal court-annexed and federal court-mandated arbitration proceedings, in the circumstances set out in the rule. And notwithstanding Rule 501, this rule applies even if state law provides the rule of decision.

(g) Definitions. In this rule:

    (1) "attorney-client privilege" means the protection that applicable law provides for confidential attorney-client communications; and

    (2) "work-product protection" means the protection that applicable law provides for tangible material (or its intangible equivalent) prepared in anticipation of litigation or for trial.

ARTICLE VI. WITNESSES

Rule 601. Competency to Testify in General

Every person is competent to be a witness unless these rules provide otherwise. But in a civil case, state law governs the witness's competency regarding a claim or defense for which state law supplies the rule of decision.

Rule 602. Need for Personal Knowledge

A witness may testify to a matter only if evidence is introduced sufficient to support a finding that the witness has personal knowledge of the matter. Evidence to prove personal knowledge may consist of the witness's own testimony. This rule does not apply to a witness's expert testimony under Rule 703.

Rule 603.   Oath or Affirmation to Testify Truthfully

Before testifying, a witness must give an oath or affirmation to testify truthfully. It must be in a form designed to impress that duty on the witness's conscience.

Rule 604.   Interpreter

An interpreter must be qualified and must give an oath or affirmation to make a true translation.

Rule 605.   Judge's Competency as a Witness

The presiding judge may not testify as a witness at the trial. A party need not object to preserve the issue.

Rule 606.   Juror's Competency as a Witness

(a) **At the Trial.** A juror may not testify as a witness before the other jurors at the trial. If a juror is called to testify, the court must give a party an opportunity to object outside the jury's presence.

(b) **During an Inquiry into the Validity of a Verdict or Indictment.**

 (1) *Prohibited Testimony or Other Evidence.* During an inquiry into the validity of a verdict or indictment, a juror may not testify about any statement made or incident that occurred during the jury's deliberations; the effect of anything on that juror's or another juror's vote; or any juror's mental processes concerning the verdict or indictment. The court may not receive a juror's affidavit or evidence of a juror's statement on these matters.

 (2) *Exceptions.* A juror may testify about whether:

 (A) extraneous prejudicial information was improperly brought to the jury's attention;

 (B) an outside influence was improperly brought to bear on any juror; or

 (C) a mistake was made in entering the verdict on the verdict form.

Rule 607. Who May Impeach a Witness

Any party, including the party that called the witness, may attack the witness's credibility.

Rule 608. A Witness's Character for Truthfulness or Untruthfulness

(a) **Reputation or Opinion Evidence.** A witness's credibility may be attacked or supported by testimony about the witness's reputation for having a character for truthfulness or untruthfulness, or by testimony in the form of an opinion about that character. But evidence of truthful character is admissible only after the witness's character for truthfulness has been attacked.

(b) **Specific Instances of Conduct.** Except for a criminal conviction under Rule 609, extrinsic evidence is not admissible to prove specific instances of a witness's conduct in order to attack or support the witness's character for truthfulness. But the court may, on cross-examination, allow them to be inquired into if they are probative of the character for truthfulness or untruthfulness of:

   (1) the witness; or

   (2) another witness whose character the witness being cross-examined has testified about.

By testifying on another matter, a witness does not waive any privilege against self-incrimination for testimony that relates only to the witness's character for truthfulness.

Rule 609. Impeachment by Evidence of a Criminal Conviction

(a) **In General.** The following rules apply to attacking a witness's character for truthfulness by evidence of a criminal conviction:

   (1) for a crime that, in the convicting jurisdiction, was punishable by death or by imprisonment for more than one year, the evidence:

   (A) must be admitted, subject to Rule 403, in a civil case or in a criminal case in which the witness is not a defendant; and

    (B) must be admitted in a criminal case in which the witness is a defendant, if the probative value of the evidence outweighs its prejudicial effect to that defendant; and

  (2) for any crime regardless of the punishment, the evidence must be admitted if the court can readily determine that establishing the elements of the crime required proving—or the witness's admitting—a dishonest act or false statement.

(b) Limit on Using the Evidence After 10 Years. This subdivision (b) applies if more than 10 years have passed since the witness's conviction or release from confinement for it, whichever is later. Evidence of the conviction is admissible only if:

    its probative value, supported by specific facts and circumstances, substantially outweighs its prejudicial effect; and

  (2) the proponent gives an adverse party reasonable written notice of the intent to use it so that the party has a fair opportunity to contest its use.

(c) Effect of a Pardon, Annulment, or Certificate of Rehabilitation. Evidence of a conviction is not admissible if:

  (1) the conviction has been the subject of a pardon, annulment, certificate of rehabilitation, or other equivalent procedure based on a finding that the person has been rehabilitated, and the person has not been convicted of a later crime punishable by death or by imprisonment for more than one year; or

  (2) the conviction has been the subject of a pardon, annulment, or other equivalent procedure based on a finding of innocence.

(d) Juvenile Adjudications. Evidence of a juvenile adjudication is admissible under this rule only if:

  (1) it is offered in a criminal case;

  (2) the adjudication was of a witness other than the defendant;

  (3) an adult's conviction for that offense would be admissible to attack the adult's credibility; and

(4) admitting the evidence is necessary to fairly determine guilt or innocence.

(e) Pendency of an Appeal. A conviction that satisfies this rule is admissible even if an appeal is pending. Evidence of the pendency is also admissible.

Rule 610. Religious Beliefs or Opinions

Evidence of a witness's religious beliefs or opinions is not admissible to attack or support the witness's credibility.

Rule 611. Mode and Order of Examining Witnesses and Presenting Evidence

(a) Control by the Court; Purposes. The court should exercise reasonable control over the mode and order of examining witnesses and presenting evidence so as to:

(1) make those procedures effective for determining the truth;

(2) avoid wasting time; and

(3) protect witnesses from harassment or undue embarrassment.

(b) Scope of Cross-Examination. Cross-examination should not go beyond the subject matter of the direct examination and matters affecting the witness's credibility. The court may allow inquiry into additional matters as if on direct examination.

(c) Leading Questions. Leading questions should not be used on direct examination except as necessary to develop the witness's testimony. Ordinarily, the court should allow leading questions:

(1) on cross-examination; and

(2) when a party calls a hostile witness, an adverse party, or a witness identified with an adverse party.

Rule 612. Writing Used to Refresh a Witness's Memory

(a) Scope. This rule gives an adverse party certain options when a witness uses a writing to refresh memory:

(1) while testifying; or

(2) before testifying, if the court decides that justice requires the party to have those options.

(b) Adverse Party's Options; Deleting Unrelated Matter. Unless 18 U.S.C. § 3500 provides otherwise in a criminal case, an adverse party is entitled to have the writing produced at the hearing, to inspect it, to cross-examine the witness about it, and to introduce in evidence any portion that relates to the witness's testimony. If the producing party claims that the writing includes unrelated matter, the court must examine the writing in camera, delete any unrelated portion, and order that the rest be delivered to the adverse party. Any portion deleted over objection must be preserved for the record.

(c) Failure to Produce or Deliver the Writing. If a writing is not produced or is not delivered as ordered, the court may issue any appropriate order. But if the prosecution does not comply in a criminal case, the court must strike the witness's testimony or—if justice so requires—declare a mistrial.

Rule 613. Witness's Prior Statement

(a) Showing or Disclosing the Statement During Examination. When examining a witness about the witness's prior statement, a party need not show it or disclose its contents to the witness. But the party must, on request, show it or disclose its contents to an adverse party's attorney.

(b) Extrinsic Evidence of a Prior Inconsistent Statement. Extrinsic evidence of a witness's prior inconsistent statement is admissible only if the witness is given an opportunity to explain or deny the statement and an adverse party is given an opportunity to examine the witness about it, or if justice so requires. This subdivision (b) does not apply to an opposing party's statement under Rule 801(d)(2).

Rule 614.   Court's Calling or Examining a Witness

(a) Calling. The court may call a witness on its own or at a party's request. Each party is entitled to cross-examine the witness.

(b) Examining. The court may examine a witness regardless of who calls the witness.

(c) Objections. A party may object to the court's calling or examining a witness either at that time or at the next opportunity when the jury is not present.

Rule 615.   Excluding Witnesses

At a party's request, the court must order witnesses excluded so that they cannot hear other witnesses' testimony. Or the court may do so on its own. But this rule does not authorize excluding:

(a) a party who is a natural person;

(b) an officer or employee of a party that is not a natural person, after being designated as the party's representative by its attorney;

(c) a person whose presence a party shows to be essential to presenting the party's claim or defense; or

(d) a person authorized by statute to be present.

ARTICLE VII. OPINIONS AND EXPERT TESTIMONY

Rule 701.   Opinion Testimony by Lay Witnesses

If a witness is not testifying as an expert, testimony in the form of an opinion is limited to one that is:

(a) rationally based on the witness's perception;

(b) helpful to clearly understanding the witness's testimony or to determining a fact in issue; and

(c) not based on scientific, technical, or other specialized knowledge within the scope of Rule 702.

Rule 702. Testimony by Expert Witnesses

A witness who is qualified as an expert by knowledge, skill, experience, training, or education may testify in the form of an opinion or otherwise if:

(a) the expert's scientific, technical, or other specialized knowledge will help the trier of fact to understand the evidence or to determine a fact in issue;

(b) the testimony is based on sufficient facts or data;

(c) the testimony is the product of reliable principles and methods; and

(d) the expert has reliably applied the principles and methods to the facts of the case.

Rule 703. Bases of an Expert's Opinion Testimony

An expert may base an opinion on facts or data in the case that the expert has been made aware of or personally observed. If experts in the particular field would reasonably rely on those kinds of facts or data in forming an opinion on the subject, they need not be admissible for the opinion to be admitted. But if the facts or data would otherwise be inadmissible, the proponent of the opinion may disclose them to the jury only if their probative value in helping the jury evaluate the opinion substantially outweighs their prejudicial effect.

Rule 704. Opinion on an Ultimate Issue

(a) **In General—Not Automatically Objectionable.** An opinion is not objectionable just because it embraces an ultimate issue.

(b) **Exception.** In a criminal case, an expert witness must not state an opinion about whether the defendant did or did not have a mental state or condition that constitutes an element of the crime charged or of a defense. Those matters are for the trier of fact alone.

Rule 705. Disclosing the Facts or Data Underlying an Expert's Opinion

Unless the court orders otherwise, an expert may state an opinion—and give the reasons for it—without first testifying to the underlying facts or data. But the expert may be required to disclose those facts or data on cross-examination.

Rule 706. Court-Appointed Expert Witnesses

(a) **Appointment Process.** On a party's motion or on its own, the court may order the parties to show cause why expert witnesses should not be appointed and may ask the parties to submit nominations. The court may appoint any expert that the parties agree on and any of its own choosing. But the court may only appoint someone who consents to act.

(b) **Expert's Role.** The court must inform the expert of the expert's duties. The court may do so in writing and have a copy filed with the clerk or may do so orally at a conference in which the parties have an opportunity to participate. The expert:

    (1) must advise the parties of any findings the expert makes;

    (2) may be deposed by any party;

    (3) may be called to testify by the court or any party; and

    (4) may be cross-examined by any party, including the party that called the expert.

(c) **Compensation.** The expert is entitled to a reasonable compensation, as set by the court. The compensation is payable as follows:

    (1) in a criminal case or in a civil case involving just compensation under the Fifth Amendment, from any funds that are provided by law; and

    (2) in any other civil case, by the parties in the proportion and at the time that the court directs—and the compensation is then charged like other costs.

(d) Disclosing the Appointment to the Jury. The court may authorize disclosure to the jury that the court appointed the expert.

(e) Parties' Choice of Their Own Experts. This rule does not limit a party in calling its own experts.

ARTICLE VIII. HEARSAY

Rule 801. Definitions That Apply to This Article; Exclusions from Hearsay

(a) Statement. "Statement" means a person's oral assertion, written assertion, or nonverbal conduct, if the person intended it as an assertion.

(b) Declarant. "Declarant" means the person who made the statement.

(c) Hearsay. "Hearsay" means a statement that:

  (1) the declarant does not make while testifying at the current trial or hearing; and

  (2) a party offers in evidence to prove the truth of the matter asserted in the statement.

(d) Statements That Are Not Hearsay. A statement that meets the following conditions is not hearsay:

  (1) *A Declarant-Witness's Prior Statement.* The declarant testifies and is subject to cross-examination about a prior statement, and the statement:

   (A) is inconsistent with the declarant's testimony and was given under penalty of perjury at a trial, hearing, or other proceeding or in a deposition;

   (B) is consistent with the declarant's testimony and is offered:

    (i) to rebut an express or implied charge that the declarant recently fabricated it or acted from a recent improper influence or motive in so testifying; or

> **(ii)** to rehabilitate the declarant's credibility as a witness when attacked on another ground; or
>
> **(C)** identifies a person as someone the declarant perceived earlier.

(2) *An Opposing Party's Statement.* The statement is offered against an opposing party and:

> **(A)** was made by the party in an individual or representative capacity;
>
> **(B)** is one the party manifested that it adopted or believed to be true;
>
> **(C)** was made by a person whom the party authorized to make a statement on the subject;
>
> **(D)** was made by the party's agent or employee on a matter within the scope of that relationship and while it existed; or
>
> **(E)** was made by the party's coconspirator during and in furtherance of the conspiracy.

The statement must be considered but does not by itself establish the declarant's authority under (C); the existence or scope of the relationship under (D); or the existence of the conspiracy or participation in it under (E).

Rule 802. The Rule Against Hearsay

Hearsay is not admissible unless any of the following provides otherwise:

- a federal statute;

- these rules; or

- other rules prescribed by the Supreme Court.

Rule 803. Exceptions to the Rule Against Hearsay—Regardless of Whether the Declarant Is Available as a Witness

The following are not excluded by the rule against hearsay, regardless of whether the declarant is available as a witness:

(1) ***Present Sense Impression.*** A statement describing or explaining an event or condition, made while or immediately after the declarant perceived it.

(2) ***Excited Utterance.*** A statement relating to a startling event or condition, made while the declarant was under the stress of excitement that it caused.

(3) ***Then-Existing Mental, Emotional, or Physical Condition.*** A statement of the declarant's then-existing state of mind (such as motive, intent, or plan) or emotional, sensory, or physical condition (such as mental feeling, pain, or bodily health), but not including a statement of memory or belief to prove the fact remembered or believed unless it relates to the validity or terms of the declarant's will.

(4) ***Statement Made for Medical Diagnosis or Treatment.*** A statement that:

    (A) is made for—and is reasonably pertinent to—medical diagnosis or treatment; and

    (B) describes medical history; past or present symptoms or sensations; their inception; or their general cause.

(5) ***Recorded Recollection.*** A record that:

    (A) is on a matter the witness once knew about but now cannot recall well enough to testify fully and accurately;

    (B) was made or adopted by the witness when the matter was fresh in the witness's memory; and

    (C) accurately reflects the witness's knowledge.

If admitted, the record may be read into evidence but may be received as an exhibit only if offered by an adverse party.

(6) ***Records of a Regularly Conducted Activity.*** A record of an act, event, condition, opinion, or diagnosis if:

    (A) the record was made at or near the time by—or from information transmitted by—someone with knowledge;

    (B) the record was kept in the course of a regularly conducted activity of a business, organization, occupation, or calling, whether or not for profit;

    (C) making the record was a regular practice of that activity;

    (D) all these conditions are shown by the testimony of the custodian or another qualified witness, or by a certification that complies with Rule 902(11) or (12) or with a statute permitting certification; and

    (E) the opponent does not show that the source of information or the method or circumstances of preparation indicate a lack of trustworthiness.

(7) ***Absence of a Record of a Regularly Conducted Activity.*** Evidence that a matter is not included in a record described in paragraph (6) if:

    (A) the evidence is admitted to prove that the matter did not occur or exist;

    (B) a record was regularly kept for a matter of that kind; and

    (C) the opponent does not show that the possible source of the information or other circumstances indicate a lack of trustworthiness.

(8) ***Public Records.*** A record or statement of a public office if:

    (A) it sets out:

        (i) the office's activities;

        (ii) a matter observed while under a legal duty to report, but not including, in a criminal case, a matter observed by law-enforcement personnel; or

> **(iii)** in a civil case or against the government in a criminal case, _factual findings from a legally authorized investigation_; and
>
> **(B)** the opponent does not show that the source of information or other circumstances indicate a lack of trustworthiness.

(9) ***Public Records of Vital Statistics.*** A record of a birth, death, or marriage, if reported to a public office in accordance with a legal duty.

(10) ***Absence of a Public Record.*** Testimony—or a certification under Rule 902—that a diligent search failed to disclose a public record or statement if:

> **(A)** the testimony or certification is admitted to prove that
>
>> **(i)** the record or statement does not exist; or
>>
>> **(ii)** a matter did not occur or exist, if a public office regularly kept a record or statement for a matter of that kind; and
>
> **(B)** in a criminal case, a prosecutor who intends to offer a certification provides written notice of that intent at least 14 days before trial, and the defendant does not object in writing within 7 days of receiving the notice—unless the court sets a different time for the notice or the objection.

(11) ***Records of Religious Organizations Concerning Personal or Family History.*** A statement of birth, legitimacy, ancestry, marriage, divorce, death, relationship by blood or marriage, or similar facts of personal or family history, contained in a regularly kept record of a religious organization.

(12) ***Certificates of Marriage, Baptism, and Similar Ceremonies.*** A statement of fact contained in a certificate:

> **(A)** made by a person who is authorized by a religious organization or by law to perform the act certified;
>
> **(B)** attesting that the person performed a marriage or similar ceremony or administered a sacrament; and

    (C) purporting to have been issued at the time of the act or within a reasonable time after it.

(13) *Family Records.* A statement of fact about personal or family history contained in a family record, such as a Bible, genealogy, chart, engraving on a ring, inscription on a portrait, or engraving on an urn or burial marker.

(14) *Records of Documents That Affect an Interest in Property.* The record of a document that purports to establish or affect an interest in property if:

    (A) the record is admitted to prove the content of the original recorded document, along with its signing and its delivery by each person who purports to have signed it;

    (B) the record is kept in a public office; and

    (C) a statute authorizes recording documents of that kind in that office.

(15) *Statements in Documents That Affect an Interest in Property.* A statement contained in a document that purports to establish or affect an interest in property if the matter stated was relevant to the document's purpose—unless later dealings with the property are inconsistent with the truth of the statement or the purport of the document.

(16) *Statements in Ancient Documents.* A statement in a document that was prepared before January 1, 1998, and whose authenticity is established.

(17) *Market Reports and Similar Commercial Publications.* Market quotations, lists, directories, or other compilations that are generally relied on by the public or by persons in particular occupations.

(18) *Statements in Learned Treatises, Periodicals, or Pamphlets.* A statement contained in a treatise, periodical, or pamphlet if:

    (A) the statement is called to the attention of an expert witness on cross-examination or relied on by the expert on direct examination; and

(B) the publication is established as a reliable authority by the expert's admission or testimony, by another expert's testimony, or by judicial notice. If admitted, the statement may be read into evidence but not received as an exhibit.

(19) *Reputation Concerning Personal or Family History.* A reputation among a person's family by blood, adoption, or marriage—or among a person's associates or in the community—concerning the person's birth, adoption, legitimacy, ancestry, marriage, divorce, death, relationship by blood, adoption, or marriage, or similar facts of personal or family history.

(20) *Reputation Concerning Boundaries or General History.* A reputation in a community—arising before the controversy—concerning boundaries of land in the community or customs that affect the land, or concerning general historical events important to that community, state, or nation.

(21) *Reputation Concerning Character.* A reputation among a person's associates or in the community concerning the person's character.

(22) *Judgment of a Previous Conviction.* Evidence of a final judgment of conviction if:

(A) the judgment was entered after a trial or guilty plea, but not a nolo contendere plea;

(B) the conviction was for a crime punishable by death or by imprisonment for more than a year;

(C) the evidence is admitted to prove any fact essential to the judgment; and

(D) when offered by the prosecutor in a criminal case for a purpose other than impeachment, the judgment was against the defendant. The pendency of an appeal may be shown but does not affect admissibility.

(23) *Judgments Involving Personal, Family, or General History, or a Boundary.* A judgment that is admitted to prove a matter of personal, family, or general history, or boundaries, if the matter:

    (A) was essential to the judgment; and

    (B) could be proved by evidence of reputation.

(24) [*Other Exceptions.*] [Transferred to Rule 807.]

Rule 804. Exceptions to the Rule Against Hearsay— When the Declarant Is Unavailable as a Witness

(a) Criteria for Being Unavailable. A declarant is considered to be unavailable as a witness if the declarant:

    (1) is exempted from testifying about the subject matter of the declarant's statement because the court rules that a privilege applies;

    (2) refuses to testify about the subject matter despite a court order to do so;

    (3) testifies to not remembering the subject matter;

    (4) cannot be present or testify at the trial or hearing because of death or a then-existing infirmity, physical illness, or mental illness; or

    (5) is absent from the trial or hearing and the statement's proponent has not been able, by process or other reasonable means, to procure:

        (A) the declarant's attendance, in the case of a hearsay exception under Rule 804(b)(1) or (6); or

        (B) the declarant's attendance or testimony, in the case of a hearsay exception under Rule 804(b)(2), (3), or (4).

But this subdivision (a) does not apply if the statement's proponent procured or wrongfully caused the declarant's unavailability as a witness in order to prevent the declarant from attending or testifying.

(b) The Exceptions. The following are not excluded by the rule against hearsay if the declarant is unavailable as a witness:

(1) *Former Testimony.* Testimony that:

    (A) was given as a witness at a trial, hearing, or lawful deposition, whether given during the current proceeding or a different one; and

    (B) is now offered against a party who had—or, in a civil case, whose predecessor in interest had—an opportunity and similar motive to develop it by direct, cross-, or redirect examination.

(2) *Statement Under the Belief of Imminent Death.* In a prosecution for homicide or in a civil case, a statement that the declarant, while believing the declarant's death to be imminent, made about its cause or circumstances.

(3) *Statement Against Interest.* A statement that:

    (A) a reasonable person in the declarant's position would have made only if the person believed it to be true because, when made, it was so contrary to the declarant's proprietary or pecuniary interest or had so great a tendency to invalidate the declarant's claim against someone else or to expose the declarant to civil or criminal liability; and

    (B) is supported by corroborating circumstances that clearly indicate its trustworthiness, if it is offered in a criminal case as one that tends to expose the declarant to criminal liability.

(4) *Statement of Personal or Family History.* A statement about:

    (A) the declarant's own birth, adoption, legitimacy, ancestry, marriage, divorce, relationship by blood, adoption, or marriage, or similar facts of personal or family history, even though the declarant had no way of acquiring personal knowledge about that fact; or

    (B) another person concerning any of these facts, as well as death, if the declarant was related to the person by blood, adoption, or marriage or was so intimately associated with the person's family that the declarant's information is likely to be accurate.

(5) [*Other Exceptions.*] [Transferred to Rule 807.]

(6) ***Statement Offered Against a Party That Wrongfully Caused the Declarant's Unavailability.*** A statement offered against a party that wrongfully caused—or acquiesced in wrongfully causing—the declarant's unavailability as a witness, and did so intending that result.

Rule 805.   Hearsay Within Hearsay

Hearsay within hearsay is not excluded by the rule against hearsay if each part of the combined statements conforms with an exception to the rule.

Rule 806.   Attacking and Supporting the Declarant's Credibility

When a hearsay statement—or a statement described in Rule 801(d)(2)(C), (D), or (E)—has been admitted in evidence, the declarant's credibility may be attacked, and then supported, by any evidence that would be admissible for those purposes if the declarant had testified as a witness. The court may admit evidence of the declarant's inconsistent statement or conduct, regardless of when it occurred or whether the declarant had an opportunity to explain or deny it. If the party against whom the statement was admitted calls the declarant as a witness, the party may examine the declarant on the statement as if on cross-examination.

Rule 807.   Residual Exception

(a) **In General.** Under the following circumstances, a hearsay statement is not excluded by the rule against hearsay even if the statement is not specifically covered by a hearsay exception in Rule 803 or 804:

(1)   the statement has equivalent circumstantial guarantees of trustworthiness;

(2)   it is offered as evidence of a material fact;

(3)   it is more probative on the point for which it is offered than any other evidence that the proponent can obtain through reasonable efforts; and

(4)   admitting it will best serve the purposes of these rules and the interests of justice.

(b) Notice. The statement is admissible only if, before the trial or hearing, the proponent gives an adverse party reasonable notice of the intent to offer the statement and its particulars, including the declarant's name and address, so that the party has a fair opportunity to meet it.

ARTICLE IX. AUTHENTICATION AND IDENTIFICATION

Rule 901. Authenticating or Identifying Evidence

(a) In General. To satisfy the requirement of authenticating or identifying an item of evidence, the proponent must produce evidence sufficient to support a finding that the item is what the proponent claims it is.

(b) Examples. The following are examples only—not a complete list—of evidence that satisfies the requirement:

    (1) *Testimony of a Witness with Knowledge.* Testimony that an item is what it is claimed to be.

    (2) *Nonexpert Opinion About Handwriting.* A nonexpert's opinion that handwriting is genuine, based on a familiarity with it that was not acquired for the current litigation.

    (3) *Comparison by an Expert Witness or the Trier of Fact.* A comparison with an authenticated specimen by an expert witness or the trier of fact.

    (4) *Distinctive Characteristics and the Like.* The appearance, contents, substance, internal patterns, or other distinctive characteristics of the item, taken together with all the circumstances.

    (5) *Opinion About a Voice.* An opinion identifying a person's voice—whether heard firsthand or through mechanical or electronic transmission or recording—based on hearing the voice at any time under circumstances that connect it with the alleged speaker.

    (6) *Evidence About a Telephone Conversation.* For a telephone conversation, evidence that a call was made to the number assigned at the time to:

(A) a particular person, if circumstances, including self-identification, show that the person answering was the one called; or

(B) a particular business, if the call was made to a business and the call related to business reasonably transacted over the telephone.

(7) ***Evidence About Public Records.*** Evidence that:

(A) a document was recorded or filed in a public office as authorized by law; or

(B) a purported public record or statement is from the office where items of this kind are kept.

(8) ***Evidence About Ancient Documents or Data Compilations.*** For a document or data compilation, evidence that it:

(A) is in a condition that creates no suspicion about its authenticity;

(B) was in a place where, if authentic, it would likely be; and

(C) is at least 20 years old when offered.

(9) ***Evidence About a Process or System.*** Evidence describing a process or system and showing that it produces an accurate result.

(10) ***Methods Provided by a Statute or Rule.*** Any method of authentication or identification allowed by a federal statute or a rule prescribed by the Supreme Court.

Rule 902. Evidence That Is Self-Authenticating

The following items of evidence are self-authenticating; they require no extrinsic evidence of authenticity in order to be admitted:

(1) ***Domestic Public Documents That Are Sealed and Signed.*** A document that bears:

(A) a seal purporting to be that of the United States; any state, district, commonwealth, territory, or insular possession of the United States; the former Panama Canal Zone; the Trust Territory of the Pacific Islands; a political subdivision of any of these entities; or a department, agency, or officer of any entity named above; and

(B) a signature purporting to be an execution or attestation.

(2) ***Domestic Public Documents That Are Not Sealed but Are Signed and Certified.*** A document that bears no seal if:

(A) it bears the signature of an officer or employee of an entity named in Rule 902(1)(A); and

(B) another public officer who has a seal and official duties within that same entity certifies under seal—or its equivalent—that the signer has the official capacity and that the signature is genuine.

(3) ***Foreign Public Documents.*** A document that purports to be signed or attested by a person who is authorized by a foreign country's law to do so. The document must be accompanied by a final certification that certifies the genuineness of the signature and official position of the signer or attester—or of any foreign official whose certificate of genuineness relates to the signature or attestation or is in a chain of certificates of genuineness relating to the signature or attestation. The certification may be made by a secretary of a United States embassy or legation; by a consul general, vice consul, or consular agent of the United States; or by a diplomatic or consular official of the foreign country assigned or accredited to the United States. If all parties have been given a reasonable opportunity to investigate the document's authenticity and accuracy, the court may, for good cause, either:

(A) order that it be treated as presumptively authentic without final certification; or

(B) allow it to be evidenced by an attested summary with or without final certification.

(4) ***Certified Copies of Public Records.*** A copy of an official record—or a copy of a document that was recorded or filed in a public office as authorized by law—if the copy is certified as correct by:

(A) the custodian or another person authorized to make the certification; or

(B) a certificate that complies with Rule 902(1), (2), or (3), a federal statute, or a rule prescribed by the Supreme Court.

(5) *Official Publications.* A book, pamphlet, or other publication purporting to be issued by a public authority.

(6) *Newspapers and Periodicals.* Printed material purporting to be a newspaper or periodical.

(7) *Trade Inscriptions and the Like.* An inscription, sign, tag, or label purporting to have been affixed in the course of business and indicating origin, ownership, or control.

(8) *Acknowledged Documents.* A document accompanied by a certificate of acknowledgment that is lawfully executed by a notary public or another officer who is authorized to take acknowledgments.

(9) *Commercial Paper and Related Documents.* Commercial paper, a signature on it, and related documents, to the extent allowed by general commercial law.

(10) *Presumptions Under a Federal Statute.* A signature, document, or anything else that a federal statute declares to be presumptively or prima facie genuine or authentic.

(11) *Certified Domestic Records of a Regularly Conducted Activity.* The original or a copy of a domestic record that meets the requirements of Rule 803(6)(A)–(C), as shown by a certification of the custodian or another qualified person that complies with a federal statute or a rule prescribed by the Supreme Court. Before the trial or hearing, the proponent must give an adverse party reasonable written notice of the intent to offer the record—and must make the record and certification available for inspection—so that the party has a fair opportunity to challenge them.

(12) *Certified Foreign Records of a Regularly Conducted Activity.* In a civil case, the original or a copy of a foreign record that meets the requirements of Rule 902(11), modified as follows: the certification, rather than complying with a federal statute or Supreme Court rule, must be signed in a manner that, if falsely made, would subject the maker to a criminal penalty in the country where the certification is signed. The proponent must also meet the notice requirements of Rule 902(11).

(13) ***Certified Records Generated by an Electronic Process or System.***
A record generated by an electronic process or system that produces
an accurate result, as shown by a certification of a qualified person
that complies with the certification requirements of Rule 902(11)
or (12). The proponent must also meet the notice requirements of
Rule 902(11).

(14) ***Certified Data Copied from an Electronic Device, Storage
Medium, or File.*** Data copied from an electronic device, storage
medium, or file, if authenticated by a process of digital identification, as shown by a certification of a qualified person that complies
with the certification requirements of Rule 902(11) or (12). The
proponent also must meet the notice requirements of Rule 902(11).

Rule 903.   Subscribing Witness's Testimony

A subscribing witness's testimony is necessary to authenticate a writing only if
required by the law of the jurisdiction that governs its validity.

ARTICLE X. CONTENTS OF WRITINGS, RECORDINGS, AND PHOTOGRAPHS

Rule 1001. Definitions That Apply to This Article

In this article:

(a) A "writing" consists of letters, words, numbers, or their equivalent set down
in any form.

(b) A "recording" consists of letters, words, numbers, or their equivalent recorded
in any manner.

(c) A "photograph" means a photographic image or its equivalent stored in any
form.

(d) An "original" of a writing or recording means the writing or recording itself
or any counterpart intended to have the same effect by the person who executed or issued it. For electronically stored information, "original" means
any printout—or other output readable by sight—if it accurately reflects the

information. An "original" of a photograph includes the negative or a print from it.

(e) A "duplicate" means a counterpart produced by a mechanical, photographic, chemical, electronic, or other equivalent process or technique that accurately reproduces the original.

Rule 1002. Requirement of the Original

An original writing, recording, or photograph is required in order to prove its content unless these rules or a federal statute provides otherwise.

Rule 1003. Admissibility of Duplicates

A duplicate is admissible to the same extent as the original unless a genuine question is raised about the original's authenticity or the circumstances make it unfair to admit the duplicate.

Rule 1004. Admissibility of Other Evidence of Content

An original is not required and other evidence of the content of a writing, recording, or photograph is admissible if:

(a) all the originals are lost or destroyed, and not by the proponent acting in bad faith;

(b) an original cannot be obtained by any available judicial process;

(c) the party against whom the original would be offered had control of the original; was at that time put on notice, by pleadings or otherwise, that the original would be a subject of proof at the trial or hearing; and fails to produce it at the trial or hearing; or

(d) the writing, recording, or photograph is not closely related to a controlling issue.

Rule 1005. Copies of Public Records to Prove Content

The proponent may use a copy to prove the content of an official record—or of a document that was recorded or filed in a public office as authorized by law—if these conditions are met: the record or document is otherwise admissible; and the copy is certified as correct in accordance with Rule 902(4) or is testified to be correct by a witness who has compared it with the original. If no such copy can be obtained by reasonable diligence, then the proponent may use other evidence to prove the content.

Rule 1006. Summaries to Prove Content

The proponent may use a summary, chart, or calculation to prove the content of voluminous writings, recordings, or photographs that cannot be conveniently examined in court. The proponent must make the originals or duplicates available for examination or copying, or both, by other parties at a reasonable time and place. And the court may order the proponent to produce them in court.

Rule 1007. Testimony or Statement of a Party to Prove Content

The proponent may prove the content of a writing, recording, or photograph by the testimony, deposition, or written statement of the party against whom the evidence is offered. The proponent need not account for the original.

Rule 1008. Functions of the Court and Jury

Ordinarily, the court determines whether the proponent has fulfilled the factual conditions for admitting other evidence of the content of a writing, recording, or photograph under Rule 1004 or 1005. But in a jury trial, the jury determines—in accordance with Rule 104(b)—any issue about whether:

(a) an asserted writing, recording, or photograph ever existed;

(b) another one produced at the trial or hearing is the original; or

(c) other evidence of content accurately reflects the content.

ARTICLE XI. MISCELLANEOUS RULES

Rule 1101. Applicability of the Rules

(a) To Courts and Judges. These rules apply to proceedings before:

- United States district courts;

- United States bankruptcy and magistrate judges;

- United States courts of appeals;

- the United States Court of Federal Claims; and

- the district courts of Guam, the Virgin Islands, and the Northern Mariana Islands.

(b) To Cases and Proceedings. These rules apply in:

- civil cases and proceedings, including bankruptcy, admiralty, and maritime cases;

- criminal cases and proceedings; and

- contempt proceedings, except those in which the court may act summarily.

(c) Rules on Privilege. The rules on privilege apply to all stages of a case or proceeding.

(d) Exceptions. These rules—except for those on privilege—do not apply to the following:

(1) the court's determination, under Rule 104(a), on a preliminary question of fact governing admissibility;

(2) grand-jury proceedings; and

(3) miscellaneous proceedings such as:

- extradition or rendition;

- issuing an arrest warrant, criminal summons, or search warrant;

- a preliminary examination in a criminal case;

- sentencing;

- granting or revoking probation or supervised release; and

- considering whether to release on bail or otherwise.

(e) Other Statutes and Rules. A federal statute or a rule prescribed by the Supreme Court may provide for admitting or excluding evidence independently from these rules.

Rule 1102. Amendments

These rules may be amended as provided in 28 U.S.C. § 2072.

Rule 1103. Title

These rules may be cited as the Federal Rules of Evidence.

Proposed Privilege Rules

Submitted to Congress In 1972 (Not Enacted)

52 F.R.D. 183

Rule 502. Required Reports Privileged by Statute

A person, corporation, association, or other organization or entity, either public or private, making a return or report required by law to be made has a privilege to refuse to disclose and to prevent any other person from disclosing the return or report, if the law requiring it to be made so provides. A public officer or agency to whom a return or report is required by law to be made has a privilege to refuse to disclose the return or report if the law requiring it to be made so provides. No privilege exists under this rule in actions involving perjury, false statements, fraud in the return or report, or other failure to comply with the law in question.

Rule 503. Lawyer-Client Privilege

(a) Definitions. As used in this rule:

    (1) A "client" is a person, public officer, or corporation, association, or other organization or entity, either public or private, who is rendered professional legal services by a lawyer, or who consults a lawyer with a view to obtaining professional legal services from him.

    (2) A "lawyer" is a person authorized, or reasonably believed by the client to be authorized, to practice law in any state or nation.

    (3) A "representative of the lawyer" is one employed to assist the lawyer in the rendition of professional legal services.

    (4) A communication is "confidential" if not intended to be disclosed to third persons other than those to whom disclosure is in furtherance of the rendition of professional legal services to the client or those reasonably necessary for the transmission of the communication.

(b) General rule of privilege. A client has a privilege to refuse to disclose and to prevent any other person from disclosing confidential communications made for the purpose of facilitating the rendition of professional legal services to the client, (1) between himself or his representative and his lawyer or his lawyer's representative, or (2) between his lawyer and the lawyer's representative, or (3) by him or his lawyer to a lawyer representing another in a matter of common interest, or (4) between representatives of the client or between the client and a representative of the client, or (5) between lawyers representing the client.

(c) Who may claim the privilege. The privilege may be claimed by the client, his guardian or conservator, the personal representative of a deceased client, or the successor, trustee, or similar representative of a corporation, association, or other organization, whether or not in existence. The person who was the lawyer at the time of the communication may claim the privilege but only on behalf of the client. His authority to do so is presumed in the absence of evidence to the contrary.

(d) Exceptions. There is no privilege under this rule:

   (1)   Furtherance of crime or fraud. If the services of the lawyer were sought or obtained to enable or aid anyone to commit or plan to commit what the client knew or reasonably should have known to be a crime or fraud; or

   (2)   Claimants through same deceased client. As to a communication relevant to an issue between parties who claim through the same deceased client, regardless of whether the claims are by testate or intestate succession or by inter vivos transaction; or

   (3)   Breach of duty by lawyer or client. As to a communication relevant to an issue of breach of duty by the lawyer to his client or by the client to his lawyer; or

   (4)   Document attested by lawyer. As to a communication relevant to an issue concerning an attested document to which the lawyer is an attesting witness; or

   (5)   Joint clients. As to a communication relevant to a matter of common interest between two or more clients if the communication was made by any of them to a lawyer retained or consulted in common, when offered in an action between any of the clients.

Rule 504.   Psychotherapist-Patient Privilege

(a) Definitions.

    (1)   A "patient" is a person who consults or is examined or interviewed by a psychotherapist.

    (2)   A "psychotherapist" is (A) a person authorized to practice medicine in any state or nation, or reasonably believed by the patient so to be, while engaged in the diagnosis or treatment of a mental or emotional condition, including drug addiction, or (B) a person licensed or certified as a psychologist under the laws of any state or nation, while similarly engaged.

    (3)   A communication is "confidential" if not intended to be disclosed to third persons other than those present to further the interest of the patient in the consultation, examination, or interview, or persons reasonably necessary for the transmission of the communication, or persons who are participating in the diagnosis and treatment under the direction of the psychotherapist, including members of the patient's family.

(b) General rule of privilege. A patient has a privilege to refuse to disclose and to prevent any other person from disclosing confidential communications, made for the purposes of diagnosis or treatment of his mental or emotional condition, including drug addiction, among himself, his psychotherapist, or persons who are participating in the diagnosis or treatment under the direction of the psychotherapist, including members of the patient's family.

(c) Who may claim the privilege. The privilege may be claimed by the patient, by his guardian or conservator, or by the personal representative of a deceased patient. The person who was the psychotherapist may claim the privilege but only on behalf of the patient. His authority so to do is presumed in the absence of evidence to the contrary.

(d) Exceptions.

    (1)   Proceedings for hospitalization. There is no privilege under this rule for communications relevant to an issue in proceedings to hospitalize the patient for mental illness, if the psychotherapist in the course of diagnosis or treatment has determined that the patient is in need of hospitalization.

(2)   Examination by order of judge. If the judge orders an examination of the mental or emotional condition of the patient, communications made in the course thereof are not privileged under this rule with respect to the particular purpose for which the examination is ordered unless the judge orders otherwise.

(3)   Condition an element of claim or defense. There is no privilege under this rule as to communications relevant to an issue of the mental or emotional condition of the patient in any proceeding in which he relies upon the condition as an element of his claim or defense, or, after the patient's death, in any proceeding in which any party relies upon the condition as an element of his claim or defense.

Rule 505.   Husband-Wife Privilege

(a)   General rule of privilege. An accused in a criminal proceeding has a privilege to prevent his spouse from testifying against him.

(b)   Who may claim the privilege. The privilege may be claimed by the accused or by the spouse on his behalf. The authority of the spouse to do so is presumed in the absence of evidence to the contrary.

(c)   Exceptions. There is no privilege under this rule (1) in proceedings in which one spouse is charged with a crime against the person or property of the other or of a child of either, or with a crime against the person or property of a third person committed in the course of committing a crime against the other, or (2) as to matters occurring prior to the marriage, or (3) in proceedings in which a spouse is charged with importing an alien for prostitution or other immoral purpose in violation of 8 U.S.C § 1328, with transporting a female in interstate commerce for immoral purposes or other offense in violation of 18 U.S.C. §§ 2421–2424, or with violation of other similar statutes.

Rule 506.   Communications to Clergymen

(a)   Definitions. As used in this rule:

(1)   A "clergyman" is a minister, priest, rabbi, or other similar functionary of a religious organization, or an individual reasonably believed so to be by the person consulting him.

(2) A communication is "confidential" if made privately and not intended for further disclosure except to other persons present in furtherance of the purpose of the communication.

(b) General rule of privilege. A person has a privilege to refuse to disclose and to prevent another from disclosing a confidential communication by the person to a clergyman in his professional character as spiritual adviser.

(c) Who may claim the privilege. The privilege may be claimed by the person, by his guardian or conservator, or by his personal representative if he is deceased. The clergyman may claim the privilege on behalf of the person. His authority so to do is presumed in the absence of evidence to the contrary.

Rule 507.   Political Vote

Every person has a privilege to refuse to disclose the tenor of his vote at a political election conducted by secret ballot unless the vote was cast illegally.

Rule 508.   Trade Secrets

A person has a privilege, which may be claimed by him or his agent or employee, to refuse to disclose and to prevent other persons from disclosing a trade secret owned by him, if the allowance of the privilege will not tend to conceal fraud or otherwise work injustice. When disclosure is directed, the judge shall take such protective measure as the interests of the holder of the privilege and of the parties and the furtherance of justice may require.

Rule 509.   Secrets of State and Other Official Information

(a) Definitions.

(1) Secret of state. A "secret of state" is a governmental secret relating to the national defense or the international relations of the United States.

(2) Official information. "Official information" is information within the custody or control of a department or agency of the government the disclosure of which is shown to be contrary to the public interest and which consists of: (A) intragovernmental opinions or recommendations submitted for consideration in the performance of decisional or policymaking functions, or (B) subject to the pro-

visions of 18 U.S.C. § 3500, investigatory files compiled for law enforcement purposes and not otherwise available, or (C) information within the custody or control of a governmental department or agency whether initiated within the department or agency or acquired by it in its exercise of its official responsibilities and not otherwise available to the public pursuant to 5 U.S.C. § 552.

(b) General rule of privilege. The government has a privilege to refuse to give evidence and to prevent any person from giving evidence upon a showing of reasonable likelihood of danger that the evidence will disclose a secret of state or official information, as defined in this rule.

(c) Procedures. The privilege for secrets of state may be claimed only by the chief officer of the government agency or department administering the subject matter which the secret information sought concerns, but the privilege for official information may be asserted by any attorney representing the government. The required showing may be made in whole or in part in the form of a written statement. The judge may hear the matter in chambers, but all counsel are entitled to inspect the claim and showing and to be heard thereon, except that, in the case of secrets of state, the judge upon motion of the government, may permit the government to make the required showing in the above form in camera. If the judge sustains the privilege upon a showing in camera, the entire text of the government's statements shall be sealed and preserved in the court's records in the event of appeal. In the case of privilege claimed for official information the court may require examination in camera of the information itself. The judge may take any protective measure which the interests of the government and the furtherance of justice may require.

(d) Notice to government. If the circumstances of the case indicate a substantial possibility that a claim of privilege would be appropriate but has not been made because of oversight or lack of knowledge, the judge shall give or cause notice to be given to the officer entitled to claim the privilege and shall stay further proceedings a reasonable time to afford opportunity to assert a claim of privilege.

(e) Effect of sustaining claim. If a claim of privilege is sustained in a proceeding to which the government is a party and it appears that another party is thereby deprived of material evidence, the judge shall make any further orders which the interests of justice require, including striking the testimony of a witness, declaring a mistrial, finding against the government upon an issue as to which the evidence is relevant, or dismissing the action.

Rule 510. Identity of Informer

(a) Rule of privilege. The government or a state or subdivision thereof has a privilege to refuse to disclose the identity of a person who has furnished information relating to or assisting in an investigation of a possible violation of law to a law enforcement officer or member of a legislative committee or its staff conducting an investigation.

(b) Who may claim. The privilege may be claimed by an appropriate representative of the government, regardless of whether the information was furnished to an officer of the government or of a state or subdivision thereof. The privilege may be claimed by an appropriate representative of a state or subdivision if the information was furnished to an officer thereof, except that in criminal cases the privilege shall not be allowed if the government objects.

(c) Exceptions.

   (1)   Voluntary disclosure; informer a witness. No privilege exists under this rule if the identity of the informer or his interest in the subject matter of his communication has been disclosed to those who would have cause to resent the communication by a holder of the privilege or by the informer's own action, or if the informer appears as a witness for the government.

   (2)   Testimony on merits. If it appears from the evidence in the case or from other showing by a party that an informer may be able to give testimony necessary to a fair determination of the issue of guilt or innocence in a criminal case or of a material issue on the merits in a civil case to which the government is a party, and the government invokes the privilege, the judge shall give the government an opportunity to show in camera facts relevant to determining whether the informer can, in fact, supply that testimony. The showing will ordinarily be in the form of affidavits, but the judge may direct that testimony be taken if he finds that the matter cannot be resolved satisfactorily upon affidavit. If the judge finds that there is a reasonable probability that the informer can give the testimony, and the government elects not to disclose his identity, the judge

on motion of the defendant in a criminal case shall dismiss the charges to which the testimony would relate, and the judge may do so on his own motion. In civil cases, he may make any order that justice requires. Evidence submitted to the judge shall be sealed and preserved to be made available to the appellate court in the event of an appeal, and the contents shall not otherwise be revealed without consent of the government. All counsel and parties shall be permitted to be present at every stage of proceedings under this subdivision except a showing in camera, at which no counsel or party shall be permitted to be present.

(3)   Legality of obtaining evidence. If information from an informer is relied upon to establish the legality of the means by which evidence was obtained and the judge is not satisfied that the information was received from an informer reasonably believed to be reliable or credible, he may require the identity of the informer to be disclosed. The judge shall, on request of the government, direct that the disclosure be made in camera. All counsel and parties concerned with the issue of legality shall be permitted to be present at every stage of proceedings under this subdivision except a disclosure in camera, at which no counsel or party shall be permitted to be present. If disclosure of the identity of the informer is made in camera, the record thereof shall be sealed and preserved to be made available to the appellate court in the event of an appeal, and the contents shall not otherwise be revealed without consent of the government.

Rule 511.   Waiver of Privilege By Voluntary Disclosure

A person upon whom these rules confer a privilege against disclosure of the confidential matter or communication waives the privilege if he or his predecessor while holder of the privilege voluntarily discloses or consents to disclosure of any significant part of the matter or communication. This rule does not apply if the disclosure is itself a privileged communication.

Rule 512. Privileged Matter Disclosed Under Compulsion or Without Opportunity to Claim Privilege

Evidence of a statement or other disclosure of privileged matter is not admissible against the holder of the privilege if the disclosure was (a) compelled erroneously or (b) made without opportunity to claim the privilege.

Rule 513. Comment Upon or Inference from Claim of Privilege; Instruction

(a) Comment or inference not permitted. The claim of a privilege, whether in the present proceeding or upon a prior occasion, is not a proper subject of comment by judge or counsel. No inference may be drawn therefrom.

(b) Claiming privilege without knowledge of jury. In jury cases, proceedings shall be conducted, to the extent practicable, so as to facilitate the making of claims of privilege without the knowledge of the jury.

(c) Jury instruction. Upon request, any party against whom the jury might draw an adverse inference from a claim of privilege is entitled to an instruction that no inference may be drawn therefrom.

Table of References to the Federal Rules of Evidence

This table lists references to each of the Federal Rules of Evidence. Page numbers in bold represent the primary discussion of that rule. Numbers in italics refer to the full text of the rule in the appendix.

Table of Cases

References are to pages.

Subject Matter Index

Page numbers in bold refer to the primary discussion of a topic.